Child Support Handbook

15th edition

Updated by Rachel Hadwen

Child Pove

CPAG promotes action for the prevention and relief of poverty among children and families with children. To achieve this, CPAG aims to raise awareness of the causes, extent, nature and impact of poverty, and strategies for its eradication and prevention; bring about positive policy changes for families with children in poverty; and enable those eligible for income maintenance to have access to their full entitlement. If you are not already supporting us, please consider making a donation, or ask for details of our membership schemes and publications.

Published by Child Poverty Action Group
94 White Lion Street, London N1 9PF

Charity No 294841

A CIP record for this book is available from the British Library

ISBN: 978 1 906076 02 3

Cover design by Devious Designs
Typeset by David Lewis XML Associates Ltd
Printed by William Clowes Ltd
Cover photo by Joanne O'Brien/Photofusion

The author

Rachel Hadwen is a freelance trainer and consultant in welfare rights and related areas. She also works for Working Families as a rights adviser to parents.

Acknowledgements

A huge debt is owed to all the authors of previous editions of the book: Alison Garnham, Emma Knights, Simon Cox, Jon Blackwell and Jacqui McDowell.

I would like to thank Jon Blackwell for checking the calculations and Nick Wikeley for his invaluable comments on the text. Thanks are due to Alison Key for editing and managing the production of the book, Katherine Dawson for the index and Paula McDiarmid for proofreading the text.

Thanks to Debbie Vialls and her colleagues at the Department for Work and Pensions, Hannah Coupe at the Child Support Agency, and Tracy Taylor and Maria Kolpa at Jobcentre Plus for answering my queries and providing access to information.

Rachel Hadwen

The law described in this book was correct at 1 June 2007.

Contents

Terms used

'She' and 'he'

As nine-tenths of people with the care of a qualifying child are women, we use 'she' to describe the person with care and 'he' to describe the non-resident parent.

However, the law applies in the same way if the person with care is a man or the non-resident parent is a woman, or if both parents are men or both women.

We recognise that in a small minority of cases the non-resident parent will be the mother and the parent with care the father and, in some cases, both will be of the same sex. However, for the sake of readability, we use 'she' for the person with care and 'he' for the non-resident parent.

'Second family'

We use the term 'second family' loosely to describe the situation where a parent of a qualifying child (in our examples, usually the non-resident parent) also has children who live with her/him. This could be a third or fourth family, or even a first family where, for example, a married man remains with his wife despite having a child with another woman. It may also apply where a parent is living with a same-sex partner who has responsibility for a child.

'Stepchild'

We use the term 'stepchild' to describe the child of a person's partner, whether or not they are a married couple or in a civil partnership.

Abbreviations

AA	Attendance allowance
CA	Carer's allowance
CAU	Central Appeals Unit
C-MEC	Child Maintenance and Enforcement Commission
CSA	Child Support Agency
CSAC	Child Support Agency Centre
CTB	Council tax benefit
CTC	Child tax credit
DCI	Departmental Central Index
DEO	Deduction from earnings order
DLA	Disability living allowance
DWP	Department for Work and Pensions
ECJ	European Court of Justice
ECHR	European Convention on Human Rights
EU	European Union
HB	Housing benefit
IB	Incapacity benefit
ICE	Independent Case Examiner
IMA	Interim maintenance assessment
IS	Income support
JSA	Jobseeker's allowance
MAF	Maintenance application form
MEF	Maintenance enquiry form
NI	National insurance
PC	Pension credit
RPC	Regular payments condition
SDA	Severe disability allowance
WTC	Working tax credit

Child support rates 2007/08

Note: many assessments in force during this year will have been calculated on the basis of earlier years' rates.

Dependent child's personal allowance

Under 19	£47.45*

Pre-6 April 2004 claims with no child tax credit

Adult's personal allowance

Single	59.15
Couple	£92.80*

* This is only used in the protected income calculation

Premiums

Family	£16.43*
Disabled child	£46.69*
Carer	£27.15
Disability (single)	£25.25
Severe disability (single)	£48.45

*Pre-6 April 2004 claims with no child tax credit

The following premiums are only used in the protected income calculation:

Disability (couple)	£36.00
Severe disability	
couple (if one qualifies)	£48.45
couple (if both qualify)	£96.90
Pensioner/enhanced/higher pensioner	
single	£59.90
couple	£88.90

Child benefit

Only or eldest child	£18.10
Other children	£12.10

Child support

Minimum payment of child maintenance ('old rules')	£6.00
Contribution towards child maintenance deducted from income support ('old rules')	£6.00

| Minimum payment of child maintenance ('new rules') | £5.00 |
| Benefit penalty | £23.66 |

Income tax (per year)

Personal allowance (under 65)	£5,225
Married couple's allowance (minimum)	£2,440
Blind person's allowance	£1,730

National insurance contributions

| Lower earnings limit | £87.00 |

11% on earnings between £100 and £670

Bands of taxable income

Lower rate – 10%	£0 – £2,230
Basic rate – 22%	£2,231 – £34,600
Higher rate – 40%	over £34,600

Part 1

Introduction

Chapter 1

Introduction to child support

This chapter covers:
1. What is child support (below)
2. The Child Support Agency (p5)
3. The future of child support (p8)
3. Using this *Handbook* (p10)

1. **What is child support**

Child support is the name given to child maintenance paid by parents who do not live with their children, where the Government calculates and enforces liability for this maintenance. Child maintenance is intended to reflect the legal responsibility of parents to provide financial support for their children. Some people make voluntary arrangements to pay maintenance, others have arrangements made following a court order, and some people have maintenance (child support) calculated by the Child Support Agency (CSA). This *Handbook* deals mainly with the rules of the child support scheme and the work of the CSA, and is intended to help parents who use the CSA and their advisers.

Since 1993 there has been a formal child support system administered by the CSA. This calculates the amount of child support people have to pay in different situations. The original complex formula for calculating child support (the 'old rules' formula) was replaced by a simpler calculation from 3 March 2003. This 'new rules' calculation mostly applies to applications made on or after this date. An even more basic system, operated by a new body, the Child Maintenance and Enforcement Commission (C-MEC), is expected to be introduced in the future (see p8).

Parents who claim certain benefits are currently treated as applying to the CSA and can lose benefit if they do not co-operate without a good reason. This rule is expected to be abolished under government proposals but, in the meantime, these parents continue to be treated as applying. Other parents may have a choice about whether to apply to the CSA, depending on their situation.

The main features of the existing child support scheme are:
• the CSA, which assesses and enforces child maintenance; *and*

- the use of a standard mechanism to set the level of child maintenance (currently under the 'old rules' formula or 'new rules' calculation); *and*
- special rules for parents claiming certain benefits if they do not live with the other parent of the child(ren) for whom they care. These parents are treated as applying for child maintenance and may face a reduction in benefit if they do not co-operate.

Responsibility for child maintenance

It is a legal principle that both parents of a child have a duty to contribute to the maintenance of that child.[1] This liability is met when a parent who does not have the main care of a child makes payments of child maintenance assessed under the formula or calculation.[2]

This duty applies whether or not:

- the child is living with the other parent or with someone else who is not legally her/his parent (see below); *or*
- the child is living with a lone parent or with a couple; *or*
- the child's parents are on benefit.

. . . .

Definitions

The following terms are used throughout this *Handbook*. For more detailed definitions, see Chapter 2.

A parent who does not live with her/his own child is a '**non-resident parent**'.

A child who does not live with both her/his parents is a '**qualifying child**'.

The person with whom the child is living and who provides her/him with day-to-day care is the '**person with care**'.

If a person with care is also a parent of the qualifying child, s/he is a '**parent with care**'.

A child living with the non-resident parent, for whom s/he or any new partner receives child benefit, is a '**relevant child**'.

We use 'he' to refer to a non-resident parent, and 'she' to refer to a person or parent with care, although we recognise that this will not always be the case.

. . . .

Calculating maintenance: 'old rules' and 'new rules'

Whether a case comes under the 'old' or 'new' rules for calculating child support is important, not only because it dictates how much maintenance should be paid, but also because there are some differences in how other aspects of child support apply – eg, enforcement. In addition, the legislative references are often different. The '**new rules**' are those that came into force on 3 March 2003 (not the proposed simplified system, which has not yet been introduced). The '**old rules**' are those which were introduced with the child support system when it started in 1993. Both sets of rules have been amended since they were introduced.

The 'old rules' use a complicated formula with several steps to work out how much maintenance should be paid (see Chapter 9). An application can be made for departure from the formula in certain circumstances (see Chapter 16). The 'new rules' use one of four rates of child support maintenance for each non-resident parent, based on his income (see Chapter 6). The calculation can be varied in certain circumstances (see Chapter 7).

Generally, if an application for child support is made on or after 3 March 2003, it is a 'new rules' case, and if the application was made before that date, it is an 'old rules' case. However, there are some exceptions to this, and some 'old rules' cases that are connected to a 'new rules' case may be converted to the new rules (see also Chapter 8). Apart from these cases, it is now unlikely that 'old rules' cases will convert to 'new rules', because the Government proposes that a third, and even more simple, calculation be introduced in the future. However, no one will be able to apply under the new system, or be transferred to it, until 2010 at the earliest.[3] In the meantime, existing cases will continue to fall under either the 'old rules' or the 'new rules'.

2. **The Child Support Agency**

The Child Support Agency (CSA) is the body set up by the Secretary of State for Work and Pensions to administer the child support scheme. It is responsible for calculating child maintenance payments and, in some cases, their collection and enforcement. This includes tracing non-resident parents and investigating parents' means. The CSA is part of the Department for Work and Pensions (DWP).

Following problems with the CSA, including delays in assessments and difficulty in enforcing payments, the Government proposes to replace it with a new Child Maintenance and Enforcement Commission (C-MEC). This will be a non-departmental public body (ie, separate from the DWP). C-MEC is not expected to be in place until 2008/09[4] and, in the meantime, the CSA will continue.

The DWP is responsible for child support policy issues and for the legislation governing the CSA's activities. The Chief Executive of the CSA issues guidance to CSA staff and is ultimately responsible for its administration.

The CSA works closely with Jobcentre Plus, which is responsible for identifying cases where a parent with care claims income support or income-based jobseeker's allowance. Jobcentre Plus also carries out any necessary interviews to establish whether a parent who has refused to co-operate has 'good cause' for doing so, and makes reduced benefit decisions if it is decided that she does not (see Chapter 4).

The CSA has wide powers to gather information. These are covered in Chapter 5. If a parent is unhappy with a child support decision, there are procedures for challenging these (see Chapter 18), and for appealing most sorts of decisions (see Chapter 19).

Structure of the Child Support Agency

The CSA is divided into six regional business units. Apart from the one for the east of England, they are all based in the areas they serve (see Appendix 1). Each business unit has a Child Support Agency Centre (CSAC), which assesses child maintenance.

Under the Operational Improvement Plan, which runs from 2006 to 2009, the CSA is working towards the following structure:[5]
* new client teams supporting new applications;
* client service teams managing ongoing cases and processing changes of cirumstances;
* debt management teams taking action when a payment is missed;
* legal enforcement teams ensuring that payment is enforced.

There should also be specialist client teams for different areas of work, usually determined by the employment status of the non-resident parent (eg, teams dealing with benefit claimants, employed clients and self-employed clients).

The CSA also has local offices around the country, called local service bases or field offices (some of these will be based in Jobcentre Plus premises). These may be used to conduct face-to-face interviews with parents.

Communicating with the Child Support Agency

The first port of call when contacting the CSA will usually be the CSAC which applies to the parent's area. You can write to or telephone the CSAC. It is advisable to keep copies of letters, and make a note of the date, time and content of telephone calls. Telephone numbers and addresses are in Appendix 1.

Dates of postage

If you fall under the 'new rules' and the CSA posts a document to you, it will usually be treated as sent on the day of posting.[6] If you send a document to the CSA, it is treated as being sent on the day the CSA receives it.

If you fall under the 'old rules', documents are treated as being sent to you by the CSA on the second day after the day of posting (unless this day is a Sunday or bank holiday).[7] If more than one document is required to be sent and they are posted on different days, or they need to be sent to different people and this is done on different days, they are treated as having been posted on the latest of the dates concerned (and so sent on the second day after this).[8] If you send a document to the CSA, it is treated as being sent on the day the CSA receives it, but in some cases the CSA can treat documents as having been sent earlier if there was unavoidable delay.[9]

It is important to bear these rules in mind, especially where time limits are concerned.

Representatives

Anyone dealing with the CSA can appoint a representative to act on her/his behalf.[10] If the person is not legally qualified, authorisation for her/him to act needs to be confirmed in writing, although if the client is with the representative during a telephone call s/he can authorise the representative verbally for the duration of the call. An authorised or legally qualified representative can complete forms, receive documents and supply information. A person with care may also choose to have payments of child support made to a representative.

A representative who understands the law and/or is experienced in dealing with the CSA may find it easier to get a quick response and clearer information from the CSA. S/he can also help you to understand your rights and what options are open to you. For information about how to find independent advice, see Appendix 4.

Representatives with legal authority to act for a CSA client (eg, someone with power of attorney, a reciever, or a mental health appointee/Scottish mental health custodian) are able to act for the client in every respect, as if they were the client.[11]

The legal help scheme (advice and assistance scheme in Scotland) can cover child support cases. A client does not have to pay back any money out of sums recovered if the money is for maintenance.

What to expect when you contact the Child Support Agency

If you contact the CSA by telephone, you should be able to get through. The Client Charter states that the CSA aims to answer the telephone within one minute.[12] If you write to the CSA, it aims to reply to your letter, resolving the issue or agreeing what will happen next, within three weeks.[13] If you have difficulty in contacting the CSA or obtaining a response within a reasonable time, you should complain. More information about standards of service and how to complain is in Chapter 21.

Face-to-face interviews

A CSA client can request a face-to-face interview with a CSA member of staff, or the CSA may decide that a face-to-face interview is needed to obtain information or resolve a parent's query. CSA guidance states that an interview should only be used where 'there is a clear business need or it is beneficial to the client'.[14] For example, you might request a face-to-face interview because of difficulties with written or telephone communication, or because English is not your first language.

In some cases, the CSA is required to hold a face-to-face interview – eg, where the results of a DNA test need to be communicated and it is important to check that the correct person has been tested.

If you are requesting a face-to-face interview, be aware that the guidance states the service should only be used if it is necessary, the most effective way to make contact, or if all other ways of progressing the case have been tried.[15] However, if you feel that your request for a face-to-face interview has not been adequately considered, or you are not happy with the service, you should think about making a complaint (see Chapter 21).

If you are going to be interviewed, the CSA will contact you to arrange this. If you have any language or access needs, the face-to-face service should accommodate these. You may be interviewed at a Jobcentre Plus office or other approved venue, your place of work or, in certain circumstances, your home. A home visit will only be arranged where there is a clear business need (eg, you are housebound or the interview would otherwise involve unreasonable travelling time) and there is no threat to the safety of the face-to-face officer. The interview will be recorded on the CSA database.[16]

Arrangements in Northern Ireland

The child support system is the same throughout the UK, but there is a separate CSA for Northern Ireland, which is part of the Department for Social Development in Northern Ireland (DSDNI). Its powers are the same as the CSA in Great Britain. The address of the Northern Ireland CSA is the same as the Eastern Business Unit that assesses cases for the eastern area of England. They are based at the same location, but they operate separately. Also part of DSDNI is the Social Security Agency, the Northern Ireland equivalent of Jobcentre Plus.

Where this *Handbook* is being used in Northern Ireland, references to the DWP should be read as references to DSDNI and references to Jobcentre Plus should be read as references to the Social Security Agency (see also p10). **Note:** some legislative references are different in Northern Ireland.

---

3. The future of child support

After several years of problems with the child support system, particularly delays in assessments and difficulties in enforcing payment, the Government has proposed a wholesale change of the system, including replacing the Child Support Agency (CSA) with a new body. None of these changes will affect parents or children before 2008 at the earliest.

The proposals include the following.
- All parents will be encouraged to make their own arrangements, with an information and support service to aid this process.

- If parents do not make their own arrangments, a simplified calcuation will be used based on gross income in the latest tax year (unless income varies by at least 25 per cent). The figures will be obtained directly from Her Majesty's Revenue and Customs.
- Parents with care who claim income support (IS) or income-based jobseeker's allowance (JSA) will no longer be treated as applying for child support.
- All parents with care will be able to keep up to £10 a week of maintenance without it affecting their IS or income-based JSA (and this disregard will be increased).
- The definition of a qualifying child will be brought into line with that for child benefit so that maintenance becomes payable for all young people for whom child benefit can be claimed (including 16–18-year-olds on certain training courses and some 19-year-olds in non-advanced education or approved training).
- The CSA will be replaced by the Child Maintenance and Enforcement Commission (C-MEC), which will calculate child support for those parents who do not make their own arrangements and will pursue non-compliant non-resident parents to enforce payment.
- Possible new powers of enforcement, including the possibility of C-MEC being able to take money from bank accounts, enforce the surrender of a non-resident parent's passport and impose a curfew on a parent who fails to pay child maintenance. The requirement to apply to court before enforcement action is taken may be removed. In some cases where successful prosecutions or court applications have been made, non-resident parents' names may be published.[17]

Existing cases

The Government proposes that parents with existing child support cases will have the choice between keeping their arrangements if they both agree, transferring to the new system, or making their own private arrangements.

Timetable for change

The Government's proposed timetable for the changes includes the following.[18]
In 2007/08:
- a Bill will be introduced in Parliament to achieve the proposed reforms;
- the new arrangements will be piloted to inform later decisions about how information and guidance services for parents will operate.

In 2008/09, C-MEC will be established. This will:
- take responsibility for existing CSA operations;
- make use of powers for enforcement and collection;
- create new information and guidance services for parents;

- remove the requirement for parents with care on IS or income-based JSA to apply for child support;
- extend the disregard on maintenance for parents on IS or income-based JSA to all 'old rules' cases by the end of 2008.

In 2009/10, parents with existing cases will be supported (by information and advice services) to choose to:
- make private arrangements; *or*
- continue with their current arrangements (if both parents agree), including accessing a cash transfer system; *or*
- become a client of the new simplified system.

In 2010/11:
- new applications from parents without existing child support cases will be accepted under the new simplified system;
- the disregard on part of child support maintenance for parents with care claiming IS or income-based JSA will be increased;
- the transfer process for existing clients who wish to be covered by the new simplified system will begin. This is expected to take around three years.

By 2012/13, it is hoped that all parents who have chosen to have their maintenance assessed under the simplified system will be covered by a single set of rules, managed by C-MEC.

4. Using this *Handbook*

This *Handbook* covers the child support scheme in England, Wales and Scotland as at 1 June 2007. Northern Ireland has a similar scheme although some of its legislative references and guidance will be different. Separate chapters detail how maintenance is worked out under the 'old' and 'new' rules. There are some references to earlier changes, but for full details of the scheme in previous years you should consult earlier editions. The other chapters cover general rules, such as how the Child Support Agency (CSA) obtains information or enforces payment, and how to challenge its decisions.

Structure of the book

Part 1 is an introduction to child support, the CSA and how to use this *Handbook*. **Part 2** explains the key principles and terms of the child support scheme, how applications are made (including for parents treated as applying) and how the CSA seeks information. Once all the information is available, the amount of maintenance can be worked out – **Part 3** does this under the 'new rules' and **Part**

4 under the 'old rules'. The transitional rules on the conversion of existing cases to the new scheme are also covered in Part 3 (Chapter 9). **Part 5** covers CSA decisions, how to change, query or challenge them (by review and appeal), collection and enforcement of maintenance, and how to complain.

The **appendices** contain useful addresses, information about reference materials and an explanation of income support premiums. For benefit rates, see pxii.

The best way to find the information you need is to use the index at the back of the book.

Footnotes

At the end of each chapter are the footnotes. These contain the legal authorities and other sources of information which support the text, and some further information. Parents and advisers can quote the reference to the CSA if the statement in the text is disputed. Appendix 6 explains the abbreviations used in the footnotes, with information on how to get hold of the sources.

Some footnotes refer to the online guidance material provided to CSA staff. These are only guidance and are *not* law. Different guidance applies to 'old rules' and 'new rules' cases. This *Handbook* also includes references to relevant caselaw, in particular child support commissioners' decisions (see p418).

Notes

1. **What is child support**
   1 s1(1) CSA 1991
   2 s1(2) and (3) CSA 1991
   3 White Paper, *A New System of Child Maintenance*, December 2006

2. **The Child Support Agency**
   4 White Paper, *A New System of Child Maintenance*, December 2006
   5 CSA Operational Improvement Plan 2006-2009
   6 Reg 2 CS(MCP) Regs
   7 Reg 1(6) CS(MAP) Regs
   8 Reg 1(8) CS(MAP) Regs
   9 Reg 1(7) CS(MAP) Regs
   10 Reg 22 CS(MCP) Regs; Reg 53 CS(MAP) Regs; DMG paras 2023-24; PG Client Communications
   11 DMG para 2025; PG, Client Communications

   12 CSA Client Charter 2006, April 2006
   13 CSA Client Charter 2006, April 2006
   14 PG, Client Communications
   15 PG, Client Communications
   16 PG, Client Communications

3. **The future of child support**
   17 Department for Work and Pensions Press Release, 15 May 2007
   18 White Paper, *A New System of Child Maintenance*, December 2006

Part 2

....

Using the Child Support Agency

Chapter 2

Who is covered by the scheme

This chapter covers:
1. The duty to maintain (below)
2. Parent (below)
3. Qualifying child (p18)
4. Person with care (p20)
5. Non-resident parent (p22)
6. Relevant child (p23)
7. Welfare of the child (p24)
8. Family (p26)
9. Habitually resident in the UK (p27)
10. The role of the courts (p28)

1. The duty to maintain

Both parents of a 'qualifying child' (see p18) are responsible for maintaining her/him.[1]

The Child Support Agency (CSA) can only require a 'non-resident parent' (see p22) to pay child maintenance for a qualifying child. A 'parent with care' (see p20) cannot be required to pay child maintenance for the child for whom s/he is caring, unless s/he is treated as a non-resident parent because s/he provides care for less time than someone else or, in some cases, for the same amount of time (see Chapter 16).

The CSA can only make a calculation (or assessment in 'old rules' cases) if the person with care, non-resident parent and qualifying child meet the rules on habitual residence (see p27).

2. Parent

A **'parent'** is a person who is legally the mother or father of the child.[2] This includes:

- a biological parent (see p16 for human-assisted reproduction);

- a parent by adoption;[3]
- a parent under a parental order (used in surrogacy cases).[4]

If a child was conceived by artificial insemination or *in vitro* fertilisation:
- the mother is the woman who gave birth to the child (wherever in the world the insemination or fertilisation took place),[5] unless an adoption order or parental order is made;[6] *and*
- the father is the man who provided the sperm, unless:
  - if the insemination was before 1 August 1991 *and* the child was born in England or Wales after 3 April 1988, the father is the mother's husband, unless he did not consent to the insemination;[7]
  - if the insemination or fertilisation was after 31 July 1991, the father is:[8]
    - the mother's husband, unless he did not consent to[9] or died before insemination;[10] *or*
    - if that was during licensed treatment services provided for the mother and a man, that man.[11] The man and woman must have received treatment services together.[12] This rule does not apply to a woman inseminated/fertilised outside the UK.[13]

This means that if an unmarried woman self-inseminated without the involvement of licensed treatment services, the donor is the father.

Note: the rules on parentage in assisted reproduction are likely to be changed in the near future under government proposals.[14]

If a person denies being the parent of a child, the Child Support Agency (CSA) must *assume* that the person is a parent of the child, unless the child has subsequently been adopted by someone else (see p17), if:[15]
- in England, Wales or Northern Ireland, a declaration of parentage or, in Scotland, a declarator of parentage, is in force about that person. This includes situations where the person with care or the CSA have applied to court for a declaration as to whether the person is a parent of the child;[16]
- in Scotland,[17] England and Wales,[18] the person is a man who:
  - was married to the mother at any time between the child's conception and birth; *or*
  - acknowledged his paternity *and* was acknowledged by the mother *and* was named as the father on the birth certificate issued in the UK;
- the person is a man who was found to be the father by a court in England or Wales in proceedings under certain legal provisions (see Appendix 3). The court decision usually states the legal provision under which it was made;[19]
- the person is a man who was found by a court in Northern Ireland to be a father in proceedings under similar legal provisions to those in Appendix 3;[20]
- the person is a man who was found by a court in Scotland to be the father in any action for affiliation or aliment;[21]

- the person is a man who refuses to take a DNA test, or where the results of the test show that he is the father (even if he refuses to accept it);[22]
- a parental order has been made in favour of that person following an application made within six months of a birth which is the result of a surrogacy arrangement.[23] Currently only married couples can apply for such an order;
- certain types of fertility treatment have been carried out by a licensed clinic and the person is treated as a parent of the child under the Human Fertilisation and Embryology Act 1990.[24]

These rules apply even if paternity was not disputed in the proceedings.[25]

If none of the above applies, the CSA cannot make a calculation until parentage is admitted by a person or decided by a court.

Since the Civil Partnership Act 2004 came into force on 5 December 2005, for most child support purposes, civil partners (including those who have adopted a child) are treated in the same way as married partners.[26] Couples living with a same-sex partner but not in a civil partnership are treated in the same way as couples of the opposite sex who are not married. However, the rules about parentage and artificial insemination/*in vitro* fertilisation currently only apply to couples of the opposite sex.[27] Couples in a civil partnership cannot apply for a parental order following the birth of a child as the result of a surrogacy arrangement. Also, the CSA does not assume that a civil partner is the other parent if a child is conceived during a civil partnership by one of the couple. However, if government proposals come into force, new rules will treat same-sex partners in a similar way to opposite-sex partners for the purpose of assuming parentage in assisted reproduction cases.[28]

An **adoption order** means that the child's biological parents (including anyone assumed to be a biological parent under the rules above) are no longer in law that child's parents.[29] This means that the liability of a biological parent to maintain her/his child ends on adoption and the parent(s) by adoption become the only people liable to maintain the child.

A person who has legal parental responsibility[30] is not necessarily a parent for child support purposes.[31] For example, a step-parent who has acquired parental responsibility (except one assumed to be a parent under the rules above) cannot be required to pay child support maintenance, but the courts could order maintenance (see p32).

A foster parent is not a parent for child support purposes because the child has been placed with her/him by a local authority (see p20).

Parentage disputes

If the parent with care does not name the other parent, or if the alleged other parent denies parentage, the CSA investigates to identify the other parent and, if possible, show that he can be assumed to be a parent under the above rules (see pp82 and 87). If the alleged non-resident parent disputes that those rules apply (eg, he says the person named in a court order is someone else), he can appeal against the CSA decision. This appeal is dealt with by a magistrates'/sheriff's court rather than by an appeal tribunal (see also pp87 and 401).[32]

However, if the alleged non-resident parent accepts that those rules apply, but disputes the correctness of the court order referred to by the CSA (ie, the court was wrong to name him as the father), he cannot dispute parentage through the CSA appeals system. Instead, he should consider applying to the court to set aside its order and/or making a late appeal against it.

If no one is assumed to be the other parent under those rules, the CSA usually tries to arrange voluntary DNA testing or applies to court for a declaration of paternity (see p91). A parent with care on income support or income-based jobseeker's allowance may face a reduced benefit decision if she refuses DNA testing (see p65).

3. **Qualifying child**

Child support maintenance is only payable for a 'qualifying child'. A child is only a **'qualifying child'** if one or both of her/his parents are non-resident parents (see p22).[33] In addition, a child only counts as a qualifying child when working out maintenance if the parent with care has applied, or been treated as applying, to the Child Support Agency (CSA) for maintenance for her/him.[34]

A **'child'** is defined as a person:[35]
* under 16; *or*
* 16–18 years old and receiving full-time, non-advanced education (see p19); *or*
* 16–17 years old, registered for work or work-based learning for young people, and has recently left education (see p20).

Even if a person falls into one of these groups, s/he is *not* a child if s/he is, or has been, married or in a civil partnership. This applies even if the marriage or civil partnership has been annulled or was never valid – eg, s/he was under 16.[36]

Note: from 10 April 2006, a person for whom child benefit is being paid is no longer necessarily a child for child support purposes. This is because child benefit is payable for a wider group of young people, including 16–19-year-olds in non-advanced education or in certain training. If a person is not a child for child support purposes, the courts may still be able to order maintenance – eg, for a dependent child at university or in training, or even beyond a young person's 19th birthday (see p32). The Government intends to extend the definition of a child in child support law in the future, so that it will cover all groups for whom child benefit can be paid.[37]

Full-time, non-advanced education

A course is **non-advanced** if it is up to A-level or higher level Scottish Certificate of Education (this includes a Scottish certificate of sixth year studies and a national diploma or certificate from BTEC or ScotVEC). Courses of degree level and above (including DipHE, Higher National Diploma, or a Higher Diploma or certificate from BTEC or ScotVEC) count as advanced education.[38]

The child must attend a recognised educational establishment (such as a school or college) *or* the education must be recognised by the CSA.[39]

The CSA must treat a child as receiving **full-time** education if the child attends a course where the weekly contact time is more than 12 hours.[40] Contact time includes teaching, supervised study, exams and practical or project work which are parts of the course. It does not include meal times or unsupervised study, whether on or off school premises.

If a child is not attending such a course (eg, where contact is for less than 12 hours) the CSA must look at all the facts and decide if the education is full time.

After leaving school or college, a child still counts as being in full-time education until the end of a fixed period after s/he leaves. The end of this period is called the 'terminal date'[41] and it coincides with the beginning of the next school term. A school leaver still counts as a child for child support up to the Sunday following this date unless s/he is 19 before that date, in which case it is the Sunday following the Monday before the 19th birthday.[42]

Time of leaving school	Terminal date
Christmas	First Monday in January
Easter	First Monday after Easter Monday
May/June	First Monday in September

If a child is under school-leaving age when s/he leaves school, s/he is treated as leaving school on the date s/he reaches that age. The terminal date is the next one after that date.[43] The upper limit of compulsory school age is, in England and Wales, the last Friday in June for a young person who will be 16 before the first day of the following September term. In Scotland, it is compulsory to be in education until 31 March if a young person's 16th birthday falls between 1 March and 30th September, or the first day of the Christmas holidays if the 16th birthday falls between 1 October and the following 28 February. If a child is entered for an external examination before s/he leaves school, the terminal date is the first one that follows the last exam.[44]

If a young person does any paid work of 24 hours or more a week before the terminal date, s/he no longer counts as a child unless the work is temporary and expected to end before the terminal date.[45]

Breaks in full-time education

Someone at school or college still counts as a child if there is a temporary break in full-time education.[46] It does not matter whether s/he is under or over 16 when education is interrupted.

Any break must be reasonable in the particular circumstances of the case. The break can be up to six months or, if it is due to physical or mental illness or disability of the child, longer. The break must not be (or likely to be) followed immediately by a period on work-based training for young people (Skillseekers in Scotland), or by education received because of the child's job.[47]

16/17-year-olds not in full-time education

A 16/17-year-old who is no longer at school or college full time still counts as a child for child support purposes if s/he is registered for work or work-based learning for young people, but has not actually started either.[48] This lasts for the 'extension period' (see below). S/he still counts as child if s/he does paid work so long as it is *either* for less than 24 hours a week *or* is temporary and expected to end before the end of the extension period.[49]

A 16/17-year-old entitled to income support or income-based jobseeker's allowance in her/his own right does not count as a child in this situation.[50]

The extension period begins on the day the person would otherwise stop being treated as a child (usually the terminal date – see p19). The date it ends depends on the terminal date. If the terminal date is after the end of the relevant extension period, there is no extension period.

The extension periods for 2007/08 are:[51]

Terminal date	Extension period ends
3 September 2007	6 January 2008
7 January 2008	30 March 2007
31 March 2008	22 June 2008
1 September 2008	4 January 2008

Note: the rules on terminal dates and the extension period are different for child benefit.

4. **Person with care**

A **'person with care'** is the person with whom the child has her/his home (see p22) and who usually provides day-to-day care (see p21) for the child.[52] There may be more than one person with care of a particular child.[53]

A person with care is usually a parent of the child or another individual but could also be, for example, an organisation such as a children's home. However, a person with care *cannot* be a local authority, or someone looking after a child who has been placed with her by the local authority.[54] The only exception to this rule is if someone in England and Wales is the child's parent and the local authority has allowed a child it looks after to live with her/him.[55]

Day-to-day care

The Child Support Agency (CSA) normally looks at how many nights of care a person provides when deciding who is a person with care.[56] To count as providing day-to-day care, a parent must provide care of at least 104 nights per year on average.[57] The amount of care can be averaged over a different period if this will be more representative of actual arrangements. The CSA adds together the time a child spends with each parent and decides who is the principal provider of care. In some cases where care is shared equally, other factors may be taken into account to determine which parent is treated as a non-resident parent – eg, the parent who does not receive child benefit.[58]

A person who is responsible for a child's daily routine may be providing day-to-day care even if some things are done by another person – eg, a childminder. It may not be necessary for a person to be *with* the child for at least 104 nights a year if she is nevertheless the person responsible for overall care during that time.

Example
A mother on night shifts leaves her son in the care of grandparents for 22 nights a month. She decides what he will eat and when he will go to bed, and each morning she dresses him and takes him to school. Using the 104 nights average, she does not provide day-to-day care, but, using the ordinary meaning of those words, she is the principal provider of day-to-day care.

In two situations, the care actually being provided does not matter. Where a child is placed with her/his parent by a local authority in England and Wales, then even though the local authority is legally responsible, the parent is treated as providing day-to-day care.[59] Where a child is a boarding-school boarder or a hospital inpatient, the person who would otherwise provide day-to-day care is treated as providing day-to-day care.[60]

Where the CSA cannot identify one person with whom the child spends the most time, it may decide that the person receiving child benefit is the person with care[61] (see also p22). The result can be that someone who would otherwise be a parent with care is treated as the non-resident parent (see p22). On the other hand, in some cases, there may be no one providing day-to-day care and so no one who can be treated as a person with care.

Home

The person with care must have a home with the child. A home is the physical place where the child lives. It is different from a household (see below). Where a child has her/his home is usually clear. A child may have more than one home, in which case the CSA decides which is the principal home.[62]

Parent with care

A **'parent with care'** is a person with care who is also a parent (see p15) of a qualifying child (see p18).[63] Currently, a parent with care who claims income support or income-based jobseeker's allowance is treated as applying for child support unless she opts out (see p38).[64]

However, where there is a shared care situation, someone who might otherwise be a parent with care may be treated as a non-resident parent (see p124 in 'new rules' cases and p299 in 'old rules' cases).

5. **Non-resident parent**

A **'non-resident parent'** ('absent parent' is the terminology used in 'old rules' cases, but we use 'non-resident parent' throughout this *Handbook* for simplicity) is a parent (see p15) who is not living in the same household (see below) as his child, and the child has her/his home with a person with care[65] (see p20) – eg, where the parents of a child have separated. In cases where people share the care of a child, a person who would otherwise be a parent with care may be treated as a non-resident parent (see p124 in 'new rules' cases and p299 in 'old rules' cases).[66] If a parent thinks that a decision identifying him as a non-resident parent is wrong, he should seek advice. If the non-resident parent begins living in the same household as the parent with care, the calculation immediately ceases to have effect.

Both parents can be non-resident parents, in which case they can both be required to pay child maintenance (see p310).[67]

Household

'Household' is not defined in child support legislation. A household is something abstract, not something physical like a home (see above). It is either a single person or a group of people held together by social ties.[68] In many cases, whether people are members of the same household is obvious. Where it is not obvious whether several people share a household, the Child Support Agency (CSA) will consider factors such as whether they have any alternative address, whether they share living areas, who pays bills and how household chores are divided.[69] No one factor on its own should be conclusive. There does not need to be any settled intention about future arrangements for a household to exist.[70]

The meaning of household has been considered in family law and social security cases as well as child support cases, and this caselaw may be used to help make child support decisions. For some of the social security caselaw, see CPAG's *Welfare Benefits and Tax Credits Handbook*.

Some guidelines from the caselaw are as follows.
- There can be two or more separate households in one house.[71] CSA staff are advised that 'household' and 'home' are different concepts and that a single home may contain a number of households.[72]
- One or more members of a household can be temporarily absent from the home without ending their membership of the household.[73]
- There does not need to be a relationship like marriage for people to share a household – eg, two sisters can form a household.[74]

Where there is a polygamous marriage there may be several partners in one household or several households.[75] The CSA will decide whether the qualifying child lives in a different household from at least one of the parents when establishing whether there is a non-resident parent.

A couple may become members of the same household even if they get back together briefly, assuming that they are hoping the relationship and, therefore, the domestic set-up will be indefinite.[76] In this case, a new household could be formed immediately, whether or not it then ceases to exist a few weeks or months later. A household can be formed as soon as people live together intending to form a household, and before they have arranged joint domestic and financial matters.

Advisers should be careful when arguing that a supposed non-resident parent shares a household with a parent with care on benefit. A decision by the CSA or an appeal tribunal that the couple share a household for child support purposes is likely to mean that the couple share a household for benefit or tax credit purposes. For more information about cohabitation decisions in benefits and tax credits, see *CPAG's Welfare Benefits and Tax Credits Handbook*.

6. **Relevant child**

A **'relevant child'** is the term used by the Child Support Agency (CSA) in 'new rules' cases for a child other than the qualifying child for whom the non-resident parent or his partner receives child benefit.[77] This can include a child who does not live with the parent all the time – eg, because s/he is at boarding school or there is a shared care arrangement for her/him.

If this relevant child is cared for by a local authority either for part or all of the time, s/he will continue to count as a relevant child if the non-resident parent or his partner receives child benefit for her/him.[78]

The number of relevant child(ren) is important because it affects the calculation of child maintenance. In 'old rules' cases, the term is not used, but children who live with the non-resident parent may affect the maintenance assessment in different ways.

Relevant non-resident child

'Relevant non-resident child' is a term used by the CSA in 'new rules' cases to refer to a child of the non-resident parent for whom an application for child support cannot be made because the non-resident parent is liable to pay maintenance under a court order for her/him.[79] This is a child who would have been considered a qualifying child if an application for child support maintenance could be made for her/him. It could be a child who does not live with the non-resident parent, or a child whose care is shared between the non-resident parent and someone else in a situation where the child would be regarded as a qualifying child but for the court order. See p28 for more information about when a court order prevents an application for child support.

The number of relevant non-resident child(ren) also affects the calculation of child maintenance in 'new rules' cases. Although the term 'relevant non-resident child' is not used in 'old rules' cases, child maintenance paid under a court order may affect the calculation.

7. **Welfare of the child**

Whenever the Child Support Agency (CSA) or Jobcentre Plus makes a discretionary decision about a case, they must take into account the welfare of any child likely to be affected by the decision.[80] This also applies to discretionary decisions made by appeal tribunals and the child support commissioners.

Many child support decisions involve choosing between alternatives, such as whether a person is habitually resident or not, but these are not usually discretionary decisions. A person has discretion only if, once s/he has decided on the facts of a case and what the law requires, s/he still has a choice about what decision to make. Examples of discretionary decisions in child support include whether to make a reduced benefit decision, or how to collect or enforce maintenance, including whether to make a deduction from earnings order.

Only the welfare of a child has to be taken into account (see definition of a child on p18), not that of any adults involved. However, it is not just qualifying children or those named in the maintenance application who must be considered. The situation of any child likely to be affected by the decision must be looked at[81] – eg, a child of the non-resident parent's new family, known under the 'new rules' as a 'relevant child', or another child of the non-resident parent who does not live with him.

The welfare of children is 'a general principle' in child support law.[82] Considerable weight should be given to this.[83] However, because there is usually no discretion about whether to make a calculation (or 'old rules' assessment), or about the amount of maintenance due, there are only a limited number of cases in which the welfare of a child can make a difference. It is important to give the CSA/Jobcentre Plus full details at the earliest stage about the effect a discretionary decision may have on a child's welfare.

'**Welfare**' includes the child's physical, mental and social welfare. For example, if a deduction of earnings order (see p443) would prevent a non-resident parent from visiting a child, that child's emotional welfare may be affected. However, an order may mean the parent with care has more money coming in, which may improve the child's physical and social welfare.

In the case of a reduced benefit decision, if there is no risk of harm or undue distress (see p61), the welfare of any child(ren) likely to be affected must always be considered.[84] However, an effect on the welfare of a child may not stop a decision being made unless there is a special factor – eg, the age or health of a child or the parent with care.[85] A reduced benefit decision cannot be made in any case if the qualifying child, parent with care or her partner is disabled and this is reflected in their benefit or tax credit payments (see p67), so it is important that the special factors which make the welfare of the child significant are considered widely, looking at all children who could be affected and considering conditions other than a disability for which benefit is paid.

Generally, the welfare of a child has to be balanced with the benefits of receiving maintenance for that child or other children. This is why it is usually only in certain situations that the welfare of a child will be deemed more important than the principle that parents should maintain their children. For example, if the non-resident parent has a child in his household who is disabled and who would be adversely affected if there were less money to spend on her/his living costs, or by the implications of enforcement action, this might mean that the welfare of the child meant certain enforcement action should not be taken. Guidance to decision makers states that in any discretionary decision, the child's best interests should always be considered.[86] However, decision makers are also reminded that, when deciding on enforcement action, the welfare of the child principle should not be applied so as to avoid full use of the CSA's powers of enforcement, unless it is genuinely appropriate,[87] and that generally, the principle should be considered along with the other principles of child support.[88]

Reasoning on the welfare of all children who could be affected has to be fully documented, and it may be useful to ask to see the welfare of the child considerations. If a decision has been made in ignorance of its effect on a child, the information should be supplied and the CSA/Jobcentre Plus asked to reconsider. It may be possible for a decision which should involve the welfare of the child principle to be revised or superseded (see Chapter 18), or appealed (see Chapter 19). If the decision cannot be appealed – eg, if it is about enforcement, a

CSA client should consider making a complaint or applying for a judicial review (see p383).

In addition to the general principle of the welfare of children expressed in child support law, the UK is also bound to comply with international obligations, including a commitment to the welfare of children under the United Nations Convention on the Rights of the Child. This means that in instances where more than one interpretation of the law is possible, the one chosen should be that which more closely complies with protecting the welfare of children.[89]

8. Family

'**Family**' is defined as a couple or a single person and any children in the same household for whom the single person or at least one member of the couple is responsible.[90]

A couple is:[91]

- a man and a woman who are married to each other and living in the same household;
- a man and woman who are living together as husband and wife but are not married to each other;
- a couple registered as civil partners who live in the same household;
- a same-sex couple living together as if they were civil partners.

The definton of family includes those living in polygamous marriages. For a discussion of when a couple are living together as husband and wife, or as civil partners, see CPAG's *Welfare Benefits and Tax Credits Handbook*. The children living with a couple or lone parent do not have to be biological or adopted children to count as family members, but foster children are not included. A person under 16 cannot be a member of a couple.[92]

Partners

A partner in the context of this *Handbook* means a married partner living with her/his spouse, a man or woman living with her/his civil partner, or someone living with a partner 'as husband and wife' or 'as if they were civil partners' (see above). Since December 2005, same-sex couples have been able to register as civil partners, and various aspects of the law have been changed to reflect this.[93] Child support legislation was amended with effect from 5 December 2005 to take account of these provisions.[94] From that date, civil partners who are parents (including those who have adopted a child) are treated, for most child support purposes, in the same way as married partners. Parents who are living with a same-sex partner but have not formed a civil partnership are treated in the same way as couples of the opposite sex who are living together but have not married. Before 5 December 2005, same-sex couples were *not* treated as partners. However, it has been decided that this treatment, which under the 'old rules' could have resulted in a non-resident parent in a same-sex partnership paying higher child support contributions than someone in an opposite sex partnership, did not constitute unlawful discrimination.[95]

The change in the law since December 2005 has several implications for same-sex couples. For example, if a same-sex partner of a parent with care applies for income support or income-based jobseeker's allowance, the parent with care is treated as applying to the Child Support Agency. There is also an effect on the amount of child support in some 'old rules' cases (eg, if the couple share housing costs or if the partner's income affects the assessment).

9. **Habitually resident in the UK**

The Child Support Agency (CSA) cannot make a maintenance calculation unless the person with care, non-resident parent and qualifying child are all habitually resident in the UK.[96] The requirement for the person with care to be habitually resident does not apply if that 'person' is an organisation.[97]

The UK means England, Scotland, Wales and Northern Ireland (including coastal islands like the Isle of Wight). It does not include the Isle of Man or the Channel Islands.[98]

Habitual residence is covered fully in CPAG's *Migration and Social Security Handbook*.

If a person is not habitually resident in the UK, see p32.

Meaning of habitual residence

A person is habitually resident if s/he is ordinarily resident and has been for an appreciable period of time.[99] For child support purposes, habitual residence is to be considered bearing in mind that the purpose of child support is the social need to require non-resident parents to contribute to the maintenance of their children.[100] Ordinary residence means 'residence for a settled purpose'.[101]

While each case is different and a decision has to take into account all of the person's circumstances and intentions, some of the most important factors to consider when deciding on habitual residence are:

- the person's normal centre of interest or connections to a particular place;
- the length, continuity and purpose of residence in the UK;
- the length and purpose of any absence from the UK; *and*
- the nature of the person's work.

If the non-resident parent is employed by the civil service, the armed forces, a UK-based company, a local authority or the NHS (including Trusts) he will be deemed habitually resident.[102]

Although the cases do not directly concern the jurisdiction of the CSA, caselaw gives the following guidelines.

- A person can habitually reside in more than one country or in none.
- Habitual residence can continue during an absence from the UK.[103]
- A person cannot be habitually resident in the UK if s/he has never been here.
- A person who leaves the UK intending never to return to reside will stop being habitually resident in the UK on the day s/he leaves.[104]
- A person held in a country against her/his will may not be habitually resident there, even after long residence (but see below).[105]
- A person unlawfully in the UK may be habitually resident.[106]

A person returning to the UK after an absence may have remained habitually resident in the UK during her/his absence.[107] When deciding whether a person has ceased to be habitually resident in the UK for child support purposes, the emphasis should be on the nature and degree of past and continuing connections with the UK and intentions for the future.[108]

Children

For a child, habitual residence depends on where the parent or person with parental responsibility lives. If there are two such people who live apart, one parent should get the consent of the other parent to a change in the residence of the child, otherwise the child may be considered to have been abducted. If there is only one person with parental responsibility, the child's residence changes with that person's.[109]

If a child has been abducted, s/he is considered still to be resident with the person with whom s/he was lawfully living, unless that person later agrees to the move.[110] Agreement might be assumed if that person does not act.[111] However, if a child is of sufficient maturity, her/his views may prevail in a child abduction case.[112]

10. **The role of the courts**

You should seek legal advice about any court proceedings. The following is not intended to be a comprehensive guide to the law.

The courts cannot make or vary an order for periodic payments of child maintenance where the Child Support Agency (CSA) has jurisdiction to make a calculation.[113] The CSA has jurisdiction if the child is a qualifying child and all the relevant parties (child and parents) are habitually resident in the UK. This applies even if the CSA *would not* in fact make a maintenance calculation.[114]

However, courts have the power to make certain orders in relation to maintenance – eg, consent orders, orders in relation to special expenses or maintenance orders where the young person is no longer considered a child by the CSA. Courts can also vary orders, unless a maintenance calculation has been made or a voluntary application is possible.[115]

The situation regarding 'consent orders' is complex. A **'consent order'** is an order made by the court with the written consent of both parties. It is legally binding and can be enforced like any other court order and cannot be changed by one party without the court's permission. This prevents an application to the CSA unless the parent with care is treated as applying because s/he is on income support (IS) or income-based jobseeker's allowance (JSA) (see Chapter 5). A consent order is useful where one party wants to prevent the other from voluntarily applying to the CSA in the future. However, if the order is made after 3 March 2003 this will only prevent an application for up to one year.

Parents who want a consent order can agree with each other what should go in it, but should seek assistance from a solicitor or law centre to turn that agreement into a draft order to be submitted to the court. This is because a consent order needs to be made as part of a formal application to the court and must refer to the family law provisions under which it is made. The wording of the order is important – eg, a consent order containing an order to provide maintenance for the parent with care and undertakings to provide maintenance for the children may not prevent a calculation by the CSA.[116] However, in some circumstances it will be right to interpret both undertakings and orders as a whole without any distinction.[117]

From 3 March 2003 a voluntary application to the CSA, whether made by an adult or by a qualifying child in Scotland (see pp37 and 38) cannot be accepted (ie, the CSA will refuse to make a calculation) if there is in force:[118]

- a written maintenance agreement made before 5 April 1993 (see p38);
- an order made before 3 March 2003; *or*
- an order made after 3 March 2003 that has been in force for less than a year.

The child support scheme does not change the court's powers in relation to other aspects of relationship breakdown – eg, contact and residence orders, maintenance for a spouse or civil partner, property division and related parentage disputes (for which see p17).

A CSA decision refusing to make a calculation can be appealed to an appeal tribunal (see Chapter 20). A court ruling that the court has no jurisdiction can be appealed or judicially reviewed (see p383).[119] No case should be outside the jurisdiction of both the CSA and the courts.

If a court order is cancelled because it was made by mistake when a CSA calculation was in force, any payments made under the order are treated as payments of child support maintenance.[120]

If a court order ceases to have effect because of a maintenance calculation (see p357), but the CSA revises the decision and decides no maintenance is payable as the previous decision was made in error, the court order revives and any child support maintenance already paid counts as paid under that order.[121]

The courts also deal with appeals about parentage (see p17).

If the Child Support Agency has jurisdiction

Until a calculation is made

Even where an application could be made to the CSA (but has not been), an agreement for periodical payments for a child (in Scotland, aliment) can be entered into.[122] However, any clause included which claims to prevent anyone from applying to the CSA is void.[123] Anyone who considers s/he would get a better deal from an agreement than under the maintenance calculation may wish to try to enter into one. If it is made into a consent order (registered agreement in Scotland) after 3 March 2003 it only stops a party to the agreement from voluntarily applying to the CSA for one year from the date it was made (see p38).[124]

The court can also use its powers to vary an existing agreement (whenever made) by *increasing* periodic child maintenance due under that agreement,[125] but not by *adding* a requirement to pay periodic child maintenance, unless the parties consent in writing.[126] A person who does not want to apply to the CSA, or who is waiting for a CSA decision, can go back to court to increase (or reduce) maintenance. This is especially important if it is unclear whether the CSA has jurisdiction (eg, the agreement does not clearly meet the rules for preventing a voluntary application), as it allows the level of child maintenance to be reconsidered quickly by the court and not left unchanged until any CSA decision is finally made.

Effect of a calculation on existing court orders and agreements

When a maintenance calculation is made, any existing court order or maintenance agreement either ceases to have effect or has effect in a modified form in relation to periodic payments.[127] The existence of a court order or agreement may mean that the amount of the calculation is 'phased in' (see p355). Where there is a court order, the CSA may make a maintenance calculation following an application from a parent with care on IS/income-based JSA, or, where the order was made after 3 March 2003 and has been in force for more than one year, a voluntary application.

These rules apply even to 'clean break' orders/agreements. There are conflicting court decisions on whether the child support scheme (or changes made to it) allows the court to re-open the capital/property part of such an order.[128] The arrangement may be self-adjusting to address the effect of any maintenance calculation which may be made. This could mean a legal charge on the transferred home so that the non-resident parent could recover any sums paid under the child support scheme from the transferred asset.[129] It could also mean an order that the non-resident parent top up any future calculation to a certain total amount of maintenance.[130]

If a child maintenance calculation is made for all of the children still covered by a court order, that order ceases to have effect on the effective date of the calculation – ie, two days after the calculation is made for applications from parents on benefits, and two months and two days after a voluntary application if the court order was made on or after 3 March 2003 and has been in force for at least a year (see p357).[131] If a maintenance assessment is made (this could only happen where a parent with care on IS/income-based JSA's application falls to be made under the 'old rules' and has not yet been decided), the court order ceases to have effect two days after the assessment is made.[132]

If the order includes provisions for additional maintenance, such as education or training expenses of a child or for a disabled child's special needs, only the elements for periodical maintenance for a qualifying child should cease to be in force. If the order is made solely for these additional expenses, it remains in force.[133] Parts of the order for matters other than periodic maintenance for the children named in the calculation (eg, other children or spousal maintenance) remain in force.[134]

In Scotland, if the CSA ceases to have power to make a calculation in respect of a child, the original order revives from the date it ceases to have that power.[135] The same is not explicitly stated for England and Wales, which means that the original order does not revive when CSA involvement ceases. However, it could be argued that it should apply since the court order has not been revoked but simply ceased to have effect for the duration of a maintenance calculation. If the original order does not revive, a new agreement or consent order will need to be negotiated. If this is no longer possible, a parent may have no other option than to use the CSA to calculate and enforce child maintenance.

Maintenance agreements are unenforceable from the effective date (see p368) of the calculation.[136] Again, this only affects the part of the agreement to pay periodic maintenance for the children named in the calculation. The agreement remains unenforceable until the CSA no longer has the power to make a calculation.[137] Any court order made after the agreement becomes unenforceable for children *not* covered by the CSA calculation can be backdated to the date of the calculation.

Notifications

As well as notifying the parties about the calculation (see p354), the CSA must notify the court in which the order was made or registered.[138] Similarly, where a court makes an order which affects, or is likely to affect, a maintenance calculation, the relevant officer of the court (see p78) must notify the CSA of this if s/he knows a calculation is in force.[139]

Additional maintenance

Even where the CSA has jurisdiction, the courts may still be able to make orders for children who are no longer qualifying children, and can still make orders for:[140]

- maintenance for stepchildren of the non-resident parent – ie, children who were accepted by him as members of his family when they used to live with him, but who are not qualifying children;[141]
- maintenance for expenses of a child's education or training for a trade, profession or vocation;[142]
- maintenance to meet expenses of a child's disability – a child counts as disabled if s/he is getting disability living allowance (DLA) or does not get DLA but is blind, deaf, without speech, or is substantially and permanently handicapped by illness, injury, mental disorder or congenital deformity.[143] The courts may even extend payments beyond the child's 19th birthday;[144]
- maintenance for a spouse or civil partner;
- maintenance from the person with care;[145] *and*
- child maintenance in excess of the maximum worked out under child support rules.[146]

The courts can backdate these maintenance orders to the effective date (see p368) of a maintenance calculation, if the application is made within six months of that date.[147] Backdating is at the court's discretion and can ensure that other maintenance is in step with child support.

The courts' power to make a lump-sum award for a child will not be used to provide regular support for the child, but only to meet a need for a particular item of capital expenditure – eg, acquiring a home.[148]

If the Child Support Agency has no jurisdiction

If the CSA does not have jurisdiction – eg, because one parent or the qualifying child is not habitually resident in the UK, the court may make and vary a maintenance order. In addition, where there is a pre-3 March 2003 court order for child maintenance, a post-3 March 2003 order which has been in effect for less than a year, or a pre-April 1993 agreement (see p38), the courts have the power to vary such orders and agreements.[149]

In the past, many courts used calculations under the 'old rules' CSA formula as a guide when setting levels of child maintenance. They may now decide to do so using the 'new rules' calculation, so parents seeking variation of an order or agreement can ask their solicitors to prepare a calculation. The calculation currently used for new CSA applications is likely to be seen as 'highly' persuasive but not legally binding on courts (as the 'old rules' formula was in the past).[150]

This principle has been emphasised in relation to the 'new rules' scheme in Scotland.[151] The courts also have the power to enforce orders and agreements, including those made by courts, in other countries.[152]

If a voluntary application to the CSA by an adult cannot be made because of a pre-April 1993 written maintenance agreement (see p38), the courts cannot make or revive an order, except with the parties' consent (see p28).[153]

Although the courts can revoke child maintenance orders, this is not usually done simply to allow an application to be made to the CSA.[154] If revocation is being considered, advice should be sought on the likely child maintenance calculation.

In England and Wales applications for maintenance are made to the family proceedings (magistrates') court, the county court or High Court. In Scotland they are made to the sheriff court or Court of Session.

If a maintenance calculation is cancelled because one of the parties moves abroad (see p361), an application for maintenance can be made to the court. If the application is made within six months of the end of the maintenance, the order can begin from that date.[155]

Notes

1. The duty to maintain
1   s1(1) CSA 1991

2. Parent
2   s54 CSA 1991
3   s39 AA 1976; s39 A(S)A 1978; s26(2) CSA 1991 Case A
4   s30 HF&EA 1990; s26(2) CSA 1991 Case B
5   s27(3) HF&EA 1990
6   ss27(1) and 29(1) HF&EA 1990
7   s27 Family Law Reform Act 1987 came into force on 4 April 1988 (there was no equivalent provision for Scotland). The father of a child born before that date is always the man who provided the sperm; *Re M(Child Support Act: Parentage)* [1997] 2 3 FCR 383, [1997] 2 FLR 90, [1997] Fam Law 536. s49(4) HF&EA 1990 came into force throughout Great Britain on 1 August 1991. See also *J v C and E (a child)* [2008] EWCA Civ 551

8   s29(2) HF&EA 1990
9   s28(2) HF&EA 1990; *Re CH (Contact: Parentage)* [1996] 1 FCR 768, [1996] 1 FLR 569, [1996] Fam Law 274
10 s28(6) HF&EA 1990
11 s28(3) HF&EA 1990
12 See *Re D (a child appearing by her guardian ad litem)* [2005] UKHL 33
13 Because such a clinic would not have a UK licence: *U v W (A-G intervening)* [1997] 3 WLR 739, [1997] 2 CMLR 431, [1997] 2 FLR 282
14 Human Tissue and Embryos (Draft) Bill 2007
15 s26 CSA 1991
16 Under s55A or 56 Family Law Act 1986, Art 32 Matrimonial & Family Proceedings (Northern Ireland) Order or s7 LR(PC)(S)A 1986
17 s26(2) CSA 1991 Case E and s5(1) LR(PC)(S)A 1986
18 s26(2) CSA 1991 Cases A1 and A2

19 s26(2) CSA 1991 Case F(a)(i) in 'relevant proceedings' under s12(5) Civil Evidence Act 1968 or affiliation proceedings
20 s26(2) CSA 1991 Case F(a)(i) in 'relevant proceedings' under s8(5) Civil Evidence Act 1968 (Northern Ireland) or affiliation proceedings
21 s26(2) CSA 1991 Case F(a)(ii) in affiliation proceedings
22 s26(2) CSA 1991 Case A3
23 s26(2) CSA 1991 Case B
24 s26(2) CSA 1991 Case B1
25 *R v Secretary of State for Social Security ex parte Shirley West*, CO/568/1998, 30 April 1999, unreported
26 CPA 2004; CP(PSS&CS)(CP)O; CPA 2004 (RACP)O
27 See also *J v C* [2006] EWCA Civ 551
28 Human Tissue and Embryos (Draft) Bill 2007
29 **EW** Part IV AA 1976 'adopted'
S Part IV A(S)A 1978 'adopted'
Both s54 CSA 1991 'parent'
30 In England and Wales, under the Children Act 1989 or in Scotland, under the Children (Scotland) Act 1995
31 s3(4) CA 1989; s3(3) Children (Scotland) Act 1995
32 Arts 3 and 4 CSA(JC)O; Art 3(1)(s) and (t) C(AP)O

3. Qualifying child
33 s3(1) CSA 1991
34 Sch 1 para 10C CSA 1991
35 s55(1) CSA 1991
36 s55(2) CSA 1991
37 White Paper, *A New System of Child Maintenance*, December 2006
38 Sch 1 para 2 CS(MCP) Regs; CCS/12604/1996
39 s55(1)(b) CSA 1991
40 Sch 1 para 3 CS(MCP) Regs
41 Sch 1 para 5(3) CS(MCP) Regs
42 Sch 1 para 5(1) CS(MCP) Regs
43 Sch 1 para 5(2) CS(MCP) Regs
44 Sch 1 para 5(6) and (7) CS(MCP) Regs
45 Sch 1 para 5(5) CS(MCP) Regs
46 Sch 1 para 4(1) CS(MCP) Regs
47 Sch 1 para 4(2) CS(MCP) Regs
48 s55(1)(c) CSA 1991; Sch 1 para 1 CS(MCP) Regs
49 Sch 1 paras 1(1)(b) and 6 CS(MCP) Regs
50 Sch 1 para 1(3)(b) CS(MCP) Regs
51 Sch 1 para 1(2) CS(MCP) Regs

4. Person with care
52 s3(3) CSA 1991
53 s3(5) CSA 1991
54 s3(3)(c) CSA 1991; reg 21 CS(MCP) Regs
55 Reg 21(1)(b) CS(MCP) Regs; s23(5) CA 1989
56 **Old rules** DMG para 2033
New rules PG, Gathering Information and Evidence, Deciding Principal Provider of Day-to-Day Care
57 **Old rules** Reg 1(2) CS(MASC) Regs, 'day to day care'
New rules Reg 1(2) CS(MCSC) Regs, 'day to day care'
58 Reg 8(2) MCSC Regs
59 Reg 13 CS(MCSC) Regs. This applies where a child is placed under s23(5) of the Children Act 1989
60 Reg 12 CS(MCSC) Regs
61 DMG para 2034
62 Reg 1(2) CS(MCSC) Regs, 'home'
63 s54 CSA 1991
64 s6(2) CSA 1991

5. Non-resident parent
65 s3 CSA 1991
66 Reg 8 CS(MCSC) Regs
67 s1(3) CSA 1991
68 *Santos v Santos* [1972] 2 WLR 889, [1972] All ER 246, CA
69 **Old rules** DMG paras 1566-73
New rules PG, Gather Information and Evidence, Household
70 CCS/2318/1997
71 CSB/463/1986
72 **Old rules** DMG para 1569
New rules PG, Gather Information and Evidence, Household
73 R(SB) 4/83
74 R(SB) 35/85
75 **Old rules** DMG para 1571
New rules PG, Gather Information and Evidence, Household
76 CCS/2332/2006

6. Relevant child
77 Sch 1 para 10C CSA 1991
78 Reg 10 CS(MCSC) Regs
79 Reg 11 CS(MCSC) Regs

7. Welfare of the child
80 s2 CSA 1991
81 CCS/1037/1995
82 s2 CSA 1991
Old rules DMG 2505
New rules PG, Specialist Areas, Welfare of the Child

83 *R v Secretary of State for Social Security ex parte Biggin* [1995] 2 FCR 595, [1995] 1 FLR 851
84 IS Guidance and Procedures, Vol 10, part 2, para 34822
85 CCS/1037/1995
86 **Old rules** DMG para 1151
   New rules PG, Specialist Areas, Welfare of the Child
87 **New rules** PG, Enforcement, Welfare of the Child
88 **Old rules** CSG para 151
89 *Smith v Secretary of State for Work and Pensions* [2006] UKHL 35

8. Family

90 Reg 1(2) CS(MCSC) Regs; the 'old rules' definition in Req 1(2) CS(MASC) Reqs is equivalent, but specifies children for whom the single person, or at least one member of the couple, has day-to-day-care.
91 Reg 1(2) CS(MCSC) Regs
92 CCS/7/1992
93 CPA 2004
94 CPA 2004; CP(PSS&CS)(CP)O; CPA 2004 (RACP)O
95 *Secretary of State for Work and Pensions v M* [2006] UKHL 11

9. Habitually resident in the UK

96 s44(1) CSA 1991
97 s44(2) CSA 1991
98 Sch 1 Interpretation Act 1978
99 *Nessa v Chief Adjudication Officer* [1998] 2 All ER 728, [1998] 2 FCR 461, [1998] 1 FLR 879, [1998] Fam Law 329, CA applying *Re J (A Minor) (Abduction: Custody Rights)* [1990] 2 AC 562, [1990] 3 WLR 492, [1990] 2 All ER 961, [1991] FCR 129, [1990] 2 FLR 442, [1991] Fam Law 57, HL; *Cruse v Chittum* [1974] 2 All ER 940; *Brokelmann v Barr* [1971] 3 All ER 29; *Langford v Athanassoglou* [1948] 2 All ER 722
100 R(CS) 5/96; CCS/7207/1995
101 *Shah v Barnet LBC* [1983] 2 AC 309, [1983] 2 WLR 16, [1983] 1 All ER 226, HL
102 s44(2A) CSA 1991; reg 7A CS(MAJ) Regs
103 *Lewis v Lewis* [1956] 1 WLR 200, [1956] 1 All ER 375
104 *Re J (A Minor) (Abduction: Custody Rights)* [1990] 2 AC 562, [1990] 3 WLR 492, [1990] 2 All ER 961, [1991] FCR 129, [1990] 2 FLR 442, [1991] Fam Law 57, HL

105 *Shah v Barnet LBC* [1983] 2 AC 309, [1983] 2 WLR 16, [1983] 1 All ER 226, HL; *Re Mackenzie* [1940] 4 All ER 310
106 *Mark v Mark* [2005] UKHL 42, [2005] WLR 111
107 R(CS) 5/96
108 R(CS) 5/96
109 *Re J (A Minor) (Abduction: Custody Rights)* [1990] 2 AC 562, [1990] 3 WLR 492, [1990] 2 All ER 961, [1991] FCR 129, [1990] 2 FLR 442, [1991] Fam Law 57, HL
110 *Re M (Minors: Residence Order: Jurisdiction)* [1993] 1 FCR 718, [1993] 1 FLR 495, [1993] Fam Law 285, CA
111 *Re A (Minors: Abduction: Acquiescence)* [1992] 2 WLR 536, [1992] 1 All ER 929, [1992] 2 FCR 97, [1992] 2 FLR 14, [1992] Fam Law 381, CA
112 *Re M (A Minor) (Abduction: Child's Objections)* [1995] 1 FCR 170, [1994] 2 FLR 126, [1994] Fam Law 366, CA

10. The role of the courts

113 s8(1) and (3) CSA 1991. It has been decided that this lack of access to the courts is not inconsistent with art 6(1) European Convention on Human Rights – see *R v Secretary of State for Work and Pensions ex parte Kehoe* [2005] UKHL 48
114 s8(2) CSA 1991
115 s8(1) and (3A) CSA 1991
116 CCS/316/1998; CCS/8328/1995
117 CCS/316/1998
118 ss4(10) and 7(10) CSA 1991; reg 2 CS(APD) Regs
119 rules 8.1(2)-(6), 10.24 and 10.25 Family Proceedings Rules
120 Reg 8(2) CS(MAJ) Regs
121 Reg 8(1) CS(MAJ) Regs
122 s9(2) CSA 1991
123 s9(4) CSA 1991
124 ss4(10) and 7(10) CSA 1991; reg 2 CS(APD) Regs
125 s9(6) CSA 1991 (applies unless a calculation is made in an s6 case, when the agreement becomes unenforceable)
126 ss8(5) and 9(5) CSA 1991
127 s10(1) and (2) CSA 1991
128 *Crozier v Crozier* [1994] 1 FLR 126; *Mawson v Mawson* [1994] 2 FLR 985
129 *Smith v McInerney* [1994] 2 FLR 1077. However, an arrangement like this might be void under s9(4) CSA 1991 because it would 'restrict the right to apply for a maintenance assessment', though the commissioner in CCS/2318/1997 thought not.

130 See the arrangement in CCS/2318/
     1997
131 Reg 3(2) CS(MAJ) Regs
132 Reg 3(2)(a), (5) and (6) CS(MAJ) Regs
133 Reg 3(3) CS(MAJ) Regs
134 Reg 3(2) CS(MAJ) Regs
135 Reg 3(4) CS(MAJ) Regs
136 Reg 4 CS(MAJ) Regs
137 Reg 4(3) CS(MAJ) Regs
138 Reg 5(1) CS(MAJ) Regs
139 Reg 6 CS(MAJ) Regs
140 s8 CSA 1991
141 **EW** MCA 1973
     S FL(S)A 1958
142 s8(7) CSA 1991
143 s8(8) and (9) CSA 1991
144 Sch 1 para 3(2)(b) CA 1989. In *C v F*
     [1997] 3 FCR 405 the court held that
     where s8(1) CSA 1991 applies, s8(8)
     CSA 1991 limits this power to children
     aged under 19. However, this seems to
     be wrong because the fact that the CSA
     1991 only applies to those aged under
     19 can hardly prevent an order being
     made under the CA 1989 for a person
     aged over 19.
145 s8(10) CSA 1991
146 s8(6) CSA 1991
147 s29(7) MCA 1973; s5(7) DPMCA 1978;
     Sch 1 para 3(7) CA 1989 as amended
     by Sch 3 paras 3, 5, and 10 CSPSSA
     2000 respectively
148 Sch 1 CA 1989; *Phillips v Pearce* [1996] 2
     FLR 230
149 ss8(3A) and 9(6) CSA 1991; *McGilchrist v
     McGilchrist* [1997] SCLR 800
150 *E v C* [1996] 1 FLR 472; *GW v RW* [2003]
     EWHC 611 (Fam), [2003] 2FLR 108
151 *Sutherland v Sutherland* [2004] GWD 20-
     436
152 MO(RE)A 1992
153 s8(3) and (3A) CSA 1991
154 s8(4) CSA 1991; *B v M (Child Support:
     Revocation of Order)* [1994] 1 FLR 342,
     [1994] 1 FCR 769, [1994] Fam Law 370
155 s29(7) MCA 1973; s5(7) DPMCA 1978;
     Sch 1 para 3(7) CA 1989

Chapter 3

Applications

This chapter covers:
1. Who can apply to the Child Support Agency (below)
2. How to apply to the Child Support Agency (p41)
3. Withdrawing or cancelling an application (p46)
4. Multiple applications (p48)

1. Who can apply to the Child Support Agency

Any person with care (see p20) or non-resident parent (see p22) can apply to the Child Support Agency (CSA) for child maintenance, unless barred by an existing maintenance arrangement (see p38).[1] In Scotland, children who are aged 12 or over can apply to the CSA for child maintenance, provided no application has been made/treated as made by the person with care or the non-resident parent.[2]

If there is more than one person with care of a qualifying child and at least one, but not all, of them has parental responsibility for the child, only those persons with parental responsibility can apply for maintenance.[3] For example, if a child is cared for partly by her/his mother who has parental responsibility, and partly by her/his grandmother who does not have parental responsibility, only the mother can apply to the CSA. Parental responsibility has the same meaning as in other areas of law.[4] Parents who were married to each other when the child was born automatically have parental responsibility which continues even if they divorce.[5] If the parents are not married, the mother can make a formal agreement giving the father parental responsibility.[6] In addition, in England and Wales, if a child's parent is married to (or in a civil partnership with) someone who is not the child's other parent (ie, a step-parent), the parent (or if both biological parents have parental responsibility, both parents) can make a parental responsibility agreement with the step-parent giving her/him parental responsibility for the child.[7] The courts can also give parental responsibility to a person(s) (including a non-parent or step-parent) who apply/ies for it.[8] In England and Wales, if an unmarried father's name appears on a birth certificate on or after 1 December 2003, he has parental responsibility. In Scotland, this applies if an unmarried father jointly registers a birth on or after 4 May 2006. Unmarried fathers who signed a birth certificate before these dates cannot acquire parental responsibility without going through one of the other routes – ie, arranging a formal agreement with the mother or applying for a court order.

Parents with care on income support or income-based jobseeker's allowance

These applicants are sometimes known as 'section 6 applicants', but in this *Handbook* we refer to them as parents with care on income support (IS)/income-based jobseeker's allowance (JSA). Such an applicant must be a *parent* (and not another person) with care who claims or receives IS or income-based JSA, even if someone else claims one of these benefits for her.[9] Such a parent can be treated by the CSA as having applied for a maintenance calculation and recovery of maintenance from the non-resident parent, unless she requests the CSA not to act.[10] A benefit penalty can be imposed for making such a request without good cause (see p55). A court order or maintenance agreement does not prevent such an application being made.[11] The Government has announced that it intends to remove the rule that requires parents on IS and income-based JSA to be treated as applying for child support unless they request the CSA not to act, probably in late 2008.[12] See CPAG's *Welfare Rights Bulletin* for updates.

Neither a non-resident parent nor another person with care can make an application for child maintenance if the parent with care or her partner is receiving IS/income-based JSA, even if she requests the CSA not to act.

Voluntary applicants

Parents with care not on IS/income-based JSA and any person with care who is not the parent of the qualifying child can choose to apply to the CSA. Qualifying children in Scotland aged 12 or over can also do so. Non-resident parents can also apply to the CSA for a maintenance calculation to be carried out. An application for maintenance is voluntary, but may be prevented by an existing maintenance arrangement or court order (see below). These applicants may be called 'section 4' or 'section 7' applicants, but in this *Handbook* we refer to them as voluntary applicants. The CSA may also talk about 'private clients'. People within this group can choose to make a voluntary maintenance agreement and even apply to court for a consent order (see p28), instead of applying to the CSA, or can decide not to apply for maintenance at all.

Written maintenance agreement

A written maintenance agreement for a child prevents a voluntary application (see above) for that child.[13] **'Maintenance agreement'** means a written agreement for making, or securing the making, of periodic payments of maintenance (or aliment in Scotland) to or for the benefit of a qualifying child.[14] An agreement only counts for this purpose if it:[15]

- was made before 5 April 1993. It does not need to have been actually in force before 5 April 1993, and it may have been varied after that date;
- is in writing. This can include an agreement made in correspondence headed 'without prejudice'.[16] While it need not be formal or prepared by lawyers, a spoken agreement is not enough, even if payments were made;[17]
- is an agreement. An offer that is never accepted in writing does not constitute a written agreement.[18] An undertaking made in court proceedings can be an agreement;[19]
- is made by the non-resident parent. The person with care does not have to be a party to the agreement. An agreement between the non-resident parent and the qualifying child does not count.[20] In practice, the agreement will usually be between the parents or their representatives;[21]
- is for periodic payments. An agreement to pay mortgage interest charges and fuel bills as they fall due can count, even though the amounts to be paid are not written down and are not at regular intervals;[22]
- is for the benefit of the child(ren). The child(ren) need not be named in the agreement and an agreement to pay the mortgage for the home where they live counts as for the benefit of those children;[23]
- is 'in force'. An agreement to pay only a nominal amount counts.[24] An agreed change to the arrangement may mean the original agreement is no longer in force.[25]

Maintenance order

A maintenance order made by a court before 3 March 2003 prevents a voluntary application for the child(ren) concerned.[26] If the order was made after 3 March 2003 and has been in force for less than one year it also prevents an application.[27] A **'court order'** only counts for this purpose if it:

- requires the making, or securing the making, of periodic payments of maintenance (or aliment in Scotland) to or for the benefit of a qualifying child.[28] Orders for payment of costs of education or training of the child, or because the child is disabled, or to 'top up' maintenance all count as maintenance orders.[29] Such top-up orders may be made in addition to any liability worked out by the CSA. For details of these, see p32. Because an order only prevents an *application* to the CSA, an order made *after* the application does not stop the CSA making a calculation ('old rules' assessment) or revising or enforcing an existing one. A court order directing capital payments (ie, not periodic payments) does not count as an order.[30] The wording of the order is important – eg, a consent order with provision for maintenance of the parent with care and undertakings to provide maintenance for the children may not prevent an application;[31]

- is in force. It may be arguable that an order is only 'in force' if it has a practical effect.[32] An order is in force where some undertakings or arrangements, such as for residence of the child, are still in effect, even though there is no further liability for maintenance payments[33] or the liability for child maintenance under the order has not yet begun.[34] If a court decides that it has no power to either vary or enforce an order, an application can be made to the CSA;[35]
- is made under one of certain legal provisions (see Appendix 3).[36] The order usually states the legal provision under which it was made.

A person who cannot apply to the CSA because of an agreement/order can:
- ask the court to vary or enforce the amount of maintenance under the order or agreement (see p30);
- where there is an agreement, agree with the other party to end the maintenance part of the agreement or possibly even unilaterally break the agreement so it is no longer in force;
- where there is an order, ask the court to revoke it so that a CSA application can be made (but see p32);
- if she is a parent with care, claim IS/income-based JSA (see p55). However, if benefit is refused before a CSA calculation is made, the CSA will cease to treat the application as having been made (because a court order or written maintenance agreement exists).[37] If a non-resident parent believes that the parent with care has made a benefit claim to obtain access to the CSA, he may want to delay providing information until the benefit claim has been determined, but should explain to the CSA why he is doing that. The CSA will notify the non-resident parent that the application has ceased to be treated as made, if it appears that the non-resident parent knew that the parent with care had been treated as applying.[38]

People with court orders or agreements can use the CSA's collection and enforcement service for amounts due under those orders/agreements, but this facility is currently only available where child support maintenance is also being collected (see p433).

Summary of who can apply to the CSA

Is there a pre-1993 written maintenance → Yes → agreement?

↓

No

↓

Is there a consent order or, in Scotland, a → YES → registered minute of agreement?

↓

No

↓

Voluntary applications may be made to the CSA by a person with care or absent parent, and by a child in Scotland.*

However, if a parent with care claims IS/income-based JSA the CSA will require her to authorise pursuit of maintenance.

There cannot be a voluntary application by a person with care or non-resident parent, or by a child in Scotland. However, if a parent with care claims IS/income-based JSA the CSA has jurisdiction.

* Alternatively, the parties may make an informal arrangement or draw up a written agreement that may be formalised into a consent order or, in Scotland, registered in the Court of Session.

---

2. **How to apply to the Child Support Agency**

Applications under the 'new rules' need not be in writing.[39] In some cases the Child Support Agency (CSA) may direct that the application must be in writing, in which case a form may be provided. Where the CSA issues a form or requests information this must be provided within 14 days unless the CSA is satisfied that there was unavoidable delay.[40] Applications in 'old rules' cases had to be made on a maintenance application form.[41] In practice, the application procedures will be slightly different depending on whether the individual is a voluntary adult applicant, a qualifying child applicant in Scotland or a parent with care on income support/income-based jobseeker's allowance who is treated as applying.

Voluntary applications

In 'new rules' cases, voluntary applications may be made orally or in writing.[42] Where there is no assessment in force, a new application will always be treated under the 'new rules'. However, there may be some cases outstanding where an 'old rules' application has not yet been decided (see p50).

The wide provisions for 'new rules' applications mean they can be made over the phone, in person, or on an application form sent to the applicant, downloaded from the CSA website, or online via the Department for Work and Pensions' e-service. Note that downloaded forms must be printed, signed and returned by post to the Child Support Agency Centre (CSAC). Signing the form confirms that the information given is correct. This is important since there are penalties for knowingly providing false information (see p81).

If the form is completed over the phone, it will be sent to the applicant to be checked. The application forms used are slightly different depending on whether it is a person with care, child in Scotland or non-resident parent who is applying. There is no time limit to return the form – if it is not returned there is no effective application (see p45). If the non-resident parent wishes to apply at a point when the parent with care has already applied, he will be directed to complete a maintenance enquiry form rather than a maintenance application form.

If the CSA requests further information or reissues the application form, the information requested should be provided within 14 days.[43] If this does not occur and the CSA is not satisfied that there was unavoidable delay this may bring forward the date of an effective application (see p45) or where no information is received, cancel the application (see p46).

The application for child maintenance form

This form may be used to gather information to pursue maintenance. It includes sections on:[44]

- personal details – name, address, national insurance (NI) number, date of birth, phone numbers and the best time to phone, armed forces service number;
- child(ren) being applied for – name, date of birth, NI number if over 16, who gets child benefit for the child, maintenance arrangements, shared care arrangements (or local authority care);
- if the parent/person with care is applying, whether the non-resident parent knows s/he is being named as the parent;
- child's education (if between 16 and 19) – school/college, course, type of course, hours a week;
- local authority details (if child is being cared for by it);
- non-resident parent details – name (other names), address or last known address and when lived there, NI number, date of birth, employment details, phone numbers, whether the parent is the father or mother of the child;
- if the parent/person with care is applying, whether the non-resident parent knows where the applicant lives;
- payment details – whether maintenance is to be collected by the CSA, preferred method and frequency of payment to the person with care, bank/building society details;
- representative details – name, address, phone numbers and the best time to phone. If the representative is not a solicitor, an attorney under a power of

attorney, Scottish mental health custodian, mental health appointee or receiver, the applicant must sign the client authority declaration on the form;
• further information – a blank page to add other relevant information.

Any relevant court order or written maintenance agreement (original documents) and the representative's authority (eg, power of attorney document) should be sent with the form and will be returned.

Signing the form confirms that all the information given is correct and complete. This is important since there are penalties for knowingly providing false information (see p81).

Parents with care on income support/income-based jobseeker's allowance

A parent with care is treated as having applied for child support maintenance when she claims income support (IS) or income-based jobseeker's allowance (JSA) or it is claimed on her behalf. This is known as a 'section 6' application.[45] It includes situations where the partner of the parent with care makes the claim.

In this section, for ease of reference, we refer to the IS claim form. However, similar provisions relate to income-based JSA claims, although the initial claim form does not ask about opting out. This will be followed up later when the parent declares that she has children whose other parent does not live with them.

The IS claim form asks for information about children and there is an accompanying leaflet which advises the claimant that her claim for benefit is also a claim for child support maintenance. The parent can ask the CSA not to act or to cease acting in relation to child support at any time – this is known as 'opting out'.[46] There is a section on the form where the parent can indicate that she wants to opt out and why. A parent with care does not have to have good cause to opt out, but should be aware that her benefit may be reduced if good cause cannot be shown.

In 'old rules' cases parents were required to co-operate and to authorise the CSA to pursue the non-resident parent for maintenance unless they opted out (rather than being treated as applying). If they now wish to opt out, they should request the CSA to stop acting. Benefit may be reduced if they do not have good cause.

If a parent with care claims IS or income-based JSA, Jobcentre Plus will arrange an interview. If a parent has indicated on the form that she has good cause or has requested to opt out, good cause will be discussed as part of this interview (see p56).

If the parent has not indicated good cause or made the request to opt out on the form, she may still opt out at any time. A good cause interview will then be carried out by Jobcentre Plus visiting staff after the request to opt out has been received.

If the parent wants to pursue child support maintenance, a child maintenance administration form will be completed at the interview. The completed form will be forwarded to the CSA. If the child maintenance administration form cannot be completed at the visit it must be completed and forwarded to the Jobcentre Plus within 14 days. In some cases, the CSA may indicate that a completed child maintenance administration form is not required – eg, there is a calculation ('old rules' assessment) currently in force and there are no new qualifying children or non-resident parents.

If a parent fails to show good cause or fails to provide information about the non-resident parent, she will be given a four-week 'cooling-off period' to consider the situation (see also p65).[47]

Applications with more than one non-resident parent

In voluntary applications, the applicant can choose to which non-resident parent she wishes to apply for child support maintenance. Thus, an application may be made for maintenance from some, but not all, non-resident parents. A parent with care on IS/JSA will be treated as applying for maintenance from all the non-resident parents of qualifying children unless she opts out. She can opt out in relation to all the non-resident parents or in relation to a specific non-resident parent; in either case, she will still be subject to a good cause interview and face a reduced benefit decision if good cause is not established (see Chapter 5).

When to apply

There are no time limits for making an application to the CSA. One can be made as soon as someone becomes a person with care or a non-resident parent, or at any later date. However, liability to pay child maintenance usually runs from the date the non-resident parent is notified and this cannot occur until an effective application (see p45) is received by the CSA. This means that delaying the application may delay the start of liability. There is no provision for applying in advance – eg, before the birth of a baby.

A benefit penalty can be imposed on a parent with care on IS/JSA who opts out without good cause or does not provide information to pursue maintenance, but only by using the full procedures, including informing the parent with care of the right of appeal (see p398).[48]

Any parent with care on IS/JSA who has not yet been contacted about child maintenance, but who wishes to apply, can do so at the CSA's discretion. This is not a voluntary application and will still be dealt with under all the provisions that usually apply to parents with care on IS/JSA. The parent should contact Jobcentre Plus and request a form, and an interview should be arranged by a visiting officer. If there is any difficulty, parents should contact the CSA, who will be able to advise them on how to proceed. They may also wish to make a complaint about Jobcentre Plus delays or other problems. See CPAG's *Welfare*

Benefits and Tax Credits Handbook for information on complaining about Jobcentre Plus.

Refusal to accept an application

The CSA may decide not to accept an application – eg, because it believes an existing maintenance agreement prevents a voluntary application or because it does not have jurisdiction. If this happens, the would-be applicant should write to the CSA explaining why she believes she is entitled to apply and ask for a written CSA decision. If a written decision is issued, she can try to appeal this to a tribunal (see Chapter 19). If this does not work or if the CSA refuses to respond in writing, a complaint (see p462) and/or judicial review (see p383) should be considered.

Effective applications

Only an effective application allows the CSA to make a maintenance calculation. An application is effective if it is made by phone or in writing according to the CSA's direction.[49] All applicants must provide information to enable the non-resident parent to be identified and traced, and the amount of child maintenance payable by him to be calculated and recovered (see Chapter 5).[50] If a parent with care on IS/JSA does not provide the information, she may receive a reduced benefit decision (see p65). If a voluntary applicant does not supply the information, the CSA may refuse to process the application (see p47).

The CSA may ask the applicant to provide further information or evidence to make an effective application; this may be done over the phone or in writing. The CSA may issue an application for child maintenance form to the applicant. If a form has been previously sent to the applicant, another may be issued. If the information or evidence is received within 14 days of the request, the application takes effect from the date the earlier application was treated as received by the CSA.[51]

For parents with care on IS/JSA, the application is usually treated as made in relation to the claim for benefit (although in some cases a person may be on benefit *before* becoming a parent with care). The relevance of the date of claim/date someone became a parent with care is only important when determining the effective date in special circumstances (see p368). To gather the information needed to pursue maintenance, Jobcentre Plus will complete a child maintenance administration form with the parent with care and forward this to the CSA. Jobcentre Plus will have conducted any further interviews and made any necessary decisions about good cause if the parent with care has opted out or failed to provide information requested (see Chapter 4).

Once an effective application has been made (or treated as made), any other relevant person (non-resident parent or person with care) is informed of the application either by phone or in writing.[52] The relevant person is asked to provide information to enable the maintenance calculation to be made. This can be done over the phone or the person may be asked to complete a form. This form is known as a child maintenance enquiry form. Non-resident parents are informed of the effective date of the calculation and rules on default maintenance decisions at the same time as they are informed of the application.[53] The CSA cannot refuse to deal with an effective application, even if it considers that processing it would be against the welfare of the children concerned.[54] If it refuses to accept an application, see p45.

For delays in dealing with applications, including where the non-resident parent is not co-operating, see p350.

Amending the application

An application can be amended at any time before a maintenance calculation is made, but not to take into account a change which occurs after the effective date (see p368).[55] For details of this and of changes after the effective date, see p351.

3. **Withdrawing or cancelling an application**

Request to cease acting by the applicant

An applicant or parent treated as applying may request that the Child Support Agency (CSA) ceases to act on her/his application for child maintenance.

This request is straightforward in a voluntary application, but a parent with care on income support (IS) or income-based jobseeker's allowance (JSA) may be subject to a good cause interview and a reduced benefit decision. The request by a parent with care on these benefits is known as 'opting out' (see p59).

The CSA cannot refuse this request, whether it is made by a voluntary applicant or parent treated as applying.[56] The request can be made at any time, whether or not a calculation (or 'old rules' assessment) has been made. For more on cancelling calculations, see p360.

Requests to cease acting can be made by phone or in writing to the CSA office processing the application, to the Child Support Agency Centre if it is not clear which office has responsibility, or to Jobcentre Plus by parents with care on IS/JSA.

An application is withdrawn or cancelled by the Child Support Agency

The CSA may withdraw or cancel an application before a calculation is made if the:
- applicant in a voluntary application does not provide information;
- qualifying child dies; or
- IS or income-based JSA ceases.

A voluntary applicant does not provide information

A voluntary application can be withdrawn or cancelled by the CSA if insufficient co-operation is received from the person with care.[57] However, if the applicant is the non-resident parent, the person with care does not wish to co-operate but the non-resident parent does not wish to withdraw the application, it will not be cancelled. A maintenance calculation will be carried out, but no maintenance can be collected and passed on to the person with care.[58]

Cases can be cancelled only where no 'effective application' has been made (see p45). If there is an effective application, a decision must be made and notified, even if it is a decision not to make a calculation (see p352). If an effective application is cancelled against the wishes of the applicant, advice should be sought.

The qualifying child dies

If a qualifying child dies before a calculation has been made, the application is treated as if it had never been made with respect to that child.[59] If the child was the only child named in the application, any calculation ceases to have effect. Otherwise, any calculation is superseded because of a change of circumstances (see p389).

Income support or income-based jobseeker's allowance ceases

An application from a parent with care who is treated as applying (see p38) can be cancelled without a request from the parent with care if the claim for benefit is refused or withdrawn before the calculation.[60] The CSA may still make the calculation but will treat the application as withdrawn or cancelled.

However, if the parent with care stops claiming IS or income-based JSA (or it stops being claimed for her) and a calculation has already been made, this will continue unless she requests that the CSA ceases to act.

The CSA will check whether there is a maintenance agreement or order in force. If there is an agreement/order that would have prevented a voluntary application, the CSA will treat the application as never made – ie, withdrawn.[61] The parent (and non-resident parent where appropriate) will be notified of this decision.[62] The parent will not need to request withdrawal, but where there is uncertainty over whether or not the agreement/order is in force, the parent should request that the CSA cease acting to ensure that this happens.

If no agreement or order is in force which could have prevented a voluntary application, the CSA will write to the parent asking her if she wishes the application to be treated as a voluntary application.[63] The parent will be given one month to reply (28 days in 'old rules' cases). If the parent does not reply, or requests that the CSA cease action, the application will be cancelled.

If the non-resident parent has already been contacted and an effective date set, a maintenance calculation will be completed. The non-resident parent will have a liability for child support maintenance for the period between the effective date and the cancellation of the application.

Short-term or fraudulent benefit claims

Jobcentre Plus treats all parents who claim IS/income-based JSA as having applied for child maintenance (unless the parent opts out), including applications made by the parent's partner, however short term the benefit claim and irrespective of allegations from the non-resident parent that the benefit claim is fraudulent.

Allegations of fraud are referred to the fraud section for investigation (see p67) but do not hold up the CSA's processing of a case. Since benefit *is* being paid, the CSA cannot consider whether the parent with care *should* be being paid.[64]

4. **Multiple applications**

If more than one application for child maintenance is made in respect of the same qualifying child, only one can go ahead.[65] Only an effective application (see p45) counts.[66] If a calculation has not yet been made, the applications are either treated as a single application or one is selected to be considered (see p49).[67] For applications made after a calculation has been made, see p50. For applications, some of which were made before 3 March 2003 (including where there is an existing 'old rules' assessment), see p50.

The decision on whose application goes ahead only determines which applicant has the power to withdraw an application or to request a cancellation of any resulting calculation. It does not affect the outcome of any calculation or have any effect on who is liable to pay any resulting child maintenance. Information included on any competing applications can be taken into account by the Child Support Agency (CSA).

If an application with priority is made by an applicant in Northern Ireland, the CSA there (see p349) deals with the application.[68]

Before a calculation has been made

The rules below apply unless a request is received to cease acting in relation to all but one of the applications.[69] See p50 if there is an existing application to which the 'old rules' apply.

Same person applies more than once

If a person applies either as a voluntary applicant or as a parent with care on income support (IS) or income-based jobseeker's allowance (JSA), and then applies again in the same circumstances before a calculation is made, both applications are treated as if they were the same application.[70]

If a parent with care applies as a voluntary applicant and again because s/he is on IS/JSA (or vice versa) before a calculation is made, the applications are treated as a single application from a parent with care on IS/JSA if this is the situation which now applies, or as a voluntary application if the parent is now not on IS/JSA.[71]

If more than one application is made by the same child in Scotland and maintenance has not yet been calculated, it counts as a single application as long as it is made in respect of the same non-resident parent and person with care.[72]

More than one applicant

The CSA decides which application to deal with as follows.[73]

Applicant	Priority application
Only one person with care	
Person with care and non-resident parent.	Person with care.
Person with care or non-resident parent applies following an application by a child in Scotland.	Person with care/non-resident parent.
More than one qualifying child applies in relation to the same person with care and non-resident parent.	Elder or eldest child.
Both parents are non-resident parents and both apply.	Treated as a single application.
More than one person with care	
Parent with care on IS/JSA makes an application and a person with care (with parental responsibility or parental rights) makes a voluntary application.	Parent with care (the other person with care is not entitled to make a voluntary application if the parent with care is on IS/income-based JSA – see p38).
More than one person with care with parental responsibility (or, in Scotland, parental rights) makes a voluntary application, and one person is treated as a non-resident parent for calculation purposes (see p298).	Person with care not treated as a non-resident parent.

More than one person with care makes a voluntary application and none of the applicants has parental responsibility/rights, or all do and either none can be treated as a non-resident parent, or even after one of the applicants has been treated as a non-resident parent under the calculation, there is still more than one application.	The principal provider of day-to-day care (see p21) in the following order of priority: the person who gets child benefit for the child(ren); the person who, in the CSA's opinion, is the principal provider of day-to-day care.

If the applications are treated as a single one under these rules, that application covers all the children named in either, and the effective date (see p368) is set by the application which was made first.[74]

If more than one person with care applies and each application refers to different children, the CSA treats each application as covering all the children mentioned in all the applications.[75] If the same person with care does not provide the principal day-to-day care for all the qualifying children mentioned in the applications, then separate calculations are made in relation to each person with care.[76]

Once the calculation is in force

No voluntary application can be made if a calculation is in force for an application treated as made by a parent with care on IS/JSA.[77] A calculation in force in respect of a person with care does not prevent the CSA making a new calculation because she becomes a parent with care on IS/JSA.[78] Once a calculation is in force, any subsequent application for maintenance made in the same circumstances (ie voluntary, or where a parent with care is on IS/JSA), in respect of the same person with care, non-resident parent and qualifying child(ren) will not be dealt with.[79] It may, however, be treated as a request for a supersession (see p389).

Applications for additional children

If there is an existing calculation and there is an application for an additional child(ren) of the same non-resident parent cared for by the same person with care, this is a relevant change of circumstances and a new calculation is made which supersedes the existing calculation.[80]

One application before 3 March 2003, and one on or after 3 March 2003

If no assessment is in force

If no assessment is in force, there are transitional provisions for determining how to proceed if there is an existing application under the 'old rules' and a further application is made under the 'new rules' in respect of the same person with care, non-resident parent or qualifying child.[81] These determine whether the applications are treated as a single application or only one is to proceed. The applications do not have to be received at exactly the same time. If one application is not determined by the time the other is received, the following rules apply.[82]

Applicant	Priority application
Person with care applies under the 'old rules' and then under the 'new rules'.	Treated as a single application.
Non-resident parent applies under the 'old rules' and 'new rules' in relation to the same qualifying child.	Treated as a single application.
Child in Scotland applies under the 'old rules' and then under the 'new rules'.	Treated as a single application.
Person with care applies under the 'old rules' or under the 'new rules' and the non-resident applies under either the 'old' or 'new' rules.	Person with care's application has priority.
Child in Scotland applies under the 'old rules' and a 'new rules' application is made by either the person with care or non-resident parent.	Person with care or non-resident parent's application has priority.
More than one child applies under either the 'old' or 'new' rules in relation to the same person with care and non-resident parent.	The application of the elder or eldest child has priority.
Parent with care on IS/JSA applies under the 'old rules' and a person with care (who has parental responsibility) makes a voluntary application under the 'new rules'.	Parent with care's application has priority.
More than one person with care with parental responsibility applies, one under the 'old rules' the other under the 'new rules', and one person is treated as a non-resident parent for calculation/assessment purposes.	The application of the person with care not treated as a non-resident parent has priority.

More than one person with care applies (as above) but none has parental responsibility or they all do and either none can be treated as a non-resident parent or, even after one of the applicants has been treated as a non-resident parent for the calculation/ assessment, there is still more than one application.	The application of the principal provider of day-to-day care in the following order of priority: the person who gets child benefit for the child(ren), otherwise the person who in the CSA's opinion is the principal provider of day-to-day care.

Whether the case is proceeded with as a 'new rules' or 'old rules' case then depends on the effective date of the application with priority or whether a maintenance assessment was previously in force in relation to the same person with care, qualifying child(ren) and non-resident parent. If an assessment was in force within the previous 13 weeks, the application is treated as an application for a maintenance assessment regardless of whether the effective date of the application is before or after 3 March 2003.[83]

A parent with care may cancel her application for a maintenance assessment and reapply after more than 13 weeks in order to have child support calculated under the 'new rules' instead. If, within 13 weeks of the cancellation of the 'old rules' assessment, the non-resident applies, his application will be dealt with under the 'old rules'. However, if the parent with care's 'new rules' application arrives before the non-resident parent's application has been assessed, the parent with care's application takes precedence under the above rules for multiple applications. The result will be to ignore the non-resident parent's application and treat the situation as a single 'new rules' application.

However, this is not a reason for the CSA to delay processing the non-resident parent's application under the 'old rules' before the parent with care's application is received. He may be entitled to compensation for the difference between his 'old rules' and 'new rules' liability (if the latter is more) for the period between the effective date of his application and the effective date of the parent with care's 'new rules' application.[84]

If a maintenance assessment is in force

If a maintenance assessment is already in force and an application is made or treated as made under the 'new rules' in relation to the same person with care, qualifying child(ren) and non-resident parent, the calculation application will not proceed.[85] It is only if the maintenance assessment has ceased, and a new application is made after at least 13 weeks, that it can be dealt with under the new rules (see Chapter 8).

If there is an existing assessment and there is an application for an additional child(ren) of the same non-resident parent cared for by the same person with care this is a relevant change of circumstances and a new assessment is made under the 'old rules' which supersedes the existing assessment.[86] If a new application is made in relation to other people, it is likely to trigger conversion (see below).

New applications that trigger conversion of an existing case

Existing cases will continue to be dealt with under the 'old rules', unless there is a related decision that causes a conversion to the 'new rules'.[87] In many cases this will be triggered by a new application from another person that involves either the non-resident parent or parent with care in the existing assessment. In addition, parents who form new partnerships with people on benefit or partners who each have maintenance but move onto benefit may be affected.

When an existing case converts to the 'new rules', transitional phasing may apply. For more information on when conversion is triggered, and on transitional phasing, see Chapter 8.

Notes

1. **Who can apply to the Child Support Agency**
   1   ss4(1) and 6(1) CSA 1991
   2   s7(1) CSA 1991
   3   ss5(1) and 54 CSA 1991
   4   As in the Children Act 1989 and the Children (Scotland) Act 1995
   5   s3(1) CA 1989; C(S)A 1995
   6   s4(1)(b) CA 1989; C(S)A 1995
   7   s4A CA 1909, as amended by s75 CPA 2004
   8   ss4(1)(a), 4A(1)(b) and 5(6) CA 1989; C(S)A 1989
   9   s6(1) CSA 1991
   10 s6(3-5) CSA 1991
   11 s9(3) CSA 1991; CCS/12806/1996; CCS/12598/1996
   12 White Paper, *A New System of Child Maintenance*, December 2006
   13 ss4(10)(a) and 7(10) CSA 1991
   14 s9(1) CSA 1991
   15 ss4(10)(a) and 7(10) CSA 1991
   16 CCS/12767/1996
   17 CCS/12797/1996
   18 CCS/11052/1995
   19 CCS/8328/1995
   20 CCS/2908/1995
   21 PG, Calculation and Decision Types, Written Maintenance Agreement
   22 CCS/8328/1995
   23 CCS/8328/1995
   24 CCS/12849/1996
   25 CCS/8328/1995
   26 ss4(10)(a) and 7(10)(a) CSA 1991; req 2 CS(APD) Regs
   27 ss4(10)(aa) and 7(10)(b) CSA 1991; reg 2 CS(APD) Regs
   28 s8(11) CSA 1991
   29 Otherwise s8(6)-(8) CSA 1991 would be unnecessary
   30 CCS/4741/1995, upheld by the Court of Appeal in *AMS v CSO* [1998] 1 FLR 955
   31 CCS/316/1998
   32 R(CS) 4/96. However, authorities differ as to whether changes in child(ren)'s residence (eg, from the parent with care to the non-resident parent) mean that an order ceases to have effect (CCS/3127/1995) or not (CCS/2567/1998). In the latter case, the commissioner suggested that it would instead be grounds to seek to vary the court order.
   33 CCS/4741/1995

34 CCS/11364/1995
35 Reg 9 CS(MAJ) Regs
36 s8(11) CSA 1991; reg 2 CS(MAJ) Regs.
Provisions repealed before 1 April 1980
are not listed.
37 s11(3) CSA 1991
38 s11(5) CSA 1991

2. How to apply to the Child Support Agency
39 Reg 3(1) CS(MCP) Regs
40 Regs 3-4 CS(MCP) Regs
41 Reg 2(1) CS(MAP) Regs
42 Reg 3(1) CS(MCP Regs
43 Reg 3(4) and (5) CS(MCP) Regs
44 CSA maintenance application forms,
CSF 001, CSF 003 and CSF 004
45 s6 CSA 1991
46 s6(5) CSA 1991
47 IS Guidance and Procedure, Vol 10 Part
2, para 34927
48 s46 CSA 1991
49 Reg 3(2) CS(MCP) Regs
50 ss4(4), 6(7) and 7(5) CSA 1991
51 Reg 3(4) CS(MCP) Regs
52 Reg 5(1) CS(MCP) Regs
53 Reg 3(2) CS(MCP) Regs
54 R(CS) 4/96; CCS/14/1994; CCS/17/
1994 and CCS/16535/1996
55 Reg 3(6-7) CS(MCP) Regs

3. Withdrawing or cancelling an application
56 ss4(6) and 6(5) CSA 1991
57 PG, Gather Information and Evidence,
Failure to Provide Requested
Information
58 PG, Applications for Child Maintenance,
PWC Does Not Wish to Co-operate
59 s11(3) CSA 1991
60 s11(3) CSA 1991
61 ss4(10) and 11(3) CSA 1991
62 s11(5) CSA 1991
63 s11(4) CSA 1991
64 *Secretary of State for Social Security v
Harmon, Carter & Cocks* [1998] 2 FLR
598, CA

4. Multiple applications
65 s5(2) CSA 1991
66 Sch 2 paras 1, 2 and 3 CS(MCP) Regs
67 s5(2) CSA 1991; reg 4 and Sch 2
CS(MCP) Regs
68 Sch 1 para 6 CS(NIRA) Regs
69 Reg 4(2) CS(MCP) Regs
70 Sch 2 para 1(1) CS(MCP) Regs
71 Sch 2 para 1(2) CS(MCP) Regs
72 Sch 2 para 2 CS(MCP) Regs

73 Sch 2 para 3(1) CS(MCP) Regs
74 Reg 4(3) CS(MCP) Regs
75 Sch 2 para 3(12) CS(MCP) Regs
76 Sch 2 para 3(13) CS(MCP) Regs
77 s4(9) CSA 1991
78 s6(12) CSA 1991
79 Sch 2 para 4 CS(MCP) Regs
80 PG, Calculation and Decision Types,
Relevant Change of Circumstances
81 Sch 3 CS(MCP) Regs
82 CCS/3868/2004
83 Reg 28(1) CS(TP) Regs
84 R(CS) 1/06
85 Sch 3 para 4 CS(MCP) Regs
86 Sch 2 para 6(1) CS(MAP) Regs
87 Reg 3 CSPSSA (Comm12)O; reg 15
CS(TP) Regs

Chapter 4

Parents treated as applying

This chapter covers:
1. Claiming income support or income-based jobseeker's allowance (below)
2. Opting out (p59)
3. Harm or undue distress (p60)
4. Reduced benefit decisions (p65))

When a parent with care applies for income support (IS) or income-based jobseeker's allowance (JSA) she is treated as applying for child support maintenance.

These provisions do not apply to parents when they transfer from IS or income-based JSA to pension credit (PC) or claim PC.

Decisions on 'good cause' for opting out of applying to the Child Support Agency are made by the Department for Work and Pensions – in practice, by Jobcentre Plus staff.

1. Claiming income support or income-based jobseeker's allowance

When a parent with care claims income support (IS) or income-based jobseeker's allowance (JSA), or if her partner makes the claim, she can be treated as applying for child support maintenance.[1]

Note: some people still receive IS or JSA that includes amounts for children or young people; if such a child or young person is a parent with care, she is *not* treated as applying for child support maintenance (see p56).

A parent with care on IS/JSA is treated as applying for maintenance even where there is an existing maintenance agreement or court order in force.

A parent with care may believe she has good reasons for not pursuing maintenance, as it would cause her, or any children living with her, undue harm or distress (see p60). This is known as 'good cause'. In this situation, the parent with care should opt out and give her reasons at the good cause interview.

A parent does not need to show good cause to opt out and she may opt out at any time, for any reason. However, a good cause interview will be arranged when a parent opts out (see p59), and if a parent does not have 'good cause', her benefit may be reduced.

Opting out means that all action on working out and pursuing maintenance ceases.

Unless the parent with care opts out (see p59) she is required to provide all the information she has, which will enable the Child Support Agency (CSA) to:[2]
- identify and trace the non-resident parent;
- calculate the amount of maintenance due from the non-resident parent;
- recover the amount due from the non-resident parent.

A parent with care is only expected to provide information 'so far as she reasonably can'.[3] If there is a reason for not giving the information requested (whether because of 'good cause', or because she does not have the information), she should make sure she explains these reasons, to help avoid a reduced benefit decision. Parents with care who do not know the name of the father should have their word accepted unless their evidence is self-contradictory or inherently improbable (see p62).

Information is gathered at a child maintenance interview, arranged by Jobcentre Plus (see below). The visiting officer has guidance on collecting information in different circumstances – eg, where the parent cannot provide the non-resident parent's full name.

The Jobcentre Plus decision maker examines any reasons for good cause and whether the parent has complied, as far as she reasonably can, with the requirement to supply information. If the decision maker decides there are no good reasons for opting out or failing to supply information, a reduced benefit decision may be made (see p65).

Where there is a dispute or uncertainty over the identity of the non-resident parent, the parent with care may be asked about DNA testing (see p91). If she refuses DNA testing she will be interviewed by Jobcentre Plus staff and, if good cause cannot be shown, a reduced benefit decision may be made (see p65).

Young parents with care

A young parent with care will not be treated as applying for child maintenance unless she can claim IS/income-based JSA in her own right. However, a young parent who is not on one of these benefits may still be able to make a voluntary application for child maintenance (see p38).

Child maintenance interview

Parents with care who claim IS or income-based JSA should be given or sent leaflet CSL302, *How Do I Get Child Maintenance if I'm on Benefits?* This explains what Jobcentre Plus will ask the parent, opting out, good cause procedures and reduced benefit decisions.

The child maintenance interview will normally be arranged by Jobcentre Plus at the parent's home. The parent does not have to be interviewed at home if she would prefer not to be – eg, she could request an interview at a Jobcentre Plus office. She can have another person present (eg, a friend or adviser) if she wishes.

At the interview the visiting officer will deal with any outstanding issues in relation to the benefit claim and take any action in relation to child support. This can include:

- gathering information for the CSA to decide whether a claimant (or her partner) is a parent with care;
- completing a maintenance administration form to gather information needed to pursue maintenance (see below);
- carrying out a good cause interview if the parent with care has opted out, regardless of whether or not good cause has been indicated on the benefit claim form (see p59).

The visiting officer should also answer the parent's questions about child maintenance, and explain how it affects benefits and what would happen if the parent started work.

The parent with care may request time to think things over. This can occur at any time – eg, while a maintenance administration form is being completed or a good cause interview is being conducted. The visiting officer will normally arrange another visit or interview in 14 days.[4] If the parent then fails to provide information, opts out or gives reasons for good cause she will be given a four-week period to provide reasons for opting out, otherwise a reduced benefit decision may be made (see p65). Parents with care who are uncertain about their position should seek advice before a visit or as soon as possible afterwards. If the parent with care is put under pressure, or extra time is refused, a complaint can be made (see p463).

Information from, or suspicions aroused at, a new claims visit can be used to begin benefit fraud investigations (see p67).

Completing the maintenance administration form

The maintenance administration form gathers information on:[5]

- the parent with care and her current partner, if any;
- children living with the parent with care;
- the non-resident parent's (or alleged non-resident parent's) details. The parent with care may be asked further questions about the non-resident parent (see p58);
- existing maintenance arrangements – eg, a court order (where and when it was made, whether it covers all or only some of the children), written maintenance agreement, any other maintenance arrangement (whether or not this is being paid), the amount and frequency of any maintenance being paid and whether there is a pre-1993 property/capital transfer.

When the parent with care signs the form she is declaring that all the information she provided is correct and complete. It is a criminal offence to fail to provide information when required, or knowingly provide false information, and penalties may be imposed (see p450). In practice, if the parent with care fails to provide information she may have a reduced benefit decision imposed, rather than a criminal penalty.

The information from the maintenance administration form is sent to the CSA to process the application.

Additional questions to identify and trace the non-resident parent

If the parent wants to pursue maintenance, but states she does not know the identity of one or more of the non-resident parents, visiting officers are encouraged to probe for information. Questions may be very personal and could be seen as intrusive. They may cover issues such as when and where the parent with care met the non-resident parent, whether they have any mutual friends, and even the non-resident parent's personal appearance. The parent with care does not have to answer, although she should be aware that if she decides not to co-operate without 'good cause', her benefit may be reduced.

Visiting officers are specially trained to deal with sensitive issues and should conduct the interview courteously. The parent with care can ask to be interviewed by someone of the same sex if she prefers. If a parent with care is not happy with the approach or manner of the visiting officer, or the general level of service from Jobcentre Plus, she could consider making a complaint (see Chapter 21).

Written record of the interview

A written record of the interview will be made by Jobcentre Plus. This may include a statement based on what the parent with care has said at the interview about why she is opting out (see p59). Before signing it, she is asked if she agrees with everything that has been written.[6] The parent with care should check that the statement includes all the points she wishes to make.

When the parent signs the statement, she is agreeing that it is a true and complete record. It is, therefore, very important to read it thoroughly so that any changes or additions can be made before it is signed. If there is a dispute about the wording or the emphasis, the parent should ask that her specific concerns be recorded. She could offer to provide a summary of her answers instead. Whether or not the parent with care does sign the statement at the interview, a copy can be requested from the visiting officer for future reference.

The visiting officer forwards the parent's statement and her/his own report as the written record to the Jobcentre Plus decision maker for a decision on whether:
- the parent has given all the information it is reasonable for her to provide; *or*
- there are reasons for good cause.

If the parent with care wants to provide any further information, she should send this to Jobcentre Plus as soon as possible after the interview. This is particularly important if she feels that the interview went badly or she wants to provide further information to assist the decision maker. Jobcentre Plus does not send her the visiting officer's report, though she should see it if a reduced benefit decision is eventually made and appealed (see p403), or if she makes a request under the Data Protection Act.

2. Opting out

A parent with care on income support (IS) or income-based jobseeker's allowance (JSA) may request the Child Support Agency (CSA) not to act in relation to child support maintenance.[7] This request is known as **'opting out'** and may be made even if it is:
- the partner of the parent with care who has claimed benefit; *or*
- a case with an 'old rules' maintenance assessment.[8]

The CSA must cease all action when a request to opt out is made. If the parent has an 'old rules' assessment the procedure will be the same. If she opts out and then opts in again within 13 weeks of a maintenance assesment being in force, the case will continue being dealt with under the 'old rules' (see also Chapter 9).

The request may be worded as a request to opt out or a request that the CSA ceases acting. In addition, the request to opt out need not be in writing and may be made to the Jobcentre Plus who will pass the information on to the CSA. Parents who are concerned may wish to contact the CSA direct.

If the reason given for the request is because:[9]
- she is no longer the parent with care of a qualifying child; *or*
- IS or income-based JSA is no longer claimed by or for her, or paid to or for her,

the CSA will cease all action and there will be no further Jobcentre Plus intervention.

Where no reasons are given or the parent indicates reasons for good cause the CSA will still cease all action immediately. The Jobcentre Plus will carry out a good cause interview (see below) and may make a reduced benefit decision where good cause is not upheld.

Good cause interview

A good cause interview may be carried out:
- at the same time as the child maintenance interview; *or*
- at a further interview if a request for 14 days' thinking time is made at the child maintenance interview (see p56); *or*
- at any other time when a parent with care opts out, regardless of whether or not reasons for good cause are given; *or*

- when a good cause decision is being reconsidered (see p63); *or*
- where a reduced benefit decision has been in force for three years and a decision needs to be made whether to make and impose a further reduced benefit decision.

A parent with care who opts out does not have to show good cause to stop the CSA acting in relation to child support maintenance. However, she may face a reduced benefit decision if good cause is not shown (see p65).

'**Good cause**' is where there is a risk of the parent with care, or any children living with her, suffering harm or undue distress (see below). If a parent with care is trying to show good cause, ideally she should seek independent advice to prepare for the interview (see Appendix 4). She may want to arrange for a friend or adviser to be present. She should think about how she is going to answer the officer's questions. This may involve writing down points she wants to make.

A full good cause interview may not be required if the parent is:

- in a refuge and provides written reasons and/or supporting evidence – eg, a letter from a caseworker, about why there is good cause. A good cause interview will not normally be required;[10]
- claiming good cause on a repeat claim in the six-month linking period where it was previously accepted in relation to the same children. A child maintenance interview will take place to confirm that relevant circumstances have not changed, but a good cause interview is not required (see p64).[11]

A female interviewing officer can be requested and should be provided if the interview covers particularly sensitive issues, such as rape.

A complaint can be made if an interview is conducted in an inappropriate way (see Chapter 21).

The good cause interview is the parent with care's opportunity to show the risk of harm or undue distress (see below) and the possible effect on the welfare of any child(ren) (see p24). The parent with care could have made a list of the points she wishes to make. This also helps in checking that the written statement is correct and complete (see p58). She may be able to supply supporting evidence (see p63) – eg, in the case of past violence.

The visiting officer will include the statement in the written record of the interview (see p58) which is forwarded to the decision maker for a decision on whether to accept good cause or make a reduced benefit decision.

3. Harm or undue distress

The risk of harm or undue distress is referred to as good cause. This section explores the meaning of the risk of harm and undue distress.

A risk of harm or undue distress

It is the *risk* of harm or undue distress that is relevant: there is no need for anything actually to have taken place in the past.[12] There does not even need to have been threats. There need only be a real risk that harm will arise.[13] The fear does not have to be of the non-resident parent, but must be as a consequence of the parent with care:[14]

- being treated as applying;
- providing sufficient information to pursue maintenance;
- taking a DNA test.

A risk of harm or undue distress caused by an unrelated event (eg, one of the parties moving in with a new partner or an ongoing contact or residency dispute) is not relevant. However, hostility around such issues is an important part of assessing whether the above actions would cause harm or undue distress. The risk could arise from a fear of violence from a new partner.[15]

For distress to be sufficient, it must be 'undue', but there is no such qualification in relation to harm, so *any* harm is sufficient. Harm is not limited to physical harm but includes psychological or emotional harm.

Meaning of terms

These terms are not defined in child support legislation and, therefore, are taken to have their ordinary English meaning.[16]

'**Harm**' means to hurt, injure or damage.

'**Undue**' means not suitable, improper, unreasonable, excessive, unjustifiable, disproportionate, illegal, or going beyond what is appropriate, warranted or natural.

'**Distress**' means strain, stress, pressure, anguish, pain, damage, danger, affliction affecting body, spirit or community, or exhausted condition under severe physical strain; distress might also mean 'lack of money or comforts'.

The following are examples of situations where good cause was accepted:

- if children were likely to be distressed by their father's visits ceasing or being curtailed, then it would probably follow that such distress would be undue;[17]
- there was a risk of undue distress to an older daughter who knew her father but not that he had another family;[18]
- there was a risk of harm or undue distress where the parent with care's written evidence stated that Child Support Agency (CSA) activity would probably result in all contact ceasing between the non-resident father and son. Relations were already strained and the father's new wife resented the contact.[19]

'**Risk of harm or undue distress**' covers a wide range of situations – eg, where a step-parent has been accepted as the father or where a couple are having a trial separation and hope to be reconciled in due course. This is borne out by the range of decisions which have been given in the past, although the majority are accepted as having a fear of violence or abuse.

If a child was conceived as a result of rape or sexual abuse, visiting officers are instructed to handle these situations with particular care and sensitivity, but they will not assume that the parent with care does not wish to apply for maintenance. In the case of a risk of violence, Jobcentre Plus staff have to ask the reasons for fearing violence in order to decide whether there are reasonable grounds for the fear (see below). Decision makers have to consider both the risk of physical harm resulting from actual violence and the risk of undue distress caused by a well-founded fear or by receiving threats.

Reasonable grounds

The decision maker must consider whether there are **reasonable grounds** for believing there is a risk of harm or undue distress.

Providing evidence of reasonable grounds

Corroboration of a parent with care's own evidence is not a necessary requirement of social security or child support law.[20] Evidence includes statements and supporting information provided orally or in writing. In some situations, because of the emphasis on preventing fraud, a Jobcentre Plus decision maker may unreasonably refuse to believe the parent with care unless there is independent evidence to support her case. If this happens, Jobcentre Plus should be asked to say why it considers the parent's evidence implausible.

If a parent appeals a decision on good cause, the appeal tribunal must give reasons for disregarding her evidence.[21] However, it may still be reasonable to do so if the evidence is inconsistent, or there is strong contradictory evidence available.

A parent should be as open and honest as possible about her grounds for good cause in order to avoid the decision maker (or tribunal) finding that her evidence cannot be accepted.

In some cases, while acknowledging that a parent has genuine fears of harm or undue distress, the Jobcentre Plus decision maker may not agree that these fears are realistic (see p61). The parent with care knows the people involved and their history and, therefore, is likely to be able to anticipate their reactions, while the decision maker does not. It is, therefore, important for the Jobcentre Plus to explain why it considers the fear is 'fanciful', and to show that its decision is not based on rumour or unfounded opinion.

If a parent's fears seems irrational or disproportionate, this cannot be taken to increase the risk of undue distress in itself, even though those fears may be genuinely held. An objective judgement has to be made about whether there is foreseeable distress which is 'unjustified or unreasonable'.[22] However, irrationality or paranoia are relevant in assessing how such distress might affect a parent.

Supporting documentation

The parent with care may be asked to produce supporting documentation. It is advisable to provide anything which may support the argument that she has good cause. However, it is recognised that not all parents will be able to provide information and this should not prejudice their case (see p62). Evidence could be a police, medical or social work report – eg, after an incidence of violence. It could be a statement from someone who knows the family and the situation – eg, a teacher, religious or community leader, youth worker, neighbour, friend or relative. It could be a statement from the parent's caseworker in a refuge. The statement should, where possible, give that person's recollection of previous events, or assessment of the attitudes or mental state of anyone involved and explain why the parent and/or child(ren) would be likely to suffer harm or undue distress.

Jobcentre Plus has no power to approach third parties to request information about the risk of harm or undue distress (see p74). However, the parent with care could give her permission for it to contact a third party on her behalf, if she prefers not to do so directly.

The decision on good cause

Decision-making staff have to weigh all the information and evidence available when making the decision. The decision maker should be able to show that all relevant evidence and factors have been taken into account.

The welfare of any child(ren) likely to be affected is always considered where good cause is not accepted for the parent with care.[23] This means that the decision maker should consider not only how the qualifing child will be affected, but also any other children whose welfare may be linked to the situation. This could include other children living with the parent with care or the non-resident parent.

The decision maker must also decide whether to set a date for a reconsideration (see below).[24]

The parent will be notified in writing of the decision on good cause.

Reconsideration of good cause

A good cause decision made after 3 March 2003 may be reconsidered at any time.[25] A case may also be reconsidered if good cause was not accepted but no further action was taken because of the welfare of the child.[26] The decision maker may set a date, any time up to three years from the date of the decision, to reconsider the case.[27] A reconsideration may be triggered earlier than this if there is a change in circumstances that indicates reconsideration is appropriate – eg, the parent with care has the non-resident parent's baby.

In some circumstances, the decision maker may decide it is *not* appropriate to reconsider the decision and accept good cause indefinitely – eg, if the qualifying child was conceived as a result of a rape, incest or sexual abuse.[28]

When a good cause decision is to be reconsidered a further visit will be arranged. The parent will be asked if she still does not wish to apply for child maintenance and, if not, to give her reasons for maintaining the request not to act. In practice, this is a further good cause interview. The visiting officer and the decision maker will have information on the reason good cause was accepted previously but the parent must re-make the case for good cause. It will not be sufficient for her to state that her reasons have not changed (unless this is because of rape/sexual abuse); the visiting officer must complete a fresh statement to support good cause. This means showing there is a current risk of undue harm or distress. Jobcentre Plus may take the view that circumstances have changed so that the original reasons for good cause being accepted are no longer valid – eg, if the relationship between the parent with care and non-resident parent has improved or the parent with care has a new partner and there is no longer a risk of violence.

'Old rules' cases where good cause was accepted before 3 March 2003 are never reconsidered. If the parent ceases to claim and then re-claims benefit, the linking period may apply (see below).

Further benefit claim if good cause was previously accepted

Good cause is accepted automatically on a new claim for benefit if a parent with care is making a repeat claim within six months of a previous claim where good cause was accepted, as long as the parent's circumstances have not changed and she still does not wish to pursue maintenance.[29] She must state at the child maintenance visit that her circumstances have not changed since the date of the last decision. This is known as the six-month linking period. In these cases a full good cause interview will not be conducted. The rule also applies to cases where good cause was accepted under the 'old rules', but although good cause will be automatically accepted on the new claim if the case is now dealt with under the 'new rules', it will also be subject to reconsideration in the future (unlike under the 'old rules').

In all other cases, the visiting officer will undertake a full good cause interview and gather information for the decision maker. The decision maker will then make a decision based on this current information. This decision may be different from a previous decision. This does not mean that previous threats are irrelevant, merely that the parent must ensure she gives full details, as no other information will be available.

If good cause was accepted previously because a tribunal or commissioner allowed the parent's appeal against a reduced benefit decision and circumstances have not changed, advice should be sought to challenge a subsequent decision on a further claim not to accept good cause. An appeal can be brought against any reduced benefit decision (see p71).

4. Reduced benefit decisions

A reduced benefit decision is considered by a Jobcentre Plus decision maker if a parent with care who is treated as applying for child maintenance:[30]

- opts out (whether or not she gives reasons for having a good cause) (see p59);
- fails to provide sufficient information to pursue maintenance;
- refuses to take a DNA test (see p91).

Note: some parents in 'old rules' cases have had their benefit reduced because of failure to co-operate. This was called a 'reduced benefit direction'. It is treated in the same way as a reduced benefit decision, and may be reconsidered if the parent provides information to support good cause. If the parent later decides to opt in and provides information to enable a maintenance calculation to be carried out, the case will be dealt with as a 'new rules' case (assuming it is more than 13 weeks since a maintenance assessment was in force).

A reduced benefit decision will not be made if the decision maker is satisfied that:

- there is good cause – ie, the parent, or any children living with her, would suffer 'harm or undue distress' (see p59) as a result of being treated as applying, providing information or taking the DNA test;[31]
- the welfare of the child would be affected (see p24).[32]

If these reasons are accepted, a good cause decision can be reconsidered at a later date and a different decision made (see p63). There are some situations where even if good cause and the welfare of the child are not accepted, the reduced benefit decision cannot be imposed (see p67).

The reduced benefit decision process

After the good cause interview the decision maker will review the written record and other evidence available.

On the basis of this s/he may:

- accept good cause/welfare of the child and notify the parent;[33]
- issue a written notice requiring the parent to provide reasons within four weeks.[34]

Unless the parent has opted out, the Child Support Agency (CSA) may contact the parent – eg, to ask for further information to identify or trace the non-resident parent (see p74).

If written notice is issued by Jobcentre Plus, the four-week period given to supply reasons begins on the day the notice is given or sent to the parent with care.[35] This time limit can be extended in special circumstances – eg, if she is in hospital.

The parent need not give further reasons for opting out in writing (ie, she may provide them over the phone or at interview) unless Jobcentre Plus specifically ask for written reasons.[36]

After the four-week period, the decision maker will re-examine the case and consider any reasons supplied. If s/he is not satisfied about good cause/welfare of the child, a reduced benefit decision can be made. There are certain circumstances in which a reduced benefit decision cannot be given (see p67).

The parent will be sent written notification of the decision.[37]

If a parent with care has opted out and good cause has been accepted, Jobcentre Plus may reconsider the case at any time (see p67).[38] This also applies where good cause was not accepted but the reason a reduced benefit decision has not been made is the welfare of a child.

A copy of the reduced benefit decision will be sent to the parent with care. The decision will state the date from when the reduced benefit decision takes effect (see p68).[39]

A reduced benefit decision will apply for 156 weeks (three years).[40] At the end of this period a further reduced benefit decision may be made (see p70).

If a reduced benefit decision has been made, the parent with care may later provide further information that affects good cause or the welfare of the child. This will trigger a reconsideration of the reduced benefit decision by Jobcentre Plus. The decision maker may decide to accept good cause or that the welfare of the child is affected and revise or supersede the previous decision.

For the circumstances in which a reduced benefit decision cannot be imposed, see pp67 and 69, and for when it ceases to be in force, see p70.

The amount of the reduction

The **standard amount** of the reduced benefit decision is 40 per cent of the income support (IS) personal allowance for an adult aged 25 or over, even if the parent is under 25.[41] Any fraction of over half a penny is rounded up, and any of half a penny or less is disregarded.[42]

For 2007/08 this means that the parent's IS/income-based jobseeker's allowance (JSA) will be reduced by £23.66 a week.

When the benefit rates are uprated in April, the amount of the reduction also increases. The level of the reduction increases from the next benefit week following the date of the uprating.[43]

If applying the reduced benefit decision would reduce the amount of benefit to nil or to below the minimum payment for that benefit, the amount is **modified** to leave the minimum amount payable.[44] The minimum payment is 10 pence for IS and income-based JSA, except where the parent is receiving IS under the trade disputes provisions, when it is £5.[45] The penalty cannot be deducted from any other benefit which may be payable with IS (eg, incapacity benefit) or with income-based JSA (eg, contribution-based JSA). Any period for which the penalty cannot be paid in full (or at all) because of these rules still counts as a period serving the penalty.

Test case rules (see p419) apply to reduced benefit decisions (and reduced benefit directions in 'old rules' cases).[46]

See p68 for when the reduction begins and ends.

When the reduced benefit decision cannot be imposed

There are certain circumstances where even though good cause/welfare of the child do not apply, a reduced benefit decision cannot be imposed. These are:[47]

- if the parent with care, or her partner, is paid IS/income-based JSA that includes a disabled child premium, a disability premium or a higher pensioner premium (this applies even if it is the partner who has the disability);
- if the parent with care, or her partner, is paid an award of child tax credit (CTC) containing an element for a disabled child or young person with a disability.

If an appropriate premium or CTC element ceases to be paid, the reduced benefit decision can be imposed.

If one of the premiums or CTC elements is awarded retrospectively and should have been payable on or before the reduced benefit decision was made, the reduced benefit decision is cancelled. However, if the element or premium only becomes payable after the date of the reduced benefit decision, that decision remains in force.

Reconsideration of a reduced benefit decision

If a reduced benefit decision has been made, the parent with care may later provide further information or reasons regarding good cause/welfare of the child. This will trigger a reconsideration of the reduced benefit decision by Jobcentre Plus.

If the parent later decides to opt in, the reduced benefit decision will cease.

If the decision maker decides to accept good cause or that the welfare of the child is affected, the decision may be revised if it is within the time limit; otherwise the decision is superseded. In either case, the reduced benefit decision ceases to be in force.[48]

Benefit fraud referrals

Jobcentre Plus and the CSA work together to try to prevent fraud. This means that where benefit fraud is suspected, information may be passed between the two organisations. However, the Department for Work and Pensions cannot give information about a person to a third party. For example, if a non-resident parent suspects a parent with care of benefit fraud or vice versa, he will not be told the outcome of any investigation.

See p81 for the possible effects of giving false information to the CSA.

The number of reduced benefit decisions

Only one reduced benefit decision can be in force at any one time in relation to a parent with care.[49] This applies to a parent with care of children by different non-resident fathers who refuses to pursue any of them. Even if she pursues one but not another, a reduced benefit decision can be imposed.

See p69 for what happens to the reduced benefit decision if a parent with care stops claiming benefit and subsequently re-claims.

Additional qualifying child

If a parent with a reduced benefit decision becomes the parent with care of another qualifying child, the parent will be treated as applying for child support maintenance. If she opts out, fails to provide information or take a DNA test and good cause/welfare of the child cannot be accepted, a reduced benefit decision may be made.

If a reduced benefit decision is in force when the further one is made, the original reduction stops and the further reduction starts the day after the original reduction ceases to be in force.[50] The new reduction is applied for a period of 156 weeks.[51] The further reduction only covers the additional child(ren) not named in the first decision. If the further reduction ceases to be in force (see p69), but the original reduced benefit decision would not have ceased to be in force, the reduction continues until 156 weeks have been served in total under that reduction.[52]

When the reduction starts

Once a reduced benefit decision has been issued, a Jobcentre Plus decision maker supersedes the relevant benefit award to or for the parent with care, and the reduction is made from the first day of the second benefit week following any such supersession.[53]

If a recent benefit claim has been made, it should be processed as normal and not held up while a decision is made about whether or not to impose a reduced benefit decision.

IS and income-based JSA are paid for seven-day periods running from the day of the week payment is made. This is known as a benefit week. A benefit week overlaps two calendar weeks (for more details, see CPAG's *Welfare Benefits and Tax Credits Handbook*). If a claimant's benefit week changes, the reduced benefit decision can be modified slightly. The reduction lasts for between 155 and 156 weeks, finishing on the last day of the benefit week which ends before the 156-week period is over.[54]

The reduction is imposed even if the parent has other deductions from benefits (but, for the minimum benefit payable, see p66).

IS and income-based JSA claimants are normally paid by direct transfer into a bank, building society or Post Office account.

When the reduction stops

A reduced benefit decision normally lasts for 156 weeks, but it can be brought to an end before the full period has been served in certain circumstances. A reduction can:

- be suspended (see below). The reduction stops for a period, but the suspended portion then has to be served unless more than 52 weeks have passed;
- cease to be in force (see p70). The reduced benefit decision stops being in force from a specified date and cannot be resurrected;
- be revised or superseded (see Chapter 18) or appealed (see p71).

Jobcentre Plus must notify the parent with care in writing that the reduction has stopped or, in certain cases, been suspended.[55] This notice does not apply to cases where the decision is suspended because a parent goes into hospital or a care home, or where it is suspended because benefit has stopped.

At the end of the 156-week period a further reduced benefit decision may be made and imposed (see p70).

Suspension of a reduced benefit decision

A reduced benefit decision can be suspended and, if appropriate, reinstated if:

- the benefit claim ceases;
- the claimant is no longer a parent with care; or
- the parent goes into hospital or a care home.

Benefit claim ceases

If the parent with care comes off IS or income-based JSA the reduction is suspended.[56] If she re-claims within 52 weeks, the suspended part of the reduction can be applied to the new benefit award.[57] The parent will be sent notification that unless she opts in or provides reasons supporting good cause within 14 days the remainder of the reduced benefit decision will be imposed.[58] If the parent opts in or gives reasons, a visit will be arranged to complete a maintenance administration form or good cause interview. The decision maker will consider the evidence and decide whether or not to reapply the reduction.

If the parent provides no reasons or the decision maker cannot accept good cause/welfare of the child, the reduced benefit decision again comes into operation at the end of the 14 days. The remainder of the 156-week reduction starts from the first day of the second benefit week following this decision.[59]

After 52 weeks off benefit, the reduction ceases to be in force – ie, it lapses. However, if the parent concerned opts out on a new claim, a new reduced benefit decision can be made and the reduction imposed for a further 156 weeks.

Claimant is no longer a parent with care

If the one and only child covered by a reduction ceases to count as a child, or the parent stops being the person who looks after the child, the reduction is suspended from the last day of the benefit week in which this change occurs.[60] For example, if a child goes to live with someone else or leaves school, the reduction is lifted from the end of the week this happens. A parent with care should tell Jobcentre Plus of any relevant changes and, if the reduction is not lifted, she should ask for a supersession of the reduced benefit decision (see p389).

If the child starts to count as a child again, or the parent resumes the care, then the unexpired portion of the reduction again applies to the benefit award.[61] On the other hand, where the reduction has been suspended for 52 weeks, it will lapse if no relevant benefit is in payment at that time.[62] If the same person becomes a parent with care again, claims a relevant benefit and opts out, a new reduced benefit decision may be made.

Parent goes into hospital or a care home

If the parent is in a care home or independent (non-NHS) hospital, or is being provided with a care home or independent health care service, a reduced benefit decision is suspended.[63] The suspension also applies where a parent's IS or income-based JSA has been calculated differently because she is detained under certain mental health legislation.

If a reduced benefit decision has been suspended for 52 weeks, the decision will lapse and cannot be re-applied.[64]

When a reduced benefit decision ceases to be in force

A reduced benefit decision ceases to be in force if:[65]
- the parent with care withdraws the request to opt out;
- the parent complies with the requirement to provide information;
- the parent consents to a DNA test;
- the CSA accepts that there are reasons for good cause or that the welfare of the child is affected. The reduction ceases from the first day in the benefit week in which the parent provides sufficient information;[66]
- a qualifying child in Scotland for whom the reduced benefit decision is in force makes an application and a calculation is made for all the qualifying children concerned. The reduction ceases from the end of the benefit week in which the information enabling the calculation to be made is received;[67]
- Jobcentre Plus decides for another reason to revise or supersede the reduced benefit decision and to end it (see pp384 and 389).

Although not stated explicitly in the legislation, when a parent moves onto pension credit (PC) from IS or income-based JSA the reduction will cease, as the provisions do not extend to PC.

Further reduced benefit decision after three years

At the end of the three-year reduced benefit period, the parent with care is again given the opportunity to provide information to pursue child support maintenance. She will be asked to opt in, take a DNA test if applicable, or provide information or reasons for good cause. The decision maker will then decide whether or not to make a further reduced benefit decision in the usual way.

The new reduced benefit decision will begin on the day after the previous reduced benefit decision ceases. This process is repeated after each three-year period. This means that a parent with care may be subject to a reduced benefit decision for many years.

Appeals

A parent with care can appeal against a reduced benefit decision (see Chapter 19) or apply for a revision or supersession (see Chapter 18).[68]

The reduced benefit decision stays in force pending the appeal tribunal's decision. A parent with care who wants to challenge the refusal to accept good cause, but cannot afford the reduction, could appeal and then:

- provide further information to enable a supersession to be carried out on the grounds that there is good cause or that the welfare of the child should be considered (see below); *or*
- opt in, provide information or take a DNA test as appropriate in the circumstances (see below).

The reduction then stops, but the appeal proceeds.

Supersessions

In some cases where a parent has a pending appeal against a reduced benefit decision, Jobcentre Plus may supersede it – eg, because the parent provides information that supports good cause/welfare of the child. In this case, the reduced benefit decision stops, but only from a later date. The parent must consider whether to withdraw the appeal or continue to get the reduced benefit decision overturned for the whole period (and so have the deducted benefit repaid). When deciding whether to continue the appeal, the possible gain of benefit being repaid should be weighed against the possibility that if the tribunal dismisses the appeal, Jobcentre Plus may look again at its decision to supersede. If an appeal is lost and this happens, seek further advice.

Appeal and opt in

If a parent with care takes this course of action she should explain that she is only opting in, providing information or taking the DNA test under protest until the tribunal decides the question of harm or undue distress, and that she still believes she has good cause but cannot afford a benefit reduction. Although a calculation may then be made, she at least has an appeal at which she can dispute the refusal to accept good cause/welfare of the child.

This course of action is not without risk. The parent may still opt out at a later stage and would be given four weeks to provide her reasons.

Outcome of the appeal

If the tribunal allows an appeal from the original reduced benefit decision or from a revision of it, the reduced benefit decision ceases to have effect from the date it started and all benefit deducted is paid to the parent with care.

If the tribunal allows an appeal from a superseded decision to impose or not to cease a reduced benefit decision, the reduced benefit decision ceases to have effect from the date that superseded decision should have had effect and benefit deducted from that date is paid.

Notes

1. Claiming income support or income-based jobseeker's allowance
1 s6 CSA 1991
2 s6(7) CSA 1991
3 s6(7) CSA 1991
4 IS Guidance and Procedure Vol 10 Part 2, para 34927
5 IS Guidance and Procedure, Vol 10 Part 2, para 32051
6 CSA *How Do I Get Child Maintenance if I'm on Benefits?*, CSL 302

2. Opting out
7 s6(5) CSA 1991
8 Reg 31 CS(MCP) Regs
9 s6(9-10) CSA 1991
10 IS Guidance and Procedure Vol 10 Part 2, paras 34513-15 and para 34922
11 IS Guidance and Procedure Vol 10 Part 2, paras 34520-21 and para 34923

3. Harm or undue distress
12 s6(7) CSA 1991
13 CCS/1037/1995
14 s46(3) CSA 1991
15 CCS/7559/1999
16 *Shorter Oxford English Dictionary; The Concise Oxford Dictionary*
17 CCS/1037/1995
18 CCS/12609/1996
19 CCS/15109/1996
20 R(SB) 33/85
21 CCS/12092/1996
22 *Secretary of State for Work and Pensions v Roach* [2006] EWCA Civ 1746

23 IS Guidance and Procedure, Vol 10 Part 2, para 34525
24 IS Guidance and Procedure, Vol 10 Part 2, paras 34937-42
25 s46(6) CSA 1991
26 IS Guidance and Procedure, Vol 10 Part 2, para 34940
27 IS Guidance and Procedure, Vol 10 Part 2, para 34941
28 IS Guidance and Procedure, Vol 10 Part 2, para 34939
29 IS Guidance and Procedure, Vol 10 Part 2, paras 34520-22 and 34923

4. Reduced benefit decisions
30 s46(1) CSA 1991
31 s46(3) CSA 1991
32 s2 CSA 1991
33 s46(4) CSA 1991
34 s42(2) CSA 1991; reg 9 CS(MCP) Regs
35 Reg 2 CS(MCP) Regs
36 s46(9) CSA 1991
37 s46(4) and (6) CSA 1991
38 s46(6) CSA 1991
39 s46(8) CSA 1991
40 Reg 11(2) CS(MCP) Regs
41 Reg 11(2) CS(MCP) Regs
42 Reg 20 CS(MCP) Regs
43 Reg 11(7) CS(MCP) Regs
44 Reg 12 CS(MCP) Regs
45 Regs 26(4) and 27(2) SS(C&P) Regs; reg 87A JSA Regs
46 ss28ZA and 28ZB CSA 1991
47 ss 46-50 CSA 1991; reg 10 CS(MCP) Regs

48 Reg 16 CS(MCP) Regs
49 Reg 11(8) CS(MCP) Regs
50 Regs 11(4) and 17(2) CS(MCP)
    Regs; reg 7B(15) SS&CS(DA) Regs
51 Regs 11 and 17(2) CS(MCP) Regs
52 Reg 17(4) CS(MCP) Regs
53 Reg 11(3) CS(MCP) Regs
54 Reg 11(6) CS(MCP) Regs
55 Reg 19 CS(MCP) Regs
56 Reg 13 CS(MCP) Regs
57 Reg 13(3) CS(MCP) Regs
58 Reg 13(6) CS(MCP) Regs
59 Regs 11(3) and 13(5) CS(MCP) Regs
60 Reg 18(1) CS(MCP) Regs; reg 7B(16)
    SS&CS(DA) Regs
61 Reg 18(3) CS(MCP) Regs
62 Reg 18(2) CS(MCP) Regs
63 Regs 14 and 15 CS(MCP) Regs
64 Regs 14(3) and 15(3) CS(MCP) Regs
65 Reg 16 CS(MCP) Regs; reg 7B(11)
    SS&CS(DA) Regs
66 Reg 7B(12) SS&CS(DA) Regs
67 Reg 7B(14) SS&CS(DA) Regs
68 s20(1)(c) and (2)(b) CSA 1991

Chapter 5

••

Information

This chapter covers:

---

1. Information-seeking powers

The Child Support Agency (CSA) has wide powers to obtain information from (among others) parents, employers, local authorities and HM Revenue and Customs.[1] In addition, the CSA can appoint inspectors who have extensive powers to obtain information (see p98). Staff at the regional Child Support Agency Centres (CSACs) (see p6) ask for information by telephone; those at local offices also conduct face-to-face enquiries. As far as possible, information is gathered by telephone, with clear guidance on when and how this should be conducted.[2] As the Operational Improvement Plan[3] states that the CSA will extend the range of information available to it, make more use of its powers to obtain information, and use private sector tracing agencies where its own staff are unsuccessful, this guidance is likely to be amended in the near future. The information in this chapter on how the CSA exercises its powers is, therefore, subject to change.

In addition, Jobcentre Plus may seek information under child support legislation – eg, when making decisions about good cause and reduced benefit decisions (see Chapter 4).

When the Child Support Agency can request information

All applicants are under a duty to provide information to identify and trace a non-resident parent, and calculate and collect maintenance.[4] The information may also be required to verify whether information already gathered is correct.[5]

••••

In many cases, all the information needed will be collected by phone. Applications need not be in writing but, where this is requested, an application for child maintenance form is provided. A parent with care on income support (IS) or income-based jobseeker's allowance (JSA) is treated as applying and, therefore, a maintenance administration form is completed with her to gather the information needed. Further information may be required to make an effective application.

After an application has been made the non-resident parent will be contacted, usually by phone, to notify him of the application and gather information.[6] In some cases, a face-to-face interview may be arranged or, if there is no phone number, a form called the 'child maintenance enquiry' is issued. The child maintenance enquiry form can be used to gather the information needed to calculate and collect maintenance (see p85). In 'old rules' cases, the original maintenance enquiry form issued sets the effective date of the maintenance assessment (see p368). A further form will not usually be issued, and as much additional information as possible will be collected by telephone.

Information can only be requested if it is necessary to:[7]
- decide whether there is a qualifying child, non-resident parent or person with care in relation to an application;
- decide whether the CSA has jurisdiction – ie, whether the qualifying child, non-resident parent, and person with care are all habitually resident in the UK (see p27);
- decide whether a written maintenance agreement made before 5 April 1993 or a court order made before 3 March 2003 is in force, or a court order made after 3 March 2003 has been in force for one year (see p38);
- decide which application has priority (see p48);
- decide, where there is more than one person with care, who has parental responsibility for a qualifying child (see p49);
- identify a non-resident parent (see p87);
- trace a non-resident parent (see p82);
- determine who is in receipt of child benefit either for a relevant child or qualifying child where a parent may be treated as a non-resident parent in shared care situations (see Chapter 15);
- calculate the amount of child maintenance;
- identify how much is payable under a court maintenance order;
- collect child support maintenance or maintenance under a court order from a non-resident parent;
- decide whether to enforce a CSA calculation or other maintenance through the courts (see p450);
- work out or collect interest on arrears (see p443);
- identify any proceedings for a court maintenance order;
- verify whether information already gathered is correct.[8]

See p77 for who can be required to give information and p81 for the effects of failing to provide it.

Information the Child Support Agency can ask for

There are no specific restrictions on the kind of information the CSA can ask for, but the law is specific about the purpose for which the information must be needed (see p75). Issues on which the CSA can require information include:[9]

- the habitual residence of the person with care, the non-resident parent and any child covered by the application to determine jurisdiction (including if the individual works abroad);
- the name and address of the person with care and non-resident parent, their marital or civil partnership status, and the relationship of the person with care to any child covered by the application;
- the name, address and date of birth of any child covered by the application, the child's marital or civil partnership status and any education the child is undergoing;
- where there is more than one person with care:
  - who has parental responsibility (or parental rights in Scotland) for any qualifying child; *and*
  - how much time is spent by that child with each person with care;
- where parentage is disputed, whether someone can be assumed to be a parent (see p15) and if not, who is the parent of a child (a parent with care on IS/ JSA can be asked to take a DNA test[10]);
- the name and address of any current or recent employer of a non-resident parent and the gross earnings derived from any such employment;
- if the non-resident parent is self-employed, the address, trading name, gross receipts and expenses, any other outgoings of the trade or business and taxable profits;
- any other income of the non-resident parent;
- how much is paid or payable under a court maintenance order or maintenance agreement;
- details of anyone who lives in the same household as the non-resident parent, their relationship to him and to each other, and the date of birth of any child of those people;
- details and statements of any account in the name of the non-resident parent, including bank and building society accounts;
- whether a person counts as a qualifying child for the purposes of child support (see p18);
- information needed to decide whether a calculation should end (see p372).

In 'old rules' cases additional information may be needed and can be required in order to work out maintenance liability, including, for example, housing costs, and the employment and income of other people who live with the non-resident parent or parent with care.[11]

Who has to give information to the Child Support Agency

Information can be required from the people listed on pp77–80. It can only be required from a person who has that information in her/his possession or can reasonably be expected to acquire it.[12] Information can also be given to the CSA when there is no obligation to provide it – eg, from a relative, neighbour, GP or landlord. However, any such voluntary disclosure of information made without the permission of the person(s) concerned could break professional codes of practice, civil contracts or the Data Protection Act 1984. Information supplied to the CSA can give rise to a libel action.[13] For information on disclosure by the CSA, see p100.

The relevant persons

The person with care, a non-resident parent (or a parent treated as non-resident for the purposes of the calculation) and in Scotland, a child applicant, must provide the information on p76 if requested.[14]

If information is not provided by a person with care or child applicant in Scotland, a voluntary application may be treated as withdrawn (see p46) or a parent with care on IS/JSA may have a reduced benefit decision imposed.

If a non-resident parent does not supply requested information, a default maintenance decision (or, in 'old rules' cases, an interim maintenance decision) may be made. There may also be penalties for failing to provide the requested information.

It is a criminal offence to fail to provide or knowingly provide false information (see p81).

Someone who denies parentage of a child

Someone who denies parentage of a child named in a maintenance application can be required to give information *only* if it is needed:[15]
* to decide whether or not all the relevant persons are habitually resident in the UK and, therefore, whether the CSA has jurisdiction to make a calculation; *or*
* to identify a non-resident parent.

This means, for example, that if the CSA only wants to identify a person as the non-resident parent, employment details would not normally be necessary and so should not be requested until parentage is established.

Employers

The current or recent employer of the non-resident parent can be required to give information *only* if it is needed to:[16]
* identify a non-resident parent;

- trace a non-resident parent;
- calculate child maintenance;
- collect child support maintenance, interest or arrears of maintenance under a court order from the non-resident parent; *or*
- decide whether to pursue a garnishee or charging order (see Chapter 20).

An employer of an alleged parent can only be required to provide information to identify and trace that parent.[17]

The same rules apply where the employer is the Crown (eg, government departments).[18]

In 'old rules' cases, the parent with care's employer may also be required to provide information which is needed in order to make a maintenance assessment.[19]

Companies or partnerships

A company or partnership for whom a non-resident parent has had a contract for services may be required to provide information, but *only* if it is needed to:[20]

- trace a non-resident parent; *or*
- calculate child maintenance.

This means, for example, a self-employed IT consultant could be traced through companies for which he provides a service and his income investigated.

Accountants

The person who acts as the non-resident parent's accountant, or who has done so in the past, can be required to give information *only* where it is needed to:[21]

- trace a non-resident parent;
- calculate child maintenance;
- collect child support maintenance, interest or arrears, or maintenance under a court order from the non-resident parent; *or*
- decide whether to pursue a garnishee or charging order (see Chapter 20).

Court officials

The following court officials can be required to give information.[22] In **England and Wales:**

- the senior district judge of the High Court Family Division or, at a district registry, the district judge;
- the district judge of a county court, or the chief clerk or other officer who may be acting on her/his behalf;[23]
- the justice's chief executive for a magistrates' court.

In **Scotland:**
- the deputy principal clerk of the Court of Session;
- the sheriff clerk of a sheriff court.

Court officials can be required to give information *only* where there is, or has been, a court maintenance order, or an application for such an order has been made but not determined, and the information is needed to:[24]
- identify how much is payable under a court maintenance order;
- collect child support maintenance or maintenance under a court order;
- identify any proceedings about a court maintenance order;
- decide whether there is in force either a pre-April 1993 maintenance agreement (see p38) or a maintenance order made after 3 March 2003 which has been in force for a year; *or*
- decide, if there is more than one person with care, who has parental responsibility for the qualifying child.

Crown employees

Some Crown employees – eg, officials of the prison services or DVLA staff, can be required to give information but *only* when it is needed to trace the non-resident parent.[25]

Government benefit departments

Any Department for Work and Pensions agency may give information held for benefits purposes to the CSA.[26]

Local authorities

Local authorities may be required to give information but *only* if it is needed to:[27]
- decide whether there is a qualifying child, non-resident parent or person with care in relation to an application;
- identify a non-resident parent;
- trace a non-resident parent;
- calculate child maintenance;
- collect child support maintenance, interest or arrears or maintenance under a court order from the non-resident parent; *or*
- decide whether to pursue a garnishee or charging order (see Chapter 20).

This applies only to the local authority for the area where one or more of the following resides or used to reside:
- the person with care;
- the non-resident parent;
- the parent treated as non-resident;
- the alleged non-resident parent; *or*
- in Scotland, a child applicant.

This means the CSA may require a local authority to give information concerning housing benefit or council tax benefit – eg, the parent's bank account details if s/he pays by direct debit.[28]

HM Revenue and Customs

HM Revenue and Customs (the Revenue) can be required to disclose the current address or details of the current employer of a non-resident parent.[29] If the parent is self-employed, this also includes details of the taxable profits, gross receipts and expenses.[30] Any information disclosed must not go any further than authorised CSA staff, unless it is about civil or criminal proceedings under the Child Support Act 1991. However, where information is obtained under the Social Security Administration Act 1992, no such restriction applies. Information may also be obtained under the Tax Credits Act 2002.[31] It is unlawful for the Revenue to give the CSA any other information.[32]

The CSA has stated in its Operational Improvement Plan that in the future it will work more closely with the Revenue to trace non-resident parents and make more use of information held by the Revenue to locate non-resident parents who owe maintenance.[33]

Credit reference agencies

Since 12 July 2006, the CSA can require information from credit reference agencies,[34] but only for the purpose of:
- enabling a non-resident parent to be identified or traced;
- enabling an assessment of the non-resident parent's 'financial standing' to be made;
- enabling an amount of overpaid child maintenance to be recovered.

When must information be supplied

If information is requested to make an effective application from the person who has made it (eg, by the re-issue of a child maintenance application or maintenance administration form or request for further information) the information must be supplied in 14 days in order to ensure that the application is treated as made on the earliest date (ie, as if the initial application had been effective).[35] The CSA can allow information to be provided by a later date if it is satisfied that the delay was unavoidable.

No deadline is specified for providing information in other circumstances, only that it must be provided as soon as reasonably practicable in the circumstances.[36] In practice, the CSA allows seven days when making a calculation and one month for a revision/supersession.[37] The decision maker can allow longer if it is appropriate to do so. See p6 for when a document is treated as sent and received.

Failing to provide and providing false information

If a person fails to provide information there are a range of consequences s/he will face.
- If she is a parent with care on IS/income-based JSA (see p38), a reduced benefit decision may be imposed (see p65).
- If she is a voluntary applicant (see p38), her application may not be processed (see p46).
- If he is a non-resident parent, a default maintenance calculation may be made.
- A criminal fine of £1,000 may be imposed.[38]

A person charged with an offence of failing to provide information may be able to avoid conviction if there is a good reason why the information cannot be provided.[39] In addition, criminal offences concerning supply of information are not applied at all if a parent with care has had a reduced benefit decision imposed.[40] However, a non-resident parent who fails to return a child maintenance enquiry form or provide information may have both a default maintenance decision and a fine imposed. This also means that if a non-resident parent makes a voluntary application and the parent with care fails to provide information she can be fined, though this would be extremely rare.

If the person knowingly provides false information, or allows it to be provided, this is also a criminal offence.[41] The CSA can go to court and a fine of up to £1,000 can be imposed. This is paid to the court, not the CSA.

The CSA must notify the person that it is a criminal offence to refuse to supply, or knowingly supply false, information.[42] All forms and requests issued contain this notification to ensure the fine may be pursued.

If a parent fails to give information, the CSA may ask another person for that information – eg, a parent's employer or accountant. As they are required to give information, the criminal sanctions apply. This gives the CSA greater powers to investigate and pursue other sources of information. The CSA has been criticised in the past for failing to seek information from other sources when the parent did not return a form despite reminders,[43] and commented that between the child's mother and the father's employer there should have been sufficient information to enable the CSA to calculate the non-resident parent's income with reasonable precision. The person approached may provide inaccurate but convincing information – eg, one parent may give details about the other's self-employed earnings which are too high; the second parent would then need to persuade the CSA of the real figures. As no indication is given in the legislation about the extent of evidence for self-employed earnings, this is left to the discretion and common sense of CSA staff or an appeal tribunal. In the case where this was decided, the tribunal was entitled to estimate the non-resident parent's net earnings on the basis of documentary evidence provided by the parent with care.[44] However, since that decision the legislation has been amended to allow the CSA to obtain details of self-employed earnings from the Revenue (see p80).

Disputing the information required

If the CSA/Jobcentre Plus requires information:
- not relevant to the reason for the request;
- of a very different kind from the examples given in the regulations;
- from a person who cannot be required to give it; *or*
- despite having sufficient information to make a full calculation,

the request should be queried. If the CSA/Jobcentre Plus insists, a challenge should be considered (see p383).

If a person in this situation refuses to give information in order to avoid a penalty, s/he should explain that decision, preferably in writing. A complaint could also be made (see p462).

2. **Contacting the non-resident parent**

If the person with care has given the non-resident parent's telephone number and the non-resident parent is named on the birth certificate and is aware of the existence of the child, he is contacted by phone.[45] If the telephone number is not known, a child maintenance enquiry form may be issued (see p85). The date of contact is the date liability for child maintenance usually starts – this is known as the 'effective date' (see p368). In some cases there have been long delays in setting the effective date and the person with care could be owed compensation. The Operational Improvement Plan commits the Child Support Agency (CSA) to speeding up its processing of applications.[46] The Client Charter states that if the parent with care gives contact details for the non-resident parent, the CSA will start gathering information from him within four weeks of the application being received.[47] If delay occurs because of CSA error, the parent can ask for compensation (see p462).

Tracing the non-resident parent

The CSA can use its information-seeking powers to identify and trace the non-resident parent. Only those persons and agencies listed on p77-80 can be required to provide information. CSA staff are advised to use the following sources of information when tracing a non-resident parent:[48]
- the applicant;
- another party;
- the telephone directory or directory enquiries;
- the Departmental Central Index (DCI) – this Department for Work and Pensions (DWP) computer network gives access to national insurance and DWP records;[49]

- the Common Enquiry Service – this gives access to other DWP computer systems, such as those for income support (IS) and jobseeker's allowance (JSA);[50]
- HM Revenue and Customs – for an address of a current employer (see p80);[51]
- the National Insurance Contributions Office, if the non-resident parent is employed or self-employed;[52]
- the army, navy, airforce or Ministry of Defence if the non-resident parent is serving in, or recently discharged from, the forces;[53]
- the Prisoner Location Service, Scottish Prison Service, Northern Ireland Prison Service;[54]
- employers, past and present.[55] If the employer does not supply the information, a warning will be given about the possibility of criminal charges, and other ways of obtaining the information have been exhausted, an inspector may be appointed;[56]
- local authorities – this method may only be used after attempts have been made to gather information from the non-resident parent;[57]
- DVLA/DVLNI – this method may only be used where all else has failed and there are special procedures for referring enquiries;[58]
- credit reference agencies – this is allowed for certain purposes (see p80).

Finding a confident address

An address is considered confident if the information on the DCI matches exactly the non-resident parent's full name, date of birth and that address, and there is no information which suggests that the non-resident parent is not living there.[59] However, in terms of establishing an effective date for a maintenance calculation, an address does not have to be certain beyond all reasonable doubt (see p357). If the DCI gives the non-resident parent the same address as the person with care, this is not considered confident.

Information from the person with care

If the person with care has not given an address for the non-resident parent, she is contacted by telephone (or if this is not possible, by letter) and, if she does not know the address, she is asked to give any information that could help trace the non-resident parent. This could include:

- middle name(s) and any other names by which he may be known;
- other addresses at which he may have lived;
- his place of work and any previous employers;
- the name and address of his accountant;
- any benefit claims made; *and*
- if he has a car, the registration or make, model, colour and other details.

In addition, a face-to-face interview may be arranged. At this, the person with care may be asked to confirm a potential address or provide further information to allow a trace to be made. A parent may be asked to give a recent photograph of the non-resident parent where DNA testing may be involved. She is asked to bring any relevant documents, such as a marriage certificate or expired passport, and is warned that the CSA may contact friends and relatives with whom the non-resident parent may be living. The CSA must preserve confidentiality where this occurs and should not disclose the CSA's interest.

At the interview the person with care could be asked other detailed questions – eg, whether the non-resident parent ever lived with the person with care. The Jobcentre Plus may have asked many of these questions of a parent with care on IS/income-based JSA at the child maintenance interview (see Chapter 4). Contact with these parents by the CSA is only likely where additional trace action is required – eg, to obtain details of the non-resident parent's car or where parentage is disputed.

In cases where the parent with care is on IS/income-based JSA, Jobcentre Plus will already have made a decision on whether the parent has provided all the information it is reasonable for her to supply (see Chapter 4). A referral back to the Jobcentre Plus will only be made if the parent with care refuses to take a DNA test or a DNA test/declaration of parentage (declarator of parentage in Scotland) indicates an alleged non-resident parent is not the parent and, therefore, details of a further possible non-resident parent are required.[60]

Initial contact with the non-resident parent

Once an effective application (see p45) has been made, or is treated as made, the CSA must give notice of that to any person(s) with care, the non-resident parent and any person treated as a non-resident parent, other than the applicant, as soon as reasonably practical.[61] The CSA will attempt to phone a non-resident parent to notify him of the application and gather information.[62] If it is not possible to phone and the non-resident parent is aware of the child, a child maintenance enquiry form may be issued. If the parent is unaware of the child or not named on the birth certificate, the CSA will try to arrange a face-to-face interview.

There are special rules for young non-resident parents (see p86).

During the initial phone call, information will be checked to confirm the identity of the individual before proceeding.[63] The non-resident parent may be asked questions to confirm jurisdiction and whether he accepts parentage.

The parent may be asked for confirmation of any court orders or information needed to make a maintenance calculation. If the parent is willing to give the information but is unable to proceed with the call, the phone interview can be carried out at a more convenient time, or a convenient time and place can be arranged for a face-to-face interview.[64]

The non-resident parent is warned that a default maintenance decision may be issued if he fails to provide sufficient information to make a calculation. At various stages he will be given the opportunity to provide more information and be given a time limit of at least seven days in which to provide it.

The child maintenance enquiry form

The CSA intends that all, or most, of the information needed to work out maintenance will be provided or collected over the phone. This means a child maintenance enquiry form will only be issued when the non-resident parent requests it or if he has not co-operated. If the non-resident parent does not know he is an alleged non-resident parent, a face-to-face interview should be arranged.

In simple terms, a form cannot be issued unless:
* a 'confident' address for the non-resident parent is established (see p83);
* an alleged non-resident parent is aware that he is considered to be the father of the child;
* an alleged non-resident parent is at least 16 years old, or under 19 and still treated as a child (however, a statement of paternity is still sought in these cases – see p86).

When a child maintenance enquiry form is issued the parent is allowed seven to 14 days to return it, depending on what stage of the procedure has been reached.[65] The CSA may only allow seven days or phone the parent after this period of time to check when the information will be returned.

Even where a form is issued the non-resident parent may instead choose to phone with the information.

Any notice sent to a non-resident parent must tell him the effective date (see p368) of any calculation to be made, and inform him about default maintenance decisions (see p352).[66]

The maintenance enquiry form asks for information on:
* personal details – name, address, other names used, phone number (work and mobile), national insurance number, date of birth, best contact times;
* whether he accepts paternity for all, or some, of the qualifying children named;
* IS/income-based JSA details if this is being claimed by or for him;
* student details if appropriate – ie, college, course, qualification, full- or part-time status (evidence is requested);
* child(ren) who live with him – ie, date of birth, national insurance number (if appropriate), who gets child benefit for the child (evidence is requested);
* details of any shared care, average per week and any other special arrangements;
* employment details – title, employer (name, address and phone number), start and end dates (if appropriate);
* income details – frequency of pay, gross pay, bonus, expenses (pay slips are requested);
* self-assessment form or tax calculation notice if the parent is self-employed;
* tax credits in payment;
* other income – eg, pension;

- other payments made to a personal or private pension;
- collection details – when the CSA wants to collect, bank details such as account number and sort code. Direct debit is the preferred method but standing order, deductions from wages, transcash or bank giro credit are also available;
- representative details, name address, phone number and best contact times (signed authorisation is needed in certain circumstances).

The form may also ask for further information. The non-resident parent will have to sign a declaration and parents are informed that failure to provide the information requested or knowingly to provide false information is a criminal offence (see p81).

Information given can be amended at any time before a calculation is made, but not about changes after the effective date.[67] For changes after the effective date, supersession should be sought.

If the form is returned fully completed and no indication is made that paternity is denied, the CSA assumes that the alleged non-resident parent accepts paternity. If a parent disputes that he is non-resident and maintains that he has day-to-day care of the child (see p21), this is not a proper reason for refusing to return the form (this decision was made in reference to the 'old rules' maintenance enquiry form but would equally apply under the 'new rules').[68]

Young non-resident parents

A face-to-face interview must always be arranged with a young non-resident parent – ie, one under 16 years of age or between 16 and 19 but still treated as a child.[69] He will be asked to confirm parentage, but no calculation can be made until he ceases to be treated as a child. An adult must be present at the interview.

If the non-resident parent is between 16 and 19 and no child benefit is being paid for him, a series of questions will be asked to establish if he is a child.[70] He can be classed as a child if he is:

- in full-time non-advanced education;
- registered for work or work-based training for young people; *or*
- working temporarily for 24 hours or more a week, due to end before the terminal date for child benefit (see p18).

The young person is no longer treated as a child, if he is under 18 and:

- in employment after the terminal date;
- in work-based training (Skillseekers in Scotland); *or*
- on IS or income-based JSA.

3. **Parentage investigations**

Where parentage is denied, a maintenance application cannot be decided unless the Child Support Agency (CSA) can assume parentage (see p15). In the vast majority of cases, it is a non-resident father disputing paternity. Paternity is also investigated where there is some doubt about it (eg, more than one possible father is named). However, in cases where the parent with care is on income support (IS)/income-based jobseeker's allowance (JSA), she may already have been asked to identify the most likely father (see Chapter 4).

Paternity investigations can take place before or after the calculation. For example, an alleged non-resident parent may deny paternity on the initial phone contact or on a child maintenance enquiry form (see p85). The dispute can be about one or all of the qualifying children. The CSA can proceed with the calculation, or collection in post-calculation cases, for those children for whom paternity is accepted or assumed while investigations are taking place for others.

In pre-calculation cases if a presumption of parentage cannot be made, the CSA cannot make a calculation until paternity has been resolved. For details of when paternity may be assumed see p15. The CSA will carry out investigations to determine if paternity may be assumed or established. This may involve interviewing both the non-resident parent and person with care; it may also include interviewing the other parent if s/he is not a person with care. The CSA may seek a DNA test or court action to establish paternity (though this is unlikely, given the presumptions and consequences of failure to take DNA tests). Court action may also be pursued by the person with care or alleged non-resident parent at any time.

In post-calculation cases the non-resident parent may dispute paternity and seek a revision. If the CSA has been able to assume paternity (see p15), it should first consider whether the non-resident parent:[71]

- is trying to avoid paying maintenance – eg, where a default maintenance decision has been made; or
- has discovered information to make him doubt paternity – eg, the parent with care tells him he is not the father.

If the presumption of parentage was based on:[72]

- a positive DNA test result;
- adoption;
- fertility treatment;
- a declaration/declarator of parentage that is still in force and the child has not been adopted;
- a declaration under section 27 of the 1991 Child Support Act;
- treating him as the father under section 28 of the Human Fertilisation and Embryology Act 1990,

the decision is not revised and the non-resident parent is advised that he may apply to the courts for a declaration/declarator of parentage. A decision to refuse to revise may be appealed, but paternity can only be established by the court (see p94).

In all other cases, the non-resident parent will be asked to provide evidence.[73] Documentary evidence is preferred. If the evidence is a previous negative DNA test or declaration/declarator of parentage, this will be sufficient proof. The calculation will be cancelled and any payments made refunded. The person with care may be re-interviewed to identify another alleged non-resident parent. In cases where a parent with care is on IS/income-based JSA this is carried out by Jobcentre Plus (see Chapter 4).

It is not sufficient in post-calculation cases simply to deny paternity; evidence must be given to raise doubt – eg, the parent with care was having another relationship when the child was conceived.[74] Where a doubt is raised the parent with care will be contacted by phone or in a face-to-face interview for her comments on the non-resident parent's evidence. If the parent with care:

- accepts that there may be doubt about paternity, a DNA test may be offered;
- disputes the non-resident parent's evidence, the decision will not be revised. The non-resident parent will be advised to obtain a DNA test or declaration/ declarator of non-parentage; the CSA will not offer a DNA test in this case.[75] He will also be informed of his right to appeal to a court.

Interviews where parentage is disputed

Interviews can be carried out by phone or face to face. Where paternity is denied after initial contact or the issue of a child maintenance enquiry form, the parent with care may be interviewed in order to establish the case to be put to the alleged non-resident parent. In other cases, sufficient information may already be available to contact the non-resident parent. However, both parties are interviewed before offering DNA tests (see p94) and, even if the parent with care has already been interviewed or paternity is assumed, she may be re-interviewed to see how she responds to the alleged non-resident parent's version of events. If the parent with care has already filled in a paternity statement she will only be re-interviewed if the alleged non-resident parent introduces new evidence.

In the case of a face-to-face interview, if the interviewee does not want to come to the local office or another local Jobcentre Plus office if that is closer, s/he can be interviewed at home or at a friend's or relative's house.

If the parent with care or alleged non-resident parent is under 16 (or under 19 and treated as a child), her/his parent or guardian must consent to the case progressing. The young person must have a face-to-face interview in the presence of a parent or guardian. A calculation is not made for a non-resident parent under 16 (or 16–19 and treated as a child), but a paternity statement is required for future use – ie, action is suspended until the young person ceases to be a child and then a calculation may be made.[76] Additional information may be sought about an alleged non-resident parent aged between 16 and 19 to determine whether or not s/he should be treated as a child – eg, details of her/his current education/training and (in 'old rules' cases only) her/his marital/civil partnership status.[77]

It is not compulsory to attend any interview, but see p77 for who can be required to provide what information.

Interview with an alleged non-resident parent

When the non-resident parent is unaware of the qualifying child, a face-to-face interview may be arranged to notify him of the application (see p88).

When paternity is denied, the alleged non-resident parent will be asked if he has documentary or verbal evidence that he is not the parent.[78] The alleged non-resident parent's evidence is recorded word for word on a paternity statement.[79] The alleged non-resident parent may ask for further time to obtain documentary evidence; seven days are usually allowed.

If documentary evidence cannot be supplied, the person with care may be interviewed to gather her evidence. If no evidence can be provided to assume paternity, the case may progress to DNA testing.

CSA guidance suggests that a non-resident parent should be asked:[80]

- whether he was in the country at any time between the date of conception and the child's birth;
- whether he had sex with the mother and, if so, over what period of time;
- where conception was assisted, was he in agreement with the treatment;
- how long the relationship lasted and whether he lived with the woman as husband and wife;
- whether or not he has had any contact with the child(ren);
- his reasons for thinking that he is not the father; *and*
- any other information which might support his view.

These questions are in guidance only, so others may also be asked. The non-resident parent need only answer such questions if he denies paternity and the information is needed to decide if he is the father.

The alleged non-resident parent is sent information about disputing parentage and the reduced-cost DNA test (see p91) before the interview. At the interview the possibility of DNA testing will be explained and the alleged non-resident parent's agreement sought.[81] The alleged non-resident parent will be told that he will be responsibile for the costs of the tests for the parent with care and child(ren), as well as his own, if he is found to be the father. He will also be told that if he is found not to be the father, he will be able to re-claim any costs he has incurred from the CSA.

If the alleged non-resident parent accepts paternity, a child maintenance form is completed at the interview.

Interviewing officers take notes and, after the interview (including a telephone interview), details of the interview are recorded.[82] If the non-resident parent wishes to make a statement, this is taken down verbatim (this must take place at an office or during a home visit).[83]

If the non-resident parent does not attend an interview, the interviewing officer attempts to arrange another and, if he does not attend the second one, the officer considers a home visit or court action at this point.[84]

Interview with a parent with care

If someone has been named as the parent of a qualifying child and denies it, the CSA contacts the parent with care to tell her of this and explain the procedures which follow. The interview can be conducted by phone or, if the parent does not want to be interviewed in this way, in the office or at her home.

The parent with care is asked if she has documentary evidence from which the CSA could assume parentage – eg, birth or marriage certificate.[85] She is also questioned about her relationship with the alleged non-resident parent at the time of conception to establish whether he could be the father.

If no evidence can be provided to assume paternity, the parent with care is asked if she is willing to take a DNA test (see p91).

The CSA will enquire about the alleged relationship and the circumstances of conception and birth. The parent with care is likely to be asked very personal questions. For example, the officer may ask about:[86]

- the place the child was born and whether the pregnancy was full term;
- whether the man is named as the child's father on the birth certificate;
- the man's reaction to the pregnancy;
- whether she and the alleged non-resident parent ever lived together and, if so, when and where;
- whether she considered them to be a couple at the time the child was conceived;
- whether the alleged non-resident parent has ever acknowledged the child;
- whether the alleged non-resident parent has ever paid any maintenance;
- whether there is, or has been, any contact with his family;
- whether she has any letters or cards acknowledging the child, or witnesses to her association with the alleged non-resident parent;
- whether the child's conception was assisted and, if so, whether the man was in agreement with the treatment;
- whether she has any photographs of him; *and*
- whether she is willing to give evidence in court.

If a person considers the question(s) inappropriate, she should ask the interviewer the point of them. If the interviewer insists, the person with care could ask to end the interview to consider whether to give the information requested. She can ask the interviewer to write down the questions and the reason for them. If, at the interview or later, she refuses to answer any of the questions, she should indicate that she has given all the information that is necessary to trace and identify the father. See p70 for refusal to give information.

The parent with care may also be asked to make a parentage statement, which is recorded word for word.[87] The parent can refuse to sign this and the refusal will form part of the evidence, along with any reasons she gives. The parent may ask for a copy of the parentage statement or reasons for failing to sign the statement. This statement is added to the report of the interview and can be used in court proceedings (see p94).

Interviewing a person with care who is not the mother

If both parents are non-resident and an alleged non-resident parent continues to deny paternity after an interview, the person with care may be interviewed.[88] The questions depend on the person with care's relationship with the alleged parents – eg, a mother or sister is likely to know the length of the relationship between the parents. She is asked for the addresses of both parents, and any letters or cards from them. She is also asked why she is looking after the child(ren), whether there is any documentation regarding the care arrangements and whether she gives her consent for the child(ren) in her care to undergo a DNA test (see below) if she has parental responsibility. A statement is prepared if the case is to go to court.[89]

DNA testing

DNA testing involves taking a cell sample from the parent with care, alleged non-resident parent and qualifying child. The test establishes the genetic fingerprint of the individual and is virtually conclusive. The test is usually done by taking a cheek cell sample, which is gathered from the inside of the mouth using a swab. It is possible for blood to be taken for the DNA test instead, but all parties must use the same method. Where young children are involved, a cheek cell sample will usually be preferred. The use of cheek cell samples means that a fear of needles could not be used as a reason not to take the test.

DNA testing is used in cases where parentage cannot be presumed and the parties involved give consent. In cases where the CSA has applied to court for a declaration/declarator of parentage the court may order DNA testing.

The CSA has special arrangements with a private testing agency called LGC Ltd and reduced testing rates may apply. There are special rules that apply where the alleged non-resident parent wishes to arrange his own test.

Consent

If there is a dispute about parentage, both the parent with care and the alleged non-resident parent are asked to agree to a DNA test. Written consent must be obtained before a test can be made.[90] If the qualifying child is under 16 the parent or guardian must give consent.

Refusal to take the test will have consequences.

- If a parent with care on IS/income-based JSA refuses to take the test herself, a reduced benefit decision may be made (see p65).[91]
- If a parent with care on benefits refuses her consent for the qualifying child to take the test, a reduced benefit decision cannot be made. If the parent accepts DNA testing for herself, but refuses her consent for the child, a court can direct DNA testing if it is in the best interests of the child, but it cannot force the child to take the test.[92]
- An alleged non-resident parent may be assumed to be the parent (see p15).[93]
- If a non-resident parent already assumed to be the parent refuses to take a test, the CSA will not revise the calculation.
- A voluntary applicant refusing consent for herself and/or a qualifying child may mean the case is closed.
- There is no guidance on when a parent or guardian of a child applicant in Scotland refuses consent, but DWP policy indicates that action may be taken to get a declaration/declarator of parentage.

The reason for any refusal must be explored. The DNA test now usually involves taking a cheek cell sample. This means that objections on medical or religious grounds which applied to blood tests may no longer be viable. A blood test can be offered as an alternative to the mouth swab. In this case, all the other parties will be tested in the same way.

If the alleged non-resident parent agrees to the test, but fails to attend the appointment, parentage will be assumed unless there are good reasons – eg, he was in hospital, did not receive test notification or was ill. If the person with care fails to attend, a reduced benefit decision may be made or the case closed.

Paying for the DNA test

The CSA offers discounted tests to alleged non-resident parents who are prepared to take it in advance. These are known as voluntary cases.[94] The cost varies depending on the number of people tested. In the latest edition of the CSA's leaflet on disputed parentage and DNA testing, the fee for testing three people in voluntary cases is £194.13.[95] The alleged non-resident parent must agree to the results being passed to the CSA.

In cases where the court directs the DNA test to be taken, the non-discounted fee is charged. Rates vary according to the number of people tested. In the latest edition of the disputed parentage leaflet, the non-discounted cost of a test for three people is £257.58.

If the alleged non-resident parent is found not to be the parent, a full refund of the cost of the test is made, as long as the parent with care confirms that the photograph of the person who attended for the test is the person she named as the father.[96]

If the alleged non-resident parent says he cannot afford to pay for the test in advance, the CSA may pay for the test initially if the alleged non-resident parent agrees to accept the results and to recoup the fee should the test show that he is the father. If the alleged non-resident parent still refuses to take the DNA test, parentage may be assumed (see p15).

The CSA can recover the costs of the test from the alleged non-resident parent if the test does not exclude him from being the parent and:[97]
- he does not now deny that he is the parent; *or*
- a court has now made a declaration that he is a parent (in Scotland, a declarator of parentage).

There are no refunds of travelling expenses for attending a DNA test.[98]

Private testing

An alleged non-resident parent may arrange the test himself either through LGC Ltd or another firm. In the meantime, the CSA may still assume parentage if the CSA test has been refused.[99] In this case there would be no discount or CSA non-discounted rate offered. Prices vary depending on which firm is used but are likely to be at least £400; this fee may not be refunded if the test proves negative.

The test must be carried out by an approved agency and proper security measures must be in place, otherwise even where the test is negative the CSA and court may not accept the result.

Tests must involve the mother; a test with only the alleged non-resident parent and the qualifying child will not be accepted. The CSA will not provide the address of the parent with care to the alleged non-resident parent or the independent testing company. If the parent with care does not consent to a private test no action can be taken against her.

DNA test results

The test results take about 12 weeks and are normally sent to the parent with care, the alleged non-resident parent and the CSA.[100]

If the alleged non-resident parent is shown to be the parent, he will also be sent notification by the CSA. The CSA will also phone the non-resident parent to gather any additional information needed, or a child maintenance enquiry form may be issued.[101] (If a form has been issued earlier, the date of liability for child maintenance is the date of the first contact – see p368.) If the alleged non-resident parent still does not accept paternity, he will have to take court proceedings to obtain a declaration/declarator of non-parentage. The CSA may make a calculation or refuse to revise because a positive DNA test is grounds to assume parentage.

If the DNA tests confirm that the person who took the test as the alleged non-resident parent is not the father, action is taken to confirm that the identity of the person tested was the alleged non-resident parent. If this is not the case, the CSA will pass the case to the fraud team if the alleged non-resident parent sent someone else, or pursue further tracing if the wrong person has been traced. If the identity is confirmed, the parent with care may be re-interviewed about any other possible non-resident parent.[102] If the parent with care is on IS/income-based JSA, Jobcentre Plus will do this.

Preparation for court proceedings

When all possible action and investigation has been completed, a CSA supervisor decides whether to apply to court for a declaration of parentage (in Scotland, declarator of parentage).[103] CSA guidance indicates that court action should be rare given the increased grounds on which to assume parentage. Examples of situations where court action may be possible include:[104]

- a DNA test is inconclusive;
- cases involving fertility treatment where the alleged non-resident parent denies he gave consent to the treatment;
- in post-calculation cases where the parent with care disputes the non-resident parent's non-conclusive evidence. In this instance, the non-resident parent must apply to court (the CSA may not be involved in this action but may be informed of the outcome).

If the CSA intends to take court action, a file is compiled detailing, for example, official documents (such as marriage certificates), interviews, statements, phone calls, correspondence, investigations and other documentary evidence, including exhibits such as a birthday card from the alleged non-resident parent to the child.[105]

If the CSA decides not to take court action, the person with care may initiate proceedings.[106] The parent with care or non-resident parent may raise court proceedings at any time.

If a case is to go to court, a proceedings file is prepared by the CSA.[107] A copy of the child's full birth certificate is obtained from the Registrar if the parent with care cannot supply one.[108] If the parent with care has mentioned potential witnesses (see p91) – eg, to confirm that she and the alleged non-resident parent were in a relationship at the time of the conception, a record is made of the witnesses' names and addresses.[109] In Scotland, two written witness statements must be obtained to attest to the sexual nature of the relationship, otherwise the case cannot proceed to court.[110] In Scotland, such files are referred to the solicitors' office at the Scottish Office (Office of the Solicitors to the Advocate General for Scotland) and, in England and Wales, to the solicitors' branch of the Department for Work and Pensions (DWP) (SolB2).[111] In England and Wales, unless the solicitor advises that the case should not go ahead, the application proceeds for a declaration of parentage that may be heard under lay representation. This means that a local CSA officer, known as the court presenting officer, presents the case to court.[112] If the case is complex or contentious a solicitor will be present. In Scotland, the solicitor presents the case.[113] Slightly different arrangements may be needed if the alleged non-resident parent is in Northern Ireland, or the case has been referred from Northern Ireland.

The hearings

The CSA *or* the person with care can apply to court for a declaration/declarator of parentage. However, if the CSA is willing to do so, the person with care should normally not also apply, because she would probably have to pay her own legal costs (and those of the alleged non-resident parent) if she loses (see p96). If the CSA suspends the case (see p94), but the person with care wants to go to court herself, she should consider taking legal advice.

The hearing normally takes place in the alleged non-resident parent's area, unless the alleged non-resident parent knows the parent with care's address or both parties and the court agree to it being held in the person with care's area.[114]

The first court hearing is known as a directions hearing (a similar preliminary hearing is heard by the sheriff in Scotland). This is an informal hearing where the parties produce the documentary evidence and the clerk to the court arranges procedure, including directions for DNA tests.[115] There is no legal obligation for the alleged non-resident parent and parent with care to attend. However, in England and Wales, if the alleged non-resident parent does not attend, the court may adjourn the hearing and ask the CSA (or, if it is her application, the parent with care) to serve notice of the hearing on him in person.

Only the courts have the power to order blood tests (including DNA tests – see p91) in any civil proceedings in which paternity is an issue.[116] If convinced that blood testing would be against the child's interests, the court should not order it.[117] A court can direct that blood tests be used to ascertain whether or not a party is excluded from being a parent of the child, but cannot force anyone to give a blood sample. It can, however, overrule a child's lack of consent if it believes it is in the child's interests.[118] However, the court may draw its own adverse inferences if a person fails to comply, depending on all the circumstances of the case.[119] Courts can only order DNA or blood testing if a party applies for it and agrees to pay. However, if that party wins the case, the court will usually order the losing party to pay costs, which can include the costs of any test. In Scotland, if an alleged non-resident parent takes action for a declaration of non-parentage or illegitimacy and the CSA does not defend the action, no expenses can be awarded against the CSA.[120]

In England and Wales, if DNA tests have been directed, a second informal hearing is arranged with the clerk once the result is obtained. If it is negative, the CSA withdraws the case.[121] If the result is positive, and the alleged non-resident parent admits he is the father, a full hearing before the magistrates takes place, if possible, on the same day. In other cases, notice of a full hearing at a magistrates'/ sheriff's court is sent to all parties. The magistrate (or sheriff) then considers whether to make a declaration/declarator of parentage on the available evidence.

Outcome of the court proceedings

The CSA prioritises cases where a declaration/declarator of parentage is issued and, if no calculation has been made, telephones the non-resident parent to gather the information needed to make a calculation.[122] If the court finds that the person is not the parent, the parent with care is approached to establish if a different alleged non-resident parent can be named.[123] In the case of a parent with care on IS/income-based JSA, this will be carried out by Jobcentre Plus and a reduced benefit decision may be made (see p65). In other cases, unless the parent can name an alternate alleged non-resident parent, the case may be closed.

The court can order any party to pay some, or all, of the legal costs of another party. Usually, the losing party is ordered to pay the other parties' costs. However, an order for costs cannot normally be made against a party who is legally aided. In addition to the costs of any test, the CSA usually asks the court to order the losing party to pay towards its own presentation costs – eg, solicitors' fees and witnesses' costs.

4. **Further investigations**

The Child Support Agency (CSA) may make further enquiries when considering an application, revision or supersession. In practice, the CSA normally makes no further investigation where:

- parentage is accepted; *and*
- information is provided to make a calculation; *and*
- any documents requested are provided – eg, copy of maintenance agreement, payslips or tax calculation notice.

Even where one parent challenges the details provided by the other, the CSA may be reluctant to make any further enquiries unless the parent can provide evidence to trigger a revision/supersession. Enquiries are normally made by telephone, if possible.

The need for evidence

Corroboration of evidence – other evidence to support what the CSA already has – is not requested unless the evidence the CSA has is self-contradictory, improbable, or contradicted by other evidence.[124] For example, if a self-employed parent says s/he has not worked for six months, this is normally accepted without any written evidence.

Evidence includes documentary, written and oral information.[125] CSA staff are advised to weigh carefully any direct, indirect or hearsay evidence. CSA guidance says that hearsay evidence (ie, evidence from one person of what another person has told her/him, or of what s/he has read) is of limited value – eg, a report from a parent with care that a non-resident parent's earnings have increased by £20 a week may be sufficient evidence to consider supersession, but insufficient on which to base a new calculation.[126] (In other words, some more reliable evidence would be needed before deciding what level of earnings to include in any superseding decision.)

Verifying information

Verification of housing costs (in 'old rules' cases) and earnings is routinely sought by the CSA.[127] However, if every effort to obtain verification of earnings has failed, the amounts provided are accepted as long as they are reasonable. Verification of benefits, other income and costs (the latter where needed to make an 'old rules' assessment) is only sought where the amounts appear to be disproportionate or there is another reason to doubt them.

Verification for CSA purposes is defined in guidance as evidence corroborating information already held.[128] CSA staff can request evidence in the form of formal documents and signed statements but should, wherever possible, collect information by phone and then seek written confirmation if necessary.[129]

Verification of earnings from a non-resident parent's employer is only requested if the employee cannot provide it (see p77).[130] A parent and any employer who fails to provide information when requested may be liable for criminal sanctions (see p81).

Self-employed earnings are usually taken from the self-assessment return to HM Revenue and Customs, or from a tax calculation notice.[131] If not supplied, attempts will be made to obtain the information through phone calls, accountants, companies or partnerships with or for whom the parent works, a face-to-face interview, an inspector's visit, or a request to HM Revenue and Customs for self-assessment details where all other means to obtain the information have failed.[132] Criminal sanctions may apply if those required to provide information have failed to do so (see p78).

When the Child Support Agency does not investigate

In some cases, the CSA fails to investigate to the satisfaction of one party. Except where one parent believes that the other should not be entitled to income support/income-based jobseeker's allowance (see p383), this situation does not usually arise until the calculation is made because the parent with care is only then notified of the non-resident parent's income (see p354). If, at any stage, a person believes that the CSA ought to make more enquiries, the CSA should be asked to do so. The most effective way is to phone the CSA explaining all the information the person has, asking what enquiries have already been made and suggesting further enquiries. Reference should be made to the CSA's power to require information (see p74) and use an inspector to conduct investigations (see below). If the CSA refuses to say what steps have been taken or to make further enquiries, judicial review may be possible (see p383). An appeal tribunal can make enquiries as soon as an appeal is made (see p404). The tribunal has more powers than the CSA and it may be easier to persuade it to use them.

A person who is dissatisfied with CSA enquiries can also make her/his own enquiries and pass the information to the CSA – eg, a person with care applying for a court order for spousal or civil partner maintenance (see p32) may obtain information about the non-resident parent's income.

The inspectors

The CSA can appoint inspectors to obtain information required.[133] The inspectors are permanently appointed and are not tied to investigations on a specific case.[134] The inspector must have a certificate of appointment, which must be produced when entering premises.[135]

If an office in Great Britain needs to appoint an inspector in Northern Ireland, or the other way around, an inspector can be appointed in the other territory.[136]

Powers of inspectors

Inspectors have the power to enter premises (except those used only as a home),[137] to make enquiries and to inspect documents.[138] Premises can include vehicles, aircraft, moveable structures and offshore installations.[139] The power to enter premises does not include any power to enter by force. Premises include ones where:[140]

- the non-resident parent is, or has been, employed;
- the non-resident parent carries out, or has carried out, a trade;
- there is information held by someone whom the inspector has reasonable grounds for suspecting has information about the non-resident parent acquired in the course of her/his own trade, profession, vocation or business.

An inspector can question any person aged 18 or over found on the premises s/he has entered[141] and request all such information and documents s/he might reasonably require from:[142]

- an occupier of the premises;
- an employer or employee working there;
- anyone else whose work or business is based at those premises;
- an employee or agent of any of the above.

An inspector can enter Crown premises in order to obtain information as long as the Queen is not in residence. Crown employees or anyone carrying out Crown functions on the premises can be questioned and asked for information in the same way as anyone else.[143]

No person is required to give any evidence or answer any question that might incriminate her/him or her/his spouse or civil partner.[144] Deliberately delaying or obstructing an inspector carrying out her/his duties is an offence. Failing or refusing to answer a question or to provide evidence requested is also an offence, unless there is a good reason for not doing so.[145] The maximum fine is £1,000.[146]

A solicitor is entitled to claim privilege as regards information about a client's confidential affairs and can refuse to give information. Also, the CSA has given assurances that the powers of inspectors will not be used in relation to other representatives, except where information is required from an employer about an employee.

There are clear directions in CSA guidance regarding further investigations if fraud or misrepresentation is suspected.[147]

5. **Duty to disclose changes**

There is no general duty to volunteer information about any changes of circumstance to the Child Support Agency (CSA). However, there are some changes which must be notified. These only apply to a person with care and only when a calculation has been made, including a nil rate. No other person has a duty to disclose any change in circumstances.

A person with care has a duty to tell the CSA if she believes that a calculation has ceased to have effect because:[148]

- the person with care, non-resident parent or qualifying child has died;
- the person with care, non-resident parent or qualifying child is no longer within CSA jurisdiction – ie, habitually resident in the UK or working for a relevant employer and treated as habitually resident (see p27);
- the non-resident parent is no longer a non-resident parent of the child or, if there is more than one, all the children named in the calculation – eg, because the child is adopted;
- a child no longer counts as a child, or as a qualifying child (see p18); or
- she has stopped being a person with care in relation to the child or, if there is more than one, all the children named in the calculation.

The person with care is required to give the reasons for her belief in writing. She may be required to give further information for a decision to be made.

The person with care is not required to inform the CSA until the change has taken place. There is no duty to disclose information to the CSA except in the circumstances described above and where the CSA has the right to request the information – eg, a non-resident parent does not have to disclose a change of income. This is different from the position for social security claims, where there is a continuing duty to disclose any relevant change.

For the effect of not disclosing information, see p81.

6. Disclosure of information by the Child Support Agency

In the course of their investigations, Child Support Agency (CSA) staff collect a lot of information and evidence about people affected by maintenance applications. Some forms of disclosure are part of the CSA's duties, such as giving information to courts, tribunals, the Department for Work and Pensions (DWP) or local authorities. Each party to a maintenance calculation must be given details of how the calculation has been worked out (see p354). The CSA may disclose information given to it by one party to another party to explain:[149]

- why an application for child maintenance or for revision or supersession has been rejected; *or*
- why an application cannot proceed or why a calculation will not be made; *or*
- why a calculation is cancelled or ceases to have effect; *or*
- how a calculation has been worked out; *or*
- why a decision has been made not to arrange for, or to stop, collection of child maintenance; *or*
- why a particular method of enforcement has been used; *or*
- why a decision has been made not to use or to stop using a deduction from earnings order (see p443) or a liability order (see p450).

The parties to an assessment are the person with care, the non-resident parent and a child applicant in Scotland. If one of those people has died, a person appointed to represent that person or a personal representative handling a revision/supersession or appeal is also a party.[150] Any request for the above information must be made in writing to the CSA, giving reasons, but the CSA can provide the information without a request.[151]

The CSA must not disclose a person's address or other information which could reasonably be expected to lead to that person being located. This disclosure can only be made when the person concerned has given written permission. (This does not apply where a case is appealed – see p403.) Also, the CSA must not disclose information which could reasonably be expected to lead to the identification of any person other than a person with care, non-resident parent, person treated as non-resident or qualifying child.[152]

The CSA can disclose any information it has to an appeal tribunal, court and, in 'new rules' cases, to anyone with a right of appeal, if it is for proceedings under the child support or benefits legislation.[153] In practice, in a child support appeal, CSA papers are included in the CSA submission sent to each party (see p403). The CSA can also disclose information to a court which has made, varied or revived a maintenance order or agreement if that information is required in relation to those proceedings or other matters arising from them.[154] The CSA can also disclose information it has to local authorities for their use in administering housing benefit or council tax benefit.[155] Otherwise, information cannot be given to third parties without the written permission of the person to whom it relates (see below). See above for dealing with representatives. Any unauthorised disclosure of information is a criminal offence (see below).

Anyone wishing to see a copy of the information on her/him held electronically by the CSA can apply in writing. Under the Data Protection Act 1984 this information must be supplied within 40 days. If anyone has concerns about the collection, retention, accuracy or use of this information, the Data Protection Registrar can be contacted.

Disclosure to other government departments

The CSA can disclose information to government departments dealing with benefits, including the DWP agencies.[156] This includes information obtained by using CSA powers or disclosed to the CSA voluntarily.

As the DWP has close links with the Home Office, disclosure may create problems for people from abroad, in particular possible illegal entrants and those subject to the public funds requirement. If there are any doubts about whether information ought to be disclosed to the CSA, you should get advice first from a law centre or independent advice centre dealing with immigration problems (see Appendix 4). You cannot be prosecuted for refusing to give information unless it was requested by the CSA or an inspector (see p98).

CSA staff can exchange information with their counterparts in Northern Ireland and *vice versa*. Once disclosed, the information is subject to local rules about unauthorised disclosure.[157]

Unauthorised disclosure

Unauthorised disclosure of information is a criminal offence. This offence applies to anyone who is or has been a child support officer, a CSA employee, a civil servant carrying out a function under the Child Support Acts (eg, a Jobcentre Plus officer helping the CSA make enquiries), staff of appeal tribunals, various ombudsmen and their staff, staff at the National Audit Office, and anyone who, whether or not a civil servant, is providing services to the DWP.[158] It does not apply to members of appeal tribunals or to child support commissioners.

It is not an offence to disclose information if:[159]
- the CSA can do so under the disclosure regulations;
- the CSA has already done so under those regulations;
- it is in the form of a summary or statistics and it cannot be related to any particular person; *or*
- the person to whom the information relates gives consent, or if that person's affairs are being dealt with under a power of attorney, by a receiver under the Mental Health Act, a mental health appointee or a Scottish mental health custodian, the attorney, receiver, custodian or appointee gives consent.

A person who has broken these rules would have a defence if s/he could prove that s/he believed s/he was making the disclosure under these rules, or believed that disclosure under these rules had already been made, and had no reason to think otherwise.[160]

On conviction, the maximum prison sentence is six months and the maximum fine is £5,000. On conviction on indictment, the maximum prison sentence is two years.[161] No prosecutions have been brought.

Disclosure of information about spent convictions, other than as part of an official duty, is also a criminal offence.[162]

Notes

1. Information-seeking powers
1 s14 and Sch 2 CSA 1991
2 PG, Client Communications, Positive Client Contact
3 CSA Operational Improvement Plan 2006-2009
4 ss4(4), 6(9) and 7(5) CSA 1991
5 Reg 3(1A) CS(IED) Regs
6 PG, Inform NRP of Application, Contacting NRP for First Time
7 Reg 3(1) CS(IED) Regs
8 Reg 3(1A) CS(IED) Regs
9 Reg 3(2) CS(IED) Regs
10 s46(1)(c) CSA 1991
11 Reg 3(2) CS(IED) Regs before amendment by CS(IEDMAJ)(A) Regs
12 Reg 2(1) CS(IED) Regs
13 *Purdew v Seress-Smith* [1992] 23 September 1992 (QBD)
14 Regs 1(2) and 2(2)(a) CS(IED) Regs
15 Reg 2(2)(b) CS(IED) Regs
16 Reg 2(2)(c) CS(IED) Regs
17 Reg 2(2)(ba) CS(IED) Regs
18 Reg 2(2)(cc) and (cd) CS(IED) Regs
19 Reg 2(2) CS(IED) Regs before amendment by CS(IEDMAJ)(A) Regs
20 Reg 2(2)(g) CS(IED) Regs
21 Reg 2(2)(f) CS(IED) Regs
22 Reg 2(3) CS(IED) Regs
23 Order 1 r3 CCR 1981
24 Reg 2(2)(e) CS(IED) Regs
25 Reg 2(2)(h) CS(IED) Regs
26 See s3 SSA 1998
27 Regs 2(2)(d) and 3(1)(a) CS(IED) Regs
28 s122D SSAA 1992
29 Sch 2 para 1 CSA 1991
30 Reg 3(2)(h) CS(IED) Regs
31 Sch 5 TCA 2002
32 s6 and Sch 1 Taxes Management Act 1970; s182 Finance Act 1989
33 CSA Operational Improvement Plan 2006-2009
34 Reg 2(h) CS(MCP) Regs; credit reference agencies are as defined by s145(8) Consumer Credit Act 1974
35 Reg 3(4) CS(MCP) Regs
36 Reg 5(1) CS(IED) Regs
37 PG, Gather Information and Evidence, Evidence Timescales
38 s14A CSA 1991
39 s14A(4) CSA 1991
40 PG, Gather Information and Evidence, Criminal Sanctions for Failing to Provide Information
41 s14A CSA 1991
42 Reg 3A CS(IED) Regs
43 CCS/16535/1996 reported as R(CS) 2/98; CCS/12686/1996 reported as R(CS) 8/98
44 CCS/7966/1995

2. Contacting the non-resident parent
45 PG, Inform NRP of Application, Contacting the NRP for the First Time
46 CSA Operational Improvement Plan 2006-2009
47 CSA Client Charter 2006 (CSA 2047)

48 PG, Specialist Areas, Basic Trace; Additional Trace
49 PG, Specialist Areas, DCI
50 PG, Specialist Areas, CES (Common Enquiry Screen)
51 PG, Specialist Areas, Inland Revenue
52 PG, Specialist Areas, NICO National Insurance Contributions Office
53 PG, Specialist Areas, Where the Employer is the Ministry of Defence
54 PG, Specialist Areas, Prison Service; Prison Addresses in Northern Ireland
55 PG, Specialist Areas, Employers
56 PG, Specialist Areas, Referring Case to Child Support Agency Inspector
57 PG, Specialist Areas, Local Authorities
58 PG, Specialist Areas, DVLA/DVLNI
59 PG, Specialist Areas, Fast Trace
60 PG, PWC in Receipt of a Prescribed Benefit
61 Regs 1(2) and 5(1) CS(MCP) Regs
62 PG, Inform NRP of Application, Contacting NRP for First Time
63 PG, Inform NRP of Application, Contacting NRP for First Time
64 PG, Inform NRP of Application, Contacting NRP for First Time
65 PG, Inform NRP of Application, NRP Co-operation
66 Reg 5(2) CS(MCP) Regs
67 Reg 5(3) and (4) CS(MCP) Regs
68 R(CS) 8/98
69 PG, Inform NRP of Application, NRP Under 16; NRP Between 16 & 19
70 PG, Inform NRP of Application, Definition of a Child

3. Parentage investigations

71 PG, Specialist Areas, Disputed Parentage Post Assessment/Calculation
72 s26 CSA 1991
73 s26 CSA 1991
74 PG, Disputed Parentage Post Assessment/Calculation
75 s26 CSA 1991
76 PG, Inform NPR of Application, NRP Under 16; NRP Between 16 & 19 Years
77 PG, Inform NRP of Application, ANRP Child Details
78 PG, Specialist Areas, ANRP Evidence Dialog
79 PG, Specialist Areas, Gathering ANRP's Statement
80 PatG, Chapter 3, para 175(1)
81 PatG, Chapter 3, para 175(2)
82 PatG, Chapter 4, para 120
83 PatG, Chapter 3, para 184
84 PatG, Chapter 4, para 162

85 PatG, Chapter 2, para 141
86 PatG, Chapter 2, para 141
87 PG, Specialist Areas, Parentage Statement
88 PatG, Appendix 4
89 PatG, Appendix 4
90 PG, Specialist Areas, Consent for DNA Test
91 s46 CSA 1991
92 PG, Specialist Areas, PWC Refuses DNA Test for the QC
93 s26, Case A3(b), CSA 1991
94 PG, Specialist Areas, DNA Test Referral
95 *What Happens if Someone Denies They are the Parent of a Child?*, CSL304, April 2007
96 *What Happens if Someone Denies They are the Parent of a Child?*, CSL304, April 2007
97 s27A CSA 1991
98 PG, Specialist Areas, DNA Test Referral
99 PG, Specialist Areas, ANRP Wants to Arrange Own DNA Test
100 PG, Specialist Areas, DNA Test Results
101 PG, Specialist Areas, Positive DNA Test Result
102 Paternity Guide, Chapter 6, para 210
103 s27 CSA 1991; PG, Specialist Areas, Court Action
104 PG, Specialist Areas, Court Action
105 PG, Specialist Areas, Gathering the Evidence for Court Proceedings
106 s27 CSA 1991
107 PG, Specialist Areas, Preparing the Case for Court Proceedings (separate guidance for England and Wales, and Scotland)
108 PG, Specialist Areas, Obtaining Birth Certificates
109 PG, Specialist Areas, Preparing the Case for Court Proceedings (England and Wales)
110 PG, Specialist Areas, Preparing the Case for Court Proceedings (Scotland)
111 PG, Specialist Areas, Authorising Court Proceedings (separate guidance for England and Wales, and for Scotland)
112 PG, Specialist Areas, Lay Representation (England and Wales)
113 PG, Specialist Areas, Authorising Court Proceedings (Scotland)
114 PG, Specialist Areas, Authorising Court Proceedings (separate guidance for England and Wales, and Scotland)
115 PG, Specialist Areas, Directions Hearing (England and Wales)
116 s20 FLRA 1969; *Re H (Paternity: Blood Test)* [1996] 2 FLR 65

117 *W v Official Solicitor* [1972] AC 24
118 s21 FLRA 1969
119 s23 FLRA 1969; *Re A (Paternity: Refusal of Blood Test)* [1994] 2 FLR 463
120 s28(2) CSA 1991; s7 LR(PC)(S)A 1986; r152 AS(CSA) (AOCSCR)
121 PG, Specialist Areas, Second Directions Hearing – DNA Cases Only (England and Wales)
122 PG, Specialist Areas, ANRP Declared to be the Parent
123 PatG, Chapter 17, para 121

4. Further investigations
124 PG, Gather Information and Evidence, Corroboration of Evidence; Self-contradictory Evidence; Uncorroborated Evidence
125 PG, Gather Information and Evidence, Types of Evidence
126 PG, Gather Information and Evidence, Hearsay Evidence
127 PG, Gather Information and Evidence, Verification Requirements; Evidence of Earnings and Income
128 PG, Gather Information and Evidence, Evidence and Verification
129 PG, Gather Information and Evidence, Collecting Evidence; Obtaining Further Evidence
130 PG, Gather Information and Evidence, Collecting Evidence
131 PG, Gather Information and Evidence, Treatment of Self-employed Earnings
132 PG, Gather Information and Evidence, Approaching Inland Revenue for Self-employed Income
133 s15(1) CSA 1991
134 PG, Gather Information and Evidence, Use of Inspectors
135 s15(8) CSA 1991
136 Sch 1 para 8 CS(NIRA) Regs
137 s14(4A) CSA 1991
138 s15(4) CSA 1991
139 s15(11) CSA 1991
140 s15(4A) CSA 1991
141 s15(5) CSA 1991
142 s15(6) CSA 1991
143 s57 CSA 1991; reg 7 CS(IED) Regs
144 s15(7) CSA 1991
145 s15(9) CSA 1991
146 s15(9) CSA 1991
147 PG, Specialist Areas, Criminal Compliance

5. Duty to disclose changes
148 Reg 6 CS(IED) Regs; ss44, 55 and Sch 1 para 16 CSA 1991

6. Disclosure of information by the Child Support Agency
149 Reg 9A(1) CS(IED) Regs
150 Reg 9A(2) CS(IED) Regs
151 Reg 9A(3) CS(IED) Regs
152 Reg 9A(4) CS(IED) Regs
153 Reg 8(1) and (2) CS(IED) Regs
154 Reg 8(3) CS(IED) Regs
155 s3 SSA 1998; PG, Gather Information and Evidence, Disclosure
156 s3 SSA 1998
157 Sch 1 para 7 CS(NIRA) Regs
158 s50 CSA 1991; reg 11 CS(IED) Regs
159 s50 CSA 1991
160 s50(3) CSA 1991
161 s50(4) CSA 1991
162 s9 Rehabilitation of Offenders Act 1974

Part 3

Amount of maintenance: 'new rules'

Chapter 6

The maintenance calculation ('new rules')

This chapter covers:
1. Maintenance calculation rates (below)
2. Net income (p114)
3. Shared care (p121)

1. Maintenance calculation rates

To carry out a child maintenance calculation the following information is needed:[1]
* the number of qualifying children;
* the number of relevant other children (see p23);
* the number of any relevant non-resident children (see p113);
* the number of persons with care;
* benefits (if any) received by the non-resident parent;
* whether the non-resident parent meets the conditions for the nil rate (see p108);
* the income of the non-resident parent (see p114);
* the number of nights (if any) that the non-resident parent has care of a qualifying child (see p125);
* the number of nights (if any) that a local authority has care of a qualifying child (see p127).

If a non-resident parent fails to provide sufficient information to calculate child support maintenance, a default maintenance decision may be made (see p352). A penalty for failing to provide information may also be imposed (see p81).

There are four rates of child support maintenance that can be applied:
* nil rate (see p108);
* flat rate (see p109);
* reduced rate (see p110);
* basic rate (see p111).

Child support maintenance will be calculated for each non-resident parent separately. This means a person with care may receive the flat rate of maintenance from one non-resident parent and an amount from the other non-resident parent worked out using the basic rate.

In all cases, the amount of child maintenance calculated is a weekly amount.[2] Rounding rules apply to the different rates as follows.[3]

- In basic rate and reduced rate cases, fractions of a pound are disregarded if less than half or rounded up to the next pound if a half or over.
- In all other cases, fractions of a penny are disregarded if less than a half or rounded up to the next penny if a half or over – ie, where there is apportionment or shared care.

There is a maximum amount of income which can be taken into account for maintenance purposes (see p121).

Apportionment

If there is more than one person with care in relation to a non-resident parent the amount of maintenance due may be apportioned between them in relation to the number of qualifying children of each person with care.[4]

Where apportionment occurs and rounding provisions would result in the total amount of maintenance being different from the total amount before any apportionment, the maintenance due is adjusted.[5] This may mean that maintenance due to one of the persons with care has to be reduced by a penny, so that no one person with care is disadvantaged. This reduction will be reallocated between the persons with care from time to time.[6]

Apportionment occurs after the calculation of maintenance at the appropriate rate and before any decrease for shared care.[7]

In basic and reduced rate cases, where an adjustment is made which reduces the non-resident parent's liability to less than £5 (eg, because of shared care or a variation), the amount payable will be £5 apportioned between the people with care.[8]

If there is more than one person with care in relation to a qualifying child, the maintenance due for this child may be further apportioned between the persons with care, but only if a request to apportion maintenance has been agreed by the Child Support Agency (CSA) (see p111).

Nil rate

This applies if the non-resident parent is:[9]

- a student;
- a child;
- a prisoner;

- a 16/17-year-old and receiving income support (IS)/income-based jobseeker's allowance (JSA) (or his partner is);
- receiving an allowance for work-based learning for young people or for Skillseekers training in Scotland. Work-based learning includes schemes such as Entry to Employment and Modern Apprenticeships. Young people may receive an education maintenance allowance or a training allowance;
- resident in a care home, independent hospital or is being provided with a care home service or/and independent health care service and who receives one of the prescribed benefits (as for the flat rate) or has the whole/part of the cost of his accommodation met by a local authority;
- a person with net income (including that from any of the prescribed benefits for the flat rate (listed below)), of less than £5 a week.

Example
Kerry is a parent with care of two children, Mia and Lewis. Her ex-partner, Craig, is in prison. In this case the nil rate applies. However, even though Craig is in prison, he is still sent a child maintenance enquiry form to complete. When he comes out of prison Kerry could ask for a supersession.

Flat rate

The flat rate of £5 applies where the non-resident parent does not qualify for the nil rate and:[10]
- his weekly income is £100 or less; *or*
- he receives one of the following:[11]
  - bereavement allowance;
  - retirement pension;
  - incapacity benefit;
  - carer's allowance;
  - maternity allowance;
  - severe disablement allowance;
  - industrial injuries benefit;
  - widowed parent's allowance;
  - widow's pension;
  - contribution-based JSA;
  - a training allowance (other than for work-based learning for young people or Skillseekers);
  - war disablement pension;
  - war widow's, war widower's or surviving civil partner's war pension;
  - payments under the Armed Forces Compensation Scheme;
  - a social security benefit paid by a country other than the UK;

- IS or income-based JSA (or his partner does);[12]
- pension credit (PC).

The flat rate can be halved for couples where the non-resident parent's partner is also a non-resident parent with a maintenance application in force, and either he or his partner receives IS, income-based JSA or PC.[13] If the non-resident parent is in a polygamous relationship and there is more than one partner, if the non-resident parent or a partner receives IS, income-based JSA or PC, the flat rate is apportioned between them.[14]

There are special rules about shared care in flat-rate cases (see p131).

Example

Craig has now come out of prison and gets income-based JSA. Kerry requests a supersession and Craig has £5 a week flat rate maintenance deducted from his benefit.

If Craig moved in with Josie and claimed income-based JSA as a couple, the flat rate of £5 would still apply and Kerry would receive £5 a week. However, if Josie were also a non-resident parent the flat rate would be halved. In this case, Kerry would receive £2.50 a week.

In the situation above, if Josie had two persons with care (Alison and Penny) each caring for one qualifying child, they would find their maintenance reduced as the flat rate applies at £2.50 and is then apportioned. Alison and Penny would each receive £1.25 each.

Reduced rate

This applies if neither the flat or nil rate applies and the non-resident parent has income of less than £200 but more than £100.[15] The flat rate of £5 is added to a percentage of the parent's income between £100 and £200.[16] This means that only the income above £100, but under £200, is used in the calculation – eg, if net income is £150 the percentage is applied to £50. The percentage depends on the number of qualifying children and the number of relevant children (ie, one for whom the non-resident parent or his partner receives child benefit[17]). Rounding is to the nearest pound.

Reduced rate percentages

Number of relevant other children	Number of qualifying children (including relevant non-resident children)		
	1	2	3 or more
0	25%	35%	45%
1	20.5%	29%	37.5%
2	19%	27%	35%
3 or more	17.5%	25%	32.5%

Step 1

Work out the net income over £100 but less than £200.

Step 2

Work out the relevant percentage depending on the number of relevant children and qualifying children. Apply this percentage to the income worked out at Step 1 and add this to £5, rounding to the nearest pound.

Step 3

If there is more than one person with care, apportion this amount between them depending on the number of qualifying children each cares for, rounded to the nearest penny. (If there is more than one person with care in relation to a qualifying child, maintenance may only be apportioned where a request to do so has been agreed by the CSA.)

- -

Example

Simon is due to pay maintenance to Fiona for two qualifying children, John and Margaret. Simon lives with a new partner, Julie, and their baby, Paul. Simon's net income is £180 a week. The reduced rate of maintenance would apply.

Step 1   Net income = £180
          Income between £100 and £200 = £80

Step 2   Relevant percentage for one relevant child and two qualifying children is 29%
          £5 + (29% x £80) = £5 + £23.20 = £28.20 (rounded to £28)

Simon is due to pay £28 maintenance to Fiona.

If the situation were as above except that Margaret was cared for by Fiona and John stayed with his grandmother, there would still be two qualifying children but now there would be two persons with care. The maintenance calculated would need to be apportioned between them.

Step 3   Each person cares for one qualifying child, so the maintenance is divided by two.
          £28 ÷ 2 = £14

Simon now pays Fiona £14 and the grandmother £14.

- -

If the non-resident parent shares the care of any of the qualifying children, the reduced rate may be decreased further by applying the shared care rules (see p121).

Basic rate

The basic rate applies if none of the other rates (nil, flat or reduced) apply.[18] Thus, if the non-resident parent has net weekly income of £200 or more, maintenance will be calculated under the basic rate. The basic rate is a percentage of net income depending on the number of qualifying children. How much is paid will also depend on the number of relevant children. There may be other relevant non-resident children who are taken into account (see p113).

Basic rate percentages

Number of qualifying children (including relevant non-resident children)	Percentage of net income	Number of relevant children	Percentage by which net income is reduced
1	15%	1	15%
2	20%	2	20%
3 or more	25%	3 or more	25%

If the non-resident parent has one or more relevant children, his net income is reduced by an equivalent percentage (as above) before the basic rate is calculated. Therefore, the basic rate may be worked out in two steps, depending on the circumstances.

Step 1

Work out the net income of the non-resident parent. Depending on the number of relevant children, reduce this by a percentage – ie, 15 per cent, 20 per cent or 25 per cent.

Step 2

Depending on the number of qualifying children, maintenance is a proportion of this remaining net income, rounded to the nearest pound.

Step 3

If there is more than one person with care, apportion this amount between them depending on the number of qualifying children each cares for, rounded to the nearest penny. (If there is more than one person with care in relation to a qualifying child, maintenance can only be apportioned where a request to do so has been agreed by the CSA.)

Example

Simon now has a net income of £240 a week. Paul is a relevant child, and John and Margaret are the qualifying children.

Step 1   Net income is £240. One relevant child means this is reduced by 15%.

15% x £240 = £36

£240 – £36 = £204

Step 2   There are two qualifying children, so maintenance is 20% of remaining net income.

20% x £204 = £40.80 (which is rounded to £41)

Simon, therefore, pays £41 in maintenance to Fiona.

If Margaret were cared for by Fiona and John stayed with his grandmother, this £41 would be split equally between Fiona and the grandmother.

Step 3 £41 is apportioned between two persons with care. Each would receive £20.50 in maintenance from Simon.

If the non-resident parent shares the care of any of the qualifying children, the maintenance calculated may be decreased further by applying the shared care rules (see p121).

Relevant non-resident children

A non-resident parent may have other children for whom child support maintenance cannot be applied because the non-resident parent is paying maintenance for them under a maintenance order (or in Scotland, registered maintenance agreement), the order of a court outside Great Britain, or under the legislation of a jurisdiction outside the UK.[19] The CSA calls these children relevant non-resident children, although they are treated like qualifying children in relation to the calculation.[20]

Where child support is payable at either the basic rate or the reduced rate, or is calculated at one of these rates after applying a variation (see Chapter 7) and would otherwise have been the flat or nil rate, the child is counted as a qualifying child.[21] The amount of maintenance calculated is then apportioned between the persons with care in relation to the number of qualifying children they care for, including any adjustment for shared care.[22] If the total amount payable by the non-resident parent would be less than £5, the non-resident will instead pay £5, apportioned between the persons with care as appropriate.[23]

No payment is actually made for the relevant non-resident child. There is also no adjustment of the notional amount worked out for the non-resident child because of the non-resident parent sharing care or the child being in local authority care for part of the time.[24]

Example
James lives with his new partner, Amanda, and her son, Liam. He has three other children. Two (Emma and Joshua) are cared for by Elizabeth, who has just claimed IS; one (Rachel) is cared for by Hilary. James has court orders for child maintenance for Emma, Joshua and Rachel. As Elizabeth is treated as applying for child maintenance on her claim for benefit and she does not opt out, a maintenance calculation will be done for her. Hilary cannot apply for child maintenance as the court order is in force (if it was made after 3 March 2003 she could apply for child maintenance had the order been in force for one year, otherwise the order must cease before she can apply). In this case:
Emma and Joshua are qualifying children.
Liam is a relevant child (even though he is not James's child, James's new partner, Amanda, gets child benefit for him).

Rachel is a relevant non-resident child.

If James had a net income of £275 a week his maintenance worked out using the basic rate would be as follows.

Step 1   £275 – (15% x £275) = £275 – £41.25 = £233.75
Step 2   25% x £233.75 = £58.44 (rounded to £58)
Step 3   Apportionment applies between Elizabeth and Hilary. Elizabeth receives two-thirds of the maintenance calculated – ie, £38.67 (when apportioning, rounding applies to the nearest penny).
          Hilary receives her normal court order maintenance.
          Note: if Hilary could apply for child maintenance, she would receive £19.33.

2. **Net income**

The non-resident parent's net weekly income includes earned income, self-employed earnings, tax credits and payments from a pension scheme, retirement annuity or other such scheme for provision of income in retirement,[25] less any relevant deductions. Only these forms of income will be included. All other income will be ignored.

Relevant week

The concept of the 'relevant week' is important in a child support calculation, particularly when calculating income.[26] The relevant week is:[27]

- on application by the non-resident parent, the seven days immediately before the application is made;
- on application in any other case, the seven days immediately before the date the non-resident parent was first given notice that an application for child support maintenance had been made, or treated as made;
- if the original decision is revised (or superseded because of ignorance, a mistake in material fact or error in law), the relevant week for the new decision is the same as the original decision;
- if the original decision is superseded because of a change in circumstances, the seven days immediately before the date on which the application to supersede was made;
- if the original decision is superseded by the Child Support Agency (CSA) on its own initiative (except for ignorance, a mistake in fact or error), the seven days immediately before the date of notification of that intention.[28]

In some cases, the CSA may make separate maintenance calculations for different periods in a particular case.[29] If this is because of changes of circumstances, the relevant week for each separate calculation made to take account of the changes is the seven days immediately before the date of notification of the change.[30]

Disregarded income

If a payment is made in a currency other than sterling, banking charges or commission for changing the payment into sterling are disregarded.[31] In addition, a payment made in a country outside the UK with a prohibition against transfer into the UK is ignored.[32]

Earnings from employment

Earnings means 'any remuneration or profit from employment' and, as well as wages, includes:[33]
- any payments for overtime;
- any profit-related pay;
- any bonus or commission;
- any royalty or fees;
- any holiday pay (except that payable more than four weeks after ending employment);
- any retaining fee;
- statutory sick pay, statutory maternity pay, statutory adoption pay and statutory paternity pay;
- pay in lieu of notice.

Earnings do not include:[34]
- payments of expenses 'wholly, exclusively and necessarily' incurred in carrying out the duties of the job;
- any tax-exempt allowance paid by an employer;
- any gratuities paid by customers (ie, tips);
- payment in kind;
- any advance earnings or loan made by the employer;
- payments made by an employer when the employee is on strike;
- payments for duties as an auxiliary coastguard, part-time firefighter, or within the lifeboat services, territorial army or reserve forces;
- payments made by a local authority to local councillors for performing their duties;
- payments made after employment ends which relate to a specific period of time, provided that a period of equal length has elapsed between the job ending and the effective date;
- earnings from a previous job if they are paid in the same week or period in which earnings from a second job are received.

Calculating normal weekly earnings

Averaged earnings are used in the child support calculation.[35] When calculating or estimating average earnings in the relevant week, the CSA considers the evidence of the person's earnings over any appropriate period, beginning not more than eight weeks before the relevant week and ending not later than the date of the calculation. The CSA may also consider cumulative earnings in the tax year in which the relevant week falls to the date of the calculation.

If the CSA believes that the amount of weekly earnings does not accurately reflect the person's normal amount of earnings, another period can be used, taking into account earnings received and those due to be received (from past, present or future employment) and the duration and pattern (or expected duration and pattern) of any employment.[36]

The CSA must be satisfied that the calculation of earnings in the relevant week produces a figure which is not normal,[37] and that the period chosen reflects the parent's usual pattern of work – eg, the amount of overtime worked or sick leave.[38] A future period can be used to take into account, for instance, earnings from a job which has not yet begun. The CSA must also consider the expected duration and pattern of any employment. A parent may want to suggest an alternative period to the CSA, giving reasons, as the CSA cannot be expected to consider this without substantial grounds and a prompt by one of the parents.[39] The CSA must use one continuous period.[40] If a bonus, commission or profit-related pay is paid during a year ending with the relevant week separately from earnings, or in relation to a longer period than other earnings, those payments are totalled over the year and divided by 52.[41]

The CSA has to take into account any change of circumstances it is aware of between the relevant week and the effective date (see p368).[42] However, it must first calculate earnings as above for the relevant week in order to determine whether there has been a material change of circumstances.[43] For changes after this date, see p351.

The calculation of earnings is one of the areas where errors are frequently made and, therefore, it should be checked carefully. Appeal tribunals must enquire into whether the process used to determine income was correctly carried out and whether the period used for the averaging of earnings gave an accurate picture.[44]

Calculating net earnings

Net earnings from employment are counted as net income in full. Net earnings mean gross earnings less:[45]

- income tax;
- Class 1 national insurance contributions;
- all of the contributions made to an occupational/personal pension scheme (unless the scheme is intended partly to pay off a mortgage on the parent's home, in which case 75 per cent of contributions).

Income tax will be the actual amount deducted, including any tax in relation to payments not included as earnings.[46]

Pension contributions are only deducted if they are made to HM Revenue and Customs (the Revenue)-approved schemes.

Earnings from self-employment

Earnings from self-employment will, in most cases, be assessed on the basis of either:[47]
- total taxable profits from self-employment submitted to the Revenue for income tax self-assessment; *or*
- the income from self-employment as set out in the tax calculation notice, or revised notice.

If only one of these pieces of information is available, the CSA may request the other.[48] If the CSA becomes aware that a revised tax calculation notice has been issued s/he may request this in preference to the other information.

Decision makers are instructed not to contact the Revenue for earnings information until all other sources have been exhausted – eg, the parent, accountant, or companies/partnerships to whom the client has provided services.[49]

The net earnings taken into account will be the total taxable profit from self-employment less:[50]
- income tax (calculated using the personal allowances and tax rates applicable at the effective date[51]);
- national insurance (Class 2 and Class 4 contributions at the rates applicable at the effective date[52]);
- all of any personal pension premiums or retirement annuity contract premiums (but 75 per cent of such premiums where the scheme is intended to pay off a mortgage).

The net weekly earnings can only be worked out based on a period not more than 24 months before the relevant week.[53]

Decision makers are reminded that if they find contradictions between information on the self-assessment form and evidence already held, they should investigate.[54] However, this does not mean that they have to use the alternative method of calculation based on gross receipts (see p118), merely that they may seek more information from accountants or the Revenue.

It is relatively rare for a case to be assessed based on gross receipts rather than using figures submitted to the evenue. The CSA will not consider revising or superseding a decision based simply on the fact that using the gross receipts method would produce a greater amount of maintenance due to the person with care than that calculated using the tax calculation notice. However, if a non-resident parent's earnings were assessed by the gross receipts method, but he now has self-assessment details or a tax calculation notice, the CSA may supersede the maintenance decision.

Earnings calculated using gross receipts less deductions

Earnings can be calculated by using gross receipts less deductions where:[55]
- the 24-month condition is not met; *or*
- the CSA accepts it is not reasonably practicable for the non-resident parent to provide the forms submitted to, or issued by, the Revenue; *or*
- the CSA believes that the earnings figure arrived at does not accurately reflect the normal weekly earnings of the earner.

If this is the case, the net earnings are the gross receipts less:[56]
- income tax;
- national insurance;
- any premiums paid in respect of a pension or retirement annuity contract (or 75 per cent of such premiums if the scheme is intended to pay off a mortgage);
- any VAT paid in excess of VAT received in the same period as that over which the earnings are assessed; *and*
- any expenses which are reasonably incurred and wholly and exclusively defrayed for the purposes of the business. If the CSA is not satisfied that the full expense was appropriate or necessary to the business, it will allow that part considered reasonable.[57] Where an expense is part business and part private (eg, a car), the CSA has to decide on the breakdown between the two uses on the evidence available.[58]

Gross earnings include all of any board or lodgings payments if this is the self-employed earner's only or main source of income.[59]

Income tax and national insurance is calculated in the same way as for taxable profit.[60]

Business expenses include:[61]
- repayments of capital on loans used to replace or repair a business asset (but not for loans taken out for any other business purpose or if the costs are met by payments from an insurance policy);
- any income used to repair a business asset;
- any payment of interest on loans taken out for business purposes (this does not include loans taken out to acquire a share of a business, nor to pay business tax liabilities).[62]

Business expenses do *not* include:[63]
- capital expenditure;
- depreciation of capital assets;
- any sum employed in setting up or expanding the business;
- any loss incurred before the period of earnings being calculated;
- any expenses incurred in providing business entertainment;
- any loss incurred in any other self-employment.

The net weekly income of the self-employed earner will be averaged over the 52 weeks up to and including the relevant week or, if the person has been self-employed for less than a year, over the period during which the person has been self-employed (including the relevant week).[64]

The self-employed person may be asked to provide other evidence of business receipts and expenses, such as business books, receipts of bills, bank statements, records of wages paid, Revenue forms and VAT bills.[65]

If the CSA believes that the above calculation would produce an amount which does not accurately represent the parent's true earnings, another period can be used.[66] This should not be used just because earnings fluctuate, receipts are irregular or come in a lump, trade is slow at times or work non-existent for a period, nor should a different period be used just because it is known that earnings will subsequently change.[67] In such cases, the CSA will take into account earnings received or due to be received, and the duration and pattern (or expected pattern) of any self-employment.[68]

Since most calculations will be based on the self-assessment form or tax calculation notice, this alternative method is only used if there has been a major change in trading which has resulted in higher or lower earnings, or if a person has been trading for less than a year.[69]

Challenging earnings of the self-employed

There have often been delays in the self-employed parent producing all the information necessary to work out the maintenance due. The CSA can impose penalties and a default maintenance decision (see p352) while waiting for the information. The person with care may want to request that this is done if there have been problems in the past. However, she cannot force the imposition of a penalty.

Under the old formula many self-employed non-resident parents received low assessments. Some persons with care alleged that the self-employed non-resident parent, sometimes with the help of an accountant, managed to disguise his true income. If a person with care wants to challenge the earnings, once a calculation has been made she can seek a revision (see p384) and ask the CSA to use an inspector (see p98) to obtain more detailed information. However, if the non-resident parent's accounts have been accepted by the Revenue, it is very unlikely that the CSA would consider it worthwhile to undertake further investigations. The CSA may also refuse to revise the calculation if the person with care cannot substantiate her allegations. This can be challenged if the belief is reasonably held as it is very difficult for one party to obtain definitive details of the other's income. The CSA is much better placed to obtain such details.

If the person with care takes the case to an appeal tribunal (see Chapter 19), she will see details of the income in the appeal papers and she may be able to argue that some of the expenses included are not reasonable or not wholly connected with the business. Tribunals may adjourn the hearing for further information to be collected. Alternatively, the tribunal can estimate net earnings based on the available evidence, including oral evidence from the person with care.[70]

The person with care can apply for a variation from the calculation on the grounds that a person's lifestyle is inconsistent with his level of income or that assets which do not currently produce income are capable of doing so (see Chapter 7).

Tax credits

Working tax credit

Working tax credit (WTC) is counted as the income of the non-resident parent if it is solely based on his work and earnings.[71] If both members of a couple are working, WTC is treated as the income of the partner with the higher earnings over the period used for assessing earnings for tax credit purposes, or halved if their earnings are equal.[72] The earnings used for determining WTC are the ones used to determine who is treated as having WTC included in their income.[73] This means that should the earnings change later, the non-resident parent could be treated as having more income than he has. For example, if he is earning more than his partner when WTC is worked out, WTC counts in full as his income. If his partner's income later increases, but he does not notify the Revenue during the tax year and waits for an end of year adjustment, he will still have WTC counted as his income even though his partner currently earns more than he does. (It is not compulsory to report changes of income during the tax year). The rate of WTC used is that payable at the effective date.[74]

Child tax credit

Child tax credit paid to the non-resident parent or his partner counts in full as income, at the rate payable at the effective date.[75]

Other income

Periodic or other payments from an occupational or personal pension, retirement annuity or other scheme to provide income in retirement count in full as income. Payments to compensate for the failure of pension schemes (Financial Assistance Scheme and Pensions Protection Fund payments) are treated in the same way.[76] Income is calculated or estimated on a weekly basis by considering the 26-week period ending in the relevant week (see p235).[77] If the income has been received during each week of the period, the total received over the 26 weeks is divided by 26. In other cases, the total received is divided by the number of complete weeks for which the payment was received. However, the CSA can use a different period if the amount produced by the above calculation does not accurately reflect actual income.[78] Furthermore, a change occurring between the relevant week and the effective date (see p368) must be taken into account by the CSA if it is aware of the change, in the same way as for earnings (see p238).

Maximum amount of net weekly income

The maximum amount of net weekly income that can be included in the calculation of child maintenance is £2,000.[79] This includes all income, whether from earnings, tax credits, self-employment or pension and other payments. Even if a variation is being applied, the amount of net income cannot exceed this maximum figure.

In simple terms this means that the maximum amount of child maintenance that can ever be paid is £500 – ie, where the non-resident parent has three or more children and no other relevant children.

Maximum maintenance payable (using the basic rate)

Number of relevant children	1 qualifying child	2 qualifying children	3 or more qualifying children
0	£300	£400	£500
1	£255	£340	£425
2	£240	£320	£400
3 or more	£225	£300	£375

3. Shared care

Shared care is the term used to describe a situation where there is more than one person looking after a particular qualifying child and those people live in different households. If the people providing care live in the same household (see p22), this is not shared care.[80]

In real terms, a number of individuals may be involved in caring for a qualifying child – eg, parents, grandparents and babysitters. For the shared care rules to apply there must be either:

- a non-resident parent who shares care (ie, looks after the qualifying child at least 52 nights a year on average) (see p125);
- a person with care (ie, with day-to-day care of a qualifying child because she cares for the child at least 104 nights a year on average) who is treated as a non-resident parent (see p124); or
- a qualifying child cared for by a local authority for part of the time (see p311).

One, or all, of these situations may apply in any individual case.

The Child Support Agency (CSA) will make a decision on shared care by looking at all the evidence. As far as possible it will seek written evidence, although oral evidence will be accepted where the parents agree.[81] Normally this information is obtained on application (ie, from relevant forms or phone contact with the person with care and non-resident parent). The CSA calculates the amount of shared care by looking at regular weekly patterns, exceptional weeks and other occasional nights.[82] It is actual care provided which counts, whether or not it is authorised or agreed. This means that contact arrangements ordered by a court or agreed to in writing are only evidence and not decisive proof of the care situation.[83] If the evidence of the person with care and non-resident parent conflicts, the CSA will, if possible, make a decision on the balance of probability.[84] Further evidence may be required to resolve the issue.

A court should determine contact arrangements and the amount of shared care without regard to the effects on child support liability.[85] Therefore, neither parent can argue that a court should vary an order due to the amount of child support payable.

Parents should keep a note of the nights the child(ren) spends with them and, in case of dispute, be willing to supply further evidence – eg, a diary. The CSA (and any subsequent appeal tribunal) must then determine the number of nights over the period spent in each person's care.[86]

What is day-to-day care

A person is treated as having day-to-day care of a child only if s/he cares for the child for at least 104 nights in the 12-month period ending with the relevant week.[87] See p235 for a definition of relevant week.

Another period ending with the relevant week may be used if that would be more representative of the current arrangement.[88] The number of nights of care in that period must be in the same ratio as 104 nights is to 12 months – ie, 52 nights in six months, 26 nights in three months, 13 nights in two months, nine nights in a month. It might be appropriate for the CSA to use a period other than 12 months because no pattern of care can be gathered from a 12-month period, or because there is an intended change. CSA guidance gives examples, including where the care arrangements have changed following a relationship breakdown or court ruling, or where the person now providing day-to-day care has been abroad, in prison, in hospital, away from home or otherwise unable to provide care.[89] If the arrangement has simply been renegotiated between the two parents, written acceptance of this should be provided so that the CSA knows that this is now the current arrangement and not a temporary change. A future period cannot be used, but if there is an intended change, a period before the relevant week may include a care distribution which is closer to the intended new arrangement, and the CSA can use this period rather than the 12 months.[90]

Example
The relevant week for Joan's maintenance application is 12.02.07 to 18.02.07. The effective date of Serge's maintenance liability is 26.03.07 (the effective date is later than

the relevant week because Joan is treated as applying and a court order is in force; this makes the effective date two days after the calculation is made). Serge is going to begin caring for Chloe (the qualifying child) two nights a week from 14.03.07. Joan confirms this change.

The CSA decides that looking at the care arrangements in the period ending with the relevant week would not give an accurate reflection of the current care arrangements, so an alternate period is used: 14.03.07 to 26.03.07 – ie, from the date of change to the effective date.

If a change occurs after the relevant week, the CSA should be informed as this may be grounds for supersession. If it refuses to use an alternative period, an appeal can be sought.

Example

A father who only looks after the children for six weeks in the school holidays would not be accepted as a person with care. However, he could request a supersession during the summer holidays on the grounds that he is now a parent with care and a shorter period should then be used to calculate who has day-to-day care to reflect the current arrangement. It is unlikely that this would be grounds for supersession if the six-week period had already been taken into account. However, if the arrangement for the holiday had not been known at the time, this may be successful. If day-to-day care were to be re-assessed over the summer holidays, the father would become the parent with care and the mother the non-resident parent. Indeed, the father may be able to apply for maintenance from the mother (in voluntary cases). (**Note:** the relevant week in this case is the seven days preceding the request for a supersession – see p389. The request, therefore, should not be made right at the beginning of the summer holiday.)

If it is held that a supersession cannot take place, the father remains the non-resident parent over the holiday when he has the children full time. He would be liable to continue paying the mother the full level of maintenance even for those weeks the children spent with him. The parents may be able to come to a voluntary arrangement to reflect the father's level of care over this time, but this may not be financially viable, especially if the mother receives income support or income-based jobseeker's allowance.

The parent does not have to provide continuous care throughout a period of 24 hours, but must provide care during the night.[91] If a child is a boarder at boarding school, a hospital inpatient, or temporarily in someone else's care, whoever would otherwise have day-to-day care is treated as providing care.[92] For example, if a babysitter or grandparent looks after the child one night a week, this would count as a night spent with the principal provider of day-to-day care. In the case of boarding school, the person who is treated as having day-to-day care for such periods need not be the person who pays the school fees.[93] However, a non-resident parent who pays school fees for a qualifying child may be able to apply for a variation (see p138).

Parent with care treated as non-resident

If there are two or more persons with care (of a child for whom an application has been made or treated as made) and at least one of them is a parent, special rules are applied.[94] In this case, a parent with care may be treated as a non-resident parent if s/he provides care:[95]

- to a lesser extent than the other parent or persons with care;
- to the same extent as the other parent but does not get child benefit; *or*
- to the same extent as the other parent and neither parent receives child benefit but the CSA decides she is not the principal provider of day-to-day care.

A lesser extent could be interpreted as meaning either for fewer *nights* a week on average or fewer *hours* a week on average. However, the CSA will normally consider the number of nights to be a determining factor.[96]

Example

Robert looks after Geraldine from Friday afternoon to Monday morning. Nikki looks after Geraldine from Monday afternoon to Friday morning. Each is a parent with care but Robert cares for Geraldine for a lesser extent so he is treated as the non-resident parent.

A year later, Robert has moved onto shift work. One week he has Geraldine four nights, the second week three nights. Nikki cares for Geraldine the rest of the time. They now share care equally but, as Nikki receives child benefit, Robert is still treated as the non-resident parent.

Note: as the right to receive child maintenance follows receipt of child benefit, this may lead to competing claims for child benefit. If more than one person who is entitled makes a claim for child benefit, an order of priority is used to decide who will receive it.[97] For example, the person with whom the child is living has priority over other claimants. If the priority rules do not decide the matter, and the entitled claimants cannot come to an agreement, HM Revenue and Customs makes the decision. Priority can be conceded by a higher priority claimant to someone else, in writing. For more information on entitlement to child benefit and the priority rules, see CPAG's *Welfare Benefits and Tax Credits Handbook*.

In cases where a parent with care is treated as non-resident, a calculation is carried out to find out how much child maintenance s/he has to pay. This is worked out in the same way as for a non-resident parent who shares care.

If the situation includes a remaining parent with care who does not have to pay child maintenance, this assignment of non-resident parenthood can result in one parent paying child maintenance to another who has equal responsibility for the child. This can be particularly contentious where neither parent receives child benefit and the CSA has had to make a decision on the principal provider of day-to-day care.[98]

Who receives maintenance

If there are two or more people in different households who both have day-to-day care of a qualifying child, either can make an application for child maintenance as long as both or neither of them has parental responsibility.[99] If only one of them has parental responsibility, the person with parental responsibility must be the applicant. This means that if the person with parental responsibility decides not to apply, the other person with care could lose out on child maintenance, unless there is an application from the non-resident parent or a child in Scotland.

If both/all the persons with care make an application, only one will be accepted, depending on the order of priority (see p48). This may include a parent with care who is subsequently treated as a non-resident parent for the calculation.

If none of the persons with care is a parent who is treated as a non-resident parent, the person whose application is accepted will receive all the maintenance calculated.[100] The applicant or other person with care may request that the payment is apportioned between them.[101] In making the decision, the CSA considers all the circumstances of the case and representations from the persons with care.[102] If agreed, the maintenance payable will be apportioned in relation to the amount of care provided. See the example on p126.

If one of the persons with care is treated as a non-resident parent this split cannot take place. The entire amount of child maintenance from the actual non-resident parent is paid to the remaining person with care. In other words, a parent with care who shares care for the lesser amount of time can never receive child maintenance from a non-resident parent, irrespective of the amount being paid.

This may seem illogical, particularly where the application has been made by the parent with care or where, although applications have been made by both persons with care, the application from the parent has been given priority (see p48). A parent with care who applies to the CSA for maintenance from the non-resident parent but ends up being deemed non-resident and paying maintenance can request a withdrawal (see p360). However, she may find that the other person with care makes another new application (if that person has parental responsibility).

When a non-resident parent shares care

A non-resident parent shares care where he looks after a qualifying child at least one night a week on average.[103] The care must be provided overnight and the non-resident parent must stay at the same address as the child.[104] This means that the care could be provided away from the non-resident parent's normal home – eg, while on holiday or at other relatives' homes.

The number of nights is averaged over the 12 months ending with the relevant week.[105] A shorter period may be used – eg, because there is no pattern for the frequency or there is an intended change in frequency.[106] The number of nights of care in that period must be in the same ratio as 52 nights is to 12 months (52 weeks) – ie, 26 nights in six months (26 weeks), 13 nights in three months (13 weeks).[107]

Qualifying child is in hospital or at boarding school

If a qualifying child is in hospital or at boarding school, any night spent there will count as a night with the person who would normally provide care at that time.[108] This includes nights normally spent with the:
- non-resident parent;[109]
- person with care;
- local authority.[110]

These nights count in determining whether the non-resident parent or local authority shares care. They are also counted when establishing who is a person with care or which parent is to be treated as non-resident.

Example

A child who has been living with his mother during the week and spending Friday nights with his father goes to boarding school. The time as a boarder would continue to be treated as if he were living with his mother. Even if the care arrangement alters so that he spends alternate weekends with his father, the nights at school still count as spent with his mother.

If the parents agree, or the periods involved are infrequent, the case may be straightforward. However, if the normal arrangements break down, a normal pattern cannot be established or the parents disagree, the CSA must make a decision on shared care.

Example

Ella is a qualifying child cared for most of the time by her mother, Sarah, although her father, Stuart, looks after her on Wednesday and Saturday nights. Over the past year Ella has undergone treatment for cancer, which has resulted in her spending periods in hospital. Because of the periods in hospital Stuart has actually only looked after Ella for 42 nights in the year. On 16 of the remaining nights that Ella should have stayed with him she was in hospital. On the other nights that Ella should have stayed with Stuart she was unwell and wanted to stay with Sarah. The CSA would have to decide whether to consider Ella as staying with Stuart for 58 nights or accept that the intention was for her to stay with Stuart on 104 nights in the year.

If, having counted these nights, a person is not a:

- person with care;
- non-resident parent who shares care;
- local authority who has part-time care,

the night is treated as if the child is in the care of the principal provider of day-to-day care.[111] For example, if a babysitter looks after a child one night a week, then the child goes into hospital, the babysitter is not a person with care, non-resident parent or local authority. Therefore, that night is treated as one normally spent with the principal provider of day-to-day care.

Shared care and part-time local authority care

There are different rules depending on which calculation rate is applied.

The effect of shared care on the basic and reduced rate

A non-resident parent (or parent with care treated as non-resident) may share care in a number of situations – ie, be:

- caring for different qualifying children at different times; or
- caring for qualifying children with more than one person with care.

There may be any number of variations and permutations. Indeed, in any one family situation there may be a number of non-resident parents and children.

If a non-resident parent, or parent with care who is treated as a non-resident parent, shares care of a qualifying child for 52 or more nights a year, the amount of maintenance he is due to pay is reduced by a suitable fraction depending on the number of nights of shared care.[112] The amount depends on the relevant band.[113]

Number of nights	Fraction to subtract
52 to 103	One-seventh
104 to 155	Two-sevenths
156 to 174	Three-sevenths
175 or more	One-half

If the non-resident parent shares care of a qualifying child for a sufficient number of nights for the one-half fraction to apply, an additional £7 decrease in maintenance must also be applied.[114] The CSA refers to this situation as equal shared care, even though the amount of time spent with each may not be the same.[115] This extra allowance where there is equal shared care is known as **'abatement'**.[116] Abatement will be applied for each child for whom equal shared care applies.

If the decreases applied because of shared care result in the non-resident parent being liable to pay the person with care less than £5, the non-resident parent will instead pay the flat rate of £5.[117] This includes the situation where the total amount of maintenance due to all persons with care is decreased to less than £5, in which case the £5 is apportioned between the persons with care in relation to the number of qualifying children. For more details on situations involving more than one person with care, see p298.

When applying the decrease for shared care, the rounding provisions apply to the nearest penny.[118]

Example: shared care with one person with care

Alex shares care of Mark with the person with care, Diane. He looks after Mark on average two nights at the weekend and a couple of weeks in school holidays. Although Alex is a parent with care he is treated as a non-resident parent as he is not the principal provider of care. Alex's net income is £240.

Step 1   Basic rate 15% x £240 = £36
Step 2   Apply decrease for shared care
          Alex shares care in the 104 – 155 band (two-sevenths).
          £36 maintenance must be decreased by 2/7 – ie, £36 – £10.29 = £25.71
Alex pays Diane £25.71.

Alex increases the amount of time he shares care of Mark to three nights one week and four nights the next. In this case, Alex shares care for over 175 nights and the one-half fraction is applied. Alex's maintenance calculated under the basic rate remains £36.
Step 2   £36 decreased by 1/2 and a further £7 subtracted – ie, £18 – £7 = £11
Because of the increase in shared care Alex pays £11 maintenance to Diane.

Alex's circumstances change and he now has income of £160.
Step 1   Reduced rate of maintenance £5 + (25% x £60) = £5 + £15 = £20
Step 2   Apply decrease for shared care
          The fraction to apply remains at one-half and there is an abatement of £7.
          (50% x £20) – £7 = £10 – £7 = £3
Step 3   Maintenance due is below £5 so Alex will pay £5 a week to Diane.

More than one qualifying child

If the person with care and non-resident parent have more than one qualifying child, the fractions that apply for shared care for each qualifying child are added together, then divided by the number of qualifying children.[119] This applies where care is shared for some, but not all, of the qualifying children or there are different shared care arrangements for each qualifying child.

Example: shared care where there is more than one qualifying child

Pat is the non-resident parent of Lea and Dylan. Both are cared for by their grandmother, Jean. Lea does not like staying with Pat and only does so occasionally. However, Dylan stays with him on Friday and Saturday nights. Both children stay with him for a few days at Christmas and during the school holidays. Pat has net income of £220.

Step 1	**Basic rate** for two children 20% x £220 = £44
Step 2	**Apply decrease for shared care**

Lea does not stay with Pat sufficient days for it to count as shared care.

Dylan is in the 104 – 155 band (two-sevenths).

The fractions which apply are added together and divided by two, as there are two qualifying children for whom Jean cares.

$(0 + 2/7) \div 2 = 2/14$

Pat's maintenance is decreased by 2/14 (ie, £6.29)

Because of the shared care Pat must pay £37.71 (£44 – £6.29) to Jean in maintenance.

Note: if Pat has costs for keeping in contact with Lea he may be able to apply for a variation (see Chapter 7).

Lea increases the amount of time she spends with her dad and now this counts as shared care.

Step 2 Lea is in the 52 – 103 band (one-seventh).

Dylan is in the 104 – 155 band (two-sevenths).

The fractions are added together and divided by two – ie, $3/7 \div 2 = 3/14$

The maintenance due is, therefore, decreased by 3/14 because of shared care.

Pat's maintenance is decreased by 3/14 (ie, £9.43)

Because of shared care Pat must pay £34.57 (£44 – £9.43) to Jean in maintenance.

Dylan stays with his dad more often and increases the amount of care, so that:

Step 2 Lea is in the 52 – 103 band (one-seventh).

Dylan is in the 175 or more band (one-half).

The decrease will be $(1/7 + 1/2) \div 2 = 9/28$; $9/28 \times £44 = £14.14$

£44 – £14.14 = £29.86. However, because care is shared equally for one qualifying child the abatement of £7 applies and maintenance due is decreased by a further £7.

Pat now pays Jean maintenance of £22.86 (£29.86 – £7).

More than one person with care

A non-resident parent may be due to pay maintenance to more than one person with care because there:

- are several qualifying children with different persons with care (known as multiple maintenance units);
- is more than one person with care in relation to a qualifying child(ren).

One or both of these situations may apply in any one case, and the non-resident parent may share care with only one or all of the persons with care. In these cases there may be apportioning and shared care adjustments made throughout the calculation.

Example: shared care in multiple maintenance units

Ivan is the non-resident parent for two children, Holly, whose parent with care is Ellen, and Jamie, whose parent with care is Laura. Ivan looks after Holly when Ellen is on night shifts, which is every other week apart from holidays, and takes her camping with him on the odd weekend. Jamie and Laura live further away so Ivan only sees Jamie for a long weekend once a month when he visits his parents and two weeks in the summer holidays. Ivan's net income is £230.

Step 1 **Basic rate** applies for two qualifying children, there are no relevant children and net income is £230.

20% x £230 = £46

There is apportionment between the persons with care. They each care for one qualifying child so halve the maintenance between them.

To Ellen for Holly = £23

To Laura for Jamie = £23

Step 2 **Apply decrease for shared care**
Maintenance paid to Ellen for Holly
Holly is in the 156 – 174 band (three-sevenths).
3/7 x £23 = £9.86
£23 – £9.86 = £13.14
Maintenance paid to Laura for Jamie
Jamie is in the 52 – 103 band (one-seventh).
1/7 x £23 = £3.29
£23 – £3.29 = £19.71

Step 3 **Total maintenance due** is £13.14 (to Ellen) + £19.71 (to Laura) = £32.85

The situation is as above but now Laura has a new job which means she is away from home on average two nights a week and the occasional weekend. Her sister (Alice) looks after Jamie and Laura asks the CSA to split the maintenance between her and Alice.

Step 1 **Basic rate** is £46.

Apportion between the persons with care (there are two qualifying children but three persons with care – Ellen for Holly, and Laura and Alice for Jamie).

To Ellen for Holly = £23

Between Laura and Alice for Jamie = £23

Alice looks after Jamie two nights a week on average (2/6 – ie, one-third).

To Alice for Jamie = £7.67 (1/3 x £23)

Laura looks after Jamie for the remaining four nights (4/6 – ie, two-thirds).

To Laura for Jamie = £15.33 (2/3 x £23)

Step 2   **Apply decrease for shared care.**
Maintenance paid to Ellen for Holly
Ivan's care for Holly is in the 156 – 174 band (three-sevenths).
3/7 x £23 = £9.86 (ie, £23 – £9.86 = £13.14)
Maintenance paid to Alice for Jamie
Ivan's care for Jamie is in the 52 – 103 band (one-seventh).
1/7 x £7.67 = £1.10; £7.67 – £1.10 = £6.57
Maintenance paid to Laura for Jamie
Ivan's care for Jamie is in the 52 – 103 band (one-seventh).
1/7 x £15.33 = £2.19; £15.33 – £2.19 = £13.14

Step 3   **Total maintenance due** is £13.14 (to Ellen) + £6.57 (to Alice) + £13.14 (to Laura) = £32.85

Overall, Ivan pays exactly the same amount of maintenance as before, but it is split between three people.

The effect of shared care on the flat rate

As with basic or reduced rate maintenance, the non-resident parent may share care with one or more persons with care. In these cases, it must be established whether the non-resident parent is liable for the flat rate because he has income of under £100.

If the answer to this question is yes, there will be no adjustment of his maintenance liability regardless of how many nights of shared care there are.

If the non-resident parent:

- is liable to pay the flat rate because he is in receipt of a relevant benefit (eg, incapacity benefit (IB) or maternity allowance – for full list, see p109) or he or his partner receives income support (IS) or income-based jobseeker's allowance (including cases where a reduced flat rate of £2.50 applies); *and*
- cares for a qualifying child for at least 52 nights a year,

the amount of child maintenance due to the person with care of that qualifying child is nil.[120]

If there is more than one person with care, the flat rate is apportioned in relation to the number of qualifying children before any adjustment for shared care is made. This may mean that the non-resident parent's liability reduces to nil for one person with care because of shared care. However, he is still liable for the remaining amounts to the other person(s) with care, in which case he will pay an amount which is less than £5. In simple terms the process is:

- **Step 1.** Check the reason why the flat rate applies.
- **Step 2.** Apportion the flat rate between the persons with care on the basis of the number of qualifying children. Where appropriate, apply any apportioning in relation to a qualifying child where there is more than one person with care.
- **Step 3.** Apply any reduction to nil because of shared care.

Note: apportioning and rounding may result in adjustments of a penny in some calculations done by the CSA – see p107.

Example

Alistair is the non-resident parent of Keith, who lives with his older brother Neil, and Katie who lives with her mum, Rachel. Alistair looks after Katie one or two nights a week but Keith and he do not get on. Both Neil and Rachel apply for maintenance. Alistair receives IB and IS.

Step 1   Alistair is due to pay maintenance at the flat rate of £5, as he receives IB and IS.

Step 2   Apportion the flat rate of £5 between the persons with care in relation to the qualifying children each cares for – ie, the amount is halved.
To Neil for Keith = £2.50
To Rachel for Katie = £2.50

Step 3   Alistair cares for Katie over 52 nights a year so the amount due reduces to nil. Alistair remains liable to pay £2.50 in maintenance to Neil for Keith.

The situation is as above but now Keith goes to stay with his grandfather two nights a week. Neil asks for maintenance to be split between them and the CSA agrees to do this.

Step 1   Remains the same.

Step 2   Rachel is due £2.50 but now the £2.50 for Keith is to be split between Neil and grandfather.
Neil looks after Keith five nights out of seven, his granddad looks after him two out of seven, therefore:
5/7 x £2.50 is due to Neil = £1.79
2/7 x £2.50 is due to grandfather = £0.72

Step 3   The amount due to Rachel reduces to nil as Alistair cares for Katie over 52 nights a year.
Alistair remains liable to pay £1.79 to Neil and £0.72 to Keith's grandfather

In total, this would mean that Alistair is due to pay £2.51. This is more than the amount before apportioning because of the rounding provisions. Therefore, in this case, the maintenance will be adjusted by one penny to one of the persons with care. Neil has his adjusted to £1.78 for a period, after which the adjustment is made to grandfather's and he will receive £0.71 and Neil will receive £1.79.

The effect of care provided in part by the local authority

This section only applies if:

- the non-resident parent is liable to pay maintenance at the basic or reduced rate (including where a variation has been made which results in the non-resident parent paying maintenance at either of these rates);[121] *and*
- the qualifying child is cared for by the local authority at least one night a week on average but not more than five (see p133).

Part-time local authority care does not affect how maintenance is worked out in flat-rate cases.

A local authority cannot be a person with care.[122] Therefore, if a child is in the care of the local authority for more than five nights a week, no child maintenance is payable by the non-resident parent because there is no person with care.

If the local authority cares for the child for 52 nights or more in the 12-month period ending with the relevant week, the maintenance to be paid by the non-resident parent will be decreased.[123] As in deciding day-to-day care, the CSA may use a period other than 12 months which it considers to be more representative of current arrangements. A future period may also be considered if the qualifying child is to go into local authority care on, or after, the effective date.[124] If an alternative period is used, the number of nights of care must be in the same ratio as 52 to 12 months.[125] (Nights spent in hospital or at boarding school which normally would have been spent in care are included – see p126.)

Local authority care only affects the calculation of maintenance when it applies to a qualifying child. If a relevant other child is in local authority care (whether full or part time), this will not affect how s/he is treated so long as the non-resident parent or his partner receives child benefit for her/him.

The decrease for part-time local authority care

If the local authority has part-time care of a qualifying child, the basic or reduced rate maintenance calculated from the non-resident parent is decreased in relation to the number of nights the qualifying child spends in local authority care.

This calculation may be carried out either on its own, where the non-resident parent does not share care, or alongside one carried out because the non-resident parent shares care (see p125).

The effect of part-time local authority care

Number of nights	Fraction to subtract
52 to 103	One-seventh
104 to 155	Two-sevenths
156 to 207	Three-sevenths
208 to 259	Four-sevenths
260 to 262	Five-sevenths

If the person with care and non-resident parent have more than one qualifying child, the fractions that apply for each qualifying child in local authority care are added together and divided by the number of qualifying children for whom maintenance is calculated.[126] This applies where the local authority cares for one or all qualifying children or there are different care arrangements for each qualifying child.

If the decrease because of part-time care by the local authority would reduce the amount of maintenance to less than £5 for the only or all persons with care, the amount due will be £5.

Example: local authority provides part-time care

Jake is the non-resident parent for Michael and Leanne. Michael has just been placed under local authority supervision, which means that over the next six months he is to spend four nights a week in a residential unit. The rest of the time he spends with his mum, Naomi. Jake has net income of £280 and currently pays maintenance of £56 (basic rate maintenance). This must be superseded because of local authority care. The CSA supersedes the decision, considering the ratio in the six-month period.

Step 1   Work out amount of maintenance due
           Basic rate 20% x £280 = £56

Step 2   Work out the decrease because of part-time local authority care
           Local authority care for Michael is in the 208 – 259 band (four-sevenths).
           The fractions which apply are added together and divided by the number of
           qualifying children – ie, (0 + 4/7) ÷ 2 = 4/14
           Jake's maintenance is decreased by 4/14 (ie, £16)

Jake now pays Naomi £40 (£56 – £16) in maintenance.

If Leanne were also in care for two nights a week:

Step 1   Same as above.

Step 2   Local authority care for Leanne is in the 104 –155 band (two-sevenths).
           Local authority care for Michael is in the 208 – 256 band (four-sevenths).
           The fractions are added together and divided by two:
           (2/7 + 4/7) = 6/7 ÷ 2 = 6/14
           Jake's maintenance decreases by 6/14 = £24

Jake now pays Naomi £32 (ie, £56 – £24) in maintenance.

The non-resident parent shares care and local authority has part-time care

If the non-resident parent shares care of a qualifying child and the local authority has part-time care of a qualifying child, in relation to the same person with care, the appropriate fractions are worked out under each provision and are added together.[127] The amount of maintenance due from the non-resident parent is then decreased by this fraction.

If this decrease would result in the non-resident parent being due to pay less than £5 to the only or all persons with care, he will pay £5.[128]

This calculation is carried out at Step 2.

Example: shared care and part-time local authority care

The situation is as in the first example above except that Leanne spends one night a week with Jake but Michael does not.

Step 2   Jake cares for Leanne in the 52 – 103 band (one-seventh).

The fractions which apply are added together and divided by the number of qualifying children:

(0 + 1/7) ÷ 2 = 1/14

Jake's maintenance because of shared care should be reduced by 1/14.

Because Michael is in local authority care the maintenance due should be reduced by 4/14. This is added to the amount because of shared care.

1/14 + 4/14 = 5/14

Jakes maintenance is reduced by £20 (5/14 x £56)

Jake now pays Naomi £36 (£56 – £20) in maintenance.

If Leanne is also in care two nights a week but still spends one night a week with Jake:

Step 2   Jake's maintenance because of shared care should reduce by 1/14 (as above).

Local authority care for Michael and Leanne should reduce maintenance by 6/14 (as in the second example above).

These fractions are added together:

1/14 + 6/14 = 7/14 = 1/2

Jake's maintenance is reduced by £28 (1/2 x £56)

Jake now pays Naomi £28 (ie, £56 – £28) in maintenance.

Notes

1. Maintenance calculation rates

1 Sch 1 CSA 1991; reg 2(5) CS(MCSC) Regs
2 Reg 2(1) CS(MCSC) Regs
3 Reg 2(2) and (3) CS(MCSC) Regs
4 Sch 1 Part 1 para 6 CSA 1991
5 Reg 6 CS(MCSC) Regs
6 Reg 6 CS(MCSC) Regs; PG Calculation and Decision Types, Apportionment
7 Sch 1 Part 1 para 1(2) CSA 1991
8 PG, Calculation and Decision Types, Apportionment
9 Sch 1 Part 1 para 5 CSA 1991; reg 5 CS(MCSC) Regs
10 Sch 1 Part 4 CSA 1991
11 Reg 4 CS(MCSC) Regs
12 Reg 4(1)(c) CS(MCSC) Regs
13 Sch 1 Part 1 para 4(2) CSA 1991; reg 4(3)(a) CS(MCSC) Regs

14 Reg 4(3)(h) CS(MCSC) Regs
15 Sch 1 Part 1 para 3 CSA 1991
16 Reg 3 CS(MCSC) Regs
17 Sch 1 Part 1 para 10C CSA 1991
18 Sch 1 Part 1(1) CSA 1991
19 Reg 11(1) CS(MCSC) Regs
20 PG, Gather Information and Evidence, Person is an NRP or NRP Partner in a Case
21 Reg 11(2) and (3) CS(MCSC) Regs
22 Reg 11(3) CS(MCSC) Regs
23 Reg 11(5) CS(MCSC) Regs
24 Reg 11(4) CS(MCSC) Regs

2. Net income

25 Sch 1 para 1 CS(MCSC) Regs
26 Sch 1 paras 3(1)(a) and 7(6) CS(MCSC) Regs
27 Reg 1(2) CS(MCSC) Regs
28 Reg 7C SS&CS(DA) Regs

29 Sch 1 Part II para 15 CSA 1991
30 Reg 1(2) CS(MCSC) Regs
31 Sch 1 para 2(a) CS(MCSC) Regs
32 Sch 1 para 2(b) CS(MCSC) Regs
33 Sch 1 para 4 (1) CS(MCSC) Regs
34 Sch 1 para 4(2) CS(MCSC) Regs
35 Sch 1 para 6(1) CS(MCSC) Regs
36 Sch 1 Part II para 6(4) CS(MCSC) Regs
37 CCS/16/1994; CCS/11873/1996
38 CCS/6810/1995
39 CCS/511/1995
40 CCS/7312/1995; CCS/556/1995;
    CSCS/1/1996; CSCS/6/1996
41 Sch 1 Part II para 6(3) CS(MCSC) Regs
42 Reg 2(4) CS(MCSC) Regs
43 CCS/2750/1995
44 CCS/556/1995
45 Sch 1 Part II para 5 CS(MCSC) Regs
46 Sch 1 Part II para 5(2) CS(MCSC) Regs
47 Sch I Part III para 7(1) CS(MCSC) Regs
48 Sch 1 Part III para 7(2) CS(MCSC) Regs
49 PG, Gather Information and Evidence,
    Approaching the Inland Revenue for
    Self-employed Income
50 Sch 1 Part III para 7(3) CS(MCSC) Regs
51 Sch 1 Part III para 7(4) CS(MCSC) Regs
52 Sch 1 Part III para 7(5) CS(MCSC) Regs
53 Sch 1 Part III para 7(6) CS(MCSC) Regs
54 PG, Gather Information and Evidence,
    Self-assessment Returns
55 Sch 1 Part III para 8(1) CS(MCSC) Regs
56 Sch 1 Part III para 8(2) CS(MCSC) Regs
57 PG, Gather Information and Evidence,
    Reasonably Incurred Expenses
58 PG, Gather Information and Evidence,
    Wholly and Exclusively Defrayed
    Expense
59 Sch 1 Part III para 10 CS(MCSC) Regs
60 Sch 1 Part III para 8(4) CS(MCSC) Regs
61 Sch 1 Part III para 8(3)(a) CS(MCSC)
    Regs
62 CCS/15949/1996
63 Sch 1 Part III para 8(3)(b) CS(MCSC)
    Regs
64 Sch 1 Part III para 9(2) CS(MCSC) Regs
65 PG, Gather Information and Evidence,
    Business Receipts *and* Business Expenses
66 Sch 1 para 9(3) CS(MCSC) Regs
67 CCS/3182/1995; CCS/6145/1995
68 Sch 1 Part III para 9(3) CS(MCSC) Regs
69 PG, Gather Information and Evidence,
    Treatment of Self-employed Earnings
70 CCS/7966/1995
71 Sch 1 Part IV para 11(1) CS(MCSC) Regs
72 Sch 1 Part IV para 11(2) CS(MCSC) Regs
73 Sch 1 Part IV para 11(2A) CS(MCSC)
    Regs
74 Sch 1 Part IV para 11(1) CS(MCSC) Regs

75 Sch 1 Part IV para 13A CS(MCSC) Regs
76 The CS(MCSC) Regs have not been
    amended to provide for this at the time
    of writing, but the DWP has stated that
    this is the intention.
77 Sch 1 Part V para 16 CS(MCSC) Regs
78 Sch 1 Part V para 16(2) CS(MCSC) Regs
79 Sch 1 para 10 CSA 1991

3. **Shared care**
80 Reg 8(1) CS(MCSC) Regs
81 PG, Gather Information and Evidence,
    PWC and NRP Provide Different
    Information
82 PG, Gather Information and Evidence,
    Calculate Shared Care
83 CCS/2885/2005
84 PG, Gather Information and Evidence,
    Contradictory Evidence
85 *Re B (A Child)* [2006] EWCA Civ 1574
86 CCS/11728/1996
87 Reg 1(2)(a) CS(MCSC) Regs
88 Reg 1(2)(b) CS(MCSC) Regs; CCS/6/
    1994
89 PG, Gather Information and Evidence,
    Alternative Period for Establishing Day-
    to-Day Care
90 Reg 7(4) CS(MCSC) Regs
91 Reg 1(2) CS(MCSC) Regs; CCS/449/
    1995
92 Reg 1(2)(b)(i) CS (MCSC) Regs
93 CCS/12686/1996
94 Reg 8 CS(MCSC) Regs
95 Reg 8(2) CS(MCSC) Regs
96 PG, Gather Information and Evidence,
    Deciding Principal Provider of Day-to-
    Day Care
97 s144(3) and Sch 10 SSCBA 1992
98 PG, Gather Information and Evidence,
    Deciding Who Should be Treated as the
    NRP
99 s5(1) CSA 1991
100 Reg 14(2)(a) CS(MCSC) Regs
101 Reg 14(2)(b) CS(MCSC) Regs
102 Reg 14(2)(c) CS(MCSC) Regs
103 Sch 1 Part 1 paras 7 and 8 CSA 1991
104 Reg 7(1) CS(MCSC) Regs
105 Reg 7(3) CS(MCSC) Regs
106 Reg 7(4) CS(MCSC) Regs
107 Reg 7(5) CS(MCSC) Regs
108 Reg 12 CS(MCSC) Regs
109 Reg 7(6) CS(MCSC) Regs
110 Reg 9(10) CS(MCSC) Regs
111 Reg 1(2)(b)(i) CS(MCSC) Regs
112 Sch 1 Part 1 para 7 CSA 1991
113 Sch 1 Part 1 para 7(4) CSA 1991
114 Sch 1 Part 1 para 7(6) CSA 1991

115 PG, Gather Information and Evidence,
Equal Shared Care and Abatement
116 PG, Gather Information and Evidence,
Equal Shared Care and Abatement
117 Sch 1 Part 1 para 7(7) CSA 1991
118 Reg 2(2) CS(MCSC) Regs
119 Sch 1 Part 1 para 7(5) CSA 1991
120 Sch 1 Part 1 para 8 CSA 1991
121 Reg 9(1) CS(MCSC) Regs
122 Reg 21(1)(a) CS(MCP) Regs
123 Reg 9(2) and (4) CS(MCSC) Regs
124 Reg 9(2)(c) CS(MCSC) Regs
125 Reg 9(5) CS(MCSC) Regs
126 Reg 9(7) CS(MCSC) Regs
127 Reg 9(8) CS(MCSC) Regs
128 Reg 9(9)(a) CS(MCSC) Regs

Chapter 7
Variations ('new rules')

This chapter covers:
1. Grounds for a variation (below)
2. Applying for a variation (p152)
3. Procedure (p153)
4. The decision (p159)

This information only applies to 'new rules' cases, including where a case has been converted to the new rules. There are additional provisions which must be read with this information in conversion cases where there is an existing departure direction or application for a departure (see Chapter 8).

An application for a variation to the maintenance calculation may be made before a calculation is made or once a maintenance calculation is in force.[1]

A variation to the calculation can only be made under a ground laid out in the legislation and only if it would be just and equitable to do so (see p158).

An application may be rejected in specific circumstances, either at preliminary consideration or at a later stage (see p154). In certain cases, the Child Support Agency may refer the application to an appeal tribunal for a determination (see p159).

If an application is successful, it may result in a maintenance calculation being made, or, where a calculation already exists, being revised or superseded with the variation incorporated (see p163).

There is no separate variation decision; the decision is whether to revise/supersede the maintenance calculation or to refuse to revise/supersede the maintenance calculation with or without a variation element. This means that any appeal is simply against the revised or superseded decision or against the refusal to revise/supersede.

1. Grounds for a variation

The grounds for a variation fall into three groups:[2]
- special expenses (see p139);
- property or capital transfers made before 5 April 1993 (see p144);
- additional cases (see p146).

Special expenses

Variation can be considered on special expenses grounds where there are:[3]
- costs of maintaining contact with the child(ren) for whom the calculation is, or will be, in force;
- costs of long-term illness or disability of a relevant child;
- prior debts, incurred before the couple separated;
- boarding school fees being paid for the child(ren) for whom the calculation is, or will be, in force;
- costs from paying a mortgage on the person with care's and child(ren)'s home.

Except for costs associated with an illness or disability of a relevant child, there is a threshold level, which must be exceeded.[4] If the net income of the non-resident parent is:
- £200 or more, the threshold is £15;
- below £200, the threshold is £10.

The threshold applies to one ground or, where there is more than one relevant ground, the sum of those costs. This also means that the first £10 or £15 of these special expenses are disregarded when calculating the variation and any subsequent adjustment to the calculation.[5] The disregard, like the threshold, does not apply to the costs associated with an illness or disability of a relevant child.

The Child Support Agency (CSA) can also substitute a lower amount for any special expenses costs that it thinks are unreasonably high or have been unreasonably incurred.[6] This may be below the threshold amount or nil. In the case of contact costs, any reduced amount must not be so low that it makes it impossible for contact to occur at the level of frequency stated in any court order, so long as those visits are taking place.[7]

Contact costs

The costs related to the non-resident parent's contact with the qualifying child can be included.[8] They can be for the non-resident parent or the child. The cost of a travelling companion can also be included – eg, because of disability, long-term illness or the young age of the child.

Costs of contact cannot include those that arise where the non-resident parent shares care of the child and that are already taken into account under the shared care provisions.[9] This means, for example, that the cost of travel to collect the child from an overnight stay which counts as a night of shared care cannot be grounds for a variation, as the the non-resident parent already has that contact taken into account in his maintenance calculation.

The costs of phone calls, day trips and upkeep of a car are not included.[10]

The following count as contact costs:[11]
- tickets for public transport;
- fuel for a private car;

- taxi fares, but only where the illness or disability of the non-resident parent or qualifying child makes it impractical to use another form of transport;
- car hire, where the cost of the journey would be less than by public transport or taxis, or a combination of both;
- accommodation costs for the parent or the child for overnight stays, where a return journey on the same day is impractical, or the pattern of care includes contact over two or more days;
- minor incidental costs, such as tolls or fees for roads/bridges. It may include parking fees and ticket reservation fees if it was necessary to incur these to maintain contact with the child.

The costs are based on an established pattern of visits, if one exists.[12] If there is no current established pattern, a previous one may be referred to if contact is to begin again, or an intended pattern, agreed between the non-resident parent and person with care. The pattern set out in a court order may also be used.

The costs are calculated as an average weekly amount. This will be based on a 12-month, or shorter, period which ends just before the first day of the maintenance period in which the variation would take effect.[13] In other cases, it can be based on anticipated costs. If it is based on a pattern which ends before the maintenance calculation, the CSA will consider the costs incurred between the effective date of the variation and the date on which it would cease (ie, the date on which the circumstances giving rise to the variation ended) and the date of the interim maintenance decision/maintenance calculation.[14]

When contact is set out in a court order, it may only specify an upper limit on visits. The CSA is advised to consider what is a reasonable balance between maintenance paid and visits made.[15] A non-resident parent who visits more often than the court order states may wish to change the order to reflect the true position.

To determine if the cost for fuel is reasonable the CSA will compare the amount claimed with an average figure.[16] The guidance uses petrol costs as at April 1999, resulting in suggested average petrol costs of 10.5p per mile. The CSA can adjust the figure to reflect changes in petrol prices. The figure is used only as a starting point for calculating whether the amount requested in the variation application is reasonable given the distance travelled.

If the non-resident parent returns from abroad and contact is only one reason for the trip, the CSA may limit costs to those of travel from his home in the UK. The CSA will only allow those costs that are a necessary and integral consequence of maintaining contact with the child.

Overnight costs only include reasonable accommodation costs where an overnight stay is necessary. They do not cover the cost of meals and sundries. The only exception is where breakfast is included as part of the accommodation cost – ie, its cost cannot be separately identified.[17]

Changes in contact may mean changes to the variation element. If contact stops, even through no fault of the non-resident parent, the calculation may be superseded to reflect this change (see p163).

Example

Bronwen has a net income of £428 and pays basic rate maintenance of £86 to Ivan for Ursula and Gretchen. She claims a special expenses cost for contact with her children, amounting to £450 over a six-month period since the girls attend boarding school. This includes travel from Northern Ireland by ferry, petrol and overnight stays in hotels, amounting to 18 nights over the six-month period.

The amounts included are deemed reasonable in the circumstances and the weekly amount is calculated:

£450 ÷ 26 = £17.30 a week on average.

This is above the threshold of £15. Therefore, a variation of £2.30 (£17.30 − £15) for contact costs may be considered.

The number of nights Bronwen sees the children is 18 (ie, less than 26 nights in six months), so the shared care rules would not result in a reduction of her maintenance.

Costs of a long-term illness or disability of a relevant child

In order to apply for a variaton, the costs of a child's long-term illness or disability may only relate to a relevant child – ie, a child for whom the non-resident parent or his new partner receives child benefit.

A long-term illness is one current at the date of the variation application or from the date the variation would take effect. It must be likely to last for a further 52 weeks or to be terminal.[18] The child is considered disabled if:[19]

- disability living allowance (DLA) is paid for her/him;
- s/he would receive DLA but for the fact s/he is in hospital; *or*
- s/he is blind or registered as blind.

Costs allowable are the reasonable additional costs of:[20]

- personal care, attendance and communication needs;
- mobility;
- domestic help;
- medical aids which cannot be provided under the NHS;[21]
- heating, clothing and laundry;
- food essential for a diet recommended by a medical practitioner;
- adaptations to the non-resident parent's home; *and*
- day care, respite care and rehabilitation.

Where an aid or appliance can be provided under the NHS (by health services or local authorities) a variation will normally not be agreed, even if the item is not available due to lack of funds at a particular time. However, a variation can be agreed where there is likely to be a serious delay in supplying an item which would prevent the child's condition from seriously deteriorating.[22] The decision maker will also consider the cost of the aid and whether it can be obtained at a cheaper price.

Any financial help towards these costs from any source, paid to the non-resident parent or a member of his household, is deducted.[23] This includes DLA but only where it relates to the expense claimed[24] (eg, if costs for personal care are claimed, DLA care component could be deducted, but not the mobility component). If DLA has been applied for but is not in payment it can be included if, when awarded, it will cover the date the variation starts. In other cases where no financial assistance is in payment, no amount will be offset against the costs.

Debts of the relationship

A non-resident parent may be repaying debts incurred *before* he became a non-resident parent (see p22) of the qualifying child (whether before or after April 1993). Repayment can count as special expenses, but only if the debt was incurred when the non-resident parent and person with care were a couple (see p26). The debts must have been taken out for the benefit of:[25]

- the non-resident parent and person with care, jointly;
- the person with care alone, if the non-resident parent is liable for the repayments;
- a person who is not a child but at the time the debt was incurred:
  - was a child;
  - lived with the non-resident parent and person with care; *and*
  - was the child of the non-resident parent, person with care or both of them;
- the qualifying child;
- any child other than the qualifying child who at the time the debt was incurred:
  - lived with the non-resident parent and person with care; *and*
  - is a child of the person with care.

Loans only count if they are from a qualified lender, or from a current or former employer.[26] Qualified lenders include banks, building societies or other registered lenders (eg, hire purchase).[27]

The following do *not* count as debts:

- debts incurred to buy something which the non-resident parent kept after the relationship ended;[28]
- a loan other than one obtained from a qualified lender, or the non-resident parent's current or former employer;[29]
- a debt for which the applicant took responsibility under a financial settlement with the ex-partner or a court order;[30]

- a debt for which a variation has previously been agreed, but which has not been repaid in the period for which the variation has been applied to the calculation;[31]
- secured mortgage repayments, except for amounts incurred to buy or repair/ improve (see p215)[32] the home of the person with care and qualifying child; *and*
- endowment/insurance premiums, except for mortgage/insurance incurred to buy or repair/improve (see p215) the home of the person with care and qualifying child.[33]

Payments or a debt taken out to pay off any negative equity on the former joint home do not count as debts, as the person with care no longer lives there.[34]

The following also do *not* count as debts:[35]

- debts of a business or trade;
- gambling debts;
- legal costs of the separation, divorce or dissolution of the civil partnership;
- credit card repayments;
- overdrafts, unless taken out for a specified amount repayable over a specified period;
- fines imposed on the applicant;
- any debt incurred to pay off one of these; *or*
- any other debt the CSA considers reasonable to exclude.

A debt incurred to pay a former debt which would have counted may be included. However, only that part which could have counted is included as special expenses.[36]

A variation is normally based on the original debt repayment period; any rescheduling of the debt is usually ignored.[37] However, if the applicant has been unemployed or ill and the creditors have agreed to extend the repayment period, the CSA can take the extended period into account. There is discretion on the length of time over which the debt may be taken as extended when setting the period for which the variation for prior debt applies to the calculation.

Boarding school fees

The maintenance element of boarding school fees incurred, or expected to be incurred, by the non-resident parent for the qualifying child may be considered.[38] Only term-time costs for non-advanced education at a recognised educational establishment can be included.[39]

If the maintenance element cannot be distinguished from other costs, the CSA can decide what to include, but this should not exceed 35 per cent of the total fees.[40]

If the non-resident parent receives financial help to pay the fees, or only pays part of the fees with someone else, a proportion of the costs are included. This is calculated in the same ratio as the maintenance element to overall fees.[41]

In all cases, a variation for boarding school fees should not reduce the amount of income to be considered for calculating maintenance by more than 50 per cent.[42]

Example

Bronwen claims special expenses for her contribution to boarding school costs for Ursula and Gretchen. She pays the school £1,500 a term – ie, £4,500 a year. Ivan pays the rest of the fees – ie, £4,500 a year. Her net income is £428.

The fees for each child per term are £1,500 and the maintenance element is £500 a term. Bronwen's contribution to maintenance is worked out as £250 a child each term – ie, £500. Over the three terms this amounts to £1,500, which is converted into a weekly figure (£1,500 ÷ 365 x 7 = £28.77). This is above the threshold of £15 so a variation for a contribution to boarding school fees of £13.77 may be considered. (If this were to be accepted, it would not reduce the net income by more than 50 per cent.)

Payments for certain mortgages, loans or insurance policies

These cover payments made to a mortgage lender, insurer or person with care for a mortgage or loan where:[43]

- it was taken out to facilitate the purchase of, or repairs/improvements to, the property by someone other than the non-resident parent;
- the payments are not made because of a debt or other legal liability of the non-resident parent for the period in which the variation is applied;
- the property was the person with care's and non-resident parent's home when they were a couple, and it is still the home of the person with care and qualifying child; *and*
- the non-resident parent has no legal/financial rights in the property – eg, a charge or equitable interest.

Payments may also be considered for an insurance/endowment policy taken out to discharge a mortgage or loan as above, except where the non-resident parent is entitled to any part of the proceeds when the policy matures.[44]

Property/capital transfers

Variation is only possible where a pre-5 April 1993 court order or written agreement was in force between the non-resident parent and the person with care and/or the child(ren) in the child maintenance application.[45] The court order must have been to transfer property/capital in lieu of maintenance for the child either wholly or in part.[46] If the court order specifies that it is in lieu of spousal maintenance only, the variation will be disallowed.[47]

The court order must be made under:[48]

- Part 2 of the Matrimonial Causes Act 1973;

- the Domestic Proceedings and Magistrate's Court Act 1978;
- Part 3 of the Matrimonial and Family Proceedings Act 1984;
- the Family Law (Scotland) Act 1985;
- Schedule 1 to the Children Act;
- Schedule 5, 6 or 7 to the Civil Partnership Act 2004; *or*
- any other prescribed enactment.

The transfer must mean that the non-resident parent has transferred any beneficial interest in the property/capital to:[49]
- the person with care;
- the qualifying child; *or*
- trustees where the trust is set up solely, or as one of its objects, to provide maintenance for the qualifying child.

Where the transfer does not satisfy any of these conditions but the CSA is satisfied that some or all of the property subsequently transferred to the person with care, the transfer will be accepted.[50]

The CSA first works out the value of the transfer, ignoring any part which was not in lieu of child maintenance.[51] (Allowance is also made for any compensating transfer from the person with care to the non-resident parent.) Unless there is evidence to show otherwise, the CSA assumes that:[52]
- the property covered by the order/agreement was held in equal shares by the non-resident parent and person with care;
- if those parties had been married, half of the value of the transfer was for the person with care's benefit, and not for the child(ren);
- if those parties were *never* married, *none* of the value of the transfer was for the person with care's benefit.

The minimum value of the transfer must be £5,000.[53]

The equivalent weekly value is then worked out. The number of years of liability is deemed to begin on the date of the order/agreement and to end on the date it sets for maintenance to end (for the youngest child if there is more than one), or, if no date is given, when the youngest child reaches 18.[54] Using that figure and the interest rate at the date of the order/agreement, a multiplier is given by a table.[55] That gives an equivalent weekly value. If using that figure in the variation would lead to an amount of maintenance of less than the child maintenance payable under the order/agreement, a lower weekly value can be set.[56]

Example

Marcus and Helene divorced in 1992, when their youngest child, Robert, was one. Marcus transferred his share in the home to Helene, in lieu of maintenance for her and the children.

Marcus applies for a variation on property transfer grounds.

7

The value of the house at that time was £46,000 but there was a mortgage of £14,000. The CSA considers that of the £16,000 transferred (£46,000 – £14,000 ÷ 2 as they each had equal shares) only £8,000 can be considered in lieu of child maintenance. This is above the threshold of £5,000.

The number of years of liability is worked out as 17 (ie, from the date of the order until Robert is 18). The interest rate for a judgment debt at the time of the order was 15 per cent. Based on the table of equivalent values this gives a multiplier of 0.00323.

The equivalent weekly value of the property transfer to be considered is £8,000 x 0.00323 = £25.84

Additional cases

There are additional cases in which a variation may be applied for by a person with care or child in Scotland. These are where the non-resident parent has:[57]

- assets over £65,000;
- a lifestyle which is inconsistent with his stated income;
- income which has not been taken into account in the calculation; *or*
- diverted income.

The effect of a variation on additional cases grounds will be to increase the net weekly income of the non-resident parent to be taken into account in the calculation.[58] The maximum net weekly income, after adding any amount for additional cases variation(s), cannot exceed the capped amount of £2,000.

If the non-resident parent is in receipt of a benefit (other than income support (IS) or income-based jobseeker's allowance (JSA)) that attracts the flat rate, even though he may not pay this because of shared care or because he qualifies for the nil rate (but not on income grounds), there are special rules regarding the maximum amount payable when a variation is agreed on additional cases grounds.[59] This is known as the 'better-buy' provision (see p161).

Assets over £65,000

The CSA must be satisfied that the asset:[60]

- is under the non-resident parent's control, or is one in which he has a beneficial interest;
- has been transferred to trustees, but the non-resident parent is the beneficiary of the trust, and the transfer was made to reduce the amount of assets which could be considered under a variation application;
- is subject to a trust of which the non-resident parent is a beneficiary.

Assets include:[61]

- money – actual cash or deposits in banks, building society, Post Office accounts, premium bonds or savings certificates;
- legal estate, interest in, or rights over, land;

- stocks and shares;
- claims it would be reasonable to enforce;
- in Scotland, monies due or an obligation owed which it would be reasonable to enforce; *and*
- any of the above located outside Great Britain.

The CSA will not count assets if:[62]
- their total value is £65,000 or less after repaying any mortgage/charge on them. Any asset in respect of which income is taken into account following the application of the next type of variation described (income not taken into account – see p148) will be deducted from the non-resident's parent's total assets before this test is applied;
- it is satisfied the non-resident parent is holding them for a reasonable purpose (eg, cash from the sale of a home that is intended to purchase a new home);
- they are compensation for personal injury;
- they are used for a trade or business (except property which produces rental income). Shares are not used in the course of a business or trade if the trade or business is not that of the non-resident parent (eg, where he has invested in a company or even owns one, but it is not his trade/business);[63]
- the asset is the home of the non-resident parent or his child; *or*
- they are payments from certain trusts (eg, Macfarlane Trust or the variant CJD compensation trust), which would be ignored if the non-resident parent were on IS.[64]

If an asset is held in joint names, the CSA assumes that each person has equal shares, unless there is evidence to suggest otherwise.[65]

The weekly value of the assets is worked out by multiplying the value of the assets by the statutory rate of interest and dividing the resulting figure by 52.[66] The statutory rate of interest is that which applies on the effective date in the non-resident parent's country of habitual residence (ie, England, Wales, Scotland or Northern Ireland); this is currently 8 per cent.[67] If the non-resident parent works abroad for a UK-based employer the rate is based on the locality of the employer. The weekly value is added to other income, including benefits and bearing in mind the better buy rules for those on benefit (see p161).[68]

Example
Graham has a net income of £480 a week and pays maintenance to Andie of £96 a week. Andie applies for a variation on the grounds that Graham has substantial assets – ie, a holiday home in Spain and savings.

The property in Spain has a value of £52,000 and Graham has savings and investments of £17,000. The total value of his assets is £69,000, which is above the threshold of £65,000. A variation may be considered using a weekly value worked out as £106.15 (ie, £69,000 x 8% ÷ 52).

> If Graham had owned the property in Spain jointly with his new partner, Nadia, the total value of his assets would have been £26,000 + £17,000 = £43,000, which is below the threshold.

Income not taken into account and diversion of income

Income not taken into account covers situations where the non-resident parent is on the nil rate (except where this is because income is below £5) or the flat rate because of receipt of a prescribed benefit (other than IS or income-based JSA), even though he may pay less because of shared care.[69] The CSA must be satisfied that the non-resident parent receives income which would be taken into account in the maintenance calculation if he were not due to pay the nil rate or the flat rate for these reasons.

A variation may also be agreed for income not taken into account if:[70]

- the non-resident parent has the ability to control the amount of income he receives from a company or business, including earnings from employment or self-employment; *and*
- the income from that company or business would not otherwise be taken into account in the maintenance calculation.

This variation could, for example, apply where income in the form of dividends is received by a company director. However, it can also apply to other forms of income received from a company or business. Reimbursement to the non-resident parent of legitimate business expenses will be ignored. The additional income received from the company or business is added to the non-resident parent's net weekly income for the purposes of the maintenance calculation. A variation where the non-resident parent can control income which would not otherwise be taken into account can only be agreed on or after 6 April 2005. Before this date, the regulations did not provide for these circumstances. Caselaw gives some guidance on the treatment of dividends under the old form of the regulations.[71]

For a variation for income not taken into account to be made, the income not taken into account must be net weekly income of over £100. This can be from either of the situations described above or, if a variation is considered under both cases, income from both can be added together.[72]

When working out the earnings of students, the total income for the year, ending with the relevant week, is added together and divided by 52 to give a weekly amount. An alternative period may be used if the CSA considers it more representative.

The weekly value of any additional income is added to other income from benefits, bearing in mind that the better-buy provision (see p161) applies to those on benefit when calculating the maximum maintenance due.[73] Benefits include those prescribed for the flat rate, except IS/income-based JSA, less any disregards.[74]

Example

Joel is a mature student who works part time in a care home. He is on the nil rate for maintenance. Kaliani applies for a variation on income not taken into account grounds. Kaliani looks after one child, Selim.

Joel's student grant and loan do not count as income, so only his part-time earnings are considered. Over the year Joel's net earnings are £9,367.80, which is converted into a weekly amount (ie, £9,367.80 ÷ 52 = £180.15). As this is over £100 a variation may be considered using a weekly value figure of £180.15. Therefore, if the variation to the calculation is agreed, instead of paying nothing Joel will now be due to pay a reduced rate of £25 (£5 + (25% x £80.15) = £25.04 rounded to the nearest pound).

Diversion of income is considered where:[75]
- the non-resident parent has the ability to control the income he receives, including earnings from self-employment; *and*
- the CSA is satisfied that the non-resident parent has unreasonably reduced the amount of income he would have received (and which would have been taken into account in the maintenance calculation or under a variation for income from a company or business – see p148) by diverting it to someone else. The diversion does *not* have to have been arranged specifically to avoid child maintenance responsibilities.

Diversion may include the following:
- to a third party, such as a new partner or close family member;
- to a business, such as where the non-resident parent takes a lower income, or to a pension scheme from which the non-resident parent will benefit later. It would, however, have to be reasonable to make a variation in such circumstances – eg, if the money is being used to develop the company, a variation should not be made;[76]
- diversion of funds towards other purposes, such as where the non-resident parent uses company assets for private use or business funds for day-to-day expenditure.

Example

Marcus runs his own import/export business, employing his new partner, Shamira, and his brother. Each has a company car, in his case a Jaguar. His brother is paid £600 a week and he and Shamira each receive £400. His ex-wife, Helene, gets basic rate maintenance of £80 for their two children. Helene applies for a variation because she thinks he is diverting income via the company, especially as Shamira does not seem to do any work.

Part of his day-to-day expenses are included in business expenses – eg, the car and business lunches. Shamira's salary could also be a token payment, as Marcus takes less from the business than he pays his brother. The CSA considers that, on balance, there could be

> diversion of income via the company and Shamira's wages. Given its contentious nature, the case is referred to an appeal tribunal.

The full amount of any diverted income will be added to net weekly income when working out maintenance.[77]

Lifestyle inconsistent with declared income

The person with care, or a qualifying child in Scotland, may apply for a variation on this ground if:[78]

- a maintenance calculation has been made, either based or not based on net weekly income (see table on p151), but not where the flat rate is payable because of receipt of IS, income-based JSA or pension credit (PC); *and*
- the CSA is satisfied that the income used (or which would have been used) in the calculation is substantially lower than that needed to support the non-resident parent's lifestyle.

However, a variation will not be allowed where it is clear that the lifestyle is paid for by:[79]

- income which is, or would be, disregarded in the maintenance calculation;
- income which could be considered under the diversion of income ground;
- income which could be considered under a variation for income not taken into account from a company or business (see p148);
- assets, or income from assets; *or*
- a partner's income or assets, except if the non-resident parent is able to influence or control the amount of income, assets or income from the assets.

A variation cannot be granted where an inconsistent lifestyle is financed by borrowing, as this would not meet the requirement that the variation decision be just and equitable (see p158).[80]

In addition to these situations, if the calculation is not based on net weekly income (see table on p151), a variation will not be allowed where the lifestyle is paid for from income of £100 or less, or which could be considered in the income not taken into account ground (see p148).[81]

Situations where lifestyle could be considered inconsistent with declared income

Non-resident parent's child maintenance based on net weekly income is or would be:	Non-resident parent's child maintenance not based on net weekly income is or would be:
– the basic rate;	– the flat rate because of receipt of a
– the reduced rate;	benefit, other than IS, income-based JSA
– the flat rate because net weekly income is £100 or less;	or PC (including if the amount paid is less than the flat rate because of shared care);
– the nil rate because net weekly income is less than £5;	– the nil rate because of receipt of benefit.
– equivalent to the flat rate because of shared care;	
– equivalent to the flat rate because of a property transfer variation, part-time care by a local authority or there is an 'old rules' case that has been converted with a property transfer departure.	

The amount of income which will be taken into account will be the difference between the amount:[82]
- the non-resident parent needs to support his overall lifestyle; *and*
- taken into account (or which would have been taken into account) in the maintenance calculation.

This includes any income from benefits (ie, except for IS/income-based JSA/PC, benefits prescribed for the flat rate, less disregards), bearing in mind the better buy rules for those on benefit (see p161).

CSA guidance indicates that this ground is most likely to be used in situations where the non-resident parent is self-employed or where it is suspected that he is working without fully declaring income for tax and national insurance purposes.[83] Before the non-resident parent is contacted, a fraud check will be made by the CSA in order not to jeopardise any ongoing fraud investigation.

It would not be enough to show that the non-resident parent pursued one extravagant activity, as there may be good reasons for this. The non-resident parent must have an overall lifestyle that, in most respects, is inconsistent with his declared income – eg, a large, expensively furnished home, expensive car, frequent foreign holidays and expensive leisure activities would all be considered. The use of declared capital to finance an otherwise inconsistent lifestyle, or a lifestyle supported by a partner's wealth or income, cannot lead to a successful variation.[84]

Example

Marcus lives with his new partner, Shamira, in a townhouse in central London. He runs his own import/export business. His ex-wife, Helene, gets basic rate maintenance of £80 for their two children. Helene applies for a variation because Marcus is able to afford to live in central London, drive a new Jaguar (changing cars every two or three years), he plays polo (keeping three ponies in stables), is a member of an exclusive golf club and he and Shamira frequently travel abroad.

Part of the expenses are included in business expenses – eg, the car and travel abroad on business trips, and the golf club membership is used for corporate entertaining. Shamira is also an employee of the company, meaning her income is under Marcus's control, though her wages are equivalent to those of other staff. The CSA considers that, on balance, his lifestyle does appear inconsistent with his income. However, it also considers that there could be a diversion of income. Given its contentious nature, the case is referred to an appeal tribunal.

Had the situation been reversed, with Shamira independently wealthy, owning the business and paying for the lifestyle, including paying Marcus's wages, the case may have been refused. Helene could appeal such a refusal, although it may be that a variation is not possible on this ground. The CSA would also have to consider whether there had been a diversion of income or assets which Marcus could control.

2. Applying for a variation

An application for a variation may be made before or after a maintenance calculation has been made.[85] Only a relevant person may apply – ie, a person with care, a non-resident parent or a qualifying child in Scotland. An authorised representative may also make an application. The Child Support Agency (CSA) also has the discretion to reinstate a previous variation without an application in certain prescribed circumstances (see p165).

The application for a variation may be made either orally or in writing.[86] This means an applicant may give details over the phone, although the CSA may ask for a written application – eg, because complicated special expenses are being asked for which could not be explained over the telephone. A form may be provided by the CSA, or the applicant can send the application in another written form which the CSA may accept as sufficient, depending on the circumstances.[87] Where a written application is required this should be provided within 14 days. If the time limit is exceeded without good cause, the effective date of the variation may be affected.

The application must state the grounds on which it is made.[88] If the application does not state the grounds, or at least give a reason, it will not be accepted as properly made.

Example

Joe applies for a variation because he believes his maintenance is too high. The CSA does not accept it as a properly made application.

Joe applies for a variation because he believes his maintenance is too high and he cannot afford it because of the high cost of pet food. The CSA accepts the application as properly made, but then rejects the application on preliminary consideration, as it is not on a regulated ground.

Joe applies for a variation because he believes his maintenance is too high because he cannot afford the kennel costs he incurs when he travels to see his children. The CSA accepts the application is properly made and it is given preliminary consideration. It rejects the application as kennel costs are not a recognised ground. However, had Joe referred to other contact costs (eg, tickets or fuel) his application would probably have proceeded.

If an application is made, but there is insufficient information to decide whether to progress it, the CSA may request further information.[89] The request may be made orally or in writing (including email).[90] The applicant is given one month from the date of notification in which to supply the information.[91] This time limit may be extended in special circumstances – eg, if the applicant is in hospital. If the information is not provided, the CSA may either reject the application or proceed with it at its discretion.[92]

An application for a variation may be amended or withdrawn at any time before a decision is made.[93] This may be done orally or in writing. No amendment can be made if the change relates to a period after the effective date of the application.[94]

3. **Procedure**

Once an application has been made the procedure is as follows:
- preliminary consideration of the application (see p154);
- unless rejected, other parties may be notified and asked to make representations ('contest') (see p155);
- an interim maintenance decision may be made (see p156);
- a regular payment condition may be imposed (see p157);
- the decision will be considered (see p158).

In addition, the case may be passed to an appeal tribunal after preliminary consideration for a determination (see p159).

The application will proceed for determination unless it has already failed.[95] It may fail (ie, the Child Support Agency (CSA) may refuse to consider it further before this point) because, for example:

- one of the grounds for rejection is established on preliminary consideration (see below);
- it is withdrawn; *or*
- the regular payment condition has not been met.

Two or more applications for a variation may be considered at the same time.[96] In addition, if appropriate, an application made on one ground may be treated as an application on a different ground.[97]

Preliminary consideration

Once an application is properly made there is a preliminary consideration of the case.[98] At this point, the CSA may reject the application and decide:

- to revise or supersede the maintenance calculation, or to refuse to revise or supersede;[99] *or*
- make the maintenance calculation, or make a default maintenance decision.[100]

Any decision carries the normal appeal rights.

Grounds for rejecting or refusing a variation

An application for a variation may be rejected because:[101]

- the requirements of the stated ground are not met;
- in special expenses cases, the threshold is not exceeded;
- in property/capital transfer cases, the £5,000 minimum value is not exceeded;
- in additional assets cases, their value does not exceed £65,000;
- in income not taken into account cases, this does not exceed £100;
- information requested by the CSA has not been provided within the one-month time limit;
- a default maintenance decision is in force;
- the application is made by the person with care or qualifying child on additional cases grounds and the capped amount of income is already applied, or the non-resident parent or his partner are in receipt of working tax credit;
- the application is made by the non-resident parent on special expenses grounds and after deducting these, net income exceeds the capped amount;
- the non-resident parent is on the flat rate as he or his partner is on income support (IS), income-based jobseeker's allowance (JSA) or pension credit (PC) (including if the partner is also a non-resident parent), but is due to pay less than the flat rate or nil because of shared care or the transitional rules on conversion;
- the non-resident parent is due to pay the flat rate (or the lower prescribed amount) under the transitional rules on conversion, or a property or capital transfer reduces maintenance below the flat rate or because of part-time care by a local authority;
- the application is made by the non-resident parent; *and*

- he is on the nil rate; *or*
- he is on the flat rate because he receives a prescribed benefit (other than IS/income-based JSA/PC) or has income of £100 or less; *or*
- he pays the flat rate of £5 (or less if apportioned) because of shared care, including care by a local authority.

In some cases, if a default maintenance decision applies, an application for a variation may contain sufficient information to revise the default decision and replace it with a maintenance calculation.

Contest

If the application has not been rejected on preliminary consideration the other relevant parties will usually be notified. However, in some situations where the CSA has discretion to reinstate a previous variation it does not need to notify or invite representations (see p165).

The notification may be done orally or in writing and must:[102]

- state the grounds on which the application has been made and provide any information or evidence the applicant has given to support it;
- invite parties to make representations about the circumstances within 14 days; *and*
- not contain information that should not be disclosed.

In practice, non-applicants are informed in writing and supplied with the evidence. Where the application has been via a phone call the evidence may be a transcript of the telephone conversation.

In some cases, the applicant may be late in supplying further evidence or information (ie, outside the one-month time limit) but the CSA may have decided to proceed with the application in the meantime and notify the other parties. This information may be passed to the other parties later and a further 14 days for representations allowed from the date of this later notification.[103] If the CSA is satisfied that it is reasonable, this time limit may be extended.[104]

The other parties may respond orally or in writing, although the CSA may require them to make a written submission. Where no contesting information is provided, the CSA may make a determination on the application as it stands.[105]

Any information which the other party provides, other than that which may not be disclosed (see p156), may be forwarded to the applicant if the CSA considers this reasonable.[106] This will only happen if the other party has contradicted the applicant's statement and the decision maker does not have sufficient evidence to decide the case, or s/he has provided supporting evidence to refute it.[107] The applicant will be given 14 days to comment on the evidence or information supplied by the other party.

Additional non-disclosure rules

There are additional rules on non-disclosure in variations cases. Supporting evidence or information from one party will not be notified to the other party if it contains:[108]

- details of an illness or disability of a relevant other child if the non-resident parent has requested that this is not disclosed and the CSA agrees;
- medical evidence which has not been disclosed to the applicant or a relevant person (person with care, non-resident parent or qualifying child in Scotland) which would be harmful to that individual;
- the address of a relevant person or qualifying child, or information which could lead to that individual or child being located, and there is a risk of harm or undue distress.

If an applicant requests that information is not disclosed, this will be discussed with her/him. It may be possible to make an amended application which does not include details s/he does not wish to be disclosed. If an applicant refuses to disclose information that is relevant for the other party to contest the application, the application can be rejected.[109] However, there may be a good reason for non-disclosure and each case should be considered on its own merits.

Contest not required

Representations from the other relevant parties are not required if:[110]

- the CSA is reinstating a variation at its own discretion (see p165);
- there is a property/capital transfer variation and a change of circumstances meant that the CSA no longer had jurisdiction, but a subsequent change means it does and an application for variation is made on a further application for a maintenance calculation;
- a variation is agreed and the non-resident parent has the maintenance calculation replaced by a default decision, but subsequently this is replaced with a maintenance calculation.

Interim maintenance decision

If an application for a variation is made before the maintenance calculation, an interim maintenance decision may be made.[111] This means an interim maintenance decision can be made if the first calculation has not been made or if the process is complete except for an outstanding variation application. The amount of the interim maintenance decision will be the maintenance calculated in the normal way, ignoring the variation. This is to allow the variation application to be considered. An interim maintenance decision may be replaced by a maintenance calculation, which is made whether or not a variation has been agreed. The effective date of the maintenance calculation will be the same as the interim maintenance decision.

The interim maintenance decision can be appealed in the normal way. However, when a maintenance calculation is made which replaces this, any appeal may lapse.[112] If the interim maintenance decision is superseded, the normal 5 per cent change in net income tolerance rule (see p390) does not apply.

Regular payment condition

A non-resident parent may have a regular payment condition imposed after the preliminary consideration.[113] It is intended that this will be used if a non-resident parent has:

- a poor payment record or arrears;
- failed to make payments while the variation application is being contested and considered; *or*
- special expenses which make it hard for him to meet the maintenance liability.

The amount due under a regular payment condition will be either the:[114]

- maintenance calculated, including that set under an interim maintenance decision; *or*
- amount of maintenance which would be due if the variation was agreed.

This means that if the CSA believes that the variation application will be successful, it may set a regular payment condition that adjusts the maintenance calculated to reflect the variation, reducing the financial burden on the parent. However, if it believes that the application will be unsuccessful and a regular payment condition is imposed, it will be set at the calculation rate.

A regular payment condition does not affect the amount of maintenance the non-resident parent is liable to pay.[115] Therefore, if the set amount is lower than the amount due there will be arrears if the variation application fails.

The condition is set independently of any other arrears arrangement the parent may have and ends either when the CSA makes a final decision on the maintenance calculation (whether or not the variation is agreed to), or when the application is withdrawn.[116]

When a regular payment condition is imposed, the non-resident parent, person with care and/or qualifying child applicant in Scotland will be sent written notification.[117] This will make it clear that if the condition is not met, the application may lapse.[118]

If a non-resident parent does not meet the regular payment condition within one month of this notification, the CSA will refuse to consider the application for a variation.[119] Written notification of this refusal will be sent to the non-resident parent, person with care and/or qualifying child applicant in Scotland.[120] A refusal to consider the application cannot be appealed.

Considering the decision

The CSA can exercise some discretion in variations to the maintenance calculation. In addition to the normal rules, the CSA must be satisfied that:[121]
- the grounds are met; *and*
- it is just and equitable to agree to the variation.

When considering the decision, the CSA must bear in mind the general principles that:[122]
- a parent is responsible for maintaining her/his children when s/he can afford to do so;
- a parent is responsible for maintaining all her/his children equally;
- the welfare of any child affected by an application for a variation must be taken into account.

A decision may be made to agree to the variation in full or to refuse it. This may result in a revision or supersession of the decision or replacement of the interim maintenance decision.[123] The revision/supersession decision is dealt with under the normal rules (see p163).

Just and equitable

Even though the grounds are met, a variation decision will only be agreed if it is just and equitable.[124] Certain factors must be taken into account when making the decision. These include:[125]
- whether agreeing to a variation would lead the non-resident parent or parent with care to give up employment;
- if the applicant is the non-resident parent, whether there is any liability to pay child maintenance under a court order or agreement prior to the effective date of the maintenance calculation; *or*
- if the non-resident parent has applied for a special expenses variation, whether he could make financial arrangements to cover those expenses or could pay for them from money currently spent on non-essentials.

This list is not exhaustive and other factors may be considered in deciding what is just and equitable.

The following must *not* be taken into account:[126]
- whether or not the child's conception was planned;
- who was responsible for the breakdown of the relationship between the non-resident parent and person with care;
- whether the non-resident parent or person with care is in a new relationship with someone who is not the qualifying child's parent;
- any contact arrangements;

- the income or assets of anyone other than the non-resident parent, and/or, if an application is made on the grounds of a lifestyle inconsistent with declared income, his partner;
- any failure of the non-resident parent to pay child maintenance under CSA arrangements, a court order or written agreement; *and*
- representations from individuals other than the person with care, non-resident parent or a qualifying child applicant in Scotland.

Referral to an appeal tribunal

Once the application has passed the preliminary consideration and contest stage, the case may be passed to an appeal tribunal for a determination on whether or not to agree to the variation.[127] This will normally only occur if a novel or particularly contentious issue is being considered.[128] At one point, almost all cases on the additional case grounds of inconsistent lifestyle and diversion of income would have been referred to a tribunal, provided they had not first been rejected or refused at the preliminary consideration stage. However, since May 2005, the CSA has begun to make decisions on these cases itself rather than routinely refer them to appeal tribunals.

The decision maker should also consider whether only a tribunal would be able to obtain the necessary evidence to determine the application, in which case the application should be referred.

An appeal tribunal considering a variation will apply the same rules as a CSA decision maker and will determine that the variation should be either agreed or refused.[129] The tribunal's determination will be passed back to the CSA to make the decision. This decision by the CSA (ie, to revise/supersede, or refuse to revise/supersede, the maintenance calculation) may then be appealed in the normal way (see p167).

4. **The decision**

A variation is an element of the maintenance calculation. The Child Support Agency (CSA) may agree to, or refuse, the application for variation. In either case, it may result in a decision to:[130]

- revise or supersede the maintenance calculation/replace the interim maintenance decision, or refuse to revise or supersede;
- make a maintenance calculation (this may replace an interim maintenance decision) or default maintenance decision.

The CSA's internal guidance indicates when to refuse to revise or supersede – eg, refusing if an application does not meet one of the grounds, or fails at preliminary consideration or later.[131]

In some cases, a variation may be agreed which makes no difference to the amount of maintenance calculated. A revision or supersession will still be carried out, as each decision gives further appeal rights.

Once a variation is made it will continue to be considered each time there is a revision or supersession of the maintenance calculation, under the normal revision/supersession rules (see Chapter 18). Because of some changes in circumstances the variation may cease to have effect, in which case the calculation may be suspended or cancelled in order to remove the variation element. When there is a further change in circumstances the variation may be reinstated by the CSA without an application. In other cases, a new request for a variation may need to be made.

Following variation to the maintenance calculation, as with other maintenance calculation decisions, the amount of maintenance paid may be affected by the special rules on court order phasing (see p355) or conversions (see Chapter 8).

The effect of the variation

The effect of the variation should not reduce the total amount of maintenance to less than £5,[132] and the maximum amount of net income that can be taken into account is the capped amount of £2,000.[133] The following sections examine the effect of a variation on different grounds, including where there is more than one ground – eg, special expenses and additional cases. The CSA calls these 'concurrent variations'.

Additional cases

If a variation is made on additional cases grounds, the amount of any additional income is added to the net income of the non-resident parent.[134] Where this would result in a net income figure above the capped amount, the net income is restricted to the capped amount of £2,000.

- -

Example

The case in the example on p149 is referred to an appeal tribunal. The tribunal determines that there should be a variation for additional income, with a weekly value of £360 for both diversion of income and a lifestyle inconsistent with declared income. This is added to Marcus's net income, as used in the maintenance calculation, of £400. His net income is now £760. The amount he is now due to pay Helene is £152.

- -

If the non-resident parent is in receipt of a benefit (other than income support (IS), income-based jobseeker's allowance (JSA) or pension credit (PC)) that attracts the flat rate, even though he may not pay this because of shared care or because he qualifies for the nil rate (but not on income grounds) there are special rules regarding the maximum amount payable when a variation is agreed on additional cases grounds.[135] This is known as the 'better-buy' provision (see p161).

Better-buy

The maximum amount of maintenance a non-resident parent on benefit (other than IS, income-based JSA or PC) will have to pay after a variation on additional cases grounds is the lesser of:[136]

- the flat rate plus the amount calculated under the normal calculation rules on additional income (exclusive of the benefit income); *or*
- the amount calculated under the normal calculation rules on total income (including any benefit that attracts the flat rate liability, less disregards).

The amounts disregarded in benefit income are:[137]

- industrial injuries benefits – constant attendance and exceptionally severe disablement allowances;
- war disablement pension – constant attendance, exceptionally severe disablement, severe occupational and mobility supplement allowances;
- service pensions – the unemployability allowances.

> *Example*
> Adam gets retirement pension of £82.05 and is due to pay Carol the flat rate of £5 for one child. He has an occupational pension of £97.50 a week and a personal pension providing a further £39 a week. Carol applies for a variation on income not taken into account grounds. As he has income over £100 the better buy calculation is carried out.
> £5 + (normal rules calculation on income of £136.50) = £5 + (reduced rate on £136.50)
> £5 + (£5 + 25% x £36.50, rounded to the nearest pound) = £5 + £14 (£5 + £9.13, rounded to the nearest pound) = £19
> Normal rules calculation on total income (ie, £82.05 + £136.50 = £218.55)
> Basic rate maintenance is 15% of £218.55 = £32.78 rounded to £33
> Better-buy will mean a variation may be considered which would result in maintenance of £19 (ie, the lesser of the two amounts).

Special expenses

The total amount of any special expenses (less any threshold amounts) is deducted from the net weekly income of the non-resident parent and the calculation is carried out as normal using this amount.[138] Where there is more than one special expense included, the amounts are aggregated and only one threshold is applied (where applicable).[139]

If the net income is the capped amount, the effect of the variation is worked out by subtracting the special expenses from the actual net weekly income.[140] If this results in a figure above the capped amount of £2,000, the special expenses variation will be refused.

> *Example*
> Bronwen has a net income of £428 and pays basic rate maintenance of £86 to Ivan for Ursula and Gretchen. She claims special expenses costs for contact with her children,

which amounts to £450 over a six-month period, and for the contribution to their boarding school fees of £1,500 a term.

Her special expenses are worked out as £17.30 for contact and £28.77 for boarding school costs, totalling £46.07. The threshold of £15 applies and £15 is deducted from the total, leaving £31.07.

This is deducted from her weekly net income (£428 – £31.07 = £396.93)

Her maintenance is now worked out in the usual way: 20% x £396.93 = £79.39 rounded to £79

Her variation for special expenses has reduced her maintenance from £86 a week to £79.

Property and capital transfers

The transfer is treated as an advance payment of maintenance.[141] Therefore, the equivalent weekly value is subtracted from the maintenance calculated to produce the amount due after a variation on property/capital transfer grounds.[142]

Example

Marcus has a property transfer variation agreed with a weekly value of £25.84. His net weekly income is £400 and under the maintenance calculation he is due to pay Helene maintenance of £80 a week for Robert and Heather. There is no reduction for shared care and so the weekly value of the property transfer is subtracted from the amount he is due to pay.

£80 – £25.84 = £54.16, the amount he must pay following the variation.

Concurrent variations

If there is more than one variation element (ie, special expenses, additional cases) to be applied, the calculation is carried out using the following steps.

Step 1

Work out the amounts of each element.

Step 2

Apply the additional cases element, capping the income at £2,000.

Step 3

Apply the special expenses element.

Step 4

Work out the maintenance due, applying any apportionment or reduction for shared care or part-time local authority care.

Step 5

Apply any property transfer element (only that which applies to the parent with care who benefited from the transfer).

Step 6

Check that the total amount of maintenance is not less than £5. If so, apportion this between the persons with care.

> *Example*
> The situation is as in the example on p145. In this instance, both the property transfer and the additional cases variation are applied to work out how much Marcus must pay Helene for Robert and Heather. His net income before variation is £400, as before.
> **Step 1** The additional cases variation is that £360 additional income should be included.
> The property transfer variation has a weekly value of £25.84.
> **Step 2** £360 + £400 = £760, which is below the capped amount.
> **Step 3** Does not apply.
> **Step 4** Basic maintenance due is 20% x £760 = £152
> **Step 5** Maintenance due is reduced by the property transfer (ie, £152 £25.84 = £126.16)
> Therefore, instead of receiving £80 from Marcus, Helene will now be due £126.16 a week

Revisions and supersessions

A variation is not a separate decision to be challenged; it is a variation of the maintenance calculation. If a variation is agreed and applied to the calculation, this decision may be challenged by seeking a revision within one month. Any changes of circumstances, whether in relation to the variation or other factors, can result in a revision or supersession of the maintenance calculation under the normal rules, depending on the circumstances (see Chapter 18). This also applies to decisions referred by the CSA to an appeal tribunal for a decision – eg, contentious cases.[143]

The variation will be taken into account in any reconsideration. However, there may be changes of circumstances which mean that the variation ceases to have effect. In certain circumstances, a previous variation to the calculation may be reinstated, without an application, at the discretion of the CSA.

Date the variation takes effect

If the ground existed at the effective date of the maintenance calculation (ie, when the non-resident parent was notified of the application or the application was treated as made), the date the variation takes effect will be the effective date of the maintenance calculation if either:

- the application is made before the calculation is made;[144] *or*
- the application is made within one month of the maintenance calculation, or meets the other normal rules applying to revisions (eg, misrepresentation or

failure to disclose information that meant the decision was to the person's advantage) or erroneous decisions.[145]

The exception to this rule is where the non-resident parent is applying for a variation on the grounds of prior debts or payments in respect of certain mortgages, loans or insurance policies, and payments towards these are treated as voluntary payments in the initial payment period.[146] In this case, the variation takes effect from the maintenance period following the date on which the non-resident parent was notified – ie, the start of the second week of liability.

If the ground did not apply at the effective date of the maintenance calculation the variation is effective from:

- the first day of the maintenance period in which the ground arose, where this is after the effective date but before the maintenance calculation is made;[147]
- the first day of the maintenance period in which the relevant person requested the variation.[148] However, if the CSA requests that the application is made in writing, and this is not supplied within 14 days, the date the request was made will be the date the application is received unless the CSA accepts that the delay was unavoidable;[149]
- the first day of the maintenance period in which the ground will arise, where the application for variation is made in advance.[150]

A case may have a number of different grounds, agreed over time, and each may have different dates from which they take effect.

Example

Tara claims maintenance. The effective date is 26 August 2003. She is notified of her maintenance calculation on 19 September 2003. She takes advice and applies for a variation on the basis that an additional cases ground applied on 26 August 2003. She makes this application on 8 October 2003 (ie, within one month of her notification of the decision). The variation is agreed and the maintenance calculation is revised on 14 November 2003, with effect from 26 August 2003.

Juan takes advice and on 3 December 2003 applies for a variation on the grounds that he has been paying off the car which they bought before splitting up and which Tara needs, as she lives in a secluded cottage. He is also just about to start paying boarding school fees for their eldest child in late December. The variation is agreed and a revision is made on 3 January 2004 in which the elements for prior debts take effect from 2 December and the boarding school fees take effect from 16 December 2003.

However, even though the variation for prior debts only applies from December, Juan could ask that the amounts he paid toward the car before the calculation was made be considered as voluntary payments to offset initial arrears. Had Juan taken advice at the same time as Tara and applied for a variation at the same time as she did on the grounds of prior debts and that his repayments on the car were voluntary payments, then there could have been a further variation to the calculation, with the decision taking effect from 26 August 2003.

When a variation ceases to have effect

A variation will cease to have effect when the ground no longer applies or any other of the reasons for refusing a variation is met.[151] For example, a variation in favour of the person with care will always cease to have effect where the non-resident parent or his partner starts to receive working tax credit.[152] When a variation ceases a supersession is carried out, which takes effect from the first day in the maintenance period in which the change occurred.

Where there is a later change, unless the CSA has discretion to reinstate the variation, a further application may need to be made.

Situations where a further application for variation is required

Ground	When variation ceases	When a further application could be made following a later change
Additional cases	Net income before any variation is greater than £2,000. The non-resident parent or his partner receives working tax credit.	Net income before variation would be less than £2,000. Neither receives working tax credit.
Special expenses	Net income after any variation is greater than £2,000.	Net income after variation would be less than £2,000.

Discretion to reinstate a previous variation

In some cases, the CSA may revise or supersede a maintenance calculation to reinstate a variation that has previously been agreed. This discretion may be applied where there is:[153]

- a change of circumstances which means the non-resident parent's liability is reduced to nil or another rate where the variation cannot be taken into account; *then*
- a subsequent change of circumstances means his liability can now be adjusted to take the variation into account.

Examples of situations where this could apply could be where:

- the non-resident parent becomes a full-time student and so becomes liable for the nil rate, but subsequently returns to a basic or reduced rate;
- a variation is agreed and on a subsequent application for revision/supersession the non-resident parent fails to provide information. Therefore, the maintenance calculation is replaced by a default decision. Later on the information required is provided and this default maintenance decision is

replaced with a maintenance calculation. The variation may then be reapplied without a fresh application.

Had the maintenance calculation ceased, this discretion would not apply. For example, if the parent had moved abroad and the CSA ceased to have jurisdiction, then s/he returns to the UK, a subsequent application would need to be made for a maintenance calculation, including an application for variation. However, in some circumstances the CSA may be able to reinstate the variation without contest (see p156).

In exercising the discretion to reinstate, the CSA must be satisfied that there has been no material change in circumstances which affects the earlier variation.[154] If this is satisfied, the previous variation can be reinstated without an application or any further contact with the relevant persons – ie, s/he is not invited to make representations. There is no obligation to investigate; therefore, decisions are made based on the information available to the decision maker. There is no time limit on the period between the variation ceasing to apply and being reinstated, as long as the circumstances that gave rise to the variation remain unchanged. This is most easily satisfied in pre-1993 property/capital transfers.

Example

Joe applies for, and obtains, a variation from his basic rate maintenance on the grounds of contact costs with his children. He is later convicted of a criminal offence and sentenced to six months in prison. He becomes liable to pay the nil rate. On his release, three months later, he again becomes liable, this time at the reduced rate. The CSA is not satisfied that the circumstances relating to eligibility are still the same and does not reinstate the variation. Joe will need to make a new application for a variation on the grounds of contact costs.

Had the variation been granted on the grounds of a pre-1993 property/capital transfer, the CSA could probably have reinstated the variation without Joe having to make a further application, as there is no reason why this ground and its effect should be altered by his intervening imprisonment.

Revision and supersession of a previously agreed variation

If a variation has been agreed, it may be subsequently revised or superseded. When a request is received to revise or supersede such a decision, the CSA may notify the other relevant parties and invite them to make representations.[155] This need not be done if the CSA thinks it would not agree to vary the calculation or that a revision/supersession would not be to the advantage of the applicant.

If contest does take place, the usual procedure is followed (see p155).[156]

The CSA may decide to revise/supersede, or not to revise or supersede, the decision and notify the applicant and any relevant parties, as appropriate.

Appealing a decision

Decisions on the maintenance calculation in response to a variation application, or where a variation element is reinstated into a maintenance calculation, may be appealed under the normal procedure. As with other appeals, if, following the appeal application, there is a revision or supersession of the appealed decision that is to the advantage of the appellant, the appeal will lapse.[157] For further details on appeals, see Chapter 20.

Notes

1 s28A(1) CSA 1991 (note the modifications under the CS(V)(MSP) Regs only apply in cases where the application is made after a maintenance calculation is in force)

1. Grounds for a variation
2 Sch 4B CSA 1991 as substituted by s6 CSPSSA 2000
3 Sch 4A para 2(3) CSA 1991 as substituted by s6 CSPSSA 2000
4 Reg 15 CS(V) Regs
5 Reg 15(1) CS(V) Regs
6 Reg 15(2) CS(V) Regs
7 Reg 15(3) CS(V) Regs
8 Reg 10(1) CS(V) Regs
9 Reg 10(4) CS(V) Regs
10 PG, Specialist Areas, Unacceptable Expenses
11 Reg 10(1) CS(V) Regs
12 Reg 10(3)(a) CS(V) Regs
13 Reg 10(3)(b) CS(V) Regs
14 PG, Specialist Areas, Frequency of Visits
15 PG, Specialist Areas, Frequency of Visits
16 PG, Specialist Areas, Travel Costs
17 PG, Specialist Areas, Accommodation Costs
18 Reg 11(2)(c) CS(V) Regs
19 Reg 11(2)(a) CS(V) Regs
20 Reg 11(1) CS(V) Regs
21 Reg 11(2)(b) CS(V) Regs
22 PG, Specialist Areas, Illness or Disability of a Relevant Other Child
23 Reg 11(3) CS(V) Regs
24 PG, Specialist Areas, Illness or Disability of a Relevant Other Child
25 Reg 12(2) CS(V) Regs
26 Reg 12(3)(k) and (6)(a) CS(V) Regs
27 Reg 12(6)(a) CS(V) Regs; s3/6(4) ICTA 1988; PG, Specialist Areas, Prior Debts
28 Reg 12(3)(a) CS(V) Regs
29 Reg 12(3)(k) CS(V) Regs
30 Reg 12(4) CS(V) Regs
31 Reg 12(3)(l) CS(V) Regs
32 Reg 12(3)(h) CS(V) Regs
33 Reg 12(3)(i) CS(V) Regs
34 PG, Specialist Areas, Prior Debts
35 Reg 12(3)(b)-(g), (j) and (m) CS(V) Regs
36 Reg 12(5) CS(V) Regs
37 PG, Specialist Areas, Prior Debts
38 Reg 13(1) CS(V) Regs
39 Reg 13(5) CS(V) Regs
40 Reg 13(2) CS(V) Regs
41 Reg 13(3) CS(V) Regs
42 Reg 13(4) CS(V) Regs
43 Reg 14(2)(a) CS(V) Regs
44 Reg 14(2)(b) CS(V) Regs
45 Sch 4B para 3(1) CSA 1991; regs 16(1) and (2) and 17(4) CS(V) Regs
46 Sch 4B para 3(2) CSA 1991
47 PG, Specialist Areas, Property Capital Transfer - Overview
48 s8(11) CSA 1991; reg 16(1)(a) CS(V) Regs; PG, Specialist Areas, Property Capital Transfer - Overview
49 Reg 16(2) CS(V) Regs
50 Reg 16(3) CS(V) Regs
51 Sch 4B para 3 CSA 1991; reg 17(1) CS(V) Regs
52 Reg 17(2) CS(V) Regs
53 Reg 16(4) CS(V) Regs
54 Sch para 1(3)(b) CS(V) Regs

55 Sch para 2 CS(V) Regs
56 Sch para 3 CS(V) Regs
57 Sch 4B para 4 CSA 1991
58 Reg 25 CS(V) Regs
59 Reg 26 CS(V) Regs
60 Reg 18(1) CS(V) Regs
61 Reg 18(2) CS(V) Regs
62 Reg 18(3) CS(V) Regs
63 CCS/1026/2006
64 Reg 18(3)(f) CS(V) Regs
65 Reg 18(4) CS(V) Regs
66 Reg 18(5) CS(V) Regs
67 Reg 18(6) CS(V) Regs; PG, Specialist
    Areas, Assets
68 Regs 18(5) and 25 CS(V) Regs
69 Reg 19(1) CS(V) Regs
70 Reg 19(1A) CS(V) Regs
71 CCS/1320/2005. See 2004/05 edition
    of this *Handbook* for the rules which
    applied before 6 April 2005.
72 Reg 19(2) CS(V) Regs
73 Regs 19(5)(a) and 25 CS(V) Regs
74 Reg 26(3) CS(V) Regs
75 Reg 19(4) CS(V) Regs
76 PG, Specialist Areas, Diversion of Income
77 Regs 19(5)(b) and 25 CS(V) Regs
78 Reg 20(1) and (2) CS(V) Regs
79 Reg 20(3) and (4)(a) CS(V) Regs
80 CCS/2018/2005
81 Reg 20(4) CS(V) Regs
82 Reg 20(5) CS(V) Regs
83 PG, Specialist Areas, Lifestyle
    Inconsistent with Declared Income
84 PG, Specialist Areas, Lifestyle
    Inconsistent with Declared Income

2. Applying for a variation

85 s28A CSA 1991 (note the modifications
    under the CS(V)(MSP) Regs take effect
    where the application is made when the
    maintenance calculation is in
    force); s28G CSA 1991
86 s28A(4) CSA 1991 (note the
    modifications under the CS(V)(MSP)
    Regs take effect where the application is
    made when the maintenance
    calculation is in force)
87 Reg 4(1) CS(V) Regs
88 s28A(4)(b) CSA 1991
89 Reg 8(1) CS(V) Regs
90 PG, Specialist Areas, Insufficient
    Information Provided
91 Reg 8(1) CS(V) Regs
92 Regs 6(2)(c) and 8(2) CS(V) Regs
93 Reg 5(1) CS(V) Regs
94 Reg 5(2) CS(V) Regs

3. Procedure

95 s28D CSA 1991 (note the modifications
    under the CS(V)(MSP) Regs take effect
    where the application is made when the
    maintenance calculation is in force)
96 Sch 4B para 5(1) CSA 1991; reg 9(9)
    CS(V) Regs
97 Reg 9(8) CS(V) Regs
98 s28B(1) CSA 1991
99 Reg 6(1) CS(V) Regs
100 s28B CSA 1991 (note the modifications
    under the CS(V)(MSP) Regs take effect
    where the application is made when the
    maintenance calculation is in force); reg
    7 CS(V) Regs
101 s28B CSA 1991 (note the modifications
    under the CS(V)(MSP) Regs take effect
    where the application is made when the
    maintenance calculation is in
    force); regs 6 and 7 CS(V) Regs
102 Reg 9(1) CS(V) Regs
103 PG, Specialist Areas, Contest – New
    Information/Evidence Received
104 Reg 9(1) CS(V) Regs
105 Reg 9(5) CS(V) Regs
106 Reg 9(4) CS(V) Regs
107 Procedures Guide, Specialist Areas,
    Contest - Contradictory Evidence
108 Reg 9(2) CS(V) Regs
109 PG, Specialist Areas, Contest –
    Information for Non-disclosure
110 Reg 9(3) CS(V) Regs
111 s12 CSA 1991
112 s28F(5) CSA 1991 (note the
    modifications under the CS(V)(MSP)
    Regs take effect where the application is
    made when the maintenance
    calculation is in force)
113 s28C CSA 1991 (note the modifications
    under the CS(V)(MSP) Regs take effect
    where the application is made when the
    maintenance calculation is in force)
114 s28C(2) CSA 1991 (note the
    modifications under the CS(V)(MSP)
    Regs take effect where the application is
    made when the maintenance
    calculation is in force); reg 31(1) CS(V)
    Regs
115 PG, Specialist Areas, Regular Payments
    Condition
116 s28C(4) CSA 1991 (note the
    modifications under the CS(V)(MSP)
    Regs take effect where the application is
    made when the maintenance
    calculation is in force)

117 s28C(3) CSA 1991(note the modifications under the CS(V)(MSP) Regs take effect where the application is made when the maintenance calculation is in force)

118 s28C(5) CSA 1991 (note the modifications under the CS(V)(MSP) Regs take effect where the application is made when the maintenance calculation is in force)

119 Reg 31(2) and (3) CS(V) Regs

120 s28C(7) CSA 1991(note the modifications under the CS(V)(MSP) Regs take effect where the application is made when the maintenance calculation is in force)

121 s28F(1) CSA 1991 (note the modifications under the CS(V)(MSP) Regs take effect where the application is made when the maintenance calculation is in force)

122 ss28E and 28F(2)(a) CSA 1991; PG, Specialist Areas, Discretion

123 ss28D(1)and 28F CSA 1991 (note the modifications on both sections under the CS(V)(MSP) Regs take effect where the application is made when the maintenance calculation is in force)

124 s28F(1) CSA 1991

125 Reg 21(1) CS(V) Regs

126 Reg 21(2) CS(V) Regs

127 s28D(1)(b) CSA 1991

128 PG, Specialist Areas, Role of Appeals Service

129 s28D(3) CSA 1991 (note the modifications under the CS(V)(MSP) Regs take effect where the application is made when the maintenance calculation is in force)

4. The decision

130 ss28B(2)and 28F(3) and (4) CSA 1991 (note the modifications to both sections under the CS(V)(MSP) Regs take effect where the application is made when the maintenance calculation is in force)

131 PG, Specialist Areas, Revising/Refusing to Revise a Maintenance Calculation to Take Account of a Variation Application; Superseding/Refusing to Supersede a Maintenance Calculation to Take Account of a Variation Application

132 Reg 27(5) CS(V) Regs

133 Reg 25 CS(V) Regs

134 Reg 25 CS(V) Regs

135 Reg 26 CS(V) Regs

136 Reg 26(1) CS(V) Regs

137 Reg 26(3) CS(V) Regs

138 Reg 23(1) CS(V) Regs

139 Reg 15(1) CS(V) Regs

140 Reg 23(2) CS(V) Regs

141 PG, Specialist Areas, Variation on the Grounds of a Property Transfer

142 Reg 24 CS(V) Regs

143 ss16(1A)(c) and 17(1)(d) CSA 1991

144 Reg 22 CS(V) Regs

145 s28G CSA 1991; reg 3A SSCS(DA) Regs

146 Reg 22(2) CS(V) Regs

147 Reg 22(1)(b) CS(V) Regs

148 s28G CSA 1991; regs 6A(6) and 7B(6) SS&CS(DA) Regs

149 Reg 4 CS(V) Regs; PG, Application Properly Made

150 Regs 6A(3) and 7B(5) SS&CS(DA) Regs

151 PG, Specialist Areas, Suspension of Variations

152 Reg 7(5)(b) CS(V) Regs

153 Reg 29 CS(V) Regs

154 Reg 9(3) CS(V) Regs

155 Reg 15B SS&CS(DA) Regs

156 Reg 15B SS&CS(DA) Regs

157 s16(6) CSA 1991

Chapter 8

Conversions

This chapter covers:
1. When 'old rules' cases convert to the 'new rules' (below)
2. The calculation and transitional phasing (p172)
3. The conversion decision (p179)
4. The linking rules (p181)
5. Revisions, supersessions and appeals (p183)
6. Conversion, benefits and collection (p189)

---

1. When 'old rules' cases convert to the 'new rules'

Apart from a situation where an 'old rules' case converts to a 'new rules' case, the two systems of calculating child support continue to operate independently. The fact that parents in the two systems are treated differently in terms of the amount of maintenance received and paid, even though their circumstances may otherwise be the same, is probably not discriminatory and does not breach human rights law.[1]

Under the proposed new system (see p3), parents will be able to choose to continue with 'old' or 'new' rules arrangements, make private arrangements or become clients of the reformed, simplified system.[2] New applications to the simplified system will not be accepted until at least 2010/11.

In effect, this means that there is no longer any intention to convert all 'old rules' cases to the 'new rules' at a future date. The current arrangements will continue, unless there is some other reason to convert a case. An 'old rules' case may convert because there is a connection to a 'new rules' case.

If an 'old rules' case converts there may be transitional phasing to increase or decrease the old amount to the new amount due (see p173).

Where an 'old rules' assessment ceases to be in force, an application may be decided under the 'new rules' if it is made more than 13 weeks after the assessment ceases. This is not a conversion as such and, therefore, transitional phasing will not apply.

Conversions

Conversion occurs where a maintenance assessment is in force and a related decision is made.[3] The related decision may be that a maintenance calculation is made or there has been a change involving a new or existing partner who also has maintenance. A conversion will occur where:[4]

- a maintenance calculation is made in respect of a person who is a relevant person (person with care or non-resident parent) in the existing assessment, whether or not this is for a different qualifying child;
- an application is made, or treated as made, that would result in a maintenance calculation but there is an assessment in force, the non-resident parent in the new application is the non-resident parent in the existing case but the person with care in the new application is different from the one in the existing case. However, if it is the common non-resident parent who applies for the maintenance calculation and the person with care in the new application does not wish to co-operate, there will be no conversion of the existing case (see also p47);
- a maintenance calculation is made in relation to person A who is a partner to person B who has a maintenance assessment, either A or B are in receipt of income support (IS) or income-based jobseeker's allowance (JSA), and A and B are either both persons with care or both non-resident parents;
- a maintenance assessment is in force in relation to person C and a maintenance calculation is in force in relation to person D, either C or D are in receipt of IS or income-based JSA, C and D are either both persons with care or both non-resident parents, and then C and D become partners; *or*
- a maintenance assessment is in force in relation to person E and a maintenance calculation is in force in relation to her/his partner F. E and F are either both persons with care or both non-resident parents and then they become entitled to IS or income-based JSA as partners.

The conversion of one case may set off a chain of conversions of other cases where the relevant person in a conversion is also a relevant person in an existing maintenance assessment.[5] The Child Support Agency (CSA) calls these 'linked cases'. This may result in a lengthy sequence of interrelated decisions that need to be made. Whenever an 'old rules' case is converted, transitional phasing may apply (see p173).

Example
Celine is the parent with care of two children, Michelle and Francis. Franco is their non-resident parent in the 'old rules' assessment. After 3 March 2003 Francis goes to live with Franco and his new partner, Helen. Franco applies, as the parent with care of Francis, for maintenance from Celine, as the non-resident parent. A maintenance calculation is made. As a relevant person in the old assessment is a relevant person in the new calculation (ie,

Celine is a person with care in the old and a non-resident parent in the new), the old maintenance assessment converts to the 'new rules' (transitional phasing may apply).

Celine is the parent with care of two children, Michelle and Francis. Franco is their non-resident parent in the 'old rules' assessment. Celine is on IS. She forms a new relationship with Bill and they move in together. Bill is also a parent with care on IS with a maintenance calculation for his daughter, Sophie. As they are both parents with care on a relevant benefit, Celine's 'old rules' case converts to the 'new rules' when Celine and Bill become partners (transitional phasing may apply to Celine's case). If Bill had been the non-resident parent instead of the person with care there would have been no case conversion.

If, in the first situation, Francis went to live with Franco before 3 March 2003, then both Celine and Franco would have 'old rules' assessments – ie, Celine as the person with care of Michelle in one assessment and Franco as the person with care of Francis in the other 'old rules' assessment. Then, if Celine moved in with Bill not only would her case convert but Franco's would as well because of the linking effect (see p181).

---

2. The calculation and transitional phasing

The new amount is worked out applying the new calculation rates, using the information that the Child Support Agency (CSA) has at the calculation date (see p170).[6] Where there are decisions outstanding on the maintenance assessment at conversion, the calculation may be carried out, and once those decisions are made, the maintenance calculation may be revised or superseded (see p183). There are additional rules for calculating the new amount at conversion where a relevant departure direction or relevant property transfer was applied to an 'old rules' case (see p176).

Where there is an interim maintenance assessment (IMA) in force when the conversion decision is being made, this may be:

- used to make the conversion decision;[7] *or*
- replaced with a default maintenance decision, if there is insufficient information to make a maintenance assessment or conversion decision.[8]

In either case, if information is subsequently provided by the non-resident parent to make a maintenance assessment, the conversion decision or default maintenance decision may be superseded.[9]

At conversion, the new rate will either be paid immediately or transitional phasing may be applied.[10] There are some situations where the new amount is always applied; in other cases, the CSA checks whether transitional phasing applies. If it does not, the new amount is paid.

When the new amount is always applied

The new amount of maintenance will be applied immediately (ie, without checking whether transitional phasing applies) if the:[11]
- 'new rules' amount is nil;
- 'old rules' amount was nil and the 'new rules' amount is the flat rate reduced to nil because of shared care (see p175);
- 'old rules' amount was more than nil but the 'new rules' amount is the flat rate (or halved flat rate where there is a partner who is a non-resident parent);
- 'old rules' amount was a Category A or D IMA;
- 'new rules' amount is a default maintenance decision.

Where none of the above apply, the CSA will check whether transitional phasing should be applied (see below). If it does not apply, the new amount will be payable.

Example

Sally is due to pay Mark maintenance at the minimum amount before conversion. After conversion she is liable for the flat rate. She pays the new amount from conversion.

Kieran pays Leah a maintenance assessment worked out under a Category A IMA. At conversion, as there is insufficient information to make a maintenance calculation, a default decision replaces the IMA and the new amount applies immediately.

If Kieran had been assessed under a Category B IMA, sufficient information would have been available to make a maintenance calculation.

Transitional phasing

Transitional phasing will apply (unless the situation is one where the new amount is always applied, see above) where the difference between the old amount and new amount is greater than the phasing amount.[12] Where there is more than one assessment in relation to the same non-resident parent, apportionment occurs, in which case the amounts referred to are those after the apportionment has been made.[13] Where there is an application from a new person with care which triggers conversion of an existing assessment (see p171), the apportionment in the new calculation will occur as normal, then the previous assessment amount is compared with the new amount due after apportionment.[14] There are special rules in some flat-rate cases (see p175).

The phasing amount depends on the net income of the non-resident parent. This is:[15]
- £2.50, if income is £100 or less;
- £5, if income is between £100 and £400; *or*
- £10, if income is £400 or more.

Net weekly income is as worked out under the 'new rules'. (This includes where a relevant departure direction is converted and treated as a variation.) If the difference between the old and new amounts is greater than the phasing amount, the old amount is increased or decreased by the phasing amount as appropriate.[16] This increase or decrease occurs on an annual basis during the transitional period. The transitional period lasts until the new amount is reached or for up to five years, unless there is a subsequent decision which affects this.[17]

Where transitional phasing applies, the **maximum transitional amount** that the non-resident parent may pay in maintenance (to all persons with care) is 30 per cent of his net income.[18] This is worked out under the normal rules plus, if there is a relevant additional cases departure, the net income is taken to be the total of the additional income and the income from prescribed benefits (excluding those disregarded). If there is an additional cases variation this means the total income after variation.[19]

In some situations, there may be a new case being calculated, and an old case converting at the same time. If this happens, apportionment of the maintenance calculation is carried out as normal. Transitional phasing may be applied to the 'old rules' case, in which case the total amount of maintenance is checked against the 30 per cent maximum. This means adding together the apportioned amount due for the 'new rules' case and the phased amount due for the 'old rules' case. If the 30 per cent maximum is breached, the maintenance is capped at this amount. The amount for the person (or persons) with care in the new case is deducted from the maximum, and the remainder is the amount due to the person (or persons) with care in the converting 'old rules' case.[20] Rounding is to the nearest penny (amounts can be adjusted where rounding would result in inequalities over time).[21]

- -

Example

Under her 'old rules' assessment Celine is due to get £68.40 in maintenance from Franco for Michelle and Francis. Franco lives with his new partner, Helen, and their son, Damien. Celine remains living on her own, but has a baby with a different non-resident parent. She applies for maintenance after 3 March 2003, and it is worked out under the 'new rules'. Franco's case will convert as a linked case. If Franco's net income is £360 a week at the conversion date, Celine's new amount from Franco is worked out under the basic rate.

| **Basic rate** | **Step 1** | 15% reduction for relevant child – ie, £360 – £54 = £306 |
| | **Step 2** | Maintenance is 20% x £306 = £61.20 (ie, £61 rounded to the nearest pound) |

Does transitional phasing apply?

The phasing amount is £5, as Franco's income is between £100 and £400. Since there is more than £5 difference between the old and new amounts transitional phasing applies. Celine is paid £63.40 (£68.40 – £5) in maintenance from Franco.

If Franco and Helen split up and Helen applied for maintenance for Damien after 3 March 2003, Celine's case would convert at this point, assuming this is before she has her third child. In this case there are now no relevant children living with Franco and three qualifying children.

Basic rate	Step 1	No reduction.
	Step 2	25% x £360 = £90
	Step 3	Apportionment between two persons with care (£90 ÷ 3 = £30)
		Helen is due to receive £30. Celine's new amount is £60.

Does transitional phasing apply?
As there is more than £5 difference between the old amount (£68.40) and the new amount (£60) phasing applies.

Year 1	£68.40 – £5 = £63.40
Year 2	£60

Therefore, the total amount of maintenance due is £93.40. This is less than the 30 per cent maximum (£108) so it does not affect maintenance.

If Celine's 'old rules' assessment was £100 a week, transitional phasing would mean:

Year 1	£100 – £5 = £95
Year 2	£95 – £5 = £90
Year 3	£90 – £5 = £85
Year 4	£85 – £5 = £80
Year 5	£60

This means Franco would pay £30 (Helen) + £95 (Celine) = £125
As this is greater than the 30 per cent maximum (£108) the calculation is adjusted. Helen still receives £30 but Celine receives £78 (£108 – £30).

Transitional amount in certain flat rate cases

If the old amount was nil and the new amount is the flat rate (because of receipt of a prescribed benefit), transitional phasing is £2.50 in the first year and then £5 in the second.[22] In cases where the non-resident parent's partner is also a non-resident parent with a maintenance calculation in force and either the non-resident parent or his partner is in receipt of income support (IS), income-based jobseeker's allowance (JSA) or pension credit (PC), transitional phasing is £1.25 in the first year and £2.50 in the second.[23]

Except where the old amount was nil, if the flat rate is due but reduces to nil because of shared care, the transitional amount due will be £2.50 in the first year and £5 in the second.[24] (In cases where the flat rate is halved because a partner is a non-resident parent, the phasing amount will be £1.25.[25]) This will occur where the non-resident parent shares care with the only (or all) person(s) with care.

If the amount due reduces to nil for some, but not all, of the persons with care, transitional phasing will only apply if:[26]
- the old amount is less than the new amount and the difference is more than £2.50; *or*
- the old amount is greater than the new amount but the new amount is less than £2.50.

Apportionment of the transitional amount takes place between those persons with care for whom the amount due does not reduce to nil because of shared care.[27]

Example

Andrew has four qualifying children. Claire and Hannah are each a person with care for one qualifying child, Millie is a person with care for two. Andrew has one child living with him and also shares care with Claire. Andrew's case converts because it is a linked case.

Under the 'old rules' he was exempt from paying the minimum amount. Under the 'new rules' he is liable for the flat rate of £5. This is apportioned between the persons with care: Hannah and Claire are due £1.25 each and Millie is due £2.50.

Because of shared care, Claire's maintenance is reduced to nil. This means £3.75 is now due in maintenance. As this is greater than the old amount and there is more than a £2.50 difference between old and new amounts, phasing is applied. The £2.50 phased amount is apportioned between Hannah and Millie: Hannah receives 83p and Millie £1.67.

Relevant departure directions and property transfers

In 'old rules' cases where there is a departure direction or an allowance for a property/capital transfer in the exempt income calculation these may be taken into consideration when working out the new amount used in the conversion calculation.[28] Only a relevant departure and relevant property/capital transfer affect the calculation.

If a departure direction can be considered as a variation, it is known as a **'relevant departure direction'**. A relevant departure direction is one for:[29]
- contact costs;
- prior debts;
- illness and disability costs of a relevant child (ie, the non-resident parent or his partner receives child benefit for the child);
- a property or capital transfer;
- diversion of income;
- when lifestyle is inconsistent with stated income; *or*
- assets, where the value of the assets is greater than £65,000.

In the case of contact costs and prior debts, the £15 and £10 threshold that applies to special expenses variations must be met for either amount or the sum of both where they apply.[30] In the case of diversion of income or an inconsistent lifestyle, the amount of income must exceed £100 in cases where the new amount would otherwise be:

- the flat rate because of receipt of a prescribed benefit (other than IS, income-based JSA or PC);
- the flat rate as above, but reduced to nil because of shared care; *or*
- the nil rate (other than on income grounds).[31]

If there is a relevant departure direction, an equivalent variation will be applied to the calculation of the new amount without any separate application for a variation.[32]

Example

Joan has a maintenance assessment with a special expenses departure direction of £22 for contact costs and £18 for travel to work costs. When her case is converted because of a linked case, her special expenses for contact costs count as a relevant transfer but her travel-to-work costs do not.

A **'relevant property transfer'** is distinct from a property/capital departure as this is where an allowance is included at the exempt income stage (see Chapter 11) of the 'old rules' assessment formula.[33] In these cases, the amount of the relevant property transfer is deducted at conversion from the net income used to work out maintenance.[34] It may be advisable, where a relevant property transfer is applied, to seek a variation on property/capital transfer grounds.[35] If this application is successful, the conversion decision will be revised or superseded depending on when the application was made.

Adjustments to the conversion calculation

The adjustment made to the conversion calculation depends on the ground under which the departure direction has been granted – ie, special expenses, additional cases or property/capital transfer. The effect of an adjustment for departure directions and relevant property transfers (or the aggregate of those that apply) are listed below and are carried out in the following order.[36]

- **Additional cases departure direction.** The amount of the departure is added to the net income figure. Where this takes net income over the capped amount of £2,000, the net income figure used is £2,000.[37] If the non-resident parent is on benefit there is a maximum amount payable – ie, a conversion 'better-buy' (see p178).
- **Special expenses departure direction.** The amount of the departure is deducted from the net weekly income.[38] Where the net income is the capped amount of £2,000, deduct the expenses from the actual net income not the capped amount. If this reduces the net income figure to below £2,000, this is

the net income figure to use in the calculation, otherwise it is the capped amount.

- **Relevant property transfer.** The amount of the transfer is deducted from the net income of the non-resident parent. Where the net income is the capped amount of £2,000 the transfer is deducted from this capped amount.[39]
- **Property/capital transfer departure direction.** The amount of the departure is deducted from the maintenance due to the person with care.[40] This deduction can only be completed after any reduction for shared care (or part-time local authority care) has been applied.[41]

If these adjustments reduce the amount of maintenance due to below the £5 flat rate, the amount due will be the £5 flat rate. This may be apportioned between the persons with care as appropriate.[42]

Conversion better-buy

If the non-resident parent is on benefit, the maximum amount payable where there is a relevant departure on additional cases grounds is the lesser of:[43]
- the flat rate plus the appropriate rate (reduced or basic) applied to the additional income under the departure; or
- the amount calculated by applying the appropriate rate to the total of the additional income under the departure and the income payable under any prescribed benefits (excluding amounts that are disregarded).

The conversion calculation is carried out in the normal way. However, the conversion better-buy provision is applied and may cap the amount to be paid.

Outstanding overpayments at conversion

In 'old rules' cases, if there has been an overpayment of child support and the amount payable under the maintenance assessment has been adjusted to reflect this (see p432), the adjustment can be applied to the new amount, or the transitional amount, which applies on conversion. This will be done if the overpayment remains on the case conversion date and the CSA considers it appropriate to apply the adjustment.[44] The usual factors when considering overpayment adjustments should be taken into account (see p432).

If the conversion decision affects more than one parent with care, the adjustment of the amount payable is only applied to the apportioned amount payable to the parent with care in respect of whom the original adjusted maintenance assessment applied.

Offsetting arrears

If there are arrears of child support due in an 'old rules' case and the CSA has allocated other payments of child support against the arrears, this attribution of child support payments can be applied to the new amount, or the transitional amount, which applies on conversion.[45] This will be done if the arrears remain outstanding on the case conversion date and the CSA has used its discretion to offset the arrears against the payment of child maintenance in accordance with the regulations, as they apply to a conversion decision (see also p431).

3. **The conversion decision**

At conversion, the Child Support Agency (CSA) carries out a conversion calculation (see p172).[46]

There is no requirement to seek more up-to-date information;[47] if the information used at the calculation date is incorrect a revision can be requested. This may be particularly important in cases where there have been significant changes, which could increase or decrease the 'old rules' maintenance assessment The policy intention is not routinely to supersede maintenance assessment decisions before conversion.

The new rate will either be paid immediately (ie, the maintenance calculation comes into force) or transitional phasing may be applied (see p173).[48] There are some situations where the new amount is always applied; in other cases, the CSA checks if transitional phasing applies and if it does not, the new amount is paid.

The effective date of the conversion decision

The effective date of the conversion decision is normally the beginning of the first maintenance period on or after the conversion date.[49] This is known as the **'case conversion date'**. If a case converts, the effective date may be the beginning of the first maintenance period on or after the effective date of the new calculation or another period depending on the circumstances.[50]

Effective date of conversion decisions

Situation	Effective date
A maintenance calculation is made in respect of a relevant person in relation to the maintenance assessment, whether or not in respect of a different qualifying child.	The beginning of the first maintenance period on or after the effective date of the new calculation.

A maintenance calculation is made in respect of person A who is a partner to person B who has a maintenance assessment. Either A or B are in receipt of income support (IS)/income-based jobseeker's allowance (JSA) and A and B are either both persons with care or both non-resident parents.	The beginning of the first maintenance period on or after the effective date of the new calculation.
An application is made, or treated as made, that would result in a maintenance calculation but there is an assessment in force. The non-resident parent in the new application is the non-resident parent in the existing case but the person with care in the new application is a different one from the one in the existing case.	The beginning of the first maintenance period on or after the date of notification of the conversion decision.
A maintenance assessment is in force in respect of person C and a maintenance calculation is in force in relation to person D. Either C or D are in receipt of IS/income-based JSA. C and D are either both persons with care or both non-resident parents. C and D become partners and the benefit decision is superseded because of this.	The beginning of the first maintenance period on or after the date that the benefit supersession decision takes effect.
A maintenance assessment is in force in respect of person E and a maintenance calculation in force in relation to partner F. E and F are either both persons with care or both non-resident parents and they become entitled to IS/income-based JSA as partners.	The beginning of the first maintenance period on or after the date from which they become entitled to IS or income-based JSA.
All other circumstances.	The beginning of the first maintenance period on or after the conversion decision.

Notification

Once the conversion decision is made, the non-resident parent, person with care and Scottish child applicant are notified in writing.[51]

This notification states the:

- new amount;
- transitional amount, if appropriate;
- length of the transitional period;
- date the conversion decision was made and the date from which it is effective;
- non-resident parent's net weekly income;
- number of qualifying and relevant children;
- adjustments for apportionment or shared care;
- details of departure directions or relevant property transfers taken into account;
- adjustments because of the maximum transitional amount rule.

The conversion decision is treated as a maintenance calculation decision so requests for revision, supersession, variation and appeal may be made.[52] However, when considering subsequent decisions there are additional rules to determine the amount of maintenance to be paid (see p185).

After notification of the conversion decision there may be an application for a departure direction or a variation (see p188).

When does the conversion end

Transitional phasing may be applied for up to five years from the case conversion date or until the maintenance calculation amount is reached.[53] Where there are subsequent decisions that result in the new amount being paid immediately (ie, nil rate or default rate), these may be applied. If the calculation is cancelled, conversion will end. However, in some cases where linking applies (see below), a second subsequent decision or new application may be dealt with as if the conversion decision still applied. This may affect the amount to be paid under any subsequent decision.

4. **The linking rules**

The linking rules cover a range of situations where an 'old rules' assessment or a transitional amount has been in force and there are applications and subsequent decisions made after 3 March 2003. Whether or not linking is applied depends on the timescales and circumstances. In each instance there are two key factors.

- A 13-week linking period is used.
- If there is another application in the interim that involves either the person with care or non-resident parent (but not both) there is no linking.

If linking applies, the rules on working out how much maintenance is paid are adjusted.

The linking rules and their effect

Scenario	Maintenance is worked out as if:
After 3 March 2003 there is an application, but within 13 weeks there was a maintenance assessment in force for the same parent with care, non-resident parent and qualifying child.	– it is a maintenance assessment. All the 'old rules', including the formula, are applied to the case.
The conversion calculation ceases to have effect, but within 13 weeks there is an application for the same parent with care, non-resident parent and qualifying child.	– the conversion calculation is still in force and subsequent decision rules are applied.
A transitional amount is being paid. There is a subsequent decision where the £5/£2.50 flat rate, nil rate for shared care or nil rate is paid. Within 13 weeks of the effective date of this, a second decision is made where none of these rates apply for the same parent with care, non-resident parent and qualifying child.	– the first subsequent decision had not been made (ie, the transitional amount is still in force) and the subsequent decision rules are applied.

Applications on or after 3 March 2003

An application for a maintenance calculation made on or after 3 March 2003 can be treated as an application for a maintenance assessment if it is:[54]
- made within 13 weeks of a maintenance assessment being in force; *and*
- in relation to the same person with care, non-resident parent and qualifying child,

unless there is a new application which includes either the 'old rules' case person with care or non-resident parent (but not both) before the new application is made, in which case there is no linking and it is dealt with as a new case.[55]

Where linking applies, maintenance is worked out using the 'old rules' maintenance assessment.

Where a new application is linked to an old assessment and there is then a new application which involves the person with care or non-resident parent, the old case will be converted and a conversion calculation will be done.

If an application is made after 13 weeks of a maintenance assessment being in force, it is treated as an application under the 'new rules' and a calculation is carried out. No transitional phasing will apply. A parent with care has a right to opt out if she wishes, and to reapply at any time, whether or not the reason for doing so is to increase her maintenance.[56]

Example

Celine is the parent with care. Franco is the non-resident parent in an 'old rules' assessment. Celine asks the CSA to stop acting (ie, she opts out). After six weeks she applies for a 'new rules' maintenance calculation. Since her 'old rules' assessment was in force within the last 13 weeks her application is treated as an application for a maintenance assessment.

If Celine opts out and waits for 14 weeks and then applies, her case will be dealt with as a 'new rules' case.

Celine opts out, but before she reapplies Franco and his partner, Helen, split up. Helen makes an application for a maintenance calculation as the parent with care with Franco the non-resident parent, three weeks after Celine opts out. Helen is a 'new rules' case and when Celine reapplies three weeks later her case is dealt with as a new case and no linking or conversion rules apply.

If Celine opts out but before she reapplies Franco applies as the parent with care of Francis, Franco is a 'new rules' case. When Celine applies six weeks later, the linking rules apply and a conversion calculation will be done. Transitional phasing may apply to her maintenance.

5. **Revisions, supersessions and appeals**

At conversion there may be decisions outstanding on a maintenance assessment or departure direction. In other cases, decisions may have been made but the time limits for challenging them may not yet have expired (see below).

Once the conversion decision has been made it may be challenged in the normal way (revision, supersession, appeal and application for variation) since it is treated as if it were a maintenance calculation.[57] Adjustments of the amounts payable under the transitional phasing rules (see p173) may also be revised or superseded.[58] However, there are some conversion decisions that cannot be revised, superseded or appealed (see p184). There are also additional rules to be applied when working out how much maintenance should be paid on any subsequent decision (see p185).

Applications may also be made for a departure direction or variation that may result in decisions being revised or superseded (see p188).

Outstanding decisions and time limits at conversion

In some cases, a decision may have been made on a maintenance assessment or departure direction and the time limit for seeking a revision or making an appeal has not expired at conversion.[59] In these cases, a revision or appeal may still be sought using the 'old rules'.

Alternatively, at the conversion date there may be outstanding decisions on:[60]
- the maintenance assessment;
- a departure direction;
- a revision or supersession (including those initiated by the Child Support Agency (CSA)[61]);
- an appeal.[62]

If this is the case, a conversion decision may be made using the information held at the conversion date.[63] In the case of an outstanding maintenance assessment this may mean an interim maintenance assessment (IMA) is made and, at conversion, a default maintenance decision becomes due. The outstanding decision may be determined using the 'old rules' as if they still applied.[64] Once the outstanding decision is made or the appeal is decided, the conversion decision may be revised or superseded.[65]

Outstanding decisions on revision and supersession may themselves be appealed when they are made using the 'old rules'.[66] This means a decision not to make a departure direction may be appealed under the 'old rules'.[67] An appeal decision may be challenged on a point of law to the child support commissioners.

Conversion and subsequent decisions

Conversion and subsequent decisions can be revised, superseded and appealed in the same way as maintenance calculations,[68] except for the following.
- There are certain conversion decisions that may not be revised, superseded or appealed (see p185).
- When appealing against a conversion decision, the time limit for making an appeal is either from the date of notification to one month after the case conversion date, or the usual one month from the notice of the decision, whichever is the later.[69] In practice, this means that the normal time limit applies unless there is advance notification of the conversion.
- The effective date of a revision or supersession of a conversion decision is either the conversion date or the date worked out under the normal rules, whichever is the later.[70]
- Notifications contain details of the amount in any subsequent decision rather than the new amount and details of any variations taken into account.
- A conversion decision may be revised or superseded because of a revision/supersession/appeal of a maintenance assessment (including an IMA) or departure direction after the calculation date.[71]
- When further decisions are made, the linking rules may be applied (see p181) and the rules on working out the amount of maintenance due on a subsequent decision are applied.

After notification of the conversion decision there may be an application for a departure direction or a variation. If this is made after the calculation date but before the case conversion date, it may result in a series of supersession decisions.

Decisions that cannot be revised, superseded or appealed

A revision, supersession and appeal will not be allowed on the grounds:[72]
- that the CSA used the information it already had at the calculation date;
- that the CSA took into account a relevant departure direction (ie, one that counts as a variation under the 'new rules');
- that the CSA failed to take into account a departure direction (ie, where it does not count as a variation under the 'new rules');
- that the CSA applied a phasing amount;
- of the length of the transitional period;
- that the CSA took into account a relevant property transfer, except where the person with care or Scottish child applicant asks for it to be removed as it did not reflect the true value of the transfer, or a relevant person applies for a variation.

How much is paid on a further decision after conversion

There are special rules on how to work out how much is paid when there are further decisions after conversion. These are applied to conversion cases where there is transitional phasing (or there has been in cases where the linking rules apply – see p181). These are in addition to the normal rules on revisions and supersessions.

When considering a revision of the conversion decision (ie, where the effective date is the case conversion date, not the revision of a later supersession) the rules for working out an initial conversion are used.[73]

Where there is a supersession of the conversion decision, or revision of such a decision, the additional rules, explained below, are used to determine the amount of maintenance to be paid.[74]

These apply to such decisions on appeal.

The amount to be paid under a further decision could be:
- the nil rate, or £5 (£2.50) flat rate (or if it is less or reduced to nil because of shared care);
- the transitional amount (see p186);
- a new transitional amount (see p186); *or*
- the subsequent decision amount.

If the decision is the nil rate, flat rate or flat rate reduced to nil because of shared care (including where the amount due is less than £5/£2.50), this is the amount that is paid and transitional phasing ceases.[75] However, if there is a subsequent decision after this and the linking rules may apply (see p181), the rules below may be applied and transitional phasing may be revived (see the example on p187).

In all other cases, the subsequent decision amount is compared with the former assessment and the new amount due under the maintenance calculation. Where there is more than one person with care the apportioning rules apply to the calculation (including any adjustments to the maximum transitional amount).[76] The subsequent decision amount and new amount are the amounts worked out using the maintenance calculation, including adjustments for apportionment and shared care, before any transitional phasing is applied. If linking applies (see p181), this may mean the new amount referred to is in a conversion calculation that has ceased to be in force or is in a previous decision. If, at the date of the subsequent decision, there was more than one person with care in relation to the same non-resident parent, but as a result of the subsequent decision there is only one, the new amount and the transitional amount used are the apportioned amount payable immediately before the subsequent decision to that person with care. The subsequent decision amount refers to the full amount payable under the subsequent decision.[77]

Unless the conditions in the table below are met, the amount due will be the subsequent decision amount. If this applies, transitional phasing ceases and cannot be revived for any further decisions and only the normal supersession rules apply.

Where the original transitional phasing or a new transitional amount applies, transitional phasing then continues until the subsequent decision amount is reached or the five-year transitional period ends, whichever is earlier (see p173).

Any further decisions in the meantime will be worked out under these rules.[78] There are provisions to allow this where the subsequent decision (Decision B) replaces an earlier subsequent decision (Decision A) or one made with an incorrect effective date, so that in effect Decision A is ignored in applying the rules.[79] However, the rules do not apply in this situation if the decision before Decision A took effect from the case conversion date.

Other cases where the amount due is not the subsequent decision amount

Condition one	Condition two	Amount due
The new amount is greater than the former assessment.	Subsequent decision is greater than new amount.	A new transitional amount is worked out, increasing the previous transitional amount by the difference between the new amount and the subsequent decision.

The new amount is greater than the former assessment.	Subsequent decision is less than or equal to the new amount and greater than the previous transitional amount.	Amount is the previous transitional amount.
The new amount is less than the former assessment.	Subsequent decision is less than the new amount.	A new transitional amount is worked out, decreasing the previous transitional amount by the difference between the new amount and the subsequent decision.
The new amount is less than the former assessment.	Subsequent decision is greater than or equal to the new amount and less than the previous transitional amount.	Amount is the previous transitional amount.

Example
Kevin is due to pay an assessment of £68. His net income is £248. When his case converts following a linked case, he is due to pay a basic rate of £50. This has transitional phasing applied, so he is due to pay £63. Four months later he gets a promotion and his ex-wife requests a supersession. As Kevin's net income has increased to £270, the 5 per cent tolerance level is breached and the CSA considers supersession. The amount he would now be due to pay is £54. The new amount of £50 was less than the assessment (Condition one) and the subsequent decision amount £54 is greater than this and less than the previous transitional amount £63 (Condition two). This means he continues to be due to pay the previous transitional amount of £63.

If Kevin's net income had increased to £325, the amount due would be £65. In this case he does not meet Condition two as this is greater than the previous transitional amount (£63). This means he is due to pay £65. There is no more transitional phasing. If Kevin reduces his working hours and his income decreases to £270, his maintenance due would be £54 with no transitional phasing applied.

If the situation were different, the linking rules may apply. If the case converts, but instead of a promotion Kevin is made redundant and claims contribution-based jobseeker's allowance, he is now due to pay at the flat rate of £5. Ten weeks later he gets a new job and has a net income of £210 a week. As this is within 13 weeks, the linking rules apply (see p181). The maintenance decision at the flat rate is ignored. The new amount in Condition one is, therefore, £50 and the subsequent decision amount is £42. As this is lower than the new amount a new transitional amount is worked out. The difference between the two, £8 (£50 – £42), is subtracted from the first transitional amount (£63). Kevin now has to pay £55 (£63 – £8). Unless there are further decisions, a year later transitional phasing will mean he becomes due to pay £50 (£55 – £5).

Applications for a departure direction or variation

After notification of the conversion decision a relevant person may apply for a variation, in which case the conversion decision may be revised or superseded accordingly (see p183).

Departure directions are slightly more complex. To be taken into account at conversion a departure direction must apply to the maintenance assessment used in the conversion calculation.

Where an application for a departure direction is made after the calculation date but before the case conversion date this may result in the maintenance assessment being superseded to take account of the departure direction and then the conversion decision would be revised to reflect the change.[80] Where it is a relevant departure direction this revision of the conversion decision will include a variation.[81] A departure direction application cannot be made after the case conversion date. However, it may be possible to seek a revision or appeal a refusal to agree a departure direction if the relevant time limits have not expired.[82] For more information on decisions and time limits outstanding at conversion, see p183.

Conversion decision made in error

If a conversion decision, or subsequent decision on a conversion, has been made and it is found that the conversion grounds did not apply (see p171), the case will be treated as if those decisions had not been made.[83] This means the maintenance assessment will be reinstated, bearing in mind any revisions, supersessions or appeals made in the meantime which would have affected that assessment.

Example

Amy's maintenance assessment is converted because of an administrative error, which is discovered two months later. When the error is discovered the maintenance assessment is reinstated. However, the non-resident parent notified changes in housing costs and travel-to-work costs that could not be taken into account under the 'new rules' but were relevant in the previous assessment. The assessment is superseded, the effective date being linked to the relevant date of notification of the changes by the non-resident parent, as there was a significant change under the 'old rules'.

6. **Conversion, benefits and collection**

All the provisions relating to 'new rules' maintenance calculations apply to old cases that convert, even though transitional phasing may apply. This section clarifies how certain issues are dealt with at conversion.

Person with care on benefit

Child maintenance bonus and child maintenance premium

Up to conversion of an existing maintenance assessment to the 'new rules', a child maintenance bonus may be accrued.[84] The child maintenance bonus may also accrue where the maintenance is paid under an agreement or order, unless maintenance is paid for a different child or under a new agreement/order for the existing child(ren), in which case the child maintenance premium will apply from an earlier date.[85] If the payment is made after 16 February 2004, and it is the first voluntary payment of maintenance since the person has been on income support or income-based jobseeker's allowance, the child maintenance premium will apply.[86]

The rules on how to claim a child maintenance bonus before the case converts remain unchanged (see p374). When a child maintenance bonus is being replaced by a child maintenance premium at conversion, it may be possible to claim the bonus that has accrued.

When the case converts, the bonus period will cease and a child maintenance premium will apply.[87] The bonus period will end the day before conversion.[88] The child maintenance premium will begin on the first day of the benefit week in which the conversion date falls.

After conversion the bonus may be claimed where the conditions are met.[89] However:

- the normal time limit for the work condition to be met is extended from 14 days to one month;[90]
- the exceptional time limits for the work condition to be met (eg, if the non-resident parent or the only qualifying child die) apply if the change in circumstances occurs before conversion.

This means that if the work condition is not met within one month of conversion, the accrued bonus may be lost. Claims must be made within 28 days, though this may be extended by up to six months where there are good reasons for a late claim. For details of the other conditions on claiming a child maintenance bonus, see p374.

Non-resident parent on benefit

A non-resident parent on benefit may be due to pay the flat rate of maintenance or a transitional amount if, under the 'old rules', he made a contribution to maintenance or was exempt. The new rules on deduction from benefit applying to conversion decisions and deductions mean that deductions may be made from benefit for maintenance and arrears (see p372). There is no appeal against deductions from benefit for flat rate maintenance or to recover arrears (see p185).

Collection and enforcement

Maintenance worked out under a conversion decision is collected and enforced in the normal way, since it is treated as a maintenance calculation.[91]

Arrears built up under the 'old rules' may be recovered using the new deduction from earnings orders or the normal enforcement action. An existing deductions from earnings order may be cancelled and a new one issued.

A payment penalty may also be imposed, but only on arrears or late payments that fall due after conversion.

Notes

1. **When 'old rules' cases convert to the 'new rules'**
   1 In CCS/1077/2006 the commissioner stated that, even if discrimination could be shown, 'it is an objective and reasonable justification that parents are treated differently as new legislation is tested as it is brought into force.' See also CSCS/15/2005 in which the commissioner decided there was no breach of the European Convention on Human Rights, even though it is now clear that the 'new rules' scheme will not be implemented for all 'old rules' cases.
   2 White Paper, *A New System of Child Maintenance*, December 2006
   3 Reg 15 CS(TP) Regs; reg 3 CSPSSA (Comm 12) O
   4 Reg 15 CS(TP) Regs
   5 PG, Migration and Case Conversion, Overview – CSR Case Conversion

2. **The calculation and transitional phasing**
   6 Reg 16(1) CS(TP) Regs
   7 Reg 3(1)(c) CS(TP) Regs
   8 Reg 3(4) CS(TP) Regs
   9 Reg 3(5) CS(TP) Regs

10 s29 CSPSSA 2000; reg 9 CS(TP) Regs
11 Reg 14 CS(TP) Regs
12 Reg 10 CS(TP) Regs
13 Reg 11(2) CS(TP) Regs
14 Reg 11(3) CS(TP) Regs
15 Reg 24 CS(TP) Regs
16 Reg 11(1) CS(TP) Regs
17 Reg 2(1) CS(TP) Regs
18 Regs 2(1) and 25(1) CS(TP) Regs
19 Reg 25(5)-(7) CS(TP) Regs
20 Reg 25(3) CS(TP) Regs
21 Reg 25(4) CS(TP) Regs
22 Reg 13(2) CS(TP) Regs
23 Reg 13(1) CS(TP) Regs
24 Reg 12(1) CS(TP) Regs
25 Reg 12(2) CS(TP) Regs
26 Reg 12(3)-(5) CS(TP) Regs
27 Reg 12(6) CS(TP) Regs
28 s29(3)(b) CSPSSA 2000
29 Reg 17 CS(TP) Regs
30 Reg 17(2) CS(TP) Regs
31 Reg 17(6) CS(TP) Regs
32 Reg 17(9) CS(TP) Regs
33 Reg 17(8) CS(TP) Regs
34 Reg 21 CS(TP) Regs
35 Reg 17(10) CS(TP) Regs
36 Regs 23 and 23A CS(TP) Regs
37 Reg 20 CS(TP) Regs

38 Reg 18 CS(TP) Regs
39 Reg 21 CS(TP) Regs
40 Reg 19 CS(TP) Regs
41 Reg 23(4) CS(TP) Regs
42 Reg 23(5) CS(TP) Regs
43 Reg 22 CS(TP) Regs
44 Reg 9A CS(TP) Regs
45 Reg 9B CS(TP) Regs

87 s23 CSPSSA 2000
88 Reg 4(7) SS(CMB) Regs
89 Reg 4(2)-(5) SS(CMPMA) Regs 2002
90 Reg 3 (1)(f)(iii) SS(CMB) Regs
91 Reg 16(2A) CS(TP) Regs

3. The conversion decision
46 Regs 3(2) and 16(1) CS(TP) Regs
47 Regs 3(2) and 16(1) CS(TP) Regs
48 s29 CSPSSA 2000
49 Reg 15(1) CS(TP) Regs
50 Reg 15(2)-(3G) CS(TP) Regs
51 Reg 3(3) CS(TP) Regs
52 Reg 16(2) CS(TP) Regs
53 Reg 2 CS(TP) Regs

4. The linking rules
54 Reg 28(2) CS(TP) Regs
55 Reg 28(2A) CS(TP) Regs
56 see comments in R(CS) 1/06

5. Revisions, supersessions and appeals
57 Reg 16(2) CS(TP) Regs
58 Reg 4A CS(TP) Regs
59 Regs 14(2)(b) and (c) and 15(b)
    CS(D&A)(A) Regs
60 Reg 5 CS(TP) Regs
61 Reg 5A CS(TP) Regs
62 Reg 8 CS(TP) Regs
63 Regs 5(b) and 8(1) CS(TP) Regs
64 Regs 14(2) and 15(1) CS(D&A)(A) Regs
65 Regs 4(3) and 8(2) CS(TP) Regs
66 Regs 14 and 15 CS(D&A)(A) Regs
67 Reg 15(1) CS(D&A)(A) Regs
68 Reg 4(1) CS(TP) Regs
69 Reg 4(5)(b) CS(TP) Regs
70 Reg 4(4)(a) CS(TP) Regs
71 Reg 4(3) CS(TP) Regs
72 Reg 7 CS(TP) Regs
73 Reg 26 CS(TP) Regs
74 Reg 27 CS(TP) Regs
75 Reg 27(6) CS(TP) Regs
76 Reg 27(7) and (8) CS(TP) Regs
77 Reg 27(7A) and (7B) CS(TP) Regs
78 Reg 27(9) CS(TP) Regs
79 Reg 27(10) CS(TP) Regs
80 Reg 6(1)(a) and (2)(a) CS(TP) Regs
81 Reg 6(1)(b) and (2)(b) CS(TP) Regs
82 Reg 15 CS(D&A)(A) Regs
83 Reg 33 CS(TP) Regs

6. Conversion, benefits and collection
84 Art 6 CSPSSA (Comm12)O
85 Art 6 CSPSSA (Comm12)O
86 Reg 1(3) SS(CMP)A Regs

Part 4

Amount of maintenance: 'old rules'

Chapter 9

The 'old rules' formula

This chapter covers:

1. Introduction

For 'old rules' cases there is a statutory, non-discretionary formula for calculating child maintenance. An 'old rules' case is generally one where the application was made before 3 March 2003 (but some cases may be transferred to the 'new rules' – see Chapter 8). The amount of the child maintenance assessment cannot be negotiated. There is a right of appeal against the assessment, but appeal tribunals are bound by the same law as the Child Support Agency (CSA – see p398), so an appeal is only likely to be successful if the CSA has made a mistake or there is room for interpretation in the law.

The amount of child maintenance payable depends largely on the circumstances and the income of both parents, but particularly the income of the non-resident parent. It may be difficult for parents and advisers to obtain all the information needed from the other parent in order to carry out an exact calculation, particularly if the other parent is the non-resident parent.

However, understanding the way in which the formula works is important for explaining the result of an assessment as well as forecasting the effect of any change of circumstances and deciding whether to seek a revision or supersession (see p381). The formula might also be used to estimate the amount of child maintenance due before the CSA notification is sent to a non-resident parent, in order to prevent a build-up of unmanageable initial arrears (see p435).

Deviation from the 'old rules' formula

A number of people have a duty to provide information to the CSA. If the CSA does not have sufficient information to carry out a full assessment, an interim maintenance assessment can be imposed (see p367). These are usually penalty assessments which are set a higher rate than the final assessment.

The formula is not used to calculate the contribution towards child maintenance if the non-resident parent is on income support (IS) or income-based jobseeker's allowance (see p200).

Non-resident parents with second families have the assessment phased in if there would be an increase in the payments of over £20 a week, compared with a pre-April 1993 maintenance agreement. The maximum phasing-in period is 18 months, so this should only apply to non-resident parents whose 'old rules' case has still not been assessed, or who still have an interim maintenance assessment (see p372).

Departure

It may be possible to request a change to the standard 'old rules' formula in certain circumstances. This is called departure. Departure is a way of taking into account a financial factor particular to that family – eg, the costs of the non-resident parent travelling to visit the children, or a partner's contribution towards housing costs. Although the decision on whether to take the factor into account (and to what extent) is discretionary, an adjusted statutory formula is then used to obtain the final assessment. See Chapter 16 for details of departure.

Weekly rates and rounding up

The child maintenance payable under the 'old rules' formula is given as a weekly rate and all stages of the calculation use weekly figures.[1] Fractions of a penny will be disregarded if less than one-half or rounded up to the next penny if equal to or more than one half-penny (except when calculating 70 per cent net income for the protected level (see p280), when any fraction of a penny is ignored).[2]

Income support rates

The formula for assessing child maintenance is based on IS components – both the personal allowances and the premiums. The 2007/08 rates are given at the front of this *Handbook*. It is important to note that although some of the rules on entitlement to allowances and premiums have changed for IS claimants, they still apply for the purpose of working out 'old rules' assessments (see Appendix 2).

The IS rates used in the calculation are those which apply on the date that the maintenance assessment comes into effect, known as the 'effective date' (see p368).[3] As the effective date is usually some time before the date on which the assessment is being made, assessments may be made in 2007/08 using a previous year's rates. Benefit rates increase in April each year. The maintenance assessment is not automatically altered at the annual April uprating of IS rates, but if a re-assessment is requested after a change of circumstances, the new rates would then be relevant. CSA policy is to carry out periodic re-assessments of maintenance payable (case checks) at various intervals, but there is no legal requirement to do so (see p392).

Changes to the formula

Since the 'old rules' formula for setting assessments was introduced in April 1993, there have been several changes to it. Unless there is a specific provision, the general rule is that the calculation must be done using the regulations which applied on the effective date (see p368) of the assessment.[4] This edition of the *Handbook* covers the formula in effect during 2007/08; make sure you refer to the appropriate earlier edition for assessments with earlier effective dates.

2. **The five steps of the 'old rules' formula**

It is tempting to skip steps of the 'old rules' formula as it is long and complex, and you might think certain steps do not apply. However, you should not skip any steps without checking them unless you are very familiar with the formula.

Although only a non-resident parent is liable to pay child maintenance, the calculation involves the income of both parents. The term 'parent' applies to both the non-resident parent and the parent with care.

As elsewhere in this *Handbook*, for the sake of simplicity the parent with care is referred to as 'she' and the non-resident parent as 'he'. However, all aspects of the formula apply in the same way if the parent with care is in fact the father and the non-resident parent the mother. If the person with care is *not* the legal parent of the child, then the income of that person does not affect the amount of child maintenance payable.

Step 1: the maintenance requirement

The maintenance requirement represents the minimum day-to-day expenses of maintaining children. However, the maintenance requirement is neither the minimum nor the maximum amount of child maintenance payable. Under the formula, a non-resident parent might be assessed as liable to pay less or more than the maintenance requirement.

The main significance of this step is that a non-resident parent pays 50 per cent of his assessable income (see Chapter 12) in child maintenance until the maintenance requirement figure has been met. At this point he pays a lower percentage of any remaining assessable income.

For full details of the maintenance requirement, see Chapter 10.

Step 2: exempt income

Exempt income represents the minimum day-to-day living expenses of the parent and covers the housing costs of the family with whom s/he lives. However, it only includes amounts for living expenses of any of the parent's *own* children who are living with her/him, *not* the living expenses of a new partner or stepchildren. An allowance in recognition of property/capital settlements pre-dating April 1993 may also be included in exempt income.

Each parent is allowed to keep income equal to the exempt income before being expected to pay any child maintenance.

For full details of exempt income, see Chapter 11.

Step 3: assessable income

Assessable income is income which is available to pay child maintenance. It is the amount of the parent's income which remains after exempt income has been taken into account. If a non-resident parent has no assessable income, he may still have to pay the minimum payment.

For full details of assessable income, see Chapter 12.

Step 4: proposed maintenance

Proposed maintenance is the amount of child maintenance the non-resident parent is expected to pay as long as it does not bring his income below the protected income level (see Step 5).

A non-resident parent pays 50 per cent of his assessable income in child maintenance until he has met the maintenance requirement figure of Step 1. Once the maintenance requirement is met, he pays 15, 20 or 25 per cent of any further assessable income, depending on the number of children for whom he is being assessed to pay maintenance.

The assessable income of the parent with care can reduce the proposed maintenance.

There is an upper limit to the amount of child maintenance payable under the formula, but it may be possible for the parties to go to court to seek additional child maintenance (see p32).

For full details of proposed maintenance, see Chapter 13.

Step 5: protected income

The protected income step ensures that a non-resident parent's disposable income does not fall below a certain level as a result of paying the proposed maintenance. At this stage the whole family's expenses and income are taken into account, including those relating to a new partner and stepchildren.

In addition, a non-resident parent is not expected to pay more than 30 per cent of his own net income.

For full details of protected income, see Chapter 14.

3. **Minimum child maintenance**

There is a standard minimum of child maintenance that a non-resident parent must pay if the formula results in an amount less than this minimum.[5]

The amount of the minimum payment is currently £6. This is calculated by rounding 5 per cent of the income support (IS) personal allowance for someone aged 25 or over (£59.15) up to the next 5 pence and doubling it.[6]

The minimum payment must be made unless the non-resident parent falls into a category which is specifically excluded (see below). This means that a non-resident parent who has been assessed under the formula as liable to pay less than £6 will have to pay child maintenance of £6 a week unless he falls into one of the exempt categories, when he would pay nothing.

Only one minimum payment is due if the non-resident parent has qualifying children being looked after by more than one parent or person with care.[7] For example, if a non-resident parent has children with two or more women with whom he does not live, or if the qualifying children are being cared for by different people in different households, the minimum payment is divided between the persons with care in proportion to the relative maintenance requirements (see Chapter 10).

Exempt non-resident parents

A few non-resident parents do not have to pay any child maintenance at all. If a non-resident parent has been assessed under the formula as having to pay £6 or less, he is exempt from paying any child maintenance if he:[8]

- has the family premium (see Appendix 2) included in the calculation or estimation of his protected income level – ie, a child is a member of his family for at least two days a week;
- is a prisoner;
- receives (or would receive if he satisfied the national insurance contribution conditions or did not receive an overlapping benefit) one of the following:
  - incapacity benefit or statutory sick pay;
  - maternity allowance or statutory maternity pay;
  - severe disablement allowance;
  - disability living allowance or attendance allowance;
  - an industrial disablement benefit;
  - a war disablement benefit or payment from the Armed Forces Compensation Scheme;
  - carer's allowance; *or*
  - payments from the Independent Living Funds;
- is under 16 years old, or under 19 and in full-time non-advanced education (ie, a child for child support purposes – see p18);

- has a net income of less than £6 (for details of what is net income, see Chapter 12). Trainees on approved training (eg, Entry to Employment or Skillseekers in Scotland) whose income consists solely of a training allowance/education maintenance allowance,[9] or students whose only income is a grant or student loan,[10] have these payments ignored when calculating net income for child support purposes. This means that they are usually exempt from paying child maintenance.

4. Non-resident parents on certain benefits

If the non-resident parent is in receipt of income support (IS), pension credit (PC) or income-based jobseeker's allowance (JSA), the formula is not used. Instead, the Secretary of State can make a deduction from the IS/PC/income-based JSA of a non-resident parent as a contribution towards child maintenance.[11] The deduction can be made from a partner's IS/PC/income-based JSA if the partner of a non-resident parent is claiming for the couple.[12]

Who cannot have the deduction made

Deductions cannot be made if the non-resident parent is exempt. In these cases a non-resident parent will pay nothing. A non-resident parent will be exempt if he:[13]

- is aged under 18; *or*
- qualifies for the family premium (see Appendix 2) and/or has day-to-day care (see p21) of any child; *or*
- receives any of the following benefits (or would receive one except for the national insurance contribution requirements or overlapping benefit rules):
  - statutory sick pay;
  - incapacity benefit;
  - severe disablement allowance;
  - attendance allowance or disability living allowance;
  - carer's allowance;
  - maternity allowance;
  - statutory maternity pay;
  - an industrial disablement benefit;
  - a war disablement benefit or payment from the Armed Forces Compensation Scheme; *or*
  - payments from the Independent Living Funds.

Amount of the deduction

A non-resident parent on IS/PC/income-based JSA who is not exempt may have an amount equal to the minimum payment (see p199) deducted from his benefit by the Department for Work and Pensions (DWP), irrespective of the age of the non-resident parent.[14] This is currently £6 a week. No more than one deduction of £6 can be made from an IS/PC/income-based JSA claim at any one time.[15] In some cases, half of this amount may be deducted. Whether the deduction is actually made by the DWP, and how much is deducted, depends on the number of other deductions of higher priority being made from benefit. For more information about how deductions are made, see p65.

Only one deduction for child support can be made, even if there is more than one person with care looking after the non-resident parent's qualifying children. In this case, the minimum payment is apportioned between the persons with care in the same ratio as their respective maintenance requirements.[16]

What the deduction is for

Technically deductions from benefit are not a payment of child support maintenance, but payments in lieu of child maintenance.[17] It is not the result of a maintenance assessment and the rules that apply to assessments do not apply to these contributions. In particular, liability for the contributions will not be backdated to the effective date and arrears will not accrue if the DWP is unable to make the full deduction because there are other deductions with higher priority.

No more than one deduction of £6 can be made from an IS/PC/income-based JSA claim at any one time,[18] and because deductions can only be made where there is a non-resident parent with current liability, no amount for child maintenance arrears can ever be deducted from these benefits. Arrears of child maintenance could still be collected by other methods (see Chapter 20), but usually the arrears will just be held in abeyance until the non-resident parent comes off IS/PC/income-based JSA. However, remember that if a non-resident parent is in receipt of contribution-based JSA, an amount can be deducted from this benefit towards arrears (see p438).

Challenging decisions

CSA decisions about the liability of non-resident parents on certain benefits can be challenged in the same way as other CSA decisions[19] – ie, by seeking a revision[20] or supersession[21] (see Chapter 18) or by appealing to a tribunal[22] (see Chapter 19). If the DWP's decision is being contested (ie, whether the non-resident parent can have £6 or some other amount deducted from his IS/PC/income-based JSA given other higher priority deductions) this can be challenged in a similar way (see CPAG's *Welfare Benefits and Tax Credits Handbook* for more details).

5. Special cases

The legislation uses the phrase 'special cases' to cover situations that are not as straightforward as where one non-resident parent has left one family and there is one person with care looking after all the children from that family.[23] However, in order to enable people to carry out calculations for all family situations, we have integrated these situations into the relevant steps of the formula – eg, where:

- both parents are non-resident (see pp206 and 269);
- more than one person with care applies for child maintenance from the same non-resident parent (see p271);
- a person cares for children of more than one non-resident parent (see pp207 and 276).

Where care of a child is being shared between different people, several modifications of the formula are necessary. Shared care under the 'old rules' is, therefore, treated separately (see Chapter 15).

Shared care is different to the situation where different children of the same family have different homes. Where the children of a family are divided between two households (eg, where one child lives with one parent and another child with the other parent), this involves two maintenance assessments. In one assessment, the first parent is the parent with care and the second parent is the non-resident parent. In the second assessment the roles are reversed. We have called this situation 'divided families' (see p275); the Child Support Agency may refer to this as 'split care'.

Notes

1. Introduction
 1 Reg 33(1) CS(MAP) Regs; reg 2(1) CS(MASC) Regs
 2 Reg 2(2) CS(MASC) Regs
 3 Regs 3(2), 9(5) and 11(5) CS(MASC) Regs
 4 Reg 2(3) CS(MASC) Regs; CCS/7312/1995

3. Minimum child maintenance
 5 Sch 1 para 7 CSA 1991
 6 Reg 13 CS(MASC) Regs
 7 Reg 22(4) CS(MASC) Regs
 8 Reg 26 and Sch 4 CS(MASC) Regs
 9 Sch 2, paras 21 and 36 CS(MASC) Regs
 10 Reg 7(3) CS(MASC) Regs

4. Non-resident parents on certain benefits
 11 s43 and Sch 1 para 5(4) CSA 1991
 12 Sch 9 para 7A(1) SS(C&P) Regs
 13 Reg 28 CS(MASC) Regs
 14 Reg 28(2) CS(MASC) Regs; Sch 9 para 7A(3) SS(C&P) Regs
 15 Reg 28(3) and (4) CS(MASC) Regs
 16 Sch 9 para 7A(2) SS(C&P) Regs
 17 s43(2)(a) CSA 1991
 18 Sch 9 para 7A(2) SS(C&P) Regs
 19 s43(3) CSA 1991
 20 Sch 4C para 1(a) CSA 1991
 21 Sch 4C para 2(1)(a) CSA 1991
 22 Sch 4C para 3(1)(a) CSA 1991

5. Special cases
 23 Part III CS(MASC) Regs

Chapter 10

The maintenance requirement ('old rules')

This chapter covers:
1. What is the maintenance requirement (below)
2. How much is the maintenance requirement (p204)
3. Both parents are non-resident (p206)
4. More than one non-resident parent (p207)

---

1. **What is the maintenance requirement**

The maintenance requirement is intended to represent the minimum weekly cost of caring for the child(ren) for whom child maintenance is being assessed.[1] The maintenance requirement is based on income support (IS) rates. For information on the conditions of entitlement to the IS premiums, see Appendix 2. Note that some of these premiums may no longer be paid with IS (for example, because parents get child tax credit instead), but are still used in the child support formula.

Both parents' incomes affect the maintenance requirement. In the case of the parent with care, a notional contribution towards the maintenance requirement is calculated, which may reduce the amount of child maintenance a non-resident parent has to pay.

The parents may not have sufficient income to be able to pay the full maintenance requirement. If this is the case, the non-resident parent pays 50 per cent of his available income, known as 'assessable income'. Equally, the maintenance requirement is not the total amount of child maintenance that may be expected from a non-resident parent. However, once the maintenance requirement is met, the non-resident parent then pays a lower percentage of any further income (see Chapters 12 and 13).

The maintenance requirement is also used where child maintenance has to be apportioned between two persons with care. This occurs where a parent is a non-resident parent for two different maintenance assessments (see p275).

Interim maintenance assessments

When the Child Support Agency does not have sufficient information from the non-resident parent to carry out an assessment, it can make an interim maintenance assessment. Where the non-resident parent is withholding information other than information about his partner or another member of the family's income, the interim maintenance assessment is set at 1.5 times the maintenance requirement (see p367).[2]

---

2. How much is the maintenance requirement

The maintenance requirement includes an allowance for each qualifying child (see p18) being looked after by that person with care. The person who is being assessed to pay child maintenance *must* be the parent (see p15) of that qualifying child. If a person with care is looking after children of different non-resident parents, a different maintenance requirement is calculated for each of the assessments (see p207).

The maintenance requirement calculation

The maintenance requirement is calculated as follows:[3]
- for each qualifying child, the amount of the income support (IS) personal allowance for a child (£47.45); *plus*
- the amount of the IS family premium (£16.43); *plus*
- a 'parent as carer' element (see also p205):
  - where at least one qualifying child is under 11 years of age, the amount of the adult IS personal allowance at the rate for a person aged 25 years or over, irrespective of the age of the person with care (£59.15); *or*
  - where none of the qualifying children are under 11 but at least one is under 14 years of age, 75 per cent of this adult allowance (£44.36); *or*
  - where none of the children are under 14 but at least one is under 16 years of age, 50 per cent of the adult allowance (£29.58); *less*
- an amount of child benefit for the qualifying child(ren) (see below).

This is the basic maintenance requirement calculation, which is adapted in situations where more than one non-resident parent is involved (see p207).

The rates used in the calculation are the IS and child benefit rates applicable at the date on which the maintenance assessment takes effect, known as the 'effective date' (see p368).[4] The figures given above are those for 2007/08.

Deduction of child benefit

The amount of child benefit deducted is:[5]
- £18.10 for the only, elder or eldest child for whom child benefit is payable; *and*

- £12.10 for all other children.

The amount of child benefit deducted from the maintenance requirement may be different from that actually paid to the person with care, perhaps because she has not claimed it or because someone else (eg, the non-resident parent) is receiving it. In such cases, the person with care should consider claiming child benefit or asking the non-resident parent to make the payment of child benefit in addition to the maintenance payment (see the example on p209). Where more than one eligible person claims child benefit, the person with whom the child lives has priority. See CPAG's *Welfare Benefits and Tax Credits Handbook* for more details.

If child benefit is not payable for a child because s/he is in the care of an institution, an amount of child benefit is still deducted.[6] However, in other situations where no one is entitled to child benefit for that child (eg, because of the rules about residence in the UK) no deduction is made. For more information about child benefit, who is entitled and when it is payable, see CPAG's *Welfare Benefits and Tax Credits Handbook*.

The parent as carer element

When the 'old rules' assessment was designed, the inclusion of the adult personal allowance was intended to represent the care costs of the child. The reduction of the allowance for children over 11 years of age is based on an assumption that care needs reduce as children grow up. This means that the maintenance requirement as a whole can reduce immediately after a child's birthday.

The parent as carer element is not maintenance for a former spouse or civil partner.[7] Spousal or civil partner maintenance is completely separate from child maintenance calculated by the Child Support Agency. Any application for maintenance for the parent with care must be made to the courts (see p28).

Couples

The personal allowance for couples is never included in the maintenance requirement. This is because the non-resident parent is not responsible for maintaining a partner of the person with care.

Children with disabilities

The disabled child premium is not included in the calculation of the maintenance requirement and neither is any related carer premium. A court may be able to consider a top-up maintenance award for a child who is disabled (see p32).[8]

The maintenance requirement calculation where there is one non-resident parent and one parent with care

The most common situation in which the maintenance requirement needs to be calculated is where there is one parent with care and one non-resident parent.

Example: maintenance requirement where there is one non-resident parent and one parent with care

Anita and Bob have two children. They split up, and Anita remains in the family home with Carol (13) and David (8).

		£
Personal allowances	Anita	59.15
	Carol	47.45
	David	47.45
Family premium		16.43
Sub-total		170.48
Less child benefit		30.20
Maintenance requirement		**140.28**

Five years later, Anita remarries. David is 13; Carol is 18 and still at school.

		£	
Personal allowances	Anita	44.36	(75% x 59.15)
	Carol	47.45	
	David	47.45	
Family premium		16.43	
Sub-total		155.69	
Less child benefit		30.20	
Maintenance requirement		**125.49**	

3. **Both parents are non-resident**

An application for maintenance can be made by a person with care who is not a parent – eg, if a child lives with her/his grandparents or another relative (see p38). Both parents of that child are then non-resident parents and liable to pay maintenance. An assessment can be carried out for each non-resident parent if an application is made in respect of her/him, and each contributes to the maintenance requirement (see p269 for the calculation of the proposed maintenance).

An application may be made for maintenance from only one of the non-resident parents. In this case the maintenance requirement for the one non-resident parent is halved.[9] However, it is not halved when an application is made for maintenance from both non-resident parents even if an assessment cannot be made for both – eg, one parent cannot be traced or is habitually resident outside the UK.

> **Example: maintenance requirement where both parents are non-resident**
> Beverley (15) lives with her grandmother, who is a widow.
>
> | | | £ | |
> |---|---|---|---|
> | Personal allowances | Grandmother | 29.58 | (50% x 59.15) |
> | | Beverley | 47.45 | |
> | Family premium | | 16.43 | |
> | Sub-total | | 93.46 | |
> | *Less* child benefit | | 18.10 | |
> | **Maintenance requirement** | | 75.36 | |
>
> This maintenance requirement will be halved to £37.68 if the grandmother applies for child maintenance only from her son-in-law and not her daughter.

4. **More than one non-resident parent**

A person with care may look after qualifying children who have different parents – eg, a mother is looking after her children who have different fathers, a grandmother is looking after children of two of her sons, or a lone parent is also looking after a friend's child. In these cases, if applications are made for child maintenance from each non-resident parent, a number of different assessments must be carried out, one for each non-resident parent.

The maintenance requirement for each non-resident parent includes only the child(ren) who are his own responsibility. However, the adult personal allowance and the family premium are divided among the non-resident parents[10] in proportion to the number of non-resident parents and not in proportion to the number of the children who are their responsibility.[11] This apportionment should occur whether or not child maintenance is being pursued from all the non-resident parents.[12] For example, a person with care may apply for child maintenance from one father and not another, or one of the parents may be resident abroad and hence outside the Child Support Agency's jurisdiction. However, a deceased parent is not treated as a non-resident parent and does not lead to any reduction in the maintenance requirement for living non-resident parents.[13]

The apportioned 'parent as carer' element is then further reduced if the children in the individual assessment are aged 11 or over – ie, 75 per cent of the apportioned amount is used if the youngest child is aged 11–13 and 50 per cent of the apportioned amount if s/he is 14 or 15 years old.[14]

· ·

Example: maintenance requirement where the children have different fathers

Zoe is a single parent and has three children, all of whom live with her. Wayne is the father of Yvonne (12) and Veronica (10). Terence is the father of Scott (3).

Wayne's assessment:

		£	
Personal allowances	Zoe	29.58	(50% x 59.15)
	Yvonne	47.45	
	Veronica	47.45	
Family premium		8.22	(50% x 16.43)
Sub-total		132.70	
Less child benefit		30.20	
Maintenance requirement		**102.50**	

Terence's assessment:

		£	
Personal allowances	Zoe	29.58	(50% x 59.15)
	Scott	47.45	
Family premium		8.22	(50% x 16.43)
Sub-total		85.25	
Less child benefit		12.10	
Maintenance requirement		**73.15**	

Two years later, Zoe is living with Bob and her four children. Wayne is the father of Yvonne (14) and Veronica (12). Terence is the father of Scott (5). Bob is the father of Ricky (1). However, as Bob is not a non-resident parent, the apportionment occurs between Wayne and Terence only. Terence's assessment remains as above.

Wayne's assessment:

		£	
Personal allowances	Zoe	22.19	(75% of 50% x 59.15)
	Yvonne	47.45	
	Veronica	47.45	
Family premium		8.22	(50% x 16.43)
Sub-total		125.31	
Less child benefit		30.20	
Maintenance requirement		**95.11**	

· ·

If a person with care is looking after children of different parents, but two of the non-resident parents are parents of the same child (ie, the person with care is *not* a parent of that child), those two non-resident parents will be treated as one person for the purposes of apportioning the relevant elements of the maintenance requirement.[15]

Example: maintenance requirement where there is more than one non-resident parent and both parents of one child are non-resident

Zoe's niece, Rebecca, who is aged 17 and still at school, comes to live with Zoe and Bob when her parents split up. Rebecca joining the household alters the maintenance requirement for the other children. For the four qualifying children Zoe is now looking after, there are four non-resident parents (Wayne, Terence, and both of Rebecca's parents). However, Rebecca's parents count as one unit for this purpose and therefore the amounts are divided by three.

Wayne's assessment:

		£	
Personal allowances	Zoe	14.79	(75% x one-third of 59.15)
	Yvonne	47.45	
	Veronica	47.45	
Family premium		5.48	(one-third of 16.43)
Sub-total		115.17	
Less child benefit		24.20	
Maintenance requirement		**90.97**	

Terence's assessment:

		£	
Personal allowances	Zoe	19.72	(one-third of 59.15)
	Scott (5)	47.45	
Family premium		5.48	(one-third of 16.43)
Sub-total		72.65	
Less child benefit		12.10	
Maintenance requirement		**60.55**	

Rebecca's parents' assessment:

	£	
Personal allowance for Rebecca	47.45	
Family premium	5.48	(one-third of 16.43)
Sub-total	52.93	
Less child benefit	18.10	
Maintenance requirement	**34.83**	

An assessment is carried out separately for both of Rebecca's parents, each using the maintenance requirement of £34.83. If Zoe chose to apply for child maintenance only from one of Rebecca's parents, the maintenance requirement would be halved to £17.42.
Note: Bob is unemployed and claiming jobseeker's allowance. Although Zoe is required to apply for maintenance for Scott, Yvonne and Veronica under the 'old rules' (see Chapter 4), she can choose whether or not to make an application for maintenance from Rebecca's parents. However, even if she chooses not to make an application for child maintenance for Rebecca, the apportionment should still take place for the other two assessments.
Note: if she chose to apply for child maintenance for Rebecca on or after 3 March 2003, this would prompt conversion of the other assessments and all her child maintenance would be dealt with under the 'new rules' (see Chapter 8).

We have assumed that Zoe has claimed child benefit for Rebecca, which means that under the child benefit regulations the higher rate applies to Rebecca and the lower rate now applies to Yvonne. As the person with whom Rebecca is living, Zoe takes priority over the mother for child benefit purposes (see p300).[16]

If Rebecca's mother had continued to claim child benefit, the higher rate would be payable for Rebecca as the only child for whom her mother is claiming. At the same time, the higher rate would still be payable for Yvonne as she is the eldest child for whom Zoe is claiming child benefit.[17] If this were the case, the child benefit of £18.10 would be deducted for both children in the calculation, even though Zoe would not actually be receiving child benefit for Rebecca.

In this scenario, if Rebecca's mother did not give £18.10 each week to Zoe, whether as child maintenance or on top of the maintenance assessment, she would no longer be entitled to child benefit.[18] In this case, the maintenance requirements would be as shown above, as child benefit would not legally be payable to Rebecca's mother, even though in practice it may still be being paid. It would be to Zoe's advantage to claim the child benefit for Rebecca in this situation.

Notes

1. **What is the maintenance requirement**
   1 Sch 1 para 1(1) CSA 1991
   2 Regs 8(3)(a) and 8A(1) CS(MAP) Regs

2. **How much is the maintenance requirement**
   3 Sch 1 para 1 CSA 1991; reg 3 CS(MASC) Regs
   4 Regs 3(2) and 4 CS(MASC) Regs
   5 Reg 4 CS(MASC) Regs
   6 Sch 1 para 1(2) CSA 1991
   7 CCS/11729/1996
   8 s8(8) and (9) CSA 1991

3. **Both parents are non-resident**
   9 Reg 19(2)(d) CS(MASC) Regs

4. **More than one non-resident parent**
   10 Reg 23 CS(MASC) Regs
   11 Reg 23(3) CS(MASC) Regs
   12 Reg 23(1) CS(MASC) Regs

13 CCS/7436/1999
14 Reg 23(2A) CS(MASC) Regs
15 Reg 23(3) CS(MASC) Regs
16 Sch 10 para 2 SSCBA 1992
17 Reg 2 CB&SS(FAR) Regs
18 s143(1)(b) SSCBA 1992

Chapter 11

Exempt income ('old rules')

This chapter covers:
1. What is exempt income (below)
2. How much is exempt income (p212)
3. Housing costs (p214)
4. Pre-April 1993 property settlements (p222)
5. Travel-to-work costs (p226)
6. Second families (p228)

1. What is exempt income

Exempt income is income a parent can keep for her/his own essential expenses before any child maintenance is expected. The expenses are based on income support (IS) rates but also include housing costs.

When the 'old rules' assessment was designed, exempt income was intended to represent the minimum day-to-day living expenses of parents and their *own* children who are living with them. If the parent has a partner, the partner's personal expenses are *not* included in exempt income. However, the housing costs for the whole family, including any partner and stepchildren, are covered in exempt income.

'**Own child**' means a child for whom the parent is, in law, a parent – ie, the biological or adoptive parent (see p15). Exempt income does *not* include amounts for any other children in the family – eg, stepchildren. Allowances for other children are not even initially included if the child is the primary responsibility of the parent – eg, where the stepchild's other parent is dead or cannot afford to pay any child maintenance. In some cases departure from the 'old rules' assessment can be sought on these grounds (see p319).

Exempt income applies to *both* the non-resident parent and the parent with care as both are liable to maintain their children. If the parent with care has any income available to maintain the children, this might reduce the non-resident parent's contribution (see Chapter 13). However, if the parent with care is on IS, pension credit (PC), income-based jobseeker's allowance (JSA) or working tax credit (WTC), it is assumed that she has no income available for child maintenance[1] and the exempt income step is carried out for the non-resident parent only. This applies both where the parent with care is the benefit claimant and where her partner is making the claim. If the non-resident parent is on IS/PC/income-based JSA, there is no need to calculate exempt income for either parent, as the formula is not used at all in this case. Instead, the non-resident parent may have deductions made from his IS/PC/income-based JSA as a contribution towards child maintenance (see p200). If the non-resident parent is on WTC, the child support calculation is still carried out unless there is also an assessment being considered or in force for a child for whom he is the parent with care (see p20).[2] If he is a parent with care in this position, he is not liable to pay any child maintenance as a non-resident parent. This does not apply if a 'new rules' calculation is being considered. If a 'new rules' calculation is carried out, the assessment as a non-resident parent will be converted and carried out as a 'new rules' calculation too. In this case, WTC is counted as income. See also Chapter 8.

If the person with care is not a parent, the exempt income step does *not* apply to her/him, as only parents have a liability to maintain their children. In this case there will usually be two non-resident parents and a maintenance assessment (including the exempt income step) is carried out for both.

2. **How much is exempt income**

Exempt income is generally calculated in the same way for parents with care as for non-resident parents.[3] Any reference to 'parent' below applies equally to the parent with care and the non-resident parent.

The rates used in the calculation are the income support (IS) rates applicable on the date at which the maintenance assessment takes effect, known as the 'effective date' (see p368).[4] The rates given below are for 2007/08.

For the qualifying conditions of the IS premiums, see Appendix 2.

The exempt income calculation

Exempt income is calculated as follows for each parent:[5]
- the amount of the IS personal allowance for a single person aged 25 or over, irrespective of the age of the parent (£59.15); *plus*
- if there is a child – ie, the parent's own child (see above) living with the parent, the amount of the IS personal allowance for such child (£47.45);**†*plus*
- if an allowance for a child is included, the amount of the IS family premium (£16.43)**†; *plus*
- if any of the children included would qualify for the IS disabled child premium, the amount of that premium for each child entitled (£46.69);**†*plus*
- if any of the children included would qualify for the IS enhanced disability premium, the amount of that premium for each child entitled (£18.76);**†*plus*

- if the parent would qualify for the IS disability premium if s/he is under 60 years old, the amount of the premium for a single person (£25.25); the disability conditions must be satisfied by the parent her/himself; *plus*
- if the parent would qualify for the IS carer premium, the amount of that premium (£27.15); *plus*
- if the parent would qualify for the IS severe disability premium, the amount of that premium (£48.45); *plus*
- if the parent would qualify for the IS enhanced disability premium, the amount of that premium (£12.30); *plus*
- housing costs (see p214); *plus*
- where applicable, an allowance for a pre-April 1993 property settlement (see p222); *plus*
- if an employee travels more than 240 kilometres a week to and from work, an amount towards travel costs (see p226).

* If the child's other parent also lives in the family and has sufficient income to help support the child, these amounts may be halved (see p228).

† These amounts will be included at a proportionate rate if the parent looks after the child(ren) for less than seven days, but at least two nights on average per week (see Chapter 15). For parents with care, this apportionment only takes place if another person also has day-to-day care of the child.[6] Special expenses can be added to exempt income after a departure direction.

Example

Bob and Anita have split up. Anita is looking after Carol and David, and remains in the family home. There is no need to calculate Anita's exempt income as she is in receipt of IS. Bob is living on his own in a bedsit, paying rent of £48 a week. He is not entitled to any housing benefit. He does not qualify for any premiums. He travels less than 240 kilometres a week to work.

Bob's exempt income is therefore:	£
Personal allowance	59.15
Housing costs	48.00
Total exempt income	**107.15**

If Bob had moved in with his parents, his exempt income would be £59.15. If Bob was in receipt of long-term incapacity benefit and living with his parents, his exempt income would then be:

	£
Personal allowance	59.15
Disability premium	25.25
Total exempt income	**84.40**

3. **Housing costs**

Housing costs for the parent and any of her/his family (see p26) living with her/him are included in exempt income. If the other party believes that the parent's partner can afford to contribute to the housing costs, s/he may be able to apply for a departure direction (see p327).

To be included in exempt income, housing costs must be eligible (see p215) and payable in respect of the parent's home (see p217). Housing costs which are excessive may not be included in full (see p220).

Responsibility for housing costs

Eligible housing costs for the parent's home are included if the parent or partner is responsible for the costs and the payment is made to a person who is not a member of the same household.[7] Therefore, if a parent lives with a new partner, the housing costs are accepted, even if they are the partner's responsibility. The amount of the housing costs included in exempt income can be reduced if it is reasonable to expect the partner to contribute.[8] Otherwise the full eligible costs are covered, and not the amount paid by the parent towards the housing costs.[9]

As well as where s/he is actually liable for the costs, a parent will be treated as responsible for housing costs if:[10]

- s/he has to meet the costs in order to live in the home; *and*
- the person liable to make the payments is not doing so; *and*
- either the parent is the former partner of the liable person or is someone else whom it is reasonable to treat as liable.

If costs are shared with another person who is not a partner, only the parent's actual share of the costs is used (unless the parent is treated as liable because the other person(s) is not paying her/his share).[11] This means that where the non-resident parent continues to pay his liability of the housing costs on the former joint home in which the parent with care remains, this amount cannot be included as the parent with care's housing costs.[12] If the non-resident parent stops paying his liability, the full amount is treated as the parent with care's housing costs.[13] If three friends are joint tenants and share the rent equally, one-third of the rent is considered to be the responsibility of the parent, unless the Child Support Agency (CSA) believes that such a division would not be reasonable – eg, one of the joint occupiers is not paying her/his share (in which case the amount the parent actually pays may be used), or they have unequal shares of the accommodation.[14] However, a parent will not be treated as responsible for housing costs which a member of their family (see p26) is not paying.[15]

Before 1 December 2005, same-sex couples were not treated as partners, and so if a same-sex partner of a parent was paying or contributing to housing costs, these costs would not automatically be treated as the parent's. Eligible housing costs from 1 December 2005 should include payments made by a same-sex partner of a parent, but exempt income for periods before that date will not include such costs, unless another rule applies allowing them to be treated as the parents's costs (see below). Although a parent argued against this, it was decided that the resulting higher child support liability was not unlawful discrimination.[16]

The parent may be treated as responsible for housing costs that s/he shares with other members of the household, even if s/he makes those payments via another member of the household and not directly.[17] This applies if:

- it is reasonable for a parent to be treated as responsible for a share of the costs; *and*
- the person with responsibility is not a close relative of the parent or her/his partner (see p22); *and*
- the person with responsibility either has an equivalent responsibility for housing costs as the parent or that person is meeting the costs because the liable person is not.

However, if a parent is a non-dependent member of a household (see p284), no housing costs are included in exempt income, even if s/he is paying a contribution for housing costs to another member of the household.[18] In order for a parent to be a non-dependant, not only can there be no commercial arrangement, but s/he has to be a member of the same *household* as the person liable to make the payments (see p22).

Where a parent is living with her/his parents as a non-dependant s/he is, therefore, clearly not entitled to have her/his contribution to the housing costs included in exempt income.[19] However, where costs are shared with other people who are not close relatives and the parent is not a non-dependant, even if the parent is contributing to housing costs on a voluntary basis it might, depending on the circumstances of the case, be arguable that it is reasonable to treat the parent as responsible for a share of the costs. This is most likely to succeed in cases where the costs have previously been shared with someone else and the parent has taken over that person's share. If the parent becomes a co-owner or joint tenant, half of the housing costs will definitely be treated as the parent's responsibility. If the parent became a sub-tenant, s/he would be responsible for the costs specified in the tenancy agreement.

Eligible housing costs

Eligible housing costs are costs which have to be incurred in order to buy, rent or otherwise secure possession of the parent's home or to carry out repairs and improvements as defined below.[20] Eligible costs are:[21]

- rent (after deduction of any housing benefit (HB)[22] – see p217);
- mortgage interest payments;
- capital repayments under a mortgage;

- premiums paid under an endowment or other insurance policy, or a personal pension plan to the extent that the policy was taken out to cover the cost of the mortgage (see p217);
- interest payments on any loans for repairs and improvements to the home taken out before the maintenance application or enquiry form is sent to the parent;
- interest payments on loans for major repairs necessary to maintain the fabric of the home and for measures which improve its fitness for occupation, such as the installation of a bath, shower, wash basin or lavatory; the provision of heating, electric lighting and sockets, drainage facilities, or storage facilities for fuel and refuse; improvements to ventilation, natural lighting, insulation or structural condition; or any other improvements considered reasonable by the CSA (the previous 'unfitness' which necessitated the improvement needs to be demonstrated[23]);
- interest payments under a hire purchase agreement to buy a home;
- payments in respect of a licence or permission to occupy the home;
- payments in respect of, or as a result of, the occupation of the home. (This is intended to cover payments made by a former licensee who occupies premises unlawfully – eg, after a notice to quit has expired.[24] It does not include property and contents insurance,[25] payments in respect of the purchase of a home[26] or council tax[27]);
- payments of ground rent or feu duty;
- payments under co-ownership schemes;
- payments of service charges if such payments are a condition for occupying the home (but see p219);
- mooring charges for a houseboat;
- site rent for a caravan or mobile home;
- payments for a tent and its site;
- payments under a rental purchase scheme;
- payments in respect of croft land;
- payments in respect of a home made to an employer who provides the home;
- payments for a Crown tenancy or licence;
- payments in respect of a loan taken out to pay off (in full or in part[28]) another loan that covered eligible housing costs;
- the fees (after deduction of any HB) if a parent or a partner lives in a care home or an independent hospital, or is being provided with a care home service or independent health care service.[29]

Repayments of an advance of salary (see also p235) used to purchase a home cannot be housing costs.[30]

Home

For the purposes of housing costs, the parent's home is either the dwelling in which the parent normally lives or, if s/he normally lives in more than one home, her/his principal home.[31] Therefore, if a non-resident parent is paying the costs of the family home in which the parent with care remains with the child(ren), these costs cannot be included in the non-resident parent's exempt income as this is not the non-resident parent's own home.[32] Before deciding which dwelling is the principal home, the facts must show that the parent does actually live in more than one home.[33]

The test of a principal home is not simply the parent's own view nor a calculation of the time spent at each home.[34] An army officer's own home where he spends his leave could be his principal home over and above army married quarters. Expenditure on army accommodation in addition to the principal home could not in this situation also be taken into account as expenses (see p236), but army officers serving abroad may be able to have the costs of both a home in the UK and quarters overseas included in exempt income.[35]

The only other exception to the rule about only including one set of housing costs is where the parent is in a care home. The residential fees can be included as well as the costs of the parent's own home if the parent has been in the residential accommodation for less than a year or if the CSA believes that the parent intends to return home.[36]

If the payments for the property cover accommodation used for other purposes (eg, business use) the CSA has to identify the proportion of the cost attributable to housing.[37]

Housing benefit

HB is subtracted from housing costs if the parent has claimed and been awarded it.[38] In this situation, the CSA will use as housing costs the weekly amount treated as eligible rent for the purposes of HB minus the amount of HB calculated by the local authority. (Because of rent restriction rules in HB, eligible rent may be less than the non-resident parent's actual rent, even allowing for the deduction of ineligible charges. For more information, see CPAG's *Welfare Benefits and Tax Credits Handbook*.)[39]

If a parent delays claiming HB until after completing the maintenance enquiry or application form, full housing costs will be included as exempt income (unless they are excessive – see p220). If a parent is awaiting a decision on an HB claim, the excessive housing costs rule does not apply, but the CSA may later seek further information about the claim.

Mortgage and other loan payments

Unlike for income support (IS), most payments connected to mortgage repayment – whether directly as capital repayments or through certain policies – are eligible housing costs for exempt income purposes.[40] However, such payments are not eligible at the protected income stage (see p284).

As well as endowment policies, other insurance policies taken out to pay off a mortgage on the home are considered to be eligible housing costs. These include premiums paid into a mortgage protection policy to cover the mortgage in the event of unemployment, sickness or disability.[41] Life assurance policies taken out with the mortgage in order to discharge the debt on death are also included.[42] However, neither building nor contents insurance is included.[43] The mortgage which any such policy is intended to discharge need not exist at the time of the assessment.[44]

Only loans for the provision of a home are eligible. A loan used to buy out a former partner's interest in a property will only be eligible if it can be shown that the loan is necessary to protect the right of occupancy.[45]

If a loan is partly for the provision of a home (see p217), only that part is an eligible housing cost.[46] If only part of the mortgage is eligible, the nature of any insurance policies should be investigated. It should not be assumed that the proportions of the premiums allowed should follow the proportion of the mortgage interest allowed.[47]

Personal pension plans taken out, at least in part, to discharge a mortgage on the parent's home are eligible housing costs.[48] If a personal pension plan has been obtained both to discharge the mortgage and to pay a pension, 25 per cent of the contributions made are included as housing costs in exempt income.[49]

If the mortgage is under £60,000, all the premiums paid to an endowment policy are eligible housing costs.[50] If the policy was also taken out to produce a lump sum and the mortgage is over £60,000, 0.0277 per cent of the mortgage is taken to be weekly housing costs, unless the CSA can ascertain what proportion of the premium is actually paid to cover the mortgage. If the parent's endowment premium is larger than this 0.0277 per cent figure, it is worth pursuing the issue of how much capital is likely to be produced, especially as many endowment policies may not produce any capital in excess of the mortgage. Any payments made in excess of those required by the mortgage agreement are not eligible housing costs.[51]

There is nothing to prevent repayments to a member of the family or friend on a loan to purchase a home being considered as housing costs, as long as a mortgage or charge has been created by depositing the title deeds or a land certificate which prevents the borrower disposing of the property without the lender's consent.[52]

Repayments made under an agreement for a loan taken out for eligible repairs and improvements (see p215) or a service charge to cover these items are included in exempt income as housing costs,[53] as are insurance policies associated with such a loan or which are taken out to pay off another loan for an eligible housing cost.[54]

Ineligible charges

Charges made for food, fuel, water or sewerage services do not count as eligible housing costs.[55] If the housing costs payments include an ineligible charge, an amount attributable to the service must be deducted.

If meals are provided, a standard weekly deduction is made:

2007/08	Aged 16 or over	For each child under 16
Full board	£21.10	£10.65
Half board	£14.05	£7.05
Breakfast only	£2.60	£2.60

If the parent provides information about the level of the fuel charge inclusive in the housing payment, this actual or estimated amount can be deducted. Otherwise standard weekly deductions are made, which for 2007/08 are: heating £15.45; hot water £1.80; cooking £1.80; and lighting £1.25. If the parent has exclusive use of only one room, the deduction for heating, hot water and/or lighting is £9.25 a week.

If the amount for water and sewerage charges is not separately identifiable, an amount will be attributed.

If other service charges are included in the rent payments, the amount deducted is any amount higher than the following, whichever is greater:[56]

- the total of eligible charges included in the rent; or
- 25 per cent of eligible housing costs.

If it is not clear what amount for ineligble service charges is included, the CSA attributes a reasonable amount. Ineligible services include:

- personal laundry service;
- sports and other leisure facilities, including TV rental and licence fees, but excluding children's play areas;
- cleaning, other than communal areas or where no one in the accommodation is able to do it;
- transport;
- medical or nursing services; and
- any other charge not connected with the provision of adequate accommodation.

Weekly amount of housing costs

The amount allowed for housing costs is usually the amount payable at the effective date (see p368), converted into a weekly amount.[57] If the costs are monthly, the amount at the effective date must be multiplied by 12 and divided by 52. Where the housing costs are paid on any basis other than weekly or calendar monthly, the CSA considers the amount and payment period of the housing costs payable on the effective date and:[58]

- divides 365 by the number of days in the payment period, rounding to the nearest whole number;
- multiplies this figure by the amount of the costs due in the payment period; *and then*
- divides this figure by 52 to give the weekly costs.

If rent is payable to a local authority or housing association on a free-week basis, the rent payable in the relevant week (see p235) is used unless that was a free week, in which case the last week which was not a free week is used.

If the housing costs are a repayment mortgage and the parent has failed to provide information on repayments and interest on the effective date but has provided a mortgage statement from the lender for a period ending less than a year before the relevant date, this statement can be used to calculate the capital repayments and, where possible, the interest payments.[59]

The calculation of housing costs should be carefully checked as this is an area where the CSA often makes mistakes.

Excessive housing costs

Excessive housing costs of a non-resident parent are not generally allowed in full. Parents are exempt from restrictions on housing costs if they:[60]

- have day-to-day care of any child;
- have claimed or been awarded HB;
- would qualify for an IS disability premium (see Appendix 2);
- remain in a home previously occupied with a former partner;
- have high housing costs because money which would otherwise be available is tied up in the former family home which is still occupied by an ex-partner;
- have been meeting high housing costs for over 52 weeks before the application for child support, and there has been no increase in those costs other than an increase in the rate of mortgage interest or rent;
- have higher housing costs than the usual restricted amount (see below) only because of an increase in the rate of mortgage interest or rent.

Departure can be sought by the other parent if the exemption applies and the housing costs are unreasonably high (see p326).

Unless exempt, eligible housing costs are otherwise only allowed up to the greater of £80 or half of the parent's net income.[61] (See p234 for the calculation of net income.) Therefore, parents who have a net income of less than £160 are allowed to include housing costs of up to £80, while those with higher net incomes can include housing costs of up to half of the parent's income.

The excessive housing costs rule does not apply to parents with care and it is unlikely that the notional income or capital rules could be used where a parent with care takes on excessive housing costs (see p250).[62]

Example

Bob goes to live with Zoe who has three children, Yvonne (12), Veronica (10) and Scott (3). Zoe's rent on a three-bedroomed council house is £45 a week. They do not receive HB. Even though it is Zoe who is legally liable for the rent, it is still an eligible cost.

Bob's exempt income is now:	£
Personal allowance	59.15
Housing costs	45.00
Total exempt income	**104.15**

Anita is now in paid employment. As long as she is not in receipt of working tax credit, her exempt income must be calculated. She lives with her two children, Carol (13) and David (8). Her mortgage is under £60,000 and the payments, including the capital repayments, are £75 a week.

		£
Personal allowances	Anita	59.15
	Carol	47.45
	David	47.45
Family premium		16.43
Mortgage payment (total)		75.00
Total exempt income		**245.48**

Anita marries Joe and together they buy a house, taking out a mortgage of £85,000. The interest payments are £495 a month and the endowment premium £108 a month – ie, £114.23 and £24.92 a week. However, as the CSA does not have information about how much of the premium is to cover the mortgage, the endowment premium is restricted to £23.55 (0.0277% x £85,000) (see p217).

		£
Personal allowances	Anita	59.15
	Carol	47.45
	David	47.45
Family premium		16.43
Mortgage payment	(£114.23 + £23.55)	137.78
Total exempt income		**308.26**

The excessive housing costs rule does not apply because there are children in the family, but Bob could consider seeking a departure (see p327) on the grounds that Joe can afford to contribute towards the mortgage.

4. Pre-April 1993 property settlements

In order for an allowance to be included in 'old rules' exempt income, the property or capital transfer must satisfy certain qualifying criteria (see below).[63] Departure can be sought where the allowance in exempt income does not properly reflect the effect of the settlement (see p327).

Unlike other elements of exempt income, this allowance applies to a parent with care only if she was the non-resident parent at the time the property was transferred.[64] Where a parent with care transferred capital to the non-resident parent or the child(ren) and the non-resident parent also transferred capital, this 'compensating transfer' may be offset against that of the non-resident parent's 'qualifying transfer'.[65]

Qualifying transfer

A qualifying transfer is one which was made:[66]

- as part of a court order or written maintenance agreement made before 5 April 1993;
- when the non-resident parent and parent with care were living separately;
- between the non-resident parent and either the parent with care or a child for whom maintenance is being assessed;
- with the effect that the recipient was given the whole of the value of the transferred property (this condition can be met where the whole value of a part share in a property or asset is transferred);[67] *and*
- without its only purpose being to replace maintenance payments (either periodic or a lump sum) for the parent with care – ie, for herself as opposed to the child(ren) – and to compensate the parent with care for the loss of any right to apply for or receive such payments, or to compensate her for a reduction in such payments. 'Loss of any right' in this context should be taken to mean 'loss of any one right' rather than 'loss of all rights'.[68] This means that where a maintenance agreement for a low or nominal sum exists, it may still be the case that the only purpose of the transfer was to compensate the parent with care for this reduced maintenance and hence the transfer will not qualify.[69]

Child Support Agency (CSA) guidance gives examples of the types of evidence which might be considered in deciding whether a transfer should be excluded by the final condition listed above (a court order, written maintenance agreement, the transfer document, and/or confirmation from building society, solicitor, accountant or property valuers).[70] All evidence produced by either party should be considered, including any documents which might expressly state that the transfer was only to compensate the parent with care for the loss of some right to spousal maintenance.[71] However, although decision makers may consider other evidence beyond the transfer agreement in order to determine the purpose of the transfer, the purpose must be 'clearly and explicitly' shown by the evidence and not inferred on the balance of probabilities.[72]

Certain transfers made under Scottish law can only be for the purpose of compensating the parent with care and, therefore, cannot be qualifying transfers,[73] but transfers made under a written maintenance agreement rather than a court order may still qualify.[74]

It is possible for the non-resident parent to transfer the whole of the asset to the parent with care, but for the lender to insist that the non-resident parent's name is retained on the mortgage – eg, where the amount of the mortgage is more than the parent with care can borrow. This does not negate the fact that the whole of the asset has been transferred to the parent with care. Even where the non-resident parent retains a partial beneficial interest in the property it may still be considered a relevant transfer.[75] If a charge is placed on the property to benefit the non-resident parent, this will be deducted when calculating the allowance.[76]

Property is defined as:[77]

- cash and savings in a bank, building society or equivalent account;
- a legal estate or an equitable interest in land (or in Scotland, an interest in land);
- an endowment or other insurance policy obtained in order to discharge the mortgage or charge on a property which was also being transferred;
- a business asset, whether in the form of money, land or otherwise, which before it was transferred was being used in the course of a business in which the non-resident parent was a sole trader, a partner or a participator in a 'close' company.[78]

It does not include other assets – eg, a car or contents of the home. The value of a trust or trust fund set up betwen the non-resident parent and parent with care, or the non-resident parent and the child, can be considered.[79]

Providing evidence

Once a non-resident parent has notified the CSA that he wants a property/capital settlement taken into account, he has to supply evidence within a reasonable time.[80] If the evidence is not produced within this time, the transfer will be treated as having no value.[81]

The non-resident parent must send written evidence to the CSA of:[82]

- a court order or maintenance agreement which required the transfer of property (this evidence must be from the same time period as the court order or agreement);
- the fact of the transfer (eg, solicitors' or building society correspondence, or a copy of a Land Registry extract);

- the value of the property transferred at the date that the court order/written agreement was made (confirmed by a building society, insurance company or firm of property valuers); *and*
- the amount of any mortgage or charge outstanding at the date that the court order/written agreement was made (confirmed by a building society, bank, solicitor or accountant).

If the parent does not have this documentary evidence, it could be contained in solicitors' files, if still available. The most difficult information to obtain may be the historical value of the asset and a charge will usually be made for such a valuation.

When the non-resident parent applies for a property/capital settlement to be taken into account, the person with care is notified and asked for any relevant information.[83] Any allowance in exempt income is not calculated until 14 days after the person with care has been contacted.

Calculating the allowance

The qualifying value of a transfer of property, land or a business asset is calculated using the following formula.[84]

$$\text{Qualifying Value} = \frac{\text{(VP-MCP)}}{2} - \text{(VAP-MCR)} - \text{(VCR)}$$

Where:

- VP is the value of the property or business asset which is (wholly or in part) transferred.
- MCP is the amount of any mortgage or charge outstanding on the property immediately prior to the date of the agreement.
- VAP is the value of any interest in the property which continues to be beneficially owned by the non-resident parent (eg, if the non-resident parent transfers three-quarters of the interest in a house to the parent with care, VAP would be one-quarter of the total value).
- MCR is the amount of any mortgage or charge on the property for which the non-resident parent remains liable immediately following the transfer (this will be the same proportion of MCP as VAP is of VP).
- VCR is the value of any charge in favour of the non-resident parent on the property immediately following the transfer.

Any change in property, land or business prices since that time is irrelevant – the above figures are based on values at the agreement date. Land or property is valued on the basis that the parent with care and the child(ren) would vacate it on completion of a sale.[85] The total net value is used irrespective of whether or not the asset was previously in joint ownership.

The qualifying value in the case of a bank or building society account is half of the balance on the date of the order/agreement, and for an endowment policy, half of the surrender value at that date.[86]

Where the evidence produced shows that the whole of the transfer was made in lieu of ongoing child maintenance, the qualifying value is twice that arrived at by the above formula (in the case of property, land or business assets)[87] or (in the case of money or endowment policies) the full value transferred.[88] If there has been more than one qualifying transfer, the qualifying values of the transfers are totalled.[89]

Transfers made by the parent with care to the non-resident parent or child(ren) which satisfy the qualifying criteria (see p222), except that they are made in the reverse direction, are called compensating transfers.[90] In addition, there is provision for the whole amount of money raised by a parent with care (eg, by taking out a loan) after the date of the court order or written agreement in order that she or her child(ren) will be entitled to the whole of the property to be taken into account as a compensating transfer.[91] This applies if a non-resident parent transfers the matrimonial home to the parent with care on the condition that she buys out his interest in the property. Otherwise, compensating transfers are valued in the same way as qualifying transfers.[92]

The value of any compensatory transfer is deducted from that of the qualifying transfer to give the relevant value.[93] The allowance included in the exempt income relates to this relevant value:[94]

Relevant value	Weekly allowance
Less than £5,000	Nil
£5,000 – £9,999	£20
£10,000 – £24,999	£40
£25,000 or more	£60

Remember that this is an allowance in the exempt income and, therefore, its inclusion does not mean that the resulting maintenance assessment will be reduced by a corresponding amount.

Example: pre-April 1993 property settlement allowance

Debbie and Steve were divorced in 1991. The family home was transferred to Debbie. At the time of the court settlement, the property was worth £58,000 and the outstanding mortgage was £22,000. Almost all the contents of the house were left with Debbie, as was the car. Instead of Steve paying maintenance for Debbie, as part of the settlement, their joint savings account of £14,200 was transferred into Debbie's name. In addition, Steve gave each of the two children £3,000.

The house contents and the car do not come within the definition of property. The savings account is not a qualifying transfer as it was payment in lieu of maintenance for Debbie.

In this case, VP = £58,000 and MCP = £22,000 (see p224). VAP, MCR and VCR are nil. The qualifying value of the transfer of the house is therefore (£58,000 – £22,000) ÷ 2 = £18,000

The qualifying value of the cash to the children is the whole actual value – ie, 2 x £3,000 = £6,000

Total qualifying value = £24,000

There is no compensating value to offset.

As the relevant value is over £10,000 but less than £25,000, the allowance included in exempt income is £40.

If the savings transferred to Debbie were only £10,000 of the £14,200 and this was not for any specified purpose, this would have been another qualifying transfer valued at £5,000.

Total qualifying value = £29,000

Debbie has to pay Steve for the funds remaining in the joint account, so there is a compensating transfer with a value of £4,200 ÷ 2 = £2,100

Relevant value = £29,000 – £2,100 = £26,900

The allowance = £60

If Steve had transferred only three-quarters of the property to Debbie (retaining one-quarter interest himself), the qualifying value of the transfer of the home would be lower. VP = £58,000, MCP = £22,000, VAP = £14,500 (25% x VP) and MCR = £5,500 (25% x MCP). VCR is nil.

The qualifying value = (£58,000 – £22,000) ÷ 2 – (£14,500 – £5,500) = £18,000 – £9,000 = £9,000

In this case, if the house were the only asset transferred, the allowance included in exempt income would be £20.

---

5. **Travel-to-work costs**

An allowance towards travel costs can be included in 'old rules' exempt income for parents in employment who travel long distances.[95] It does not apply to self-employed parents.

As well as buying petrol or a ticket, travel-to-work costs include contributing to the costs of someone other than the employer who pays for transport, or paying someone else to provide the transport.[96] The allowance does not apply if an employer either provides transport (including a company car) for any part of the journey between home and the workplace, or pays for any part of the travel-to-work cost.[97] If an employer has made a loan to the parent, increases the amount of pay, or makes a payment which would be taken into account as part of net income (see p235), this is not classed as an employer paying for the transport.

Calculating the allowance

The parent must supply the required information.[98] The Child Support Agency (CSA) calculates or, where this is not possible, estimates:[99]

- the straight-line distance (ie, as the crow flies), rounded to the nearest kilometre, between the parent's home and workplace;
- the number of journeys made between home and the workplace over a period of whole weeks which it thinks is representative of the parent's normal pattern of work (disregarding any two journeys made between the home and workplace within a period of two hours); *and*
- the number of journeys multiplied by the distance and divided by the number of weeks in the period used.

No allowance is included if this figure comes to less than or equal to 240 kilometres. However, where it is over this, 6 pence is included for each kilometre over 240.[100]

If the allowance does not reflect the real travel costs, either party can apply for a departure direction (see pp322 and 327).

Example: exempt income including travel costs

Steve has remarried and has a net income for child support purposes of £380 a week. He and his wife, Lisa, have a mortgage of just under £60,000 and make monthly interest and endowment premium payments totalling £416 a month. They have no children.

Steve commutes five days a week to London with a straight-line distance from home to work of 132.3km. 10 journeys x 132.3km = 1323 a week.

Days of annual leave or sickness are ignored.

This gives 1083 kilometres over 240 and thus an allowance of 1083 x 6 pence = £64.98 a week.

Steve's exempt income:	£	
Personal allowance	59.15	
Mortgage in full*	96.00	
Property settlement allowance	40.00	(from the first part of the previous example)
Travel-to-work costs	64.98	
Total exempt income	**260.13**	

*Although the housing costs are over £80, they are not considered excessive as half of Steve's net income is £190 a week (see p220).

More than one workplace

There are special rules to deal with parents who work at more than one workplace, whether for one employer or in more than one job.[101] If the pattern of work is irregular in a job, the CSA can select one of the workplaces or another location connected with the employment and assume that each day the parent travels to and from this deemed workplace.[102]

Otherwise, the CSA must calculate the straight-line distances between any of the workplaces between which the parent travels, as well as between the home and each of the workplaces.[103] The pattern of journeys is obtained over a representative period as above. Each distance is multiplied by the number of times that journey is made over the period, and the total number of kilometres is divided by the number of weeks in the period.

6. **Second families**

We use the term 'second family' loosely to describe the situation where a parent is living with a partner and children. The children may be her/his own and/or the partner's. We recognise that the word 'second' is not precise, as the family could be a parent's third or fourth family, or indeed a first family, for example, where the qualifying children are children of a relationship formed after a marriage, and the parent continues to live with her/his spouse and children of the marriage.

We have already looked at the general position of second families as regards the 'old rules' exempt income calculation. Partners and children who are not the parent's children are not considered when including personal allowances and premiums at this stage. However, a child of the parent is included and that child may have another parent who is liable to maintain her/him. If the other parent is non-resident, then the child is a qualifying child and there is the possibility of receiving child maintenance.

Alternatively, if the other parent is also living in the family, then the 'old rules' exempt income calculation can be adjusted to recognise the other parent's liability to maintain the joint child. In other words, if a parent is living with her/his own child and the child's other parent, then the partner may be able to help support the child. This will reduce the parent's responsibility for their joint child included in exempt income. If the partner has sufficient income, this will halve the amounts for the joint child in the exempt income calculation.

The partner can refuse to disclose her income, in which case it is assumed that she can afford to help support her children and their allowances are halved.

This assessment will need to be done not only where the non-resident parent has a second family, but also where a parent with care has had a child with a current partner. This is the only time in the formula that the income of the parent with care's partner is involved.

Can the partner afford to maintain a joint child?

Before including the full allowance and premiums for a joint child in the parent's exempt income, the net income of the partner must be assessed. The partner's net income is calculated in the same way as the parent's net income when working out her/his assessable income (see Chapter 12), with just one difference.[104] The income of any of the partner's own children is *not* included. This means that maintenance for any of her own qualifying children from their non-resident parent (ie, stepchildren in the second family) is ignored.

To assess whether a partner can help support a joint child(ren), compare the amount of her/his net income with the total of:[105]

- the income support (IS) personal allowance for a person aged 25 or over (£59.15); *plus*
- half the amount of the IS personal allowance for each child; *plus*
- if the child(ren) would qualify for the IS disabled child premium (see Appendix 2), half the amount of that premium for that child(ren); *plus*
- half the amount of the IS family premium, except where the family premium would be payable in respect of another child who is included in exempt income (£8.22); *plus*
- any contribution the partner is expected to make towards housing costs after a departure direction (see p327).

No personal allowances are included for any other children of the partner.

If the partner's net income is higher than the figure above, s/he can afford to contribute to their joint child's support. Therefore, the parent's exempt income will include only half the child's personal allowance, and half of any disabled child premium and (if there is no other child included in the exempt income), only half the family premium.[106]

Example: exempt income with a joint child

Bob and Zoe have a baby, Ricky. They are still living in the same house with a rent of £45 a week and Zoe's other three children (see p221).

Zoe stays at home full time. Her only income is child benefit and maintenance for Yvonne and Veronica, both of which are ignored. Therefore, Zoe cannot afford to contribute to Ricky's upkeep and Bob's exempt income will include the full allowances for Ricky.

Bob is not the father of Yvonne, Veronica and Scott, and therefore they are not included in the exempt income calculation.

Bob's exempt income:		£
Personal allowances	Bob	59.15
	Ricky	47.45
Family premium		16.43
Housing costs		45.00
Total exempt income		**168.03**

Zoe begins paid work and brings home £95 a week.
Her earnings are compared with:

Personal allowances	Zoe	59.15
	Ricky (half)	23.73
Family premium (half)		8.22
Total		**91.10**

Note: half the family premium is allowed in Zoe's means test as the family premium is only included in Bob's exempt income for Ricky. There is no other child included in exempt income.

Zoe's other three children are not taken into account.

No departure application has been made for Zoe's contribution towards housing costs.

As her earnings are higher than £91.10, Zoe is seen as being able to contribute to the maintenance of Ricky. Therefore, Bob's exempt income is adjusted.

Bob's exempt income:		£
Personal allowances	Bob	59.15
	Ricky (half)	23.73
Family premium (half)		8.22
Housing costs		45.00
Total exempt income		**136.10**

Family premium

If the only children who are included in the parent's exempt income are joint children with the current partner, whether or not the family premium is included in full or halved in the exempt income depends solely on the net income of the partner. When calculating whether the partner can afford to help support the children, half the family premium is included in the amount with which the partner's net income is compared, as in the above example.

However, if there is another child in the family who is the parent's, but not the partner's child, s/he will be included in the exempt income calculation of her/his parent. Therefore, the family premium is payable in full for this other child and the question of halving the family premium does not arise. The family premium is therefore excluded from the amount with which the partner's net income is compared when calculating whether she can support half the joint child.[107]

Example: exempt income with a joint child and a qualifying child

The situation is the same as in the above example except that Bob's daughter, Carol (15), has come to live with Bob and Zoe.

Zoe's earnings would now be compared with:

		£
Personal allowances	Zoe	59.15
	Ricky (half)	23.73
Total exempt income		**82.88**

Half of the family premium is not included as Bob is entitled to the full family premium in his exempt income for Carol, and between the two partners there cannot be more than one family premium.

As her earnings are higher than £82.88, Zoe is seen as being able to contribute to half the maintenance of Ricky. Therefore, Bob's exempt income is adjusted.

Bob's exempt income:		£
Personal allowances	Bob	59.15
	Carol	47.45
	Ricky (half)	23.73

Family premium (in full)	16.43
Housing costs	45.00
Total exempt income	**191.76**

If Carol only comes to stay some of the time, her personal allowance may be included in Bob's exempt income, but at a reduced rate, depending on how often she stays with him (see Chapter 15).

For a detailed explanation of the family premium in exempt income where there is a joint child and a shared-care child, see p302.

Notes

1. What is exempt income
1 Sch 1 para 5(4) CSA 1991; regs 10A and 10B CS(MASC) Regs
2 Sch 1 para 5(4) CSA 1991; reg 10A CS(MASC) Regs

2. How much is exempt income
3 Reg 10 CS(MASC) Regs
4 Reg 9(5) CS(MASC) Regs
5 Sch 1 para 5 CSA 1991; reg 9(1)CS(MASC) Regs
6 Reg 10(b) CS(MASC) Regs

3. Housing costs
7 Reg 14 and Sch 3 para 4(1)(b) and (c) CS(MASC) Regs
8 Reg 40(7) CSDDCA Regs
9 CCS/6741/1995; CCS/2852/1995; DMG para 5300
10 Sch 3 para 4(2)(a) CS(MASC) Regs
11 Reg 15(3) CS(MASC) Regs
12 CSCS/8/1995; CCS/8189/1995
13 CCS/13698/1996
14 DMG paras 5525-27
15 Reg 15(3) CS(MASC) Regs
16 Secretary of State for Work and Pensions v M [2006] UKHL 11
17 Sch 3 para 4(2)(b) CS(MASC) Regs
18 Reg 15(4) CS(MASC) Regs
19 CSCS/2/1994; CSCS/5/1995
20 Sch 3 para 4(1)(a) CS(MASC) Regs

21 Sch 3 paras 1, 2, 2A and 3 CS(MASC) Regs; CCS/12/1994 and CCS/2750/1995
22 Reg 15(2) CS(MASC) Regs
23 CSCS/3/1996
24 DMG para 5310, 9
25 CSCS/1/1994; R(CS) 3/96
26 CCS/11252/1995
27 CSCS/13/1995
28 CCS/12897/1996
29 Regs 9(1)(h) and 11(1)(i) CS(MASC) Regs
30 CCS/11252/1995
31 Reg 1(2) CS(MASC) Regs
32 CSCS/8/1995; CCS/8189/1995
33 CCS/19/1994
34 CCS/4/1994; R(CS) 2/96
35 CCS/4305/1995
36 Regs 1(2), 9(1)(h) and 11(1)(i) CS(MASC) Regs
37 Sch 3 para 5 CS(MASC) Regs; DMG paras 5501-07
38 Reg 15(2) CS(MASC) Regs
39 Reg 15(2) CS(MASC) Regs; DMG para 5450
40 Sch 3 para 3 CS(MASC) Regs
41 Sch 3 para 3(4) CS(MASC) Regs; CCS/12598/1996
42 DMG para 5350; Sch 3 para 3 CS(MASC) Regs
43 CSCS/1/1994; DMG para 5410
44 CCS/1321/1997
45 CCS/11591/1995

46 Sch 3 para 4 CS(MASC) Regs
47 CCS/2750/1995
48 Sch 3 para 3(5A) and (5B) CS(MASC) Regs
49 Sch 3 para 3(5B) CS(MASC) Regs
50 Sch 3 para 3(5) and (5A) CS(MASC) Regs
51 Sch 3 para 3(6) CS(MASC) Regs
52 CCS/9/1995
53 Sch 3 para 3(2A) CS(MASC) Regs
54 Sch 3 para 4A CS(MASC) Regs
55 Sch 3 para 6 CS(MASC) Regs
56 Sch 3 para 6(d) CS(MASC) Regs
57 Reg 16(1) CS(MASC) Regs
58 Reg 16(2)(d) CS(MASC) Regs; DMG para 5603
59 Reg 16(2) CS(MASC) Regs
60 Reg 18(2) CS(MASC) Regs
61 Reg 18(1) CS(MASC) Regs
62 CCS/6/1995

4. Pre-April 1993 property settlements
63 Reg 9(1)(bb) and Sch 3A CS(MASC) Regs
64 Reg 10(a) CS(MASC) Regs
65 Sch 3A paras 1, 8 and 9 CS(MASC) Regs
66 Sch 3A para 1(1) CS(MASC) Regs
67 Sch 3A para 1(1)(d) CS(MASC) Regs; CCS/14368/1997; CCS/97/1997
68 CCS/97/1997
69 Sch 3A para 1(1)(d) CS(MASC) Regs
70 DMG para 3177
71 DMG para 3178
72 CCS/97/1997
73 Family Law Act (Scotland) 1985
74 CSCS/1/1998; CSCS/2/1998
75 DMG para 3168
76 DMG para 3186
77 Sch 3A para 1(1) and (2) CS(MASC) Regs
78 as defined by ss414 and 415 ICTA 1988
79 DMG para 3183
80 Sch 3A para 2(2) CS(MASC) Regs
81 Sch 3A para 2(2) CS(MASC) Regs
82 Sch 3A para 2(1) CS(MASC) Regs
83 Sch 3A para 3 CS(MASC) Regs; DMG para 3158
84 Sch 3A para 4(1) CS(MASC) Regs; DMG para 3185
85 Sch 3A para 4(2) CS(MASC) Regs
86 Sch 3A para 5 CS(MASC) Regs
87 Sch 3A para 6(a) CS(MASC) Regs
88 Sch 3A para 6(b) CS(MASC) Regs
89 Sch 3A para 7 CS(MASC) Regs
90 Sch 3A para 1 CS(MASC) Regs
91 Sch 3A para 8A CS(MASC) Regs
92 Sch 3A para 8 CS(MASC) Regs

93 Sch 3A para 9 CS(MASC) Regs
94 Sch 3A para 10 CS(MASC) Regs

5. Travel-to-work costs
95 Reg 9(1)(i) and Sch 3B CS(MASC) Regs
96 Sch 3B para 1 CS(MASC) Regs
97 Sch 3B paras 21-23 CS(MASC) Regs
98 Sch 3B para 2 CS(MASC) Regs
99 Sch 3B paras 3-6 CS(MASC) Regs
100 Sch 3B paras 7, 14 and 20 CS(MASC) Regs
101 Sch 3B paras 8-20 CS(MASC) Regs
102 Sch 3B paras 8(2) and 15(2) CS(MASC) Regs
103 Sch 3B paras 9-13 and 16-19 CS(MASC) Regs

6. Second families
104 Reg 9(2) CS(MASC) Regs
105 Reg 9(2)(c) CS(MASC) Regs
106 Reg 9(1)(f) and (g) CS(MASC) Regs
107 Reg 9(2)(c)(iv) CS(MASC) Regs

Chapter 12

Assessable income ('old rules')

This chapter covers:
1. What is assessable income (below)
2. What is net income (p234)
3. Calculating assessable income (p253)

1. What is assessable income

Assessable income is the parent's income remaining after basic living expenses (represented by exempt income – see Chapter 11) have been accounted for. A proportion of this remaining income is used to contribute towards child maintenance payments (see Chapter 13). In the case of the parent with care this is a notional contribution which can have the effect of reducing the maintenance payable by the non-resident parent.

Assessable income is the parent's net income minus exempt income.[1]

This step of the formula is carried out in the same way for non-resident parents and parents with care[2] and, therefore, any reference to parent in this chapter applies to both. It does not apply to a person with care who is not the parent of the qualifying child.

It is useful to calculate the non-resident parent's assessable income first because if he has no assessable income there is no need to calculate that of the parent with care (see p253).

A parent who is in receipt of income support (IS), pension credit (PC) or income-based jobseeker's allowance (JSA) is treated as having *no* assessable income.[3] If only the parent with care is on IS/PC/income-based JSA, the assessable income step must be done for the non-resident parent alone. If the non-resident parent is on IS/PC/income-based JSA, the formula calculation is not carried out at all and instead the non-resident parent may have a deduction from his benefit (see p430). If the benefit claim of one party is thought to be fraudulent, this can be challenged by the other party (see p383).

Parents with care who are on working tax credit (WTC) are treated as having no assessable income.[4] This, as for IS/PC/income-based JSA, applies whether the benefit is being paid to the parent herself or to her partner. A non-resident parent on WTC is only treated as having no assessable income if he is also a parent with care and either there is a maintenance assessment in force for his qualifying child(ren) or an application for an assessment is being considered.[5] (But if a maintenance calculation is made as a parent with care, this will convert the non-resident parent's maintenance assessment to the 'new rules', under which WTC is included as income.)

2. **What is net income**

Net income under the 'old rules' is the total income of the parent taken into account when assessing how much child maintenance the parent can afford to pay.

Net income includes earnings, benefits and other income.[6] The types of income that come within each of these categories are clearly defined in the regulations.[7] Certain types of income are ignored in full or in part.[8] The rules about income are similar, but not identical, to those for income support (IS).

The net income of a parent's partner is calculated using these rules when assessing whether s/he can afford to contribute to the support of any joint child in the exempt income calculation (see p276).[9]

These rules for calculating net income are also used when working out the family's total income at the protected income stage of the formula (see Chapter 14). However, there are a few exceptions,[10] which we explain here and in Chapter 14.

If any income which is normally received at regular intervals is not received, it can be treated as though it has been received as long it is due to be paid and there are reasonable grounds for believing that the payment will actually be made.[11]

Capital itself is not taken into account, although any income generated from the capital does count as income (see p247).

In certain cases, a parent can be treated as having income (or capital which is a source of income) which s/he does not possess if the Child Support Agency (CSA) believes the parent deprived her/himself of it with the intention of reducing her/his assessable income (see p250).

Verification of income is expected (see p97).

Whose income is included

A partner's income is *not* included in the net income when calculating assessable income. This is commonly misunderstood (see p281 for the way in which a partner's income may affect the assessment). Where a source of income is held jointly and the proportions are not known or defined, the income available is divided equally between the people who are entitled to receive it.[12]

The income of the parent's own child living in the household can be treated as though it were the income of the parent (see p249).[13]

Relevant week

The concept of the 'relevant week'[14] is important in child support assessments, particularly when calculating income.

For the parent who is not the applicant, the relevant week is the seven days immediately before the date that the maintenance enquiry form (see p85) is sent to him. For the applicant, the relevant week is the seven days immediately before the maintenance application form (see p42) is submitted to the CSA. For the purpose of calculating earnings only, if the CSA has not been able to make an assessment (except perhaps an interim maintenance assessment – see p367), but is later supplied with the information required, the relevant week is the seven days immediately before the date on which the required information or evidence was received.[15]

If a decision is revised (or if it is superseded because of ignorance or a mistake about a material fact), the relevant week of the new decision is the same as that for the original decision. If a decision is superseded on other grounds, the relevant week is the seven days immediately prior to the application for a supersession (or the seven days prior to the date of notification if the CSA supersedes on its own initiative).[16] See Chapter 18 for more information on grounds for revision and supersession of decisions.

Earnings from employment

Earnings mean 'any remuneration or profit derived from employment' and, as well as wages, include:[17]
- any payments for overtime;
- any profit-related pay;
- any bonus or commission (including tips);
- any holiday pay (except any payable more than four weeks after the job ends);
- payment in lieu of notice;
- statutory sick pay, statutory maternity pay, statutory adoption pay and statutory paternity pay;[18]
- any payment for expenses not 'wholly, exclusively and necessarily incurred' in actually carrying out the job (these include payments made to cover travelling expenses from home to work and the care costs of any other member of the family);
- allowances paid to local councillors for local authority duties, as opposed to expenses 'wholly, exclusively and necessarily incurred';
- payment for duties as an auxiliary coastguard, part-time firefighter, or with the lifeboat services, territorial army or reserve forces relating to a period of less than one year (such payments for a period of one year or more are disregarded);[19]
- awards of compensation for unfair dismissal;
- certain employment protection payments;

- any retaining fee;
- remuneration, but not share dividend or debenture interest (which is other income), paid to a director of a limited or unlimited registered and incorporated company (as opposed to a sole trader or partner who is self-employed – see p238).[20]

Where an employee is also a director of a company, money drawn from a director's current account or loan account could be either income or capital. If it is income, it may or may not be earnings, depending on whether it is 'derived from that employment'. A decision about this money needs to be fully explained following an investigation of the facts.[21]

The CSA should not simply adopt HM Revenue and Customs' estimate (eg, of expenses) and should carry out an independent examination of the facts, but CSA staff would have to consider carefully before taking a different position.[22] Non-taxable allowances are not automatically excluded as earnings for child support purposes.[23]

Earnings do *not* include:[24]

- occupational pension payments (these count as other income – see p244. For how payments made into a pension scheme are treated, see p238);
- payments for expenses 'wholly, exclusively and necessarily' incurred in carrying out the duties of the job (see below);
- payments in kind;
- any advance of earnings or loan made by an employer to an employee (such a payment is also disregarded as other income,[25] and any repayments made will be included as earnings, not deducted from them[26]);
- payments made after employment ends which relate to a specific period of time, provided that a period of equal length has elapsed since the payment was received;
- earnings from a previous job where they are paid in a week or a period that earnings from a second job are received;
- payments made by an employer when an employee is on strike;
- any tax-exempt allowance paid by an employer to an employee;
- a compensation payment negotiated and made on the termination of employment[27] (with the exception of any payment in lieu of notice – see above);
- the value of free accommodation provided by an employer (although the CSA may consider the issue of notional earnings – see p250 – if the actual earnings are low in relation to the job performed).[28]

Payments made by the parent for expenses can be deducted from her/his earnings where the employer did not reimburse them,[29] but only if the expenses were incurred 'in the performance of duties'. It is possible that part of a payment (eg, towards a telephone rental or travel costs) could be 'wholly, exclusively and necessarily' incurred.[30]

A local overseas allowance paid to members of the armed forces abroad is disregarded,[31] whereas a rent or mortgage allowance paid by an employer (eg, to a police officer,[32] an army major in the UK,[33] or a civil servant[34]) would normally be taken into account as earnings, except where the housing expenses are necessarily incurred in the performance of their duties.[35] For the same reason, meals allowances are to be treated as earnings.[36]

Calculating normal weekly earnings

Averaged earnings are used in the child support calculation.[37] When calculating or estimating average earnings at the relevant week (see above), the CSA considers the evidence of the parent's earnings over any appropriate period, beginning no more than eight weeks before the relevant week and ending by the date of the assessment. It may also consider cumulative earnings to date in the tax year covering the relevant week.

If a parent has claimed or been paid working tax credit (WTC)/child tax credit (CTC) on any day during the eight weeks before the relevant week or up to the date the assessment is made, the CSA can use the amount of earnings taken into account in the WTC/CTC calculation even though those earnings may relate to a period outside that normally used for a child support assessment.

CSA staff are advised to give reasons for the assessment period chosen for calculating earnings and to record fully how the decision was made.[38]

If the parent is a student (see p245), earnings are averaged over 52 weeks ending with the relevant week, or as many weeks as the parent has been a student if this is shorter.[39]

If the CSA believes that the amount of weekly earnings arrived at does not accurately represent the parent's normal earnings, any other period can be used, taking into account earnings received and those due to be received.[40] The CSA must be satisfied first that the calculation of earnings at the relevant week produces a figure which is not normal,[41] and then that the period chosen reflects the parent's usual pattern of work, taking into account how aspects such as sick leave and overtime may affect normal earnings.[42] A future period can be used to ensure the usual pattern is reflected – eg, earnings from a job which has not yet begun. The CSA must also consider the expected duration and pattern of any employment. A parent may want to suggest an alternative period to the CSA, giving reasons, as the CSA cannot be expected to consider an alternative period without substantial grounds and a prompt by one of the parents.[43] The CSA must use one continuous period.[44]

If a bonus, commission or profit-related pay is paid separately from earnings or in relation to a longer period than other earnings during a year ending with the relevant week, those payments are totalled over the year and divided by 52 weeks.[45] Such a payment cannot be disregarded on the grounds that it distorts normal earnings.[46]

The CSA has to take into account any change of circumstances it is aware of between the relevant week and the effective date (see p368).[47] However, it must first calculate earnings in the usual way for the relevant week in order to determine whether there has been a material change of circumstances.[48] For changes after this date, see p351.

The calculation of earnings is one of the areas where errors are frequently made and, therefore, should be checked carefully. A commissioner has held that an appeal tribunal must enquire into whether the process used to determine income was correctly carried out and whether the period used for the averaging of earnings gave an accurate picture.[49]

Calculating net earnings

Net earnings from employment are counted as net income in full. Net earnings mean gross earnings *less*:[50]

- income tax;
- Class 1 national insurance contributions;
- half of any contributions made to an occupational pension scheme; *and*
- half of any contributions made towards a personal pension scheme (unless that scheme is intended partly to pay off a mortgage on the parent's home, in which case 37.5 per cent of such contributions). Certain retirement savings plans do not come within this provision,[51] but regular contributions under a retirement annuity contract may be deducted.[52]

The amount of tax and national insurance actually paid is usually deducted.[53] However, where earnings are being estimated, the amount to be deducted as income tax is calculated using the personal allowances and the tax rates applicable at the relevant week (see p235).[54] Similarly, the amount to be deducted as Class 1 national insurance contributions will be calculated by using the appropriate percentage rate applicable in the relevant week.

Earnings from self-employment

Earnings from self-employment will, in most cases, be assessed on the basis of total taxable profits from self-employment submitted to HM Revenue and Customs for income tax self-assessment.[55] This includes earnings which fall under the self-employment, partnerships and land and property sections of the self-assessment form. If a parent cannot provide the submission to HM Revenue and Customs, but can provide a tax calculation notice, the total taxable profit from self-employment will be taken from the tax calculation notice instead.[56] Total taxable profits are those *before* any deduction for capital allowances, and so may differ from actual entries on the self-asessment form or tax calculation form.[57] If the CSA becomes aware of a revision by HM Revenue and Customs of the total taxable profit from self-employment, the revised figure should be taken into account.[58]

The intention is that self-employed parents will send the CSA copies of their self-assessment forms or tax calculation notices voluntarily. Where the CSA is satisfied that it is not reasonably practicable for a parent to provide the taxable profit figure, the earnings will be calculated under the rules applying before 4 October 1999 (see below).[59]

The earnings taken into account are the total taxable profit from self-employment less tax, national insurance and half of pension premiums (37.5 per cent of the premium where the scheme is intended to pay off a mortgage).[60] The tax, national insurance and pension premium deductions from self-employed earnings are calculated using the rates applicable at the effective date.

If self-employed earnings are assessed using taxable profits submitted to HM Revenue and Customs, those profits must relate to a period of not less than six months and not more than 15 months ending within two years of the relevant week.[61] If there is more than one such period, the figure used will be the taxable profits relating to the latest period.[62] If the CSA believes that the earnings figure arrived at in this way does not accurately reflect the normal weekly earnings of the earner (eg, because there are no periods to which a taxable profit relates which meet the criteria), then self-employed earnings will be assessed in the same way as they were prior to 4 October 1999.[63]

The use of self-assessment details is intended to simplify the assessment of self-employed earnings. However, if a decision maker finds contradictions between information on the self-assessment form and evidence already held, this may be grounds for further investigation.[64]

Some parents with care who were previously assessed on the basis of their non-resident parent's taxable profit may find that the non-resident parent now provides self-assessment information. This may result in a lower assessment as the allowances against profit are more generous under income tax rules than the CSA rules for calculating taxable profit. At the time of writing, capital allowances cannot be deducted in the assessment of net income,[65] so this difference is not as great as it was. However, the Government has stated that it intends to change the law so that non-resident parents are allowed to deduct capital allowances.[66]

If a person with care has had her maintenance reduced because of the use of self-assessment records, she could raise the issue with her MP, or complain to the CSA and ask for compensation.

Earnings from self-employment not calculated from taxable profit

Where the CSA is satisfied that it is not reasonably practical for a self-employed parent to provide a taxable profit figure (see above) or where the taxable profit figure does not reflect her/his normal weekly earnings, earnings will be assessed on the following basis (these are the rules which applied to all self-employed assessments prior to 4 October 1999).

In these cases, earnings mean the gross receipts of the business. They include any business start-up grant which is paid for in the same period as the receipts, unless it was ended by the relevant week, in which case it is disregarded.[67] Payments received for providing board and lodging accommodation are counted as other income (see p244) unless they provide the largest part of the parent's income, when they are treated as earnings from self-employment.[68] If a parent is a childminder, only one-third of her gross receipts count as earnings.[69]

Net earnings to be included as net income are the gross receipts of the business less:[70]

- income tax (calculated for the chargeable earnings using the personal allowance and the tax rates applicable on the effective date – see p368);
- national insurance contributions (Class 2 and Class 4 contributions at the rates applicable on the effective date[71]);
- half of any premium on a personal pension scheme (unless that scheme is intended partly to pay off a mortgage on the parent's home, in which case 37.5 per cent of the contributions are deducted) or on a retirement annuity contract;
- any VAT paid in excess of VAT received in the same period as that over which the earnings are assessed;
- any expenses which are reasonably incurred for the purposes of the business. If the CSA is not satisfied that the full expense was appropriate or necessary to the business, it will allow that part considered reasonable.[72] Where an expense is part business and part private (eg, a car), the CSA has to decide on the breakdown between the two uses on the evidence available. CSA staff are given examples of how to deal with apportionment.[73] They may well follow the apportionment used by HM Revenue and Customs. CSA staff are also given guidance on what may be allowable business expenses.[74]

Business expenses include:[75]

- repayments of capital on loans used to replace or repair a business asset (but not for loans taken out for any other business purpose);
- any income used to repair a business asset;
- any payment of interest on loans taken out for business purposes (this does not include loans taken out to acquire a share of a business, nor to pay business tax liabilities).[76]

Business expenses do *not* include:[77]

- capital expenditure;
- depreciation of capital assets;
- any sum employed in the setting up or expansion of the business;
- any loss incurred before the period of earnings being calculated;
- any expenses incurred in providing business entertainment;
- any loss incurred in any other self-employment.

There are separate rules and guidance for share fishermen, to reflect the different ways in which their expenses may be shared .[78]

If a profit and loss account is provided for a period of at least six months (but no longer than 15 months) which ended within the last two years, it can be used to calculate average weekly earnings.[79] The two years end on the date on which the assessment takes effect – ie, the effective date (see p368). The CSA may decide to wait if accounts will shortly be available and impose a Category C interim maintenance assessment in the meantime. However, it is important that accounts which include income received after the effective date are not used.[80]

If there is more than one such profit and loss account covering different periods, the account covering the latest period will be used unless the CSA is satisfied that this latest account is not available for reasons beyond the parent's control.[81] Not being available includes where an accountant or another government department (eg, HM Revenue and Customs) holds them without a date set for their return, the Official Receiver has the accounts, or they have been destroyed, lost or stolen.

A trading account or balance sheet (or both) may be requested in addition to the profit and loss account, if it is appropriate to the type of self-employment.[82] The accounts do not need to be prepared by accountants or even typed. However, if they do not contain the required information, the CSA may request other evidence of gross receipts.

Where no appropriate profit and loss account is available, earnings for the self-employed will be averaged over the previous 52 weeks or, if the person has been self-employed for less than a year, over the period during which the person has been self-employed up to an including the relevant week (see p235).[83] The self-employed person is asked to provide other evidence of business receipts and expenses, such as business books, receipts of bills sent and paid, bank statements, records of wages paid, HM Revenue and Customs forms and VAT bills.[84]

Unless the assessment period is the period of the profit and loss account being used, the actual gross receipts and expenses falling in the assessment period should be taken into account. Some of these may relate to work done or expenses incurred outside the assessment period, but they should be included if payment was received or made during the assessment period.[85]

If the CSA believes that either or both of the above calculations produce an amount which does not accurately represent the parent's true earnings, another period can be used.[86] This may happen where there has been a major change in trading which has resulted in higher or lower earnings or where a person who has been trading for less than a year has not established a regular pattern of trading.[87] This should not be used just because earnings fluctuate, receipts are irregular or come in a lump sum, trade is slow at times or work non-existent for a period, nor should a different period be used just because it is known that earnings will subsequently change.[88]

Self-employed parents on tax credits

If a self-employed parent has claimed or been paid WTC/CTC on any day during the eight weeks before the relevant week or up to the date the assessment is made, the CSA may use the amount of earnings taken into account in the WTC/CTC calculation even though those earnings may relate to a period different from those described on p241.[89]

Challenging self-employed earnings

There have often been delays in the self-employed parent producing all the information necessary to carry out the assessment. The CSA can impose a Category C interim maintenance assessment while awaiting the information, but this is rare. The person with care may want to request that this is done.

Many self-employed non-resident parents have, in the past, received low assessments, and some persons with care may allege that the self-employed non-resident parent, perhaps with the help of an accountant, has managed to disguise his true income. Once an assessment has been made, the person with care can seek a revision of the assessment (see p384) and ask the CSA to use an inspector (see p98) in order to obtain more detailed information. However, if the non-resident parent's accounts have been accepted by HM Revenue and Customs, it is very unlikely that the CSA would consider it worthwhile to undertake further investigations. The CSA may also refuse to revise the assessment if the person with care cannot substantiate her allegations. This refusal can be challenged if the belief that income is too low is reasonably held, as it is very difficult for one party to obtain definitive details of the other's income. The CSA is much better placed to do this.

If the person with care takes the case to an appeal tribunal, she will see details of the income in the appeal papers, and she may be able to argue that some of the expenses included are not reasonable or not wholly connected with the business (see p241). She should also consider the notional earnings rules (see p250) and, if relevant, suggest the tribunal makes a finding on this issue. Tribunals may adjourn the hearing and instruct the CSA to collect further information. Alternatively, the tribunal can estimate net earnings based on the available evidence, including oral evidence from the person with care.[90] It can also consider data about earnings in different sectors (and in particular localities) – eg, the *New Earnings Survey*, to estimate the likely self-employed earnings in particular jobs.[91]

The person with care can apply for departure from the assessment on the grounds that a person's lifestyle is inconsistent with his level of income or that assets which do not currently produce income are capable of doing so (see p325).

Benefits

Benefits paid by the Department for Work and Pensions count as income for the purposes of net income, although some of these are disregarded in full or in part.[92] Remember that if income support (IS)/income-based jobseeker's allowance (JSA) or pension credit (PC) is received by the parent or her/his partner, the parent is treated as having no assessable income (see p234) and the formula is not used.

The amount of benefit to be taken into account is the weekly rate applying on the effective date (see p368).[93]

Whose benefit?

The income of a partner is not included when working out a parent's net income. Some non-means-tested benefits contain an extra amount for a partner, called an adult dependency increase. The amount paid in respect of that dependant is treated as the dependant's income, not the claimant's[94] – ie, if the parent is the claimant, s/he is treated as not receiving the adult dependency increase and, if the partner is the claimant, the parent is assumed to have income equal to the increase paid to the partner in respect of her/him. If a parent receives a non-means-tested benefit which includes a dependency increase for a child, this is treated as the income of the child (see p249). These rules also apply to adult and child dependency increases paid with a war disablement, war widow's, war widower's or surviving civil partner's pensions.[95]

Child benefit

Child benefit is ignored when working out net income.[96] When calculating total family income for protected income purposes, child benefit is counted in full.[97]

Benefits ignored in full

The following benefits are ignored in full:
- housing benefit;[98]
- council tax benefit;[99]
- disability living allowance (or a mobility supplement);[100]
- attendance allowance (or constant attendance allowance or exceptionally severe disablement allowance paid because of industrial injury or war injury);[101]
- social fund payments;[102]
- guardian's allowance;[103] *and*
- Christmas bonus.[104]

Payments made to compensate for the loss of benefits are also disregarded.[105] Special war widows' payments granted in 1990 are likewise disregarded in full.[106]

Benefits ignored in part

A total of £10 a week of a war disablement pension, war widow's or war widower's pension, or a payment made to a parent under the Armed Forces Compensation Scheme is disregarded.[107] However, only £20 a week in total can be disregarded from a combination of war pensions, regular charitable/voluntary payments(see p245) and student income (see p248).

Other income

Unless specified below, all other income is taken into account on a weekly basis by considering the 26-week period ending in the 'relevant week' (see p235).[108] If the income has been received during each week of the period, the total received over the 26 weeks is divided by 26. In other cases, the total received is divided by the number of complete weeks for which the payment was received. However, the CSA has the discretion to use a different period if the amount produced by the above calculation does not accurately reflect actual income. Furthermore, a change occurring between the relevant week and the effective date (see p368) must be taken into account by the CSA if it is aware of the change, in the same way as for earnings (see p238).

Other income includes any payments received on a periodic basis which are not earnings, benefits, or a child's income, as well as the following types of payment. It does not include a non-resident parent's payments towards his share of a parent with care's housing costs.[109] Some payments are taken into account in full or in part, while others are ignored completely. Payments which are ignored as earnings cannot be taken into account as other income.

Working tax credit

WTC is usually treated as the income of the parent who qualifies for the payment through her/his normal engagement in remunerative work.[110] Where a couple both meet the conditions for WTC, it is all treated as the income of the non-resident parent provided his earnings are higher than his partner's during the period used to calculate earnings for the maintenance assessment. If the earnings are equal, half the amount of the WTC counts as the income of the non-resident parent. If the non-resident parent's earnings are less than the other person's then WTC is not counted as his income.

Child tax credit

All payments of CTC are ignored in full.[111]

Payments from occupational or personal pension schemes

These and any analogous payments are taken into account in full.[112]

Income from rent

Different provisions apply, depending on the type of income from the property.

- Payments made towards household expenses by a non-dependant (see p284) are completely ignored.[113]
- The first £20 a week of a payment from a boarder is disregarded, as is 50 per cent of any amount over £20 (as long as this is not the largest part of a parent's income when it would be treated as earnings from self-employment).[114] A boarder is someone who is liable to pay for board and lodging which includes at least one meal a day.

- Payments from a person who is liable to pay for accommodation in the parent's home (but who is not a lodger or a non-dependant) are treated as income. However, there is a disregard of £19.45 (or £4 if the payment is not inclusive of heating).[115]
- Payments for the use of a property which is not the parent's home are taken into account as other income, unless the parent is self-employed. In this case, the income is treated as part of the gross receipts of the business. If the parent is not self-employed, the amounts to cover income tax,[116] mortgage interest, interest on loans for repairs and improvements, council tax and water charges can be deducted from the amount received as rent.[117] It is not clear whether other expenses necessary to obtain the rental income (eg, servicing gas fires) may also be deducted, but there is nothing in the guidance for decision makers to suggest that they can.[118]

Student income

A student is defined as someone following a full-time course of study at an educational establishment and, if under 19 years old, the course must be advanced education – ie, above A level or Scottish Higher.[119] This can include sandwich courses. There is no definition of full time and it does not relate to the number of hours the student actually attends. The CSA attaches great weight to evidence from the educational establishment.[120] Once a course has begun, a person continues to be treated as a student until either the course ends or s/he leaves it.

Unless they have income in addition to an educational grant (including any contribution due) or student loan, students are treated as having no net income and, hence, are exempt from having to pay child maintenance.[121]

In other cases, income paid to a student as a grant, grant contribution, covenant income or student loan, is taken into account, except that which is:[122]

- intended to meet tuition fees or examination fees;
- intended to meet additional expenditure as a result of a disability;
- intended to meet expenditure connected with residential study away from the educational establishment;
- made on account of the student maintaining a home away from the educational establishment;
- intended to meet the cost of books and equipment, or, if not specified, £361 (this increases at the start of each academic year);
- intended to meet travel expenses.

The amount of a student's grant, covenant income and loan are apportioned equally between the weeks for which they are payable.[123] Five pounds a week can be deducted from covenant income and £10 a week from loan income, although not more than £10 a week can be deducted in total where both types of income are received.[124] Any amount disregarded under this provision counts towards the

£20 disregard for war pensions (see p243) and charitable/voluntary payments (see p248).[125]

Financial assistance or awards from an education authority for courses of further education are disregarded.[126]

New Deal for 18–24-year-olds

Payments from an employer under the New Deal Employment option are treated as earnings (see p234). This also applies to payments from an employer under the Voluntary Sector and Environmental Task Force options.[127] Participants in other New Deal options, or where options include a work placement rather than actual employment, are likely to receive a training allowance. This is taken into account, but most New Deal participants will receive income-based JSA and will, therefore, not be assessed under the formula (see p199).

Training allowances

Training allowances are taken into account (but see below), except for the training premium, travelling expenses or any living away from home allowance.[128]

Work-based learning for young people

These training schemes for young people aged under 19 include apprenticeships, other work-based training and (in Scotland) Skillseekers training. Trainees who are not employees receive a training allowance or an education maintenance allowance, depending where in the UK they are training. Young people on these schemes who have no income other than their training allowance or education maintenance allowance are taken to have no net income and are exempt from paying any child maintenance (see p199).[129] Trainees who are employees have their earnings taken into account in the usual way (see p235).

Maintenance for a parent

This income is taken into account in full. There is a specific rule used to calculate the amount of maintenance to be taken into account. It is calculated by averaging the payments received in the 13 weeks preceding the assessment over the number of weeks for which a payment was due.[130] Although there is caselaw which says that payments of maintenance to a parent with care by a non-resident parent cannot be counted as the parent with care's income,[131] this approach is not reflected in guidance to CSA staff[132] and the CSA continues to regard such payments as income.

Child maintenance

Child maintenance from a non-resident parent for the qualifying child for whom the assessment is being carried out is ignored when calculating the income of the parent with care.[133]

Except at the protected income stage (see p282), the CSA treats maintenance paid to a parent for any other child as the child's income. This may still be included in net income, but there are separate rules covering when and how much of the child's income can be taken into account as the parent's income (see p249).

In the calculation of protected income, any maintenance being paid for other children under a court order is deducted from the liable person's income, as long as an application cannot be made to the CSA (see p37).[134] See p282 for further details.

Lump-sum maintenance

There is provision to disregard other maintenance payments in full, whether child support maintenance or other forms, if they are not income.[135] However, as all payments received on a periodic basis are income, this disregard appears only to apply to irregular maintenance payments. It does not apply to maintenance payments made periodically.[136]

Payments made by local authorities towards a child's living costs

Payments made by a local authority where it is looking after a child and has placed the child with a family, relative or other suitable person, including a foster parent, are ignored completely.[137] Payments made by local authorities to promote the welfare of children being looked after, or who were formerly in their care, are also ignored.[138]

Payments made as a contribution towards the maintenance of a child living with the family as a result of a residence order are ignored to the extent that they exceed the personal allowances and any disabled child premium included for the child in the exempt income calculation (see p212).[139]

Adoption allowances

A payment for an adopted child is disregarded:[140]
- to the extent that it exceeds the personal allowance and any disabled child premium for the child, if child maintenance is *not* being assessed for that particular child;
- only up to the amount of any income of the child which is included as income of the parent, if child maintenance is being assessed for that child.

Income from capital

A payment is capital and not income if it is not paid in respect of a particular period, it is paid without reference to any past payment, and it is not intended to form part of a series of payments.[141] Such capital payments are not taken into account. However, the interest, dividend or any other income produced by capital is taken into account as income and is calculated by dividing the total received over 52 weeks by 52.[142] If this gives a figure which the CSA decides is not representative of the income produced, it can use another period.

Where capital is jointly held and the shares are unknown, any income from the capital is divided equally between the joint owners.[143] If capital is divided on divorce, dissolution of a civil partnership or separation and it is intended for the purchase of a new home or furnishings, income from that capital will be ignored for one year.[144]

Although CSA staff are given examples of what may constitute capital and ownership, there is no guidance on the calculation of income from different types of capital.[145] It is the actual income received which must be taken into account, although in some cases this may be apportioned (ie, if capital is jointly owned).

Prisoners' pay

Unless they have another source of income, prisoners receiving only prisoners' pay will be assumed to have no net income and will be exempt from paying child support.[146]

Regular charitable or voluntary payments

These are disregarded in full if they are intended and used for any items *other than* food, ordinary clothing, household fuel, housing costs or council tax.[147] There has to be a mutual understanding between the donor and the recipient as to the purpose of the payment, but this does not need to be a formal agreement.[148] If the payment is for school fees, it is not counted as income at all even if part of the school fees relates to one of the specified items – eg, school meals.[149]

If the payment is for one of these specified items, the first £20 will be disregarded, although no more than £20 in total can be disregarded from the total of a student's income (see p245), a war pension (see p243) and such voluntary payments.[150] See p282 for the position if the voluntary or charitable payment is made direct to a third party.

This provision does not apply to payments made by non-resident parents which are treated as maintenance (see p246).

Other disregarded income

The following will also not be taken into account as income:
- any income tax payments;[151]
- payments in kind (except for self-employed earners);[152]
- payments made instead of Healthy Start vouchers;[153]
- all NHS health benefits such as fares to hospital;[154]
- payments for prison visits;[155]
- payments made by a local authority to help a child take advantage of a course of study or educational facilities, including a scholarship, or an assisted place;[156]
- payments under a mortgage protection insurance policy to the extent that they exceed the interest, capital payments and any further mortgage protection premiums;[157]

- payments of expenses to unpaid voluntary workers (as long as the expenses cannot be treated as notional earnings);[158]
- payments made to assist a person with a disability to obtain or keep employment;[159]
- payments made to a person under the relevant community care provision to enable her/him to obtain community care services;[160]
- payments made by a local authority for welfare services or housing services;[161]
- payments made by a health authority, local authority or voluntary organisation for a person who is temporarily a member of the household in order to receive care;[162]
- compensation for personal injury and any payments made from a trust fund set up for that purpose[163]
- payments from the Macfarlane Trust, Independent Living (1993) Fund or Independent Living (Extension) Fund;[164]
- payments from the Family Fund;[165]
- payments (other than those for lost earnings and benefits) made to jurors and witnesses for court attendance;[166]
- certain home income annuities purchased when aged 65 or over;[167]
- charges for converting payments in another currency to sterling;[168]
- amounts payable outside the UK where transfer to the UK is prohibited;[169] *and*
- payments to a person as a result of holding the Victoria or George Cross.[170]

Children's income

If the parent has a child of her/his own living with her/him for at least 104 nights a year, the income of that child may be included in the parent's net income.[171] This does not have effect where the child is *not* a child of the parent whose income is being assessed. If a parent of the qualifying child has, for example, stepchildren or grandchildren living with her/him, the income of these children does not count in calculating net income at assessable income stage, but it is taken into account at the protected income stage.

The child's income is taken to be her/his own parent's income when calculating both net income for assessable income purposes and total family income for protected income purposes. However, the child's income is *not* included when calculating the net income of her/his parent's partner in order to find out whether the partner can help support a joint child included in the exempt income (see p276).[172]

What counts as the child's income

Child maintenance already being received for a qualifying child who is the subject of the assessment being undertaken is ignored in full.[173] Child dependency increases of any benefit received by an adult are income of the child which is included in the parent's net income, if applicable.[174]

The following are *not* included when calculating the child's income and are, therefore, not part of a parent's net income.[175]

- a child's earnings;
- payments by a non-resident parent to the child for whom maintenance is being assessed;
- interest payable on arrears of child maintenance;
- payments from a discretionary fund which benefit the child, as long as they do not cover food, ordinary clothing/footwear, household fuel or housing costs.

How much of the child's income counts as the parent's

The first £10 a week of any income of a child is ignored.[176] In addition, once the child's income is treated as that of her/his parent, the same disregards apply as for the parent's own income.[177]

How much of the child's net income is taken into account as her/his parent's income depends on whether the child is the subject of the maintenance assessment. If the child is *not* the subject of the maintenance assessment, her/his income up to the amount of the personal allowance (and any disabled child premium) included in the exempt income calculation in respect of that child is counted as the parent's income.[178] Income above that amount is disregarded.

If the child is the subject of the maintenance assessment, the child's income counts in full if s/he is the only child for whom an assessment is being made.[179] Where there is more than one child, each child's income is counted up to the level of the child's proportion of the maximum child maintenance payment (see p266) – ie, a share of the maintenance requirement plus 1.5 times the basic rate of the family premium and the personal allowance.[180]

At the protected income stage of the formula, the rules about how much of the child's income is taken into account are different (see p282).

Notional income

Parents can be assumed to have income which they do not possess.[181] Such 'notional income' is treated in the same way as if it were actual income.[182] In practice, this provision is not used very often, and parents who are contesting the other party's income may want to remind the CSA that notional income should be considered.

Notional earnings

The issue of notional earnings arises where a person has done some work without being paid or at an insufficient rate for the job for an employer who could afford to pay full wages.[183] This cannot apply if the employer is a charity or voluntary organisation, or a member of the parent's family. The estimated forgone income is treated as earnings if the CSA decides that the principal purpose of the person doing the work without pay or for reduced pay was to reduce her/his assessable

income. To estimate an appropriate level of forgone earnings the decision maker has to consider:[184]
- the nature of the service from which the employer benefits;
- the comparable rate of pay;
- the means of the employer.

If the question of notional earnings is raised, the parent should let the CSA know her/his motives for doing the work. For example, notional earnings will be an issue where a parent is paid via a personal service company at less than the market rate.[185] In such a case, if the principal purpose was for business and tax reasons, notional income cannot be included.[186]

Deprivation of income or capital

If the CSA decides that a parent has intentionally deprived her/himself of income in order to reduce her/his assessable income, an amount equal to that income will be included in her/his net income.[187]

This rule applies equally to capital which would have been a source of income – eg, where shares are given away or sold at less than their market value.[188] Lump sum voluntary contributions towards a retirement annuity contract may count as deprivation of capital.[189] The CSA has to estimate a notional income from the notional capital, and guidance to CSA staff suggests that it may be reasonable to use rates of interest paid by high street banks and building societies.[190] When the CSA has decided that a certain sum is notional capital, that capital is reduced after 52 weeks by an amount equal to the income which would have been generated from that capital over the year.[191]

Deprivation refers both to income or capital that a person has disposed of or failed to obtain – eg, by failing to apply for a benefit. However, it does not apply to contribution-based JSA if IS is payable, nor to a payment from a discretionary trust or a trust set up with personal injury compensation.[192] Apart from social security benefits and WTC, other examples given to CSA staff of payments which could be acquired include unclaimed Premium Bond wins.[193] Where income would have been available to a parent on application, an estimated amount is included in her/his net income from the date on which it could be expected to have been paid.[194]

The CSA is most likely to identify a potential deprivation of income or capital where it finds that a source of income previously declared is no longer included.[195] The first question to be considered is whether the parent has actually disposed of the income or capital, and the onus is on the parent to prove s/he no longer has the resource.[196] CSA staff are given examples of deprivation of capital, although it is emphasised that these may not have been done for the purposes of reducing assessable income – eg, making a lump-sum payment, putting money into a trust which cannot be revoked, gambling, using capital to fund an extravagant lifestyle or purchase personal possessions.[197] Deprivation can apply to a parent who has transferred assets to a new partner or possibly to a self-employed parent who is paying his partner a reasonable salary but not drawing much himself. Once it is shown s/he no longer possesses it, the intention behind the deprivation has to be examined and on the balance of probabilities the CSA must decide whether the aim was to reduce assessable income for child support purposes.[198]

This rule is similar, but not identical, to those for means-tested benefits (see CPAG's *Welfare Benefits and Tax Credits Handbook*) and an adviser should, therefore, consider whether any social security commissioners' decisions could be cited as persuasive. Although it may be argued that the reduction of assessable income need not be the only, or even principal, motive, the CSA has to be able to show that it is satisfied that such an intention existed and that it was a significant purpose for the parent's actions. The onus of proof remains with the CSA.[199]

When deciding whether reducing assessable income was a significant factor in the disposal of the resource, CSA staff are advised to consider all the parent's reasons and the timing of the action.[200] If deprivation of capital is an issue, the CSA will consider whether the parent was aware that reducing capital would reduce the maintenance assessment.

This deprivation rule cannot be used against a parent who refuses an offer of employment,[201] but it might be applied to a non-resident parent who gave up his job.[202] It would have to be shown that by leaving the employment he had intentionally deprived himself of income, and that he did so with the intention of reducing his assessable income.

Deprivation is probably not applicable to a case where a parent has taken out a higher mortgage which reduces her/his assessable income.[203] A non-resident parent in this situation needs to consider the excessive housing costs rule (see p318). On the other hand, the use of capital as a deposit to buy a property could possibly be considered to be deprivation and motives would need to be examined.

Payments to third parties

If a payment is made on behalf of a parent or a child to a third party, it will only be treated as the parent's income if it is a payment for food, ordinary clothing or footwear, household fuel, housing costs or council tax.[204] For example, if a grandparent paid the parent's fuel bill direct to the fuel company, this would be notional income, whereas paying the telephone bill would not. Some of this notional income can be disregarded as a voluntary payment if made regularly (see p248).

A payment made by a partner to meet her/his own liability (eg, for a mortgage to a building society) is not made on behalf of the parent or child.[205] The same applies to payments made by an ex-partner for his own liability towards the former joint home in which the parent with care remains, whereas payments made by him towards her part of the mortgage count as the parent with care's income (see also p246).[206]

3. **Calculating assessable income**

Assessable income is the parent's total net income less her/his exempt income. For details of exempt income, see Chapter 11.

If the parent's exempt income is higher than her/his net income, assessable income is taken to be nil.[207] If his assessable income is nil, the non-resident parent may still have to make the minimum payment of child maintenance. There is, however, no need to continue with the steps of the formula in this case as the maintenance due will either be the minimum payment of £6 or nil (see p199). If a non-resident parent's net income is itself less than £6, he is exempt from paying child maintenance.[208]

If the parent with care's assessable income is nil, the proposed maintenance step is carried out with just the non-resident parent's assessable income.

Example: assessable income of a non-resident parent

Bob is living in a bedsit on his own. His exempt income is £107.15 (see p212). His income is £154 a week in earnings after tax, national insurance and £12 weekly superannuation contribution. Only half his superannuation is taken into account when calculating Bob's net earnings for child support purposes, which are £154 + £6 = £160

Bob's net income is, therefore, his net earnings = £160

	£
Net income	160.00
Less exempt income	107.15
Assessable income	**52.85**

Bob moves in with Zoe and her three children (see p220).

	£
Net income	160.00
Less exempt income	104.15
Assessable income	**55.85**

Bob is in receipt of long-term incapacity benefit (IB) of £98.45 and lives with his parents (see p212).

	£
Net income	98.45
Less exempt income	84.40
Assessable income	**14.05**

If Bob were receiving the higher rate short-term IB of £72.55, his assessable income would be nil. He would be exempt from the minimum payment (see p199) and would receive a nil assessment. No further calculation would be required.

Example: assessable income of a parent with care

While Anita is on income support (IS) or working tax credit (WTC), she is automatically treated as having no assessable income.

Anita receives child benefit of £30.20 (this is ignored in net income). Bob has been paying £30.50 a week in maintenance for Carol (13) and David (8). This is not taken into account as income because it is maintenance for the qualifying children – ie, the children for whom the re-assessment is being carried out.

Anita is now bringing home £265 a week (after tax, national insurance and a £15 superannuation contribution). She is entitled to child tax credit (CTC) (which is ignored as income) but not to any WTC. Only half of the superannuation payment can be taken into account (ie, £7.50) and, therefore, her net earnings for exempt income purposes are now £272.50 a week.

	£
Earnings	272.50
Total net income	272.50
Less exempt income (from p220)	245.48
Assessable income	**27.02**

Anita remarries. She brings home £195 a week after tax, national insurance and a £15 superannuation contribution. Her husband, Joe, earns £205 a week.
Net income is now £202.50. Joe's income is not taken into account.

	£
Net income	202.50
Less exempt income (from p221)	308.26
Assessable income	**Nil**

Example: Bob and Zoe have a baby

Bob is now living with Zoe, their son Ricky and three stepchildren (aged 13, 11 and 4 years old). The exempt income is £168.03 (see p228). Bob's net earnings are £260 a week. Any income of Zoe's is not taken into account, including the maintenance of £20 a week for her daughters. The couple receive £158 CTC a week, which is ignored.

	£
Earnings (Bob)	260.00
Total net income	260.00
Less exempt income	168.03
Bob's assessable income	**91.97**

Zoe begins paid work, bringing home £95 a week. The total net income remains at £260, as Zoe's earnings are not taken into account at this stage. However, her earnings have affected the exempt income (see p228) as she is now helping to support Ricky.

	£
Total net income	260.00
Less exempt income	136.10
Bob's assessable income	**123.90**

As the increase in their annual income is less than £25,000, it will not affect their final entitlement to CTC for the current tax year. In the next tax year, assuming no further changes in income, it will be taken into account and reduce their tax credits. In the meantime, the tax credit calculation will be affected by Ricky's first birthday and, if Zoë works 16 hours or more a week, by the childcare element (if they use eligible childcare). This does not affect assessable income, but it may affect the calculation at the protected income stage.

Notes

1. What is assessable income
1 Sch 1 para 5(1) and (2) CSA 1991
2 Regs 8 and 10 CS(MASC) Regs
3 Sch 1 para 5(4) CSA 1991; Reg 10B CS(MASC) Regs
4 Reg 10A CS(MASC) Regs
5 Reg 10A(2) CS(MASC) Regs

2. What is net income
6 Reg 7(1) CS(MASC) Regs
7 Sch 1 CS(MASC) Regs
8 Sch 2 CS(MASC) Regs
9 Reg 9(2)(c) CS(MASC) Regs
10 Reg 11(2) CS(MASC) Regs
11 Reg 7(5) CS(MASC) Regs
12 Reg 7(4) CS(MASC) Regs
13 Sch 1 para 9(a) CSA 1991; reg 7(1)(d) CS(MASC) Regs
14 Reg 1(2) CS(MASC) Regs
15 Sch 1 para 2(3A) CS(MASC) Regs
16 Reg 1(2) CS(MASC) Regs
17 Sch 1 para 1(1) CS(MASC) Regs
18 Sch 1 para 1(1)(gg) CS(MASC) Regs
19 Sch 2 para 48B CS(MASC) Regs
20 DMG paras 4107-22
21 CCS/2287/2006; CCS/3499/2004; CCS/3671/2002
22 CCS/2750/1995; CCS/318/1995
23 CCS/11364/1995; R(CS) 2/96; CCS/4/1994; CCS/10/1994; CCS/12598/1996; CCS/1321/1997; CCS/2320/1997; CCS/2561/1998; CCS/5352/1995
24 Sch 1 para 1(2) CS(MASC) Regs
25 Sch 2 para 6 CS(MASC) Regs
26 CCS/11252/1995; CCS/5352/1995
27 CCS/3182/1995
28 DMG para 4102
29 R(CS) 2/96 (CCS/4/1994)
30 CCS/12073/1996
31 CCS/318/1995
32 CCS/10/1994; CCS/12598/1996; CCS/1321/1997; CCS/2320/1997; CCS/2561/1998
33 CCS/5352/1995
34 CCS/11242/1995
35 CCS/12769/1996
36 CCS/6807/1995
37 Sch 1 para 2(1) CS(MASC) Regs
38 DMG paras 4051-52 and 4073
39 Sch 1 para 2(3) CS(MASC) Regs
40 Sch 1 para 2(4) CS(MASC) Regs
41 CCS/16/1994; CCS/11873/1996
42 DMG paras 4069-72; CCS/6810/1995
43 CCS/511/1995
44 CCS/7312/1995; CCS/556/1995; CSCS/1/1996; CSCS/6/1996
45 Sch 1 para 2(2) CS(MASC) Regs
46 CCS/5079/1995
47 Reg 2(3) CS(MASC) Regs
48 CCS/2750/1995
49 CCS/556/1995
50 Sch 1 para 1(3) CS(MASC) Regs
51 CSCS/5/1994
52 CCS/3542/1998
53 Sch 1 para 1(3) CS(MASC) Regs
54 Reg 1(2A) CS(MASC) Regs
55 Sch 1 para 2A(1) CS(MASC) Regs
56 Sch 1 para 2B(1)(a) CS(MASC) Regs

57 *Smith v Secretary of State for Work and Pensions and another* [2006] UKHL 35
58 Sch 1 para 2B(1)(b) CS(MASC) Regs
59 Sch 1 para 2C CS(MASC) Regs
60 Sch 1 para 2A(2) CS(MASC) Regs
61 Sch 1 para 5A(1) CS(MASC) Regs
62 Sch 1 para 5A(2) CS(MASC) Regs
63 Sch 1 para 5A(3) CS(MASC) Regs
64 DMG para 4244
65 *Smith v Secretary of State for Work and Pensions* [2006] UKHL 35
66 House of Commons Select Committee on Work and Pensions, *Fourth Report,* 7 March 2007, para 122
67 Sch 1 para 3(1) and (2)(a) CS(MASC) Regs
68 Sch 1 para 3(2)(b) CS(MASC) Regs; DMG para 4601
69 Sch 1 para 4 CS(MASC) Regs
70 Sch 1 para 3(3) CS(MASC) Regs
71 Sch 1 para 3(6) and (8) CS(MASC) Regs
72 DMG para 4287
73 DMG paras 4289-91
74 DMG paras 4327-42
75 Sch 1 para 3(4)(a) CS(MASC) Regs
76 CCS/15949/1996
77 Sch 1 para 3(4)(b) CS(MASC) Regs
78 Sch 1 para 3(7) CS(MASC) Regs; DMG paras 4410-18
79 Sch 1 para 5(2) CS(MASC) Regs
80 CCS/1938/2006
81 Sch 1 para 5(2A) CS(MASC) Regs
82 DMG paras 4251-53
83 Sch 1 para 5(1) CS(MASC) Regs
84 DMG paras 4218-20
85 Sch 1 para 5(2) CS(MASC) Regs; DMG paras 4281-82
86 Sch 1 para 5(3) CS(MASC) Regs
87 DMG paras 4240-41
88 CCS/3182/1995; CCS/6145/1995
89 Sch 1 para 5(5) CS(MASC) Regs
90 CCS/7966/1995
91 CCS/13988/96; CCS/2901/02
92 Sch 1 para 6 CS(MASC) Regs; reg 10B CS(MASC) Regs
93 Sch 1 para 6(3) CS(MASC) Regs
94 Sch 1 para 7(1) CS(MASC) Regs
95 Sch 1 paras 9A and 22(1B) CS(MASC) Regs
96 Sch 2 para 16 CS(MASC) Regs
97 Reg 11(2)(a)(i) CS(MASC) Regs
98 Sch 2 para 7 CS(MASC) Regs
99 Sch 2 para 7 CS(MASC) Regs
100 Sch 2 para 8 CS(MASC) Regs
101 Sch 2 para 9 CS(MASC) Regs
102 Sch 2 para 11 CS(MASC) Regs
103 Sch 2 para 48A CS(MASC) Regs
104 Sch 2 para 10 CS(MASC) Regs

105 Sch 2 paras 8 and 12-15 CS(MASC) Regs
106 Sch 2 para 40 CS(MASC) Regs
107 Sch 2 para 18 CS(MASC) Regs
108 Sch 1 para 16 CS(MASC) Regs
109 Sch 1 para 15 CS(MASC) Regs
110 Sch 1 para 14B CS(MASC) Regs
111 Sch 2 para 48D CS(MASC) Regs
112 Sch 1 para 9 CS(MASC) Regs
113 Sch 2 para 35 CS(MASC) Regs
114 Sch 2 para 24 CS(MASC) Regs
115 Sch 2 para 22 CS(MASC) Regs
116 Sch 2 para 2 CS(MASC) Regs
117 Sch 2 para 23 CS(MASC) Regs
118 CCS/5310/1995; CCS/3542/1998; DMG para 4669
119 Reg 1(2) CS(MASC) Regs; DMG paras 4962 and 4965
120 DMG para 4966
121 Regs 7(3)(b) and 26(1)(b)(v) CS(MASC) Regs
122 Sch 1 paras 11 and 12 CS(MASC) Regs; DMG para 4937
123 Sch 1 para 16(3) CS(MASC) Regs
124 Sch 1 para 16(4) CS(MASC) Regs
125 Sch 2 para 20 CS(MASC) Regs
126 Sch 2 paras 36 and 36A CS(MASC) Regs
127 DMG paras 4150-53
128 Sch 2 para 21 CS(MASC) Regs
129 Regs 7(3)(a) and 26(1)(b)(v) CS(MASC) Regs; DMG para 4002
130 Sch 1 paras 14 and 16(2) CS(MASC) Regs
131 CCS/13698/1996; CCS/13923/1996
132 DMG paras 4610-11
133 Sch 2 para 28 CS(MASC) Regs
134 Reg 11(2) CS(MASC) Regs
135 Schs 1 para 15 and 2 para 44 CS(MASC) Regs
136 CCS/4514/1995
137 Sch 2 para 29 CS(MASC) Regs; the payments are made under the Children Act 1989, the Social Work (Scotland) Act 1968 or the Boarding and Fostering Out of Children (Scotland) Regulations 1985
138 Sch 2 para 31 CS(MASC) Regs; these payments are made under the Children Act 1989
139 Sch 2 para 26 CS(MASC) Regs
140 Sch 2 para 25 CS(MASC) Regs
141 DMG para 4615
142 Sch 1 para 16(5) and (6) CS(MASC) Regs; DMG para 4614
143 Reg 7(4) CS(MASC) Regs
144 Sch 2 para 45 CS(MASC) Regs; CCS/4923/1995
145 DMG paras 4613-31
146 Regs 7(3) and 26(1)(b) CS(MASC) Regs

147 Sch 2 para 19 CS(MASC) Regs; DMG para 4699
148 R(SB) 53/83; CCS/15/1994
149 Sch 1 para 31 CS(MASC) Regs
150 Sch 2 paras 19 and 20 CS(MASC) Regs
151 Sch 2 para 2 CS(MASC) Regs
152 Sch 2 para 46 CS(MASC) Regs
153 Sch 2 para 17 CS(MASC) Regs
154 Sch 2 para 33 CS(MASC) Regs
155 Sch 2 para 42 CS(MASC) Regs
156 Sch 2 para 36 CS(MASC) Regs
157 Sch 2 para 27 CS(MASC) Regs
158 Sch 2 para 48 CS(MASC) Regs
159 Sch 2 para 34 CS(MASC) Regs
160 Sch 2 para 48C CS(MASC) Regs
161 Sch 2 para 48D CS(MASC) Regs
162 Sch 2 para 30 CS(MASC) Regs; this refers to payments made under s93(1) and (2) Local Government Act 2000 or s91(1) Housing (Scotland) Act 2001
163 Sch 2 para 5 CS(MASC) Regs
164 Sch 2 para 38 CS(MASC) Regs
165 Sch 2 para 47 CS(MASC) Regs
166 Sch 2 para 39 CS(MASC) Regs
167 Sch 2 para 37 CS(MASC) Regs
168 Sch 2 para 3 CS(MASC) Regs
169 Sch 2 para 4 CS(MASC) Regs
170 Sch 2 para 41 CS(MASC) Regs
171 Sch 1 Part IV CS(MASC) Regs
172 Reg 9(2)(c) CS(MASC) Regs
173 Sch 2 para 28 CS(MASC) Regs
174 Sch 1 paras 7 and 22 CS(MASC) Regs
175 Sch 1 para 23 CS(MASC) Regs
176 Sch 1 para 23 CS(MASC) Regs
177 Sch 1 para 24 CS(MASC) Regs
178 Sch 1 para 21 CS(MASC) Regs
179 Sch 1 para 19 CS(MASC) Regs
180 Sch 1 para 20 CS(MASC) Regs
181 Reg 7(1)(e) and Sch 1 Part V CS(MASC) Regs
182 Sch 1 para 32 CS(MASC) Regs
183 Sch 1 para 26 CS(MASC) Regs; DMG para 4831
184 DMG paras 4850-51
185 CCS/4912/1998
186 CCS/3675/2004
187 Sch 1 para 27 CS(MASC) Regs
188 CCS/4912/1998; DMG para 4875
189 CCS/3542/1998
190 DMG paras 4902-03
191 Sch 1 para 30 CS(MASC) Regs; DMG para 4911
192 Sch 1 para 28 CS(MASC) Regs
193 DMG para 4901
194 Sch 1 para 29 CS(MASC) Regs
195 DMG paras 4808 and 4889

196 R(SB) 38/85; DMG paras 4811 and 4890
197 DMG para 4891
198 CCS/8172/1995; DMG paras 4885 and 4892-94
199 R(SB) 38/85
200 DMG paras 4893-94
201 CCS/7967/1995
202 CCS/4056/2004
203 CCS/6/1995
204 Sch 1 para 31 CS(MASC) Regs; DMG paras 4865 and 4868
205 CCS/6/1995
206 CSCS/8/1995; CSCS/1/1996; CCS/ 8189/1995

3. **Calculating assessable income**
207 Sch 1 para 5(3) CSA 1991
208 Reg 26(1)(b)(v) CS(MASC) Regs

Chapter 13

Proposed maintenance ('old rules')

This chapter covers:
1. What is proposed maintenance (below)
2. How much is proposed maintenance (p259)
3. The 50 per cent calculation (p260)
4. The additional element calculation (p263)
5. Maximum child maintenance (p266)
6. Both parents are non-resident (p269)
7. More than one person with care (p271)
8. Divided families (p275)
9. More than one non-resident parent (p276)

1. What is proposed maintenance

'Proposed maintenance' is not a term which is used in the legislation. We use it to describe the amount of child maintenance that, given the maintenance requirement and the assessable income of the parents, the non-resident parent would be expected to pay. There is no specific legal term for this amount; it is already referred to in the legislation as 'the amount of the assessment'. However, the proposed maintenance step is not the end of the maintenance assessment. The protected income calculation still has to be done and this may reduce the amount of child maintenance payable. Therefore, a term is needed for this intermediate stage. The Child Support Agency uses the phrase 'the non-resident parent's notional assessment'.

Although the proposed maintenance figure may be reduced by the protected income calculation, it will never be increased. No non-resident parent ever pays more than the proposed maintenance figure.

There is a lot of misunderstanding about the way in which the income of a partner of the non-resident parent affects the maintenance assessment. At the protected income stage (see Chapter 14) the partner's income *is* taken into account in order to assess whether the family as a whole can afford the proposed maintenance. However, the partner's income *cannot* increase the assessment above the proposed maintenance which is arrived at using the non-resident parent's net income (see p234). The income of the partner is also used to decide whether she can help support their own children (see p228). If the partner objects to providing income details, the non-resident parent could consider the option of withholding the information and accepting a Category B interim maintenance assessment.

2. How much is proposed maintenance

Proposed maintenance is based on the assessable incomes of both parents. In some situations a deduction rate of 50 per cent assessable income is used and in others, a more complex calculation must be carried out. The 50 per cent calculation gives an amount of proposed maintenance which is smaller than the maintenance requirement figure (from Step 1). The additional element calculation applies where the parents have higher incomes and the maintenance requirement figure is met. The calculation for proposed maintenance becomes increasingly complex with more complex family situations.

To illustrate the principles of proposed maintenance, we first give an overview of the calculation (see below). To help readers through this step of the formula, we then identify the four situations, beginning with the most straightforward, in which the calculation of proposed maintenance varies:

- the 50 per cent calculation of proposed maintenance where the parent with care has no assessable income (see p260);
- the 50 per cent calculation of proposed maintenance where both parents have assessable income (see p261);
- the additional element calculation of proposed maintenance where the parent with care has no assessable income (see p263);
- the additional element calculation of proposed maintenance where both parents have assessable income (see p266).

These calculations are adapted if both parents are non-resident, or where there is more than one non-resident parent or more than one parent with care.

Overview of proposed maintenance

There are two alternative calculations.

- The 50 per cent calculation if the maintenance requirement is not met.
- The additional element calculation if the maintenance requirement is met.

To decide which to use, first do the 50 per cent calculation:[1]
- Add together both parents' assessable incomes (if the parent with care is on income support, income-based jobseeker's allowance, pension credit or working tax credit, her assessable income is nil).
- Take 50 per cent of the joint assessable income.
- Compare the figure obtained with the maintenance requirement (from Step 1 as calculated in Chapter 10).

If 50 per cent of the joint assessable income is less than or equal to the maintenance requirement, the proposed maintenance is 50 per cent of the non-resident parent's assessable income.[2]

If 50 per cent of the joint assessable income is higher than the maintenance requirement, the additional element calculation must be done. This involves two components of proposed maintenance: a basic element and an additional element (see p263).[3] The end result is that the non-resident parent pays less than 50 per cent of his assessable income overall, but more than the maintenance requirement.

The general rule is that 50 per cent of the parents' assessable income goes towards child maintenance until the maintenance requirement is met.[4] Once the maintenance requirement is met, the non-resident parent continues to pay maintenance. However, only 15, 20 or 25 per cent of his remaining assessable income is paid as maintenance and only up to a maximum amount.[5]

Both parents are liable to maintain their child(ren) and, therefore, both their assessable incomes must be taken into account when calculating whether the maintenance requirement has been met. Although the assessable income of the parent with care may reduce the proposed maintenance, she will never end up paying child maintenance herself.

If the assessable income of the non-resident parent is nil, then the proposed maintenance is nil and the minimum payment rules must be considered (see p199). The non-resident parent either pays £6 or is exempt. Similarly, if the proposed maintenance is less than £6, the non-resident parent pays the minimum payment of £6 unless he is exempt. In these cases there is no need to calculate the protected income level as the proposed maintenance cannot be further reduced.

3. **The 50 per cent calculation**

Once assessable income has been calculated for both parents, the next step is to check whether the 50 per cent calculation is applicable. If the parent with care has assessable income, see p261.

The parent with care has no assessable income

In most cases the parent with care will have no assessable income – eg, because she is on income support (IS) or working tax credit (WTC).

---

50 per cent calculation if the parent with care has no assessable income
- Take 50 per cent of the non-resident parent's assessable income.
- Compare the figure obtained with the maintenance requirement (from Step 1 as calculated in Chapter 10).

If 50 per cent of the non-resident parent's assessable income is less than or equal to the maintenance requirement, the proposed maintenance is this figure – ie, 50 per cent of his assessable income.[6]

If 50 per cent of the non-resident parent's assessable income is higher than the maintenance requirement, the additional element calculation is used to obtain proposed maintenance (see p263).

In these cases, the proposed maintenance calculation ends at this point, and the protected income calculation must now be done (see Chapter 14).

Example: 50 per cent calculation if the parent with care has no assessable income

Anita is on IS and, therefore, has no assessable income.

The maintenance requirement is £140.28 (see p205).

Bob is living on his own and has assessable income of £52.85 (see p253). As Anita has no assessable income, the first stage is to take 50 per cent of Bob's assessable income.

50 per cent of Bob's assessable income = 50% x £52.85 = £26.43

This is less than £140.28 (the maintenance requirement) and, therefore, £26.43 is the proposed maintenance for Carol and David.

Bob is living with Zoe, three stepchildren and his baby son. His assessable income is £91.97 (see p253).

50 per cent of Bob's assessable income = 50% x £91.97 = £45.99

This is less than £140.28 (the maintenance requirement) and, therefore, £45.99 is the proposed maintenance.

Note: the maintenance payable may be reduced by the protected income step.

The parent with care has assessable income

Even when the parent with care has assessable income, this income does not necessarily affect the proposed maintenance. If, together, the parents do not have enough joint assessable income for half of it to meet the maintenance requirement, the non-resident parent pays half of his own assessable income. This is exactly what he would have paid anyway had the parent with care had no assessable income.

50 per cent calculation if the parent with care has assessable income

- Add both parents' assessable incomes to give joint assessable income.
- Take 50 per cent of the joint assessable income.
- Compare the 50 per cent figure with the maintenance requirement (from Step 1 as calculated in Chapter 10).

If 50 per cent of the joint assessable income is less than or equal to the maintenance requirement, take 50 per cent of the non-resident parent's own assessable income to give proposed maintenance.

If 50 per cent of the joint assessable income is higher than the maintenance requirement, the additional element calculation must be done (see p265).

A parent with care's income does not reduce the maintenance she receives unless her notional contribution towards the maintenance requirement *plus* the non-resident parent's proposed maintenance is over the maintenance requirement. The level of the joint assessable income is the deciding factor. The higher the assessable income of a non-resident parent, the sooner the assessable income of the parent with care will reduce the maintenance payable (see p265).

Example: 50 per cent calculation if both parents have assessable income

Anita is now working full time and has assessable income of £27.02 (see p253).
Bob's assessable income = £52.85 (see p253)
Joint assessable income = £52.85 + £27.02 = £79.87
50 per cent of joint assessable income = 50% x £79.87 = £39.94
This is well below the maintenance requirement of £140.28 (see p205) and so Bob pays 50 per cent of his own assessable income (assuming the protected income calculation allows it).
Proposed maintenance = 50% x £52.85 = **£26.43 a week**.
This is the same amount of proposed maintenance as when Anita had no assessable income (see p261). In this case, Anita takes home £265 a week. Although this is more than Bob, who takes home £154, her income still does not affect the level of proposed maintenance for David and Carol.

If Bob had net earnings for child support of £380 a week (rather than £160 as in the previous example), his assessable income would be £272.85
Anita's assessable income = £27.02
Joint assessable income = £27.02 + £272.85 = £299.87

50 per cent of joint assessable income = 50% x £299.87 = **£149.94**
This is above the maintenance requirement of £140.28 and so the additional element calculation would have to be done to calculate the proposed maintenance (see p265). Anita's assessable income, although still £27.02, would now reduce the proposed maintenance. This is because Bob's assessable income is higher and together they meet the maintenance requirement.

4. **The additional element calculation**

An alternative calculation is used to obtain the proposed maintenance if half of the parents' joint assessable incomes is more than the maintenance requirement.

Proposed maintenance is composed of a basic element and an additional element. Likewise, the non-resident parent's total assessable income is composed of basic assessable income and additional assessable income.

The basic assessable income contributes towards the basic element at the rate of 50 per cent. The additional assessable income contributes towards the additional element at a lower rate, up to a maximum amount. The deduction rate is 15 per cent if there is one qualifying child, 20 per cent if there are two, and 25 per cent if there are three or more qualifying children in the assessment.[7]

The assessable incomes of both parents are taken into account in calculating the basic proposed maintenance. However, to illustrate the principle of what is a complex calculation, we first address the situation where only the non-resident parent has assessable income.

The parent with care has no assessable income

If 50 per cent of the non-resident parent's assessable income is higher than the maintenance requirement, ignore the 50 per cent figure and continue as described below.

If the parent with care has no assessable income, the basic element equals the maintenance requirement.[8] As basic assessable income contributes towards the basic element at the rate of 50 per cent, the non-resident parent must (in order to meet the maintenance requirement) use up assessable income equal to twice the maintenance requirement. Additional assessable income which is not used up in meeting the maintenance requirement contributes towards the additional element at the rate of 15, 20 or 25 per cent.

The non-resident parent thus pays more than the maintenance requirement, but overall less than 50 per cent of his assessable income.

When proposed maintenance has been obtained using the additional element calculation, this figure must be compared with the maximum amount (see p266).

Additional element calculation if the parent with care has no assessable income

To calculate the proposed maintenance if only the non-resident parent has assessable income and the 50 per cent calculation has shown that it more than meets the maintenance requirement:

- Multiply the maintenance requirement (the basic element) by two to give the basic assessable income.
- Deduct the basic assessable income from the total assessable income to give the additional assessable income.
- Take:
  - 15 per cent if there is one qualifying child; *or*
  - 20 per cent if there are two qualifying children; *or*
  - 25 per cent if there are three or more qualifying children,

  of the additional assessable income to give the additional element.
- Add the basic element (the maintenance requirement) to the additional element to give the proposed maintenance.

Example: additional element calculation where the parent with care has no assessable income

Jeremy has just left his wife, Evie, who has no income of her own other than child benefit and child tax credit. They have four children, Francis (14), Georgina (12), Henry (8) and Isobel (4), who are all living with Evie.

The maintenance requirement is therefore:

		£
Personal allowances	Evie	59.15
	Francis	47.45
	Georgina	47.45
	Henry	47.45
	Isobel	47.45
Family premium		16.43
Sub-total		265.38
Less child benefit (see p204)		54.40
Maintenance requirement		**210.98**

Jeremy has an assessable income of £600 a week.

50% x £600 = £300

This is above the maintenance requirement of £210.98. Therefore, to calculate proposed maintenance, do the additional element calculation:

Basic element = £210.98 (the maintenance requirement)

Basic assessable income = 2 x £210.98 = £421.96

Additional assessable income = £600 − £421.96 = £178.04

Additional element = 25% x £178.04 = £44.51 (the 25 per cent deduction rate is applicable as there are four qualifying children)
Proposed maintenance = £210.98 + £44.51 = **£255.49**
Check whether this figure is above the maximum child maintenance payable (see example on p267).

The parent with care has assessable income

Both parents contribute towards the maintenance requirement if they can afford to do so, although in the case of a parent with care this is a notional transaction. If the parents together cannot meet the maintenance requirement, the income of the parent with care does not affect the maintenance assessment (see p261).

However, if 50 per cent of the parents' joint assessable income more than meets the maintenance requirement, the parent with care's assessable income reduces the non-resident parent's proposed maintenance. Each parent contributes towards the maintenance requirement in proportion to her/his assessable income. The parent with care's notional contribution towards the maintenance requirement reduces the amount of the non-resident parent's assessable income required to meet that maintenance requirement. Therefore, the non-resident parent begins paying at the lower deduction rate earlier than he otherwise would have done.

The additional element calculation is used to work out the proposed maintenance; the basic element does not now equal the full maintenance requirement, but only the proportion of the maintenance requirement that the non-resident parent has to contribute.[9] Once the basic element has been calculated, the rest of the calculation is the same as before.

The parent with care's assessable income can reduce the proposed maintenance below the maintenance requirement, but cannot reduce the non-resident parent's proposed maintenance to zero. The non-resident parent still pays at least some contribution towards the maintenance requirement and then a percentage of his additional assessable income.

Additional element calculation if parent with care has assessable income
To calculate proposed maintenance if the parents have joint assessable incomes, half of which more than meets the maintenance requirement:
- Add together both parents' assessable incomes to give their joint assessable income.
- Multiply the maintenance requirement by the non-resident parent's assessable income divided by the joint assessable income (ie, the non-resident parent's proportion of the joint assessable income) to give the basic element (ie, the non-resident parent's contribution to the maintenance requirement).
- Multiply the basic element by two to give the basic assessable income.

- Deduct the basic assessable income from the non-resident parent's total assessable income to give his additional assessable income.
- Take:
  - – 15 per cent if there is one qualifying child; *or*
  - – 20 per cent if there are two qualifying children; *or*
  - – 25 per cent if there are three or more qualifying children,

  of the additional assessable income to give the additional element.
- Add the basic element to the additional element to give the proposed maintenance.

Example: additional element calculation if both parents have assessable incomes
Evie has now taken a paid job. Her exempt income is high as it includes allowances for the four children and a significant mortgage. Although she is earning £26,000 a year, her assessable income is only £70 a week (she is not entitled to any working tax credit). Jeremy's assessable income is still £600 a week.
The maintenance requirement is still £210.98 (see p263).
Joint assessable income = £70 + £600 = £670
50 per cent of the joint assessable income is £335, which more than meets the maintenance requirement. Therefore, the additional element calculation of proposed maintenance has to be done:
Basic element (the proportion of the maintenance requirement that Jeremy has to pay) = £210.98 x (£600/£670) = £188.94
Basic assessable income = £188.94 x 2 = £377.87
Additional assessable income = £600 – £377.87 = £222.13
Additional element = £222.13 x 25% = £55.53
Proposed maintenance = £188.94 + £55.53 = **£244.47**
Check whether this figure is above the maximum child maintenance payable (see p267).

5. **Maximum child maintenance**

There is an upper limit on the amount of child maintenance payable for a child under the child support formula.[10] No further child maintenance is deducted from assessable income once the maximum is being paid.

When the maximum is being paid, the parties could go to court to seek any further maintenance. The courts can consider further weekly child maintenance in the context of any other arrangements which have been made for the children (see p28).

Like proposed maintenance, maximum child maintenance is composed of a basic element and an additional element. The basic element is the same as the basic element of proposed maintenance, whereas the additional element relates to the number and age of the qualifying children.[11]

Again, like proposed maintenance, the calculation varies slightly if the parent with care has assessable income.

The parent with care has no assessable income

When the parent with care has no assessable income, the basic element of maximum child maintenance equals the maintenance requirement. The maximum amount of child maintenance equals the maintenance requirement plus the additional element.

The additional element equals 1.5 times the total of the income support (IS) personal allowance for each child and the amount of the IS family premium for each child.[12]

Example: maximum child maintenance if the person with care has no assessable income

Assuming Evie has no assessable income of her own, the maximum Jeremy would have to pay for the four children, Francis (14), Georgina (12), Henry (8) and Isobel (4), is as follows: The maintenance requirement is £210.98 (see p261).

	£
Additional element = 1.5 x [(4 x £47.45) + (4 x £16.43)] = 1.5 x £255.52 =	383.28
Basic element	210.98
Additional element	383.28
Maximum child maintenance	**594.26**

Therefore, the proposed maintenance of £255.49 is less than the maximum.

In order to pay the maximum amount, Jeremy would have to have an assessable income of at least (£210.98 x 2) + (£383.28 x 4) = £1,955.08 a week.

The parent with care has assessable income

The non-resident parent is responsible only for paying the proportion of the maximum child maintenance which corresponds to his proportion of joint assessable income.

The basic element of the maximum child maintenance is the proportion of the maintenance requirement which the non-resident parent must contribute. It is calculated as for the additional element calculation for proposed maintenance – ie:

- *add* together both parents' assessable incomes to give their joint assessable income;

- *multiply* the maintenance requirement by the non-resident parent's assessable income divided by joint assessable income.

To calculate the additional element:
- multiply the total of the IS personal allowance for each child and the family premium for each child by 1.5; *then*
- multiply this figure by the non-resident parent's assessable income divided by the joint assessable income.

The maximum child maintenance equals the basic element plus the additional element.

Alternatively, there is a short cut for this calculation. Multiply the maximum amount, as calculated, where the parent has no assessable income by the non-resident parent's proportion of the joint assessable income.

Example: maximum child maintenance if the parent with care has assessable income

To check whether the proposed maintenance calculated in the example on p265 (£244.47) is above the maximum:

Evie's assessable income = £70

Jeremy's assessable income = £600

Joint assessable income = £670

The maintenance requirement = £210.98

Basic element = £210.98 x (£600/£670) = £188.94

Additional element = 1.5 ([4 x £47.45] + [4 x £16.43]) x (£600/£670) = £383.28 x (£600/£670) = £343.24

Maximum child maintenance = basic element plus the additional element = £188.94 + £343.24 = **£532.18**

(Alternatively, multiply the maximum figure from the example on p267 by Jeremy's proportion of joint assessable income: £594.26 x (£600/£670) = £532.17; the slight difference is due to the rounding up of the basic element and additional element figures).

Jeremy therefore pays the proposed maintenance of £244.47.

Evie's income has reduced the assessment by just £11.02.

6. **Both parents are non-resident**

If the person with care is not a parent, this usually means that there are two non-resident parents. If an application is made for maintenance from both parents, an assessment is carried out for each non-resident parent. The same maintenance requirement is used in both assessments (see p207).

When calculating the proposed maintenance for each parent, the other non-resident parent's assessable income is used where the parent with care's income would normally be taken into account – ie, to give joint assessable income.[13] In other words, the parents will together contribute towards the maintenance requirement at the rate of 50 per cent of assessable income and, once the maintenance requirement is met, each will pay a lower percentage of their own additional assessable income.

Example: proposed maintenance if both parents are non-resident

Zoe is looking after her 17-year-old niece, Rebecca, whose parents have separated. Zoe's income is not taken into account as she is not Rebecca's mother.

The maintenance requirement = £34.83 (see example on p207)

50 per cent calculation

Her mother's assessable income = £14.50

Her father's assessable income = £23.90

Joint assessable income = £38.40

50 per cent of joint assessable income = £19.20

This is less than the maintenance requirement.

Proposed maintenance from her mother = 50% x £14.50 = £7.25

Proposed maintenance from her father = 50% x £23.90 = £11.95

The additional element calculation

Her mother's assessable income = £52

Her father's assessable income = £84

Joint assessable income = £136

50 per cent of joint assessable income = £68

This is more than the maintenance requirement.

Therefore, the additional element calculation has to be done. The 15 per cent deduction rate is used as Rebecca is the only qualifying child in the assessment.

Mother's proposed maintenance:

Basic element = £34.83 x (£52/£136) = £13.32

Basic assessable income = £13.32 x 2 = £26.64

Additional assessable income = £52 – £26.64 = £25.36

Additional element = £25.36 x 15% = £3.80

Proposed maintenance from mother = £13.32 + £3.80 = £17.12

Father's proposed maintenance:

Basic element = £34.83 x (£84/£136) = £21.51

Basic assessable income = £21.51 x 2 = £43.02

Additional assessable income = £84 – £43.02 = £40.98

Additional element = £40.98 x 15% = £6.15

Proposed maintenance from father = £21.51 + £6.15 = £27.66

Note: the basic proposed maintenance from both parents is the maintenance requirement – ie, £13.32 + £21.51 = £34.83

An application is made for maintenance from the mother only. The maintenance requirement is therefore halved to £17.42

With assessable income of £14.50, the mother still cannot meet the maintenance requirement and, therefore, she pays 50% x £14.50 = £7.25. This is the same as in the 50 per cent calculation.

With assessable income of £52, the mother can now meet the maintenance requirement on her own (50% x £52 = £26). The basic element is the maintenance requirement of £17.42.

Basic assessable income = £17.42 x 2 = £34.84

Additional assessable income = £52 – £34.84 = £17.16

Additional element = £17.16 x 15% = £2.57

Proposed maintenance = £17.42 + £2.57 = £19.99

The total proposed maintenance for a child with two non-resident parents is the same as if there were one non-resident parent (with assessable income equal to the joint assessable income of the two non-resident parents) and a parent with care with no assessable income. However, with two non-resident parents the total liability is split between the parents in proportion to their assessable incomes.

If an application is made for maintenance from both parents and the Child Support Agency (CSA) does not have the information about the other parent's income within the fortnight given to provide it (see p80), it is assumed that this second non-resident parent has no assessable income when calculating the first non-resident parent's proposed maintenance.[14] When this information is available, a fresh assessment will be carried out.[15]

The regulations do not distinguish between non-resident parents who live separately from one another and those who, although they are no longer living with their child, still live together as a couple. Therefore, in the case of a couple being assessed, two separate assessments would be carried out following the same basic rules up to this stage (ie, net income and exempt income would be calculated separately for each parent), even though between the two assessments the same housing costs would be included twice.

The person with care who is not a parent of the qualifying children may be looking after children who have different parents. For example, a grandmother may be looking after two grandchildren, one the child of her son and the other the child of her daughter. This involves two maintenance requirements. The proposed maintenance steps for the two children are completely separate and each can be carried out for both the non-resident parents of each child (see above). In theory, the grandmother could receive child maintenance from four non-resident parents.

---

7. **More than one person with care**

'More than one person with care' does not refer to the situation where a child is looked after for part of the time by one person and the rest of the time by another; we call that 'shared care' (see Chapter 15).

Here, we cover the situation where different children of a non-resident parent are being looked after by different people. This includes where the non-resident parent has two or more families by different women with whom he does not live and also where the children of one family are split between two carers, perhaps with one child living with the mother and the other with grandparents. The non-resident parent is equally liable to maintain all the qualifying children and must pay child maintenance to each of the persons with care who makes an application.[16]

The more than one person with care situation involves applications for maintenance for *different* children from the *same* non-resident parent.

Sharing out the proposed maintenance

If the children of a non-resident parent are in the care of two or more people and a maintenance application has been made by more than one of those persons with care, the proposed maintenance has to be shared between the persons with care.[17] This is achieved by dividing the non-resident parent's assessable income between the maintenance assessments in the same proportions as their maintenance requirements.[18] Where an allowance for a pre-April 1993 property settlement has been included in exempt income (see p222), an adjustment is made when apportioning the assessable income. The proposed maintenance step is then carried out separately for each application using the relevant portion of assessable income.

Only one protected income calculation (see Chapter 14) is carried out for the non-resident parent, using the total amount of proposed maintenance for all the assessments.[19] Where the total maintenance worked out for all the persons with care is less than £6 (see p199), the minimum payment is divided between the persons with care in proportion to the maintenance requirements.[20]

. . . .

Example: 50 per cent calculation if there is more than one parent with care

Wayne is the father of Yvonne (12) and Veronica (10) who live with Zoe. Zoe has no assessable income. She has been receiving £20 a week child maintenance from Wayne. Zoe's maintenance requirement for Yvonne and Veronica is £102.50 (see p207).

Wayne's girlfriend, Lauren, has recently had his baby, Keith. Wayne is not living with Lauren who is claiming income support (IS) as a single parent.

Lauren's maintenance requirement is:		£
Personal allowances	Lauren	59.15
	Keith	47.45
Family premium		16.43
Sub-total		123.03
Less child benefit		18.10
Total maintenance requirement		**104.93**

Joint maintenance requirement is £102.50 + £104.93 = £207.43

Wayne's total assessable income is £40 a week.

For calculating Zoe's child maintenance, Wayne's assessable income =
£40 × £102.50/£207.43 = £19.77

For calculating Lauren's child maintenance, Wayne's assessable income =
£40 × £104.93/£207.43 = £20.23 (or £40 – £19.77 = £20.23)

Proposed maintenance = 50 per cent assessable income

For Zoe: 50% × £19.77 = £9.89

For Lauren: 50% × £20.23 = £10.12

Subject to the protected income calculation, Wayne is paying £20.01 in total, but divided between the two parents with care.

When Lauren makes an application for child maintenance, Zoe's child maintenance will be reduced from £20 to £9.89 a week. Zoe receives less than half the maintenance paid by Wayne, although she has two of his children and Lauren has only one younger child (see below).

. . . .

By dividing the non-resident parent's assessable income in proportion to the different maintenance requirements, persons with care responsible for a larger number of children will usually receive a greater amount of child maintenance. However, in the above example, Zoe's maintenance requirement is smaller than would usually be expected for two children. She is receiving only half of certain allowances in the maintenance requirement, as her other child, Scott, has a different non-resident father (see p207).

The division in the proposed maintenance occurs only if both of the persons with care involved actually make an application for child maintenance from the same non-resident parent.[21]

Where one assessment is already in force when the second application involving the same non-resident parent is made (eg, when his second marriage breaks down) the first assessment is reduced from the date the assessment to the second person with care takes effect (see p356).[22]

Pre-April 1993 property settlements

Before dividing the non-resident parent's assessable income between the persons with care, any allowance for a pre-April 1993 property settlement (see p222) is added on to the assessable income.[23] Once this has been apportioned, the property settlement allowance (if any) relevant to that person with care is deducted from her portion of assessable income.

Example: more than one parent with care and a property settlement allowance
The situation is as in the example on p271 except that Wayne has an allowance of £20 included in his exempt income in recognition of the capital settlement he made to Zoe at the time of their divorce in 1992.
Assessable income to be apportioned = £40 + £20 = £60
For Lauren's child maintenance, Wayne's assessable income =
£60 x £104.93/£207.43 = £30.35
Proposed maintenance for Lauren = 50% x £30.35 = £15.18
For Zoe's child maintenance, Wayne's assessable income =
(£60 x £102.50/£207.43) – £20 = £9.65
Proposed maintenance for Zoe = 50% x £9.65 = £4.83
(The minimum payment of £6 applies only where the total payments due from an non-resident parent to all persons with care work out at less than £6.)
Again, Wayne continues to pay £20.01 a week in total, although Zoe sees her maintenance reduced from £20 to £4.83 when Lauren applies to the CSA.

The additional element calculation

The additional element calculation of proposed maintenance when there is more than one person with care is done in the same way as when there is only one person with care, except that a proportion of the non-resident parent's assessable income is substituted for his total assessable income.

Example: additional element calculation if there is more than one person with care
Jeremy has left his wife, Evie, who has no income of her own. Of their four children, Francis (14), Georgina (12), Henry (8) and Isobel (4), the three youngest are living with Evie, but Francis is living with Jeremy's brother and sister-in-law. Jeremy has an assessable income of £600 a week.
The income of Jeremy's brother is irrelevant as he is not Francis' parent. Francis now has two non-resident parents who are liable to maintain him. Evie is now a non-resident parent in respect of Francis, but as she is on IS, she has no assessable income. Because she has children living with her, she is exempt from the deductions from IS.

Jeremy must pay his brother child maintenance for Francis as well as paying Evie child maintenance for Georgina, Henry and Isobel. Both the brother and Evie have made applications for child maintenance.

Evie's maintenance requirement:

		£
Personal allowances	Evie	59.15
	Georgina	47.45
	Henry	47.45
	Isobel	47.45
Family premium		16.43
Sub-total		217.93
Less child benefit		42.30
Total maintenance requirement		**175.63**

Francis' maintenance requirement:

Personal allowances	Adult (half)	29.58
	Francis (14)	47.45
Family premium		16.43
Sub-total		93.46
Less child benefit		18.10
Total maintenance requirement		**75.36**

(The adult personal allowance is halved since Francis, the only qualifying child in the assessment, is 14 years old – see p204.)

Joint maintenance requirement = £175.63 + £75.36 = £250.99

Jeremy's £600 assessable income has to be split between the two assessments in proportion to their maintenance requirements.

Evie's child maintenance:

Jeremy's assessable income = £175.63/£250.99 x £600 = £419.85

Proposed maintenance = 50% x £419.85 = £209.93

This is above the maintenance requirement of £175.63; therefore the additional element calculation must be done (as on p263):

Basic assessable income = £175.63 x 2 = £351.26

Additional assessable income = £419.85 – £351.26 = £68.59

Additional element = £68.59 x 25% = £17.15

Proposed maintenance = £175.63 + £17.15 = £192.78

When Francis leaves home, Evie's maintenance falls from £255.49 a week (see p263) to £192.78

Note: if Evie had assessable income, then the additional element calculation would follow that on p267, using £419.85 as Jeremy's assessable income.

Child maintenance for Francis:

Jeremy's assessable income = £600 x £75.36/£250.99 = £180.15

Proposed maintenance = 50% x £180.15 = £90.08

This is above the maintenance requirement of £75.36; therefore:

Basic assessable income = £75.36 x 2 = £150.72

Additional assessable income = £180.15 – £150.72 = £29.43

Additional element = £29.43 x 15% = £4.41

Proposed maintenance = £75.36 + £4.41 = £79.77

Jeremy is paying £79.77 to his brother and £192.78 to Evie, a total of £272.55. This is £17.06 more than he paid to Evie when the four children were living together. The non-resident parent usually ends up paying more in total when there are two or more applications. This is because he is paying a larger amount of his assessable income at the 50 per cent rate, as he now has two or more maintenance requirements to meet.

8. **Divided families**

We use the term 'divided family' to cover the situation where some children of a family are in the care of the mother and the others in the care of the father. The Child Support Agency may use the term 'split care'. This situation could involve two separate maintenance applications and assessments. If only one of the parents applies for maintenance, then only that application will be assessed. The calculations do not involve any variation from the basic formula.

This is not the same situation as where the care of the same child(ren) is shared between the parents ('shared care' – see Chapter 15).

Example: two proposed maintenance calculations for a divided family

Carol (now 15) does not like her stepfather, Joe, and decides that she wants to live with Bob and Zoe's family – Yvonne (14), Veronica (12), Scott (5) and Ricky (1). David (10) is still living with Anita and Joe.

Therefore, Anita is the non-resident parent for Carol and Bob is the non-resident parent for David.

Maintenance requirement for Carol (15) = £75.36

Maintenance requirement for David (10) = £104.93

Although Carol is older, her maintenance requirement is lower as the carer element is halved because she is over 14.

Anita's exempt income = £260.81

(Anita's exempt income is as in the example on p221, but without the £47.45 for Carol)

Anita's assessable income = £270 (net income) – £260.81 = £9.19

Bob's exempt income = £191.76

Bob's assessable income = £260 (net income) – £191.76 = £68.24

Joint assessable income = £9.19 + £68.24 = £77.43

50 per cent of joint assessable income = £77.43 x 50% = £38.72

The 50 per cent joint assessable income figure (£38.72) is lower than the maintenance requirement for David (£104.93) and that for Carol (£75.36).

Proposed maintenance from Bob = 50% x £68.24 = £34.12

Proposed maintenance from Anita = 50% x £9.19 = £4.60

The protected income calculation (see p291) shows that both Anita and Bob can afford these amounts. Therefore, Bob in effect pays Anita: £34.12 – £4.60 = £29.52 a week.

If either or both of the maintenance requirements had been lower than 50 per cent joint assessable income, then the proposed maintenance would have been obtained using the additional element calculation (see p266).

9. **More than one non-resident parent**

A person with care may be looking after children of different non-resident parents. Here we look at the situation where the person with care is a parent of all the qualifying children. The situation where the person with care is not the parent of the qualifying child(ren) is dealt with on p269 – ie, both parents are non-resident.

If a parent with care is looking after children of different non-resident parents and applies for maintenance from more than one non-resident parent, then more than one maintenance assessment has to be done. If the parent with care has no assessable income, the two (or more) assessments will not alter from the basic formula.

Example: proposed maintenance from more than one non-resident parent where the parent with care has no assessable income

Zoe has applied for maintenance from her ex-husband, Wayne, for Yvonne (14) and Veronica (12), and from Terence for Scott (5). She is living with Bob and has no income of her own other than child benefit and child tax credit. This means that her net income is nil and, therefore, her assessable income is nil.

Child maintenance from Wayne:

Step 1: Maintenance requirement = £102.50 (see example on p207)

Step 2: Exempt income

Wayne, Zoe's ex-husband, lives on his own in a rented flat. His rent is £65 a week.

	£
Personal allowance	59.15
Housing costs	65.00
Total exempt income	**124.15**

Step 3: Assessable income £
Total net income 160.00 (net earnings)
Less exempt income 124.15
Assessable income **35.85**

Step 4: Proposed maintenance = 50% x £35.85 = £17.93
This is below the maintenance requirement of £102.50.
Therefore, the proposed maintenance is **£17.93**.
(You may remember that Wayne had a son with Lauren. However, she has now married Sean and moved to Eire where the CSA has no jurisdiction.)

Child maintenance from Terence:
Step 1: Maintenance requirement = £73.15 (see example on p207)

Step 2: Exempt income
Terence is married to Dipa and, although they have three children, only Rana, 17 and still at school, counts as a dependant. They have a mortgage of £34.18 a week. Dipa receives carer's allowance for looking after her mother, but this is not enough income to support half of Rana. They get working tax credit (WTC) of £27.64 and £45.84 child tax credit.

		£
Personal allowances	Terence	59.15
	Rana	47.45
Family premium		16.43
Housing costs		34.18
Total exempt income		**157.21**

Step 3: Assessable income
190.21 (net earnings)
27.64 WTC
Total net income 217.85
Less exempt income 157.21
Assessable income **60.64**

Step 4: Proposed maintenance = 50% x £60.64 = £30.32
This is below the maintenance requirement of £73.15.
Therefore, the proposed maintenance for Scott is **£30.32**.
The protected income calculations now have to be done to see whether Wayne and Terence can afford these amounts (see example on p287).

The parent with care has assessable income

If the parent with care has assessable income and makes an application for child maintenance from more than one non-resident father, then a proportion of her assessable income is taken into account for each of the assessments. Her assessable income is divided between the maintenance assessments in proportion to the maintenance requirements.[24] This apportioning will only happen if an application is made for maintenance from more than one non-resident parent.

> **Example: more than one non-resident parent and parent with care has assessable income**
>
> Jeremy left his wife, Evie, when he discovered that her youngest child, Isobel (4), was not his daughter. Evie is also looking after his three children, Francis (14), Georgina (12) and Henry (8). Evie decided to apply for child maintenance from Isobel's father, Max, as well as from Jeremy.
>
> **Maintenance requirement for Francis,**
>
> | **Georgina and Henry:** | | £ | |
> |---|---|---|---|
> | Personal allowances | Evie | 29.58 | (half of 59.15) |
> | | Francis | 47.45 | |
> | | Georgina | 47.45 | |
> | | Henry | 47.45 | |
> | Family premium | | 8.22 | (half of 16.43) |
> | Sub-total | | 180.15 | |
> | *Less* child benefit | | 42.30 | |
> | **Total maintenance requirement** | | **137.85** | |
>
> **Maintenance requirement for Isobel:**
>
> | Personal allowances | Evie | 29.58 | (half of 59.15) |
> |---|---|---|---|
> | | Isobel | 47.45 | |
> | Family premium | | 8.22 | (half of 16.43) |
> | Sub-total | | 85.25 | |
> | *Less* child benefit | | 12.10 | |
> | **Total maintenance requirement** | | **73.15** | |
>
> Joint maintenance requirements = £137.85 + £73.15 = £211
>
> Evie's total assessable income is £70. This has to be shared between the two assessments in proportion to the maintenance requirements.
>
> **Proposed maintenance from Max: 50 per cent calculation**
>
> Evie's assessable income used in this assessment = £70 x £73.15/£211 = £24.27
>
> Max's assessable income is £42.50
>
> Max and Evie's joint assessable income = £24.27 + £42.50 = £66.77
>
> 50% x £66.77 = £33.39
>
> This is less than the maintenance requirement of £73.15
>
> Therefore, proposed maintenance is 50 per cent of Max's own assessable income: 50% x £42.50 = **£21.25**
>
> **Proposed maintenance from Jeremy: additional element calculation**
>
> Evie's total assessable income is £70

Her assessable income used in this assessment = £70 x £137.85/£211 = £45.73

Jeremy's assessable income is now £235

Jeremy and Evie's joint assessable income = £45.73 + £235 = £280.73

50% x £280.73 = £140.37

This is more than the maintenance requirement of £137.85 and, therefore, an additional element calculation has to be done:

Basic element − £137.85/£280.73 x £235 = £115.40

Basic assessable income = £115.40 x 2 = £230.80

Additional assessable income = £235 − £230.80 = £4.20

Additional element = £4.20 x 25% = £1.05

Proposed maintenance = £115.40 + £1.05 = **£116.45**

Subject to the protected income stage, Evie will receive £21.25 from Max and £116.45 from Jeremy.

Notes

2. How much is proposed maintenance
1 Sch 1 para 2(1) CSA 1991
2 Sch 1 para 2(2) CSA 1991
3 Sch 1 para 2(3) CSA 1991
4 Sch 1 para 2 CSA 1991; reg 5 CS(MASC) Regs
5 Sch 1 para 4 CSA 1991; reg 6 CS(MASC) Regs

3. The 50 per cent calculation
6 Sch 1 para 2(2) CSA 1991

4. The additional element calculation
7 Sch 1 para 4(1) CSA 1991; reg 6(1) CS(MASC) Regs
8 Sch 1 para 3 CSA 1991
9 Sch 1 para 3 CSA 1991

5. Maximum child maintenance
10 Sch 1 para 4(2) CSA 1991
11 Sch 1 para 4(3) CSA 1991
12 Reg 6(2) CS(MASC) Regs

6. Both parents are non-resident
13 Reg 19(2) CS(MASC) Regs
14 Reg 19(3) CS(MASC) Regs
15 Reg 19(4) CS(MASC) Regs

7. More than one person with care
16 Reg 22(5) CS(MASC) Regs
17 Reg 22(1) CS(MASC) Regs
18 Reg 22(2) CS(MASC) Regs
19 Reg 22(3) CS(MASC) Regs
20 Reg 22(4) CS(MASC) Regs
21 Reg 22(1)(a) CS(MASC) Regs
22 Reg 22(1)(b) and (2A) CS(MASC) Regs
23 Reg 22(2) CS(MASC) Regs

9. More than one non-resident parent
24 Reg 23(4) CS(MASC) Regs

Chapter 14

Protected income ('old rules')

This chapter covers:
1. What is protected income (below)
2. Basic protected income (p283)
3. Total protected income (p285)
4. The maintenance payable (p287)
5. Change of circumstances (p291)

1. **What is protected income**

Protected income is income which cannot be used for paying child maintenance.[1] At the end of the protected income calculation, the amount of maintenance payable will be known. It will either be the proposed maintenance figure or a reduced amount. The non-resident parent never ends up paying more than the proposed maintenance. This step should be carried out for all non-resident parents. The only time it does not apply is where the proposed maintenance is £6 or less (see p199).

There are two forms of protection for non-resident parents. One prevents them having to pay an excessive proportion of their own income as child maintenance, and the other considers the needs of the whole family.

30 per cent cap

A non-resident parent never has to pay more than 30 per cent of his net income (see p234).[2] His partner's income is ignored. If the proposed maintenance is greater than this, it will be reduced to 30 per cent of net income. In other words, 70 per cent net income is a protected level of income; all non-resident parents (except a few of those making the minimum payment) are left with at least 70 per cent of their own net income. This applies even where a non-resident parent is paying more than one Child Support Agency (CSA) assessment (see p289). Also, if a non-resident parent is paying maintenance for other children under a court order, whether inside or outside the UK, this can be deducted from net income at the protected income stage (see p282).[3]

Example

Bob is living with his parents, and is liable to pay maintenance for Carol and David. His net earnings are £160 a week.

Step 1: Maintenance requirement = £140.28 (see p205)

Step 2: Exempt income (personal allowance) = £59.15

Step 3: Assessable income = £160 – £59.15 = £100.85

Step 4: Proposed maintenance = 50% x £100.85 = £50.43 (less than the maintenance requirement)

Step 5: Protected income = 30% x £160 = £48

The maintenance is, therefore, reduced to £48, before proceeding with the rest of the protected income step.

Two years later, Bob is living with Zoe, their son Ricky and Zoe's three other children. His net income is £260 (see p253) and the proposed maintenance is £45.99 (see p261).

30% x £260 = £78

The proposed maintenance is less than 30 per cent net income and remains at £45.99.

Even where the proposed maintenance has been capped at 30 per cent net income, the second protected income calculation is carried out, as the maintenance payable may be further reduced. When carrying out this second calculation, substitute the capped maintenance for proposed maintenance where the latter is more than 30 per cent net income.

Total protected income

This second part of the protected income calculation is intended to prevent the non-resident parent and his family being left below the income support (IS) level as a result of paying child maintenance.[4] The 'family' is the same as that used for means-tested benefits (see p26 for a detailed definition).

What is total family income

'Total family income' includes the incomes of all members of the non-resident parent's family (see p26).[5] The CSA calls total family income 'disposable income'. We do not use this term at this stage as disposable income is also used to specify the income remaining after proposed maintenance has been paid.

Income for total family income purposes is calculated in the same way as net income (see Chapter 12) except that:[6]

- child benefit is included in full as income;
- child tax credit (CTC) is included in full as income, whether it is payable to the non-resident parent or his partner;
- part of payments under a mortgage protection insurance policy which exceed the mortgage interest repayments are disregarded; *and*

- with the exception of child maintenance, which is counted in full as the parent's income, the income of any child is included as income up to the amount of the personal allowance for that child and any disabled child premium included in the protected income calculation. As at exempt income stage, children's earnings and the first £10 a week of other income are disregarded.

Child maintenance paid

If a non-resident parent or his partner is paying maintenance for a child under a court order where an application to the CSA cannot be made (see p38), the amount of that payment is deducted from total family income.[7] The effect is to protect the payments under the court order at the possible expense of the proposed maintenance resulting from the CSA application. This certainly applies where the person with care receiving the maintenance under the court order is not the parent of the child or where she is not receiving one of the specified benefits (see p37). Arguably, it also applies where a parent with care on benefit has refused to make an application to the CSA (eg, to preserve the court order) and the non-resident parent is now being assessed for his liability to maintain other children. It also applies where the non-resident parent or his partner is paying any child maintenance due under a court order made outside Great Britain.[8] However, no account is taken of voluntary payments, whether made in this country or abroad. In the former situation, the non-resident parent should consider making an application to the CSA as he may be better off with two CSA assessments.

Example: total family income
The proposed maintenance from Bob to Anita for Carol and David is £45.99 (see example on p261). Can he afford it?
Bob is living with Zoe and four children – Yvonne (14), Veronica (12), Scott (4) and Ricky (baby). Bob has net earnings of £260 (see p253). Zoe receives weekly maintenance of £20 for Yvonne and Veronica, CTC of £158 and child benefit of £54.40.

	£
Earnings (net)	260.00
Maintenance for Yvonne and Veronica	20.00
CTC	158.00
Child benefit	54.40
Total family income	**492.40**

What is total protected income

Total protected income is the level below which the non-resident parent's or second family's income must not fall. To make the calculation more manageable, we have separated the total protected income level into basic protected income (see below) and additional protected income (see p285).

The basic protected income is based on IS rates, and it includes personal allowances, premiums, an amount towards high travel-to-work costs, housing costs for all members of the non-resident parent's family, and £30 as a margin above IS. The family is allowed additional protected income of 15 per cent of any family income over and above the basic protected level.

Maintenance payable

The total protected income level is compared with the family's income remaining were the proposed maintenance, or capped maintenance if it is lower, to be paid. If the family's income would be brought below the total protected income level by paying the proposed maintenance, the maintenance due is reduced. The child maintenance is then payable at an amount which would leave the family with disposable income equal to the protected income level.[9] However, the maintenance due cannot be reduced to less than the minimum payment[10] unless the non-resident parent is exempt (see p199).

If the family would have income remaining over the protected income level after paying the proposed maintenance, then the non-resident parent is due to pay the proposed maintenance, or the capped maintenance if that is lower. In other words, the non-resident parent pays the *lowest* of:

- 30 per cent of his net income; *or*
- the amount which would leave his family with disposable income equal to the total protected level; *or*
- the proposed maintenance from Step 4.

2. **Basic protected income**

Basic protected income includes income support (IS) personal allowances and any relevant premiums for all the members of the family, whether the family receives IS or not (including where IS is received for adults but child tax credit is received for children). See Appendix 2 for the qualifying conditions and 2007/08 rates of the premiums.

Basic protected income is:[11]

- the amount of the IS personal allowance for someone aged 25 or over (£59.15) *or* if the non-resident parent has a partner, the IS personal allowance for a couple both aged 18 or over (£92.80); *plus*
- for each child in the family, the amount of the IS personal allowance for a child (£47.45);* *plus*
- the amount of any IS premiums for which the conditions are satisfied* (note that, unlike at exempt income stage, pensioner premiums are included); *plus*
- housing costs for the whole family (see p284); *plus*

- council tax liability less any council tax benefit (CTB – see p285); *plus*
- an allowance towards high travel-to-work costs of a non-resident parent (see p285); *plus*
- a standard margin of £30.

*A proportion of the full rate of the personal allowances and any premiums will be used if a child lives in the household for between two and six nights a week.[12]

Housing costs

The rules for assessing housing costs are the same as those used at the exempt income stage (see p215),[13] except that:
- if there is a mortgage, only interest payments are allowed;[14]
- if the non-resident parent is living as a non-dependant in someone else's house, an amount is included as housing costs (see below);[15]
- excessive housing costs are the higher of £80 or half the total family income.[16] Housing costs will be restricted to this figure unless the non-resident parent is exempt from that rule – eg, because the family includes a child (see p220).

The non-resident parent is a non-dependant

A non-resident parent may be a non-dependant if he lives in a household with people who are not 'family' (see p26). He is *not* a non-dependant if he, or a partner, is:[17]
- a co-owner or joint tenant of the home;
- employed by a charitable or voluntary body as a resident carer;
- liable to make a commercial payment in order to live in the home. It will not be considered a commercial arrangement if payments are made to a close relative in the household; a close relative is a parent, son, daughter (including step-relatives and in-laws), brother and sister, and any of their partners.

The weekly amount to be included in protected income is given below.[18]

Working 16 or more hours a week and with a gross income of:	£
£353 or more	47.75
£283 to £352.99	43.50
£213 to £282.99	38.20
£164 to £212.99	23.35
£111 to £163.99	17.00
Below £111	7.40
Not working 16 hours a week	7.40

When calculating gross income, disability living allowance/attendance allowance is ignored.[19]

Council tax

If the non-resident parent is the only person, other than a partner, who is liable to pay council tax in respect of the home for which housing costs are included, the weekly council tax (less any CTB) is included in basic protected income. However, if there are other people resident in the home, the amount of council tax included is either:[20]

- the weekly liability divided by the number of liable people; *or*
- the weekly amount actually paid by the non-resident parent where he is required to pay more than his share because another liable person has defaulted.

If the non-resident parent lives in Northern Ireland, liability for rates replaces council tax. Likewise, if the person with care has applied to the Child Support Agency (Northern Ireland) but the non-resident parent lives in Great Britain, council tax is used.[21]

High travel-to-work costs

This allowance applies for non-resident parents who travel more than 240 kilometres a week to and from work.[22] The allowance is calculated in exactly the same way as at exempt income stage (see p226). It does not apply to partners.

3. **Total protected income**

In order to obtain total protected income, additional protected income has to be calculated. To do this, basic protected income must be compared with total family income.

Where the total family income *exceeds* the basic protected income, an addition is made to the basic protected income.

Deduct the basic protected income from the total family income to give the excess family income. The additional protected income equals 15 per cent of this excess family income.[23] This figure is added to basic protected income to give total protected income.

Where the total family income is *below* the basic protected income, there is no additional protected income. Any payment of child maintenance will bring the family's disposable income below the protected income level. Therefore, the non-resident parent will either pay the minimum amount (£6) or be exempt from paying altogether (see p199).

Example: total protected income

The situation is the same as in the example on p280, with Bob living with his parents. He is contributing towards the household but is not a co-owner of the home, nor liable to pay council tax. He travels less than 240 kilometres a week to and from work.

Basic protected income:	£
Personal allowance	59.15
Housing costs (as a non-dependant)	17.00
Margin	30.00
Basic protected income	**106.15**

Additional protected income:	
Total family income	160.00
Less basic protected income	106.15
Excess family income	53.85
Additional protected income (15% x £53.85)	**8.08**

Total protected income:	
Basic protected income	106.15
Plus additional protected income	8.08
Total protected income	**114.23**

Two years later, Bob lives with Zoe and the situation is the same as in the example on p282. Their rent is £45 a week and the council tax liability is £1,050.92 a year. Bob and Zoe are not entitled to housing benefit or council tax benefit.

Basic protected income:		£
Personal allowances	Couple	92.80
	Yvonne	47.45
	Veronica	47.45
	Scott	47.45
	Ricky	47.45
Family premium		16.43
Housing costs		45.00
Council tax liability		20.21
Margin		30.00
Basic protected income		**394.24**

Additional protected income:	
Total family income	492.40
Less basic protected income	394.24
Excess family income	98.16
Additional protected income (15% x £98.26)	**14.72**

Total protected income:	
Basic protected income	394.24

Plus additional protected income	14.72
Total protected income	**408.96**

4. **The maintenance payable**

There are two methods of calculating the maintenance payable. We cover first the full logic of the step and then a short cut.

The family's disposable income which would remain after paying child maintenance is obtained by subtracting the proposed maintenance (Step 4) from the total family income. If the proposed maintenance has been capped at 30 per cent net income (see p280), this capped amount is used instead of the proposed maintenance.

If the disposable income is *higher* than the total protected income, the parent can afford to pay the full proposed/capped maintenance. Maintenance payable is the proposed/capped maintenance figure. Where the proposed maintenance has been capped, it cannot be increased back to the originally proposed level.

If the disposable income is initially *below* the total protected income, the maintenance payable is reduced until the disposable income equals the total protected income.[24] Therefore, the maintenance payable is the total family income minus the total protected income.

The minimum payment rule still applies (see p199).[25]

The alternative way of arriving at the maintenance payable is to cut out the disposable income step and in all cases to deduct total protected income from total family income to give an alternative proposed maintenance. This is compared with proposed maintenance from Step 4 and also 30 per cent of net income; the non-resident parent pays whichever figure is smallest.

Example: maintenance payable

The proposed maintenance from Bob to Anita for Carol and David has been capped at £48 (see p280) and Bob's total protected income is £114.23 (see p285).

	£
Total family income	160.00
Less capped maintenance	48.00
Disposable income would be	**112.00**

As this is below the total protected income level, the capped maintenance is reduced. Bob can only afford to pay:

Total family income	160.00
Less total protected income	114.23
Maintenance payable	**45.77**

Two years later, when Bob is living with Zoe, the proposed maintenance is £45.99 (see p280)

Total family income (from p282)	492.40
Less proposed maintenance	45.77
Disposable income would be	**446.63**

This is more than the total protected income of £408.96 (see example on p285) and, therefore, the proposed maintenance is paid.

Example: protected income from start to finish

A few months later, child maintenance from Zoe's ex-husband, Wayne, for Yvonne and Veronica and from Terence for Scott is being assessed (see example on p276). The proposed maintenance from Wayne is £17.93 and from Terence £30.32. Can each of them afford it?

Wayne lives on his own in a rented flat. He earns on average £160 net a week and only travels a few kilometres to work. His rent is £65 a week and his council tax is £6 a week. He is not entitled to any council tax benefit or housing benefit. The 30 per cent cap does not reduce the proposed maintenance as: 30% x £160 = £48. Therefore, the proposed maintenance remains at £17.93.

	£
Basic protected income:	
Personal allowance	59.15
Housing costs	65.00
Council tax	6.00
Margin	30.00
Basic protected income	**160.15**
Total family income	160.00
Less basic protected income	160.15
Excess family income	0.00
Additional protected income (15% x £0)	**0.00**
Total protected income	**160.15**

Wayne's total family income is already slightly below his total protected income. Payment of the proposed maintenance of £17.93 would leave Wayne with a disposable income of £142.07, considerably below his total protected income. As Wayne's family income is below his total protected income there is no disposable income from which to pay maintenance. However, Wayne is not exempt from the minimum maintenance payment and, therefore, he is liable to pay £6 a week.

Terence is married to Dipa and they have one dependent daughter, Rana (17), who lives with them. Their mortgage is £34.18 a week, half of which is capital repayments. Their council tax is £9.32 a week. Terence is self-employed and his net earnings average £190.21 a week. Dipa receives carer's allowance of £48.65 and child benefit of £18.10 a week. They get £27.64 working tax credit (WTC) and child tax credit of £45.84 per week.

The 30 per cent cap does not reduce the proposed maintenance as: 30% x £217.85 (earnings plus WTC) = £65.35. Therefore, the proposed maintenance remains at £30.32.

Basic protected income:		£
Personal allowances	Couple	92.80
	Rana	47.45
Family premium		16.43
Carer premium		27.15
Housing costs (mortgage interest)		17.09
Council tax		9.32
Margin		30.00
Basic protected income		**240.24**
Total family income:		
Net earnings		190.21
Carer's allowance		48.65
Child benefit		18.10
Working tax credit		27.64
Child tax credit		£45.84
Total family income		**330.44**
Less basic protected income		240.24
Excess family income		90.20
Additional protected income	(15% x £90.20)	**13.53**
Total protected income		**253.77**
Total family income		330.44
Less proposed maintenance		30.32
Disposable income		**300.12**

As disposable income is above the total protected income, the maintenance payable is the proposed maintenance of £30.32.

More than one person with care

If a non-resident parent is being assessed to pay child maintenance to two or more persons with care for different qualifying children, only one protected income step is carried out on the total proposed maintenance. Both the 30 per cent cap and the total protected income check are carried out for this total.[26] If the non-resident parent cannot afford the total proposed maintenance, the amount he can afford is divided between the persons with care in proportion to their proposed maintenance.

Example: protected income step for more than one person with care

Lauren has returned to the UK. She claims income support and applies for child maintenance for Wayne's son, Keith. Wayne is also the father of Zoe's daughters. His net wages are now £174, his rent is now £67.

Step 1: Maintenance requirement

	£	
Zoe	95.11	(see p207)
Lauren	104.93	(see p271)
Total	**200.04**	

Step 2: Wayne's exempt income = £126.15
Step 3: Wayne's assessable income = £47.85
(Neither parent with care has any assessable income)
Step 4: Proposed maintenance
Zoe: (£95.11 x £47.85/£200.04) x 50% = £11.38
Lauren: (£104.93 x £47.85/£200.04) x 50% = £12.55
Total proposed maintenance = £11.38 + £12.55 = £23.93
Step 5: Protected income
Check whether the total proposed maintenance is more than 30 per cent net income:
30% x £174 = £52.20
The total proposed maintenance of £23.93 is less than this and, therefore, does not need to be capped. Now carry out the second protected income calculation.

	£
Personal allowance	59.15
Housing costs	67.00
Council tax	6.00
Margin	30.00
Basic protected income	**162.15**
Total family income	174.00
Less basic protected income	162.15
Excess family income	11.85
Additional protected income (15% x £11.85)	1.78
Total protected income (£162.15 + £1.78)	**163.93**
Total family income	174.00
Less total proposed maintenance	23.93
Disposable income	**150.07**

This is below the total protected income (£163.93), so Wayne cannot afford to pay the proposed maintenance.

	£
Total family income	174.00
Less total protected income	163.93
Maintenance payable	**10.07**

The maintenance is split between Zoe and Lauren in proportion to their proposed maintenance:
Zoe: £10.07 x £11.38/£23.93 = £4.79
Lauren: £10.07 x £12.55/£23.93 = £5.28

Note: Lauren ends up with a greater proportion of the maintenance, even though she has one young child and Zoe has two older children. In this case, as neither of them has assessable income, the difference is entirely due to the maintenance requirement rules.

5. **Change of circumstances**

An increase in the total family income of a second family on the protected income level can result in an increase in the maintenance payable to the first family. This arises because the total protected income level only increases by 15 per cent of any increase in family income. The net effect of a £1 a week increase in total family income is an 85 pence increase in the child maintenance payable to the first family. This begins as soon as the maintenance payable is £6 a week and only ceases once the maintenance due reaches the capped or proposed maintenance level.

This recycling effect is the same, irrespective of whether the income is the non-resident parent's or a partner's. There is no exception for income specifically meant for stepchildren in the second family – eg, child maintenance paid for them. The theory is that an increase in the income of the non-resident parent's partner means that she is better able to support herself and her own children. This in turn releases more of the non-resident parent's income away from supporting his partner and his stepchildren and into paying maintenance to his own children. However, this distinction may not be obvious to second families, who are likely to perceive it as unfair.

Once the proposed maintenance level is due, a £1 increase in the non-resident parent's income results in an increase of between 50 pence and 15 pence in the maintenance assessment. The partner's income then no longer increases the assessment at all (except to a limited extent in some instances where there is a joint child see p228).

If the proposed maintenance has been capped, then increases in the partner's income do *not* increase the maintenance payable. While the maintenance remains capped, a £1 increase in the non-resident parent's own net income produces a 30 pence increase in the assessment.

Example: change in total family income
Zoe decides to take a job, earning £95 net a week. Bob is still taking home £260 a week. When their tax credit award is reassessed (Zoe's earnings will not affect their tax credits until the following tax year), they are now entitled to £112.64 a week (Ricky has had his first birthday). Zoe now receives child maintenance as assessed in the example on p287.
Step 1: Maintenance requirement = £140.28 (see p205)
Step 2: Bob's exempt income = £136.10
Step 3: Bob's assessable income = £123.90 (see p253)

Step 4: Proposed maintenance = 50% x £123.90 = £61.95
(Anita has no assessable income)
Step 5: Protected income
To check whether the proposed maintenance is less than 30 per cent net income (see p253): 30% x £260 = £78
Therefore, the proposed maintenance remains at £61.95.

	£
Bob's earnings	260.00
Zoe's earnings	95.00
Maintenance from Wayne	6.00
Maintenance from Terence	30.32
Child benefit	54.40
Child tax credit	112.64
Total family income	558.36
Less basic protected income (see p285)	394.24
Excess family income	164.12
Additional protected income (15% x £164.12)	**24.62**
Total protected income (£394.24 + £24.62)	**418.86**

If the proposed maintenance were paid, disposable income would be:

Total family income	558.36
Less proposed maintenance	£61.95
Disposable income	**496.41**

This is higher than the total protected income (£418.86) and, therefore, the proposed maintenance is the maintenance payable. Bob is now paying Anita £61.95 instead of £45.99 (see p287). Although Bob and Zoe's total family income has increased by £65.86, their disposable income after maintenance has been paid has increased by £49.68. Since the proposed maintenance is being paid, any wage increase of Zoe's will not increase Bob's maintenance assessment any further.

It would not be to Bob's advantage to ask for a supersession of the assessment on the grounds of change of circumstances (see p389).

For two reasons, not every change of circumstances will immediately affect the amount of child maintenance payable. First, the person concerned does not have to request a supersession if there is a change in her/his circumstances. It is optional. Second, if a supersession is requested and undertaken, the general rule is that the maintenance in payment will only be altered if the new assessment is at least £10 more or less than the assessment in force. However, a new assessment which is reduced by only £1 or more or increased by £5 or more from the previous assessment will always take effect if it leaves the non-resident parent's family on the protected income level (see p390). Therefore, cases which involve a non-resident parent on the protected income level will be changing more frequently than cases where the full amount of the proposed maintenance is being paid.

Example: change in family composition

Bob's daughter Carol (now 15) moves, leaving Anita, to live with Bob and Zoe. Child benefit increases to £66.50. Child tax credit increases to £148.03. Otherwise, the situation is as in the above example.

David (10), Bob's son, still lives with Anita and her husband, Joe. Anita has net earnings of £270 and Joe has net earnings of £295. Anita's child benefit entitlement is now £18.10. Their mortgage interest payments are £114.23 a week, the endowment policy premium is £24.92 a week, and council tax £14.50 a week.

See the example on p275:

Proposed maintenance from Anita for Carol = £4.60

Proposed maintenance from Bob for David = £34.12

Protected income calculation for Bob

The 30 per cent cap does not reduce the proposed maintenance as:

30% x £260 = £78

Basic protected income:		£
Personal allowances	Couple	92.80
	Carol	47.45
	Yvonne	47.45
	Veronica	47.45
	Scott	47.45
	Ricky	47.45
Family premium		16.43
Housing costs		45.00
Council tax liability		20.21
Margin		30.00
Basic protected income		**441.69**
Total family income:		
£445.72 (from p282 without child tax credit) + £148.03 (child tax credit) + £12.10 (child benefit)		605.85
Excess family income (£605.85 – £441.69)		164.16
Additional protected income (15% x £164.16)		24.62
Total protected income (£441.69 + £24.62)		466.31
Total family income		605.85
Less proposed maintenance		34.12
Disposable income		**571.73**

This is above the total protected income of £466.31 and, therefore, Bob can afford to pay the proposed maintenance of £34.12.

Protected income calculation for Anita

Basic protected income:		£
Personal allowances	Couple	92.80
	David	47.45
Family premium		16.43
Housing costs (mortgage interest only)		114.23
Council tax liability		14.50
Margin		30.00
Basic protected income		**315.41**
Total family income:		
Anita's earnings		270.00
Joe's earnings		295.00
Child tax credit		10.50
Child benefit		18.10
Total family income		**593.60**
Less basic protected income		315.41
Excess family income*		278.19

*At this point it is already clear that Anita will pay the proposed maintenance, but we continue with the calculation for completeness.

Additional protected income (15% x £278.19)	41.73
Total protected income (£315.41 + £41.73)	357.14
Total family income	593.60
Less proposed maintenance	4.60
Disposable income	**589.00**

This is well above the total protected income of £357.14 and, therefore, Anita can afford to pay the proposed maintenance.

Note: the formula works in such a way as to leave Anita and Joe with disposable income of £589 when they have the care of one child, whereas Bob and Zoe are left with £571.73 when they are looking after five children.

Notes

1. What is protected income
1 Sch 1 para 6 CSA 1991
2 Regs 11(6)-(6A) and 12 CS(MASC) Regs
3 Reg 12(1)(c) CS(MASC) Regs
4 Reg 11(1)-(5) CS(MASC) Regs
5 Regs 11(1)(l) and 12(1)(a) CS(MASC) Regs
6 Reg 11(2) CS(MASC) Regs
7 Reg 11(2)(a)(ii) CS(MASC) Regs
8 Reg 11(2)(a)(v) CS(MASC) Regs
9 Reg 12(2) CS(MASC) Regs
10 Reg 12(3) CS(MASC) Regs

2. Basic protected income
11 Reg 11(1)(a)-(kk) CS(MASC) Regs
12 Reg 11(3) and (4) CS(MASC) Regs
13 Reg 11(1)(b) CS(MASC) Regs
14 Sch 3 para 3(1) CS(MASC) Regs
15 Reg 11(1)(b) CS(MASC) Regs
16 Reg 18(1)(b) CS(MASC) Regs
17 Reg 1 CS(MASC) Regs; reg 3 HB Regs or reg 3 HB(SPC) Regs
18 Reg 74(1) and (2) HB Regs or reg 55(1) and (2) HB(SPC) Regs
19 Reg 63(9) HB Regs
20 Reg 11(1)(j) CS(MASC) Regs
21 Sch 1 para 5(4) CS(NIRA) Regs
22 Reg 11(1)(kk) CS(MASC) Regs

3. Total protected income
23 Reg 11(1)(l) CS(MASC) Regs

4. The maintenance payable
24 Reg 12(2) CS(MASC) Regs
25 Reg 12(3) CS(MASC) Regs
26 Reg 22(3) CS(MASC) Regs

Chapter 15

Shared care ('old rules')

This chapter covers:
1. What is shared care (below)
2. Care shared between separated parents (p298)
3. Care shared between a parent and another person (p307)
4. Care shared between two people who are not parents (p310)
5. Three persons with care (p311)
6. Care provided in part by the local authority (p311)
7. The maintenance requirement is met in full (p312)

---

1. **What is shared care**

We use the term 'shared care' to describe a situation where there is more than one person looking after a particular child and those people live in different households. If the people providing care live in the same household (see p22), this is not shared care.[1] The legislation only acknowledges shared care where more than one person has 'day-to-day care' of a child.

Day-to-day care

There is no definition of 'day-to-day care' set down for deciding whether someone is a person with care. Therefore, an everyday definition can be used (see p21). A person who is not a parent can apply to receive child maintenance only if s/he has day-to-day care of a child. Parents with care and non-resident parents can both apply for a maintenance assessment, although there are some exceptions (see p37) as well as rules governing which application takes precedence (see p48). There can be more than one person with care of a child.

However, for the purposes of shared care in the maintenance formula, a person will be treated as having day-to-day care of a child only if s/he cares for the child for at least 104 nights in the 12-month period ending with the 'relevant week'.[2] See p235 for a definition of relevant week. If 12 months have not passed since there was a shared care situation, or since the parents separated, this does not mean that there is no pattern – see p297.[3]

Another period, ending with the relevant week, may be used if that would be more representative of the current arrangement.[4] The number of nights of care in that period must be in the same ratio as 104 nights is to 12 months – ie, 52 nights in six months, 26 nights in three months, 13 nights in two months, nine nights in a month. Examples in Child Support Agency (CSA) guidance of situations where it might be appropriate to use a period other than the previous 12 months include a recent relationship breakdown, a court ruling on residence or contact, or the person now providing day-to-day care having been abroad, in prison, in hospital, away from home or otherwise unable to provide care.[5] If the arrangement has simply been renegotiated between the two parents, written acceptance of this should be provided so that the CSA knows that this is now the current arrangement and not a temporary change. A future period cannot be used. The period should generally end with the relevant week, but does not have to.[6] Therefore, if a change occurs after the relevant week, a supersession will usually have to be sought (see p389).

The parent does not have to provide continuous care throughout a period of 24 hours, but must usually be providing care during the night.[7] Where a child is a boarder at boarding school or a hospital inpatient, whoever would otherwise have day-to-care is treated as providing care. The person who is treated as having day-to-day care for such periods need not be the person who pays the school fees.[8] Parents should keep a note of the nights the child(ren) spends with them and, in case of dispute, be willing to supply further evidence – eg, a diary. The CSA – and any subsequent appeal tribunal – must determine the amount of day-to-day care provided by each person on the basis of available evidence.[9]

Fewer than 104 nights in the year

If a non-resident parent is providing some care, but to a lesser extent than that described as day-to-day care, he is still liable to pay child maintenance and the level of care he provides is not acknowledged by the child support formula. Therefore, such a non-resident parent is expected to contribute the same amount of child maintenance as if he were not looking after the child at all. This means, for example, that fathers who have their children to stay every other weekend will pay the same level of maintenance as those who do not.

A father who looks after the child(ren) for all of the school holidays would not be accepted as a person with care if the time spent with the children was assessed over 12 months. However, the father could request a supersession during the summer holidays on the grounds that he is now a parent with care and a shorter period should then be used to calculate who has day-to-day care in order to reflect the current arrangement. It is unlikely that this would be grounds for supersession if the six-week period had already been taken into account when averaging over the year for the current assessment. However, if the arrangement for the holiday had not been known at the time, this may be successful. If not, an appeal should be considered (see p398).

If day-to-day care were to be re-assessed over this shorter period, the father would become the parent with care and the mother the non-resident parent. Indeed, the father could then apply for maintenance from the mother. **Note:** the period used to assess day-to-day care ends with the relevant week which precedes the request for a supersession – see p389. Therefore, the request should not be made right at the beginning of the summer holiday.

On the other hand, if it is held that a supersession cannot take place, such a father technically remains the non-resident parent over the holiday when he has the child(ren) full time. He would be liable to continue paying the mother the full level of maintenance even for those weeks the children spend with him. Parents in such a situation could try to come to some voluntary arrangement whereby the mother pays back some or all of the maintenance, but this may not be financially possible, especially if she is in receipt of income support.

More than one person with care

Where there are two people in different households who both have day-to-day care of a qualifying child, either can make an application for child maintenance as long as both or neither has parental responsibility (see p15) for the child.[10] If only one of them has parental responsibility, the person with that responsibility must be the applicant. This means that if the person with parental responsibility decides not to apply, the other person with care could lose out on child maintenance.

If both persons with care can, and do, make an application, only one will be accepted (see p48).[11] Which application is accepted is largely a technicality, however, as this does not change the status of the people involved nor the way in which the assessment is carried out. It does, though, affect who can cancel the assessment (see p360).

The basic formula is varied to take into account the fact that there is more than one person with care. The way in which the formula is adjusted depends on which people share the care.

2. Care shared between separated parents

Where it is accepted that both parents have day-to-day care (ie, there is a shared care situation), one of the parents with care still has to be treated as a non-resident parent in order to make an assessment.[12] CPAG tried to challenge this rule in the past, but a child support commissioner (see p414) decided that this is the correct interpretation of the law.[13]

Where parents share care, only a parent who provides day-to-day care as defined above – ie, care of at least 104 nights out of 12 months or the equivalent (see p296) – can be deemed non-resident (see below). In almost all cases, the parents with care will both be providing care for at least 104 nights out of 12 months and, therefore, one has to be deemed non-resident. However, in some cases, although care is shared according to its everyday meaning, but both parents are not providing day-to-day care according to the definition. For example, if the mother provides care during the day but the children sleep at their father's home, each cares for the children an equal number of hours a week, but because they are not providing day-to-day care, the shared care rules cannot be used to deem one of them non-resident. No maintenance assessment should be carried out. In a case like this, the CSA may try to argue that the mother is the non-resident parent because she does not have day-to-day care; if this happens, she should appeal on the basis that the day-to-day care definition only legally has to be used in establishing whether there is shared care, not in deciding whether someone is a person with care, when a different definition can be used (see p296).

In cases where a parent with care is treated as non-resident, an assessment is carried out to find out how much child maintenance s/he has to pay to the other parent. As the remaining parent with care does not have to pay child maintenance, this can result in one parent paying child maintenance to another who has equal responsibility for the child.

Who is treated as the non-resident parent

The parent who provides day-to-day care to a 'lesser extent' is treated as the non-resident parent.[14] A **'lesser extent'** could be interpreted as meaning either for fewer *nights* per week on average or fewer *hours* per week on average. The number of nights will be considered first by the Child Support Agency (CSA), but it should be argued on the basis of hours if this would give a fairer result. Indeed, it could be said that nights involve less care than days. For example, if one parent had a school-age child from 4pm Friday to 8.30am Monday (three nights), this could be argued to be as much care as the other parent who is with the child from 4pm Monday to 8.30am Friday (four nights). It might be possible to argue that the degree of responsibility, as well as the amount of time, is relevant to determining the extent of the care – eg, who buys the child's clothes, who attends school functions or arranges visits to the dentist. These issues need not be raised if both parents agree that the number of nights of care fairly determines the question.

It is helpful if parents keep a record of the time the children spend in each household, especially if there are changes to the usual pattern of care. The extent of care is measured over the period explained on p296, usually the last year or since a change in the arrangements.

If the parents provide care for an equal amount of time, the parent who does *not* receive child benefit is treated as the non-resident parent.[15] As the right to receive child maintenance follows the receipt of child benefit, this may lead to competing claims for child benefit. If more than one person make a claim for child benefit, an order of priority is used or, if this does not apply, HM Revenue and Customs makes a (non-appealable) decision.

For more information on the priority rules for child benefit, see CPAG's *Welfare Benefits and Tax Credits Handbook*.

If care is shared equally and neither parent receives child benefit, the CSA decides who is the principal carer.[16]

Example: shared care and a deemed non-resident parent

Marcia and Nathan are divorced. They have two children, Oscar (7) and Patrick (5). Every fortnight the children spend five nights with Nathan. The rest of the time they live with Marcia.

Marcia has the children 9 out of every 14 nights = 234 nights a year.

Nathan has the children 5 out of every 14 nights = 130 nights a year.

Do both parents have day-to-day care? Yes.

But Nathan looks after the boys to a lesser extent. Therefore, Nathan is deemed a non-resident parent and an assessment is carried out to decide how much child maintenance he should pay to Marcia.

Marcia remains a parent with care and has no liability to pay child maintenance.

There may be cases where each child of a family spends a different amount of time with the two parents – ie, the mother may be deemed the non-resident parent for one child and the father for the other. If this is the case, the situation is similar to that of a divided family in which different children live full time with different parents (also known as 'split care', see p275). Two completely separate assessments are carried out: if the mother cares for the daughter for the greater amount of time, the daughter's child maintenance will be assessed with the father as the deemed non-resident parent; child maintenance for the son, who spends more time with the father, will be assessed with the mother as the deemed non-resident parent.

Calculating child maintenance

When two parents share care, there is a remaining parent with care and a deemed non-resident parent (see p299). The five steps of the formula described in Chapters 10 to 15 are still applicable in calculating how much maintenance the deemed non-resident parent must pay. However, the standard formula is adjusted to take into account the time that the so-called non-resident parent looks after the child(ren).

Step 1: maintenance requirement

Only one maintenance requirement is calculated (see Chapter 10).

Example: maintenance requirement

The situation is as described in the above example. Marcia has remarried and looks after Oscar (7) and Patrick (5) for nine nights every fortnight.

Maintenance requirement with Marcia as parent with care:

		£
Personal allowances	Marcia	59.15
	Oscar	47.45
	Patrick	47.45
Family premium		16.43
Sub-total		170.48
Less child benefit		30.20
Maintenance requirement		**140.28**

Step 2: exempt income

When calculating the exempt income of the parents, a proportion of the personal allowance for the child (plus any disabled child premium) is included to reflect the average number of nights a week the parent does have care of the child.[17] Similarly, only a proportion of the family premium is allowed unless another of the parent's children lives in the household all week (see below for the situation where there is another child).[18] See the example on p312 where the care of more than one child is shared, but the children spend a different number of nights with the parent.

For full details of exempt income, see Chapter 11.

Example: exempt income for shared care when no child lives in the household for seven nights a week

Marcia looks after Oscar and Patrick for an average of 4.5 nights a week.
Nathan looks after Oscar and Patrick for an average of 2.5 nights a week.
Marcia married Gareth recently. Their mortgage payments are £120 a week.

Marcia's exempt income:

		£	
Personal allowances	Marcia	59.15	
	Oscar	30.50	(for 4.5 days)
	Patrick	30.50	(for 4.5 days)
Family premium		10.56	(for 4.5 days)
Housing costs		120.00	
Total exempt income		**250.71**	

Nathan lives on his own when the children are not with him. His privately rented flat costs £75 a week. He lives within a few kilometres of his work.

Nathan's exempt income:

		£	
Personal allowances	Nathan	59.15	
	Oscar	16.95	(for 2.5 days)
	Patrick	16.95	(for 2.5 days)

Family premium	5.87	(for 2.5 days)
Housing costs	75.00	
Total exempt income	**173.92**	

See the example on p312 for the apportionment of premiums where the children spend a different number of nights with each parent.

Premiums where there is a shared-care child and another child

This section only applies if there is a child who lives in the household all week, as well as child(ren) who are there part time. If the household includes only the children whose care is shared and stepchildren, the premiums are apportioned as above. Go to Step 3.

If another child of the parent lives in the household for seven nights a week, this child can be either another qualifying child or a joint child with a new partner. The family premium is either included in full or halved.[19] It will be included in full if:

* the parent qualifies for the family premium for the shared child(ren) (ie, receives child benefit for her/him, or where no one receives child benefit, has claimed child benefit or is the person with whom the child usually lives); we call this shared-care children 'with child benefit'; *or*
* there is another qualifying child (of that parent) in the household; *or*
* a new partner cannot support the joint child (see p228).

The following outlines the various permutations.
* A lone parent with shared-care children (with or without child benefit) and another qualifying child: full family premium.
* A parent with shared-care children (with child benefit) and a joint child with a new partner: full family premium. Note that the personal allowance for the joint child is halved if the new partner can contribute to her/his support.
* A parent with shared-care children (no child benefit) and a joint child with a new partner: the family premium is halved if the new partner can contribute to the support of the joint child, but is included in full if the partner cannot (see p228).

Example: exempt income if there is shared care and a joint child

Marcia still has the qualifying children, Oscar and Patrick, 9 out of 14 nights (an average of 4.5 nights a week) and receives child benefit for them. Marcia and her husband, Gareth, now have a baby daughter, Megan. Gareth earns £450 a week. Their mortgage payments are £120 per week.

Marcia's exempt income:

		£	
Personal allowances	Marcia	59.15	
	Oscar	30.50	(4.5 days)
	Patrick	30.50	(4.5 days)

Megan (half*)	23.73
Family premium (in full**)	16.43
Housing costs	120.00
Total exempt income	**280.31**

* As Gareth earns £450 a week, he can afford to contribute to his daughter's maintenance and, therefore, only half of Megan's personal allowance is included (see p228 for details of the means test).

** Because Megan lives in the household all week, the family premium is not apportioned according to how many nights Oscar and Patrick stay. Instead, consideration has to be given to whether Marcia is entitled to the family premium as a result of looking after Oscar and Patrick. As she receives child benefit for them, she is entitled to the full rate of the premium. (If her ex-husband received the child benefit, Marcia would not be due the full family premium for them. Consideration would then be given to Megan and, since Gareth can afford to maintain half of Megan, the family premium would be halved.)

Step 3: assessable income

This step is exactly the same as for other situations (see Chapter 12).

Example: assessable income

Before the birth of her daughter, Marcia's income is net earnings of £145 a week. Her husband's earnings are not taken into account in the net income calculation and neither is any child benefit.

Marcia's assessable income:	£
Net income	145.00 (net earnings)
Less exempt income	250.71 (from example on p301)
Assessable income	**Nil**

Nathan takes home £220 a week, after £10 superannuation is deducted. Only half of the superannuation is taken into account (see p238).

Nathan's assessable income:	£
Net income	240.00 (net earnings)
Less exempt income	173.92 (from example on p301)
Assessable income	**66.08**

Step 4: proposed maintenance[20]

The proposed maintenance step is carried out in full for each parent in order to obtain the proposed maintenance from the deemed non-resident parent and a notional proposed maintenance from the remaining parent with care. When calculating the proposed maintenance from each parent, the assessable income of the other parent is taken into account in the same way as if both were non-resident parents (see the example on p269).

The amount of the deemed non-resident parent's proposed maintenance and the notional amount of proposed maintenance from the remaining parent with care are then added together to give the joint proposed maintenance. The deemed non-resident parent is taken to have already contributed a proportion of the maintenance in kind. His assumed contribution is the proportion of the joint proposed maintenance that is equivalent to the proportion of time the children spend with him. The proportion of time the parent spends with his children is given in terms of the average number of nights per week divided by seven. The average number of nights per week does not have to be a round figure; it is calculated to two decimal figures – eg, if a deemed non-resident parent has the child one week in three, the average number of nights per week is 2.33. If there is more than one child, the total average number of nights per week is divided by the number of children – eg, if a father has one child two nights a week and another child four nights a week, the average number of nights per week is three.

This contribution in kind is then subtracted from the non-resident parent's proposed maintenance to give an adjusted proposed maintenance figure. If this produces a figure less than zero, no child maintenance is payable.[21] The non-resident parent has more than contributed his proportion of the total proposed maintenance in kind by providing a certain amount of care.

The minimum payment rule (see p199) applies to an adjusted proposed maintenance figure of between £0 and £6.[22] Therefore, all deemed non-resident parents calculated to pay child maintenance of up to £6 are exempted from the payment (as they have at least part of the family premium included in their protected income calculation).

Example: proposed maintenance

As Marcia has no assessable income, the proposed maintenance is 50 per cent of Nathan's assessable income (see p303):

50% x £66.08 = £33.04

This is less than the maintenance requirement of £140.28 (see p300), so £33.04 is the proposed maintenance.

As there is no proposed maintenance from Marcia, the joint proposed maintenance is also £33.04.

Nathan contributes a proportion of the care:

2.5 + 2.5/(7 x 2) nights in the average week = 35.71%

(2 represents the number of children for whom care is shared.)

As he contributes 35.71% of the care, he is taken as contributing 35.71% of the joint proposed maintenance in kind:

35.71% x £33.04 = £11.80

Nathan is deemed to have contributed £11.80 and is, therefore, due to pay the remainder of his proposed maintenance (if protected income allows).

Adjusted proposed maintenance = £33.04 – £11.80 = £21.24

(If the caring roles were reversed and Nathan had the children for 4.5 nights a week, the proposed maintenance from Marcia, as a deemed non-resident parent, to Nathan would be nil, as Marcia has no assessable income.)

The above example gives the most straightforward shared care situation where only the deemed non-resident parent has assessable income and even then not enough to meet the maintenance requirement. See p312 for an example of the additional element calculation where both parents have assessable income.

However, any of the situations explained in Chapter 13 can apply to the assessments carried out for parents sharing care. In effect, two separate assessments are being carried out up to Step 4 to give a proposed maintenance from the deemed non-resident parent and a notional proposed maintenance from the parent with care. First, arrive at the proposed maintenance for each parent in the same way as for non-resident parents before adding together the two amounts of proposed maintenance to give the joint proposed maintenance. Only at this stage is the non-resident parent's proposed maintenance reduced in recognition of his payment in kind.

The shared care calculation is complicated, but there is a certain amount of logic to it. Both parents have a liability to maintain and, in theory, maintenance is due from each of them for the nights that the child spends with the other parent. For the child there is a notional amount of maintenance available per week. Imagine the joint proposed maintenance divided by seven to give a daily rate of maintenance. Each night of care provided is equivalent to having paid this amount of maintenance. A deemed non-resident parent has to make payments of child maintenance if the amount equivalent to the number of nights' care he contributes does not exceed his portion of the proposed maintenance.

However, the calculation can mean that the parent with a lower income who has the child for less time can end up paying maintenance to a parent with a higher income. Although this is equally true in standard cases, in cases of shared care the deemed non-resident parent may find that he does not have what he considers to be sufficient income left for those days when he is responsible for the child. In such a situation, the deemed non-resident parent on a low income will never receive any maintenance from a parent with care with a higher income. Parents may find this difficult to understand, and it may lead to competing claims for child benefit (see p299).

It may also be difficult to accept that a parent with care on income support (IS) or income-based jobseeker's allowance (JSA) who is required to apply for maintenance can be deemed a non-resident parent and thus not entitled to any child maintenance at all. A parent with care on these benefits who is deemed to be non-resident does not, however, have deductions for contributions to child maintenance from IS/JSA.

Step 5: protected income

Protected income is still the final stage of the calculation (see Chapter 14).[23] The deemed non-resident parent may not be able to afford the proposed adjusted maintenance. When assessing the basic protected income, the allowances for the child are adjusted as for exempt income (see p301) to represent the proportion of the average week that a child spends with the non-resident parent.[24] If there is more than one shared care child and they spend different nights with the family, the family premium is included in proportion to the average number of nights per week that at least one qualifying child is in the household.[25] However, if another child lives in the household on a full-time basis, the premium is included in full.

Example: shared care and protected income

Nathan lives on his own when his children are not with him. His rent is £75 a week and his council tax is £342 a year. He earns £240 net a week. He has Oscar and Patrick for five nights per fortnight. Can Nathan afford to pay the proposed maintenance of £21.24 (see p303)?

The 30% cap does not reduce the proposed maintenance as:

30% x £240 = £72

Therefore, the proposed maintenance remains at £21.24.

Basic protected income:		£	
Personal allowances	Nathan	59.15	
	Oscar	16.95	(for 2.5 days)
	Patrick	16.95	(for 2.5 days)
Family premium		5.87	(for 2.5 days)
Housing costs		75.00	
Council tax		6.58	
Margin		30.00	
Basic protected income		**210.50**	
Additional protected income:			
Total family income		240.00	(net earnings)
Less basic protected income		210.50	
Excess total family income		29.50	
(15% x £29.50)		4.43	
Total protected income		**214.93**	
(£210.50 + £4.43)			
Total family income		240.00	
Less proposed maintenance		21.24	
Disposable income		**218.76**	

This disposable income is above the total protected income level of £214.93. Nathan can pay the proposed maintenance of £21.24 a week.

3. Care shared between a parent and another person

Once again, both the parent and the other person involved must provide day-to-day care (see p296) and live in different households. The way in which this situation is treated depends on which person with care provides day-to-day care to the lesser extent (see p299).

The parent provides care for less time

Where there are two persons with care but the one who is a parent of the child provides care for less time, the parent with care, for the purposes of the formula, is again deemed to be non-resident.[26] Therefore, there is no longer a parent with care, but a person with care and a deemed non-resident parent.

In most cases, the second parent will also be involved as a non-resident parent. For example, the grandmother has the child Monday night to Thursday night (the person with care), the mother has the child Friday to Sunday nights (deemed non-resident parent) and the father has the child for only two weeks in the summer (non-resident parent).

Both non-resident parents are liable to pay maintenance to the person with care. Therefore, two separate assessments are carried out, one for each of the liable parents as long as an effective application has been made in each case. The person with care who is actually going to receive the child maintenance cannot apply if she (eg, the grandmother) does not have parental responsibility while the deemed non-resident parent (eg, the mother) does have that responsibility (see p15).

How child maintenance is calculated

In the case of the non-resident parent who does not participate in the care of the child, the assessment is the same as it would be if there were no shared care arrangement. The fact that the care of the child is shared between two people does not affect the amount that the non-resident parent can afford to pay. However, where an application is only made against the non-resident parent, and not the parent with care, the maintenance requirement is not halved as it would be when an application is made against one of two truly non-resident parents (see p206).[27]

At the proposed maintenance step of the calculation, the assessable income of the deemed non-resident parent is added to the actual non-resident parent's assessable income to give the parents' joint assessable income, in the same way as if both parents were truly non-resident (see p269).

The deemed non-resident parent's calculation follows that described above for a deemed non-resident parent sharing care with the other parent. The only difference is that instead of adding a notional proposed maintenance for the parent with care, the actual proposed maintenance of the non-resident parent is used to obtain joint proposed maintenance.[28] Where there is no non-resident parent (eg, he has gone abroad or is deceased) or where the non-resident parent's assessable income is unknown (eg, he has not been traced) the deemed non-resident parent just pays child maintenance for those days for which she is not caring for the child(ren).[29]

Example: care shared between a parent to a lesser extent and another person to a greater extent

Gran, who is a widow, has Beverley (15) for four nights a week and her mother has her for the remaining three nights. As the mother looks after Beverley for less time than Gran, the mother is deemed to be non-resident. The mother has parental responsibility and receives child benefit.

The maintenance requirement is £75.36 (see example on p206)

The mother's assessable income is £42 a week. (When working out her exempt income, 3/7ths of the personal allowance for Beverley and 3/7ths family premium are included.)

The non-resident father's assessable income = £57

Parents' joint assessable income = £42 + £57 = £99

50% of joint assessable income = £49.50

This is below the maintenance requirement and, therefore, the 50 per cent calculation applies to each parent.

Father's proposed maintenance = 50% x £57 = £28.50

Mother's proposed maintenance = 50% x £42 = £21

Joint proposed maintenance = £28.50 + £21 = £49.50

The mother provides three out of seven nights' care = 42.86%

This is equivalent to paying 42.86% of £49.50 = £21.22 a week maintenance.

The mother's adjusted proposed maintenance: £21 – £21.22 = nil

As she is exempt from the minimum payment, she is not liable to pay any child maintenance as her contribution in kind outweighs the financial contribution.

Assuming the protected income calculation allows it, the father pays £28.50 a week to the grandmother, but nothing to the mother.

See p312 for the assessment where the parents have higher assessable incomes.

If the father emigrated or no application was made against him, the mother would pay 4/7ths of her proposed maintenance to the grandmother, assuming that the protected income calculation did not reduce this.

The mother's proposed maintenance would still be £21. She is still providing care three nights a week or 42.86% of the proposed maintenance in kind: 42.86% x £21 = £9

This leaves her with adjusted proposed maintenance of £21 – £9 = £12 a week to the grandmother. The protected income calculation has to be carried out and would include 3/7ths of Beverley's personal allowance and 3/7ths family premium.

Maintenance paid by the non-resident parent cannot be split between two persons with care where one is a deemed non-resident parent. The entire amount of child maintenance from the non-resident parent is paid to the remaining person with care. In other words, a parent with care who shares care for the lesser time can never receive child maintenance from a non-resident parent, no matter the size of the bill being paid.

This may seem illogical, particularly where the application has been made by the parent with care or where, although applications have been made by both persons with care, the application from the parent has been given priority (see p48). A parent with care who applies to the Child Support Agency (CSA) for maintenance from the non-resident parent, but ends up being deemed non-resident and paying maintenance, might therefore decide to have the assessment cancelled (see p360). However, if she is on income support (IS) or income-based jobseeker's allowance (JSA) and the qualifying child(ren) are part of her family for benefit purposes, cancelling is not currently an option unless she is prepared to accept a reduction in benefit (see p59).

The parent provides care for greater amount of time

If a parent does a greater proportion of the caring than another person with care, she remains a parent with care for the purposes of the maintenance assessment.[30] This also applies where the parent provides care to the same extent as someone else, but the parent receives the child benefit. There is no deemed non-resident parent. Instead, there is usually a parent with care, another person with care and a non-resident parent. It can also cover the rare situation where a person cannot technically be a person with care even though s/he is providing care of at least two nights a week on average (see p20).

If only one of the persons with care has applied for a maintenance assessment, that person will receive all the child maintenance payable by the non-resident parent.[31] This also applies where both persons with care have made an application, but only one has been accepted. There is an order of priority on which applications will be accepted (see p49). It also covers cases where the second carer cannot make an application – eg, s/he does not have parental responsibility or s/he does not share a home with the child.

However, if a request is made to the CSA by *either* of the people looking after the child(ren), the child maintenance may be divided between the two of them in proportion to the day-to-day care provided.[32] The ratio of care provided does not have to be calculated on the basis of the number of nights a child spends with the carer. An alternative method could be argued for if this would give a fairer division of the maintenance (see p298).

There is no specific format needed for a request for maintenance to be divided. It is advisable to state in writing on the maintenance application form, or in a letter, that part of the maintenance should go to another person. There is no time limit for making the request.

The decision to share the child maintenance assessment between the persons with care is a discretionary decision made by the CSA on behalf of the Secretary of State for Work and Pensions. The CSA must consider the interests of the child, the current care arrangements and all representations received about the payment proposals.[33] The decision cannot be appealed.

The alternative is for the persons with care to come to a voluntary arrangement, but this may not be possible if the person who has applied is a parent with care on IS or income-based JSA.

> **Example: care shared between a parent to a greater extent and another person to a lesser extent**
> If the caring responsibilities of the grandmother and mother in the example on p307 are swapped, so that the mother has Beverley for four nights a week, the calculation is as follows:
> The mother now remains the parent with care and the grandmother is still a person with care. (This also applies where care is shared equally but the mother is in receipt of child benefit.)
> The father's proposed maintenance remains £28.50 a week.
> However, this time the mother will receive the full amount if she makes the application for maintenance and there is no request to split the payment. If there is such a request and it is granted, then the mother will receive 4/7ths – ie, £16.29 – and the grandmother the remainder – ie, £12.21 a week.

4. **Care shared between two people who are not parents**

The situation may arise where two people living in different households each have day-to-day care (see p296) of a child of whom neither is the parent. The same rules apply as those where care is shared between a parent for the greater part of the time and another person for the rest of the time (see p309)[34] – ie, if a request is made by either person, the maintenance payable by each non-resident parent may be divided between the carers in proportion to the amount of care being provided. If no request is made, the full amount goes to the applicant.

In this situation, it is likely that there are two non-resident parents and, therefore, maintenance could be paid by both. If one of the persons with care chooses to apply for maintenance from only one of the non-resident parents, there is no reason why the second person with care cannot apply for child maintenance from the other non-resident parent.

5. **Three persons with care**

As a person with care has to look after the child for a minimum of two nights a week on average, there can be no more than three persons with care for any child. However, there may be a combination of parents and others providing the care as follows (in each case the first person provides the greatest amount of care and the third, the least).

- Parent, parent, other person – this situation is not covered specifically, although the intention must be to deem the second parent non-resident and for maintenance to be paid by him to the applicant.
- Parent, other person, parent – the second parent is deemed non-resident and maintenance is paid by him to the applicant.
- Other person, parent, parent – the first parent is deemed non-resident and maintenance is paid by him to the applicant, as well as by the second actual non-resident parent.
- Parent, other person, other person – the applicant receives maintenance from the non-resident parent or it may be apportioned on request.
- Other person, parent, other person – this is not explicitly covered, but we presume that the intention is that the parent would be deemed non-resident; there would, of course, be a second parent who is non-resident.
- Other person, other person, parent – the parent with care will be deemed non-resident and there would also be a second parent who is non-resident.
- Three other people – maintenance from both non-resident parents may be apportioned on request.

6. **Care provided in part by the local authority**

A local authority cannot be a person with care.[35] Therefore, if a child is in the care of the local authority for seven nights a week, no child maintenance is payable by the non-resident parents. There may be cases where a child is not being provided with care by the local authority all the time, but only for part of the time. If the local authority care provides less than day-to-day care (see p296), such a level of care can be ignored.

However, if the care provided by the local authority amounts to day-to-day care, child maintenance is not payable for any night that the child is in that local authority care.[36] Instead, the person with care who looks after the child for the remainder of the time receives reduced child maintenance from the non-resident parent. The maintenance payment is reduced to correspond to the number of nights per week that the child is in that person's care – eg, if the child is in local authority care for five nights a week, the person with care will receive two-sevenths of the amount of the maintenance assessment from the non-resident parent.

Where there is more than one qualifying child and the local authority provides some day-to-day care for at least one of the children, again the maintenance payable is reduced.[37] For example, a person with care looks after two children: one spends the whole week with the person with care, the other child spends four nights in local authority care and three nights with the person with care. To work out the maintenance payable in these circumstances, calculate the total number of nights spent with the person with care per week, and divide this by seven times the number of qualifying children. In this case 10 (7+3) out of 14 (7x2) nights are spent with the parent with care. The maintenance payable is ten-fourteenths (or 71.43 per cent) of the maintenance assessed.

7. **The maintenance requirement is met in full**

The calculations described earlier in this chapter hold true when the maintenance requirement is met in full. If 50 per cent of the parents' joint assessable income is greater than the maintenance requirement, the additional element calculation has to be done. See Chapter 13.

Example: care shared by parents
This is the same family as in the examples on pp300-06.
Oscar (now aged 9) now spends every other week with Nathan, while Patrick (6) still spends five days a fortnight with him. Marcia still receives child benefit for both boys and, therefore, Nathan is still deemed to be a non-resident parent of Oscar as well as Patrick. A calculation, therefore, has to be done to assess how much Nathan pays Marcia. However, in assessing Nathan's actual contribution, a notional contribution from Marcia has to be calculated.
Nathan's take-home earnings have risen to £362 a week and his superannuation contribution is now £50 a week.
Marcia has increased her hours and now earns £360 net a week. Her husband, Gareth, earns £450 net a week. Their mortgage payments are £120 a week. Their daughter Megan is two years old.
Step 1: the maintenance requirement = £140.28 (see p300)
Step 2: exempt income
Marcia's exempt income is as on p302 except that Oscar's personal allowance is now included for 3.5 days (£23.73) instead of 4.5 days = £273.54
Nathan's exempt income:

		£	
Personal allowances	Nathan	59.15	
	Oscar	23.73	(for 3.5 days)
	Patrick	16.95	(for 2.5 days)
Family premium*		8.22	(for 3.5 days)

Housing costs		75.00
Total exempt income		**183.05**

* The family premium is included in proportion to the average number of nights a week that care is provided for a child. In this case, Patrick stays with Nathan on nights that Oscar is there – ie, care is provided for at least one child for an average of 3.5 nights a week and for the other 3.5 nights Nathan is on his own. However, if the children stayed different nights, 6/7ths of the premiums would be included.[38]

Step 3: assessable income

Marcia's assessable income:		£
Net income	Earnings	360.00
Less exempt income		273.54
Assessable income		**86.46**
Nathan's assessable income:		
Net income	Earnings*	387.00
Less exempt income		183.05
Assessable income		**203.95**

* Only half of the superannuation is taken into account.

Step 4: proposed maintenance

Joint assessable income = £86.46 + £203.95 = £290.41
50% x £290.41 = £145.21.

This is above the maintenance requirement of £140.28 and, therefore, an additional element calculation must be done (see p265).

Marcia's notional proposed maintenance:

Basic element = £140.28 x £86.46/£290.41 = £41.77
Basic assessable income = £41.77 x 2 = £83.54
Additional assessable income = £86.46 – £83.54 = £2.92
Additional element = 20% x £2.92 = £0.59
Notional proposed maintenance = £41.77 + £0.59 = £42.36

Nathan's proposed maintenance to Marcia:

Basic element = £140.28 x £203.95/£290.41 = £98.51
Basic assessable income = £98.51 x 2 = £197.02
Additional assessable income = £203.95 – £197.02 = £6.93
Additional element = 20% x £6.93 = £1.38
Proposed maintenance = £98.51 + £1.38 = £99.89
Joint proposed maintenance = £42.36 + £99.89 = £142.25

Nathan contributes in kind = $\frac{3.5 + 2.5}{7 \times 2}$ = 42.86% of the care.

This is equivalent to £60.97 (42.86% x £142.25)
Nathan's proposed maintenance after taking into account his portion of the care = £99.89 – £60.97 = £38.92 a week.

This is below the maximum payment (see p266).

Step 5: protected income
This follows the example on p306, except that now Nathan's income has risen, and half Oscar's personal allowance and half the family premium are included (see p306).

There could be times when there is more then one child and because the care is shared in different ways for the different children, each parent would be the person with care for one child and the deemed non-resident parent for the other. In this case, two shared care calculations would have to be carried out. This would happen in the situation described in the above example if Nathan were in receipt of the child benefit for Oscar.

Example: care shared between a parent and another person
Gran has Beverley (15) for four nights a week and her mother has her for the remaining three nights. The mother is, therefore, deemed to be a non-resident parent. When the mother's assessable income was £42 and the father's was £57, the mother's child maintenance liability was nil while the father's proposed maintenance was £28.50 (see p307).
The mother's assessable income has increased to £100
Joint assessable income = £100 + £57 = £157
50 per cent of joint assessable income = 50% x £157 = £78.50
This is above the maintenance requirement of £75.36 (see p206) and so an additional element calculation has to be done.
Father's proposed maintenance:
Basic element = £75.36 x £57/£157 = £27.36
Basic assessable income = £27.36 x 2 = £54.72
Additional assessable income = £57 – £54.72 = £2.28
Additional element = £2.28 x 15% = £0.34
Proposed maintenance = £27.36 + £0.34 = £27.70

Mother's proposed maintenance:
Basic element = £75.36 x £100/£157 = £48
Basic assessable income = £48 x 2 = £96
Additional assessable income = £100 – £96 = £4
Additional element = £4 x 15% = £0.60
Proposed maintenance = £48 + £0.60 = £48.60
Joint proposed maintenance = £27.70 + £48.60 = £76.30
The mother provides care three out of seven nights = 42.86% of the care. This is equivalent to paying 42.86% of £76.30 – ie, £32.70 a week maintenance. The mother's adjusted proposed maintenance = £48.60 – £32.70 = £15.90

Assuming the protected calculations allow these figures, Gran now receives £15.90 from the mother and £27.70 from the father, a total of £43.60 (instead of the £28.50 from the non-resident father).

If the non-resident father's assessable income had been £157 and the mother's £100 a week, again an additional element calculation would have been done.

Father's proposed maintenance would be £55.77

Mother's proposed maintenance would be £35.52

Joint proposed maintenance = £55.77 + £35.52 = £91.29

The mother provides care three out of seven nights = 42.86% of the care.

This is equivalent to paying 42.86% x £91.29 = £39.13 a week maintenance.

The mother, therefore, does not have to pay any maintenance as her contribution in kind (£39.13) outweighs her financial liability (£35.52). Despite the fact that her assessable income is the same, her liability has been reduced to nil as a result of the increased liability of the father.

The father still has to pay his proposed maintenance, assuming this does not bring his disposable income below the protected income level. The maintenance of £55.77 is paid to the grandmother.

Notes

1. What is shared care
1 Regs 20(1)(a) and 24(1)(a) CS(MASC) Regs
2 Reg 1(2) CS(MASC) Regs
3 CCS/2885/2005
4 Reg 1(2) CS(MASC) Regs; CCS/6/1994
5 DMG para 6022
6 CCS/128/2001
7 Regs 1(2) and 20(1) CS(MASC) Regs; CCS/449/1995
8 CCS/12686/1996
9 CCS/11728/1996
10 s5(1) CSA 1991
11 s5(2) CSA 1991

2. Care shared between separated parents
12 Reg 20(2) and (3) CS(MASC) Regs
13 CCS/13455/1996
14 Reg 20(2)(a) CS(MASC) Regs

15 Reg 20(2)(b)(i) CS(MASC) Regs
16 Reg 20(2)(b)(ii) CS(MASC) Regs
17 Reg 9(4) CS(MASC) Regs
18 Reg 9(3) CS(MASC) Regs
19 Reg 9(1)(f) and (2)(c)(iv) CS(MASC) Regs
20 Reg 20(3) and (4) CS(MASC) Regs
21 Reg 20(5) CS(MASC) Regs
22 Reg 20(6) CS(MASC) Regs
23 Reg 20(6) CS(MASC) Regs
24 Reg 11(3) and (4) CS(MASC) Regs
25 DMG paras 3201-03

3. Care shared between a parent and another person
26 Reg 20 CS(MASC) Regs
27 Reg 19(1) CS(MASC) Regs
28 Reg 20(4)(i) CS(MASC) Regs
29 Reg 20(4)(ii) CS(MASC) Regs
30 Reg 24(1) CS(MASC) Regs

31 Reg 24(2)(a) CS(MASC) Regs
32 Reg 24(2)(b) CS(MASC) Regs
33 Reg 24(2)(c) CS(MASC) Regs

4. **Care shared between two people who are not parents**
34 Reg 24 CS(MASC) Regs

6. **Care provided in part by the local authority**
35 Reg 51 CS(MAP) Regs
36 Reg 25 CS(MASC) Regs
37 Reg 25(3) CS(MASC) Regs

7. **The maintenance requirement is met in full**
38 Reg 9(3) and (4) CS(MASC) Regs

Chapter 16

Departures ('old rules')

This chapter covers:
1. Grounds for departure (p318)
2. Applying for departure (p328)
3. Procedure (p329)
4. Considering departure (p332)
5. The departure direction (p333)

The Child Support Agency can 'depart' from the standard formula (see Chapters 10–15) in special cases, but only once a maintenance assessment has been made (see Chapter 17). There can be no departure from a Category A or C interim maintenance assessment (IMA) (see p367).[1] A non-resident parent cannot request a departure from a Category D IMA.[2] Not all types of departure can be used with a Category D IMA where the person with care applies, or with a Category B IMA.[3]

There can be no departure if, on the date from which any departure direction would have effect (see p340):[4]
- the non-resident parent was being paid income support (IS), income-based jobseeker's allowance (JSA) or pension credit (PC), or one of those benefits was being paid for him; *or*
- the person with care was being paid IS, income-based JSA, PC or working tax credit, or one of those benefits was being paid for her. This only applies to a departure application by:
  – the person with care for special expenses (see p318); *or*
  – the non-resident parent on additional cases grounds (see p325).

A departure direction can only be made for one of the specified reasons (see p318), and only if it would be just and equitable to do so (see p332). Departure can mean changes to the amounts used in the standard formula to work out the assessment.

1. **Grounds for departure**

Grounds for departure fall into three groups.
- **Special expenses** (see below) that the standard formula does not take into account – this is mostly used by non-resident parents.
- **Additional cases** (see p325) because of the under-use of available income/ assets or unreasonably high outgoings – this is mostly used by persons with care.
- **Property and capital transfers** made before April 1993 (see p327).

Special expenses

Departure is possible if the applicant has:[5]
- travel costs of contact with the child(ren) named in the assessment (see below);
- costs of supporting a stepchild and other children in the family (see p319);
- travel-to-work costs not taken into account in the assessment (see p322);
- costs of a long-term illness or disability (for himself or his dependant) (see p323);
- debts incurred before the couple separated (see p323); *or*
- pre-April 1993 financial commitments from which it would be impossible or unreasonable to withdraw (see p324).

The first £15 of the total of contact costs, travel-to-work cost, debts and pre-1993 financial commitments is disregarded.[6] Remember that there can be no departure for special expenses (or for any other reason) if the non-resident parent is on income support (IS), income-based jobseeker's allowance (JSA) or pension credit (PC), or the person with care is on IS or income-based JSA, PC or working tax credit (WTC).

Contact costs

Only the non-resident parent's costs of contact with the child(ren) named in the assessment count.[7] The contact costs of a parent with shared care who is treated as a non-resident parent (see p299) are not treated as special expenses, and a departure would not be granted for such costs.[8]

Only travel costs count, not the cost of treats or overnight stays. Travel costs can be for the non-resident parent travelling to see the children, or the children travelling to see him. Costs incurred for the purpose of maintaining contact may include costs of some travel once the non-resident parent and child(ren) are together – eg, taking the child from the person with care's home to the non-resident parent's home. However, the cost of travel to the cinema from the person with care's home will not normally be considered.

Only the following count as travel costs:[9]
- the cost of a ticket by public transport (eg, train, coach, boat or plane);
- the cost of fuel by private vehicle – there is no allowance for repairs;

- the cost of taxi fares, but only for a non-resident parent whose disability or illness makes it impracticable for him to use another form of available transport.[10] Any financial assistance he receives towards contact costs is offset from the fare.[11]

Minor incidental costs also count. These may include bridge tolls, parking and ticket reservation fees.[12]

The costs are based on an established pattern of visits if one exists.[13] If there is no established pattern, the non-resident parent and person with care must have agreed a pattern of future contact. This will be used.[14]

The Child Support Agency (CSA) can decide that contact costs are unreasonably high or unreasonably incurred – eg, because the method of travel is too expensive, and may substitute lower amounts than those provided.

Where visits are frequent, the CSA may only allow travel costs of some of them. The CSA must allow enough costs for visits specified in a court order, as long as those visits are being made.[15] Non-resident parents who visit more often than the court order states may wish to change the order to reflect the true position.

Changes in contact may mean changes in any departure direction. If contact stops, even through no fault of the non-resident parent, the departure direction will be cancelled.[16]

The first £15 of these costs (or the total of these and other costs) is disregarded.

Costs of supporting a stepchild

If a non-resident parent or person with care supports a child who is part of her/his household (see p22), but of whom s/he is not the parent (see p15), an amount for those costs may be allowed.[17] This amount is set by a formula (see below). This ground cannot be used by a departure applicant subject to a Category B interim maintenance assessment (IMA).[18]

A 'stepchild' is one who:[19]

- counts as a member of the applicant's family. This is limited to children of:
    - the applicant's current partner; *and*
    - the applicant's former partner who live in the applicant's household every night of the week; *and*
- was part of the applicant's family and household before 5 April 1993; *and*
- remained part of that family and household from 5 April 1993 continuously to the effective date of the proposed departure direction (see p340).[20]

The expenses allowed depend upon the support for the stepchild from her/his non-resident parent and, if the applicant's partner is the child's parent, from that partner. The **cost** of the stepchild is based on the amount excluded from exempt income and is the:[21]

- IS personal allowance for a child of that age; *plus*

- IS family premium if the family contains no children of whom the applicant is the parent. Where special expenses are sought for more than one stepchild, the family premium is divided equally between them;[22] *plus*
- IS disabled child premium if the stepchild would qualify.

If the care of the stepchild is shared between the applicant's current partner and the stepchild's other parent, the cost is reduced by the proportion of time the child spends away from the applicant's household.[23]

No expenses are allowed if maintenance payable to or for the stepchild by her/his non-resident parent is more than the cost, whether the maintenance is a deduction from his IS/income-based JSA (see p200) *or* is under an order or written agreement for maintenance or a maintenance assessment.[24] The CSA can ignore maintenance payable (but not deductions due) if, for example, the stepchild's non-resident parent cannot be found.[25]

If maintenance is less than the cost, the **allowable amount** is the cost less any maintenance payable (unless ignored) or deductions.[26]

If the applicant's partner is *not* the stepchild's parent, the maximum special expenses allowed is the allowable amount.[27]

Where special expenses are sought for stepchildren of different parents, a separate allowable amount is worked out for each child (or group of children who have the same parents), and the allowable amount is the total of those amounts.[28]

If the applicant's partner is the stepchild's parent, her ability to support the child is taken into account in a similar way to the joint child calculation for exempt income (see p228). Her **net income** is worked out as if it were a non-resident parent's assessable income (see Chapter 13) plus child benefit for the stepchildren and any income of her children (except earnings) above £10.[29] Her **outgoings** are:[30]

- the IS personal allowance for a person aged 25 or over (regardless of the partner's actual age); *plus*
- any partner's contribution for joint child(ren) assumed under the standard formula (see p228); *plus*
- the allowable amount (see above); *plus*
- any partner's contribution to housing costs assumed under an existing departure direction (see p327).

If the partner's net income is more than her outgoings, no costs are allowed.[31] If it is less, maximum special expenses are the allowable amount.[32]

Example

Bob has been assessed to pay £45.99 for Carol and David (p287). He lives with his partner, Zoe, their child, Ricky, and three stepchildren so departure is possible if the stepfamily was formed before April 1993. Zoe receives maintenance of £20 a week for Yvonne (14) and Veronica (12), but nothing for Scott (5).

The **allowable amount** is worked out for each non-resident parent.

Wayne's children:		£
Personal allowances	Yvonne	47.45
	Veronica	47.45
Total (no family premium applies as there is a joint child, Ricky)		94.90
Less maintenance due		20.00
Allowable amount		**74.90**

Terence's child:		
Personal allowance	Scott	47.45
(no family premium applies as there is a joint child, Ricky)		
No maintenance due		
Allowable amount		**47.45**
Total allowable amount (£74.90 + £47.45)		**122.35**

	£
Zoe's **net income** is child benefit	54.40
Personal allowance	59.15
Total allowable amount	122.35
Outgoings	**181.50**

Zoe's income is less than her outgoings so the maximum special expenses is the total allowable amount of £122.35 (WTC counts as Bob's income and not Zoe's because he is the partner in employment). A departure direction for a special expense of £122.35 can, therefore, be made (but see p334). However, if Zoe had refused to accept maintenance for Scott, the departure decision maker may decide that departure would not be fair.

Zoe had recently applied for a CSA assessment: the departure decision maker may not make a decision until that application is decided.

Some months later the CSA issues assessments of £6 from Wayne and £30.32 from Terence. Also, Zoe is now working and when Bob's liability is reassessed it rises to £61.95. The new allowable amount is:

	£
Wayne's children (total personal allowances)	94.90
Less child support due	6.00
Allowable amount	**88.90**
Terence's child (personal allowance)	47.45
Less child support due	30.32
Allowable amount	**17.13**
Total allowable amount (£88.90 + £17.13)	**106.03**

Zoe's maintenance has increased from £20 to £36.32, and the total allowable amount has gone down by £16.32. Zoe's **net income** is now:

	£
Child benefit	54.40
Earnings	95.00
Net income	**149.40**

WTC is still not treated as her income because it is paid to the partner who works at least 16 hours a week – ie, Bob. Because Zoe is now treated as able to support the joint child (see example on p228) her **outgoings** are considered to be higher.

Personal allowances		£
	Zoe	59.15
	Ricky (half)	23.73
Family premium (half)		8.22
Allowable amount		106.03
Partner's contribution to housing costs		Nil
Total		**197.13**

Zoe's net income is lower than this, so a departure direction for the reduced allowable expenses of £106.03 can be made. However, had Zoe's income been higher it would have failed.

Travel-to-work costs

If the travel-to-work costs of a non-resident parent or person with care are not adequately covered by the broad-brush allowance in the formula (see p226), a departure can be made. As the formula allowance works on straight-line distances, those who travel around estuaries or mountains, or are in rural areas may benefit. Those whose reasonable public transport costs are more than 6 pence per straight line kilometre may also benefit. Self-employed people can benefit for travel costs which are not tax-deductible.[33]

Travel costs allowable are the same as for contact costs (see p318), except that taxi fares are allowable regardless of disability, but only where the journey is unavoidably taken at a time when no other reasonable type of transport is available.[34] Minor incidental costs count. Costs can be reduced or refused where they are considered high or unreasonably incurred.[35]

The travel cost special expenses allowance replaces the formula allowance (see p226). There is a £15 disregard on the total of travel-to-work costs and certain other special expenses (see p318). Disabled people's parking costs should be claimed as costs of a long-term disability, rather than travel-to-work costs (see p318), in order to avoid the disregard.

Example

Steve (see p226) has an allowance of £64.98 included in his exempt income for travel to work. However, Steve's season ticket to London is £5,100 a year, or £98 a week. Even with the first £15 disregarded this is greater than the allowance. The departure decision maker has decided that a direction is reasonable because Steve lives in Leicestershire in order to be near his two children and he has not been able to find an equivalent job nearer to home. The special expense of £83 replaces the broad-brush allowance of £64.98. See p334 for the re-calculated assessment.

Costs of a long-term illness or disability

Special expenses include costs of a long-term illness or disability of the non-resident parent or person with care and/or his/her dependant(s).[36] Long-term illness is one that is current at the date of the departure application and which is likely to last for a further 52 weeks or to be terminal.[37] Dependant means:[38]

- the departure applicant's partner (see p26);
- a child (see p18) of the applicant or partner, living with the applicant, except a child named in the assessment to which the departure application applies (see also p32 for additional maintenance).

Costs allowable are the reasonable costs of:[39]

- personal care, attendance and communication needs;
- mobility;
- domestic help;
- medical aids which cannot be provided under the NIIS;[40]
- heating, clothing and laundry;
- food essential for a diet recommended by a medical practitioner;
- adaptations to the applicant's home; *and*
- day care, respite care and rehabilitation.

Any financial help towards these costs from any source is deducted.[41] This includes disability living allowance (DLA) and attendance allowance (AA). If a DLA/AA claim has been made, the CSA will wait for that decision before deciding on departure.[42] If no claim has been made, but the CSA considers that the disabled person may be entitled, the CSA will notify the applicant, who has six weeks in which to claim. If no claim is made, the CSA deducts the highest rate of the appropriate component(s) of DLA (or AA if appropriate) from the costs.[43] The CSA has a discretion to ignore DLA/AA awarded to a dependant.[44]

Debts of the relationship

A non-resident parent or person with care may be repaying debts incurred *before* the non-resident parent became a non-resident parent (see p22) of the child named in the assessment (whether before or after April 1993). Repayment can count as special expenses, but only if the debt was incurred when the departure applicant and ex-partner were a couple (see p26) and was for the benefit of:[45]

- the departure applicant and an ex-partner, jointly;
- the ex-partner alone, if the applicant is liable for the repayments;
- a child (see p18) of the applicant and/or ex-partner, who lived with the applicant and ex-partner at the time the debt arose; *and/or*
- a child named in the assessment to which the departure application applies.

Ex-partner includes any ex-partner of the non-resident parent (not just the parent with care), but, if the person with care applies for departure only the non-resident parent counts as an ex-partner.[46]

Loans only count if they are from a bank, building society or other registered lender, or from the departure applicant's current or former employer.[47] The following do *not* count as debts:

- debts incurred to buy something that the applicant kept after the relationship ended;[48]
- a debt for which the applicant took responsibility under a financial settlement with the ex-partner or a court order;[49]
- secured mortgage repayments; *and*
- endowment/insurance premiums,[50] except for mortgage/insurance incurred to buy or repair/improve (see p215)[51] the home of the parent with care and child named in the assessment.

The following also do *not* count as debts:[52]

- debts of a business or trade;
- gambling debts;
- legal costs of the separation, divorce or dissolution of a civil partnership;
- credit card repayments;
- overdrafts, unless taken out for a specified amount repayable over a specified period;
- fines imposed on the applicant;
- any debt incurred to pay off one of these (except for business/trade debts); *or*
- any other debt the CSA considers it reasonable to exclude.

Debts incurred to pay off a debt which would have counted also count.[53] However, any direction is based upon the repayment period and rate of the original debt.[54]

The first £15 of the total of allowable debts of the relationship and certain other special expenses is disregarded (see p318).

Any departure direction is for the debt repayment period.[55] If the applicant cannot meet the repayments, the direction can be extended, but only if the creditor agreed to extend time for repayment because of:[56]

- the applicant's unemployment or incapacity for work; *or*
- a substantial fall in the applicant's income.

Pre-April 1993 financial commitments

Special expenses can include other financial commitments of the non-resident parent – eg, hire purchase or school fees. Commitments like those on p323 do not count. The only commitments that count are those:[57]

- made before 5 April 1993;
- from which it would be impossible or unreasonable to withdraw; *and*
- where an order or written agreement for maintenance was made before 5 April 1993 for all the non-resident parent's children (see p18) (including at least one child named in the assessment) *and* that order/agreement was in force on both

the date the commitment was made and on 5 April 1993.[58] There can be more than one order/agreement for different children.

Additional cases

This can be used by a person with care who is not a parent. However, for convenience, we refer to 'parent'.

Grounds for departure are if:[59]

- a parent's lifestyle is inconsistent with the level of her/his income;
- a parent's assets could produce some or more income;
- a parent has diverted her/his income so it is not taken into account in the formula;
- the housing costs used in the formula are unreasonably high;
- it is reasonable for a parent's partner to contribute towards the couple's housing costs;
- travel-to-work costs used in the formula are unreasonably high; *or*
- travel-to-work costs should be disregarded completely.

There can be no departure on additional cases grounds if the non-resident parent is on IS or income-based JSA *or* if he is the departure applicant and the person with care is on IS, income-based JSA or WTC (see p317). However, it is possible that information about undeclared income will be passed to Jobcentre Plus (see p101) and/or the case referred to CSA to consider whether there is notional income (see p250).

> **Example**
> A non-resident parent has a large well-furnished house in a stockbroker belt, with several cars in the drive and a lifestyle which suggests wealth. He is a director of his own company and pays a modest salary to himself and to his new partner. His declared income is only a few pounds above the mortgage so the assessment is nil. He is not subject to the excessive housing cost rule (see p220) nor to the minimum payment (see p199) as the couple have a child. The person with care could seek a departure on the grounds that:
> • the non-resident parent's lifestyle is incompatible with his declared income;
> • the non-resident parent's partner should contribute to housing costs; *and*
> • the housing costs are unreasonably high.
> If the new partner does not do much work for the business, the non-resident parent's income may have been unreasonably diverted to her.

Lifestyle inconsistent with income

Departure is possible where a parent's overall lifestyle requires substantially higher income than the amount of her/his income on which the maintenance assessment is based.[60] This cannot be done if the lifestyle is paid for:[61]

- from the parent's capital; *or*
- by her/his partner, unless the parent can influence the amount of the partner's income (eg, as employer). If s/he cannot, the CSA can consider whether the partner could contribute to housing costs (see p327).[62]

The CSA is unlikely to investigate a parent's lifestyle. If there appear to be grounds for investigation, it may refer the case to an appeal tribunal, which could direct the parties to provide evidence (see p405).

If departure is directed, notional extra income will be set (see p339).

Under-use of assets

A parent may be under-using her/his money or property. Departure can only happen if the total value of the assets found to be under-used (less any mortgage or charge) is £10,000 or more.[63] This can apply if s/he is the beneficiary of, or can control:[64]

- an asset which does not produce income but could do so;
- an investment producing less income than is reasonable;
- a claim to money (eg, a debt or legal action) which it is reasonable to enforce; *and/or*
- an asset which it would be reasonable to sell.

This also applies to any trust funds of which the parent is a beneficiary.[65]

The CSA can ignore assets which are to be used for a reasonable purpose.[66] The parent's home would not normally be treated as an asset for the purpose of this ground, but any second or holiday homes could be considered.

If an under-used asset exists, any departure direction will set the notional extra income which the asset could produce. The asset is assumed to produce income at the judgment rate: currently 8 per cent.[67] Any actual income from the asset is deducted from that notional income.

Diversion of income

Departure is possible where a parent can control her/his income *and* has unreasonably reduced her/his income (as worked out for the standard formula) by diverting it to other people or other purposes.[68] For example, a non-resident parent's company pays him no salary but pays his partner an inflated one.

Unreasonable housing costs

If a parent's housing costs are more than the amount normally allowed under the formula but s/he is exempt from that restriction (see p220), departure is possible if those costs are unreasonably high.[69] Departure only removes the exemption, so weekly housing costs still cannot be set at less than £80 or half the parent's net income, whichever is greater.[70]

Partner's contribution towards housing costs

Departure is possible if a parent has a partner who occupies the home and it is reasonable for that partner to contribute towards housing costs.[71] The CSA will decide what proportion the partner should pay, considering the parent's income and the partner's income.[72] This can be 100 per cent, especially if a Category B IMA is in force and/or the parent is withholding information about her/his partner's income.[73]

Unreasonable travel to work costs/allowance

Departure is possible where travel costs allowed under the formula (see p226):
- are unreasonably high – eg, the parent shares a car;[74] *or*
- ought not to be allowed because the parent can pay maintenance assessed without an allowance for part or all of those costs.[75]

Property and capital transfers

The broad-brush formula allowance for pre-1993 property transfers (see p222) may not result in a proper reflection of the effect of that transfer in the amount of child support maintenance. Also, some parents cannot use that allowance – eg, because of lack of evidence. Departure allows for a more flexible approach. Property is not defined (as it is for the broad-brush allowance – see p222) so it includes things such as household items and shares. It is not a ground for departure, however, from a Category D IMA.[76]

Departure is possible if:[77]
- before 5 April 1993 a court order or written agreement was in force between the non-resident parent and the person with care and/or the child(ren) named in the assessment; *and*
- in connection with that order/agreement, property which the non-resident parent owned (or had the benefit of) was transferred to that person with care or that child, or to a trust for payment of the normal day-to-day living expenses of that child; *and either*:
  - that transfer reduced the non-resident parent's maintenance liability (not child support) *and* the effect of that transfer is not properly reflected in the current maintenance assessment; *or*
  - that transfer did *not* reduce the non-resident parent's maintenance liability (not child support) *but* the current maintenance assessment is reduced because of that transfer *and* that reduction is inappropriate because of the purpose of the transfer – eg, it was for spousal maintenance.

No departure can be made if:
- the change in maintenance would be less than £1;[78] *or*
- the transfer was temporary and ends before the effective date of the direction.[79]

To see if the broad-brush property allowance fairly reflects the child maintenance forgone, the CSA first works out the value of the transfer, ignoring any part which was not in lieu of child maintenance. Unless there is evidence to show otherwise, the CSA assumes that:[80]

- the property covered by the order/agreement was held in equal shares by the non-resident parent and person with care;
- if those parties had been married, half of the value of the transfer was for the person with care's benefit, and not for the child(ren);
- if those parties were *never* married, *none* of the value of the transfer was for the person with care's benefit.

The equivalent weekly value is then worked out. The number of years of liability is deemed to begin on the date of the order/agreement and to end on the date it sets for maintenance to end (for the youngest child if there is more than one), or, if no date is given, when the youngest child reaches 18.[81] Using that figure and the interest rate on judgment debts at the date of the order/agreement, a multiplier is given by a table.[82] That gives an equivalent weekly value which replaces the broad-brush allowance (see p222). If that would lead to a departed assessment of less than the child maintenance payable under the order/agreement, a lower weekly value can be set. The weekly value of a transfer of less than £5,000 is nil.[83]

The result is difficult to predict (see p337). The assessment may be increased or reduced, irrespective of who applied for departure.

---

2. **Applying for departure**

Once an assessment has been made, a person with care, non-resident parent or child applicant in Scotland may apply for a departure direction.[84] This applies to any assessment – whether made on initial application or after a revision or supersession – but not to all categories of interim maintenance assessment (see p317). Information about departure is provided with an assessment.

The Child Support Agency (CSA) can provide an application form on request, or a letter can be accepted if it has all the information required by the form.[85] The applicant should fill in the form as fully as possible. The date of the application is the date it is received by the CSA, unless there was unavoidable delay.[86] The date of the application affects the effective date of any direction (see p340).

If the application is not accepted because it is not properly made, the CSA can send it back (or send a form) to the applicant. If it is properly made within 14 days of the day the CSA sends it back, it counts as made when the defective application was made.[87]

An application cannot be made before the assessment is made.[88] Even if the reason for departure is in the maintenance application form or maintenance enquiry form, a separate application must still be made.

A departure applicant can be represented by any other person.[89]

A departure application can be withdrawn or amended by the applicant at any time before it is decided.[90] S/he may want to do this after seeing the other party's information. However, a person considering applying may want to try to work out what any departure would be *before* applying. This is because a departure may work against the applicant.

3. **Procedure**

Departure applications on several grounds or by both parties will be considered together to ensure that the outcome is just and equitable (see p332). Each party may have a departure direction granted (on multiple grounds) and applied to the assessment.

Preliminary consideration

The decision maker will carry out a preliminary consideration of each application before asking the other party for information.[91] If the application has no chance of success, it will be refused.[92]

The Child Support Agency (CSA) may ask the applicant for further information, which must be provided within one month (longer may be allowed if the CSA is satisfied that this is reasonable).[93] If it is not, and the decision maker is satisfied on the available evidence that a departure direction should not be given, the application may be refused without the other party being asked for information.[94]

Because the decision maker wants the assessment to be correct *before* departure is considered, s/he may pass the case to other CSA staff for revision or supersession before completing the preliminary consideration (see p341).

There is a right of appeal against refusal on preliminary consideration (see p343).

If the case passes the preliminary consideration, but the decision maker considers that a direction is unlikely to be given, s/he can decide the application without asking the other party for information.[95] However, if the decision maker then considers a direction should be made, s/he must ask for that information before making a decision (see below).[96]

Information

If the application passes the preliminary consideration, the CSA must (unless a direction is unlikely to be made) write to the other party (or parties if the maintenance application was by a Scottish child):[97]

- notifying her/him that the departure application has been made;
- sending details of the grounds for the application and any relevant information the applicant has given (but see below); *and*
- asking for representations about the application to be made within 14 days.[98]

If representations are sent, the CSA may send them to the applicant asking for comments.[99] However, this is only likely to happen where the evidence provided by the parent contradicts that supplied by the applicant, and the CSA cannot make a decision based on the evidence available. The contradictory evidence may then be copied to the other party for comments.[100] Any party can send further information to the CSA at any time. If a response cannot be made within 14 days, the information available should be sent with a request for more time to provide the rest. The CSA is unlikely to make its own enquiries so each party must make their own case. On appeal, the tribunal can require information to be provided (see p400).

Where one party does not know the whereabouts of another party or a child named in the maintenance assessment and that party has not agreed to disclosure, then that address and any information which could reasonably be expected to lead to them being located will not be disclosed unless:[101]

- that address/information is necessary to decide the departure application; *and*
- there is no risk of harm or undue distress to that party/child if disclosure were made.

Undisclosed medical evidence will not be sent to a person if it would harm her/his health.[102]

Regular payments condition

If a non-resident parent applies for departure, the CSA can impose a regular payments condition (RPC).[103] This will only normally be done where the non-resident parent has persistently failed to pay maintenance due and only once the application has passed a preliminary consideration (see p329). A person with care who knows a departure application has been made can ask the CSA to make an RPC.

Decisions about an RPC may be initiated by the CSA debt management section, but the decision maker decides whether to impose the RPC and the rate at which it should be paid. An RPC will usually be set at the rate of the current assessment.[104] The exception is where the departure application is for special expenses for travel costs, contact costs or illness/disability.[105] If this applies, the RPC will be set for a lower amount on the assumption that a departure direction has been made for those expenses, unless the non-resident parent has exaggerated or claimed unreasonable expenses.[106]

The CSA notifies the non-resident parent and person with care of any RPC and the effect of failing to comply.[107] If the non-resident parent fails to comply, he will usually be contacted and the RPC may be re-negotiated.

If this does not work, the CSA can decide that the non-resident parent has failed to comply with the RPC. Written notice of this is sent to the non-resident parent and person with care. If the CSA decides that the non-resident parent has failed to comply with the RPC within 28 days of the notice, the departure application lapses.[108]

An RPC does not affect the amount of maintenance the non-resident parent is *liable* to pay. Even if he complies with the RPC, if this is less than the amount of the current assessment, there will be arrears if the departure application fails (see p435).

The RPC will end once the departure decision has been made.

Revision or supersession of the assessment

A departure application can be made even if a revision or supersession of the existing assessment has been applied for.[109] An assessment can also be revised or superseded while a departure application is being considered. In a case where a fresh assessment is made on a revision or supersession the decision maker may direct that the departure application lapse, unless the applicant asks for it to stand.[110] See Chapter 18 for revisions and supersessions.

If the application shows a ground for changing the assessment (eg, a mistake or a change of circumstances), the case will be considered for revision or supersession.

Where an assessment is revised or superseded (see p341) the departure decision maker treats that fresh assessment as the current assessment when considering departure.

Decision on the application

If the decision maker decides the application (rather than referring it to a tribunal) s/he must notify the parties of that decision and the reasons for it.[111] If the decision is to make a direction, the notification must state the way in which maintenance is to be worked out as a result of the direction. The CSA will then make a new assessment, taking into account the instructions in the departure direction (see p333). The decision on the departure direction and the maintenance assessment after the departure is taken into account can both be appealed.It is, therefore, important to be clear which decision is being appealed to the tribunal. For more information on appeals, see Chapter 19.

Referral to an appeal tribunal

Once a departure application has passed the preliminary consideration and the parties' representations have been sought, a decision maker can refer it to an appeal tribunal instead of deciding it her/himself.[112] Many departure cases will be complex or difficult, but these should normally be decided by a decision maker. A referral to tribunal might be made if, for example:

- the case raises new points – ie, ones which have never arisen in a departure case before; *or*
- the case is very contentious – eg, both parties have solicitors and the evidence is completely contradictory; *or*
- only an appeal tribunal will be able to obtain the necessary evidence.

An appeal tribunal considering a referral is subject to the rules which apply to a decision maker and will either give a direction or refuse to give one.[113] However, the procedure will be similar to an appeal and the tribunal's decision can be appealed on a point of law (see p414).

4. **Considering departure**

A departure direction can only be made if it would change the amount of the assessment by £1 or more.[114] The possible effect of 'old rules' phasing-in (see p355) is ignored.[115]

Discretion to make a direction

When considering whether and how to make a direction, the departure decision maker must:[116]

- treat parents as responsible for maintaining their children when they can afford to do so;
- treat parents as responsible for maintaining all their children equally;
- ignore the fact that all, or part, of the income of the person with care (or her partner) includes (or would, on departure, include) income support, income-based jobseeker's allowance, working tax credit, housing benefit or council tax benefit, or that child maintenance might be taken into account for benefit entitlement.

Just and equitable

Even though the grounds for departure are met and the assessment would change by £1 or more, a direction will only be made if it would be just and equitable to do so – ie, fair to all concerned.[117] The decision maker will first work out what direction would be appropriate and how it would affect the assessment. When considering whether it would be fair to make that direction, the decision maker must consider:[118]

- the financial circumstances of the non-resident parent, including any liability to pay maintenance before the assessment's effective date;

- the financial circumstances of the person with care (but ignore her receipt of certain benefits – see p332);
- whether a direction would lead to the non-resident parent or person with care giving up employment;[119]
- where the application is for special expenses, whether the applicant could have made financial arrangements to cover those expenses, or could pay for them from money s/he is spending on non-essentials.

This may mean taking into account circumstances for which either party could have sought a direction, even if s/he did not. For example, since contact costs have an effect on the financial circumstances of the non-resident parent, it may be just and equitable to take these into account when deciding on departure, even if the departure application was about something else (and may have been made by the person with care).[120] However, if such circumstances are taken into account, it must be made clear to all parties on what basis the departure has been decided.

The decision maker must *not* take into account:

- the circumstances of the child's conception;
- the reasons for the breakdown of the relationship;
- the fact that either party is now involved in a new relationship;
- any contact arrangements;
- the failure of the non-resident parent to pay maintenance under the CSA assessment or any previous arrangement; *nor*
- any representations made by a person other than the person with care, the non-resident parent or a Scottish child applicant.

Discretion should only rarely be used to refuse a departure direction outright. However, it may well be used to reduce the amount of the direction. Both parties are seen as responsible for organising their lives so as to support their children. If parties have unreasonably taken on new responsibilities (eg, a second family), failed to reduce outgoings (eg, re-schedule debts) or failed to increase their income (eg, through work), the CSA may decide that it is not just and equitable for a departure direction to be made.

5. **The departure direction**

A direction is not a new assessment. It is a direction to reassess child maintenance on a different basis.[121] The Child Support Agency (CSA) must comply as soon as reasonably practicable.[122]

The direction cannot take maintenance above the formula maximum (see p266) or below the £6 weekly minimum (see p199).[123] A non-resident parent cannot fall below the protected income level (see Chapter 14), though the direction may change that level (see below).[124]

Phased assessments

If the assessment is being phased in (see p355), special rules apply. If the effective date of the departure direction (see p340) is the *same* as that of the assessment, the direction is applied to the formula assessment.[125] The CSA then applies any phasing to that departed assessment.

If the effective date of the departure direction is *later* than that of the assessment, the direction is applied to the formula assessment. This proposed departed assessment is then compared with both the formula assessment and the phased assessment. If the proposed departed assessment is:[126]

- higher than the formula assessment, the difference between them is added to the phased assessment to give the actual departed assessment;
- less than the formula assessment but more than the phased assessment, then departure has no effect and the phased assessment is used; *or*
- less than the phased assessment, the proposed departed assessment is used.

Special expenses directions

The direction states an amount for special expenses. The CSA includes this in the applicant's exempt income and any protected income.[127] Expenses for a stepchild do not change protected income because they are already included (see p289).[128] If the direction is for travel-to-work costs (see p322), any amount for those already included in exempt income or protected income is replaced by the amount stated in the direction.[129]

If the direction reduces the non-resident parent's assessable income, the departed assessment is *the lowest of*:[130]

- the assessment current on the direction's effective date (see p340);
- 50 per cent of his assessable income after departure (see Chapter 12); *and*
- protected income level (see Chapter 14). This applies regardless of the maintenance requirement or the number of children.

If the direction would also change the figures to be used because of over-generous provision (see p325), the same calculation is done assuming those changes have taken effect.[131] For the rules if a direction for property/capital transfer is also made, see p337.

If a non-resident parent is liable to more than one person with care (see p271), his total liability is set by these rules.[132] The amount of each departed assessment will be the same proportion of total liability as it would be if liability were based on the maintenance requirements.[133]

Example: special expenses – debts and travel costs

Steve has been assessed to pay £62.18 a week to Debbie as maintenance for Paul (17), Grace (15) and Lewis (10). In July 2006, Steve applies for departure on the grounds of travel-to-work costs, debts of the relationship and pre-April 1993 commitments. He does not apply on the ground of the property settlement (see p225) as he wants first to ask his solicitor whether it would be to his advantage.

Steve is awarded special expenses of £83 travel-to-work costs (see p322). He divorced in 1991 and has already cleared some debts, but there remains one debt of the relationship and another commitment pre-dating the divorce. The total repayments amount to £34.60 a week: there is no £15 disregard as this has already been applied to the travel costs.

Debbie has net earnings of £210 and assessable income of £28.60. These were taken into account under the formula but, on departure, Steve simply pays 50 per cent of his own assessable income (as long as this is below the current assessment).

Steve's exempt income:		£
Personal allowance		59.15
Mortgage (in full – see p226)		96.00
Property settlement allowance		40.00
Travel-to-work costs		83.00
Debt repayments		34.60
Total		**312.75**
Steve's net income for child support purposes		380.00
Steve's assessable income (£380 – £312.75)		**67.25**
Proposed maintenance (50% x £67.25)		**33.63**
Protected income:		
Personal allowance	Couple	92.80
Mortgage (interest only)		78.46
Council tax		15.00
Travel-to-work costs		83.00
Debt repayments		31.60
Standard margin		30.00
Basic protected income		**333.86**

Total family income: Steve's new wife, Lisa, has net earnings of £280, so total family income = £380 + £280 = £660. This is far above protected income so Steve can afford the proposed maintenance of £33.63.

The departure direction has, therefore, reduced the assessment from £62.18 to £33.63.

Because the 50 per cent taper applies right up the income range, there comes a point where a non-resident parent's income is too high to benefit from departure (see example on p336).

Example: the well-off and special expenses

Jeremy has been assessed to pay £255.49 a week for his four children (see p264). He applies for departure on two grounds – contact costs and the commitment of school fees for the children. The children stay with Jeremy every other weekend. He collects and returns them in his car. This is cheaper than four return train fares: the petrol used is £38 a weekend. As this is £19 a week, the £15 disregard leaves a special expense of £4.

All four children are in private education, but the commitments for Henry (8) and Isobel (4) were made after 1993. The decision maker could decide that it would not be unreasonable to move Georgina (now 13) to another school whereas Francis (14) has already begun his GCSE courses.

The decision maker decides that, in principle, special expenses of £80 a week should be allowed for the next 18 months. Jeremy's exempt income would be increased by £4 + £80 = £84.

His assessable income would be now £516 (instead of £600).

The proposed maintenance after the departure would be: 50% x £516 = £258. As this is higher than the current maintenance assessment of £255.49, no departure direction is given.

If, instead, Jeremy had net income of £600 a week and assessable income of £430 a week, the current assessment would be:

Basic element = maintenance requirement = £210.98 (see p264)
Basic assessable income = 2 x £210.98 = £421.96
Additional assessable income = £430 – £421.96 = £8.04
Additional element = £8.04 x 25% = £2.01
Proposed maintenance = £210.98 + £2.01 = £212.99

The 30% protected income is less, so the assessment is capped at £180 (total protected income does not affect the assessment).

If Jeremy were awarded special expenses of £84, his assessable income would be £430 – £84 = £346.

Proposed maintenance = 50% x £346 = £173, which is less than the previous assessment of £180.

The protected income needs checking again as special expenses are now included:

	£
Personal allowance	59.15
Mortgage (interest only)	123.08
Council tax	21.00
Travel-to-contact costs	4.00
Pre-1993 commitments	80.00
Standard margin	30.00
Basic protected income	**317.23**

His total family income = £600 net earnings
Excess income = £600 – £317.23 = £282.77
15% x £282.77 = £42.42

Total protected income = £317.23 + £42.42 = £359.65

Jeremy can, therefore, afford to pay the £173 assessment without his disposable income falling below £359.65 a week.

Even if Evie applies for departure for excessive housing costs, none can be made because these are less than half Jeremy's net income.

Property/capital transfer directions

The direction states the weekly value of the transfer (see p327). Any property settlement allowance in exempt income (see p222) is removed, even if the weekly value is nil.[134] Proposed maintenance (see Chapter 13) is then reduced by the amount of any transfer value and the protected income level worked out again.[135] Maintenance payable cannot be below the £6 minimum (see p199).[136]

If a special expenses direction is also made, any property settlement allowance is removed from assessable income and the special expenses calculation is then carried out (see p334).[137] The result is then reduced by the transfer value (if any).[138]

If a non-resident parent is liable to more than one person with care (see p271) the transfer value is deducted from the assessment for the person with care or for the child for whom the transfer was made.[139]

The removal of the allowance from exempt income continues after the direction ends because it has compensated for the transfer.[140]

Where the transfer was to trustees and the weekly value is more than nil, any child maintenance from that trust is disregarded from the parent with care's assessable income.[141]

Example: property transfer direction

Hamish and Kirsty divorced in February 1993, when their only child, Angus, was two. The house, then worth £31,000, was transferred to Kirsty with a mortgage of about £9,000. From April 1995, Kirsty's assessment was reduced when Hamish was given an allowance of £40 in his exempt income. Kirsty has remarried, has a baby and has no net income of her own. Hamish is single.

The current assessment is:

	£
Maintenance requirement	45.78
Hamish's exempt income:	
Personal allowance	59.15
Housing costs	45.00
Property settlement allowance	40.00
Total	**144.15**

Hamish's net income = £205 a week net earnings.

Assessable income = £205 − £144.15 = £60.85

Proposed maintenance = £60.85 x 50% = **£30.43** (less than the maintenance requirement). Protected income shows that Hamish can afford this.

The purpose of the capital transfer was unspecified. Kirsty believes it was in lieu of spousal maintenance forgone and to provide a home for Angus. Hamish also had to pay £15 a week under a court order as maintenance for Angus. The departure decision maker decides that the property transfer in lieu of child maintenance was £6,000. Given that Angus was to be dependent for at least another 14 years from the date of the order, a transfer of £6,000 does not amount to £20 a week child maintenance in advance as implied by the £40 allowance.

No date was set in the order for maintenance payment to end, so it is deemed to end when Angus turns 18. The number of years of liability is, therefore, 16. The interest rate for judgment debt was 14 per cent at the time of the order so the table gives a multiplier of 0.00320: £6,000 x 0.00320 = £19.20. This is, therefore, the equivalent weekly value.

Hamish's exempt income = £59.15 + £45 = £104.15

Hamish's net income = £205 a week net earnings.

Assessable income = £205 – £104.15 = £100.85

Proposed maintenance = (£100.85 x 50%) = £50.43 (more than the maintenance requirement of £45.78)

Therefore, proposed maintenance is

£45.78 + 15% x (£100.85 – (£45.78 x2)) = £47.17

Protected income shows that Hamish can afford this.

The amount under the departure direction is then deducted: £47.17 – £19.20 = £27.97

If Hamish's net income is £315, but exempt income the same (£144.15), the current assessment would be:

Assessable income = £315 – £144.15 = £170.85

£170.85 x 50% = £85.43 (more than maintenance requirement of £45.78).

Therefore proposed maintenance =

£45.78 + 15% x (£170.85 – (£45.78 x 2)) = £57.67

Protected income shows that he can afford this.

With a property transfer direction of £19.20 (where the £40 allowance in exempt income does not apply).

Assessable income = £315 – £104.15 = £210.85

Proposed maintenance = £45.78 + 15% x (£210.85 – (£45.78 x 2)) = £63.67

The amount under the departure direction is deducted:

£63.67 – £19.20 = £44.47

The departure has in fact ended up reducing the assessment by £13.20

Additional cases directions

If departure is on the grounds of *lifestyle inconsistent with income, under-use of assets* or *diversion of income*, the direction states a figure of notional income to be added to net income (see p211) and so is also included in protected income (see p283).[142]

If *housing costs are unreasonably high*, the direction states the costs that are considered reasonable, and this replaces actual housing costs for exempt income (see p214) and protected income (see p284).[143] The limit of half income/£80 still applies.

If the *partner is to contribute to housing costs*, the direction states the proportion of costs by which housing costs are to be reduced (which may be 100 per cent).[144] Housing costs are reduced by that proportion for exempt income, but not for protected income (see p284). If the direction also states that housing costs are unreasonably high (see above), housing costs used in exempt income are reasonable costs reduced by the stated proportion. The limit of half income/£80 still applies.

If *travel-to-work costs are unreasonably high or should be disregarded*, the direction states the amount of costs allowed (which may be nil). This replaces any travel costs included in exempt income or protected income.[145]

If a direction for special expenses has been given and one for over-generous provision is then sought (or vice versa), the case is reconsidered as if a single application were made on both grounds (see p325).[146]

Example: housing costs relating to the partner

A departure direction (see p334) reduced Steve's assessment from £62.18 to £33.63 a week. Debbie, his ex-wife, then applies for departure on the ground that Steve's second wife, Lisa, can contribute towards the couple's housing costs.

Lisa has net earnings of £280 compared with Steve's net earnings of £380. However, once Steve's travelling expenses of £83 a week are taken from his earnings, both partners have roughly the same amount to contribute towards the joint mortgage. Therefore, the departure decision maker decides Lisa can afford to contribute half the mortgage payments.

Therefore, Steve's exempt income is now:

	£
Personal allowance	59.15
Mortgage (half of £96)	48.00
Property settlement allowance	40.00
Travel-to-work costs	83.00
Debt repayments	34.60
Total	**264.75**

Steve's assessable income = £380 – £264.75 = £115.25
Proposed maintenance = 50% x £115.25 = £57.63
The protected income calculation remains as on p334 and, therefore, Steve can afford £57.63 (which is still slightly below the original assessment).

Note: the 50 per cent calculation is used because of the special expenses departure; if only the housing costs departure had been made, proposed maintenance would have been calculated in the usual way (see Chapter 13).

Effective date of the direction

Normally, the effective date of a departure direction is:[147]
- the maintenance assessment's effective date, if the departure application is made within one month of the notification of the current assessment (see p354). If there was unavoidable delay the CSA can treat the application as received in time;[148] *otherwise*
- the first day of the maintenance period in which the departure application was received.

However, if the reason for departure is a change of circumstances after the assessment's effective date, the effective date of the direction is:
- the first day of the maintenance period after the change of circumstances, if the departure application is made within one month of the notification of the assessment (see p354);[149] *otherwise*
- the first day of the maintenance period in which the departure application was received.[150]

If the direction is for contact costs and there was no established pattern of visits at the date of the application (see p328), the effective date is the first day of the first maintenance period after *either* the date the parents have agreed that pattern is to start *or*, if there is no agreed date, the date of the direction.[151]

Normally, a direction can only be made for the current assessment when the departure application was made. However, in some cases an application cannot be made while the assessment is current because notification was not sent until after the period covered by the assessment – eg, because it is made for a past period. The departure decision maker can still make a direction for that assessment, as if it were the current one, if:[152]
- a departure direction is given for the current maintenance assessment; *and*
- s/he considers that a direction would have been made for the assessment for the earlier period if an application had been made.

Duration of the direction

The direction may last for a specified period (eg, a 30-week repayment period) or until a specified event (eg, a child leaves school).[153] A direction may require the CSA to make a fresh assessment on a later change of circumstances and specify how that assessment is to be made.[154]

Changing the direction

The rules on changing a decision on departure are similar to those on changing a decision on the assessment itself (see Chapter 18). Any decision of the CSA (or one referred to an appeal tribunal regarding departure can be revised[155] or superseded.[156] This would appear to include a decision that regular payments conditions have not been complied with. Where it is considered that an application for departure is defective, there is no formal notified decision and this may only be challenged by judicial review. Refusal and rejection of applications may be revised. The 'test case' rules (see p419) also apply to revisions and supersessions of departure decisions.[157]

The rules on who can initiate a revision/supersession, on what grounds and when are summarised below.

Change of decision	Grounds	Initiated by	Time limit
Revision	Any	CSA/Any party*	1 month
Revision	Official error	CSA	No limit
Revision	Misrepresentation	CSA	No limit
Supersession	Change of circumstances	CSA/Any party*	No limit
Supersession	Erroneous in point of law	CSA/Any party*	No limit
Supersession	Ignorance/Mistake as to fact	CSA/Any party*	No limit

*'Any party' includes any parent with care, non-resident parent or Scottish child applicant of the assessment to which the departure relates.

Disputing decisions

Any party to an assessment can apply to have a departure direction decision revised. This includes decisions made on referral to an appeal tribunal (see p331). The CSA can also act to revise a decision on any grounds within one month of notification of the original decision.[158] In addition, the CSA can also act to revise a decision at any time where that decision was made as a result of official error (see p386)[159] or where the original decision was wrong because a person misrepresented or failed to disclose a material fact (see p386) and the decision was, therefore, more advantageous to that person.[160] Revision cannot occur if a material change of circumstances has occurred (or is expected to occur) since the original decision;[161] in this case supersession may be possible. Revision is not possible where the original decision is being appealed to an appeal tribunal and the revised decision (if made) would be less advantageous to the person making the appeal.[162]

An application for revision must normally be made within one month of notification of the decision.[163] Where an application for revision is made and the CSA informs the applicant that the revision will not be made because there is insufficient evidence or information, the applicant has one month from the date of this notification to re-apply with the required information.[164] The one-month time limit may be extended where the CSA accepts that it is reasonable to grant an extension. The application for the decision to be revised must have merit and there must have been special circumstances which meant that it was not practicable for the application to have been made within the one-month limit.[165] The longer the extension requested, the more compelling the relevant special circumstances would need to be.[166] An application for an extension must be made within 13 months of notification of the original decision.[167] When deciding whether to grant an extension the CSA will take no account of an applicant's ignorance or misunderstanding of the law relating to her/his case, nor will account be taken of a commissioner's or court's new interpretation of the relevant law (see p385).[168] Applications for extension which are refused cannot be renewed.[169]

The revised decision normally takes effect on the same date as the original decision.[170] If the effective date from which the original decision takes effect is wrong, the revised decision takes effect from the correct date.[171] If, on revision of the decision, the CSA decides that a departure direction should not have been given, the direction will be cancelled.[172]

Supersession of a decision on departure

A decision relating to departure may be superseded if there has been a material change of circumstances since the original decision was made. Any party to the assessment can apply for a supersession on this ground or, where the CSA becomes aware of a relevant change of circumstances, it can act on its own initiative.[173] A party to the assessment can also apply for a supersession if s/he expects that a material change of circumstances is going to occur.[174] No supersession on a change of circumstances will be made if the amount of child maintenance payable would be changed by less than £1.[175] Decisions may also be superseded (either on application by a party or on the initiative of the CSA) where the original decision was made in ignorance of (or based on a mistake as to) a material fact[176] or (apart from decisions given on appeal) where the original decision was wrong in point of law.[177] Decisions to refuse or reject an application for departure and decisions to cancel a departure direction cannot be superseded,[178] nor can any decision which can be revised (see p341).[179]

A superseding decision normally takes effect on the first day of the maintenance period (see p360) in which the application for supersession is made.[180] This also applies where the CSA supersedes a decision on its own initiative on the basis of information or evidence contained in an unsuccessful application for revision or supersession.[181] If an application is made because of an anticipated change of circumstances, the new decision takes effect from the first day of the maintenance period immediately after the maintenance period in which the change of circumstances is expected to occur.[182] If the CSA supersedes a decision on its own initiative because it becomes aware of a change of circumstances following a revision or supersession of a social security decision, the superseding decision takes effect from the first day of the maintenance period in which the social security decision maker became aware of the change of circumstances.[183]

If, on supersession, the CSA decides that a departure direction should no longer have effect, the direction will be cancelled.[184]

Correction of accidental errors

A minor accidental error can be corrected by the departure decision maker at any time, without making a fresh direction. The parties must be notified and the normal time for appealing starts to run again (see Chapter 20).[185]

Change to the assessment

If the assessment is changed on revision or supersession, the direction normally applies to any fresh assessment. This may not mean there is a decision on departure that may be appealed at this stage. It has been recommended that the Secretary of State should always give a departure decision when making a new assessment to allow the party appeal rights.[186] Where this does not occur and an appeal relates in part to the continuation of the departure direction, the tribunal does not have jurisdiction to deal with the departure issue and should refer the case to the CSA as a request for supersession of the departure, which would lead to a decision that carried appeal rights.

In some cases, the CSA may replace the existing assessment with an interim maintenance assessment (IMA) (see p367). If the direction could not have been made for that IMA (see p317), the direction is suspended.[187] The suspension continues until the IMA is replaced by an assessment for which the direction could have been made.

If an assessment is cancelled or ceases to have effect (see p372), the direction normally ceases to have effect and does not apply to any later assessment.[188] However, if the cancellation is because of the CSA ceasing to have jurisdiction, and the CSA later gets jurisdiction again for the same parties and at least one of the same children, a property transfer direction has effect again from the effective date of any new assessment.[189] This only applies where a party moves away from the UK and then returns or where the parents reconcile but later split up again.

Appealing the decision

Decisions on departure can be appealed to a tribunal.[190] Any party to the assessment can appeal. The time limit and procedures for appealing are the same as for other appeals (see p401).[191] Any decision with respect to a departure application can be appealed.[192] This includes a decision to refuse an application and one to make a direction. A decision that an application is defective can only be challenged via judicial review. Where more than one departure direction is appealed and those departure directions relate to the same maintenance assessment, a tribunal can consider both appeals at the same time.[193]

When making an appeal it is important to distinguish whether the appeal is against the direction and/or any fresh maintenance assessment. See Chapter 19 for further details of appeals.

Notes

1 Reg 10(1)(a) CSDDCA Regs	39 Reg 15(1) and (2) CSDDCA Regs
2 Reg 10(1)(c) CSDDCA Regs	40 Reg 15(6)(c) CSDDCA Regs
3 Reg 10(1)(b) and (c) CSDDCA Regs	41 Reg 15(3) CSDDCA Regs
4 Reg 9 CSDDCA Regs	42 Reg 15(4)(a) CSDDCA Regs
	43 Reg 15(3)(b) and (4)(b) CSDDCA Regs;
1. Grounds for departure	see also reg 32(6) CSDDCA Regs
5 Sch 4B para 2 CSA 1991	44 Reg 15(4A) CSDDCA Regs
6 Reg 19 CSDDCA Regs	45 Reg 16(1) CSDDCA Regs
7 Reg 14(1) CSDDCA Regs	46 Reg 16(5)(b) CSDDCA Regs
8 Reg 14(4) CSDDCA Regs	47 Reg 16(2)(k) and (5)(c) CSDDCA Regs;
9 Reg 14(1) CSDDCA Regs	s376(4) ICTA 1988
10 Reg 14(1)(c) and (6) CSDDCA Regs	48 Reg 16(2)(a) CSDDCA Regs
11 Reg 14(5) CSDDCA Regs	49 Reg 16(3) CSDDCA Regs
12 Reg 14(1) CSDDCA Regs	50 Reg 16(2)(h) and (i) CSDDCA Regs
13 Reg 14(1) CSDDCA Regs	51 Reg 16(5)(d) CSDDCA Regs
14 Reg 14(7) CSDDCA Regs	52 Reg 16(2)(a)-(g), (j) and (m) CSDDCA
15 Reg 14(3) CSDDCA Regs	Regs
16 Reg 32F(b) CSDDCA Regs	53 Reg 16(4) CSDDCA Regs
17 Reg 18 CSDDCA Regs	54 Reg 37(4) CSDDCA Regs
18 Reg 10(1)(b) CSDDCA Regs	55 Regs 16(2)(l) and 37(3) CSDDCA Regs
19 Sch 4B para 2(6) CSA 1991; reg 18(8)(a)	56 Reg 37(3) CSDDCA Regs
CSDDCA Regs	57 Reg 17 CSDDCA Regs
20 Reg 18(1) and (2)(a) CSDDCA Regs	58 Reg 17(1)(a) CSDDCA Regs
21 Reg 18(4) CSDDCA Regs	59 Sch 4B para 5 CSA 1991; regs 23-29
22 Reg 18(4B) CSDDCA Regs	CSDDCA Regs
23 Reg 18(4A) CSDDCA Regs	60 Reg 25 CSDDCA Regs
24 Reg 18(2)(b) CSDDCA Regs	61 Reg 25(2) CSDDCA Regs
25 Reg 18(7) CSDDCA Regs	62 Reg 25(3) CSDDCA Regs
26 Reg 18(3) CSDDCA Regs	63 Reg 23(2)(a) CSDDCA Regs
27 Reg 18(3) CSDDCA Regs	64 Reg 23(1)(a) CSDDCA Regs
28 Reg 18(7A) CSDDCA Regs	65 Reg 23(1)(b) and (c) CSDDCA Regs
29 Reg 18(5) CSDDCA Regs	66 Reg 23(2)(b) CSDDCA Regs
30 Reg 18(6) CSDDCA Regs	67 Reg 40(2) and (3) CSDDCA Regs
31 Reg 18(2)(c) CSDDCA Regs	68 Reg 24 CSDDCA Regs
32 Reg 18(3) CSDDCA Regs	69 Reg 26 CSDDCA Regs
33 Reg 13(3) CSDDCA Regs	70 Reg 40(6) CSDDCA Regs
34 Reg 13(1) CSDDCA Regs	71 Reg 27 CSDDCA Regs
35 Reg 13(2) CSDDCA Regs	72 Reg 40(7) CSDDCA Regs
36 Reg 15(1) and (6)(a) and (b) CSDDCA	73 Reg 40(9) CSDDCA Regs
Regs	74 Reg 28 CSDDCA Regs
37 Reg 15(6)(b) CSDDCA Regs	75 Reg 29 CSDDCA Regs
38 Reg 15(5) CSDDCA Regs	76 Reg 10(1)(c) CSDDCA Regs

77 Sch 4B paras 3(1) and 4(1) CSA
1991; regs 21(1) and (2) and 22(4)
CSDDCA Regs
78 Reg 21(5)(a) CSDDCA Regs
79 Reg 21(5)(b) CSDDCA Regs
80 Reg 22(2) CSDDCA Regs
81 Sch para 1(3)(b) CSDDCA Regs
82 Reg 22(3) and Sch CSDDCA Regs
83 Sch para 3 CSDDCA Regs

2. Applying for departure
84 s28A(1) CSA 1991
85 s28A(2) and (3) CSA 1991; reg 4(1)
CSDDCA Regs
86 Reg 2 CSDDCA Regs
87 Reg 4(4)-(8) CSDDCA Regs
88 s28A(1) CSA 1991
89 Reg 4(9) and (10) CSDDCA Regs
90 Reg 5 CSDDCA Regs

3. Procedure
91 s28B CSA 1991
92 s28B(2) CSA 1991; reg 7 CSDDCA Regs
93 Reg 6 CSDDCA Regs
94 Reg 8(4) CSDDCA Regs
95 Reg 8(1) CSDDCA Regs
96 Reg 8(4A) CSDDCA Regs
97 Reg 8(1) and (3) CSDDCA Regs
98 Reg 8(5) CSDDCA Regs
99 Reg 8(6) CSDDCA Regs
100 Reg 8(7) CSDDCA Regs
101 Reg 8(2)(b) CSDDCA Regs
102 Reg 8(2)(a) CSDDCA Regs
103 s28C(1) CSA 1991
104 s28C(2)(a) CSA 1991
105 Reg 45 CSDDCA Regs
106 Reg 45(1)-(3) CSDDCA Regs
107 s28C(3) CSA 1991
108 s28C(6)(b) CSA 1991; reg 45(4)
CSDDCA Regs
109 s28A(4) CSA 1991
110 s28B(6) CSA 1991
111 s28F(8) CSA 1991; reg 8(9)(a) and
(10)(a) CSDDCA Regs
112 s28D(1)(b) CSA 1991
113 s28D(3) CSA 1991

4. Considering departure
114 s28F(4)-(5) CSA 1991; reg 7 CSDDCA
Regs
115 Reg 44(4) CSDDCA Regs
116 s28E(2) and (4) CSA 1991; reg 12
CSDDCA Regs
117 s28F(1)(b) CSA 1991
118 s28F(2) and (3) CSA 1991; reg 30
CSDDCA Regs
119 Reg 1 CSDDCA Regs
120 CCS/1131/2005

5. The departure direction
121 s28F(6) CSA 1991
122 s28G(1) CSA 1991
123 Sch 1 paras 4(2) and (3) and 7 CSA
1991. A direction does not change the
way these work.
124 Sch 4B para 6(6) CSA 1991
125 Reg 44(1) and (2) CSDDCA Regs
126 Reg 44(1) and (3) CSDDCA Regs
127 Regs 37(1) CSDDCA Regs
128 Reg 38(2) CSDDCA Regs
129 Regs 37(2) and 38(3) CSDDCA Regs
130 Reg 41(1)-(5) CSDDCA Regs
131 Reg 42A(1)-(6) CSDDCA Regs
132 Reg 43(1) CSDDCA Regs
133 Reg 43(2) CSDDCA Regs
134 Reg 39(1)(a) and (c) and (6) CSDDCA
Regs
135 Reg 39(1)(b) CSDDCA Regs
136 Reg 39(2) CSDDCA Regs
137 Reg 42(1) and (2) CSDDCA Regs
138 Reg 42(3) CSDDCA Regs
139 Reg 43(3) CSDDCA Regs
140 Reg 39(3) CSDDCA Regs
141 Reg 39(3) CSDDCA Regs
142 Reg 40(2)-(5) CSDDCA Regs
143 Reg 40(6) CSDDCA Regs
144 Reg 40(7) CSDDCA Regs
145 Reg 40(10) CSDDCA Regs
146 Reg 42A(7) and (8) CSDDCA Regs
147 Reg 32(1)(a) and (2)(a) CSDDCA Regs.
Different rules apply for assessments in
force on 2 December 1996 if the
application was made before 2
December 1997 – see 1997/98 edition
of this Handbook.
148 Reg 32(2)(b) CSDDCA Regs
149 Reg 32(1)(b) CSDDCA Regs
150 Reg 32(4) CSDDCA Regs
151 Reg 32(3A) CSDDCA Regs
152 Reg 46 CSDDCA Regs
153 s28G(2) CSA 1991
154 Sch 4A para 5 CSA 1991
155 Reg 32A CSDDCA Regs
156 Reg 32D CSDDCA Regs
157 s28ZA and Sch 4C para 1(a)(i) CSA 1991
158 Reg 32A(1)(f) CSDDCA Regs
159 Reg 32A(1)(c) CSDDCA Regs
160 Reg 32A(1)(d) CSDDCA Regs
161 Reg 32A(2)(a) CSDDCA Regs
162 Reg 32A(2)(b) CSDDCA Regs
163 Reg 32A(1)(a) CSDDCA Regs
164 Reg 32A(1)(b) CSDDCA Regs
165 Reg 32B(4) CSDDCA Regs
166 Reg 32B(5) CSDDCA Regs
167 Reg 32B(3)(a) CSDDCA Regs
168 Reg 32B(6) CSDDCA Regs
169 Reg 32B(7) CSDDCA Regs

170 s16(3) CSA 1991
171 Reg 32C CSDDCA Regs
172 Reg 32F(a) CSDDCA Regs
173 Reg 32D(2)(a) and (3)(a)(i) CSDDCA
    Regs
174 Reg 32D(3)(a)(ii) CSDDCA Regs
175 Reg 32D(6) CSDDCA Regs
176 Reg 32D(2)(b) and (4) CSDDCA Regs
177 Reg 32D(5) CSDDCA Regs
178 Reg 32D(10) CSDDCA Regs
179 Reg 32D(9) CSDDCA Regs
180 s17(4) CSA 1991; reg 32E(2) CSDDCA
    Regs
181 Reg 32E(5) CSDDCA Regs
182 Reg 32E(4) CSDDCA Regs
183 Reg 32E(3) CSDDCA Regs
184 Reg 32F(b) CSDDCA Regs
185 Reg 34A CSDDCA Regs. This does not
    say the error must be minor, but its
    terms suggest it does not cover major
    errors.
186 CCS/1641/2001
187 Reg 35(4) CSDDCA Regs
188 Reg 35(1) CSDDCA Regs
189 Reg 35(2) CSDDCA Regs
190 Sch 4C para 3(4) CSA 1991
191 Regs 31, 32 and 33 SS&CS(DA) Regs
192 Sch 4C para 3(1)(a) CSA 1991
193 Reg 45 SS&CS(DA) Regs

Part 5

Decisions, enforcement and challenges

Chapter 17

Maintenance decisions

This chapter covers:

This chapter does not contain information on the conversion of 'old rules' maintenance assessments to the new rules. For information on conversion decisions, see Chapter 8. For information on revision and supersession decisions, see Chapter 18.

Where there are multiple applications under the 'old' and 'new' rules, the Child Support Agency (CSA) decides which application to proceed with. For more information on how the CSA decides applications, see Chapter 3.

1. Making the initial maintenance decision

Once an effective maintenance application has been made and the Child Support Agency (CSA) has obtained, or tried to obtain, the necessary information, it can:[1]

- make a maintenance calculation;
- make a default maintenance decision (see p367); *or*
- refuse to make a maintenance calculation (p352).

Details of the case are entered onto the CSA computer and maintenance is calculated automatically.

Relationship with Child Support Agency Northern Ireland

For child support cases, there are two territories: Great Britain and Northern Ireland (see p8). If the person with care, non-resident parent and qualifying child do not all reside in the same territory, the application is dealt with by the CSA of the territory where the person with care lives.[2] If more than one application names the same non-resident parent, those applications are dealt with by the CSA of the territory where the person with care named in the first application received by the CSA lives.[3] Where a case has been allocated to a CSA by these rules and the person with care applies again, naming a further non-resident parent, that application is dealt with by the CSA already dealing with the earlier case(s).[4]

These rules do not apply if an application is made by a child in Scotland (see p37). Instead, that application and any others naming the same non-resident parent are dealt with by the CSA for the territory where the person with care of the child applicant lives.[5]

Any calculation made under these rules must take into account the rules of the other territory.[6] Because the rules for the two territories are very similar, this should not make any difference.

Waiting for the calculation decision

If the person with care can provide contact details for the non-resident parent, the CSA aims to make an accurate decision within 12 weeks of an application, but some cases may take 26 weeks.[7] Where the CSA has to trace the non-resident parent, it is likely to take longer before it can make a decision.

Delays in dealing with applications

Even though it is intended that much of the contact with parents to collect and check information needed to make a maintenance calculation and collect payments is done by phone there may still be a delay between the application and a decision.

Applicants are contacted at certain stages during the progress of the case – eg, to let them know about negotiations with the non-resident parent about collection or where the applicant has made a complaint. The CSA has also said that it will do more to let its clients know about progress on a case, and it is reviewing and revising letters sent to clients so that they 'have a better understanding of what is happening with their case'.[8] However, you should continue to contact the CSA regularly for progress reports.

Delay after the non-resident parent is contacted about the application does not normally put off the starting date of any calculation (see p356), but the date of the decision on maintenance may be delayed. Liability under an order or agreement continues and these remain enforceable. Other non-resident parents should consider putting money aside or making voluntary payments (see p436). Parents who are already contributing voluntarily should check if such payments might be used to offset initial arrears (see p432).

If the non-resident parent is not co-operating, the CSA should make a default maintenance decision (see p352) and may impose a criminal sanction. If the person with care is told by the CSA that the non-resident parent is causing the delay by failing to provide information and the CSA has not made a default maintenance decision, the person with care should write to the CSA requesting that one be made. If this does not happen, a complaint should be made (see p462).

Withdrawing the application

If an application is withdrawn or treated as withdrawn (see p46) (or a parent with care on income support (IS) or income-based jobseeker's allowance (JSA) opts out) before the CSA makes a decision, the CSA cannot make a calculation. If a calculation *is* made after withdrawal, it can be challenged (see Chapter 19).

The application cannot be withdrawn after a decision has been made, but the applicant can ask the CSA to cease acting, in which case the calculation can be cancelled (see p360). In other cases, the decision may be revised or superseded (see Chapter 19).

Change of circumstances

Unlike under social security law, there is no general requirement to notify the CSA of changes. However, the person with care is required to notify the CSA of some changes (see p99) and the non-resident parent must inform it of changes when a deduction from earnings order is in force (see p445).

However, any party may want to tell the CSA of changes or new information about the case – eg, the parent with care may have discovered that the non-resident parent has a second job which she believes has not been disclosed to the CSA.

If the CSA is told about a change or given new information that relates to *before* the effective date (see p368), it has discretion on whether to take this information into account. This can be done in the initial calculation or by making two or more calculations for the different periods.[9]

If the date or period normally used is before the effective date (eg, for earnings) and the CSA knows about a relevant change which happened after that date or period but before the effective date, it must take that change into account.[10] If the change is after the normal 'relevant week' (see p235), the relevant week for each later calculation is the week before the date the CSA was notified of the relevant change.[11]

Any information about a change *after* the effective date but before the maintenance calculation can lead to a series of calculations.[12] The effective date of each such maintenance calculation will be the beginning of the maintenance period in which the change occurred or is expected to occur.[13]

Once a calculation is made, the person with care has a duty to notify the CSA of certain changes that happen after that (see p99). These may result in a revision or supersession, depending on when the change is notified and its significance (see Chapter 18).

Refusal to make a calculation

The CSA *must* refuse to make a calculation if:

- the application was made by a person who is *not* a non-resident parent, a person with care or, in Scotland, a qualifying child aged 12 or over (see p37);
- it is a voluntary application and there is a pre-3 March 2003 court order (registered agreement in Scotland) or written agreement (see p38);
- it is a voluntary application and there is a post-3 March 2003 court order (registered maintenance agreement in Scotland) that has been in force for less than one year (see p38);
- it is a voluntary application made by the non-resident parent or the person with care, and the parent with care is on IS or income-based JSA;
- not all the parties are habitually resident in the UK (see p27);
- there is no non-resident parent, either because both parents live in the same household as the child (see p22) or because the CSA does not accept that the person named is a parent of the child (see p15); *or*
- there is no qualifying child (see p18).

The CSA can also refuse to make a calculation pending the outcome of a test case (see p419). Otherwise, the CSA must make a calculation.

If there is a change of circumstances so that one of these situations applies for a period beginning after the effective date (see p368), the CSA makes a calculation that ends on the date of the change.

If the only child (or all the children) dies before the calculation is made, the CSA can treat the application as if it had not been made.[14] The CSA cannot refuse to make a calculation just because it has insufficient information or because it may affect the welfare of a child.[15] The CSA may make a default maintenance decision (see p352). If the CSA refuses to make a calculation, the applicant (and, if the applicant is a child in Scotland, any person with care or non-resident parent who had been notified of the application) must be notified in writing of the decision, the right of appeal (see Chapter 19) and how to seek a revision and supersession (see Chapter 18).[16]

A fresh application may be made after the refusal – eg, if there is a change of circumstances such as the non-resident parent returning to live in the UK.

2. **Default maintenance decisions**

If the Child Support Agency (CSA) does not have enough information to make a maintenance calculation, or to revise or supersede a decision, it may make a default maintenance decision.[17] A default maintenance decision can also be made at conversion (see p172). (In 'old rules' cases prior to conversion, where there is not enough information to make a full assessment, an interim maintenance assessment may be made, see p367.)

The amount of the default maintenance decision is based on the number of qualifying children applied for.[18]

- £30 if there is one qualifying child;
- £40 if there are two qualifying children; *or*
- £50 if there are three or more qualifying children.

This amount may be apportioned if there is more than one person with care. (Any relevant non-resident children are ignored.[19])

Court order phasing may be applied to a default maintenance decision (see p355).

The effective date of a default maintenance decision is the same as it would have been for a maintenance calculation decision (see p368).

Notification of a default maintenance decision must state the effective date, the default rate, the number of qualifying children, details of any apportionment, revision/supersession/appeal rights and the information needed to make a maintenance calculation.[20]

When a default maintenance decision ends

A default maintenance decision may be revised at any time – eg, when it is replaced by a maintenance calculation.[21] If the default decision is replaced with a maintenance calculation, the date from which this revision takes effect depends on the circumstances.[22]

- If the total amount of maintenance for the relevant period is greater than the default maintenance decision, the date the revision takes effect is the date of the default maintenance decision.
- If the total amount of maintenance for the relevant period is less than the default maintenance decision, the date the revision takes effect is the first day of the maintenance period in which the information needed to make the calculation was provided.

Example

Paul was contacted on 7 April 2004 about Cassandra's application for maintenance for his two daughters, Hannah and Ella. He refused to provide information to calculate maintenance.

A default maintenance decision was made for £40 with an effective date of 7 April 2004. Paul took advice from an advice agency and he provided information on 29 April 2004 which enabled the CSA to calculate maintenance.

If Paul's maintenance is based on net income of £190, he is due to pay £37 a week at the reduced rate. As this is less than the default maintenance decision, he is due to pay £40 a week for the period 7 April to 27 April and £37 a week from 28 April when the default maintenance decision is revised by the maintenance calculation.

> If Paul's maintenance is based on net income of £220, he is due to pay £44 a week at the basic rate. As this is greater than the default maintenance decision, it is revised and the maintenance calculation of £44 takes effect from 7 April 2004.

If the CSA is satisfied that the failure to provide information is not the parent's fault and that s/he tried her/his best to provide it, the date the revision takes effect is the date of the default maintenance decision.[23]

> If Paul had been in hospital and did not return the child maintenance enquiry form sent to him on 7 April 2004, a default maintenance decision of £40 would be applied from 7 April 2004. If, on leaving hopsital on 16 May 2004, Paul contacted the CSA and the CSA accepted the failure to provide information was not his fault, then based on his net income being £190, the maintenance calculation of £37 would revise the default decision with effect from 7 April 2004.

'Relevant period' means the period for which the default maintenance decision applied.[24]

In other circumstances – eg, the person with care stops being the person with care, normal revision and supersession rules apply (see Chapter 18).

3. **Notification of decisions**

The Child Support Agency must notify the person with care, non-resident parent and Scottish child applicant once a maintenance calculation or interim maintenance decision has been made.[25] This also includes default maintenance decisions (but see p355). There are similar rules regarding notification of revision and supersession decisions (see Chapter 18).

The notification of the maintenance calculation or interim maintenance decision *must* include information on:[26]

- the effective date (see p368);
- the net weekly income of the non-resident parent;
- the number of qualifying children;
- the number of relevant other children;
- the weekly rate;
- any variations;
- any adjustments for apportionment, shared care by the non-resident parent or part-time local authority care, or maintenance to another relevant non-resident child; *and*
- revision, supersession and appeal.

Notification of a default maintenance decision must state the effective date, the default date, the number of qualifying children, details of any apportionment, revision/supersession/appeal rights and the information needed to make a maintenance calculation.[27]

Unless there is written permission, the notification should not contain:[28]

- the address of anyone else other than the recipient or information that could lead to her/him being located; *or*
- information on anyone other than persons with care, non-resident parents or qualifying children.

If there are errors or someone disagrees with the decision, s/he may seek a revision (see p384) or appeal (see Chapter 19).

If there is a court order for maintenance, the court is notified of the calculation (see p31). In addition, where court order phasing applies the amount due may be replaced by a transitional amount (see p356).

4. Court order phasing of calculations

If weekly liability under the calculation is higher than under an existing court order or agreement, the calculation can be introduced in up to three stages.

A calculation may *only* be phased in if:[29]

- a court order or maintenance agreement (see below) in relation to one or more qualifying children was in force on 4 April 1993 and remained in force until the date the calculation was made;
- the calculation exceeds that due under the old order/agreement; *and*
- either the non-resident parent is a member of a family or there is a reduction for shared care to the basic or reduced rate.

Any payments in kind or to third parties are ignored when determining the old amount. Arrears are also ignored – it is the weekly liability that counts.[30]

Maintenance agreements which count for phasing must have been:[31]

- made in writing (see p38); *or*
- evidenced in writing,

and must meet all the other requirements of a maintenance agreement (see p38).

Court orders which count for phasing must have been made under:[32]

- one of the provisions listed in Appendix 3 for court maintenance orders;
- section 151 of the Army Act 1955;
- section 151A of the Air Force Act 1955;
- articles 1(b) or 3 of the Naval and Marine Pay and Pension (Deductions for Maintenance) Order 1959.

The Child Support Agency will seek verification of the order or written maintenance agreement, which could be an original document or a copy.[33] In some instances, confirmation may be obtained by Jobcentre Plus.

Where court order phasing applies, instead of the calculation amount a transitional amount is paid.[34] The transitional amount is:[35]

- for the first 26 weeks, the old amount *plus* the greater of £20 and a quarter of the difference between the calculation and the old amount;
- for the next 26 weeks, the old amount *plus* the greater of £40 and half of the difference between the calculation and the old amount; *and*
- for the last 26 weeks of the phasing-in period, the old amount *plus* the greater of £60 and three-quarters of the difference between the calculation and the old amount.

The maintenance payable becomes the calculation amount if the transitional amount would be larger than that.[36] Therefore, it is only where the difference between the old amount and the calculation amount is more than £60 a week that the phasing-in period lasts the full 18 months.

Revision and supersession where there is phasing

Where phasing applies and there is a subsequent decision, the following amount is payable:[37]

- if the subsequent decision is less than the calculation amount and less than or equal to the transitional amount, the subsequent decision;
- if the subsequent decision is less than the previous calculation but more than the transitional amount, the transitional amount;
- if the subsequent decision is higher than the previous calculation, the transitional amount is increased by the same amount as the increase between the calculation and the subsequent decision.

5. When the first maintenance calculation begins

The date a maintenance calculation takes effect is called the **'effective date'** (see below).[38] There are different rules for effective dates after a supersession (see Chapter 18), for calculations replacing default maintenance decisions (see p352) and where there is conversion of an 'old rules' case (see p359). For effective dates in 'old rules' cases prior to conversion, see p368.

The effective date

Unless there is a maintenance order in force in relation to all the qualifying children (see p384), the effective date of the calculation depends on who made the application. However, where there is, or has been, a maintenance calculation (or 'old rules' maintenance assessment) in force special rules may apply (see p358).

If the application is made before 3 March 2003 but the effective date under the 'old rules' is after 3 March 2003 the case is dealt with as a 'new rules' case (unless the linking rules apply). However, the effective date remains that worked out under the 'old rules'.[39]

If the application was made by the **person with care, a Scottish child applicant or treated as made by a parent with care on benefit,** the effective date is:[40]

- the date the non-resident parent is notified of the application; *or*
- if the non-resident parent has intentionally avoided notification, the date on which notification would have been given but for the avoidance.

The non-resident parent is normally notified of the application by phone. In some cases a maintenance enquiry form may be issued (see p74). In this case, notification is treated as given or sent on the day it is given or posted.[41] Notification is treated as occurring if the maintenance enquiry form is sent to the non-resident parent at his last known or last notified address. A commissioner's decision has stated that it is for the Child Support Agency (CSA) to decide whether an address is sufficiently reliable to send a maintenance enquiry form; it does not have to be beyond reasonable doubt that it is the non-resident parent's current address.[42]

The non-resident parent cannot delay the effective date of a calculation by disputing paternity. The CSA does not make a calculation until the issue of paternity is resolved (see p17) but, if it later decides that the alleged non-resident parent is the father, the calculation is then backdated to the effective date.

If the **non-resident parent** made the application, the effective date of the first calculation is the date of the effective application (see p368).[43]

If there are multiple applications for child maintenance and these are treated as a single application (see p48), the effective date is set by the earlier or earliest application.[44]

Court orders

The following rules apply where there is, or has been, a maintenance order in force for all of the qualifying children named in the calculation.[45] This means that where the order covers one but not all of the qualifying children the normal rules regarding the effective date applies to those qualifying children.

The following rules apply in relation to court orders regardless of whether a maintenance calculation or default maintenance decision is being made.[46]

If the application is treated as made by a parent with care on benefit and the order is in force on the date the calculation is made, the effective date is two days after that.[47]

If the decision is in response to a voluntary application and an order made on or after 3 March 2003 has been in force for one year, the effective date is two months and two days after the application is made.[48]

In either case, if the order ceases to have effect after the application is made, the effective date is the day after the order ceased to have effect.[49]

Liability for maintenance continues until the order stops being in force, so the non-resident parent should continue making payments while awaiting the calculation. If a calculation is made following a voluntary application, an order made on or after 3 March 2003 has been in force for at least a year, and the non-resident parent makes payments due under the order but after the effective date of the maintenance calculation (and so will have been making them retrospectively after the order ceased to have effect), these will be treated as payments of child support maintenance (see also p435).[50] For collection and enforcement of arrears, see Chapter 20.

Effective dates in special cases

The effective date may be set earlier or later than under the normal rules in certain circumstances where there is, or has been, a maintenance calculation in force.

Condition	Effective date
A maintenance calculation is in force, the non-resident parent in the new application is the non-resident parent in the current calculation and the application is in respect of a different person with care and qualifying child.	The beginning of the maintenance period in the existing case which is not more than seven days after the non-resident parent is notified of the new calculation.[51]
A maintenance calculation is in force and the person with care in the new application is the non-resident parent in the current calculation.	The beginning of the maintenance period in the existing case which is not more than seven days after the non-resident parent in the new application is notified of that application.[52]
A maintenance calculation was in force within eight weeks of the application in relation to the same non-resident parent and qualifying child(ren) but a different person with care.* (This does not apply if the parent with care on benefit opts out.)	The date on which the previous maintenance calculation ceased to have effect.[53]

A maintenance calculation is in force, a new application is made in respect of the same non-resident parent but a different parent with care and the previous maintenance calculation ceases to have effect before a decision is made on the new application. (This does not apply if the parent with care is on benefit and opts out.)	If the non-resident parent has been notified before the previous calculation ceases to have effect, the day after it ceases to have effect. If the non-resident parent is not notified until after the previous calculation ceases to have effect, the date of notification.[54]
A maintenance calculation was in force within the eight weeks preceding the application and the parent with care and non-resident parent have swapped roles in relation to all the qualifying child(ren) concerned – ie, the person with care in the old calculation is the non-resident parent in the new application.* (This does not apply if the parent with care on benefit opts out.)	The date on which the previous maintenance calculation ceased to have effect.[55]

* In cases where a parent with care on benefit is treated as making an application, the date that the application is made means whichever is the later of the following:[56]
– the date of the claim for income support (IS) or income-based jobseeker's allowance (JSA) made by or on behalf of the parent with care; or
– the date that the parent with care (or her partner) reports a change in circumstances to the Secretary of State or HM Revenue and Customs that relates to an existing claim for IS/income-based JSA, the effect of which is that the parent with care is treated as applying for maintenance.

If there is, or has been, an 'old rules' maintenance assessment in force

If an 'old rules' maintenance assessment is, or has been, in force, the case may be dealt with under the 'old rules' or 'new rules' depending on who is involved and when the application is made.

Applications for a maintenance calculation after 3 March 2003 but within 13 weeks of an assessment being in force involving the same person with care, non-resident parent and qualifying child(ren) may be treated as an application for a maintenance assessment.[57] In these circumstances, the effective date is set in relation to the 'old rules'.

Otherwise, the effective date of the new maintenance calculation is dealt with under the:

• normal effective date rules; or
• special cases rules explained above, as if references to the calculation were to the assessment.[58]

However, if there is a maintenance assessment in force that converts to the 'new rules' early (eg, because of an application from another person with care), there are special rules for working out the effective date of the conversion decision for that existing assessment (see Chapter 8).

Maintenance periods

Child maintenance is calculated on a weekly basis, although it is not always paid weekly (see p428). It is payable in respect of successive seven-day periods with the first period beginning on the effective date.[59]

The only exception is where, when the calculation is made, there is already a calculation in force for the same non-resident parent but for a different child and person with care. In that case, the maintenance periods of the new calculation begin on the same day of the week as the existing calculation.[60]

After a supersession, any fresh calculation comes into effect on the first day of the maintenance period (see p394).

6. **When a maintenance calculation ends**

A maintenance calculation continues until the Child Support Agency (CSA):
- cancels it following a request (see below);
- revises it (see p384);
- supersedes it because it has ceased to have effect (see p361); *or*
- supersedes it for another reason (see p389).

In some cases the calculation is replaced by another, while in others no further calculation is made. Any arrears remaining after a calculation ends may still be collected (see Chapter 20). Also, if an application is made for children of the non-resident parent who are not named in the existing calculation, the new calculation replaces the old one.

Request to cancel a calculation

A maintenance calculation must be cancelled when the applicant (a person with care not on income support (IS)/income-based jobseeker's allowance (JSA), a non-resident parent or a qualifying child in Scotland) or parent treated as applying (a parent with care on IS/JSA) requests the CSA to cease acting.[61] Such a request by a parent with care on benefit is known as opting out and a reduced benefit decision may be made (see p65).

The request may be made verbally or in writing. If the request is made, the CSA must stop all action, including collection and enforcement of arrears, though the person may, if s/he wishes, specifically ask for action in relation to arrears to continue.

Living together

When the request is made, reasons need not be given. However, if the reason is because the parent with care and non-resident parent are living together the CSA should be told. This is because once the parties all share a household, the non-resident parent is no longer non-resident (see p22), so the child is no longer a qualifying child and the calculation ceases to have effect (see below).[62] Both parents should inform the CSA, though the CSA will seek other verification.[63] If there is a suspicion of fraud, Jobcentre Plus may be informed.

The calculation ceases to have effect

Some changes of circumstances lead to a cancellation, whether or not a request is made. The CSA may be aware of a change from, for example, a request or a notification by the parent with care under her duty to do so (see p99) or from the Department for Work and Pensions. The CSA *must* supersede the decision and cancel a calculation (including a default decision) if the calculation ceases to have effect. The calculation will cease to have effect if:[64]

- the non-resident parent or person with care dies;
- the only, or all, qualifying child(ren) is no longer a qualifying child(ren); *or*
- the non-resident parent ceases to be a parent of the only, or all, the qualifying child(ren).

This means cancellation occurs, for example, when:

- a child aged 16 or over leaves school or becomes too old to count as a child;
- the qualifying child, non-resident parent and parent with care start living together;
- the qualifying child goes to live with someone else and as a result the person with care no longer counts as a person with care;
- the qualifying child is adopted, in which case the non-resident parent is no longer a parent; *or*
- the non-resident parent is no longer considered a parent because of the results of a DNA test or a declaration of parentage.

Where the maintenance calculation has been made from an application by a child in Scotland and that child is no longer a child, the CSA must notify the person with care, non-resident parent and other children over 12.[65]

Other cancellations

The CSA must cancel the calculation if the person with care, non-resident parent or qualifying child is no longer habitually resident in the UK (see p27).[66]

A non-resident parent who has successfully contested paternity will have any maintenance calculation cancelled and, if he has paid maintenance, may obtain a refund.

If a voluntary applicant (or a parent with care who was treated as applying because she was on IS/JSA and who would now count as a voluntary applicant) fails to provide the CSA with enough information to make a revision or supersession decision, the CSA *may* cancel the calculation.

Date cancellation has effect

If the calculation is cancelled because it ceases to have effect or because of another relevant change, the cancellation takes effect from the first day in the maintenance period in which the change occurred. This includes where:

- the person with care is no longer the person with care for the child(ren) named in the calculation;[67] *or*
- a party is no longer habitually resident in the UK;[68] *or*
- the person with care, non-resident parent or qualifying child dies;[69] *or*
- the non-resident parent ceases to be a parent.[70]

If the cancellation is because the non-resident parent is not considered to be the parent because of a DNA test or declarator of parentage, the effective date is the date of the original maintenance calculation.[71]

Cancellation following a request

A calculation is cancelled with effect from the first day of the maintenance period in which the request was received *or* a different date depending on the reason for the cancellation.[72] A later date may be appropriate if an applicant has requested that the calculation ends on a later date.

If a parent who was on IS/income-based JSA stops claiming and requests the CSA to stop acting, the effective date is the first day of the maintenance period after the request is made.[73] This means that had the parent made the request to opt out while on benefit the maintenance calculation would have been cancelled from the first day of the maintenance period in which the request was made. If a calculation is cancelled because the non-resident parent and parent with care are living together, and both request the cancellation, it takes effect from the first day of the maintenance period in which the later request to cancel the calculation is made.[74]

Notification of the cancellation decision

When the CSA cancels a calculation or refuses to cancel one, it must notify the non-resident parent, person with care and Scottish child applicant of that decision, and must also provide information on the right of appeal and on revisions and supersessions.[75]

If the maintenance calculation has been made following an application from a child in Scotland and that child is no longer a qualifying child, the CSA must notify the person with care, non-resident parent and other children over 12 who are potential child applicants.[76]

7. **How a maintenance calculation affects means-tested benefits**

In this section, the effect of receiving child support maintenance on means-tested benefits is covered. The benefits affected are: income support (IS), income-based jobseeker's allowance (JSA), housing benefit (HB) and council tax benefit (CTB). Other social security benefits, including pension credit (PC), and tax credits are not affected.

Child maintenance paid by a non-resident parent is not taken into account when calculating his, or his partner's, means-tested benefits. However, deductions for flat rate maintenance or arrears may be taken from a non-resident parent's benefits when the Child Support Agency (CSA) requests this to be done.[77] For full details of how means-tested benefits are calculated, including the effect of maintenance other than child support, see CPAG's *Welfare Benefits and Tax Credits Handbook*. For the benefit penalty for non-co-operation by a parent with care on IS or income-based JSA, see p65.

Income support/income-based jobseeker's allowance

The following covers special provisions within these benefits in relation to child maintenance. Payments of child maintenance may be made direct to the person with care or via the CSA.

Housing costs

Full mortgage interest is not usually included in the calculation for the first 26 or 39 weeks of any IS/income-based JSA award. Nevertheless, the benefit calculation includes 100 per cent of eligible mortgage interest if:[78]

- a person with care stops being entitled to IS/income-based JSA as a result of receiving child maintenance; *and*
- when that happened, she was receiving IS/income-based JSA including 100 per cent eligible mortgage interest; *and*
- her maintenance calculation is later reduced or ended because:
  - the child support regulations are changed; *or*
  - the calculation is an interim maintenance assessment (IMA) under the 'old rules' and it is ended and not replaced or is replaced by another IMA/default decision or by a full assessment/calculation; *and*
- she then claims IS/income-based JSA within 26 weeks of the date she stopped being entitled to either benefit.[79]

Child maintenance premium

From 3 March 2003 a person with care on IS/income-based JSA who is paid child maintenance under the 'new rules' will have a child maintenance premium applied when working out her/his benefit.[80] Where an 'old rules' case converts to the 'new rules' the child maintenance premium may replace a child maintenance bonus (see p374). The premium also applies if maintenance is first paid on or after 3 March 2003 under an agreement or court order,[81] or paid from 16 February 2004.[82]

Just because the parent was paid, or due to be paid, maintenance for a different child or under an earlier agreement/order does not preclude the premium from being applied. In some circumstances, this may mean a parent ceases to accrue a bonus and instead will have a premium applied. She may claim the bonus if she meets the relevant conditions (see p374).

A person with care on IS/income-based JSA who is paid child maintenance under the 'new rules' will have up to £10 a week ignored when working out her benefit entitlement.[83] This means that where maintenance paid is £6, only £6 will be ignored. The maintenance may be made in respect of one child or more, but the amounts are aggregated and only up to £10 will be ignored. The child maintenance premium applies whether maintenance is paid directly to the parent with care or via the CSA. Payments can be made under a CSA calculation, maintenance order, written maintenance agreement or voluntarily.[84] This includes where the CSA makes a payment in lieu of maintenance and the non-resident parent is on the flat rate of maintenance.[85]

Payment direct to the person with care

The parent with care may ask that payments of maintenance are not made via the CSA but direct from the non-resident parent. For how to request a change to the collection service, see p427. Payments of child maintenance, including lump sums, are treated as income and are taken into account when assessing entitlement to IS/income-based JSA on a weekly basis.[86] Payments are treated as income in the week they are received by the parent with care, except that child maintenance due before the benefit award is always treated as paid in the week it was due – ie, before the award began.[87]

Payments made regularly are converted into a weekly amount to work out IS/income-based JSA – eg, where payments are made monthly, multiply by 12 and divide by 52.[88] Where payments are made at irregular intervals, each payment is divided over the weeks since the previous payment.[89]

If the child maintenance premium applies, up to £10 of the maintenance is ignored. The remainder counts in full as income and benefit is, therefore, reduced by this amount.

Jobcentre Plus should not assume that child maintenance is paid as soon as the CSA sends notification of the calculation. Benefit should not be reduced until payments begin.

Once a person with care's benefit has been reduced because of maintenance payments, if a payment due direct from the non-resident parent is missed, she should ask the Jobcentre Plus for extra benefit to be paid for that period. The

Jobcentre Plus should do this without waiting for the CSA to enforce payment of maintenance. The person with care can contact the CSA to chase missing payments and to have payments made to the CSA (see Chapter 20).

Payment to the Child Support Agency

The CSA usually arranges to collect maintenance so that the non-resident parent does not have to pay direct to the person with care. The CSA normally keeps any payments made by the non-resident parent for a person with care on IS/income-based JSA,[90] apart from up to £10 a week (the child maintenance premium), which is paid to the person with care.

Payment of arrears

Non-resident parents are encouraged by the CSA to pay arrears direct to the CSA, which then keeps the arrears up to the amount of IS/income-based JSA paid because the maintenance was not paid on the due date.[91] Any balance is passed to the person with care. If the arrears are collected by the CSA, they should be passed on in full to the person with care.

If the non-resident parent pays arrears direct to the person with care, the full amount of overpaid benefit for the period when that maintenance was due can be recovered from her by the Jobcentre Plus.[92]

Arrears of child support should usually be treated as income for IS and income-based JSA, but there may be difficulty in working out the period covered by the arrears and this treatment may be open to argument.[93]

Loss of income support/income-based jobseeker's allowance

Persons with care lose IS/income-based JSA when the child maintenance paid (after the child maintenance premium) increases their income over the benefit applicable amount. If the person with care is only a few pounds over the benefit level, she may find herself worse off because of the loss of passported benefits – eg, free school meals, full health service benefits (see below) and access to the social fund.

A person with care who is not a parent of the qualifying child is a voluntary applicant (see p38) and can, therefore, ask for the calculation to be cancelled (see p360). She could then be deemed to have notional income for IS/income-based JSA (see CPAG's *Welfare Benefits and Tax Credits Handbook*), but in practice, it would be difficult for Jobcentre Plus to work out the level of notional income as it would not have the necessary information.

The loss of passported benefits could have a greater effect than a reduced benefit decision (see p65) for a parent with care on benefit (see p360), particularly one with school-age children. Where benefit entitlement is low and a reduced benefit decision is imposed the amount of the reduction may be modified to retain the minimum amount of benefit. If the claim ends and maintenance is not paid on time, a new IS/income-based JSA claim can be made. If Jobcentre Plus delays a decision on the claim in order to allow the CSA to enforce maintenance, make a complaint (see Chapter 21). Jobcentre Plus cannot take into account child maintenance that has not yet been paid (see p363).

Housing benefit and council tax benefit

There are no special rules for child maintenance when calculating HB/CTB, except that £15 weekly is disregarded as income for persons with care who are not in receipt of IS/income-based JSA, or the guarantee credit of PC.[94] The disregard applies to all forms of maintenance paid by a former partner or a parent of a child, but only if there is a child in the HB/CTB claimant's family. Only £15 is disregarded from total maintenance paid.

If there is a change in the amount of child maintenance received, the person with care should tell the local authority benefits section. Persons with care claiming HB/CTB who are not on IS/income-based JSA cannot be treated as applying to the CSA. However, a local authority might use the notional income rules and decide that a claimant who does not apply to the CSA has deprived herself of child maintenance.[95] In practice, this would be extremely difficult for the authority to do, as it would not have enough information to work out the maintenance calculation that would be made.

For the notional income rules, see CPAG's *Welfare Benefits and Tax Credits Handbook*.

Health service benefits

People on IS/income-based JSA or the guarantee credit of PC are automatically exempt from all NHS charges. Others may be entitled to full or partial reductions of charges on low-income grounds. This covers prescriptions, dental treatment, sight tests, glasses, wigs, fabric support and fares to hospital.

For these purposes, where child maintenance payments are made:

- regularly, income is the weekly equivalent of payments; *or*
- not regularly, income is the total payments in the 13 weeks before the claim, divided by 13.

There is no disregard. For full details, see CPAG's *Welfare Benefits and Tax Credits Handbook*.

8. Taxation of child maintenance

Person with care

Child support maintenance is not taxable income.

Non-resident parent

From 6 April 2000 maintenance, including child support maintenance, no longer qualifies for tax relief.

9. Existing 'old rules' cases

Existing cases continue to be dealt with under the legislation prior to reform, except for some provision for parents with care on benefit – eg, they can ask the Child Support Agency (CSA) to cease acting in both 'new' or 'old' cases. For full details of the 'old rules', see Chapter 14 in the 2002/03 edition of this *Handbook*.

This section outlines the areas where there are differences between the 'new rules' and 'old rules' on maintenance decisions and provides an overview of the relevant provisions.

The following are minor differences between the 'old' and 'new' rules.

- Notifications under the 'old rules' are treated as given or sent by the CSA two days after posting, apart from the issue of a maintenance enquiry form, which is treated as given or sent on the day that it is posted.
- Cancellations are now possible by 'old rules' parents with care on income support (IS)/income-based jobseeker's allowance (JSA) – ie, they can opt out (see p59). There are several other differences for parents with care on benefit (see p363).

Some provisions are completely different.

- Interim maintenance assessments (IMA – see below) are made under the 'old rules' where there is insufficient information to make an assessment. Default maintenance decisions apply to 'new rules' cases only. At conversion, an IMA may convert to a maintenance calculation or default maintenance decision (see p352).
- The effective dates of a maintenance assessment or IMA have different rules (see p368).
- A person with care on benefit may accrue up to £5 a week child maintenance bonus (see p374). The child maintenance premium does not apply to 'old rules' cases. When a case converts, the premium may apply, but any bonus may be claimed if the conditions are met.

Interim maintenance assessments

If the CSA does not have sufficient information to make a full assessment using the formula, or to decide whether to revise or supersede a decision, it may make an IMA rather than a full assessment.[96] The decision to make an IMA is discretionary, so the CSA must take into account the welfare of any child(ren) affected by the decision (see p24).

There are four types of IMA.[97] For IMA commencement see p370, for cancellation see p372, and for revisions and supersessions see Chapter 18.

Interim maintenance assessments

Category	When it is applied	How it is worked out
A	A non-resident parent has failed to provide information about his own circumstances (not any new partner).	One-and-a-half times the maintenance requirement.
B	Either the person with care or non-resident parent has failed to provide information about the income of their new partner, or about other members of their family.	Calculated as a full assessment except that in exempt income it is assumed a new partner can help maintain a joint child and there is no protected income calculation, although the 30 per cent cap may apply.
C	The non-resident parent is self-employed and is unable to provide information about earnings.	Normally £30, but may be less.
D	A Category A IMA is in force but on the information available it appears that a full assessment would be higher.	Calculated as a full assessment, except: – there is no protected income, nor a 30 per cent cap; – no housing costs are allowed; exempt income is the adult personal allowance only; *and* – when working out income, there is no disregard of payments to personal or occupational pension schemes or to pension schemes intended to provide capital sums to discharge a mortgage.

For full information, see the 2002/03 edition of this *Handbook*.

The effective date of an assessment

Under the 'old rules' there are different rules on setting the effective date of assessments, IMAs and maintenance assessments replacing IMAs. In some cases the CSA may set an interim effective date.

Effective date of assessments

Circumstances	Effective date
Application by person with care or qualifying child in Scotland.[98]	Eight weeks from the date on which the maintenance enquiry form (MEF) is given or sent to a non-resident parent as long as, within four weeks of being sent the MEF, he returns it with his name, address and written confirmation that he is the parent of the child(ren) named in the maintenance application form (MAF). *Otherwise* the date the non-resident parent was actually given or sent the MEF.
Application by non-resident parent.[99]	Eight weeks from the date on which the application was received by the CSA as long as the non-resident parent provides his name, address and written confirmation that he is the parent of the child(ren) named in the MAF as part of the MAF or provides these details within four weeks of the date of the application. *Otherwise* the date an effective MAF (see p45) is received.
In either case where there is a court order in force for at least one of the qualifying children on the date the assessment is made.[100]	Two days after the date the assessment is made. The order for maintenance ceases to have effect from the effective date (see p30).[101]
The court order ceases (not because of an IMA) before the assessment is made and after the MEF/MAF is received, depending on the applicant.[102]	The day after the order ceased to be in force.
Another assessment is already in force and an application by a different person with care is then made.[103]	The CSA may treat the new application as received up to eight weeks earlier than the date it was actually received, but no earlier than the date on which the previous assessment ended.[104]

An assessment made following an application from a qualifying child in Scotland has been cancelled at the child's request or because s/he is no longer a child and an application for children who were qualifying children under the previous assessment has been made.[105]

The CSA may treat the new application as received up to eight weeks earlier than the date it was actually received, but no earlier than the date on which the previous assessment ended.[106]

An assessment is in force for a non-resident parent and a different person with care then applies for child maintenance.

The first day of the first maintenance period (see p360) not more than seven days after the parties are notified of the second assessment.[107] If this would make the effective date fall within the eight-week period and the non-resident parent meets the rules for that period (see p368), the effective date is the first day of the first maintenance period after the eight-week period.[108]

If there are multiple applications for child maintenance and these are treated as a single application, the effective date is set by the earlier or earliest application.[109]

Effective date of interim maintenance assessments

Circumstances	Effective date
Category A or C unless there is a court order in force.	The first day after it is made which falls on the same day of the week as the day the MEF was actually given or sent to the non-resident parent or, where the non-resident parent is the applicant, the day the MAF was received by the CSA (but see the exception below).[110]
Category B unless there is a court order in force.	The date the MEF was actually given or sent to the non-resident parent or, where the non-resident parent is the applicant, the day the MAF was received by the CSA (but see exception below).[111]
There is a court order in force.	See normal effective date rules.

Superseding IMA with another Category A, C or D IMA.	The first day of the maintenance period in which the CSA decides to make the new IMA.[112]
Superseding IMA is a Category B IMA.	Where the cancelled IMA (or the first cancelled IMA, if there is more than one) had caused a court order to cease to have effect, the effective date of that (or that first) IMA.[113] *Otherwise* the day the MEF was actually given or sent to the non-resident parent or, where the non-resident parent is the applicant, the day the MAF was received by the CSA.[114]

The exception to these rules is that, if the effective date set by them would fall within the eight-week period and the non-resident parent meets the rules for that period for a full assessment (see p356), the effective date is set by those rules.[115]

Effective date of a maintenance assessment replacing an interim maintenance assessment

If the CSA:
- has sufficient information to make a full assessment for the *whole of the period* beginning with the usual effective date (see p368), the IMA ceases to have effect on the first day of the maintenance period (see p360) in which the CSA received the information.[116] The CSA revises (see p384) the IMA decision.[117] The amount payable under the IMA becomes that of the full assessment;[118] *or*
- has sufficient information to make a full assessment for *only part of that period*, the IMA ceases to have effect on the first day of the maintenance period in which the CSA received the information.[119] The CSA supersedes the IMA decision.[120] The effective date of the full assessment is also that date.[121] The amount payable under the IMA remains that of the IMA.[122]

If the information which enables the CSA to make a full assessment is that IS or income-based JSA has been awarded, the CSA is treated as receiving that information on the day benefit became payable.[123]

Interim effective date

If the CSA does not have sufficient information to make a full assessment from the usual effective date (see p368), but has enough to make one running from a later date, it can make a full assessment from that later date.[124] The interim effective date is the first day of the maintenance period (see p370) in which the CSA received the information.[125]

If the CSA later receives sufficient information to make a full assessment from the usual effective date, the assessment already made for the later period then has effect from the usual effective date instead.[126]

Cancelling assessments

The information on ending assessments is the same as that under the 'new rules' except for the following.

- From 3 March 2003, any applicant (including a parent with care on benefits) under the 'old rules' may ask the CSA to stop acting. The calculation will be cancelled, although a parent with care on IS or income-based JSA may have a reduced benefit decision made and imposed (see p65).
- Under the 'old rules', if a Scottish child applicant is no longer habitually resident in Scotland the assessment is cancelled.[127] This takes effect from the first day in the maintenance period in which the change occurred.
- Under the 'old rules', the CSA had discretion, in some cases, on when to set the effective date of the cancellation – eg, if the person with care and non-resident parent are living together.[128] Guidance indicates that effective dates are now set in the same way under both 'old' and 'new' rules.
- Before cancelling a calculation, the CSA must, if possible, give written notice to the person with care, non-resident parent and any Scottish child applicant of intention to cancel the calculation, and allow 14 days from the date the notice is sent before cancelling.[129]
- The full amount of the assessment is due for the maintenance period in which the cancellation date falls,[130] except if a Category A or D IMA is cancelled, when it is only due to the cancellation date.[131]
- An IMA must be cancelled when the CSA has enough information to make a full assessment. Otherwise the only provision for cancellation is when the CSA accepts that the non-resident parent was unavoidably delayed in providing the information. The effective date of the maintenance assessment is as under the normal rules. However, where the new decision is another category of IMA, the date is:[132]
  - for a Category A or D IMA, the first day of the maintenance period in which the CSA decides to make the new IMA; or
  - for a Category B IMA, the day the MEF was given or sent to the non-resident parent or if the non-resident parent is the applicant, the day the MAF was received by the CSA.

Court order phasing of assessments

The definition of maintenance agreement and court order are the same as in court order phasing for 'new rules' cases, but the legislative references are slightly different.[133] Evidence of the order must be provided.

In the regulations there are two similar types of phasing, which we call 'original phasing' and '1994 phasing'. As phasing can last for a maximum of 18 months, it should only apply to 'old rules' cases which have had considerable delays in assessment, or for which there is still an IMA.

For full information on court order phasing and supersession of decisions where court order phasing applies, see the 2002/03 edition of this *Handbook*.

Original phasing

This has existed since April 1993 and the reduced amount payable is known as the **'modified amount'**.[134] It does not apply to a Category A IMA.[135] It applies where:[136]

- the old maintenance order/agreement covered all the children named in the assessment; *and*
- the non-resident parent is responsible for maintaining a child (see p18) living with him who is not named in the assessment; *and*
- the assessment is £60 or less.

The weekly modified amount is the weekly amount due under the old order/agreement *plus* £20.[137] This continues for a year, but ends before that if one of the above conditions is no longer met.

1994 phasing

This was introduced on 7 February 1994 and the reduced amount payable is known as the **'transitional amount'**.[138] It does not apply to a Category A or D IMA.[139] It applies where:[140]

- the old maintenance order/agreement covered at least one child named in the assessment; *and*
- the non-resident parent was a member of a family (see p26) which included at least one child on the effective date (see p368) and is still a member of a family with a child; *and*
- original phasing does not apply;[141] *and*
- the assessment does not replace a Category A or D IMA made after 22 January 1996.[142]

If the assessment is £60 or less, the transitional amount is the amount under the old order/agreement *plus* £20.[143] This lasts for 52 weeks.

If the assessment is more than £60 a week, the transitional amount is:[144]

- for the first 26 weeks, the old amount *plus* the greater of £20 and a quarter of the difference between the assessment and the old amount;
- for the next 26 weeks, the old amount *plus* the greater of £40 and half of the difference between the assessment and the old amount; *and*
- for the last 26 weeks of the phasing-in period, the old amount *plus* the greater of £60 and three-quarters of the difference between the assessment and the old amount.

The maintenance payable becomes the assessment amount if the transitional amount would be larger than that. Therefore, it is only where the difference between the old amount and the assessment amount is more than £60 a week that the phasing-in period lasts the full 18 months.

Which type of phasing applies

CSA guidance covers only 1994 phasing, implying that original phasing cannot be applied. However, the provisions remain in force.[145] This is only likely to matter if a Category D IMA is made or replaced, because only original and not 1994 phasing can apply to a Category D IMA. If the wrong (or no) phasing is applied, an appeal can be made (see Chapter 19).

Revisions and supersessions

Where original phasing applies and the assessment decision is revised (see p384) or superseded (see p389) and the conditions for phasing are still met, phasing continues until the 52-week period ends.[146]

Where 1994 phasing applies (or where original phasing applies and there is a change of circumstances), then the following amount is payable:[147]

- if the fresh assessment is less than the modified/transitional amount, the fresh assessment;
- if the fresh assessment is less than the previous assessment but more than the modified/transitional amount, the modified/transitional amount;
- if the fresh assessment is higher than the previous assessment, the modified/ transitional amount is increased by the same amount as the increase between the two formula assessments.

Child maintenance bonus

The child maintenance bonus is not available to cases under the 'new rules', or where maintenance is first paid under an agreement or court order after 3 March 2003.[148] Persons with care who were entitled to a child maintenance bonus on 3 March 2003 will continue to be entitled to a bonus, unless:[149]

- in 'old rules' cases, the case converts early to the 'new rules' (see p170);
- in cases where maintenance is paid under a voluntary agreement or court order (in Scotland registered agreement), either maintenance is paid for a different child or there is a new agreement or order for the existing child(ren).

If the child maintenance bonus is replaced by a child maintenance premium, see p363.

A person caring for a child(ren) builds up a child maintenance bonus for weeks in which maintenance for the child (not just child support maintenance) is paid or payable to her and in which she or her partner is entitled to IS or income-based JSA.[150] This does not include where the urgent cases rate is being paid because she is treated as if she were receiving income due to her.[151]

This bonus normally builds up at a rate of £5 a week. It can be claimed as IS or income-based JSA when the person with care (or partner) finds work (or more work/pay) and so comes off IS/income-based JSA. There are special rules for people approaching state retirement age (see p377).

Decisions about the child maintenance bonus are made by Jobcentre Plus. The usual IS/income-based JSA rules apply to revisions, supersessions and appeals about bonus decisions. The overpayment rules also apply (see CPAG's *Welfare Benefits and Tax Credits Handbook*).

Conditions for child maintenance bonus

To build up the bonus, the person with care must:[152]
- live with a qualifying child for whom she gets child maintenance (the child may be temporarily absent for up to 12 weeks[153]);
- be entitled (or her partner is) to IS/income-based JSA (even if not paid); *and*
- have not yet reached the day before her 60th birthday (or, for a man on income-based JSA, his 65th birthday).[154]

This is known as a bonus period.

The child maintenance paid by the non-resident parent must be either:[155]
- child support;
- under a court order or an agreement, including an informal agreement; *or*
- a deduction from IS/income-based JSA as a contribution to child maintenance (see p200).

If there is a break (eg, because of loss of entitlement) two bonus periods may be linked,[156] if the break is either:[157]
- a period of 12 weeks or less;
- a period throughout which maternity allowance is payable to the person claiming the bonus; *or*
- any period of two years or less throughout which incapacity benefit, severe disablement allowance or carer's allowance is payable to the person claiming the bonus.

The bonus is payable if the person:
- meets the work condition within the time limits and because of that ceases to be entitled to IS/income-based JSA[158] (the bonus must also be claimed); *or*
- has reached or is approaching retirement age (see special rules below).

There are special rules if the person with care dies which allow someone else to acquire the bonus (see p376).

To meet the work condition:
- the person (or her/his partner) must take up or go back to work, earn more from employment, or increase her/his hours sufficiently to bring benefit entitlement to an end.[159]

Note: a person involved in a trade dispute who then returns to work does not count under these rules as 'going back to work'.[160]

The time limit for meeting the work condition:

- is 14 days from the end of the bonus period,[161] but it can be extended if:
  - the non-resident parent dies, ceases to be habitually resident and/or is found not to be the parent of the qualifying child (ren), to 12 weeks from the date of that event (or where there is more than one – the first);[162]
  - the person cares for only one child and that child dies, to 12 months from the date of death.

Note: where the child maintenance bonus is replaced by a child maintenance premium the time limit is amended (see p189).

Claims must be made:

- by sending or delivering a claim form to Jobcentre Plus;[163] *and*
- within 28 days of the day after IS/income-based JSA ends.[164] This can be extended to up to six months, if there are good reasons.[165]

There are special rules for:

- a person approaching retirement age who does not meet the work condition. The 28 days begin on the day after her 60th birthday (or, for a man on income-based JSA, his 65th birthday);[166]
- a person who dies after a bonus becomes payable but without having claimed it. Another person can apply to Jobcentre Plus to be appointed to claim the bonus, but must do so within six months of the death. This is extendable to up to 12 months in exceptional circumstances.[167]

For more details and examples, see the 2002/03 edition of this *Handbook*.

Amount of the child maintenance bonus

The total child maintenance bonus is the *lowest* of the following:

- £5 for each week in which at least £5 maintenance was due,[168] *plus* for any other week in which less than £5 maintenance was due, the amount due in that week;[169]
- the total maintenance paid during the bonus period.[170] This includes any maintenance retained by the CSA.[171] Any maintenance paid but not declared to the Jobcentre Plus and so not taken into account for benefit purposes does not count towards the bonus;[172]
- £1,000.[173]

This means that if you qualify for a bonus at the end of an unbroken bonus period (including any linked periods), the bonus is the whole amount built up, with the maximum bonus payable £1,000. The minimum is £5.[174]

The bonus is paid as IS or income-based JSA – whichever benefit the person was entitled to when the bonus stopped being built up.[175]

If the person with care dies

If a person with care dies, the bonus built up passes to the new person with care if:[176]

* the deceased person with care was entitled (or her partner was entitled) to IS/income-based JSA in the 12 weeks before the death;
* the new person with care was not a person with care before the death;
* the new person with care is a close relative of the deceased person with care ie, a parent, step-parent, parent-in-law, son, stepson, son-in-law, daughter, stepdaughter, daughter-in-law, brother or sister, or the partner of any of those people (from 5 December 2005, step-relatives and in-laws include those formed by civil partnerships); *and*
* the new person with care (or her partner) becomes entitled to IS/income-based JSA within 12 weeks of the day the deceased person with care (or her partner) was last entitled to IS/income-based JSA.

Only the current bonus period passes to the new person with care, not any linked period.[177]

Retired people

Special rules apply to a person who is entitled to IS/income-based JSA on the day before her 60th birthday (or, for a man on income-based JSA, his 65th birthday) and to some people approaching that age.

The bonus stops building up on the day before a person's 60th birthday (or, for a man on income-based JSA, his 65th birthday).[178] The bonus is then payable without a claim being needed.

If IS/income-based JSA entitlement stops in the 12 weeks before that date, and the person does not meet the work condition, the bonus is payable but a claim must be made.[179]

If a man's entitlement to income-based JSA stops after the age of 60 but before pensionable age, but he then becomes entitled to pension credit (PC), the bonus is payable without a claim being needed.[180] This only applies if entitlement to PC begins within 12 weeks of income-based JSA entitlement ending, or it begins during a connecting period (for more information about connecting periods for the child maintenance bonus, see CPAG's *Welfare Benefits and Tax Credits Handbook*).

Other benefits, tax credits and tax

The bonus does not count as income for IS, income-based JSA, working tax credit, child tax credit, housing benefit (HB) and council tax benefit (CTB).[181] It is disregarded as capital for 52 weeks from the date it is received if the claimant is under 60 or if s/he or her/his partner is on IS or income-based JSA.[182] It does not count as income or capital for PC, HB or CTB if the claimant is 60 or over and neither s/he nor her/his partner is on IS or income-based JSA. None of the deductions which can be made from IS/income-based JSA (eg, for fuel) can be made from a bonus.[183]

The bonus is not subject to income tax.[184]

Notes

1. Making the initial maintenance decision
1 s11 CSA 1991
2 Sch 1 Art 5(5) CS(NIRA) Regs
3 Sch 1 Art 5(1) CS(NIRA) Regs
4 Sch 1 Art 5(3) CS(NIRA) Regs
5 Sch 1 Art 5(2) and (6) CS(NIRA) Regs
6 Sch 1 Art 5(4) and (7) CS(NIRA) Regs
7 CSA Charter, February 2007
8 CSA Operational Improvement Plan 2006-2009
9 Sch 1 para 15 CSA 1991
10 Reg 2(4) CS(MCSC) Regs; CCS/2750/1995
11 Reg 1(2)(c) CS(MCSC) Regs
12 PG, Calculation and Decision Types, Taking Account of Changes That Happen at Different Times
13 Reg 25(5) CS(MCP) Regs
14 Reg 6 CS(MCP) Regs
15 R(CS) 2/98
16 Reg 10(1) and (4) CS(MAP) Regs

2. Default maintenance decisions
17 s12(1) CSA 1991
18 Reg 7 CS(MCP) Regs
19 PG, Calculation and Decision Types, Calculate a DMD
20 Reg 23(2) CS(MCP) Regs
21 s16(1B)CSA 1991; reg 3A(5) SS&CS(DA) Regs
22 Reg 5A(2) SS&CS(DA) Regs
23 Reg 8A(2)(a) SS&CS(DA) Regs
24 Reg 5A(3) SS&CS(DA) Regs

3. Notification of decisions
25 Reg 23 CS(MCP) Regs
26 Reg 23(1) CS(MCP) Regs
27 Reg 23(2) CS(MCP) Regs
28 Reg 23(3) CS(MCP) Regs

4. Court order phasing of calculations
29 Reg 30 CS(TP) Regs
30 Reg 30 CS(TP) Regs
31 Reg 30(a)(iii) CS(TP) Regs
32 Reg 30(a)(i) and (ii) CS(TP) Regs
33 PG, Gather Information and Evidence, Court Order Details Dialog; Court Order and WMA Verification Levels
34 Reg 31 CS(TP) Regs
35 Reg 31(2) CS(TP) Regs
36 Reg 31(3) CS(TP) Regs
37 Reg 32 CS(TP) Regs

5. When the first maintenance calculation begins
38 Reg 1(2) CS(MCP) Regs
39 Reg 31(2) CS(MCP) Regs
40 Regs 1(2) and 25(3) and (4) CS(MCP) Regs
41 Reg 2 CS(MCP) Regs
42 CCS/2288/2005
43 Reg 26(2) CS(MCP) Regs
44 Reg 4(3) CS(MCP) Regs
45 Regs 26 and 27 CS(MCP) Regs
46 PG, Calculation and Decision Types, Effective Date of a New Rules Calculation
47 Reg 27 CS(MCP) Regs
48 Reg 26 CS(MCP) Regs
49 Reg 28 CS(MCP) Regs
50 Reg 8A CS(MAJ) Regs
51 Reg 7B(21) SS&CS(DA) Regs
52 Reg 29(1)(b) CS(MCP) Regs
53 Reg 29(1)(a) CS(MCP) Regs
54 Reg 29(1)(d) CS(MCP) Regs
55 Reg 29(1)(c) CS(MCP) Regs
56 Reg 29(2) and (3) CS(MCP) Regs
57 Reg 28(1) CS(TP) Regs
58 Reg 31(1) CS(MCP) Regs
59 s4A CSA 1991
60 Reg 7B(21) SS&CS(DA) Regs

6. **When a maintenance calculation ends**

61 ss4(5),6(5) and 7(6) CSA 1991
62 PG, Withdraw/Cancel Application and Close Case, User Initiated – Reason and Effective Date for Withdrawal/Cancellation
63 PG, Withdraw/Cancel Application and Close Case, Non-resident Parent and Parent with Care Living Together Verification Levels
64 Sch 1 para 16 CSA 1991
65 Reg 24 CS(MCP) Regs
66 s44(1) CSA 1991
67 Reg 7B(17A) SS&CS(DA) Regs
68 Reg 7B (18) SS&CS(DA) Regs
69 Reg 7B(17) SS&CS(DA) Regs
70 Sch 1 para 16(1)(c) CSA 1991
71 s16(3) CSA 1991
72 s17(4) CSA 1991
73 Reg 7B(19) SS&CS(DA) Regs
74 Reg 7B(20) SS&CS(DA) Regs
75 Reg 15C(5) SS&CS(DA) Regs
76 Reg 24 CS(MCP) Regs; reg 15C(5)(b) SS&CS(DA) Regs

7. **How a maintenance calculation affects means-tested benefits**

77 s43 CSA 1991; Sch 9B SS(C&P) Regs
78 Sch 3 para 14(2) IS Regs; Sch 2 para 13(2) JSA Regs
79 Reg 32 IS Regs; Sch 2 para 18(1)(c) JSA Regs
80 Art 6 CSPSSA (Comm 12)O
81 Reg 1 SS(CMPMA) Regs 2000
82 Reg 1 SS(CMP)A Regs
83 Sch 9 para 73 IS Regs as substituted by reg 2 SS(CMP)A Regs; Sch 7 para 70 JSA Regs as substituted by reg 3 SS(CMP)A Regs
84 Sch 9 para 73(4) IS Regs as substituted by reg 2 SS(CMP)A Regs; Sch7 para 70 JSA Regs as substituted by reg 3 SS(CMP)A Regs
85 Reg 60A IS Regs; reg 125 JSA Regs
86 Reg 60B IS Regs; reg 126 JSA Regs
87 Reg 60D IS Regs; reg 129 JSA Regs
88 Reg 60C(2) and (3) IS Regs; reg 128(2) and (3) JSA Regs
89 Reg 60C(4) IS Regs; reg 128(4) JSA Regs
90 s74A SSAA 1992
91 Reg 8 CS(AIAMA) Regs
92 s74(1) SSAA 1992; reg 7(1)(b) SS(PAOR) Regs
93 *Secretary of State for Work and Pensions v Menary-Smith* [2006] EWCA Civ 1689

94 Sch 5 para 47 HB Regs or Sch 5 para 20 HB(SPC) Regs; Sch 4 para 48 CTB Regs or Sch 3 para 20 CTB(SPC) Regs
95 Reg 42(2) HB Regs or reg 41(8) HB(SPC) Regs; reg 32(2) CTB Regs or reg 31(8) CTB(SPC) Regs

9. **Existing 'old rules' cases**

96 s12(1) CSA 1991
97 Reg 8 CS(MAP) Regs
98 Reg 30(2)(a) CS(MAP) Regs
99 Reg 30(2)(b) CS(MAP) Regs
100 Reg 3(5) CS(MAJ) Regs
101 Reg 3(6) CS(MAJ) Regs
102 Reg 3(8) CS(MAJ) Regs
103 Reg 3(1) CS(MAP) Regs
104 Reg 3(3) CS(MAP) Regs
105 Reg 3(2) CS(MAP) Regs
106 Reg 3(3) CS(MAP) Regs
107 Reg 33(6) and (7) CS(MAP) Regs
108 Reg 33(9) CS(MAP) Regs
109 Reg 4(3) CS(MAP) Regs
110 Reg 8C(1)(a) CS(MAP) Regs
111 Reg 8C(1)(b) CS(MAP) Regs
112 Regs 9(4) and 23(13) CS(MAP) Regs
113 Reg 9(5) and (6) CS(MAP) Regs
114 Reg 9(3) CS(MAP) Regs
115 Reg 8C(1)(d) CS(MAP) Regs
116 Reg 8D(5) CS(MAP) Regs
117 Reg 17(3)(a) CS(MAP) Regs
118 Reg 30A(2) CS(MAP) Regs
119 Reg 8D(6) CS(MAP) Regs
120 Reg 20(6) CS(MAP) Regs
121 Reg 30A(1) CS(MAP) Regs
122 Reg 8D(2) CS(MAP) Regs
123 Reg 8D(8) CS(MAP) Regs
124 Reg 30A(4) CS(MAP) Regs
125 Reg 30A(3) CS(MAP) Regs
126 Reg 30A(6) CS(MAP) Regs
127 Sch 1 para 16(5) CSA 1991; reg 7(1) CS(MAJ) Regs; reg 32A(1) CS(MAP) Regs
128 Sch 1 para 16(7) CSA 1991
129 Reg 32B CS(MAP) Regs
130 Reg 33(5) CS(MAP) Regs
131 Reg 8D(4) CS(MAP) Regs
132 Reg 9(1) CS(MAP) Regs
133 Sch para 7(1)(a)(iii) CSA(Comm3)O; reg 7(1)(a) CS(MATP) Regs
134 Sch para 6 CSA(Comm3)O
135 Sch para 7(2) CSA(Comm3)O
136 Sch para 7(1) CSA(Comm3)O
137 Sch paras 6 and 8 CSA(Comm3)O
138 Reg 6(1) CS(MATP) Regs
139 Reg 7(2)(a) CS(MATP) Regs
140 Reg 7(1) CS(MATP) Regs
141 Reg 7(2)(b) CS(MATP) Regs
142 Reg 7(2)(c) CS(MATP) Regs

143 Reg 8(2)(a) CS(MATP) Regs
144 Reg 8(2) CS(MATP) Regs
145 Reg 7(2)(b) CS(MATP) Regs
146 Sch para 8 CSA(Comm3)O
147 Sch para 12 CSA(Comm3)O; reg 11 CS(MATP) Regs
148 Art 6 CSPSSA(Comm12)O as substituted by Art 2 CSPSSA(Comm13)O
149 Art 6 CSPSSA(Comm12)O as substituted by Art 2 CSPSSA(Comm13)O
150 s10 CSA 1995; reg 4(1) SS(CMB) Regs
151 Reg 4(1) and (9) SS(CMB) Regs
152 Reg 4(1) SS(CMB) Regs
153 Reg 4(6) SS(CMB) Regs
154 Reg 8(1) and (3) SS(CMB) Regs
155 Reg 1(2) SS(CMB) Regs
156 Reg 4(2) SS(CMB) Regs
157 Reg 4(3) SS(CMB) Regs
158 Reg 3(1)(d) SS(CMB) Regs
159 Reg 3(1)(c) SS(CMB) Regs
160 Reg 3(2) and (3) SS(CMB) Regs
161 Reg 3(1)(iii) SS(CMB) Regs
162 Reg 3(1)(f)(ii) SS(CMB) Regs
163 Reg 10(1), (2) and (92) SS(CMB) Regs
164 Reg 10(1)(b) SS(CMB) Regs
165 Reg 11(4) SS(CMB) Regs
166 Reg 10(1)(d) SS(CMB) Regs
167 Reg 13 SS(CMB) Regs
168 Reg 5(1)(a)(i) SS(CMB) Regs
169 Reg 5(1)(a)(ii) SS(CMB) Regs
170 Reg 5(1)(b) SS(CMB) Regs
171 Reg 4(1)(c)(ii) SS(CMB) Regs
172 Reg 5(3) SS(CMB) Regs
173 Reg 5(1)(c) SS(CMB) Regs
174 Reg 5(5) SS(CMB) Regs
175 Reg 12 SS(CMB) Regs
176 Reg 7 SS(CMB) Regs
177 Reg 7(1) SS(CMB) Regs
178 Reg 8(1) SS(CMB) Regs
179 Reg 8(4) and (5) SS(CMB) Regs
180 Reg 8(2) SS(CMB) Regs
181 Reg 14 SS(CMB) Regs
182 Sch 10 para 7 IS Regs; Sch 8 para 12 JSA Regs; Sch 5 para 48 HB Regs; Sch 5 para 50 CTB Regs
183 Schs 9 para 1 and 9A para 1 SS(C&P) Regs; reg 16(8) SS(PAOR) Regs; reg 4 Social Fund (Recovery by Deductions from Benefits) Regs 1988
184 s617(2)(ad) ICTA 1988

Chapter 18

•••

Revisions and supersessions

This chapter covers:
1. Changing decisions (below)
2. Revisions (p384)
3. Supersessions (p389)

•••

This chapter does not include information on revisions and supersessions outstanding at conversion. These are covered in Chapter 8. Conversion decisions themselves may be revised or superseded as described in this chapter.[1] However, the amount of any maintenance to be paid (eg, transitional amount) will be worked out using the rules described in Chapter 8.

•••

---

1. Changing decisions

Most decisions can be changed or challenged by revision or supersession. However, there are some decisions that cannot (see p383).

A revision or supersession normally happens because the Child Support Agency (CSA) is told that something is wrong or has changed since the decision was made. The CSA may also initiate a revision or supersession itself.

The table on p382 is a quick guide to when decisions are revised and superseded. Put simply, the main difference between revision and supersession is that:

- a revision means the decision which is wrong or has been challenged is itself changed;
- a supersession means that a new decision is made with effect from a later date.

If a decision is challenged within one month, it may be revised, but outside this time period a decision will only be revised in special circumstances – eg, there has been official error (see p386). If these special circumstances are not met it may mean that the decision is not revised; instead, it may be superseded.

Quick guide to revisions and supersessions

Why is the decision being challenged?	When?	What can be done?
The decision is wrong for any reason.	Within a month of being told the decision.	The decision can be revised.
The CSA made a mistake ('official error'), was misled or did not know about something that would have affected the decision.	At any time.	The decision can be revised. If the CSA did not know something or was misled, the decision can only be revised in certain circumstances (see p384). If these do not apply, the decision can be superseded.
The decision is wrong for any reason (except someone not being a parent of a child to whom a calculation relates).	Later than one month after being told the decision.	The decision may be superseded but the person can ask for a late application for revision to be considered (see p385).
Something that affects the decision has changed.	At any time.	The decision can be superseded.
The CSA has not dealt with the case properly.	At any time.	The person may make a complaint (see p383).

Variations are an element of the calculation. This means that any change relating to a variation element can give rise to a revision or supersession of the maintenance calculation.

For changing reduced benefit decisions, see p69. For changing deductions of maintenance from income support (IS)/income-based jobseeker's allowance (JSA) and pension credit, see p430.

Decisions of appeal tribunals and child support commissioners (see Chapter 19) can also be superseded or revised, but only in certain circumstances (see pp385, 389 and 420).

Jobcentre Plus makes some decisions related to child support, principally reduced benefit decisions. Applications to change these should be made to Jobcentre Plus. This chapter refers to applications to change a CSA decision, but where the decision is made by Jobcentre Plus, information should be read as such. For more information on Jobcentre Plus decision making see CPAG's *Welfare Benefits and Tax Credits Handbook*.

If a non-resident parent thinks the revision/supersession may reduce the amount of his calculation, he may try to negotiate lower payments pending the decision, although this is usually difficult (see p438).

For the CSA approach to parentage disputes, see p17.

Challenging decisions that cannot be revised or superseded

Most of these are in the areas of information gathering, collection and enforcement. Deduction from earnings orders can be appealed to a court (see p443). Judicial review may also be possible (see below).

Further information can be given to the CSA and the officer asked to reconsider. If the officer refuses to change the decision, a complaint can be made. There may be other occasions that do not involve a decision, but where the behaviour of CSA staff, or others acting for the CSA, is unsatisfactory – eg, intimidating or unnecessarily intrusive questioning, or unwarranted demands for evidence and documentation. In these cases, a complaint can be made.

Complaints should initially be made through the CSA's own complaints system before being taken further if necessary – eg, to the Independent Case Examiner (see Chapter 21).

Judicial review

A person affected by a decision or action of a public body or one of its officers can ask the High Court to carry out a judicial review of the decision or action. The court can 'set aside' the decision and also order the decision maker to consider it again in a lawful way. Judicial review cannot usually be brought where there is a right to raise the issue in an appeal to a tribunal, commissioner or court. Otherwise, judicial review may be sought of a decision of the CSA (eg, on enforcement) or of an appeal tribunal or child support commissioner (eg, to refuse to grant leave to appeal) that cannot be appealed. Legal advice *must* be taken as soon as possible after the decision is made. Legal aid may be available.

Judicial review can succeed if there is:[2]

- illegality – where the decision maker makes an error in law – eg, does something s/he has no power to do; *or*
- irrationality – where a decision maker fails to have regard to a relevant matter or has regard to an irrelevant matter, or where a decision is 'so outrageous in its defiance of logic or of accepted moral standards that no sensible person who had applied his mind to the question could have arrived at it'; *or*
- procedural unfairness.

Challenging decisions about benefit entitlement

Some CSA decisions depend upon a decision of Jobcentre Plus. In particular, a person in receipt of IS or income-based JSA is due to pay the minimum rate (see p199) or the flat rate (see p109). As long as Jobcentre Plus pays one of these benefits, even if the non-resident parent has other income, there can be no application for a variation on additional income grounds (see p148). A parent who believes that the other parent should not be allowed to claim IS/income-based JSA (eg, because s/he is working full time) cannot directly challenge a Jobcentre Plus decision to award that benefit. However, s/he can make an allegation by raising it with the CSA. The CSA reports it to Jobcentre Plus, which investigates. Jobcentre Plus reports the result to the CSA but not to the person who made the allegation. The person who made the allegation cannot appeal to an appeal tribunal against the Jobcentre Plus decision,[3] although judicial review could be sought.

2. Revisions

The CSA can revise a decision if a person applies within one month (or longer if special circumstances exist – see p385), applies for a variation within one month (provided the grounds for variation existed from the date of the decision under revision) or if the Child Support Agency (CSA) initiates the revision. A revised decision normally has effect from the date of the original decision had effect.

Information on revisions of decisions made by Jobcentre Plus is the same as that for CSA decisions, except that applications are made to Jobcentre Plus.

Decisions that can be revised

Most child maintenance decisions can be revised, including:[4]
- a decision to make or refuse to make a maintenance calculation, including an interim maintenance decision and default maintenance decision (see p367);
- a decision to make a reduced benefit decision. This is a Jobcentre Plus decision;
- a decision of an appeal tribunal to make or refuse to agree a variation to a maintenance calculation;
- a decision to adjust maintenance payable or to cancel an adjustment (see p432);[5]
- any of those decisions made on supersession (see p389).[6]

It may also be possible to revise other sorts of CSA decisions, depending on how the CSA (and, eventually, appeal tribunals and commissioners) interpret the rules. A person who disputes a CSA interpretation of these rules should seek advice. Decisions that may be possible to revise include:
- a decision to treat a maintenance application as withdrawn when a parent with care on benefits becomes a voluntary applicant (see p46);[7]
- a decision to refuse to cancel or to suspend a reduced benefit decision (see p69);[8]
- a decision to impose a regular payments condition on a variation applicant (see p330).[9]

When a decision can be revised

The CSA can revise a decision if, within **a month** of notification of the decision:[10]
- the CSA starts action leading to a revision;
- a person (person with care, non-resident parent or Scottish child applicant) applies for a revision;
- a person applies for a variation; *or*
- the revision is refused because of insufficient information or evidence, the person reapplies (or a longer period if there are sufficient reasons) and provides sufficient information or evidence to revise.

Outside this one-month time period the CSA can revise a decision if:[11]
- an appeal is made in time (or within the time allowed for late appeals if the application meets those conditions – see p402) and the appeal has not yet been determined (see below);
- the decision arose from 'official error' (see p386);
- the decision was wrong because of a misrepresentation or failure to disclose a material fact (see p386) *and*, because of that, the decision was more advantageous to the person who misrepresented or failed to disclose;
- a late application is accepted;[12]
- the decision was made under the rules about a pending test case decision which has now been given (see p419);[13]
- the decision is wrong because a person with respect to whom the maintenance calculation has been made was not, at the time the calculation was made, a parent of a child to whom the calculation relates.[14]

If an appeal is lodged, the CSA checks to see whether the decision should be revised (see p384).

A decision *cannot* be revised because of a change in circumstances after the date the decision was made, or because of an expected change.[15] Instead, the decision may be superseded (see p389).

For revision of default maintenance decisions, see p353.

Under the test case rules (see p419), the CSA may refuse to follow the law as decided by the commissioners or courts, or even suspend a decision on revision while an appeal is being brought in another case.

Late applications

Because supersession (see p389) cannot usually lead to a decision being backdated to the original effective date, a late application for revision (which can) may need to be made. However, in case it should not be accepted, an application for a supersession can be made at the same time, if appropriate. For example, a decision may be based on the wrong mortgage payment details. If the person concerned missed the deadline for applying for a revision, s/he can make a late application (giving special reasons – see below) and also apply for a supersession on the grounds of mistake of fact (see p389).

The CSA can extend the one-month period for applying for a revision if it considers that:[16]

- it was not practicable to apply within one month because of 'special circumstances' (see below);
- the application for revision has merit; *and*
- it is reasonable to grant the application.

'**Special circumstances**' are not defined, but they are *not* the same as the special circumstances needed for bringing a late appeal (see p402). However, ignorance of, or a mistake about, the law, including time limits, or a new interpretation of the law by a commissioner or court are *not* special circumstances and must be ignored when considering the application.[17] The person applying for a revision must apply for an extension at the latest within 13 months of the notification.[18] However, if the person applying for the revision has asked for written reasons for the decision s/he is seeking to revise (see p401), the 13 months can be extended. If the statement of reasons is provided within one month of notification of the decision, the 13-month period is extended by 14 days. If the statement of reasons is provided after one month, the 13 months plus 14 days runs from the date it is provided.[19] The longer the delay in applying for a revision, the more compelling the special circumstances must be.[20]

An application for an extension must identify the decision that it is sought to revise and explain why an extension should be granted.[21] An application that is refused may not be renewed,[22] though the CSA may have power to reconsider a refusal to extend.[23] Judicial review of a refusal to extend time may be possible (see p383).

Official error

'**Official error**' is a mistake made by an officer of the CSA, Jobcentre Plus or designated authority, which was not caused or contributed to by anyone outside the CSA, Jobcentre Plus or designated authority.[24] This includes mistakes of law (see p391), except those only shown as an error by a child support commissioner or court, as well as mistakes of fact, such as:

- a mistake of arithmetic;
- a wrong assumption about a person's circumstances, where there was no evidence for it;
- a mistake made because CSA staff did not pass information or evidence to the officer who made the decision, when they should have done.

Misrepresentation and failure to disclose

A '**misrepresentation**' is a written or spoken statement of fact which is untrue.[25] This applies to an untrue statement, even if the person making it believes it to be true – ie, 'innocent misrepresentation'.[26]

There is only a 'failure to disclose' a fact if there is a legal duty to report that fact to the CSA.[27] Therefore, a person who is asked to give information but leaves it out has failed to disclose that information. However, if the person is not asked for the information, there can be no failure to disclose unless it is one of the facts a parent with care must always report (see p99). There is no general duty to report changes of circumstances to the CSA (see p99).

The decision that the CSA wishes to revise must have been wrong because of a fact that was misrepresented or not disclosed and the decision was more advantageous to the person who misrepresented or failed to disclose.[28] Therefore, if the CSA ignored that fact or if that fact made no difference, the CSA cannot base a revision on misrepresentation or failure to disclose.

Example
When Amy applied for maintenance she also applied for a variation on the ground that Shaun had assets over £65,000. However, the variation was not agreed and her maintenance calculation was made without this element, based on the information Shaun provided. A few months later Amy discovers that Shaun inherited a property from his aunt a few weeks before her application for maintenance. She informs the CSA, it investigates and confirms that he failed to disclose this when he was asked to provide information for the variation element. Because he failed to disclose the inheritance his maintenance calculation is less than it would have been with the variation element. Since there was failure to disclose that resulted in a decision that was more advantageous to him, the CSA revises the original maintenance calculation.

However, had Shaun only inherited the property some time after he was asked for information in relation to the variation application the CSA could not decide that he had failed to disclose information. In this case, the maintenance calculation cannot be revised, but it may be superseded if Amy asks for a variation to be considered.

Procedure for revising

A notification of a decision sets out how to ask the CSA to revise that decision.[29] The revision request may be made by telephone. However, unless the issue is straightforward, it is still best to follow up any telephone call with a letter to the CSA confirming the reason for the request.

There is no general requirement for the CSA to notify the parties that it is considering a revision or to inform one party that the other has applied for a revision. However, where an application for variation has passed preliminary consideration[30] or there is a request for a revision of a calculation with a previously agreed variation,[31] the other parties may be contacted and asked for their representations.

The rules about disclosure apply to the information given in any notification (see p100).

Where a revision has been requested the burden of proof is on the applicant.[32] In cases where the applicant fails to provide sufficient information to make a decision, the CSA may ask her/him to provide further information within an agreed time limit. In this situation the CSA may decide to:

- close the case, if a person with care who is not on benefits is not co-operating; *or*
- make a default maintenance decision, if the non-resident parent is failing to co-operate; *or*
- refuse to revise the decision.

If a default decision would be less than the current maintenance calculation the CSA may refuse to revise rather than make a default maintenance decision. For further information on default maintenance decisions, see p352.

If a parent with care on benefit comes off benefit before the application is determined there are special provisions regarding notifications and treating the application as never made.

If a revision is considered because an appeal has been lodged, unless the revised decision would be worse for the appellant, the revision is carried out and the appeal lapses.[33] The appellant could then decide to appeal against the revised decision, within the usual time limits. If the revised decision does not benefit the appellant, it is still carried out but the appellant is asked whether s/he wishes the appeal to go ahead against the revised decision and if so, whether s/he wants to make further representations (see p406).

The revised decision

The revised decision normally has the same effective date as the decision it replaces.[34] However, if the effective date of that decision was wrong, the revised decision has the effective date that the replaced decision should have had.[35]

Notification

If the decision is revised, whether or not this results in a fresh or new maintenance calculation (including a default maintenance decision), the parties must be notified of the decision and given the usual details (see p354).[36] If there is more than one person with care in relation to a non-resident parent, this means all must be notified. The normal rules on information disclosure apply.[37]

If the request for revision is refused, only the applicant may be informed, unless the other parties have been contacted – eg, where there has been a request for a variation. Notification of the decision includes reasons for refusal and details of appeal rights.[38]

The time limit for appealing runs from the date of the notice of the revised decision or refusal to revise.[39]

3. **Supersessions**

The Child Support Agency (CSA) can supersede a decision at any time if certain rules are met, with or without an application. Usually a decision is superseded because of a change in circumstances. A superseded decision normally takes effect from the date of the application for supersession or, if none, the date the decision under revision has effect. Unlike in social security cases, there is no duty to tell the CSA of all changes of circumstances (see p99 for changes which must be notified). An application for a variation to the maintenance calculation may be treated as a request for a supersession (see p331).

Information on supersession of decisions made by Jobcentre Plus is the same as for CSA decisions, except that applications are made to Jobcentre Plus.

Decisions that can be superseded

Most child support decisions (whether made by the CSA, Jobcentre Plus, appeal tribunal or commissioner) may be superseded, including:[40]
- a decision to make a maintenance calculation, including a default maintenance decision and interim maintenance decision (see p354);
- a decision to make a reduced benefit decision (see p65). This is a Jobcentre Plus decision;
- a decision of an appeal tribunal which was made on a CSA referral of a variation application (see p331);
- a decision to make, or refuse to make, a departure direction;[41]
- a decision to adjust maintenance payable or to cancel an adjustment for overpayments of maintenance or voluntary payments (see p432);[42]
- any of those decisions made on revision (see p384).

It may also be possible to supersede other sorts of CSA decisions, depending on how the CSA (and, eventually, appeal tribunals and commissioners) interpret the rules. For decisions which may be possible to revise, see p384.

When a decision can be superseded

The CSA can *normally* supersede a decision if:[43]
- a material change of circumstances has taken place (or is expected to take place) since the effective date of the decision and there would be a significant change in the amount of the calculation;
- the decision was made in ignorance of, or was based on a mistake about, a material fact;
- there is an application for a variation to the calculation; *or*
- the decision was made by the CSA (*not* by an appeal tribunal or commissioner) and it is wrong in law (see p391).

Any information on evidence on which a superseding decision is to be based must be known to the CSA and not based on supposition.[44] If a change of circumstances has taken place or is expected, this must be based on fact and not on probability.

However, the CSA cannot supersede a decision:

- which can be revised instead (see p384);[45]
- refusing to make or cancelling a maintenance calculation.[46] A further application for a maintenance calculation should be made instead.

The CSA can initiate a supersession even though a party has already applied for one[47] – eg, where the CSA is aware of a change of circumstances which has not been raised in the supersession application. The CSA may supersede to reinstate a previously applied variation.

The CSA also carries out periodic case checks. In some cases a notified change of circumstances can be treated as a periodic case check instead of a request for a supersession (see p393).

Under the test case rules, the CSA may refuse to follow the law as decided by the commissioners or courts, or even suspend a decision on supersession, while an appeal is being brought in another case. See p419 for details.

When a decision cannot be superseded

A decision cannot be superseded unless there is a change of 5 per cent or more in the non-resident parent's net income used in the calculation.[48] The CSA refers to this as the 'tolerance level'. In some cases, this net income tolerance rule does not apply. The net income tolerance rule does not apply if the superseding decision:[49]

- is on the outcome of a variation application;
- affects a variation ground in a maintenance calculation, or revised/superseded such a decision;
- is made on an interim maintenance decision, or on the revised/superseded decision;
- is made on a decision to adjust, or cease to adjust, amounts due to take account of overpayments of maintenance or voluntary payments, or on the revision/ supersession of such a decision;
- is because the non-resident parent or his partner have gone on or off benefit – ie, benefits that count for the flat rate (other than income support (IS)/income based jobseeker's allowance (JSA)) or child benefit;[50]
- is made following an application for a supersession on more than one ground, and the grounds which do not relate to the net income of the non-resident parent lead to a superseding decision. The change in income can also be taken into account.[51]

Some of these exceptions to the tolerance rule do not apply in 'old rules' cases. For further information, see the 2002/03 edition of this *Handbook*.

The tolerance rule is not applied to other changes of circumstances – eg:[52]

- relevant children joining or leaving the household;
- applications for other qualifying children;
- changes in shared care arrangements;
- changes notified by a third party (eg, Jobcentre Plus);
- a qualifying child dies or ceases to be a child;[53]
- the person with care, non-resident parent or qualifying child are no longer habitually resident in the UK;[54] *or*
- the person with care and non-resident parent start living together.[55]

Where an application for a supersession is made to which the tolerance rule would apply, and a further application is then made on a ground(s) which does not relate to the net income of the non-resident parent, a superseding decision can be made as if the two applications had been made at the same time (ie, so that the change in income can be taken into account).[56]

Wrong in law

A decision is 'erroneous in point of law' if:[57]
- when making the decision, the CSA misinterpreted or overlooked part or all of an Act of Parliament, a regulation or relevant caselaw;
- there is no evidence to support the decision;
- the facts are such that no reasonable person applying the law could have come to such a conclusion;
- there is a breach of natural justice – ie, the procedure used led to unfairness or the CSA officer who took the decision appeared to be biased;[58]
- the CSA has not given enough reasons for the decision;
- when exercising a discretion, the CSA took into account something irrelevant or ignored something relevant – eg, the welfare of the child (see p24).[59]

A decision is wrong in law if the regulation under which it is made was not made lawfully. Such a regulation is said to be *ultra vires* (outside the powers). The courts, appeal tribunals and commissioners can decide that a regulation is *ultra vires*,[60] and appeal tribunals and commissioners have done so in benefit cases.

A decision is also wrong in law if it is contrary to European law (European Union (EU) law and the European Convention on Human Rights (ECHR)). EU law will rarely be relevant to child support issues. Commissioners have decided that European law on the equal treatment of men and women in social security matters do not apply to child support.[61]

ECHR law is more likely to be relevant. Courts and commissioners are required to interpret Acts of Parliament consistently with the ECHR as far as it is possible to do so.[62] Neither courts nor commissioners can use the ECHR to overrule an Act of Parliament, but the courts can issue a declaration of incompatability.[63] However, courts and commissioners can use the ECHR to override regulations which are incompatible with the provisions of the ECHR. It is unlawful for courts, commissioners or tribunals to act in a way which is incompatible with an ECHR right.[64] In practice, few challenges using these principles have succeeded so far.

Otherwise, the CSA, Jobcentre Plus, tribunals and commissioners cannot override or ignore the Acts or regulations.

Procedure for superseding

A party to the calculation can apply for a supersession at any time. There are no time limits, but any superseding decision usually runs from the date of the application (see p394). If an application is made, the CSA must consider it and supersede if the conditions set out above are met.

The CSA can initiate a supersession itself, so it must take into account the welfare of the child (see p24) when considering whether to do so. The CSA learns of some changes automatically from the Jobcentre Plus or may do so from a third party.

If the CSA is considering supersession on its own initiative in a 'new rules' case, it must give 28 days' notice to the relevant parties – ie, person with care, non-resident parent and/or Scottish child applicant.[65] The CSA can give notice of its intention to supersede orally (eg, by telephone) or in writing.[66] Where more than one method of notification is used, the earliest date is treated as the date of notification. Where the parties are notified on different dates the latest is counted as the date of notification.[67]

In an 'old rules' case, the CSA should notify parties who 'could be materially affected' where it is proposing to make a superseding decision.[68] However, a commissioner has decided that in some circumstances it may not be necessary for notice to be given in an 'old rules' case, as the effective date is separately determined,[69] and that failure to notify does not mean that a subsequent supersession is invalid.[70] A request for information may be sufficient notice that the CSA is proposing to supersede in an 'old rules' case, although both parties should still be notified. Notification may be oral or written, and the date of written notification is the date it is handed or sent to a person.[71]

If the supersession is in relation to an application for a variation that has passed preliminary consideration,[72] or a supersession of a previously agreed variation,[73] the other relevant parties may be contacted. Otherwise, the other party may not be notified of the application for a supersession. The normal rules about disclosure apply to the information given in any notification (see p100).[74]

The CSA does not have to check all the facts again so can (and usually will) limit its consideration to the issues raised in any application and/or on its own initiative.[75] Information that is provided may need to be verified in the normal way (see Chapter 5). If the tolerance rule is breached, or there are other relevant changes, a decision to supersede will be made.

Periodic case checks

The CSA carries out a **periodic case check** on each calculation. The 'normal' period within which a check should be carried out is every two years. However, a longer or shorted period can be decided by the CSA decision maker, depending on the likelihood that changes will occur.[76] The tolerance rule does not apply to periodic case checks.[77]

A periodic case check may be requested by any party but the CSA may decide not to conduct one – eg, because the non-resident parent remains on IS/income-based JSA. A case check is not a supersession, but if the information gathered shows there are grounds for supersession the CSA will start the procedure for a supersession. A change of circumstances which occurs within 26 weeks of a later periodic case check may be treated as part of the case check rather than a grounds for a separate supersession.

When a periodic case check is due or the CSA decides to conduct one, each party should be given 28 days' notice of any resulting supersession.[78] This notification may be oral or in writing, with the date of notification being the earliest if more than one method is used. If the parties are notified on different dates the notification is counted from the latest. The parties are invited to tell the CSA about any changes within 14 days. If the parties do not respond, or no relevant changes are notified, no further action is taken. If changes are reported these may need to be verified.

If the information does not show there are grounds for supersession, the CSA does not make a new decision, so no notification need be issued. However, where there is a supersession decision, notification continues in the normal way (see p395).

The effective date of any supersession depends on how the periodic case check was initiated.

- If it was initiated by the CSA, the effective date is the first day of the maintenance period that contains the 28th day from the date of notification of the periodic check.[79]
- If a change of circumstances was treated as a periodic case check, the effective date is the first day of the week in the maintenance period on, or prior to, the date the change of circumstances was notified.[80]

The superseding decision

The CSA may decide that:
- there are no grounds for supersession and refuse to supersede;
- there are grounds for supersession but the maintenance calculation remains unchanged;
- there are grounds for supersession and the maintenance calculation is changed; *or*
- the maintenance calculation should be cancelled.

Effective date of the superseding decision

The general rule is that a supersession takes effect from the first day in the maintenance period in which the decision is made, or the application for supersession/variation was made.[81] However, the effective date may be from a different date in certain circumstances, as shown in the table below. There are special rules for supersession decisions relating to reduced benefit decisions (see p65), periodic case checks (see p393) and cancellations. A commissioner has decided, in relation to an 'old rules' case, that a supersession can only have effect once the CSA knows or becomes aware of the information or evidence on which the new decision is to be based.[82]

Circumstances	Effective date
An application for an anticipated change in circumstances.	The first day in the maintenance period in which the change is expected to occur.[83]
The relevant circumstance is an expected variation ground.	The first day in the maintenance period in which the ground is expected to occur.[84]
There is a further qualifying child in relation to the same non-resident parent and person with care.	If the application for supersession is made by the non-resident parent, the date of the request.
	If the application for supersession is made by the person with care, or a maintenance calculation is made in response to an application from a child in Scotland, the date of notification to the non-resident parent.[85]
	However, if either of these dates falls on the first day of the maintenance period in relation to the existing calculation, this will be the effective date.
The non-resident parent (or his partner) claims benefit and notifies the CSA within a month of the award.	If benefit commences on or before notification, the first day in the maintenance period in which the parent notified the CSA.[86]
	If benefit commences after notification, the first day in the maintenance period in which entitlement begins.[87]

Ignorance or mistake where the non-resident parent (or his partner) had claimed benefit before notice of the maintenance calculation and, if benefit is payable, the CSA is notified within one month of the award.	If benefit commences on or before notification, the first day in the maintenance period in which the parent notified the CSA.[88] If benefit commences after notification, the first day in the maintenance period in which entitlement begins.[89]
The decision being superseded was made by an appeal tribunal or commissioner; *and* the supersession is because of a misrepresentation or failure to disclose a material fact; *and* that misrepresentation/ failure meant the decision was more favourable to the person who misrepresented/failed to disclose.	The date the tribunal/commissioner decision took, or was to take, effect.[90]
The CSA is superseding on its own initiative.	The first day of the maintenance period that is 28 days after the date of notification of this intention to the parties involved.[91] However, if the decision is superseded on the basis of information or evidence in relation to decisions about the relationship between the CSA and maintenance orders/ agreements, the first day of the maintenance period in which the information or evidence was brought to the attention of the CSA.[92]
The supersession is due to a change in circumstances brought to the attention of another agency with authority to act under the Child Support Act – ie, Jobcentre Plus.	The first day in the maintenance period in which information or evidence was first brought to the relevant officer.[93]

Notification

If the decision results in a supersession, whether or not a new maintenance calculation is made (including an interim maintenance decision or default maintenance decision), the parties must be notified of the decision and given the usual details (see p354).[94] The notice must also state how to seek a revision, supersession and appeal.[95]

If the decision is to refuse to supersede, notification will be given including the reasons for refusal and appeal rights.[96]

If the CSA intends to cancel the case it may notify each party and, where the reason for cancellation is a child applicant in Scotland ceasing to be a qualifying child, inform other potential child applicants.[97]

Whether to request supersession

Before requesting a supersession because of a change, you should try to work out whether a fresh calculation would be higher or lower. You only need tell the CSA about the changes in your favour. If the change only relates to one party, the CSA may not tell the other person, but if it does, that party might tell the CSA about other changes. These may cancel out the effect of the changes which led you to ask for a supersession.

If you believe the other person's circumstances have changed (eg, a non-resident parent no longer has children living with him) you can ask for a supersession and for the CSA to investigate (see Chapter 5). The CSA does not have to, but any changes it is aware of must be taken into account when it decides whether or not to supersede.

Notes

1 Reg 4(1)(a) CS(TP) Regs

1. Changing decisions
2 *Council of Civil Service Unions v Minister for the Civil Service* [1984] 1 WLR 1174, [1984] 3 All ER 935
3 s12(2)(b) SSA 1998; reg 25 SS&CS(DA) Regs

2. Revisions
4 s16 CSA 1991
5 Reg 3A(6) SS&CS(DA) Regs
6 s16 1A(a) CSA 1991
7 s11(3) CSA 1991
8 Regs 16, 17 and 18 CS(MCP) Regs
9 s28C CSA 1991
10 Reg 3A(1)(a), (b) and (d) SS&CS(DA) Regs
11 Reg 3A(1)(c) and (e) SS&CS(DA) Regs
12 Reg 4 SS&CS(DA) Regs
13 Reg 3A(5A) SS&CS(DA) Regs
14 Reg 3A(1)(f) SS&CS(DA) Regs
15 Reg 3A(2) SS&CS(DA) Regs
16 Reg 4(4) SS&CS(DA) Regs

17 Reg 4(6) SS&CS(DA) Regs
18 Reg 4(5) SS&CS(DA) Regs
19 Reg 4(3)(b) SS&CS(DA) Regs
20 Reg 4(7) SS&CS(DA) Regs
21 Reg 4(3) SS&CS(DA) Regs
22 Reg 4(7) SS&CS(DA) Regs
23 See CIS/93/1992
24 Reg 1(2) SS&CS(DA) Regs
25 R(SB) 9/85
26 R(SB) 2/92 (*Page and Davis v CAO*); PG, Calculation and Decision Types, Misrepresentation or Failure to Disclose Information
27 CCS/15846/1996
28 Reg 3A(c) SS&CS(DA) Regs
29 Reg 23(4) CS(MCP) Regs
30 Reg 9 CS(V) Regs
31 Reg 15B SS&CS(DA) Regs
32 PG, Calculation and Decision Types, Burden of Proof
33 s16(6) CSA 1991; reg 30(1) and (2)(f) SS&CS(DA) Regs
34 s16(3) CSA 1991
35 Reg 5A SS&CS(DA) Regs

36 Reg 15C SS&CS(DA) Regs
37 Reg 15C(3) SS&CS(DA) Regs
38 Reg 15C(9)-(11) SS&CS(DA) Regs
39 s16(5) CSA 1991; reg 31(2) SS&CS(DA) Regs

3. Supersessions

40 s17(1) CSA 1991
41 s28H and Sch 4C para 1(a) CSA 1991
42 Reg 6A(9) SS&CS(DA) Regs
43 Reg 6A(2)-(6) SS&CS(DA) Regs
44 CCS/162/2006
45 Reg 6A(7) SS&CS(DA) Regs
46 Reg 6A(8) SS&CS(DA) Regs
47 Reg 6A(2) and (5) SS&CA(DA) Regs
48 Reg 6B(1) SS&CS(DA) Regs
49 Reg 6B(4) SS&CS(DA) Regs
50 Regs 6B(4)(e) and 7B(2)-(3) SS&CS(DA) Regs
51 Reg 6B(3) SS&CS(DA) Regs
52 PG, Calculation and Decision Types, When Tolerance is Applied – New Rules Cases
53 Regs 6B(4)(e) and 7B(17) SS&CS(DA) Regs
54 Regs 6B(4)(e) and 7B(18) SS&CS(DA) Regs
55 Regs 6B(4)(e) and 7B(20) SS&CS(DA) Regs
56 Reg 6B(5) SS&CS(DA) Regs
57 R(A) 1/72; R(SB) 11/83
58 R v Gough [1993] AC 646, [1993] 2 WLR 883, [1993] 2 All ER 724
59 Wednesbury Corporation v Ministry of Housing and Local Government (No.2) [1965] 3 WLR 956, [1965] 3 All ER 571
60 CAO v Foster [1993] AC 754, [1993] 2 WLR 292, [1993] 1 All ER 705
61 R(CS) 3/96; R(CS) 2/95; CCS/17/1994. These concerned the application of Art 141 of the EC treaty (formerly Art 119), and Council Directives 75/117 and 79/7. The Sex Discrimination Act 1975 also has no effect: CCS/6/1995
62 under s3 HRA 1998, in force 1 October 2000
63 s4 HRA 1998
64 s6 HRA 1998
65 Reg 7B(7) SS&CS(DA) Regs
66 Reg 7B(8)(b) SS&CS(DA) Regs
67 Reg 7B(8)(a) SS&CS(DA) Regs
68 Reg 24 CS(MAP) Regs.
69 Reg 23(2) CS(MAP) Regs; CCS/162/2006
70 CCS/162/2006
71 Reg 23(8) CS(MAP) Regs;
72 Reg 9 CS(V) Regs
73 Reg 15B SS&CS(DA) Regs

74 Reg 15B SS&CS(DA) Regs
75 s17(2) CSA 1991
76 PG, Calculation and Decision Types, Periodic Case Checks
77 PG, Calculation and Decision Types, Periodic Case Checks
78 Regs 7B(7)-(8) and 7C SS&CS(DA) Regs
79 Reg 7B(7) SS&CS(DA) Regs
80 PG, Calculation and Decision Types, Effective Date of a Periodic Case Check
81 s17(4) CSA 1991
82 CCS/162/2006
83 Reg 7B(5) SS&CS(DA) Regs
84 Reg 7B(6) SS&CS(DA) Regs
85 Reg 7B(17B) SS&CS(DA) Regs
86 Reg 7B(3)(a) SS&CS(DA) Regs
87 Reg 7B(3)(b) SS&CS(DA) Regs
88 Reg 7B(2)(a) SS&CS(DA) Regs
89 Reg 7B(2)(b) SS&CS(DA) Regs
90 Reg 7B(9) SS&CS(DA) Regs
91 Reg 7B(7) SS&CS(DA) Regs
92 Reg 7B(1) SS&CS(DA) Regs
93 Reg 7B(1) SS&CS(DA) Regs
94 Reg 15C SS&CS(DA) Regs
95 Reg 15C(4) SS&CS(DA) Regs
96 Reg 15C(9)-(11) SS&CS(DA) Regs
97 Reg 15C(5) SS&CS(DA) Regs

Chapter 19

Appeals

This chapter covers:

This chapter does not include information on appeals outstanding at conversion (see Chapter 8). However, conversion decisions themselves may be appealed as described in this chapter.[1]

Most child maintenance decisions, whether they are made by the Child Support Agency (CSA) or Jobcentre Plus, can be appealed to an independent appeal tribunal run by the Tribunals Service. An application for a variation can also be referred to the tribunal by the CSA.[2] A tribunal decision can be appealed on a question of law to a child support commissioner.

In this chapter we refer to CSA decisions. Appeals against Jobcentre Plus decisions are progressed in the same way under child support legislation. However, the appeal is made to Jobcentre Plus and the case will be prepared and presented by Jobcentre Plus staff (see CPAG's *Welfare Benefits and Tax Credits Handbook*).

1. Appeal tribunals

An appeal tribunal usually consists of a legal member sitting alone.[3] This is a person qualified as a lawyer.[4] If the appeal raises difficult issues about financial accounts, the tribunal includes a financially qualified member – ie, a chartered or certified accountant.[5] The President of the Social Security and Child Support Appeals Tribunals decides who is on the panel and who hears each sort of appeal.[6] The President can also appoint one extra member to sit on any appeal,[7] but this is expected to happen only rarely. If there is more than one member, the legal member is the chairperson.

Who can appeal

Decisions that can be appealed[8]

A decision about whether maintenance is payable and if so, how much (including default and interim maintenance decisions) or, in 'new rules' cases, a decision to supersede a calculation.

A refusal to make a maintenance calculation (including default and interim maintenance decisions), or, in 'new rules' cases only, a refusal to supersede.

In 'old rules' cases, a decision to cancel or refuse to cancel a maintenance assessment or interim maintenance assessment,[10] and a decision to make, or refuse to make, a departure direction.

A reduced benefit decision (this is a Jobcentre Plus decision).

A decision to impose penalty payments or payment of fees.

An adjustment, or cancellation of an adjustment, to the amount paid due to overpayment of maintenance or voluntary payments.[13]
A supersession decision, whether as originally made or as revised.[14]
A decision made on revision or a decision which has not been revised following an application.

Who can appeal[9]

The person who made the application or requested the supersession (to whom the decision applies). If the application is made by a Scottish child, the person with care, non-resident parent or child can appeal.

The person who requests a cancellation or departure direction can appeal the refusal to cancel the assessment or make a departure direction. Any relevant person (ie, parent with care, non-resident parent or Scottish child applicant) can appeal against other 'old rules' decisions.

The parent with care once benefit has started to be reduced.[12]

The parent required to pay the penalty or person required to pay the fees.

Any relevant person – ie, person with care, non-resident parent or Scottish child applicant. If someone has applied for a revision and the decision is not revised, the time limit for appealing runs from the date the notice of the decision not to revise is issued.[15]

Conversion decisions are, therefore, open to appeal, since these are supersession decisions.

The Child Support Agency (CSA) may decide that some reported changes are ones which it needs to act on but do not constitute an application for supersession – eg, a change of address which does not affect the assessment. Where there is no new decision to appeal the person may instead seek a late appeal from the original decision (see p402) or may even consider judicial review (see p383).

The CSA may also refer a variation application to an appeal tribunal in certain cases (see p331). Appeal tribunals can also consider departures in 'old rules' cases.

Parties to the appeal

Except for appeals about a refusal to make a calculation and reduced benefit decisions, each party to the calculation has the right of appeal. Only the CSA and a person who has a right of appeal can take part in the appeal.[16]

This means in the case of reduced benefit decision appeals the non-resident parent is *not* contacted and takes no part.

Otherwise, regardless of who appealed, all parties have the same rights, except that only the appellant can ask to withdraw the appeal. Because an appeal can be withdrawn without the consent of any other party (see p407), it is best for each party who wishes to challenge the decision to bring their own appeal. The appeals can be heard together.

A party is not obliged to take part in the appeal, except if directed to provide evidence (see p405) or to attend as a witness (see p409).

What the tribunal can do

The tribunal looks afresh at the issues raised as the situation stood up to the date of the CSA decision under appeal.[17] It cannot consider any circumstances which exist only in relation to a period after that date. It can consider any evidence and arguments, including those rejected or overlooked by the CSA and those which have not been used before.[18] The tribunal has no duty to consider any issue not raised in the appeal.[19] However, the tribunal is 'inquisitorial', which means it can raise legal arguments and factual questions on its own initiative, if appropriate.[20] It is, however, bound by the legislation, unless this is itself unlawful (see p391). It is also bound by caselaw (see p418), unless the test case rules apply (see p421). If the tribunal reaches a different conclusion from that of the CSA, it allows the appeal (see p411).

If the appeal is against a refusal to revise/supersede, the tribunal must decide whether a revision/supersession can be carried out. When considering this, the tribunal looks at the facts as they were when the CSA refused to revise/supersede, even if the CSA did not know those facts.[21] Unless there was a basis for a revision/supersession at that time, a later change of circumstances is irrelevant.[22] A request for supersession on the basis of the later change (see p389) should be made instead.

On a reduced benefit decision appeal, the tribunal itself exercises discretion considering the welfare of the child, and decides whether a decision *should* be imposed on all the evidence now available, not simply whether the Jobcentre Plus was *entitled* to impose a decision.[23]

Change of circumstances

When deciding the appeal, the tribunal cannot take into account any change of circumstances that occurred after the date of the decision under appeal.[24] (This does not apply to an appeal made before 21 May 1998.[25]) If the tribunal decides to allow the appeal because the decision was wrong on the facts at the time it was made, it cannot go on to direct how the CSA should deal with a later change of circumstances. Supersession could be sought instead.

Parentage disputes

If the appellant disputes parentage of a child named in the maintenance application, that appeal must be made to a court, not the tribunal (see p17).[26] If there are other grounds of appeal apart from parentage, a separate appeal should be made on those grounds to the tribunal.[27] If both sorts of grounds are raised on an appeal to a tribunal, it can only deal with the non-parentage grounds.[28] Likewise, a court considering an appeal appears to be limited to parentage issues. If a person raises parentage grounds for the first time at the tribunal hearing, s/he must make a separate appeal to a court on those grounds, or apply for a revision or supersession (see Chapter 18).[29] For parentage disputes before the appeal stage is reached, see pp17 and 87.

2. Procedure

When the Child Support Agency (CSA) makes a decision, each person must get a notice of that decision and information on the right of appeal.[30] If no reasons are given for the decision, the person can request written reasons within one month of the notice,[31] and the CSA must issue them within 14 days of receiving the request, or as soon as practicable afterwards.[32]

If a person is informed of a CSA decision, but the CSA does not accept there is any right of appeal, s/he can make an appeal so that the tribunal can decide whether there is a right of appeal (see p406).

How to appeal

An appeal must be made within one month of notice of the decision, *unless* a request for a written statement of reasons for the decision is made, when the time limit is one month plus 14 days.[33] If the statement is not provided within the one-month period, the time limit is extended to within 14 days of the statement being provided.[34] See p402 for extensions of time.

Notification is deemed to happen on the day the notice is issued by the CSA.[35] If the decision is a revision, supersession or refusal to revise, time runs from the date the notice of that decision is issued.[36]

Where an accidental error in a decision has been corrected, written notification must be given of that correction.[37] If this occurs, any days before this notice is given are ignored when calculating the time limit for appealing.[38]

An appeal must be received by a CSA office within the time limit.[39]

Appeals must:[40]

• be made on a CSA appeal form (or be accepted as sufficient by the CSA);

- be signed either by the appellant or a person whom s/he has authorised in writing to represent her/him;
- identify the decision being appealed; *and*
- give the grounds for the appeal.

The appeal form is passed to the CSA's Central Appeals Unit (CAU). If the CAU considers that the form/letter meets these rules, it prepares a submission on the appeal (see p403). The appeal is only sent to the Tribunals Service when this submission has been prepared. The CSA Client Charter states that the stage of either revising the decision (see p406) or submitting the appeal to the Tribunals Service will take an average of 10 weeks.[41] The appeal is handled by the appropriate Tribunals Service regional office (see Appendix 1). The Client Charter states that the Tribunals Service will investigate and notify the CSA of a decision within 19 weeks of submission.[42]

The appeal form or letter has sufficient information

The CSA can forward to the tribunal a written appeal which is not on the appeal form (or which is, but is not fully completed) if it contains sufficient information for the appeal to proceed.[43] However, if the form is not used or is not properly completed, the CSA may return it to the appellant for completion or ask for further information.[44] If the appellant returns the completed form/information within 14 days of the CSA request (or a longer period if the CSA accepts) the appeal is treated as made on time.[45] If the appellant does not do this, the CSA refers the appeal form/letter (with any relevant documents or evidence) to a legal member to decide if it meets the rules for appeals.[46] The decision must be notified to the appellant and the CSA.[47] The member can hold an oral hearing to consider this (but is very unlikely to do so).[48] Any information received by the CSA after the referral is made but before the member's decision is given must be referred to the member, who must take it into account.[49]

Appeal is out of time

A CSA decision maker may allow a late appeal, but only if s/he is satisfied it is in the interest of justice.[50] Where s/he is not satisfied, the application for late appeal is passed to the Tribunals Service, for a legally qualified tribunal member to make a decision.

A legal member may extend the time for appealing so that the appeal can be considered, if s/he is satisfied that:[51]
- the appeal has reasonable chances of success; *or*
- it is in the interest of natural justice.

A written application seeking an extension must be made, which meets the rules for appeal forms/letters.[52] The rules for insufficient information apply to applications for an extension of time.[53] No appeal may be made more than one year after the date the time for appealing ran out.[54]

The interests of justice may be served if it was not practicable to make the application in time because of special circumstances – ie:[55]

- the applicant, her/his partner or dependant died or had a serious illness;
- the applicant is not resident in the UK;
- normal postal services were disrupted; or
- other wholly exceptional special circumstances.

The later the appeal, the more compelling the special circumstances must be.[56] When considering this, the member (or CSA) must *not* take into account any mistake made by the applicant (or her/his representative) about the law or a time limit *or* an interpretation of the law by a commissioner or court which is different from the way the CSA had understood and applied the law.[57]

The rules are the same as those for late appeals to an appeal tribunal in a social security case. The rules for late appeals to a social security commissioner are different (see p414).

When appealing late, give as many details of special reasons as possible, but do not delay appealing to do this.

If the legal member refuses to extend time, there is no right to have this decision reconsidered.[58] There is no appeal against a refusal to extend time. It is not clear if such a refusal can be 'set aside' (see p413).[59]

Preparing a case

The tribunal may be the first chance for an independent evaluation of the decision under appeal. It may also be the last chance because there can only be an appeal to a commissioner on a point of law. Therefore, each party should make sure that the tribunal knows the facts and arguments about the case.

Papers provided by the Child Support Agency

The CSA prepares a written statement of the facts and law involved in the decision under appeal (known as a 'submission'). If the CSA considers the appeal is misconceived (see p406), only a short submission is prepared. The CSA should attach copies of all relevant evidence, including correspondence and documents.[60]

The CSA asks the parties whether they consent to waive the confidentiality rules (see p100).[61] This does not apply to an appeal against a Jobcentre Plus reduced benefit decision, where there is only one party. A refusal to consent must be received within 14 days or disclosure may follow. If one (or both) party refuses to consent, parts of the papers (ie, addresses) are blacked out. A commissioner's decision has stated that this evidence must be kept confidential from the other parent but not necessarily from the tribunal, which should see all the evidence relevant to the issues it has to decide.[62] In addition, evidence is not required to be 'blacked out' (also known as editing or masking) if it is known to the other party – eg, each parent already knows where the other lives.

A party can remind the CSA not to include papers on its file which are irrelevant to the appeal – eg, an earlier dispute about parentage when the current appeal is about a variation. Also, the legal member can be asked to direct the CSA not to include them.

The submission is prepared by the CAU, which gathers information from the computer system and copies of relevant documentation

If the CSA officer preparing the submission accepts that the decision is wrong, s/he revises it (see p384). The appeal either lapses or continues (see p406). The Client Charter states that the stage of preparing the submission (or revising the decision) will take an average of 10 weeks.[63]

Considering the facts and law

Each party should:

- read the CSA submission to see whether the CSA now accepts some of the arguments previously rejected or ignored. However, just because the CSA accepts part of a person's case does not mean that the tribunal will, especially if the other party disputes it;
- check the law using this book and other sources (see Appendix 5). If the CSA quotes a commissioner's decision, consider getting a copy (see p418). The Tribunals Service does not have copies of unreported decisions. If an unreported decision is to be used by the CSA, a copy should be supplied to you. If you wish to quote an unreported decision, you should supply copies to everyone, preferably by sending a copy to the tribunal clerk in advance of the hearing. (If appealing to commissioners, you must send this within 14 days of the hearing.[64]) A party can quote the CSA's internal procedural guidance but it is not legally binding;
- check the documents attached to the submission. If anything relevant is missing, ask the CSA to send it to the Tribunals Service.

If the CSA delays producing a submission, the legal member can be asked to direct that the appeal be heard. This may mean that the tribunal will not have all the evidence the CSA has. However, a party can ask the legal member to direct the CSA (see p405) to provide copies of all the papers, explaining why those papers are needed.

Further evidence

Each party should consider:

- whether s/he has (or can get) any further relevant written evidence. This can be sent to the tribunal at any stage, but it is best to do this soon after the submission is sent out so papers can be copied to the other parties. If evidence or unreported commissioners' decisions are produced at the hearing or sent in shortly before, this may cause a postponement (see p407) or an adjournment (see p411);

- how to tell the tribunal about the facts and law at the hearing. A party can 'give evidence' – ie, say what s/he has seen and heard. For example: 'I look after the child from Friday night to Monday night' may be the best evidence of those facts;
- whether to call any witnesses at the hearing (see p409);
- whether to send a letter setting out what s/he thinks is in dispute and what the correct answers are. This is important if those points are not in the grounds of appeal or if the party has changed her/his mind about something.

Obtaining information and evidence

A party may want another person to provide further information or documents and the legal member can make a direction for the other person to provide this.[65] If so, it is best to send a prepared list to the Tribunals Service which is as precise as possible. For example, the parent with care may believe the non-resident parent has received a pay increase; she decides to ask for 'pay-slips from February to May 2006 (inclusive)'.

To get a direction, the party concerned writes to the Tribunals Service (see Appendix 1) asking the legal member to direct the person to 'produce the documents' in the list and to 'provide further particulars' – ie, the answers to the questions in the list. The letter to the Tribunals Service should explain the steps taken to get this information and why it is relevant.

The legal member can direct any 'party' (see p400) to provide evidence or information. A person who is not a party (eg, an employer) cannot be directed to provide evidence, but can be ordered to attend as a witness and produce documents (see p409). This should be done before the full hearing, so the parties can consider that evidence. It may be possible to direct a non-party to provide further particulars.

The legal member usually decides about directions without a hearing, but one may be held.[66] The chairperson may also make a direction when no one has requested it. A copy of any direction is sent to all the parties.

There is no legal requirement to comply with the direction. However, if a person fails to comply without a good explanation, the tribunal hearing the appeal may decide that s/he has something to hide and so may disbelieve that person's evidence. If the person is the appellant, the appeal can be struck out (see p406). A party can ask the High Court in England and Wales to order a person to comply with a direction.[67] Such an order has been made against a bank in a child support appeal. A person who fails to comply with an order can be fined and/or sent to prison by the Court. The Court of Session in Scotland cannot do this.

There is no appeal from a direction or a refusal to make one, but the legal member can be asked to reconsider her/his decision.

Ending an appeal without a right to a full hearing

There are three ways an appeal can end without the parties having a right to a full hearing. If a party dies, the appeal does not end. The CSA can appoint a person to continue an appeal in the place of the person who has died.[68]

Lapsed appeals

If an appeal is made, the CSA reconsiders the decision under appeal. This should take an average of 10 weeks.[69] If the CSA decides to revise (see Chapter 18) that decision, the appeal lapses unless the revised decision is worse for the appellant than the original decision. If the revised decision is favourable, the appeal lapses (see also p387).[70] A decision is favourable if it results in the appellant having any financial gain (including one which accrues in the future).[71] A decision which results in no actual change does not cause the appeal to lapse.

If the appeal lapses, the appellant can appeal against the revised decision. The usual time limits apply (see p401).

If the appeal does not lapse, it is treated as an appeal against the revised decision.[72] The appellant is asked whether s/he wishes the appeal to go ahead and, if so, for further representations.[73] Unless s/he withdraws the appeal, the tribunal hears it unless the CSA again revises the decision, this time more favourably to the appellant (when the appeal lapses).[74]

If there is a dispute about whether the revised decision is more favourable (eg, the appellant is worse off in the short term, but the CSA says s/he will be better off in the long term), a party can ask for a tribunal hearing to decide whether the appeal has lapsed.

Striking out appeals

An appeal can be struck out (ie, dismissed without consideration) by the clerk of the appeal tribunal if:
- the appellant fails to 'prosecute' the appeal – ie, pursue it properly.[75] This includes making a late appeal where an extension of time is not made (see p402);
- the appellant has failed to notify the clerk whether or not s/he wishes to have an oral hearing (see p407);[76]
- the appellant fails to comply with a direction of the tribunal or clerk, but only if s/he has been notified that striking out may result.[77]

A failure of a party other than the appellant cannot lead to striking out.

The clerk can always decide to refer any matter which needs determining in a decision to strike out to a legal member instead.[78] Written notice of the decision to strike out and how to seek reinstatement is sent to the appellant.[79]

An appeal which has been struck out because of a failure to notify about an oral hearing can be **reinstated** by the clerk if the appellant provides written reasons within one month why s/he thinks the appeal should not have been struck out and the clerk is satisfied that there are reasonable grounds for reinstating the appeal.[80] If the clerk is not satisfied that there are reasonable grounds, the appeal is passed to a legally qualified member to make a decision.

A legal member may reinstate any struck-out appeal if:[81]

- the appellant makes representations within one month of the decision to strike out being issued and the member considers there are reasonable grounds for reinstating the appeal;
- the conditions for striking out for want of prosecution or failure to comply are not met; *or*
- even though those conditions are met, it is not in the interests of justice to strike out on those grounds.

A commissioner's decision has held that a decision to strike out can be appealed to a social security commissioner.[82]

In social security cases, 'out of jurisdiction' appeals may be struck out by the tribunal clerk.[83] However, at the time of writing this does not apply to child support appeals.[84]

Withdrawing appeals

The appellant has the right to withdraw an appeal at any time, and the CSA can withdraw a variation referral at any time.[85] If the appellant gives written notice that s/he does not want the appeal to continue before the appeal is forwarded to the Tribunals Service, all action ceases on the appeal.[86] An appeal/referral is withdrawn by oral notice at the hearing or, at any time before a decision is given on the appeal, by written notice to the tribunal clerk.[87] The other parties are notified of the withdrawal in writing if it was not withdrawn at a hearing at which they were present.[88]

There is no need for the chairperson/other parties to consent to a withdrawal. This may cause injustice where another party is relying on the appeal to decide a point in her/his favour. Such a person should make a late appeal if s/he is a party to the proceedings (see p402).

A withdrawn appeal cannot be reinstated, but any of the parties can appeal the same CSA decision again, though an extension of time is likely to be needed (see p402).[89]

3. **Oral hearings**

The tribunal can hold an oral hearing of any appeal, application or referral. A hearing *must* be arranged if any party requests one, unless the appeal is struck out (see p406).[90] In the case of an appeal or referral (but not an application), the tribunal clerk writes to each party directing them to state on the approved form if a hearing is wanted.[91] In the case of an appeal, this notice warns an appellant (not all parties) that the appeal can be struck out if s/he does not reply (see p406).[92] If the appeal is struck out, it can be reinstated by the clerk or legal member. The time limit for the reply is 14 days from the date the form is issued.[93] The clerk can extend this, but it is important to reply in time if possible. However, a party who wants a hearing should always ask for one, no matter how late. If no party requests a hearing in time, the chairperson can still direct a hearing if s/he considers one is needed to decide the appeal.[94] If not, the appeal is decided on the papers and a decision notice is issued (see p410).

It is usually best to ask for a hearing.

If both parties have appealed the same decision, those appeals must be heard together.[95] Two variation applications about the same maintenance application or calculation can also be heard together.[96]

The tribunal clerk must give the parties at least 14 days' notice of the time and place of the hearing, ending the day before the hearing (unless that party has waived her/his right to this).[97] A party can ask for the hearing to be postponed.[98] This is done by writing to the Tribunals Service, explaining in detail why a postponement is needed. The clerk can decide the request or pass it to a legal member to decide.[99] If a postponement is refused, the clerk notifies the person who applied in writing and the papers about the request and refusal are put before the tribunal.[100] The clerk or tribunal member can postpone a hearing at any time with or without a request.[101]

Good reasons for a postponement include that the appellant needs, but cannot get, representation. However, if there have been previous postponements or the request is made very late, a refusal is likely. If this happens, the tribunal hearing the case can be asked to adjourn (see p410).

Members of the tribunal

The tribunal hearing the appeal is usually made up of one legal member, but can also have one or two other members. If there is more than one member, the legal member acts as the chairperson. A commissioner has recommended that where an appeal involves the accounts of the self-employed or company directors that an accountant should be included as a panel member.[102]

The tribunal clerk is not a member and cannot take part in the hearing, but can be present during the tribunal's consideration and make some directions – eg, striking out (see p406) and postponing.

Where there is a panel, a member, other than the chairperson, may attend the hearing via live television link.[103] This can only occur where the chairperson gives permission.

Attending the hearing

Every party has the right to be present.[104] This includes attendance via a live television link, if the tribunal member (if s/he sits alone) or chairperson gives permission.[105]

The Child Support Agency (CSA) may be represented by a member of staff from a local office, called a **presenting officer,** but this will usually be via television link rather than in person. A commissioner has decided it is bad practice for that to be a CSA official who has been involved in the case.[106] A party may be represented by a lawyer or lay person, whether the party attends the hearing in person or not.[107]

The hearing can go ahead in the absence of one, several, or all of the parties.[108] However, a commissioner has said that the tribunal should only exceptionally go ahead without the presenting officer.[109] The CSA's Central Appeals Unit (CAU) receives notice of a schedule of hearings 15 working days in advance; other parties to the appeal receive similar notice.

The Tribunals Service intends every hearing venue to have separate waiting rooms for the non-resident parent, parent with care and presenting officer. If another party or witness may be violent, the tribunal clerk should be told as soon as possible and asked what steps will be taken.

The hearing is usually held in the appellant's area. Expenses, including travel expenses, subsistence and some compensation for loss of earnings, are paid to those who attend a tribunal as a party, witness or unpaid representative.[110] The clerk pays travel and subsistence on the day, unless these are high. Travel expenses can be paid in advance.

A party for whom it is difficult to attend the hearing (eg, because of disability) should inform the tribunal clerk. An alternative venue may be possible, but convenience to the other parties to the appeal will also have to be considered.

Witnesses

Any person can come voluntarily to a hearing to give evidence if the tribunal member (if s/he sits alone) or the chairperson allows her/him to be present.[111] However, sometimes a person may not want to come. The chairperson (or single member) can summon or, in Scotland, cite, witnesses to the hearing and require them to answer any relevant questions or produce documents.[112] The witnesses must be in Great Britain, be given 14 days' notice and be paid their necessary expenses for attending.[113] Before issuing a summons, the chairperson must take into account the need to protect intimate personal and financial circumstances, commercial sensitivity, confidential information and national security.[114] However, since almost all child support cases involve intimate circumstances and confidentiality, those alone ought not to prevent a summons being issued.

A witness cannot be required to give evidence which a court could not compel her/him to give at a civil trial.[115] This means that:

- neither diplomats nor the Queen can be summoned as witnesses;[116]
- if a person claims public interest immunity, the tribunal has to decide whether the public interest in the secrecy of the evidence outweighs the importance of disclosure.[117] This means that HM Revenue and Customs documents *may* be disclosed.[118]

These rules do not seem to prevent questions to a witness about criminal offences which s/he or her/his spouse or civil partner may have committed or about their convictions, because those rules apply only to criminal trials.[119]

CSA staff may be witnesses – eg, about what was said at an interview.

If a party wants information or documents from a person and the chairperson will not issue a direction, or that person is wanted at the hearing to be asked questions, a summons can be applied for. A written application should be sent to the Tribunals Service, stating the information or documents wanted, why this will help the tribunal decide the case and why this is the only way of getting the information or documents. This is particularly important where the witness is a CSA staff member, because the chairperson may be reluctant to summon her/him. If only documents are wanted, the person can be summoned to produce them at a hearing arranged only for that purpose, so they can then be copied to the parties.

There is no legal requirement to comply with a summons or citation, but the tribunal may treat a failure to comply in the same way as it would a failure to comply with a direction (see p405). The High Court in England and Wales has the same powers as for a direction (see p405).

A person named in a summons or citation can write to the chairperson asking her/him to vary it or set it aside.[120] There is no appeal against a summons or citation or a refusal to issue one, but judicial review can be used (see p383).

Conduct of the hearing

The hearing is usually in public, unless the tribunal member or chairperson decides that it should be held in private:[121]
- to protect the privacy or family life of one of the parties;
- in the interest of national security, morals, public order or children; *or*
- because publicity would not be in the interest of justice.

Even when held in private, the following can attend but not take part: the clerk, the President of the Appeal Tribunals or anyone acting on her/his behalf in training, supervising or monitoring tribunal members, any member of the Council on Tribunals or Scottish Committee of the Council of Tribunals and anyone training to be a tribunal member or clerk.[122] If all the parties present and the chairperson (or single member) agree, any other person can attend a private hearing. Usually, only the tribunal, clerk and the parties are there.

Where one of the parties to the appeal or a panel member are attending via a live television link, that link should of a suitable standard to allow the person not present to see and hear the proceedings and be seen and heard themselves.[123]

Tribunals hearing child support appeals use the same members and staff as other appeal tribunals. The tribunal tries to be informal. Its member(s) usually sit on one side of a table. The clerk shows the parties into the room and they usually sit on the other side of the table, with the presenting officer between them. The chairperson/single member introduces everyone and explains the tribunal's role. If anyone's role is unclear, the chairperson/single member should be asked for clarification.

Every party has the right to address the tribunal, give evidence, call witnesses and put questions to any other party, the presenting officer or witnesses.[124] The order in which the parties present their cases is up to the chairperson/single member.[125]

The CSA is there to explain the decision, not to argue for the CSA. The presenting officer has a role, for example, to inform the tribunal about CSA procedures. It is rare for the presenting officer to call any witnesses. The tribunal may require any witness, including a party, to take an oath or affirm[126] It is Tribunals Service policy to arrange an interpreter, if requested, in good time; this should be requested on the pre-hearing enquiry form.

The tribunal can appoint an expert if a very difficult question arises[127] The expert gives evidence at the hearing like a witness and/or writes a report which is sent to the tribunal and all the parties.[128] The expert is drawn from the panel of tribunal members,[129] but does not take part in making the decision in the case in which s/he acts as an expert.

The chairperson/single member must keep a record of the proceedings.[130]

The tribunal is not allowed to carry out a physical examination of any person.[131]

The tribunal can adjourn a hearing at any point – eg, if the appeal is not reached or not decided on the day of the hearing.[132] If evidence has been taken, a new tribunal hearing the case must be made up of either exactly the same, or entirely different, members.[133]

Hearings can take one hour or longer. Smoking is not allowed.

4. **Decisions**

After all the evidence and submissions, the tribunal members consider the case. They normally do this with only the clerk present.[134] However, in rare cases they may be observed by the President, someone acting on her/his behalf, a member of the Council on Tribunals or Scottish Committee of the Council of Tribunals and, if all the parties present and the chairperson (or single member) agree, any other person.[135] An observer cannot take part in the tribunal's discussion or decision.

The decision is taken unanimously or by a majority.[136] If there are two members, the chairperson has a casting vote.[137] It is almost always announced to the parties at the hearing. The decision must be recorded in a written notice.[138] If it is not given at the hearing, a copy of the decision notice is sent to the parties later.[139] This can be done by email; if so, for the purposes of the time limits that run from the issue of the decision notice, a properly addressed copy of the decision notice is effective from the date it is sent.[140]

If the tribunal decides the decision appealed was wrong, it allows the appeal. When it allows an appeal, the tribunal can send the case back to the Child Supprt Agency (CSA) to be implemented.[141] Where there are problems with the directions of the tribunal the CSA may request clarification and/or a full statement of reasons.[142] These ought to resolve all the issues on the appeal, but the tribunal does not usually work out any fresh maintenance calculation.[143] Alternatively, the CSA may ask for the decision to be set aside or corrected, or may decide to appeal to a commissioner.

A tribunal considering a variation referral (see p331) deals with the application as if the tribunal were the CSA.[144] This means the tribunal decision is to agree to or refuse a variation to the maintenance calculation, either revising/superseding the decision or refusing to do so.

The decision notice does not give full reasons. It must tell the parties of their right to apply for a statement of reasons and how to appeal to a commissioner. A party has one month from when the decision notice was given/sent to ask the clerk for a full statement of reasons.[145] This must be done in writing and received by the clerk within the time limit. A party considering an appeal to a commissioner should always ask for a full decision. The one-month period can be extended by a legal member for the same reasons as extending time for a late appeal (see p402), except that the maximum period is three months from the date the decision notice was issued.[146] When working out the time limit, days before a notification of a correction or refusal not to set aside is sent are ignored (except if the determination not to set aside the decision was because of a refusal to extend the time for applying).[147] If a dispute arises about the evidence given at the hearing, a party should ask for the chairperson's/member's record of proceedings. This must be done within six months of the date of the decision, or of the date of the statement of reasons, any correction of the decision, any refusal to set aside or a determination for leave to appeal against the decision. The decision notice and statement of reasons must also be kept for this time. If there is an appeal, or an application for leave to appeal, against the decision within the six months, the record of proceedings must be kept until the documents are sent to the commissioners' office, and a party can apply for them before that date.[148]

If the CSA considers that a tribunal decision is given in ignorance or mistake of fact there may be grounds to set aside the decision (see p413).[149]

Accidental errors in a decision notice can be corrected by the clerk or legal member.[150] Written notice of the correction must be given to the parties.[151] The CSA must follow the tribunal's directions, including any fresh calculation required, and only then revise that decision (see Chapter 18).[152] Once the Tribunals Service has notified the CSA of the decision, any necessary revision of child maintenance will take an average of one week.[153] Each party should check that the CSA follows the tribunal's decision (including any directions). If the CSA does not, judicial review (see p383) can force the CSA to implement the decision. If the decision is not clear, a correction or appeal to a commissioner should be considered.

If any party is dissatisfied with the tribunal decision, s/he can appeal on a point of law to a child support commissioner (see p414).

Setting aside decisions

A tribunal decision can be set aside by a legal member if it appears just to do so because:[154]

- a document relating to the proceedings in which the decision was made was not:
  - sent to or received at an appropriate time by one of the parties or her/his representative; *or*
  - received at an appropriate time by the tribunal which made the decision; *or*
- a party or a representative was not present at the hearing. This does not apply to a party who did not ask for a hearing, unless setting aside is manifestly required by the interests of justice[155] – eg, if the tribunal decided the appeal on a point raised for the first time at the hearing.

Following an application for leave to appeal to the commissioners, the chairperson may set aside the decision if:[156]

- s/he considers that the decision was erroneous in law; *or*
- each of the principal parties (Secretary of State, parent with care and non-resident parent)[157] expresses the view that the decision is erroneous in law.

An application to set aside a tribunal decision must be made in writing to the clerk to the tribunal within one month of the decision being given or sent to the parties, or a full statement of reasons being given or sent, whichever is the later.[158] This time limit may be extended to one year in certain circumstances – eg, due to serious illness or residence abroad.[159] Each of the parties is asked to comment in writing on the application before a determination is made on the application to set aside.[160] The determination, and reasons for it, is sent to the parties.[161] If a decision is set aside, then another tribunal hearing is arranged and the case re-heard in full. This can be by the original tribunal or a different one. If the application to set aside is refused there is no right of appeal against the determination. A dissatisfied applicant may apply for judicial review or leave to appeal against the decision of the tribunal.[162] When an application to set aside a decision is refused, the legal member may treat it as an application for written reasons for the decision (see p411), subject to the usual time limits.[163]

It is not clear if a refusal to extend time for appealing to a tribunal or for applying to set aside a tribunal decision can itself also be set aside.

5. **Child support commissioners**

Any party can appeal against a decision of an appeal tribunal to a child support commissioner on the ground of an error of law (see p391).[164] The decision is erroneous in law, for example, if the Child Support Agency (CSA) failed to put a relevant document in the case papers before the tribunal, even though the tribunal is not at fault.[165] An appeal can be made by the CSA. Only a final decision can be appealed, but this includes a decision made without a hearing (see p407). A tribunal determination to set aside its decision (or a refusal to set aside) cannot be appealed; judicial review (p383) may be possible.[166]

An appeal *cannot* be made only on the grounds that further evidence shows that the tribunal was wrong or that circumstances have changed. These should be dealt with by supersession (see Chapter 18).

A commissioner is a very experienced lawyer. Almost all commissioners are full time, dealing also with social security appeals. In very difficult cases, a tribunal of three commissioners decides the case.

If there is an error of law, the commissioner sets aside the tribunal's decision. S/he will then:[167]

- if appropriate, make further findings of fact (this is unusual where relevant facts are disputed) *and* give the appropriate decision (eg, make a maintenance assessment);[168] *or*
- give the decision the tribunal should have given, which may be to the same effect as the decision appealed; *or*
- refer the case to the CSA or a tribunal, giving directions for its determination. If the CSA has appealed the tribunal decision, the commissioner cannot refer the case to the CSA.[169]

Northern Ireland has its own child support commissioners and a chief child support commissioner.[170]

How to appeal

Obtaining leave (permission) to appeal is the first stage of appealing to a commissioner. An application for leave to appeal must be made in writing to the tribunal chairperson at the Tribunals Service (see Appendix 1) within one month of the date the tribunal's statement of reasons was issued.[171] The time limit for requesting a statement of reasons is one month after the tribunal's decision notice was issued (see p411). When working out the time limit for appealing to the commissioners, days before notification of correction of a decision or a determination not to set aside a decision are ignored (except where the decision was not to set aside because of a refusal to extend the time for applying).[172] There is no right of appeal against a correction, only against a corrected decision.

If the CSA applies for leave, a copy of its application is sent to the other parties, who have one month to send written comments to the chairperson, who must take them into account.[173]

Any notices or documents in connection with an appeal to the commissioners that are sent to any parties to the appeal can be delivered in person, sent by post, or, if certain conditions are satisfied, by email, or in any other way if directed by a commissioner. Email can only be used if the recipient has informed the person sending the email that s/he is willing to accept notification or information electronically, has provided an email address, and, if s/he wishes, specified the electronic format in which documents must be sent. For the purposes of time limits, a document is effective from the date it is sent, by whatever means.[174]

The application for leave to appeal may be determined by the chairperson or by:[175]

- a salaried, legally qualified member, if the chairperson was a fee-paid, legally qualified tribunal member; *or*
- another legally qualified member if this is impractical or it would cause undue delay for the application to be determined by the person who was the chair.

The chairperson/legally qualified member may decide to grant leave, set aside the tribunal decision as erroneous in law or refuse leave. The decision on the application is sent to all the parties.[176] If s/he gives leave to appeal, the appellant must send a notice of appeal to the commissioner's office within one month of the notification of leave to appeal.[177] Any notices or documents for a commissioner should either be delivered to the office in person or sent by post, fax, or, where the office has given written permission in advance, by email.[178] If s/he sets aside the decision the case will be referred to the original tribunal for a redetermination or to a different tribunal.[179] If the chairperson refuses leave to appeal, an application for leave to appeal can be made to the commissioner within one month of the notification refusing leave.[180]

If no application is made to the chairperson within time, the chairperson can admit a late application up to one year after the month ran out, but only if there are special reasons.[181] If the chairperson then refuses to give leave or if the notice of appeal or application for leave is not sent in time to the commissioner, the commissioner can admit a late application up to one year after the month ran out (or, within one month of the claimant's refusal, if later) but only if there are special reasons.

'**Special reasons**' are not defined and so are wider than the reasons needed for a late appeal *to* the tribunal (see p402). Special reasons for late commissioner applications/appeals can be much wider. All the circumstances should be taken into account, not only the length of the delay in submitting the application for leave.[182] For full details on special reasons see CPAG's *Welfare Benefits and Tax Credits Handbook*. When appealing late, give as many details of the reasons as possible, but do not delay appealing to do this.

An application for leave or notice of appeal must state the grounds of appeal and have the tribunal's decision and, if separate, the statement of reasons (see p412), attached.[183] The Tribunals Service can provide a form for applications and appeals, but this does not have to be used. A copy of any application for leave made to the commissioner is sent to the other parties.[184]

For the addresses of the commissioners' offices see Appendix 1.

The commissioner usually considers applications for leave without a hearing. If leave is refused, no reasons have to be given, and a short written decision is sent to the parties. A refusal of leave can be judicially reviewed (see p383).

An application for leave can be withdrawn at any time before a decision is made, by writing to the office it was sent to.[185] An appeal may be withdrawn by the appellant, but only with the commissioner's permission.[186] A commissioner is unlikely to allow an appeal to be withdrawn if another party supports the appeal. An application for leave made to a commissioner or an appeal which has been withdrawn can be reinstated with the commissioner's permission.[187]

The written procedure

Unlike the tribunal, on a commissioner's appeal the parties are expected to explain their cases mostly in writing. If leave is granted, the papers which were before the tribunal are sent to all the parties. These are in a particular order and are numbered, and should be checked to see that all the documents are included and whether there are any new ones.

If it is not the CSA's appeal, the CSA is asked to comment in writing within one month of the papers being issued. The CSA may support the appeal, but it is the reasons for doing so which matter. For example, the CSA may support an appeal because the tribunal did not make all necessary findings of fact and give adequate reasons, but propose that the commissioner give a decision to the same effect, or even to worse effect, as far as one or both of the other parties are concerned.

The other parties are then given one month to comment. The appellant is then given one month to comment on everyone else's observations.

Before commenting, consider whether it would be best to have the case go back to another tribunal or the CSA, or instead be decided by the commissioner. However, where there is a dispute of relevant fact, the commissioner is likely to send the case back to a tribunal.

Oral hearings

If one party's case is not fully supported by the CSA or there is a point of law on which the commissioner might decide against that party, that party should request an oral hearing.[188] The CSA or another party can also request a hearing. The commissioner usually grants a request for an oral hearing, unless it is clear that the matter can be resolved on the papers alone. The CSA is almost always legally represented and other parties should consider getting expert representation (see Appendix 4). If a party is granted legal services funding s/he must send proof of funding (ie, funding notice or legal aid certificate in Scotland) to the office and notify all other parties that funding has been granted.[189]

Oral hearings are usually heard in London or Edinburgh, but are also heard in some other large cities. Plenty of notice is given and travel expenses are paid.[190] The hearings are usually in public but, unless the other party brings observers, it is very unlikely that anyone else will be there.[191] Any person or organisation who is entitled to be present at the hearing, including any representatives, can be present via a live television link if the commissioner directs that this can be done.[192] The hearing is more formal than a tribunal. While oral evidence can be given, it is uncommon. The commissioner can postpone or adjourn a hearing and usually does so if it would help a parent get representation. The commissioner may summon witnesses; the rules are the same as for the tribunal (see p409).[193]

Decisions

At the end of an oral hearing, a commissioner may announce a decision,[194] although it is more common for the decision to be notified to the parties later (called 'reserving' the decision). In any case, the written decision is later sent to all the parties.[195] The decision must not contain the surname of the child concerned in the appeal or, as far as is practicable, any other information which may lead to the child being identified.[196] An accidental error in a decision can be corrected at any time. Written notice of any correction must be sent to the parties.[197]

A commissioner's decision can be set aside if:[198]

- a document was not received at an appropriate time by one of the parties, a representative or the commissioner;
- a party or a representative was not present at the hearing.

An application for setting aside must be made within one month of notification of the decision.[199]

Jurisdictional issues may result in the commissioner's decision being void and of no effect, as occurred in a previous joined decision, under the 'old rules'.[200] This situation arose where the CSA implemented the appeal tribunal decision (ie, the one under appeal to the commissioner), then this was replaced by a number of fresh assessments on review. As the subsequent assessments had the same effective date as the original decision they completely replaced it and so the commissioner had no jurisdiction. This could also apply in 'new rules' cases.

Caselaw

Commissioners' decisions are legally binding on tribunals and the CSA. Decisions have a reference number which shows the country in which they were made and the year the file was opened at the commissioners' office (not the year in which the decision was made). CCS 3/1997 is from England or Wales, CSCS 3/1997 is from Scotland and CSC 3/1997 is from Northern Ireland. The first number is the individual file number.

The most important cases are chosen to be reported by the chief commissioner. These are called 'reported decisions' and are given a new number – eg R(CS) 1/95. Scottish decisions are not expressly identified as Scottish once they are reported. Up to and including 2001, decisions could be starred by the commissioner giving the decision to indicate that it might be useful or of general importance. These were given a 'star' number. Some starred decisions were subsequently reported and given a new number, as above. If you are citing an unreported decision, use its original number, whether or not it is starred. If you are citing a reported decision, use the 'R' number.

British decisions are binding on the CSA and tribunals throughout Great Britain. Where there are conflicting decisions, a reported decision carries more weight,[201] but starring does not matter. Where there is no British decision on the point, a Northern Irish decision is very persuasive. Where there is no child support commissioner's decision, a social security commissioner's decision on the point (eg, a similar regulation) is persuasive.

Social security decisions follow the same numbering system as child support – eg, income support decisions are numbered CIS 3/1997 or R(IS) 4/96.

Commissioners, tribunals and the CSA are bound by judgments of the House of Lords and, in England and Wales, the High Court and Court of Appeal, and, in Scotland, the Court of Session. A commissioner is not bound by her/his own previous decisions or those of other commissioners, though they usually follow long-standing decisions. A commissioner will follow a decision of a tribunal of commissioners unless there are good reasons for not doing so. The exception is where the test case rules apply (see p419).

Many decisions are available at www.osscsc.gov.uk and can be downloaded free of charge. Commissioners' decisions that are not available online can be purchased from the appropriate commissioners' office.

Further appeal

Appeals on a point of law can be made from a commissioner's decision to the Court of Appeal or, in Scotland, the Court of Session.[202] Applications for leave to appeal must be made first to the commissioner within three months of being notified of her/his decision.[203] If the decision or record of the decision is corrected, or if an application for a decision to be set aside is refused (other than because the application is made outside the time limit – see p411), the time for appealing runs from the date written notice of the correction, or of the refusal to set aside, is sent. Legal advice should be sought if possible. See CPAG's *Welfare Benefits and Tax Credits Handbook*.

6. **Test case rules**

Special rules apply if a court decision on a 'test case' is pending or a commissioner's or court decision on a test case has been made. A 'test case' is one in which a person is challenging the Child Support Agency's (CSA's) interpretation of the law, even if it is the CSA's appeal from a tribunal, commissioner or court decision and even if the person does not consider the case to be a test case.

These rules apply to maintenance calculation decisions, reduced benefit decisions, revision and supersession decisions and appeals in relation to a different matter by child support commissioners or courts. Even though they are not limited to revision and supersession cases, they are dealt with here because that is when they will most often arise. Similar rules apply to appeals (see p421).

Test case pending

If a test case is decided against the CSA, then normally the CSA has to follow the law, as decided in that case, in all other cases (see p418). However, if an appeal is pending before a child support commissioner or court, then, in any case which might be affected by the decision to be given in that appeal, the CSA can:[204]

- suspend a decision on the application, revision or supersession until the test case appeal has been decided; *or*
- make a decision on the assumption that the test case appeal has already been decided and has been decided against the person who applied for the decision (ie, the calculation, revision or supersession), but *only if*:[205]
    - the CSA would otherwise have to make a calculation (including one on revision or supersession) leading to the parent with care becoming entitled to income support (IS) or a higher rate of IS; *or*
    - the non-resident parent is employed or self-employed.[206]

An appeal is pending before a court if:[207]

- an appeal (including a judicial review) about child support has been made to the High Court, Court of Session, Court of Appeal or House of Lords, but has not been determined;
- an application for permission to make such an appeal (or judicial review) has been made, but has not been determined;

- the CSA has certified in writing that it is considering making such an appeal or application *and* the time for appealing/applying has not expired *and* the CSA considers that the appeal might result in the non-resident parent having no, or less, liability for child maintenance.[208]

An appeal also counts as pending if a court (but not a commissioner) has referred a question to the European Court of Justice (ECJ) for a preliminary ruling.

If the CSA does not make an application/appeal in time, it can no longer suspend making a decision. The time limits for making applications/appeals are as follows.

- Applying to a commissioner for permission to appeal to the Court of Appeal/ Court of Session: three months from the date the commissioner's decision is issued (see p418).[209]
- Applying to the Court of Session/Court of Appeal for permission to appeal from a commissioner to it (or appealing to one of those courts with permission of the commissioner): four weeks from the date the commissioner's decision is issued.
- Applying to the Court of Session/Court of Appeal for permission to appeal to the House of Lords: this is usually done at the end of the hearing in which the court gives its judgment.
- Applying to the House of Lords for permission to appeal to it: one month from the date the order of the Court of Session/Court of Appeal is sealed.[210]
- Appealing to the House of Lords with permission of the Court of Session/Court of Appeal: three months from the date it is sealed.[211]
- Applying to the High Court/Court of Session for permission to apply for judicial review: three months from the date of the decision for High Court challenges. There is no time limit to apply to the Court of Session, but an application should be made as soon as possible.

A decision to suspend or make a decision on the assumption that the CSA will win the test case is a discretionary one. The CSA must, therefore, have regard to the welfare of the child when making it.

Test case decisions

If a commissioner or court interprets child support law, the CSA normally has to apply the commissioner's/court's interpretation of the law in the period before that decision was given. This would usually require the CSA to supersede all decisions which are affected.

However, if the commissioner/court rejected the CSA's interpretation of the law, that test case decision only has effect from the date it is given by the commissioner/court.[212] For the period before that date, the CSA (and any appeal tribunal or commissioner) assumes that it was right in its (or the child support officer's) interpretation of the law when making the original decision which led to the appeal.[213] This includes cases where the test case appeal began with an appeal tribunal's decision on a *referral* of an application for a variation to the maintenance calculation (see p331). This rule applies:

- to maintenance calculations and reduced benefit decisions;[214]
- even where the application for a revision or supersession was made before the test case decision was given and regardless of whether the person applying raised that issue of law;[215]
- even where the commissioner/court decides that a regulation is *ultra vires* (see p391).[216] If this decision is made because the regulation is inconsistent with the European Convention on Human Rights (see p391), this rule may also breach that Convention;[217]
- even to decisions of the ECJ.[218] This rule is unlawful under European Community law, except in a case where the ECJ has itself decided that its decision only has effect from the date it is given.[219]

This rule does *not* apply to:

- an application for maintenance made before 1 June 1999 or a reduced benefit decision;[220]
- a revision of any decision made before 1 June 1999;[221]
- a supersession of any decision made before 1 June 1999;[222]
- a decision in a case where the CSA had suspended a decision under the test case pending rules (see p419);[223]
- a revision or supersession decision in a case where the CSA had required the tribunal or commissioner to refer the case to the CSA, or deal with it on the assumption that the test case had already been decided against the appellant (see below).[224]

Test case rules affecting appeals

If a test case pending before a court may affect a similar case awaiting a decision from an appeal tribunal or commissioner, or there is a possiblility that the CSA may appeal, the CSA may:[225]

- direct the tribunal/commissioner to refer the similar case to the CSA. The CSA makes no decision until the test case is decided. It then revises the CSA decision under appeal or supersedes the tribunal decision under appeal; *or*
- directs the tribunal/commissioner to deal with the case itself. The tribunal/commissioner *must* then either:
  - 'stay' the appeal (ie, postpone its decision) until the test case is decided; *or*
  - decide the appeal on the assumption that the test case appeal has already been decided and has been decided against the person who appealed to the tribunal in the similar case. If the test case is later decided in that person's favour, the CSA supersedes the tribunal/commissioner decision in the similar case.

Notes

1 Reg 4(1)(b) CS(TP) Regs
2 s28D(1)(b) CSA 1991

1. Appeal tribunals

3 Reg 36(1) SS&CS(DA) Regs
4 Sch 3 para 1 SS&CS(DA) Regs; s7(2) SSA 1998
5 Reg 36(3) and Sch 3 para 4 SS&CS(DA) Regs
6 s5 SSA 1998; reg 36(3) SS&CS(DA) Regs
7 s7(1) SSA 1998; reg 36(5) SS&CS(DA) Regs
8 s20(1) CSA 1991
9 s20(2)CSA 1991
10 s20(3) CSA 1991
11 Sch 4C para 3(1) and (4) CSA 1991
12 s20(6) CSA 1991
13 Reg 30A SS&CS(DA) Regs
14 Reg 30A SS&CS(DA) Regs
15 Reg 31(2) SS&CS(DA) Regs
16 Reg 1(3)(b) SS&CS(DA) Regs is limited to the CSA and, under (b), those who have a right of appeal under the CSA 1991
17 s20(7) CSA 1991
18 CCS/16351/1996
19 s20(7)(a) CSA 1991
20 CSCS/2/1994; CCS/12/1994
21 CSCS/2/1994; CSCS/3/1994
22 CCS/511/1995
23 CCS/15109/1996. CCS/6096/1995 was wrong to decide otherwise (the point was not argued).
24 s20(7)(b) CSA 1991
25 s20(5) CSA 1991
26 **Old rules** Arts 3 and 4 CSA(JC)(O)
 New rules Arts 3 and 4 CSA(JC)(O) 2002
27 CCS/16351/1996
28 CCS/16351/1996
29 We consider that the Northern Ireland commissioner in CSC/1/1994 and CSC/3/1994 was wrong to say it was too late to appeal to a court once an appeal was sent to the tribunal. That commissioner assumed that there could only be one notice of appeal, and not two, as CCS/16351/1996 decides: one to the tribunal and one to the court raising the issues not raised before.

2. Procedure

30 Reg 28(1) SS&CS(DA) Regs
31 Reg 28(1)(b) SS&CS(DA) Regs
32 Reg 28(2) SS&CS(DA) Regs
33 Reg 31(1) SS&CS(DA) Regs
34 Reg 33(1)(c) SS&CS(DA) Regs
35 Reg 2(b) SS&CS(DA) Regs
36 Reg 31(2) SS&CS(DA) Regs
37 Reg 9A SS&CS(DA) Regs
38 Reg 9A(3) SS&CS(DA) Regs
39 Reg 33(1)(b) and (2)(d) SS&CS(DA) Regs
40 Reg 33(1) SS&CS(DA) Regs
41 CSA Client Charter 2007
42 CSA Client Charter 2006
43 Reg 33(4) and (5) SS&CS(DA) Regs
44 Reg 33(3) SS&CS(DA) Regs
45 Reg 33(7) SS&CS(DA) Regs
46 Reg 33(8)(a) SS&CS(DA) Regs
47 Reg 33(8)(b) SS&CS(DA) Regs
48 It is not clear whether there is a duty to hold an oral hearing (under reg 39 SS&CS(DA) Regs) but we consider that one can be directed under reg 38(2) SS&CS(DA) Regs
49 Reg 33(9) SS&CS(DA) Regs
50 Reg 32(2) SS&CS(DA) Regs
51 Reg 32(4)(b) SS&CS(DA) Regs
52 Reg 32(2) and (3) SS&CS(DA) Regs
53 Reg 33 SS&CS(DA) Regs
54 Reg 32(1) SS&CS(DA) Regs
55 Reg 32(5) and (6) SS&CS(DA) Regs
56 Reg 32(7) SS&CS(DA) Regs
57 Reg 32(8) SS&CS(DA) Regs
58 Reg 32(9) SS&CS(DA) Regs; CIS/93/1992
59 Regs 38(1) or 57(1) SS&CS(DA) Regs might apply
60 CCS/12682/1996
61 Reg 44 SS&CS(DA) Regs
62 CCS/1086/2005
63 CSA Client Charter 2007
64 Social Security and Child Support Commissioners of Great Britain, Practice Memorandum No.2, 31 December 2004
65 Reg 38(2) SS&CS(DA) Regs
66 Reg 38(2) SS&CS(DA) Regs
67 Order 38 r19, Supreme Court Rules
68 Reg 34 SS&CS(DA) Regs

69 CSA Client Charter 2007
70 s16(6) CSA 1991
71 Reg 30(2)(f) SS&CS(DA) Regs
72 Reg 30(3) SS&CS(DA) Regs
73 Reg 30(4) SS&CS(DA) Regs
74 Reg 30(5) SS&CS(DA) Regs
75 Reg 46(1)(b) SS&CS(DA) Regs
76 Reg 46(1)(d) SS&CS(DA) Regs
77 Reg 46(1)(c) SS&CS(DA) Regs
78 Reg 46(3) SS&CS(DA) Regs
79 Reg 46(2) SS&CS(DA) Regs
80 Reg 47(1) SS&CS(DA) Regs
81 Reg 47(2) SS&CS(DA) Regs
82 CCS/292/2000
83 Regs 1(3) and 46(1)(a) SS&CS(DA) Regs
84 Because the definition of 'out of
    jurisdiction' appeals in reg 1(3)
    SS&CS(DA) Regs only applies to appeals
    against decisions specified in Sch 2 of
    those regs (via reg 27), Sch 2 SSA
    1998, Sch 7 para 6(2) CSPSSA 2000 and
    reg 16 HB&CTB(D&A) Regs. No child
    support decisions are listed in these
    provisions.
85 Reg 40(1) SS&CS(DA) Regs
86 Reg 33(10) SS&CS(DA) Regs
87 Reg 40(2) SS&CS(DA) Regs
88 Reg 40(2) and (3) SS&CS(DA) Regs
89 R(IS) 5/94

3. Oral hearings
90 Reg 39(4) SS&CS(DA) Regs
91 Reg 39(1) SS&CS(DA) Regs
92 Reg 39(2) SS&CS(DA) Regs
93 Reg 39(3) SS&CS(DA) Regs
94 Reg 39(5) SS&CS(DA) Regs
95 CCS/13450/1996
96 Reg 45 SS&CS(DA) Regs
97 Reg 49(2) and (3) SS&CS(DA) Regs
98 Reg 51(1) SS&CS(DA) Regs
99 Reg 51(1) SS&CS(DA) Regs
100 Reg 51(2) SS&CS(DA) Regs
101 Reg 51(3) SS&CS(DA) Regs
102 CCS/872/2000
103 Reg 49(7)(b) SS&CS(DA) Regs
104 Reg 49(7) SS&CS(DA) Regs
105 Reg 49(7)(b) SS&CS(DA) Regs
106 CCS/1037/1995
107 Reg 49(8) SS&CS(DA) Regs
108 Reg 49(4) and (5) SS&CS(DA) Regs;
    CSCS/7/1995
109 CCS/2618/1995
110 Sch 1 para 4 SSA 1998
111 Reg 49(11) and (10) SS&CS(DA) Regs
112 Reg 43 SS&CS(D&A) Regs
113 Reg 43(1) SS&CS(DA) Regs
114 Reg 43(3) SS&CS(DA) Regs

115 Reg 43(2) SS&CS(DA) Regs. This refers
    to 'action', which means a civil, not
    criminal, trial. Scottish law applies if the
    hearing is in Scotland.
116 Sch 1 Arts 31(2) and 37(1)-(3)
    Diplomatic Privileges Act 1964; Sch 1
    Art 44(1) Consular Relations Act 1968;
    Sch 1 paras 9, 14 and 20-23
    International Organisations Act 1968
117 See Keane, *The Modern Law of Evidence,*
    Oxford University Press and *Cross on
    Evidence,* Oxford University Press
118 *Lonrho plc v Fayed* [1994] QB 749,
    [1994] 2 WLR 209, [1994] 1 All ER 870
119 see s80 Police and Criminal Evidence Act
    1984; s1 Criminal Evidence Act 1898
120 Reg 43 SS&CS(DA) Regs
121 Reg 49(6) SS&CS(DA) Regs
122 Reg 49(9) SS&CS(DA) Regs
123 Reg 49(13) SS&CS(DA) Regs
124 Reg 49(7) and (11) SS&CS(DA) Regs
125 Reg 49(1) SS&CS(DA) Regs
126 Reg 43(5) SS&CS(DA) Regs
127 s7(4) SSA 1998
128 Reg 50 SS&CS(DA) Regs
129 s7(5) SSA 1998
130 Reg 55(1) SS&CS(DA) Regs
131 Reg 52 SS&CS(DA) Regs
132 Reg 51(4) SS&CS(DA) Regs; President's
    Protocol No. 15
133 President's Protocol No. 15

4. Decisions
134 Reg 49(12) SS&CS(DA) Regs
135 Reg 49(12) SS&CS(DA) Regs
136 s7(3)(b) SSA 1998
137 s7(3)(c) SSA 1998
138 Reg 53(2) SS&CS(DA) Regs
139 Reg 53(3) SS&CS(DA) Regs
140 Reg 57AA SS&CS(DA) Regs
141 PG, Specialist Areas, Tribunal Decision
    Received from AS
142 PG, Specialist Areas, Consideration of
    the AS Decision
143 CCS/5310/1995; see also CCS/4741/
    1995
144 s28D(3) CSA 1991
145 Reg 53(4) SS&CS(DA) Regs
146 Reg 54 SS&CS(DA) Regs
147 Reg 53(4a) SS&CS(DA) Regs
148 Reg 55(3)-(4) SS&CS(DA) Regs
149 PG, Specialist Areas, Application for
    Setting Aside
150 Reg 56(1) SS&CS(DA) Regs
151 Reg 56(2) SS&CS(DA) Regs
152 CCS/11260/1995
153 CSA Client Charter 2007
154 Reg 57(1) SS&CS(DA) Regs

155 Reg 57(2) SS&CS(DA) Regs
156 s23A CSA 1991
157 s23A CSA 1991
158 Reg 57(3) SS&CS(DA) Regs
159 Reg 57(6)-(11) SS&CS(DA) Regs
160 Reg 57(4) SS&CS(DA) Regs
161 Reg 57(5) SS&CS(DA) Regs
162 R(SB) 55/83
163 Reg 57(4A) SS&CS(DA) Regs

5. Child support commissioners

164 s24(1) CSA 1991
165 CCS/12682/1996 applying *R v Leyland Justices ex parte Hawthorne* [1979] QB 283 and following R(SB) 18/83
166 Only decisions, and not determinations, can be appealed: *Bland v Supplementary Benefit Officer* [1983] 1 All ER 537; R(SB) 12/83
167 s24(3) CSA 1991
168 As in CCS/5310/1995
169 s24(3)(c) and (d) CSA 1991
170 s23 CSA 1991
171 Regs 10(1) and 12 CSC(P) Regs
172 Reg 10(7) CSC(P) Regs
173 Reg 10(2)-(4) CSC(P) Regs
174 Reg 8(1) and (1A) CSC (P) Regs
175 Reg 10(6) CSC(P) Regs
176 Reg 10(4) CSC(P) Regs; reg 58(4) SS&CS(DA) Regs
177 Reg 15(1) CSC(P) Regs
178 Reg 8(2) CSC(P) Regs
179 s23A CSA 1991
180 Reg 11(2) CSC(P) Regs
181 Reg 10(5) CSC(P) Regs
182 *Howes R (on the application of) v Secretary of State for Work and Pensions* [2007] EWHC 559 (Admin) 29 March 2007. In this case the commissioner did not fully consider the claimant's earlier attempts to appeal.
183 Regs 12(2) and 14(2) CSC(P) Regs
184 Reg 12(3) CSC(P) Regs
185 Reg 24(1) CSC(P) Regs
186 Reg 24(2) CSC(P) Regs
187 Reg 24(3) CSC(P) Regs
188 Reg 21(2) CSC(P) Regs
189 Reg 9A CSC(P) Regs
190 Sch 4 para 3 SSA 1998
191 Reg 22(5) CSC(P) Regs
192 Reg 22(6A) and (6B) CSC(P) Regs
193 Reg 23 CSC(P) Regs
194 Reg 26(4) CSC(P) Regs
195 Reg 26(3) CSC(P) Regs
196 Reg 26(5) CSC(P) Regs
197 Reg 27 CSC(P) Regs
198 Reg 28(1) CSC(P) Regs
199 Reg 28(2) CSC(P) Regs

200 CCS/2731/1997; CCS/3753/1997
201 R(I) 12/75
202 s25 CSA 1991
203 Reg 30 CSC(P) Regs

6. Test case rules

204 s28ZA(1) and (2) CSA 1991
205 Reg 23(3) and (5) SS&CS(DA) Regs
206 As defined in s2(1) SSCBA 1992
207 s28ZA(4) and (5) CSA 1991
208 s28ZA(4)(c) CSA 1991; reg 23(4) SS&CS(DA) Regs
209 Reg 30(1) CSC(P) Regs
210 para 2.1 House of Lords Practice Directions on Civil Appeals
211 para 2.1 House of Lords Practice Directions on Civil Appeals
212 s28ZC(1) and (3) CSA 1991; reg 7B(10) SS&CS(DA) Regs
213 s28ZC(1) and (6) CSA 1991
214 s28ZC(3) CSA 1991
215 s28ZC(5) CSA 1991
216 s28ZC(4) CSA 1991
217 Art 13 ECHR requires an effective remedy for violations
218 s28ZC(6) CSA 1991
219 Case C-35/97 *Commission v France* [1998] ECR I-5325
220 s28ZC(1)(b)(i) CSA 1991
221 s28ZC(1)(b)(ii) CSA 1991
222 s28ZC(1)(b)(iii) CSA 1991
223 s28ZC(2)(a) CSA 1991
224 s28ZC(2)(b) CSA 1991
225 s28ZB CSA 1991

Chapter 20

Collection and enforcement

This chapter covers:
1. Payment of child maintenance (p426)
2. Collection of other payments (p433)
3. Arrears (p435)
4. Deduction from earnings orders (p443)
5. Enforcement (p450)
6. Existing 'old rules' and conversion cases (p456)

The Child Support Agency (CSA) can arrange the collection and enforcement of child support maintenance[1] and certain other maintenance payments (see p433).[2] This service has been free to all CSA clients since April 1995.[3] Fees are unlikely to be introduced by the existing CSA, but may be introduced by the new Child Maintenance and Enforcement Commission in the future (see Chapter 1).

Once the calculation has been made, a collection schedule is set up. If the payments schedule breaks down and arrears accrue, debt management procedures may be put in place, or the CSA may decide to take enforcment action.

Within the limits of the regulations, decisions about how payment is enforced are discretionary, so there is scope for negotiation between CSA staff and the individuals involved. If there are instructions or practices for dealing with a type of case in a certain way, it may be helpful to remind the CSA of these. If guidance is not helpful, the CSA can be reminded that it is not binding, and the individual officer dealing with the case may apply discretion. As the decisions are discretionary, the welfare of any child likely to be affected must be taken into account by the CSA (see p24).

The amount of maintenance calculated cannot be altered except by revision, supersession, appeal or variation (departure under the 'old rules'). The CSA does not suspend current collection just because the non-resident parent states that he cannot afford to pay. However, the CSA may agree to lower payments if a revision, supersession, appeal or variation/departure is pending (see p438).

There is no right of appeal to an appeal tribunal about a decision concerning collection and enforcement (see p399 for which CSA decisions can be appealed). A deduction from earnings order can, in limited circumstances, be appealed to a magistrates' court (see p443) and judicial review may be possible for other decisions (see p383). The Independent Case Examiner (see p466) can consider complaints about the CSA's exercise of discretion once the CSA's internal complaints procedure has been followed (see Chapter 21). For regular payment conditions imposed because a departure application has been made, see p330.

1. Payment of child maintenance

If a maintenance calculation has been made and the Child Support Agency (CSA) is collecting and enforcing the maintenance, it has discretion to decide:

- the method by which the non-resident parent pays;[4]
- the person to whom it is paid;[5]
- if payments are made through the CSA or someone else, the method by which payment is made to the person with care;[6]
- the timing of payments;[7] *and*
- the amount of payments towards arrears.[8]

Before making these decisions, the CSA must, as far as is possible, give the non-resident parent and the person with care an opportunity to make representations, and must take these into account.[9] In every case, the CSA must notify the non-resident parent in writing of the amounts and timing of payments due, to whom he must make payment, how he must pay and details of any amount that is overdue and remains outstanding.[10] This notice is sent as soon as possible after the calculation is made and again after any change in the details in the notice.[11] A copy is sent to the person with care. Where the payments are to be made directly between the two parties, the CSA takes no further action regarding collection unless the person with care notifies the CSA that the non-resident parent has failed to comply as directed. Therefore, the parties can agree between them to use another method or frequency of payment.

If there are arrears and the CSA has imposed a penalty payment, see p441.

Who is paid

The CSA can require the non-resident parent to pay child maintenance:[12]

- directly to the person with care;
- directly to a Scottish child applicant;
- to, or via, the CSA (this cannot be required in all cases); *or*
- to, or via, another person.

The CSA prefers the non-resident parent to make payments directly to the person with care, except if the parent with care is on income support (IS) or income-based jobseeker's allowance (JSA).[13] This is known as 'maintenance direct'. Once the CSA has calculated the amount of maintenance owed, the parents make their own payment arrangements. Letters are sent by the CSA telling each parent the amount of arrears and the date regular payments should start. These direct payments are not monitored by the CSA. If the payment arrangement breaks down, the parent with care can request to use the collection service (see below).

Although some non-resident parents and, indeed, some persons with care, may want to have payments made to a third party (eg, their mortgage lender) the CSA does not usually accept these as being child maintenance payments. However, any such payments made between the effective date and the date of calculation may be considered as voluntary payments to offset any initial arrears.

The collection service

When child maintenance payments are to be made to or via the CSA, this is referred to as the collection service. Any party to a case can request that payment be via the CSA.[14] The CSA normally provides the collection service if an applicant requests it, even where the other party does not.

In the case of parents with care on IS or income-based JSA (see p38), the collection service is applied automatically.[15] In practice, this means that the parent is not asked if she wishes to use the collection service when she completes the child maintenance administration form. She may request to change to direct payments from the non-resident parent, and all options should be explained to her. However, if the non-resident parent is on benefit, the collection service has to be used; direct payment is not possible because maintenance is paid by a deduction from benefit. In the case of voluntary applicants (see pp37 and 38), the CSA can only provide the collection service on the request of one of the parties to the calculation.[16] This can be done when the application is made, when each party is asked if they wish to use the CSA to collect maintenance or arrange payments direct.

The collection service can be requested at a later date – eg, if payments become irregular. The request can be made verbally or in writing. The CSA has the discretion to collect arrears already due when the request is made.[17]

Where payments are made to the CSA, only payments actually received by the CSA can be passed on. The CSA aims to make the first payment to the person with care within six weeks of making initial payment arrangements with the non-resident parent. Once maintenance is received from the non-resident parent, the CSA 'will make maintenance payments to parents with care within a week'.[18]

The collection service has a number of advantages.

- It removes the need for direct contact between the non-resident parent and person with care.
- If the person with care is on IS/income-based JSA, her benefit payments will not be affected if the non-resident parent does not pay the CSA (see p428).
- If the person with care is not on IS/income-based JSA, the collection service is supposed to ensure regular payments by starting enforcement action (see p450) as soon as payments are missed, although this does not always happen.

The following are disadvantages.

- A payment statement is only issued periodically or on request (see p431) and these are often considered to be inaccurate. The parties should, therefore, always keep their own records and evidence of payments. The majority of accounts are in arrears and many persons with care and some non-resident parents are unhappy with the level of service from the CSA.
- The CSA negotiates collection and arrears schedules with the parents and may agree to an arrears arrangement, notwithstanding objections from the person with care.

Person with care on benefits

If a parent with care is on IS/income-based JSA, the CSA may require payments for ongoing liability to be made via the CSA from when the calculation is made, especially if there is evidence that the non-resident parent will not be a reliable payer. If the person with care is not a *parent* with care, this is only usually done if s/he requests the collection service or the non-resident parent requests it. Arrears are always collected and retained by the CSA where the person with care or her/his partner is (or was during the relevant period) in receipt of IS/income-based JSA (see p365).[19]

If payments are made via the CSA, the claimant receives one credit transfer from Jobcentre Plus that includes both IS/income-based JSA and child maintenance. If the non-resident parent does not make a payment to the CSA, the person with care's benefit is still paid, but there is no maintenance element. For when arrears of child maintenance are paid later, see p365.

For the effect of child maintenance on IS/income-based JSA, see p363.

In some cases, the calculation may be cancelled because the parent with care opts out (see p59). At this point arrears may remain in lieu of benefit already paid that the CSA may collect. In practice, however, the CSA is unlikely to do so. CSA policy guidance states that all action, including collection of arrears, should cease when the parent with care opts out. If collection does continue, this should be challenged and advice sought.

Method of payment

The non-resident parent can make payments by standing order, direct debit, automated credit transfer, credit card, debit card, cheque, postal order, voluntary deductions from earnings arrangements, or cash.[20] A debit card means one that can be used as a substitute for a cheque – ie, where the non-resident parent's bank account is debited instantly, such as a Switch card.[21] If the collection service is being used, the CSA prefers payment by direct debit.[22] The CSA can direct a non-resident parent to take all reasonable steps to open a bank or building society account.[23] However, there is no penalty if he fails to do so. Some non-resident parents pay by deductions from benefit (see p200).

When deciding the method of payment, the CSA must take into account any representations from the parties.[24]

The CSA can accept payment by cheque, bankers draft, postal order, cash and foreign currency, but it does not encourage the use of these methods.[25] Non-resident parents who wish to pay in one of these ways should insist on doing so. So long as payments are made when due, no deduction from earnings order should be made.

Where payment is made via the CSA, the person with care is paid by automated credit transfer wherever possible, and if not, by cheque (although in theory cash is also possible, it is not used).[26] The person with care is asked to provide details of a bank, building society or Post Office account. If she does not have an account, or experiences difficulty opening one, she should contact the CSA national helpline on 08457 133133.

Deductions from benefit: new rules

If a non-resident parent on benefit is required to pay child maintenance at the flat rate (see Chapter 6) the CSA may request Jobcentre Plus to make a deduction for maintenance.[27] Deductions can be made from:[28]

- IS;
- income-based JSA;
- contribution-based JSA;
- maternity allowance;
- bereavement benefits;
- widows' benefits;
- retirement pension;
- incapacity benefit;
- carer's allowance;
- severe disablement allowance (SDA);
- industrial injuries schemes benefits;
- war disablement pension;
- pension credit (PC).

If someone should pay at the flat rate, but a variation has been made which results in the reduced or basic rate being payable, deductions can be made towards the new amount of maintenance calculated.

If both the non-resident parent and his partner are:[29]

- on IS or income-based JSA; *and*
- each is a non-resident parent,

the £5 flat rate deduction will be split between them so that each contributes £2.50 to their respective persons with care.[30] (In polygamous relationships where there is more than one new partner who is also a non-resident parent the £5 is apportioned between all the non-resident parents.[31])

The CSA requests the deduction and Jobcentre Plus must make it in full wherever possible. The parent must be left with at least 10 pence a week.[32] Partial deductions will not be made. In addition, priority debt rules do not apply to deductions for child support maintenance under the 'new rules'. This means the deduction for child support is always made, whatever other deductions are due.

Both the person with care and non-resident parent are notified that deductions are to be made.

If there are arrears of maintenance, a £1 deduction towards arrears may be made from the benefits listed above, except IS, income-based JSA or PC (see p438)

Deductions from benefit: old rules

When an application is received by the CSA and it is found that the non-resident parent is on IS/PC/income-based JSA, both parties will be notified as to whether or not deductions from benefit are a possibility. If the non-resident parent is not exempt from deductions, the Department for Work and Pensions (DWP) will be sent notification requesting that a deduction is made. This is binding on the DWP, unless there are other deductions being made from the benefit which take precedence.[33]

Direct deductions for contributions of child maintenance cannot be made from any benefit other than IS/PC/income-based JSA, unless contribution-based JSA, IB, SDA or retirement pension are paid together with IS/PC/income-based JSA.[34] After the deductions are made, the claimant must be left with at least 10 pence a week.[35]

There is a maximum amount which can be deducted from IS/PC/income-based JSA for various payments.[36] The contribution for child maintenance has a lower priority than any of the other possible deductions.[37] Therefore, in some cases where non-resident parents have other deductions, it will not be possible to deduct the full £6 for the contribution to child maintenance. The DWP can deduct half of the £6 contribution.[38] For more information about deductions from benefit, see CPAG's *Welfare Benefits and Tax Credits Handbook*.

If full deductions from IS/PC/income-based JSA are not possible, arrears of child maintenance contributions do *not* accrue.

The DWP will tell the CSA whether deductions are possible. The CSA, in turn, notifies the non-resident parent and the person with care if deductions are going to begin. The £6 is paid to the person with care via the CSA.[39] The CSA notifies her of the way in which the payments will be made. If the person with care is on IS/PC/income-based JSA, the contribution is generally paid with the benefit (see pp363 and 428). Otherwise, the person with care usually receives payments on a quarterly basis.

If there are arrears of maintenance, these can be deducted from contribution-based JSA only (see p438).

Timing of payments

The CSA decides the day and frequency of payments,[40] but asks for the person's preference. When deciding the day and the interval for payment by the non-resident parent, the CSA must take into account:[41]

- the day on which, and the interval at which, the non-resident parent receives his income;
- any other relevant circumstances of the non-resident parent;
- time for cheques to clear, if applicable, and for payments to be transferred to the person with care; *and*
- any representations of the parties, in particular the preference of the non-resident parent.[42]

Unless undue hardship would be caused to the non-resident parent or the person with care, the frequency of payments to the person with care will be the same as the frequency set for the non-resident parent's payments (but see p444 for deduction from earnings orders).[43]

Unless payments are to be by direct debit or standing order, the non-resident parent is advised to make each payment three to four days before the due date in order to ensure that payments are received on time and avoid arrears. Clearance times are allowed for each method of payment, but the CSA aims to make payments to the person with care within a week of receiving them from the non-resident parent.[44] In some cases, if there is delay in passing payment to the person with care, she may be entitled to compensation, including interest on the money she would have had at an earlier date if the maladministration had not occurred (see also Chapter 21).[45]

Payment statements

Statements of the CSA account can be supplied when a request is made by a person with care, non-resident parent or child in Scotland.[46] Statements can be important when contesting the level of arrears. However, both parties should keep records and evidence of payments made and received, given the high level of errors on CSA accounts.

Overpayments

An overpayment can arise either because the amount of the maintenance due for a past period has been reduced, there has been a CSA error or the non-resident parent has paid more than the regular payment due. The CSA has a discretion about allocating the overpayment,[47] including setting it against any arrears of child maintenance resulting from a previous calculation.[48] In practice, the CSA sets the overpayment against arrears and any other liabilities, then checks to see if there is an irregular first collection in the current maintenance schedule which can be reduced by allocating the overpayment.[49]

If there is a surplus remaining after current maintenance, arrears and other liabilities have been met, the non-resident parent may have the amount he pays adjusted or a refund made.[50] An adjustment is the preferred option.

If the CSA receives an unexpected payment from the non-resident parent, it will check to determine the reason for this – eg, it could be for an overdue collection to offset arrears or an amount towards a future collection.[51] Following this investigation the amount may be allocated to – eg:[52]

- current and overdue collections, plus any other arrears;
- arrears scheduled in the future;
- an advance collection;
- voluntary payment, if received in the initial payment period; *or*
- early payment – ie, with the intention that the person with care gets a maintenance payment early.

The CSA cannot pass on financial gifts from the non-resident parent to the person with care.[53] Any such payments must be refunded.

Refunds can only be made if there are no overdue collections or arrears on the case.[54]

The CSA should refund overpayments made because of CSA error – eg, where a person was told to pay more than the calculation required. In such cases, the non-resident parent may also wish to complain and seek compensation (see Chapter 21).

Adjustments

If an overpayment remains after offsetting against regular maintenance, arrears and other liability, the CSA can reduce the amount payable to compensate the non-resident parent for the overpayment.[55] Adjustments may also be made where there are overpayments of voluntary payments in the initial payment period.[56]

When making this discretionary decision, the CSA must consider, in particular:

- the circumstances of the non-resident parent and person with care;
- the welfare of any children (see p24);
- the amount of the overpayment in relation to the amount of the current calculation; *and*
- the period over which it would be reasonable to recoup it.

The amount payable cannot be reduced below the flat rate (see p199).[57]

Where the amount of an adjusted calculation changes because of a revision, supersession or variation, the adjustment applies to the fresh calculation, unless the CSA considers that this would be inappropriate, in which case it can either change the amount of the adjustment or cancel it.[58]

The non-resident parent, person with care and any Scottish child applicant must be notified of an adjustment or cancellation of an adjustment.[59] The decision to make or cancel an adjustment can be revised or superseded by the CSA (see Chapter 18) or appealed to an appeal tribunal (see Chapter 19).[60]

Recovery of overpayments from the person with care

If the CSA reimburses an overpayment to a non-resident parent, it can recover from the person with care any maintenance overpaid to her.[61] This includes overpaid voluntary payments.[62] The CSA cannot enforce recovery of overpayments because of CSA administrative error, but the person with care will be asked if she is prepared to repay.

Recovery of overpayments is a discretionary decision, so the welfare of any children likely to be affected by reimbursement must be taken into account (see p24). The CSA cannot recover the overpayment if:[63]

- the person with care was on IS or income-based JSA at any time during the period she was overpaid; or
- the person with care was on IS/income-based JSA on any of the dates reimbursement to the non-resident parent was made; or
- either of the above apply, if the non-resident parent made voluntary payments.

The overpayment is, therefore, collected from any current maintenance; where there is no ongoing maintenance other collection arrangements can be made.[64]

2. **Collection of other payments**

The Child Support Agency (CSA) can collect and enforce other forms of maintenance where child support maintenance is being collected.[65]

The power to collect other maintenance is discretionary. However, the CSA may agree to requests to collect other types of maintenance for parents with care on income support or income-based jobseeker's allowance and, where the court order was made after April 1993, for voluntary applicants. The CSA can only collect other maintenance that falls due after the CSA gives the non-resident parent written notice that the other maintenance will be collected.[66]

The following payments under a court order (see p32) can be collected by the CSA:[67]

- additional child maintenance in excess of the CSA maximum;
- maintenance for a child's education or training;
- maintenance paid to meet the expenses of a child with a disability;
- maintenance paid for a stepchild – ie, a child living with the person with care who used to live with the non-resident parent and was accepted by him as a member of his family;
- spousal or civil partner maintenance for a person with care of a child for whom child support maintenance is being collected.

The methods used by the CSA for collecting and enforcing other types of maintenance are the same as for child support maintenance.[68] Where a non-resident parent is paying more than one type of maintenance, and pays less than the total amount required, he should stipulate how the amounts are to be allocated. The CSA will allocate as requested, except that where arrears of child support maintenance are specified, current child support maintenance will be paid before arrears. If the non-resident parent does not stipulate, the CSA will allocate according to the following order of priority:[69]

- current child support maintenance liability;
- regular child maintenance;
- arrears of child support maintenance to the person with care;
- arrears of other child maintenance to the CSA; *and*
- other liabilities, with the oldest first.

Where arrears of child support maintenance are due to the CSA and others are due to the person with care, the priorities are the same as for overpayments caused by a change in the amount of the calculation (see p431).

Where there is more than one person with care, the CSA will apportion the payment between them.[70] This means that the non-resident parent cannot choose to pay one parent but not the other.

Collection of fees, court costs and penalty payments

Although fees have not been charged for CSA services since April 1995 (see p425), any outstanding fees from previous years are still collected.[71] For liability to pay fees from 1993 to 1995 and their collection and enforcement, see p369 of the 1995/96 edition of this *Handbook*.

If the CSA applies to court for a decision on whether a person is a parent and the court decides that he is, the court can order him to pay the CSA's costs in bringing the case, including the cost of any DNA tests which have been carried out (see p95). Also, a non-resident parent may have agreed to pay DNA test fees to the CSA without a court order (see p91).

The CSA may also have imposed a penalty payment on the non-resident parent for failure to pay.

The CSA will negotiate with the liable person about payment of these other liabilities.[72] It will initially request the full amount due, but payments by instalment may be agreed.

Fees and costs can only be enforced through court action. The rules for enforcement of maintenance (see p450) do not apply. The court is the sheriff court in Scotland and the county court in England and Wales. If the case is contested, a hearing is arranged in the court with jurisdiction for the area in which the parent lives. A money judgment can be enforced by the usual debt enforcement procedures.

3. **Arrears**

The Child Support Agency (CSA) acts on arrears only if the collection service (see p427) is being used. If a person with care has not requested the collection service, she should consider doing so if a payment is missed. The CSA should then pursue all outstanding arrears.

Initial arrears

As the first calculation is usually made after its effective date, there are always initial arrears. The exception is where a court order is in force and an application is treated as made by a parent with care on benefit, when the effective date is two days after the day the calculation is made (see p357). (In some cases where the effective date has been deferred under the 'old rules' this may also be the case.) If a court order made on, or after, 3 March 2003 has been in force for more than a year and there is a voluntary application to the CSA, the effective date is two months and two days from the date of the application. If the non-resident parent has continued to make payments due under the order beyond the effective date, these payments will be treated as payments of child support.[73] This helps to avoid additional liability for child support where, for whatever reason, it takes the CSA longer than two months and two days to make the maintenance calculation, so that when it is made, its effective date (and, therefore, the date the court order ceases to have effect) is in the past. If the payments made under the court order are at a higher rate than those due under the calculation, this will be treated as an overpayment of child support and the maintenance calculation can be adjusted accordingly.

The CSA prefers to notify the non-resident parent about the collection schedule, including initial arrears, by telephone.[74] The parent can request and negotiate changes to the schedule. Written confirmation of the collection schedule is issued once the non-resident parent has agreed to it. Where telephone contact is not possible the CSA will write to the non-resident parent.

The written notification states:[75]
- the amount due and to whom it is to be paid;
- how it is to be paid – ie, method, day and interval between payments;
- any amounts that are overdue and outstanding.

The CSA requests payment of the initial arrears as a lump sum.[76] If a non-resident parent cannot pay this all at once he may negotiate an agreement to pay in instalments or a collection schedule to cover both the initial payment and ongoing liability (see p437).

A parent who fails to make payment of the outstanding arrears within seven days of written notification of the amount due may face financial penalties and further enforcement action.

A parent who thinks the calculation is wrong may be able to seek a revision or make an appeal. If he objects to the way the CSA is dealing with collections he may make a complaint (see Chapter 21).

Voluntary payments made in the initial period

Voluntary payments made by the non-resident parent through the CSA (or, where the CSA agrees, to the person with care or a third party) after the effective date but before the calculation is made and notified may be offset against arrears of child maintenance.[77]

Only the following types of payment can be offset:[78]

- in lieu of child support maintenance;
- in respect of a mortgage or loan on the child's home, or for repairs or improvements to the property;
- rent on the child's home;
- mains gas, water or electricity at the child's home;
- council tax payable at the child's home;
- repairs to the heating system at the child's home; *or*
- repairs to the child's home.

Payments can be made by cash, standing order, cheque, postal order, debit card or other method/arrangement from an account of the non-resident parent or on his behalf (eg, credit card).[79]

If the payments are made to the CSA they will be passed on to the person with care (in voluntary applicant cases) or held by the CSA (in cases where the parent with care is on income support (IS) or income-based jobseeker's allowance (JSA)). Once the calculation has been made, the voluntary payments will be offset against the initial arrears.

If the payments are made direct to the person with care or a third party, the CSA will check with the person with care if payments have been made.[80] This is normally done by phone. If the person with care confirms the payments were made, this is usually accepted without any further need for proof. If there is a dispute over whether a payment has been made, the CSA will ask the non-resident parent to provide proof. Payment can be verified by bank statements, duplicates of cashed cheques, receipts, paid bills/invoices, or written or oral statement from the person with care.[81] Once the non-resident parent provides proof of payment, the person with care must be able to show that this has not been received in order for it not to be considered as a voluntary payment.[82] It is in the interest of both parties to ensure payments are recorded, and the CSA should explain to the non-resident parent the importance of keeping a record and provide a form on which to do so.

If either party disagrees with a decision about offsetting, a complaint can be made (see Chapter 21).

If offsetting means that there is an overpayment, the calculation may be adjusted to compensate the non-resident parent or a refund may be made (see p432).

Negotiating an arrears agreement

If the non-resident parent is in arrears, the CSA will seek an arrears agreement.[83]

Negotiations with the CSA may begin on notification of the collection schedule or at a later date if the non-resident parent has difficulty making ongoing payments. However, the CSA does not normally agree to defer payment of current liability, though it may do so if a revision, supersession or appeal is pending.

Limitations on the level of payments or how quickly the arrears must be cleared are not specified in child support law. Although CSA staff always begin by requesting full payment of the outstanding arrears, an arrears agreement may be reached to pay the amount in instalments. The maximum amount that the CSA will propose for arrears collection is 5 per cent of net income.[84] There is no minimum amount and the parent may arrange to pay more than 5 per cent to reduce the arrears more quickly, but if he defaults, the agreement to pay more than 5 per cent cannot be enforced. In making this discretionary decision the CSA should consider the:[85]

- needs of the non-resident parent or any new family;
- representations of the non-resident parent about hardship; *or*
- needs of the person with care and the qualifying child.

If a non-resident parent has other priorities (eg, fuel) or other large debts, he should seek independent money advice. Existing agreements with other creditors may have to be renegotiated to take into account the CSA calculation. However, it is important to keep the CSA informed so that it does not assume that the non-resident parent is refusing to come to an agreement. If there is a change of circumstances, the non-resident parent may find it hard to pay the current liability and an arrears agreement in full while the change is processed. The CSA may accept a reduced payment but this does not alter the parent's liability and enforcement action may be taken on the arrears that accrue. The CSA may suspend the debt temporarily pending investigations.[86] The arrears agreement may also be adjusted to include missed payments.

The CSA can use other methods of recovery, such as a deduction from earnings order (see p443). Therefore, CSA staff are unlikely to agree to a non-resident parent making low payments over a very long period. It is in his interests to come to an agreement if he wishes to avoid further payment penalties and enforcement action. If he has children living with him, the welfare of those children must be taken into account.

Repayments may be spread over several years. Although this may help non-resident parents who are in financial hardship, it is very late payment to the person with care. She may want to make representations to the CSA. No interest will be paid to the person with care in respect of arrears, even though the arrears may have accrued because of CSA delay and error, and/or the non-compliance of the non-resident parent.

The parent with care and qualifying children are not consulted about the level at which arrears are collected, but will be informed when the decision has been made. This practice may be contrary to the European Convention on Human Rights' protection of private property,[87] but there has been no reported caselaw on this point (see also p442 on the fact that a person with care cannot directly enforce the payment of child support).

Revision, supersession or appeal pending

The CSA can suspend collection of arrears if a revision, supersession, variation or appeal is pending. If the calculation is likely to be reduced, the CSA may agree to suspend collection of some of the ongoing payments. However, this does not often happen; the CSA prefers to speed up its consideration of the case.

A non-resident parent who requests a revision, supersession or appeal and is having problems paying the current maintenance or any arrears should make representations to the CSA for lower regular payments.

Payment of arrears

Arrears do not have to be paid by the same method as continuing child maintenance payments. For example, arrears could be collected via the CSA, while ongoing payments are made to the person with care. However, in practice the CSA prefers to use the same method of payment for both.

The CSA collects arrears if IS/income-based JSA is paid to or for the person with care. The CSA keeps the part of the arrears payments that would not have been passed to the parent with care had it been made when due.[88] Payments of arrears are allocated between the CSA and person with care in the same way as overpayments (see p431).

Collection of arrears from a non-resident parent on benefit

In 'new rules' cases, if the non-resident parent is in receipt of one of the following contribution-based benefits a deduction of £1 may be made towards arrears. This is in addition to a deduction for flat-rate maintenance. These deductions are separate to other deductions made from benefit and are not affected by priority rules on which deductions should be made first. The £1 deduction can be made from the following benefits, except where IS, income-based JSA or pension credit (PC) are also being paid to the non-resident parent or his partner:[89]

- contribution-based JSA;
- maternity allowance;
- bereavement allowance;
- widowed parent's allowance;
- war widow's pension;

- widow's pension;
- widowed mother's allowance;
- reduced earnings allowance;
- industrial death benefit and retirement allowance;
- retirement pension;
- incapacity benefit;
- carer's allowance;
- severe disablement allowance;
- industrial injuries schemes benefits;
- war disablement pension.

This means that arrears action in 'new rules' cases will be suspended against non-resident parents on IS/income-based JSA/PC. If a person with care believes that the arrears action should be pursued in some other way, she should contact the CSA and explain her reasons. If the CSA is unwilling to take action, a complaint may be made (see Chapter 21).

In 'old rules' cases, a deduction for arrears can only be made from contribution-based JSA, at a maximum of one third of the age related amount payable (eg, £19.71 a week for a non-resident parent aged 25 or over in 2007/08).[90] In 'old rules' cases, the priority rules on deductions from benefit do apply and therefore the deduction may not be made where certain other deductions take priority (eg, for arrears of council tax). For more information on the priority rules on deductions from benefit, see CPAG's *Welfare Benefits and Tax Credits Handbook*.

Starting recovery action

The CSA may begin to consider recovery action when:
- a payment from the non-resident parent to the CSA is not received;
- the person with care notifies the CSA that a payment due has not been received; *or*
- the person with care requests an increase in IS/income-based JSA because child maintenance has not been paid.

The CSA contacts the non-resident parent to investigate the situation.[91] Contact is normally by telephone. The non-resident parent may request an appointment at a local office if he wishes to discuss payment face to face with CSA staff.

If the non-resident parent intends to pay the amount, the CSA may:[92]
- accept a delayed payment, setting two further days for receipt (normally only two delayed payments are allowed in any 12-month period); *or*
- reschedule the amount to include it within the arrears.

If the non-resident parent indicates that he is having difficulty in making the payments, this may be because of a change of circumstances.[93] The CSA will collect information to check whether or not there should be a supersession. Occasionally, it may also decide to suspend collection.[94]

If the non-resident parent refuses to pay, the CSA will inform him of its powers to collect and enforce maintenance. The CSA may discuss imposing a payment penalty to encourage the non-resident parent to pay the maintenance due.

To avoid payment penalties and other methods of recovery, the non-resident parent should come to an agreement (see p437) as soon as possible and comply with that agreement. The CSA has discretion over the agreements reached with non-resident parents about debt recovery. However, where a parent fails to come to a voluntary agreement or breaks it, the CSA may then impose payment penalties. The CSA may enforce a deduction from earnings order (DEO) at up to 40 per cent of net income and/or take further enforcement action.

Arrears notice

If the non-resident parent has missed one or more child maintenance payments, the CSA must send him an arrears notice itemising the amounts owed. The notice also explains the regulations about arrears and requests payment of the outstanding amount.[95] The notice can be issued automatically unless a previous notice has been issued in the last 12 weeks.[96] The CSA will then contact the non-resident parent to discuss the issue.

The non-resident parent should check that the amount owed is correct and tell the CSA of any mistakes. There have been high levels of mistakes on accounts in the past. Therefore, if there is a concern that the balance is incorrect, the non-resident parent should ask for a payment statement (see p431) and compare this with his own record. While doing this, it is important that he keeps the CSA informed so that a penalty payment and a deduction from earnings order (DEO) are not imposed in the meantime.

The non-resident parent can contact the CSA to negotiate payment by instalments (see p437). Once an arrears notice has been served, another does not have to be sent if arrears remain uncleared unless the non-resident parent has paid all arranged payments for a 12-week period.[97]

When the non-resident parent defaults

If the non-resident parent fails to keep to an arrears agreement:
- a penalty payment may be imposed; *and*
- a DEO (see p443) or other method of enforcement may be considered (see p450).

In all cases, a non-resident parent who wants to co-operate should try to renegotiate an agreement in good time before a change in his circumstances – eg, redundancy. If the non-resident parent has paid regularly and the change would produce a reduction in the amount due, the CSA may accept a lower amount. Arrears may be temporarily suspended where personal circumstances make it difficult or insensitive to enforce recovery – eg, he is unemployed, sick or in prison.[98]

Penalty payments

In 'new rules' cases, the power exists to impose a penalty payment on a non-resident parent who is in arrears with his child maintenance payments.[99] In practice, this power is not used and, at the time of writing, late payment penalties are not imposed, although it is possible that they could be if the CSA changes its policy. All references to late payment penalties have been removed from CSA leaflets and letters to its clients.[100]

Delays in collection and enforcement

Despite CSA steps to avoid debts building up, many cases may accumulate arrears. The intention under the new scheme is for the CSA to take action more quickly to respond to failure to pay and impose financial penalties to encourage payment or establish arrears agreements. The Operational Improvement Plan also states that the CSA will take 'quicker and firmer action' where non-resident parents default, including increasing the use of deduction from earnings orders, and the number of non-resident parents brought to court,[101] and this has had some success in increased collection rates.

Persons with care who are concerned at the speed of pursuit and who want quicker action should contact the CSA by phone, letter or in person. A person with care may want to explain any effect the lack of arrears action has on the welfare of the child(ren). In particular, a person with care may want to request that a DEO be issued and, if there is undue delay, make a complaint (see Chapter 21). If a DEO or another form of enforcement is refused, the person with care should be given the reasons for this. As well as making a complaint, it is possible that judicial review (see p383) could also be considered.

If there are arrears of over £100 that have built up because of CSA maladministration, the person with care may be eligible for an advance payment (see below). This may be in addition to any payment of compensation (see p457).

There are persons with care who, as a result of the payment of child maintenance, are no longer on IS/income-based JSA because their income, including child maintenance, is now too high. If child maintenance is not paid, a fresh benefit claim should be made.

Advance payments

An advance payment of maintenance is not compensation. The payment is to ensure the person with care is not worse off as a result of maladministration by the CSA.[102] Essentially, it is advance payment of arrears that the CSA is collecting from the non-resident parent. The decision on whether or not to make an advance payment is discretionary. It can only be considered where the:

- arrears of maintenance because of CSA maladministration are £100 or more;
- non-resident parent is making regular maintenance payments;

- non-resident parent has made, and is paying, an arrears agreement and it would take more than 26 weeks to pay these arrears;
- CSA is satisfied that the non-resident parent would have complied with the calculation but for the maladministration; *and*
- person with care has shown an interest in progressing the case during the period of delay.

There must be clear evidence that there has been maladministration by the CSA for an advance payment to be considered. Maladministration may include:[103]

- rudeness;
- delay;
- refusal to answer reasonable questions;
- knowingly giving advice which is misleading or inadequate;
- incompetence;
- bias because of, for example, gender or ethnicity; *or*
- disregard of guidance that should be followed.

The CSA may consider payment on its own initiative or at the request of the person with care. If an advance payment is to be made, the amount is the arrears of maintenance due as a result of the maladministration plus interest, but only where interest is £10 or more. Allowances are made for normal processing time so only that time over and above the normal processing time is considered. Payment is usually in the form of a lump sum, paid either directly into the person's bank account or by cheque.[104] The person with care must sign a declaration agreeing that the CSA retains child support payments subsequently made in respect of the period of arrears and to refund any relevant direct payments.

If a decision is made not to make a payment, there is no right of appeal. The person with care may provide further information to support her case, complain (see Chapter 21), contact her MP or possibly seek judicial review (see p383).

Enforcement by the person with care

While there is no provision in child support legislation for the parent with care to bring her own court action against the non-resident parent for the child support maintenance due, it may be possible for the parent to raise an action to recover the amount owed to her. In practice, however, such action may be difficult. The House of Lords has decided that the lack of direct access to the courts by a person with care to enforce child support payments from a non-resident parent does not breach the right to a fair hearing under the European Convention of Human Rights[105](although it is understood that this decision is being challenged in the European Court of Human Rights).

If the person with care has lost out because of CSA delay or maladministration, it may be possible to sue the CSA for negligence. Anyone considering doing either of the above should seek legal advice. Using the complaints procedure is more likely to be an effective means of obtaining redress within a reasonable timescale (see Chapter 21).

Interest

Interest can only be charged on arrears of child maintenance accrued before 17 April 1995.[106] Interest can continue to accrue on arrears outstanding at 17 April 1995 at 1 per cent over the base rate and new demands for interest may still be issued – eg, where a non-resident parent defaults on an arrears agreement for amounts due before 17 April 1995. However, in practice, the collection of interest takes a lower priority than current liability for, and arrears of, maintenance. For details about charging and the enforcement of interest, see the 1997/98 edition of this *Handbook*, p390.

4. **Deduction from earnings orders**

The Child Support Agency (CSA) may make a deduction from earnings order (DEO). This is an order to the non-resident parent's employer to make deductions from his earnings and pay them to the CSA.[107]

CSA staff are instructed to make a voluntary DEO if the non-resident parent chooses it (see p428).[108] If possible, a DEO is also made if the account is in arrears and the non-resident parent does not respond to enquiries, refuses to make an arrears agreement or persistently defaults on an agreement.[109] Persons with care have complained in the past that the CSA is slow to make DEOs. However, as part of the Operational Improvement Plan, the CSA plans to increase the use and effectiveness of DEOs, using this method earlier and more frequently, for either non-resident parents who default or those who 'indicate that they are unlikely to pay'.[110] The Client Charter states that if the non-resident parent has a job, but either fails or refuses to pay, the CSA 'will aim to obtain payment via a DEO within four months of making initial payment arrangements.[111]

The best way for a non-resident parent to avoid a DEO is to negotiate an arrears agreement (see p437) and keep to it wherever possible. However, making ongoing liability payments in full may be enough to prevent a DEO being made. A non-resident parent's objection to a DEO is likely to be outweighed if it is unlikely that regular payments would be made using a different method.

The decision to make a DEO is discretionary and the welfare of any children must be considered (see p24).[112] If warned of a DEO, the non-resident parent should tell the CSA, preferably in writing, how any child(ren) would be affected. Any challenge should be by judicial review (see p383) and/or via the complaints procedure (see Chapter 21), rather than by appealing to a court (see p449).

A DEO can be made while the non-resident parent is awaiting a revision, supersession or appeal. Staff should consider the grounds of the revision, supersession or appeal before making a DEO. They may check the likelihood and timing of any change in the calculation, and arrange for that consideration to be 'fast-tracked'. A non-resident parent can also make representations about the amount and method of payments (see pp428 and 438). The CSA may accept lower payments, but this will not remove its right to impose a DEO.

A DEO cannot be made if the employer is based outside the UK and has no place of business in the UK,[113] but a DEO can be made in Great Britain against an employer in Northern Ireland and *vice versa*.[114]

A DEO cannot be made if the non-resident parent is in the armed forces. Instead, the CSA can request the armed forces to make deductions for child maintenance under armed forces law, known as a DER, which sets limits on the amounts which can be deducted.[115]

If the full amount requested by the CSA cannot be deducted from earnings, the CSA uses other methods to collect and enforce the remainder.

If a deduction from earnings order is made

A DEO is an instruction to the employer of a non-resident parent to make deductions from his earnings.[116] A copy of the DEO must be served on the employer and the non-resident parent.[117] The employer has to comply with the DEO within seven days of receiving it.[118] Failure to take all reasonable steps to comply with a DEO is an offence punishable by a fine of up to £500.[119]

The DEO must state:[120]

- the name and address of the non-resident parent;
- the name of the employer;
- the non-resident parent's place of work, the nature of his work, his employee number and national insurance number (if known by the CSA);
- the normal deduction rate(s) (see p456) and the date on which each takes effect;
- the protected earnings proportion;
- the address to which the deductions are to be sent.

The CSA national helpline (see Appendix 1) provides further information for employers. The CSA leaflet *What is My Role in Helping My Employees Pay Child Maintenance?* (CSL313) also provides guidance to employers on deductions. If an employer is implementing a DEO incorrectly and the non-resident parent is disputing this, the non-resident parent should ask the CSA to intervene.

Date of payment

The employer must pay the CSA monthly by the 19th of the month following the month in which the deduction is made.[121] This means that there is always a delay before the person with care receives the first payment from the CSA. Because the employer makes monthly payments, the person with care receives monthly payments, even if the non-resident parent is having weekly deductions. These monthly payments may not always be for the same amount (see pp447 and 457).

The payment by the employer may be made by credit transfer, cheque or any other method to which the CSA agrees.[122] The DEO reference number must be given so that the CSA can identify the person with care.

The employer commits a criminal offence punishable by a fine of up to £500 if s/he fails to take all reasonable steps to pay the CSA on time.[123]

Providing information

In each of the following cases, any notice that is sent from the CSA will be treated as though it was given or sent on the day that it was posted.[124]

Failure to take all reasonable steps to comply with any of the following requirements to provide information to the CSA is an offence punishable by a fine of up to £500.[125]

The non-resident parent

The non-resident parent must provide the name and address of his employer, the amount of earnings and anticipated earnings, place of work, nature of work and any works number within seven days of being asked to do so in writing by the CSA.[126] Once a DEO is in force, a non-resident parent must inform the CSA within seven days of leaving employment or becoming employed or re-employed.[127]

The employer

An employer must inform the CSA in writing within 10 days of being served with a DEO if s/he does not, in fact, employ the non-resident parent.[128] If a non-resident parent who is subject to a DEO leaves his job, the employer must notify the CSA within 10 days of his leaving.[129] If an employer finds out that a DEO is in force against an employee (eg, on becoming his employer), s/he must notify the CSA within seven days of becoming aware of this information.[130]

The employer must inform the non-resident parent in writing of the amount of each deduction no later than the date of the deduction or, if not practicable, by the following payday.[131] Although child support law imposes no penalty on an employer who fails to do this, employment protection law requires the employer to give the non-resident parent a written statement of deductions on or before the payday.[132] Where the deduction will always be the same amount, this can be done by a standing statement given at least annually.[133] If the employer does not give notice of the deduction, the non-resident parent may complain to an employment tribunal, which can order the employer to pay the non-resident parent a fine up to the total amount of the unnotified deductions, even if paid on to the CSA.[134] This fine would not affect deductions already paid to the CSA.

For other duties about providing information, see p77.

Earnings

Earnings include wages, salary, fees, bonus, commission, overtime pay, occupational pension or statutory sick pay, any other payment made under an employment contract and a regular payment made in compensation for loss of wages.[135] Earnings do not include a payment by a foreign government or the government of Northern Ireland,[136] or a payment to a special member of a British reserved armed force.[137] Net earnings means, in this context, the amount remaining after tax, national insurance and contributions towards a pension scheme have been deducted.[138]

How much is deducted

The DEO states a **normal deduction rate** and a **protected earnings proportion**.[139] These rates should usually correspond to the pay periods of the non-resident parent – ie, at a weekly rate if paid weekly and a monthly rate if paid monthly.[140] More than one normal deduction rate can be set, each applying to a different period.[141]

Normal deduction rate

The normal deduction rate is the amount that will be deducted each payday as long as net earnings are not brought below the protected earnings proportion. The normal deduction rate can include not only current maintenance liability but also an amount for any arrears, penalty payments (interest in rare cases – see p443) and fees due. There are no special rules on how quickly the CSA should seek to clear the liability. This is normally negotiated and CSA guidance sets limits for payments towards arrears (see p437).

Protected earnings proportion

The protected earnings proportion is the level below which earnings must not be reduced by the deductions. The protected earnings proportion is 60 per cent of net earnings.[142]

Administering a deduction from earnings order

The employer can deduct a charge for administrative costs each time a deduction is made under the DEO.[143] This means that employees paid weekly can be charged more for administrative costs. The additional amount must not exceed £1 per deduction and can be made even where this would bring earnings below the protected earnings proportion.

Each payday the employer should make a deduction from net earnings at the normal deduction rate plus any administration charge, unless deducting the normal deduction rate would reduce net earnings below the protected earnings proportion. If this would be the case, the amount of the deduction is the excess of net earnings over the protected earnings proportion. In addition, an administration charge may be deducted.[144]

If the employer fails to make a deduction, or the deduction is less than the normal deduction rate, arrears build up and are deducted at the next payday in addition to the normal deduction, applying the same rules for protected earnings.[145]

If, on a payday, the non-resident parent is paid for a period longer than that for which the normal deduction rate is set, the deduction is increased in proportion to the length of the pay period.[146]

Such fluctuations in deductions may mean that the person with care receives irregular payments.

Example

The non-resident parent is due to pay child maintenance of £48 a week and his net earnings are £240 a week. When a DEO is considered there are arrears of £432 and penalty payments of £26.40. The DEO shows a normal deduction rate of £60 (maintenance due + 5 per cent net income) and a protected earnings proportion of £144. His employer can deduct £1 administrative costs for weeks in which a deduction is made.

Payday	Net pay	Child support due	Deduction	Pay	DEO unpaid
	£	£	£	£	£
5/7	240	60	61	179	
12/7	250	60	61	189	
19/7	160	60	17	143	44
26/7	160	104	17	143	88
2/8	240	148	97	143	52
9/8	250	112	107	143	6
16/8	250	66	67	183	
23/8	240	60	61	179	
30/8	120	60	Nil	120	60
6/9	240	120	97	143	24
13/9	240	84	85	155	
20/9	250	60	61	189	
27/9	240	60	61	179	

In the week 19/7 the full deduction cannot be made, as this would take income below the protected earnings proportion. A deduction is made of £16 plus a £1 administration fee. The amount of the DEO outstanding is added to the next amount due on 26/7. As earnings are again low, the full deduction cannot be taken and is carried forward.

In the week 30/8 earnings are too low for a deduction to be made, and, therefore there is no deduction and no administrative charge.

Payment to the person with care

The employer has to pass the month's payments to the CSA by the 19th of the following month. When this has reached the CSA's account, the payment should be passed on to the person with care within 10 days – unless it is retained because the person with care is on IS/income-based JSA (see p428). When the person with care comes off IS/income-based JSA, the current liability will be due to her, but some (or all) of the arrears may be retained in lieu of IS paid for an earlier period.

Example
Following on from the previous example, the parent with care would receive the following payments.

Month	Payment to CSA by the 19th of the month	Current liability paid (£48 a week due)	Arrears paid (assigned to oldest debt)
	£	£	£
July	Nil	Nil	Nil
August	156	156	Nil
September	328	192	136
October	300	192	108

By the time the parent gets her first payment from the DEO in August she is owed £624 (£432 + £192 (July)), but because of the fluctuating earnings of the non-resident parent she will receive less than the maintenance due. It is only in September that she begins to obtain arrears of maintenance, even though the DEO was put into place in July.

Priority of orders

A DEO takes priority over an attachment of earnings order for a judgment or administration debt (non-priority debts), and any arrestment of earnings under Scottish law.[147] In England and Wales, when a DEO is served on an employee who is already subject to an attachment of earnings order for a priority debt (eg, council tax or fine), the earliest has priority.[148]

Any deductions under a lower priority order are taken from the net earnings left after deductions under the first order have been made.[149]

Reviews, cancellations and lapsed orders

The CSA must **review** a DEO if there is a change in the amount of the calculation or if any arrears, penalty payments (interest in some cases – see p443) and fees included have been paid off.[150] This does not apply where a normal deduction rate that takes into account the change has already been specified (see p456). A DEO can be changed on this review.[151] The employer must comply with the change within seven days of a copy of the new DEO being served on her/him.[152] The usual penalties for failure to comply apply.

The CSA can **cancel** the DEO if:[153]
- no further payments are due under it;
- the DEO is ineffective or there appears to be a more effective way of collecting the payments;
- the DEO is defective (see p449) or does not comply with some other procedural provision in the legislation;

- the CSA did not have, or has ceased to have, jurisdiction to make a DEO; *or*
- a DEO being used to enforce a default maintenance decision or interim maintenance decision is no longer appropriate given the compliance or attempted compliance of the non-resident parent.

The CSA must send written notice of cancellation to the non-resident parent and employer.[154]

A DEO **lapses** when a non-resident parent leaves the employment.[155] The CSA can revive it if he finds a new job with the same or a different employer.[156] If it is revived, copies of the notice must be served on the non-resident parent and new employer.[157] Any shortfall under the DEO prior to the revival cannot be carried over to the revived DEO.[158]

Appeals

A non-resident parent can appeal against a DEO to the magistrates' court in England and Wales or sheriff's court in Scotland.[159] The appeal must be made within 28 days.[160] An appeal can only be made on the grounds that the order is defective (see below) or that the payments made to the non-resident parent are not earnings (see p445).[161] If the CSA has not properly exercised its discretion in making a DEO, judicial review can be sought (see p383) and/or a complaint made first to the CSA and then, if not resolved, to the Independent Case Examiner (see Chapter 21).

A DEO is **defective** if it is impracticable for the employer to comply with it because it does not include the correct information required.[162] Many DEOs have included incorrect information (such as errors in names, addresses and dates) but an appeal will not succeed on this basis if the employer can still comply with the DEO. Although some early appeals were upheld because the DEO was unsigned, there is no requirement in the regulations for a signature.

In Scotland, the form of the application is laid out in the child support rules.[163] In England and Wales, a complaint is made against the Secretary of State for Work and Pensions (who acts through the CSA). As there is no specific form given, we suggest that the Scottish wording is followed as an example, but including, 'This complaint is made under section 32(5) of the Child Support Act 1991 and regulation 22 of the Child Support (Collection and Enforcement) Regulations 1992.'

Once the complaint or application is made, the court notifies the CSA. The CSA checks the DEO and contacts the employer to check the earnings. If the DEO is based on the wrong amounts, the CSA varies and reissues it. If the case does get as far as a court hearing, the magistrate/sheriff may quash the DEO or specify which payments, if any, constitute earnings.[164] The court cannot question the maintenance calculation itself.[165]

Even if the court quashes the DEO, it cannot order the CSA to repay deductions to the non-resident parent.[166] Because of this, where deductions are being made from payments that are not earnings, or on the basis of an incorrect normal deduction rate or protected earnings proportion, it may be better to challenge the DEO by judicial review.

Either party can be represented by a lawyer. The CSA can (and does) instead appoint its own staff to conduct DEO appeals and appear at related hearings before magistrates in England and Wales or a sheriff in Scotland.[167] The non-resident parent can also be represented by a lay person, if the sheriff accepts s/he is suitable. An authorised lay representative does not have the full rights of a legal representative, but may be entitled to expenses.

5. **Enforcement**

The Client Charter states that where the non-resident parent has still not paid four months after initial payment arrangements were made, the case should be referred to the Child Support Agency's (CSA's) specialist enforcement unit.[168]

A case should be considered for enforcement action as soon as it is clear that:[169]

- the non-resident parent has missed payments and there is no acceptable explanation of this; *or*
- a deduction from earnings order (DEO) cannot be implemented or has proved ineffective.

To take enforcement action, the CSA must obtain a **liability order**.[170] The CSA cannot get an injunction (inhibition in Scotland) to prevent the non-resident parent from disposing of assets or removing them out of the jurisdiction before a liability order is made.[171] When making any discretionary decision about enforcement, the CSA must consider the welfare of any children likely to be affected (see p24).

From 12 July 2006, a liability order can be sought no matter how old the debt, except for amounts that became due on or before 12 July 2000.[172]

Debts that are older than six years on 12 July 2006 cannot be enforced and will be recovered by other methods, such as a deduction from earnings order (DEO). The six years do not begin to run until the non-resident parent is notified of the assessment or calculation. Although an assessment can be backdated, liability does not exist until the assessment is made.[173]

Obtaining a liability order

If a DEO is inappropriate (eg, because the non-resident parent is not employed) or one has been made but proved ineffective, the CSA may apply to the magistrates' court in England and Wales, or sheriff's court in Scotland, for a liability order.[174] A liability order provides the CSA with legal recognition of the debt, and allows the CSA to take further enforcement measures.

If the court decides that the payments are due but have not been made, it must make the order.[175] The court cannot question the maintenance calculation itself.[176] The great majority of liability orders have been against self-employed non-resident parents.[177]

An order (including one made in Northern Ireland) can be enforced anywhere in the UK.[178]

Either party can be represented by a lawyer. The CSA can (and does) instead appoint its own staff to apply for liability orders and appear at related hearings before magistrates in England and Wales or a sheriff in Scotland.[179] The non-resident parent can also be represented by a lay person, if the sheriff accepts s/he is suitable. An authorised lay representative does not have the full rights of a legal representative, but may be entitled to expenses.

If the court makes the order, it can (and usually will) order the non-resident parent to pay the CSA's legal expenses.

England and Wales

The CSA must give the non-resident parent seven days' notice of its intention to seek a liability order.[180] The notice must state the amount of maintenance outstanding, including any penalty payments. If the non-resident parent makes an arrangement to pay, the action may be stopped, but where there is a history of broken agreements the CSA may pursue a liability order.[181] The application must be made to the court with jurisdiction for the area in which the non-resident parent lives and within six years of the date the amount became due.[182] The non-resident parent will be sent a summons giving 14 days' notice of the hearing. The magistrates decides whether or not to issue the liability order, but cannot consider whether the non-resident parent is liable or the assessment/calculation has been properly made.[183] If an appeal against the CSA is pending, however, the magistrates' court might decide to adjourn.

The magistrates may decide not to issue an order if the non-resident parent appears to be co-operating. However, the CSA will still ask for the order to be granted on the understanding that it will not be enforced if the non-resident parent continues to co-operate.[184] If the non-resident parent does not attend, the CSA may still obtain the order unless it is defective. If the non-resident parent attends, the magistrate may adjourn to allow more time.

The form of the court order in England and Wales is set out in the regulations. The order must specify the outstanding amounts of child support maintenance, penalty payments, fees (interest in some cases – see p443) and other forms of maintenance.[185]

Scotland

A CSA litigation officer can sign the liability order application instead of a solicitor.[186] Court officials serve notice of the application on the non-resident parent.[187] The non-resident parent has 21 days to object to the liability order being made. This should be done in writing by returning the notice stating the grounds of the objection and enclosing evidence. If objections are received, a hearing is held. Even if the non-resident parent does not attend, the sheriff must still consider his objections.[188] As in England and Wales, the sheriff court cannot consider whether the non-resident parent is liable, nor whether liability has been correctly calculated. An extract of the liability order may be issued 14 days after the order is actually made. All the forms used in this procedure are included in the child support rules.[189]

Enforcing a liability order in England and Wales

The CSA can decide to levy distress or take action in the county court. The Operational Improvement Plan states that the CSA will utilise the full range of sanctions available, including driving licence removal, imprisonment or seizure of assets, where appropriate.[190]

Distress

If a liability order has been made, the amount specified on the order can be enforced in England and Wales by distress (ie, seizure) and sale of goods.[191] The bailiff levying distress must either carry written authority to hand to the non-resident parent, or leave at the address where distress is to be levied a copy of the relevant regulations and a memorandum setting out the amount to be levied.[192] If payment is made in full, the levy of the goods or the subsequent sale will not take place.[193]

Certain items cannot be seized. These are:[194]
- tools, books, vehicles and other items necessary for work; *and*
- clothing, bedding, furniture, household equipment and provisions necessary to meet the basic domestic needs of the non-resident parent and any member of his family who lives with him; *and*
- any money, promissory notes, bond or other securities for money belonging to the non-resident parent.

Charges can be made at each of the stages involved in distress proceedings[195] – eg, a £10 charge for sending a letter, a charge for making a visit to the property (the maximum for this charge is £12.50 if the amount owed is less than £100, or if the amount is more than £100, £12.50 plus 4 per cent of the next £400 due, 2.5 per cent of the next £1,500, 1 per cent of the next £8,000 and 0.25 per cent of anything more).

Any person aggrieved by the levy, or by an attempt to levy distress, can appeal to the magistrates' court by making a complaint to the court.[196] If the court is satisfied that the levy was irregular, it may order the goods to be returned if they have been seized, and order compensation in respect of any goods sold.

County court action

Once a liability order has been made, the CSA can arrange for the county court to record the order as if it were a judgment debt.[197] This record is publicly available and damages the non-resident parent's credit rating. The CSA can also use the county court to recover any amount that remains unpaid.[198] This means applying for a charging order or using third party debt proceedings.

A **charging order** allows a debt to be registered against certain assets, such as land, stocks, shares and any interest the non-resident parent may have in a trust. If a charge is registered and the assets are sold, the debt due under the liability order can be recovered from the proceeds of the sale. In some cases it may not be possible to register a charge, in which case a caution against dealings may be obtained to prevent the property from being sold without the CSA's knowledge. Once a charge or caution has been registered the CSA can consider applying to the courts for an order of sale.

A **third party debt order** can be obtained by the CSA if it is aware that the non-resident parent has a bank account or is owed money by a third party. The order freezes funds in the account and requires that person to release funds to the CSA up to the amount of the liability order.

Enforcing a liability order in Scotland

In Scotland, a liability order can be enforced by diligence.[199] The form of the demand for payment sent by the sheriff's court is given in the child support rules.[200] It states the sum owed, including court charges, and specifies that further action will be taken if payment is not made within 14 days (28 days if the non-resident parent is outside the UK). Otherwise, there are no procedures specific to child maintenance. The procedures are the same as for any other debt enforced in Scotland following the granting of a liability order.[201]

The liability order may be enforced by inhibition of sale of property and arrestment of bank accounts.[202]

Disqualification from driving or imprisonment

The CSA may take action for disqualification from driving or imprisonment where all other methods of recovery have failed.[203]

Before taking action every attempt must be made to contact the non-resident parent. Where no phone contact has been successful during the enforcement action, a face-to-face visit may be appropriate.

When considering whether to take this action the CSA should consider:[204]

- the welfare of any child(ren) affected;
- whether all the appropriate procedures have been followed;
- any serious ill-health of the non-resident parent or member of his family;
- whether the action could affect future regular maintenance;
- whether the CSA could be considered insensitive in pursuing action;

- whether the non-resident parent has sufficient funds to pay the debt;
- whether the non-resident parent is under 18 and would count as a child for child support purposes (commitment to prison will not be an option here, but disqualification from driving can still be considered); *or*
- whether the non-resident parent is on benefit.

If it is decided not to pursue the action, the person with care should be informed.[205] The case will be reviewed in three months time to consider further enforcement action.

Action for committal or disqualification from driving

In England and Wales, if distress and/or county court proceedings have been tried, or in Scotland diligence via arrestments or inhibitions on sale, but an amount is still due under the liability order, the CSA can apply to the court to issue either a warrant committing the non-resident parent to prison or an order disqualifying him from driving.[206] The hearing must take place in the presence of the non-resident parent.[207] The court can summon him to appear in court and produce his driving licence.[208] If he does not appear, the court may issue a warrant (citation in Scotland) for his arrest.[209] The CSA can make representations to the court on whether to issue a warrant or order disqualification.[210] The non-resident parent may reply to these.

The court must enquire into the non-resident parent's means, whether he needs a driving licence to make a living and whether there has been 'wilful refusal or culpable neglect' on his part.[211] Only if there has been, can the court commit the non-resident parent to prison or disqualify him from driving;[212] the decision whether to do so is at the discretion of the court. A non-resident parent should seek advice in preparing a statement of his income and outgoings.[213] A written statement from an employer will be accepted as proof of earnings.[214] The CSA can appoint its own staff to apply for committal and appear at related hearings before magistrates in England and Wales or a sheriff in Scotland.[215]

Imprisonment

If the court decides that there has been wilful refusal or culpable neglect and committal is appropriate, a warrant for imprisonment will be issued.[216] A warrant for imprisonment cannot be issued against a non-resident parent who is under 18.[217]

Instead of immediate committal, the court usually fixes a term of imprisonment and postpones it on conditions, usually of regular payments.[218] A warrant of commitment is issued stating the total amount outstanding, including child maintenance, penalty payments, fees (interest in some cases – see p443), court costs and any other charges.[219] If the amount is paid in full, the non-resident parent will not be imprisoned.

The maximum period of imprisonment is six weeks.[220] If, after the warrant has been issued, part-payment is made, the period of imprisonment is reduced by the same proportion as that by which the debt has been reduced.[221]

The court cannot write off the arrears, so if full payment is not made, arrears will still exist following the period of imprisonment. In this case, the CSA will look at the circumstances again to check whether any earlier enforcement options would be appropriate, and should consider applying for a further liabilty order.[222] If a warrant is not issued or the court does not fix a term of imprisonment, the CSA can renew the application at a later date on the grounds that the non-resident parent's circumstances have changed.[223]

Disqualification from driving

If the court decides that there has been wilful refusal or culpable neglect and disqualification from driving is appropriate, an order will be issued.[224] The order may be issued but its implementation suspended on conditions – eg, regular payments. The order will state the amount outstanding, including child maintenance, interest, court costs and any other charges.[225] If the amount is paid in full, the order is revoked.

The maximum period of disqualification is two years.[226] If after the order has been issued part-payment is made, the period of disqualification is reduced.[227] If the amount is paid in full, the order is revoked. If at the end of the period of disqualification the arrears have not been paid in full, the CSA may apply again for imprisonment or disqualification.[228]

Bankruptcy

The CSA does not pursue bankruptcy (sequestration in Scotland), but a non-resident parent may have child support maintenance arrears when he is made bankrupt.[229]

In England and Wales, the CSA can take action to obtain a liability order including amounts due before the date of the bankruptcy.

In Scotland, a liability order can only recover amounts due after the date of the sequestration.

In either case, the CSA may decide not to enforce the order because it may not be practical – eg, a charging order/inhibition of sale may not be effective, as any property may already have been sold to pay off creditors. The CSA may secure a liability order to remind the non-resident parent that he cannot avoid his maintenance responsibility.

Bankruptcy/sequestration may not prevent the CSA considering action for committal to prison or disqualification from driving – eg, the non-resident parent may have a steady income and it would be up to him to show in court that he cannot afford to meet his child support liability.

---

6. Existing 'old rules' and conversion cases

Existing 'old rules' maintenance assessments are collected and enforced in much the same way as 'new rules' maintenance calculations – involving negotiations, deduction from earnings orders, liability orders and action for committal or disqualification from driving. Some differences are indicated in the rest of this chapter – eg, how deductions from benefit can be made. However, there are some other important differences which we outline here.

The legislation applied to existing 'old rules' is that prior to its reform by the Child Support, Pensions and Social Security Act 2000 and associated regulations. On conversion the case comes under the reformed legislation.

Penalty payments do not apply to 'old rules' cases; once the case converts, the 'new rules' penalty payments may be applied. This means that penalty payments can only be made in respect of missed or late payments after the date of conversion.

Voluntary payments under the 'new rules' are governed by statute – ie, there is law which stipulates how they are dealt with. In 'old rules' case the Child Support Agency (CSA) exercises discretion in how it treats such payments. A complaint may be possible if a parent is not happy with the way in which they are treated (see Chapter 21).

Deduction from earnings orders (DEOs) are calculated and applied in a slightly different way. At conversion, any old arrears uncollected under the previous order may be included in a new one issued under the 'new rules'.

Certain non-resident parents with a maintenance assessment may make a deferred debt agreement under the **temporary compensation scheme**. This agreement may continue in force after conversion. If it is discharged, the person with care may be eligible for a **deferred debt compensation payment** (see p457).

Deduction from earnings orders

Deductions made are based on the **normal deduction rate** and the **protected earnings rate**.

Normal deduction rate

The normal deduction rate is the amount that will be deducted each payday as long as net earnings are not brought below the protected earnings rate. The normal deduction rate can include current maintenance liability and amounts for arrears and interest due. No arrears or interest can be included if they would have brought the non-resident parent's disposable income, on the date the current assessment was made, below the protected income level (not the protected earnings rate) *minus* the minimum payment (see p199).[230] This does not apply if the current assessment is an interim maintenance assessment (IMA – see p367). See Chapter 14 for protected income level and disposable income.

Protected earnings rate

The protected earnings rate is the level below which earnings must not be reduced by the deductions. Unless a Category A or D IMA is in force, it is set at the exempt income level (see Chapter 11).[231] Where a Category A or D IMA is in force, the protected earnings rate is either:[232]

- if the CSA knows something of the non-resident parent's circumstances:
  - the income support (IS) single or couple personal allowance;
  - the IS personal allowance for any children under 16 living with him;
  - any relevant IS premiums (see Appendix 2); *plus*
  - £30; *or*
- otherwise, the IS adult personal allowance plus £30.

Where there is no assessment in force, the protected earnings rate is the exempt income level for the last assessment. If the non-resident parent satisfies the CSA that his circumstances have since changed, the protected earnings rate is the exempt income level he would have if his assessment were superseded.[233] If the last assessment was a Category A or C IMA, the protected earnings rate is still worked out as for IMAs.

Administering a deduction from earnings order

The rules are almost identical to those described in this chapter – ie, each payday the employer:

- should make a deduction from net earnings at the normal deduction rate. If this reduces earnings below the protected earnings rate the deduction is adjusted and the unpaid amount is carried forward to the next payday;[234]
- may deduct up to £1 as an administrative charge. This can be made even if this would bring earnings below the protected earnings rate.[235]

However, in addition to these rules, if on any payday net earnings are below the protected earnings rate, no deduction or charge can be made. When this occurs, the difference between net earnings and protected earnings is carried over and treated as additional protected earnings on the next payday.[236] For an illustration of how this operates in practice, see Example 18.1 in the 2001/02 edition of this *Handbook*.

If two or more DEOs have been issued, the employer should deal with the earliest first.[237]

Temporary compensation payment scheme (deferred debt)

From 31 January 2001 a temporary compensation payment scheme was introduced to allow the CSA to reduce the arrears liability of a non-resident parent in certain circumstances.[238] In CSA terminology this means that the arrears were classed as a deferred debt. The scheme only applied to parents with assessments made before certain dates (the latest being 1 April 2005), and who had at least six months' arrrears, at least half of which were caused because of unreasonable delay by the CSA.

If a non-resident parent entered and kept to an agreement to pay regular maintenance and repay the arrears, the CSA could reduce the amount of arrears to be repaid.[239] Throughout the period of the agreement the parent was still liable for the full amount, which could be enforced immediately if he defaulted, unless the default was outside his control or due to exceptional circumstances. For more information about what happened if a non-resident parent defaulted, see the 2006/07 edition of this *Handbook*. Agreements could only be made before 1 April 2005 and all had to expire before 1 April 2006.[240]

The CSA could make a deferred debt compensatory payment to the person with care, in respect of all or some of the arrears which were not to be collected if the non-resident parent kept to the agreement. This was a discretionary decision. For more information about deferred debt compensation payments, see the 2006/07 edition of this *Handbook*. While technically the deferred debt was not written off, it would not be enforced by the CSA if the non-resident parent kept to the agreement for the full period.

Notes

1 s29(1) CSA 1991
2 s30(1) CSA 1991
3 Reg 3(3A) CSF Regs as revoked by reg 4 CS(CEMA) Regs

1. Payment of child maintenance
4 Reg 3 CS(C&E) Regs
5 Reg 2 CS(C&E) Regs
6 Reg 5 CS(C&E) Regs
7 Reg 4 CS(C&E) Regs
8 Reg 5 CS(AIAMA) Regs
9 Reg 6 CS(C&E) Regs
10 Reg 7(1) CS(C&E) Regs
11 Reg 7(2) CS(C&E) Regs
12 s29 CSA 1991; reg 2 CS(C&E) Regs
13 PG, Collections, Methods of Collection (MOCs) Available to the NRP
14 PG, Collections, Non-maintenance Direct
15 s29(1)(a) CSA 1991
16 s29(1)(b) CSA 1991
17 PG, Collections, Failure of Maintenance Direct Reported by the PWC

18 CSA Client Charter 2007
19 Reg 8 CS(AIAMA) Regs
20 Reg 3(1) CS(C&E) Regs
21 Reg 3(1A) CS(C&E) Regs
22 PG, Collections, Non-maintenance Direct
23 Reg 3(2) CS(C&E) Regs
24 Reg 6 CS(C&E) Regs
25 PG, Collections, Non-maintenance Direct
26 Reg 5(1) CS(C&E) Regs; PG, Payments
27 s43 CSA 1991
28 s43 CSA 1991; Sch 9B SS(C&P) Regs
29 Sch 4 para 4(2) CSA 1991; reg 4(2) CS(MCSC) Regs
30 Reg 4(3)(a) CS(MCSC) Regs
31 Reg 4(3)(b) CS(MCSC) Regs
32 Reg 35(l) SS(C&P) Regs; Sch 9B SS(C&P) Regs
33 Sch 9 para 7A(1) SS(C&P) Regs
34 Sch 9 paras 1 and 2(1)(f) SS(C&P) Regs
35 Sch 9 para 2(2) SS(C&P) Regs
36 Sch 9 para 8 SS(C&P) Regs

37 Sch 9 para 9 SS(C&P) Regs
38 Sch 9 para 7A(4) SS(C&P) Regs
39 Sch 5 para 9 CS(MASC) Regs
40 Reg 4(1) CS(C&E) Regs
41 Reg 4(2) CS(C&E) Regs
42 Reg 6 CS(C&E) Regs
43 Reg 5(3) CS(C&E) Regs
44 CSA Client Charter 2007
45 PG, Payments, Compensation Payments
46 PG, Services of the CSA, Post April 2002
47 Reg 9 CS(AIAMA) Regs
48 Reg 10(1)(a) CS(AIAMA) Regs
49 PG, Collections, Calculating the
    Overpayment Recovery Schedule
50 Reg 10 CS(AIAMA) Regs; PG,
    Collections, Calculating the
    Overpayment Recovery Schedule
51 PG, Receipt Assignments and Allocation,
    Determine the Reason for the
    Unexpected Receipt
52 PG, Receipt Assignments and Allocation,
    Manually Allocate Unexpected Receipt
53 PG, Receipt Assignments and Allocation,
    Receipt Intended as a Gift
54 PG, Receipt Assignments and Allocation,
    Refunds
55 Reg 10(1)(b) CS(AIAMA) Regs
56 Reg 10(3A)(b) CS(AIAMA) Regs
57 Reg 10(4) CS(AIAMA) Regs
58 Reg 10(2) and (3) CS(AIAMA) Regs; regs
    3A(6) and 15D SS&CS(D&A) Regs
59 Reg 11 CS(AIAMA) Regs; reg 15C(6)
    SS&CS(DA) Regs
60 Regs 12, 13, 14, 15 and 16 CS(AIAMA)
    Regs; regs 3A(6), 6A(9) and 30A
    SS&CS(DA) Regs
61 s41B CSA 1991
62 s41B(1A) CSA 1991
63 Regs 10A(1) and 10B CS(AIAMA) Regs
64 s41B(6) CSA 1991; reg 10A(2)
    CS(AIAMA) Regs

2. Collection of other payments
65 s30 CSA 1991; CS(CEOFM) Regs
66 Reg 5 CS(CEOFM) Regs
67 Reg 2 CS(CEOFM) Regs
68 Regs 3 and 4 CS(CEOFM) Regs
69 s30(3) CSA 1991; PG, Receipt
    Assignments and Allocation,
    Allocation Rules
70 PG, Receipt Assignments and Allocation,
    Receipt Received for Multiple Cases
71 Reg 6(3) CS(CEMA) Regs
72 PG, Collections, Negotiating other
    Liabilities

3. Arrears
73 Reg 8A CS(MAJ) Regs 1992
74 PG, Collections, Notifying the NRP of
    the Collection Schedule
75 Reg 7 CS(C&E) Regs
76 PG, Arrears Management, Arrears
    Amount
77 s28J CSA 1991 as inserted by s20
    CSPSSA 2000
78 Reg 3(b) CS(VP) Regs
79 Reg 3(a) CS(VP) Regs
80 Regs 2(2) and 4(b) CS(VP) Regs; PG,
    Collections, Payments made as
    Maintenance Direct to the PWC
81 Reg 4(a) CS(VP) Regs
82 PG, Collections, Conflicting Evidence
83 Reg 5(10) CS(AIAMA) Regs
84 PG, Arrears Management, Arrears
    Amount
85 PG, Arrears Management, Arrears
    Amount
86 PG, Arrears Management, Suspending
    Debt
87 First protocol, Art 1 ECHR
88 s41(2) and (2A) CSA 1991; reg 8
    CS(AIAMA) Regs
89 s43 CSA 1991; Sch 9B SS(C&P) Regs
90 Sch 9 para 7B SS(C&P) Regs
91 PG, Arrears Management, Contact NRP
    to Investigate Late/Non-payment
92 PG, Arrears Management, Contact NRP
    to Investigate Late/Non-payment
93 PG, Arrears Management, Contact NRP
    to Investigate Late/Non-payment
94 PG, Arrears Management, Suspending
    Debt
95 Reg 2 CS(AIAMA) Regs
96 PG, Arrears Management, Investigating
    Late/Non-payment of Liability
97 Reg 2(4) CS(AIAMA) Regs
98 PG, Arrears Management, Suspending
    Debt
99 s41A CSA 1991
100 Independent Case Examiner for the
    Child Support Agency, Annual Report
    2006/2007
101 CSA Operational Improvement Plan
    2006-2009
102 PG, Payments, Advance Payment of
    Maintenance
103 PG, Payments, Maladministration
104 PG, Payments, Making the Advance
    Payment Amount to the PWC
105 *R v Secretary of State for Work and
    Pensions ex parte Kehoe* [2005] UKHL 48
    (1 July 2005); the case concerned Art
    6(1) ECHR
106 Reg 4(1) CS(AIAMA) Regs

4. **Deduction from earnings orders**

107 s31 CSA 1991
108 PG, Collections, Non-maintenance Direct
109 PG, Arrears Management, Considerations before Imposing a DEO
110 CSA Operational Improvement Plan 2006-2009
111 CSA Client Charter 2007
112 *R v Secretary of State for Social Security ex parte Biggin* [1995] 2 FCR 595, [1995] 1 FLR 851
113 PG, Arrears Management, DEO/DER, Employer Outside CSA Jurisdiction
114 Sch 1 para 10 CS(NIRA) Regs
115 CSA(CA)O; Army Act 1955; Air Force Act 1955; Naval Forces Act 1947; Merchant Shipping Act 1970
116 s31(5) CSA 1991
117 s31(6) CSA 1991
118 s31(7) CSA 1991
119 s32(8)-(11) CSA 1991
120 Reg 9 CS(C&E) Regs
121 Reg 14(1) CS(C&E) Regs
122 Reg 14(2) CS(C&E) Regs
123 s32(8) and (11) CSA 1991; reg 25(aa) CS(C&E) Regs
124 Reg 1(3)(b) CS(C&E) Regs
125 s32(8) and (11) CSA 1991; reg 25(ab) and (b) CS(C&E) Regs
126 Reg 15(1) CS(C&E) Regs
127 Reg 15(2) CS(C&E) Regs
128 Reg 16(1) CS(C&E) Regs
129 Reg 16(2) CS(C&E) Regs
130 Reg 16(3) CS(C&E) Regs
131 Reg 13 CS(C&E) Regs
132 s8(2)(b) ERA 1996
133 s9 ERA 1996
134 s12(3)-(5) ERA 1996
135 Reg 8(3) and (4) CS(C&E) Regs
136 Reg 8(4)(a) CS(C&E) Regs
137 Reg 8(4)(b) CS(C&E) Regs
138 Reg 8(5) CS(C&E) Regs
139 Reg 9 CS(C&E) Regs
140 Regs 10(1) and 11(1) CS(C&E) Regs
141 Reg 9(d) CS(C&E) Regs
142 Reg 11(2) CS(C&E) Regs
143 Reg 12(6) CS(C&E) Regs
144 Reg 12(20) CS(C&E) Regs
145 Reg 12(4) CS(C&E) Regs
146 Reg 12(3A) CS(C&E) Regs
147 Reg 24(2)(a) CS(C&E) Regs
148 Reg 24(2)(b) CS(C&E) Regs
149 Reg 24(2)(a) and (3) CS(C&E) Regs
150 Reg 17 CS(C&E) Regs
151 Reg 18 CS(C&E) Regs
152 Reg 19 CS(C&E) Regs
153 Reg 20(1) CS(C&E) Regs
154 Reg 20(2) CS(C&E) Regs
155 Reg 21(1) CS(C&E) Regs
156 Reg 21(4) CS(C&E) Regs
157 Reg 21(5) CS(C&E) Regs
158 Reg 21(6) CS(C&E) Regs
159 Reg 22(1) CS(C&E) Regs
160 Reg 22(2) CS(C&E) Regs
161 Reg 22(3) CS(C&E) Regs
162 Reg 8(1) CS(C&E) Regs
163 Rule 5 and form 6 AS(CSR)
164 Reg 22(4) CS(C&E) Regs
165 s32(6) CSA 1991
166 *Secretary of State for Social Security v Shotton* [1996] 2 FLR 241
167 ss48 and 49 CSA 1991; rule 6 AS(CSR)

5. **Enforcement**

168 CSA Client Charter, February 2007
169 PG, Enforcement, Deciding if Debt Enforcement Action is Suitable
170 PG, Enforcement, Applying for a Liability Order
171 *DSS v Butler* [1995] 1 WLR 1528, [1995] 4 All ER 193
172 Reg 28(2) and (2a) CS(C&E) Regs
173 *R Sutherland (on the application of) v Secretary of State for Work and Pensions* [2004] EWHC 800 (Admin), 25 March 2004
174 s33 CSA 1991
175 s33(3) CSA 1991
176 s33(4) CSA 1991
177 HC *Hansard*, 2 February 1996, col990
178 Reg 29 CS(C&E) Regs; rule 3 AS(CSR)
179 ss48 and 49 CSA 1991; rule 6 AS(CSR)
180 Reg 27 CS(C&E) Regs
181 PG, NRP Responds to the Warning Letter
182 Reg 28 CS(C&E) Regs
183 *Farley v CSA and another* [2006] UKHL 31 (28 June 2006)
184 PG, Enforcement, NRP Responds to the Warning Letter
185 Reg 29(1) and Sch 1 CS(C&E) Regs
186 *Secretary of State for Social Security v Love* [1996] SLT 78
187 Rule 2 AS(CSR)
188 *Secretary of State for Social Security v Nicol* [1996] SLT 34
189 Forms 1-4 AS(CSR)
190 CSA Operational Improvement Plan 2006-2009
191 s35 CSA 1991
192 Reg 30(2) CS(C&E) Regs
193 Reg 30(4) and (5) CS(C&E) Regs
194 s35(3) and (4) CSA 1991
195 Reg 32 and Sch 2 CS(C&E) Regs
196 Reg 31 CS(C&E) Regs
197 s33(5) CSA 1991

198 s36 CSA 1991
199 ss38(1)(a) and 58(9) CSA 1991
200 Rule 4 and form 5 AS(CSR)
201 under Part II Debtors (Scotland) Act 1987
202 s38(1)(b) CSA 1991
203 s39A CSA 1991
204 PG, Enforcement, Is Commitment to Prison or Disqualification from Driving Appropriate
205 PG, Enforcement, Deciding Not to Apply for Commitment to Prison/ Driving Licence Action
206 ss39A(2) and 40(1)-(11) CSA 1991
207 s39A(3) CSA 1991
208 Reg 35(1) CS(C&E) Regs
209 s40(11) CSA 1991
210 s39A(4) CSA 1991
211 s39A(3) CSA 1991; PG, Enforcement, Court Hearing
212 s40A(1) CSA 1991
213 ss40(5) and 40A(3) CSA 1991
214 ss40(11) and 40A(8) CSA 1991; req 35(2) CS(C&E) Regs
215 ss18 and 49 CSA 1991
216 ss40 and 40B CSA 1991
217 ss40(5) and 40A(3) CSA 1991
218 ss40(3) and 40B(1) CSA 1991
219 Sch 3 CS(C&E) Regs
220 ss40(7) and 40A(5) CSA 1991
221 Reg 34(5) and (6) CS(C&E) Regs
222 Enforcement Guide, Chapter 7, If Commitment to Prison/ Disqualification Proceedings Unsuccessful
223 Reg 33(3) CS(C&E) Regs
224 s40B CSA 1991
225 Reg 35(4)-(5) and Sch 4 CS(C&E) Regs
226 s40B(1) CSA 1991
227 s40B(5) CSA 1991
228 s40B(7) CSA 1991
229 PG, Enforcement, NRP Bankrupt (England and Wales); Sequestration (Scotland)

6. **Existing 'old rules' and conversion cases**
230 Reg 10 CS(C&E) Regs
231 Reg 11(2) CS(C&E) Regs
232 Reg 11(3) CS(C&E) Regs
233 Reg 11(4) CS(C&E) Regs
234 Reg 12(4) CS(C&E) Regs
235 Reg 12(2) CS(C&E) Regs
236 Reg 12(5) CS(C&E) Regs

237 Reg 24(1) CS(C&E) Regs
238 Reg 2(2) CSPSSA(Comm 13)O
239 s27(3) CSPSSA 2000
240 s27(5) CSPSSA 2000 as modified by reg 2 CS(TCPS)(MA) Regs

Chapter 21

Complaints

This chapter covers:
1. Complaining to the Child Support Agency (p465)
2. Complaining to Jobcentre Plus (p465)
3. Complaining to the Independent Case Examiner (p466)
4. Using an MP (p467)
5. Complaining to the Ombudsman (p467)

There are many reasons why people using the Child Support Agency (CSA) may wish to complain. Complaints are obviously appropriate in situations where there has been rudeness, discrimination, poor administration (eg, lost papers) and delays. They may also be appropriate in situations where the CSA (or Jobcentre Plus) has a discretion about how to act – eg, where enforcement action is not taken.

A complaint is a separate process to an appeal or revision request, and does not necessarily lead to a decision being changed. However, it may be appropriate where the decision is one with no right of appeal. In some of these cases, judicial review may also be possible (instead of, or as well as, making a complaint). Legal advice should be sought if a judicial review is being considered (see also p383). In some cases, an appeal may be appropriate as well as a complaint – eg, if parent thinks a maintenance calculation has been wrongly calculated and appeals against the decision, but also wishes to complain about delay in making the calculation.

It is important to be clear which organisation has caused the problem. In most cases this will be the CSA. However, interviews conducted with parents on income support or income-based jobseeker's allowance are carried out by Jobcentre Plus. Complaints about staff at these interviews, access arrangements for them, delays in decisions on 'good cause' and any other Jobcentre Plus function should be directed at Jobcentre Plus. If a parent (or qualifying child in Scotland) has appealed, and there are delays or poor administration on the part of the Tribunals Service, the complaint should be directed to the Tribunals Service. For information about making complaints to the Tribunals Service, see CPAG *Welfare Benefits and Tax Credits Handbook.*

1. **Complaining to the Child Support Agency**

Most complaints involving child support will be made to the Child Support Agency (CSA). Complaints are likely to fall into two groups.

- Complaints about standards of service, including delays, staff communications, poor administration and lost papers.
- Complaints about how discretionary decisions are made – eg, failure to follow guidance, following it too strictly or failing to take all the relevant circumstances into account. It may be appropriate to seek advice on whether judicial review is also appropriate.

A parent (or qualifying child in Scotland) should begin her/his complaint by contacting the person who has been dealing with her/his case, or the manager of that person. This information should be on letters sent by the CSA. The complaint can be made either by telephone or in writing, but records of all communications should be kept in case it is necessary to take the complaint further.

If the CSA officer concerned, or her/his manager, cannot resolve the complaint, the complainant can take things further by contacting the complaints resolution team at the office handling the case. All contact details of Child Support Agency Centres (CSACs) are in Appendix 1, or on the CSA website. Contact details should also be given on any letters which have been sent. An outline of the procedure, and useful information about the CSA's standards of service, is given in the CSA Client Charter leaflet.[1] More detailed information about the complaints procedure is also given in the leaflet *How Do I Complain About the Service I Get From the Child Support Agency?* (CSL 308).

If, after going through this procedure, a complainant is not satisfied that the complaint has been resolved, s/he can contact the Independent Case Examiner (see p466). A complainant can only do this if:

- s/he has received a final reply from or on behalf of the Chief Executive of the CSA; *and*
- no more than six months have passed since s/he received that final reply. Usually, this reply will be from a senior CSA manager.

When complaining to the CSA, it may be useful to quote its standards of service. These may also be useful when considering whether, or at what point, to make a complaint.

Standards of service

It is useful to refer to the CSA's standards of service when making a complaint or considering whether to make one. A summary of standards of service can be found in the CSA's Client Charter.[2]

Many of the standards are mentioned elsewhere in this *Handbook*. This is not an exhaustive list.

- The CSA aims to start gathering information from the non-resident parent within four weeks of maintenance application, if it has contact details.
- The CSA aims to make an accurate decision on an application within 12 weeks (but in some cases a decision may take up to 26 weeks).
- Where the collection service is being used, the CSA aims to make payments to the person with care within a week of receiving the money from the non-resident parent.
- The CSA aims to answer telephone calls within one minute.
- The CSA aims to respond to letters, and either resolve complaints or agree on the next course of action, within three weeks of receiving them.

Performance targets are also set for the CSA by the Secretary of State for Work and Pensions and published in the Department for Work and Pensions (DWP) business plan. These are broad targets for the whole of its caseload, and so may be less useful to complainants. They include long-term targets such as aiming to have payment made via the collection service, or a maintenance direct arrangement agreed by non-resident parents in 66 per cent of cases (across 'old' and 'new' rules) by 31 March 2008.[3] The Operational Improvement Plan contains other long-term targets towards which the CSA is working.[4]

Compensation

If a parent (or qualifying child in Scotland) has lost out because of CSA error, delay or standard of service, it may be appropriate to request compensation or a special payment when making a complaint. *Ex-gratia* payments can be made where someone has suffered an actual financial loss, significant delay or has been caused severe distress or inconvenience. A complainant has no legal right to these payments, but it can sometimes be useful to make it clear that financial compensation would help to resolve the complaint. Where a complainant is not offered compensation and believes that it should have been offered, s/he can consider taking the complaint further.

Special payments may be appropriate where there has been:
- significant delay in issuing forms, making calculations or reviewing liability. It is useful to refer to the Client Charter when assessing how severe the delay has been;
- delays or errors in enforcement;
- delays in passing maintenance to the person with care;
- wrong identification of non-resident parents;
- financial loss because of CSA error – eg, in bank, postal or telephone charges;
- other examples of gross inconvenience, embarrassment, breach of confidentiality or severe distress.

The publication *Financial Redress for Maladministration* applies to the CSA as it does to other parts of the DWP. This guide is available from the DWP website (see Appendix 1) and should also be provided in CSACs. It gives guidance on circumstances in which financial compensation should be paid, and how much is appropriate.

2. **Complaining to Jobcentre Plus**

As part of the Department for Work and Pensions, Jobcentre Plus has a similar complaints procedure to the Child Support Agency (CSA). Parents with care on income support or income-based jobseeker's allowance may have a complaint about the way in which Jobcentre Plus has dealt with them – eg, the procedure in 'good cause' interviews or delays in communication. Non-resident parents may have a complaint about the way in which their maintenance payments have (or have not) been deducted from their benefit.

It is important to remember that some decisions carry the right of appeal, and a parent can request a revision or appeal against them. It may be necessary to do this as well as, or instead of, appealing. For example, a parent can appeal against a reduced benefit decision made by Jobcentre Plus.

Decisions about the payment of benefit do not carry the right of appeal. A non-resident parent on benefit may disagree about the rate of maintenance he should be paying (and therefore with the deduction being made from his benefit). If so, he should appeal to the CSA about the maintenance decision. Any complaint to Jobcentre Plus would be about the administration of the deductions.

The Jobcentre Plus complaints procedure is described in the leaflet *Tell Us What You Think*. A complainant should begin by speaking to the person s/he has been dealing with, or the manager of that person. If this does not resolve matters, the district manager or delivery manager for the office concerned should be contacted. The third stage of the process, if the complaint is still not resolved, is to write to the Chief Executive of Jobcentre Plus. The Chief Executive will ensure that the complaint is fully considered by an appropriate senior officer.

Like the CSA, Jobcentre Plus can make compensatory payments if these are seen as appropriate. More information about compensation payments is provided in CPAG's *Welfare Benefits and Tax Credits Handbook*.

If a complainant has gone through every stage of the Jobcentre Plus complaints procedure and is still not satisfied, s/he can complain to the Independent Case Examiner (see p466), or, via her/his MP, to the Parliamentary Ombudsman.

3. Complaining to the Independent Case Examiner

The Independent Case Examiner's office (ICE) is a body set up to help resolve the situation where people feel that certain government agencies have not dealt with them fairly or resolved complaints to their satisfaction. ICE is an independent referee, completely separate from the Child Support Agency (CSA) or any other government department. ICE was set up to deal with complaints about the CSA, but since April 2007 it also deals with complaints about several other government agencies and businesses, including Jobcentre Plus and the Northern Ireland Social Security Agency.

A complainant can only go through ICE after using the CSA's (or other agency's) complaints procedure in full. A final response from the agency is normally a reply from the Chief Executive, or on her/his behalf (eg, from a senior manager in the CSA). The complaint to ICE should be made within six months of the CSA's final response. ICE cannot look at complaints made after this date.

ICE cannot consider a complaint which is being investigated, or has been investigated, by the Parliamentary Ombudsman (see p467). A complainant may have the choice of complaining directly to the Ombudsman via an MP, but the Ombudsman's office will usually encourage people to use ICE first.

Complaints can be made in writing or by telephone on 0845 606 0777. There is a form which complainants can use, attached to the ICE leaflet *Our Service and Standards*. The complainant should include all relevant facts, including the CSA office s/he is complaining about, details of the complaint and the CSA's response. ICE can give complainants further advice on making their complaint if required.

ICE will investigate and decide whether or not it can accept the complaint. If it can, the first attempt will be to settle the complaint by suggesting ways in which the CSA and the complainant can come to an agreement. If this fails, ICE prepares a formal report setting out how the complaint arose and how it believes it should be settled. If it makes a recommendation of action to the CSA, this is almost always followed. ICE aims to clear cases within 34 weeks.[5] Other details of its standards of service are available in its leaflet or at www.ind-case-exam.org.uk.

4. Using an MP

It may be appropriate for a parent (or qualifying child in Scotland) to consult her/his MP at any stage of the complaints process. An MP may be able to provide advocacy or other support to get the matter resolved more quickly. However, consulting an MP is particularly important if the complainant has been through the complaints process of the Child Support Agency (or Jobcentre Plus) without a satisfactory resolution, and even more so if s/he has used the Independent Case Examiner, but still wants to take matters further.

An MP may be able to advise on whether taking the complaint further is worthwhile. It may be that the complainant is unhappy about an aspect of child support law, in which case a complaint is not appropriate. Whether the issue concerns law or procedure, an MP may be willing to take matters further to try and get legislation changed or practice improved. The MP may also (or in addition) refer the complaint to the Parliamentary Ombudsman (see below).

A parent can find out who her/his MP is by using a constituency locator on the internet, or by ringing the House of Commons information service on 020 7219 4272. Most MPs have surgeries held locally where they meet constituents. Alternatively, the complaint can be passed to the MP in writing.

5. **Complaining to the Ombudsman**

The Parliamentary and Health Service Ombudsman investigates complaints about a range of government departments and other public bodies. The complainant should first give the organisation a full chance to respond to the complaint and put things right. For complaints about the Child Support Agency (and, from April 2007, Jobcentre Plus), a complainant has the option of first using the Independent Case Examiner (ICE) (see p466). This avoids the need to contact her/his MP. The Ombudsman's office will encourage people to use ICE first.

The first stage of using the Ombudsman is to send the complaint to the relevant MP who will decide whether or not to pass it on to the Ombudsman. Normally, the Ombudsman will not investigate if the complaint is passed to an MP more than 12 months after the complainant became aware that s/he had a good reason to complain – ie, that there was a need to take the complaint further.

If the complaint is investigated, the MP will be sent a full report. The Ombudsman may recommend an apology and possibly compensation. Ombudsman reports can also lead to changed practices and procedures in the agencies under investigation.

More information about the Ombudsman is available at www.ombudsman.org.uk, or from the helpline on 0845 015 4033.

Notes

1. **Complaining to the Child Support Agency**
   1 CSA Client Charter 2007
   2 CSA Client Charter 2007
   3 DWP Business Plan 2007-2008
   4 CSA Operational Improvement Plan 2006-2009

3. **Complaining to the Independent Case Examiner**
   5 *Our Service and Standards,* Independent Case Examiner, June 2006

Appendices

Appendices

Appendix 1
Useful addresses

Department for Work and Pensions
www.dwp.gov.uk

Child Support Agency

Chief Executive
Stephen Geraghty
PO Box 55
Brierley Hill
Dudley
West Midlands DY5 1YL
Tel: 0845 7133133
www.csa.gov.uk

Complaints
The Office of the Chief Executive
(M0801)
Durham House
Washington
Tyne and Wear NE38 7SF

Child Support Agency Centres

Hastings CSAC
(South East Business Unit)
Ashdown House
Sedlescombe Road North
St Leonards on Sea
East Sussex TN37 7NL

Offices covered:
Acton, Brixton, Lewisham,
Tunbridge Wells, London Highgate,
Croydon, Bloomsbury, Bromley,
Ilford, Canterbury, Colchester,
Basildon, Wandsworth, Woolwich

Plymouth CSAC
(South West Business Unit)
Clearbrook House
Towerfield Drive
Bickleigh Down Business Park
Plymouth
Devon PL6 7TN

Offices covered:
Bristol, Crownhill (Plymouth),
Exeter, Gloucester, Guildford,
Hounslow, Isle of Wight, Poole,
Portsmouth, Southampton,
Swindon, Taunton, Truro,
Weymouth, Worthing

Dudley CSAC
(Midlands Business Unit)
Postal address:
2 Weston Road
Crewe CW98 1BD

Offices covered:
Birmingham, Chester, Hanley,
Lichfield, Stockport, Banbury, Milton
Keynes, Shrewsbury, Telford

Birkenhead CSAC
(Wales and North West Business Unit)
Postal address:
2 Weston Road
Crewe CW98 1BD

Offices covered:
North West: Barrow-in-Furness, Blackpool North, Bury, Carlisle, Huyton (Liverpool), Kendal, Lancaster, Penrith, Salford, Skelmersdale, St Helens, Wirral, Workington

Wales: Aberystwyth, Anglesey, Caernarfon, Cardiff, Haverfordwest, Holyhead, Newport, Pontypridd, Rhyl, Swansea, Wrexham

Belfast CSAC (GB)
(Eastern Business Unit)
Great Northern Tower
17 Great Victoria Street
Belfast
Northern Ireland BT2 7AD
The Northern Ireland Agency has the same address.

Offices covered:
Ipswich, Cambridge, Peterborough, Great Yarmouth, King's Lynn, Norwich, St Albans, Northampton, Leicester, Nottingham, Lincoln, Sutton-in-Ashfield, Doncaster, Huddersfield, Bradford, Hull, Scarborough, Pontefract, Grimsby

Falkirk CSAC
(Scotland and North East England Business Unit)
Parklands
Callendar Business Park
Callendar Road
Falkirk FK1 1XT

Offices covered:
Aberdeen, Campbeltown, Darlington, Dundee, Edinburgh, Falkirk, Galashiels, Inverness, Irvine, Leeds, Middlesborough, Mosspark, Newcastle upon Tyne, Northshields, Oban, Sunderland, Wick

Local rate telephone lines

National enquiry line (for general enquires)	08457 133 133
Hastings CSAC:	
'old rules'	08457 134 000
'new rules'	08456 090 052
Plymouth CSAC:	
'old rules'	08457 137 000
'new rules'	08456 090 072
Dudley CSAC:	
'old rules'	08457 131 000
'new rules'	08456 090 062
Birkenhead CSAC:	
'old rules'	08457 138 000
'new rules'	08456 090 082
Belfast (GB) CSAC:	
'old rules'	08457 132 000
'new rules'	08456 090 092
Belfast	
Northern Ireland CSA:	
'old rules'	08457 139 896
'new rules	08456 080 022
Falkirk CSAC:	
'old rules'	08457 136 000
'new rules'	08456 090 042
Welsh language enquiry line	08457 138 091

The Tribunals Service

From April 2006, the Appeals Service, which previously administered child support and social security appeals, became part of a new government agency, the Tribunals Service. Local administrative

arrangements for child support
appeals are not be affected. More
information can be found at
www.tribunals.gov.uk.

The President
Social Security and Child Support
Appeals
Fox Court
14 Grays Inn Road
London WC1X 8HN
Tel: 020 7712 2600

Tribunals Service regional offices (for child support and social security appeals)

Leeds
York House
York Place
Leeds LS1 2ED
Tel: 0113 251 9500

Liverpool
36 Dale Street
Liverpool L2 5UZ
Tel: 0151 243 1400

Newcastle
Manor View House
Kings Manor
Newcastle upon Tyne NE1 6PA
Tel: 0191 201 2300

Sutton
Copthall House
9 The Pavement
Grove Road
Sutton
Surrey SM1 1DA
Tel: 020 8710 2900

Birmingham
3rd Floor
Auchinleck House
Birmingham B15 1DL
Tel: 0121 634 7200

Nottingham
Albion House
5-13 Canal Street
Nottingham NG1 7EG
Tel: 0115 924 1774

Cardiff
Eastgate House
Newport Road
Cardiff CF24 0YP
Tel: 02920 662180

Glasgow
Wellington House
134-136 Wellington Street
Glasgow G2 2XL
Tel 0141 354 8400

Offices of the Social Security and Child Support Commissioners

England and Wales
3rd Floor
Procession House
55 Ludgate Hill
London EC4M 7JW
Tel: 020 7029 9850
www.osscsc.gov.uk

Scotland
George House
126 George Street
Edinburgh EH2 4HH
Tel: 0131 271 4310
www.ossc-scotland.gov.uk

Northern Ireland
  Headline Building
  10–14 Victoria Street
  Belfast BT1 3GG
  Tel: 028 9033 2344

Independent Case Examiner
  PO Box 155
  Chester CH99 9SA
  Tel: 0845 606 0777
  Minicom: 0151 801 8888
  www.ind-case-exam.org.uk

Office of the Parliamentary Commissioner for Administration
  Millbank Tower
  Millbank
  London SW1P 4RP
  Tel: 0845 015 4033
  www.ombudsman.org.uk

Constituency Locator
House of Commons
  www.locata.co.uk/commons

Appendix 2
Income support premiums

Premiums are added to income support (IS) personal allowances and are intended to help with the extra expenses associated with age, disability or children. The premiums are used in the child support formula irrespective of whether the parent is in receipt of IS, although not all apply at each stage. **Note:** although some of the rules below no longer apply to all IS claimants, they are still relevant for working out 'old rules' assessments.

Family premium	£16.43
Disabled child premium	£46.69
Carer premium (per carer)	£27.15
Disability premium	
Single	£25.25
Couple	£36.00*
Severe disability premium	
One qualifies	£48.45
Two qualify	£96.90*
Enhanced disability premium	
Single	£12.30
Couple	£17.75
Child	£18.76
Pensioner premium	
Single	£59.90*
Couple	£88.90*

*These amounts are only ever used at the protected income stage.

Family premium

A person is entitled to family premium if her/his family includes a child, even if s/he is not the child's parent. It does not matter how much capital a child has. For child support purposes, a child is taken to be a member of the household if the adult has 'day-to-day care' of that child. If a child does not live in the household full time, a proportion of the family premium can be included in exempt income and protected income (see Chapter 15). Only one family premium is payable regardless of the number of children a person has.

If a child who is in the care of or being looked after by a local authority, or who is in custody, comes home for part of a week, a proportion of the premium is payable, according to the number of days the child is at home.

Disabled child premium

A person is entitled to a disabled child premium for each child who gets disability living allowance (DLA) or who is blind. A child is treated as blind if s/he is registered as blind and for the first 28 weeks after s/he has been taken off the register on regaining her/his sight. For how to qualify for DLA, see CPAG's *Welfare Benefits and Tax Credits Handbook*.

If DLA has stopped because the child is in hospital, this premium continues as long as the child continues to be treated as a member of your family. See CPAG's *Welfare Benefits and Tax Credits Handbook* for more details. If the child does not live in the household full time, a proportion of the premium is included in exempt income and in protected income (see Chapter 15).

If a child has over £3,000 capital, there is no entitlement to this premium.

Carer premium

A person qualifies for this if s/he or her/his partner is getting carer's allowance (CA), or would get it but for the overlapping benefit rules – ie, because s/he is receiving another 'earnings replacement' benefit paid at a higher rate. For example, a woman getting CA who at 60 is awarded retirement pension at a higher rate than CA continues to qualify for the premium as long as the person being cared for continues to get the higher or middle rate care component of DLA or attendance allowance (AA).

A double premium is awarded where both the person concerned and her/his partner satisfy the conditions for it.

See CPAG's *Welfare Benefits and Tax Credits Handbook* for more details on the premium and conditions of entitlement for CA.

Disability premium

A person can get a disability premium if s/he is under 60 (note that in the exempt income step of the child support formula, the age rule does not apply) and:

- s/he (or her/his partner) is getting a qualifying benefit. These are DLA (or an equivalent benefit paid to meet attendance needs because of an injury at work or a war injury), disability or severe disability element of working tax credit, war pensioner's mobility supplement, incapacity benefit (IB) paid at the long-term rate or when terminally ill, or severe disablement allowance (SDA). A person or her/his partner must be getting the benefit for her/himself, not on behalf of someone else – eg, as a parent or an appointee. In some situations,

entitlement to the premium continues after the person stops receiving the qualifying benefit – see CPAG's *Welfare Benefits and Tax Credits Handbook*;
- s/he (or her/his partner) is registered as blind with a local authority (England and Wales) or regional or islands council (Scotland); if sight is regained, s/he will still qualify for 28 weeks after s/he is taken off the register;
- s/he (or her/his partner) has an NHS invalid trike or private car allowance because of disability;
- s/he is 'incapable of work' (or exempt from the 'all-work test') and either entitled to statutory sick pay or has been incapable for at least:
  - 196 days if certified as 'terminally ill' – ie, it can reasonably be expected that s/he will die within six months due to a progressive disease;
  - 364 days in all other cases, provided s/he has claimed IB (it is not necessary to send in medical certificates).

Breaks in incapacity/entitlement of up to 56 days (104 weeks if a 'welfare to work beneficiary') are included in these periods. For more on incapacity for work, see CPAG's *Welfare Benefits and Tax Credits Handbook*.

Entitlement to the disability premium stops when someone has been in hospital for more than 52 weeks.

At the protected income stage of the child support calculation, couples will get the disability premium at the couple rate provided either of them qualifies under one of the first three of the above rules. But they will only get the premium under the last condition if the person who qualifies is the parent being assessed for child maintenance.

Severe disability premium

A person can get this premium if:
- s/he is receiving AA (or the equivalent war pension or industrial injury benefit), or the higher or middle rate care component of DLA (or extra-statutory payments to compensate for not receiving any of these). If s/he is part of a couple, they must both be getting one of these benefits or the partner who does not get AA/DLA must be registered or treated as blind; *and*
- no non-dependant aged 18 or over is living with her/him (see below); *and*
- no one is getting CA for looking after her/him.

A couple who are both severely disabled only get the single rate if someone is getting CA in respect of one of them or one of them qualifies only because s/he is registered or treated as blind.

Non-dependants aged 18 or over

The following people living with a person do not count:
- a partner (but s/he must be getting AA/DLA or be blind);
- anyone aged under 18;

- anyone staying in a person's home who normally lives elsewhere;
- a person (who may be her/his partner) employed by a charitable or voluntary body as a resident carer for a person or her/his partner if s/he pays for that service (even if the charge is only nominal);
- a person receiving AA or the higher or middle rate care component of DLA;
- a person who is registered blind or treated as blind;
- a person, or her/his partner, who jointly occupies her/his home and is either a co-owner with the person or her/his partner, or jointly liable with them to make payments to a landlord in respect of occupying it;
- a person, or any member of her/his household, who is liable to pay on a commercial basis for occupying the dwelling (eg, tenant or licensee), unless s/he is a close relative;
- a person, or any member of her/his household, to whom a person or her/his partner is liable to make such payments on a commercial basis, unless s/he is a close relative.

If someone (other than those listed above) comes to live with a person in order to look after her/him or her/his partner, her/his severe disability premium will only remain in payment for the first 12 weeks.

For more detail of these rules, see CPAG's *Welfare Benefits and Tax Credits Handbook*.

Enhanced disability premium

The enhanced disability premium applies if the person or a member of her/his family receives the highest rate of the DLA care component and is aged under 60.

The following people cannot qualify:

- children or young people with more than £3,000 in capital;
- a claimant who has been a hospital inpatient for more than 52 weeks; *or*
- a claimant whose partner has been a hospital inpatient for more than 52 weeks.

Pensioner premium

There are three pensioner premiums, all paid at the same rate:

- pensioner premium if a person or her/his partner is aged 60–74 inclusive;
- pensioner premium (also known as an enhanced pensioner premium) if a person or her/his partner is 75–79 inclusive;
- higher pensioner premium if a person or her/his partner is aged over 80 or satifies other conditions detailed below.

Each of these can be paid at a couple rate if one partner fulfils the age condition. If a person or her/his partner is sick or disabled, check to see if the higher pensioner premium described on p479 applies.

Higher pensioner premium

A person can get this if:

- s/he or her/his partner is 80 or over; *or*
- s/he was getting a disability premium as part of her/his IS at some time during the eight weeks (104 weeks for 'welfare to work beneficiaries') before s/he was 60 and has continued to get IS since the age of 60 (breaks of up to eight (or 104) weeks are ignored). Couples can qualify under this rule regardless of which partner meets the condition; *or*
- s/he or her/his partner is aged 60–79 *and* either of them receives a qualifying benefit (as for the disability premium but including AA), is registered blind, or has an NHS trike or private car allowance. If a person stops getting IB or SDA to change to retirement pension, the higher pensioner premium still applies if there is a continuous entitlement (apart from breaks of eight weeks (104 weeks for 'welfare to work beneficiaries') or less) to IS.

Entitlement to the higher pension premium stops if someone has been a hospital inpatient for more than 52 weeks.

For more details on the premium and who is a 'welfare to work beneficiary', see CPAG's *Welfare Benefits and Tax Credits Handbook*.

Appendix 3

Statutes

A man is assumed to be the father of a child for child support purposes if he is found to be the father by a court in England or Wales in proceedings under the following.

s42 National Assistance Act 1948
Affiliation Proceedings Act 1957
s6 Family Law Reform Act 1969
Guardianship of Minors Act 1971
Children Act 1975
Child Care Act 1980
Children Act 1989
s26 Social Security Act 1986
s4 Family Law Reform Act 1987
s105 Social Security Administration Act 1992

A maintenance order only prevents a s4 or s7 application to the Child Support Agency if it was made in proceedings under the following.

Conjugal Rights (Scotland) Amendment Act 1861
Court of Session Act 1868
Sheriff Courts (Scotland) Act 1907
Guardianship of Infants Act 1925
Illegitimate Children (Scotland) Act 1930
Children and Young Persons (Scotland) Act 1932
Children and Young Persons (Scotland) Act 1937
Custody of Children (Scotland) Act 1939
National Assistance Act 1948
Affiliation Orders Act 1952
Affiliation Proceedings Act 1957
Guardianship of Minors Act 1971
Part II Matrimonial Causes Act 1973
Guardianship Act 1973
Children Act 1975

Supplementary Benefits Act 1976
Domestic Proceedings and Magistrates' Courts Act 178
Part II Matrimonial and Family Proceedings Act 1984
Family Law (Scotland) Act 1985
Schedule 1 Children Act 1989
Social Security Act 1986
Social Security Administration Act 1992
Schedule 5, 6 or 7 Civil Partnership Act 2004

The court order usually states the legal provisions under which it was made.

Appendix 4
Information and advice

It is often difficult for unsupported individuals to get a positive response from the Child Support Agency. You may be more successful if you have taken advice about your rights or have an adviser assisting you. The following agencies may be able to help.

- Citizens advice bureaux (CABx) and other local advice centres provide information and may be able to represent you. You can find your nearest CAB from www.citizensadvice.org.uk.

- Law centres can help with advice and representation, but may not cover child support problems and may limit their help to people who live and work in certain areas. You can check if you are near a law centre from www.lawcentres.org.uk

- Solicitors can give free legal advice to people on low incomes under the 'legal help' scheme (advice and assistance scheme in Scotland). This does not cover the cost of representation at an appeal hearing, but can cover the cost of preparing written submissions and obtaining evidence such as medical reports. However, solicitors do not always have a good working knowledge of the child support rules and you may need to shop around until you find one who does.

- www.clsdirect.org.uk can be used to find high quality legal advisers in England and Wales, including advice agencies and solicitors.

- Local authority welfare rights workers provide an advice and representation service for benefit claimants in many areas.

- Lone-parent organisations may offer help and advice about child support, or it may help to talk to other parents about their experiences. For details of your local group and for helpline advice contact: Gingerbread (helpline 0800 018 4318); Single Parent Action Network (0117 951 4231); One Parent Families (helpline 0800 018 5026); One Parent Families Scotland (helpline 0808 801 0323).

- There are some groups supporting parents who may be able to provide advice. These include National Association for Child Support Action, PO Box 4454, Dudley, West Midlands DY1 9AN. You can write or email enquiries@nacsa.co.uk.

- Many trade unions provide advice to members on child support.

- Local organisations for particular groups may offer help – eg, unemployed centres, claimants' unions, centres for people with disabilities.

Representation at appeal tribunals

Some parents may find it difficult to obtain representation at appeal hearings. Although many parents, especially with the help of Chapter 19, will be perfectly able to present their own cases, it can be invaluable to obtain objective independent advice which draws on the legislation. An advice centre which has a copy of the legislation (see Appendix 5) and experience of representing at tribunals in other sorts of cases (eg, social security) may be able to provide a representative for a child support appeal to an appeal tribunal.

Child Poverty Action Group

Unfortunately, CPAG is unable to deal with enquiries, either from advisers or members of the public, on child support issues.

Appendix 5
Useful publications

Stationery Office books are available from Stationery Office bookshops or can be ordered from The Stationery Office, Post Cash Department, PO Box 29, Norwich NR3 1GN (tel: 0870 600 5522; fax: 0870 600 5533; email: customer.services@tso.co.uk; web: www.tso.co.uk). Many publications listed are available from CPAG. See below for order details, or order from www.cpag.org.uk/publications.

1. Caselaw and legislation
Social Security Case Law – Digest of Commissioners' Decisions
D Neligan (Stationery Office, looseleaf in two volumes).

CPAG's Welfare Benefits and Tax Credits Law Online
(CPAG) Includes all social security and tax credits legislation, updated and consolidated throughout the year; over 2,500 commissioners' decisions, most with commentary; guidance; the *Welfare Benefits and Tax Credits Handbook* updated throughout the year with links to the relevant legislation, decisions and caselaw. £45 + VAT per concurrent user (bulk discounts available). More information and free seven-day trial at http://onlineservices.cpag.org.uk

CPAG's Child Support Law Online
(CPAG) Includes all child support legislation, updated and consolidated throughout the year;

the *Child Support Handbook* updated once a year in line with the print edition, with links to the relevant legislation, commissioners' decisions and caselaw. £26 + VAT per concurrent user (bulk discounts available). More information at http://onlineservices.cpag.org.uk

CPAG's Housing Benefit and Council Tax Benefit Law Online
(CPAG) Includes complete housing benefit and council tax benefit legislation, updated and consolidated throughout the year; commentary from *CPAG's Housing Benefit & Council Tax Benefit Legislation* (Findlay), updated twice a year in line with the print edition, with links to commissioners' decisions, court cases and other relevant material. £97 + VAT per user (bulk discounts available). More information at http://onlineservices.cpag.org.uk

The Law Relating to Social Security
(Stationery Office, looseleaf, 12
volumes) All the legislation but
without any comment. Known as the
'Blue Book'. Also available at
www.dwp.gov.uk/advisers.

The Law Relating to Child Support
Consolidated legislation without any
commentary. Shows the law as it
applies both before and after the
'new rules' changes come into force
for a particular case. Also known as
the 'Orange Volumes'. Available at
www.dwp.gov.uk/advisers.

Social Security Legislation, Volume I:
Non-Means-Tested Benefits
D Bonner, I Hooker and R White
(Sweet & Maxwell) Legislation with
commentary. 2007/08 edition
(October 2007): £84 for the main
volume, reduced to £75.70 if you are
a CPAG member and order from
CPAG before 30 June 2007, or at full
price from July.

Social Security Legislation, Volume II:
Income Support, Jobseeker's Allowance,
State Pension Credit and the Social Fund
J Mesher, P Wood, R Poynter, N
Wikeley and D Bonner (Sweet &
Maxwell) Legislation with
commentary. 2007/08 edition
(October 2007): £84 for the main
volume, reduced to £75.70 if you are
a CPAG member and order from
CPAG before 30 June 2007, or at full
price from July.

Social Security Legislation, Volume III:
Administration, Adjudication and the
European Dimension
M Rowland and R White (Sweet &
Maxwell) Legislation with
commentary. 2007/08 edition
(October 2007): £84 for the main
volume, reduced to £75.70 if you are
a CPAG member and order from
CPAG before 30 June 2007, or at full
price from July.

Social Security Legislation, Volume IV:
Tax Credits, Child Trust Funds and
Employer Paid Social Security Benefits
N Wikeley and D Williams (Sweet &
Maxwell) Legislation with
commentary. 2007/08 edition
(October 2007): £84 for the main
volume, reduced to £75.70 if you are
a CPAG member and order from
CPAG before 30 June 2007, or at full
price from July.

Social Security Legislation – updating
supplement to Volumes I, II, III & IV
(Sweet & Maxwell) The spring 2008
update to the 2007/08 main
volumes: £50, reduced to £45 if you
are a CPAG member and order from
CPAG before 30 June 2007, or at full
price from July.

CPAG's Housing Benefit and Council
Tax Benefit Legislation
L Findlay, R Poynter, S Wright and C
George (CPAG) Legislation with
detailed commentary. 2007/08
(20th) edition (December 2007): £95
including Supplement. Reduced to
£88 per set if ordered before 30 June
2007. The 19th edition (2006/07) is
still available, £93 per set. Also

available as part of *CPAG's Housing Benefit and Council Tax Law Online* (see p484).

Child Support: The Legislation
E Jacobs and G Douglas (Sweet & Maxwell) 8th edition main volume (October 2007): £82, reduced to £79 if you are a CPAG member and order from CPAG before 30 June 2007, or at full price from July.

The Social Fund: Law & Practice
T Buck (Sweet & Maxwell) 3rd edition (late 2007): £82, also available from CPAG if you are a CPAG member.

2. Periodicals

Welfare Rights Bulletin
(CPAG, bimonthly). Covers developments in social security law, including commissioners' decisions, and updates CPAG's *Welfare Benefits and Tax Credits Handbook*. The annual subscription is £30 but it is sent automatically to CPAG Rights and Comprehensive members (contact CPAG for details).

Articles on social security can also be found in *Legal Action* (Legal Action Group, monthly magazine), *The Adviser* (Citizens Advice, bi-monthly magazine) and the *Journal of Social Security Law* (Sweet & Maxwell, quarterly).

3. Child Support Agency publications

For guidance issued to CSA staff, see Appendix 6.

A full list of CSA leaflets is available on the CSA website. Leaflets and most other CSA publications can be obtained from the national enquiry line: 08457 133 133. Many leaflets and other publications are also available at www.csa.gov.uk. The following is only a selection of the publications available. Some of the leaflets listed have 'old rules' equivalents with different titles and numbers.

Child Support: your child maintenance interview (CSL100)

What Happens if Someone Denies They are the Parent of a Child? (CSL304)

How Do I Complain About the Service I Get From the Child Support Agency? (CSL308)

What is My Role in Helping My Employees Pay Child Maintenance? (CSL313)

Child Support Agency Client Charter 2007 (CSA2047)

Child Support Agency Operational Improvement Plan 2006-2009

Child Support Agency Business Plan 2007/8 (CSA2091)

4. Other publications: child support

This section lists other publications on child support, including some relevant leaflets, but only includes the most recent research, reports and commentary. For earlier research and reports on child support, please see previous editions of this *Handbook*.

Our Services and Standards: Independent Case Examiner for the Child Support Agency (ICE SAS) (available from www.csa.gov.uk or www.ind-case-exam.org.uk)

Independent Case Examiner's Annual Report 2006/07 (available from www.ind-case-exam.org.uk)

DWP White Paper, *A New System of Child Maintenance*, CM 6979, December 2006 (available from www.dwp.gov.uk).
Many organisations, including CPAG, One Parent Families and Citizens Advice, have responded to the White Paper. Their comments can be found on their respective websites.

House of Commons Select Committee for Work and Pensions, Fourth Report of 2006/07, *Child Support Reform*, 7 March 2007 (available from www.parliament.uk)

N Wikeley, *Child Support Law and Policy*, Hart Publishing, 2006

5. Other publications: general

Tell Us What You Think (TELLUSA5JP)(available from Jobcentre Plus offices and www.jobcentreplus.gov.uk)

Department for Work and Pensions Business Plan 2007/08 (available from www.dwp.gov.uk)

Welfare Benefits and Tax Credits Handbook
£35/£8.50 for claimants (2007/08, April 2007). Also available as part of *CPAG's Welfare Benefits and Tax Credits Law Online*.

Personal Finance Handbook
£15 (2nd edition, September 2007)

Paying for Care Handbook
£18.50 (5th edition, December 2005)

Student Support and Benefits Handbook: England, Wales and Northern Ireland
£12 (5th edition, October 2007)

Benefits for Students in Scotland Handbook
£12 (5th edition, October 2007)
Available free online at www.scottishhandbooks.cpag.org.uk, funded by the Scottish Executive.

Council Tax Handbook
£16 (7th edition, autumn 2007)

Debt Advice Handbook
£18 (7th edition, October 2006)

Fuel Rights Handbook
£17 (14th edition, autumn 2007)

Migration and Social Security Handbook
£21 (4th edition, March 2007)

Guide to Housing Benefit and Council Tax Benefit
£22.50 (summer 2007)

Disability Rights Handbook
£20 (May 2007)

The Young Persons Handbook
£15.95 (3rd edition, summer 2007)

Welfare to Work Handbook
£24.95 (3rd edition, summer 2007)

For CPAG publications and most of those in Sections 1 and 5 contact: CPAG, 94 White Lion Street, London N1 9PF, tel: 020 7837 7979, fax: 020 7837 6414. Order forms are available at www.cpag.org.uk/publications. Postage and packing: free for orders up to £10 in value; for order value £10.01–£100 add a flat rate charge of £3.99; for order value £100.01–£500 add £5.99; for order value £500+ add £9.99.

Appendix 6

Abbreviations used in the notes

AC	Appeal Cases	FLR	Family Law Reports
All ER	All England Reports	HC	High Court
App	Appendix	HL	House of Lords
Art(s)	Article(s)	para(s)	Paragraph(s)
CA	Court of Appeal	QB	Queen's Bench Reports
CCR	County Court Rules	r(s)	Rule(s)
Ch	Chapter	Reg(s)	Regulation(s)
col	Column	s(s)	Section(s)
DC	Divisional Court	SCLR	Scottish Civil Law Reports
ECJ	European Court of Justice	Sch(s)	Schedule(s)
ECR	European court Reports	SLT	Scots Law Times
FamD	Family Division	Vol	Volume
FCR	Family Court Reports	WLR	Weekly Law Reports

1. The legislation

Acts of Parliament

Unless information in this *Handbook* specifically relates to 'old rules' cases, legislative references are for 'new rules' cases only. Provisions for 'old rules' cases are as the law stood before the Child Support, Pensions and Social Security Act 2000 came into force. Full legislative referencing for 'old rules' cases can be found in the 2001/02 and 2002/03 editions of this *Handbook*.

AA 1976	Adoption Act 1976
A(S)A 1978	Adoption (Scotland) Act 1978
CA 1989	Children Act 1989
CPA 2004	Civil Partnership Act 2004
CSA 1991	Child Support Act 1991
C(S)A 1995	Children (Scotland) Act 1995

CSPSSA 2000	Child Support, Pensions and Social Security Act 2000
DPMCA 1978	Domestic Proceedings and Magistrates' Courts Act 1978
ERA 1996	Employment Rights Act 1996
FL(S)A 1958	Family Law (Scotland) Act 1958
FLRA 1969	Family Law Reform Act 1969
HF&EA 1990	Human Fertilisation and Embryology Act 1990
HRA 1998	Human Rights Act 1998
ICTA 1988	Income and Corporation Taxes Act 1988
LR(PC)(S)A 1986	Law Reform (Parent and Child) (Scotland) Act 1986
MCA 1973	Matrimonial Causes Act 1973
MO(RE)A 1992	Maintenance Orders (Reciprocal Enforcement) Act 1992
SSA 1998	Social Security Act 1998
SSAA 1992	Social Security Administration Act 1992
SSCBA 1992	Social Security Contributions and Benefits Act 1992
TCA 2002	Tax Credits Act 2002

Regulations and other statutory instruments

Unless information specifically relates to 'old rules' cases, legislative references in this *Handbook* are correct for 'new rules' cases only. Most 'new rules' statutory instruments have 'old rules' equivalents. For example, the CS(MAP) Regs are the 'old rules' equivalent of the CS(MCP) Regs. Full legislative referencing for 'old rules' cases can be found in the 2001/02 and 2002/03 editions of this *Handbook*.

AS(CSA)(AOCSCR)	The Act of Sederunt (Child Support Act 1991) (Amendment of Ordinary Cause and Summary Cause Rules) 1993 No.919
AS(CSR)	The Act of Sederunt (Child Support Rules) 1993 No.920
C(AP)O	The Children (Allocation of Proceedings) Order 1991 No.1677
CB&SS(FAR) Regs	The Child Benefit and Social Security (Fixing and Adjustment of Rates) Regulations 1976 No.1267
CP(PSS&CS)(CP)O	The Civil Partnership (Pensions, Social Security and Child Support)(Consequential, etc. Provisions) Order 2005 No.2877
CPA 2004(RACP)O	The Civil Partnership Act 2004 (Relationships Arising Through Civil Partnership) Order 2005 No.3137
CS(AIAMA) Regs	The Child Support (Arrears, Interest and Adjustment of Maintenance Assessments) Regulations 1992 No.1816
CS(APD)	The Child Support (Applications: Prescribed Dates) Regulations 2003 No.194

CS(C&E) Regs	The Child Support (Collection and Enforcement) Regulations 1992 No.1989
CS(CEMA) Regs	Child Support (Collection and Enforcement and Miscellaneous Amendments) Regulations 2000 No.2001/162
CS(CEOFM) Regs	The Child Support (Collection and Enforcement of Other Forms of Maintenance) Regulations 1992 No.2643
CS(D&A)(A) Regs	The Child Support (Decisions and Appeals)(Amendment) Regulations 2000 No.3185
CS(IED) Regs	The Child Support (Information, Evidence and Disclosure) Regulations 1992 No.1812
CS(IEDMAJ)(A) Regs	Child Support (Information, Evidence and Disclosure and Maintenance Arrangements and Jurisdiction) (Amendment) Regulations 2000 No.2001/161
CS(MAJ) Regs	The Child Support (Maintenance Arrangements and Jurisdiction) Regulations 1992 No.2645
CS(MAP) Regs	The Child Support (Maintenance Assessment Procedure) Regulations 1992 No.1813
CS(MASC) Regs	The Child Support (Maintenance Assessments and Special Cases) Regulations 1992 No.1815
CS(MATP) Regs	The Child Support (Miscellaneous Amendments and Transitional Provisions) Regulations 1994 No.1227
CS(MCP) Regs	The Child Support (Maintenance Calculation Procedure) Regulations 2000 No.2001/157
CS(MCSC) Regs	The Child Support (Maintenance Calculation and Special Cases) Regulations 2000 No.2001/155
CS(NIRA) Regs	The Child Support (Northern Ireland Reciprocal Arrangements) Regulations 1993 No.584
CS(TCPS)(MA) Regs	The Child Support (Temporary Compensation Payment Scheme) (Modification and Amendment) Regulations 2002 No.1854
CS(TP) Regs	The Child Support (Transitional Provisions) Regulations 2000 No.3186
CS(V) Regs	The Child Support (Variations) Regulations 2000 No.2001/156
CS(V)(MSP) Regs	The Child Support (Variations)(Modification of Statutory Provisions) Regulations 2000 No.3173
CS(VP) Regs	The Child Support (Voluntary Payments) Regulations 2000 No.3177

CSA(CA)O	The Child Support Act 1991 (Consequential Amendments) Order 1993 No.785
CSA(JC)O	The Child Support Appeals (Jurisdiction of Courts) Order 1993 No.961 (L.12)
CSA(JO)O 2002	The Child Support Appeals (Jurisdiction of Courts) Order 2002 No.1915
CSC(P) Regs	The Child Support Commissioners (Procedure) Regulations 1999 No.1305
CSDDCA Regs	The Child Support Departure Directions and Consequential Amendments Regulations 1996 No.2907
CSF Regs	The Child Support Fees Regulations 1992 No.3094
CSPSSA(Comm3)O	The Child Support, Pensions and Social Security Act 2000 (Commencement No.3) Order 2000 No.2994
CSPSSA(Comm12)O	The Child Support, Pensions and Social Security Act 2003 (Commencement No.12) Order 2003 No.192
CSPSSA(Comm13)O	The Child Support, Pensions and Social Security Act 2000 (Commencement No.13) Order 2003 No.346
CTB Regs	The Council Tax Benefit (General) Regulations 2006 No.215
CTB(SPC) Regs	The Council Tax Benefit (Persons who have Attained the Qualifying Age for State Pension Credit) Regulations 2006 No.216
HB Regs	The Housing Benefit (General) Regulations 2006 No.213
HB(SPC) Regs	The Housing Benefit (Persons who have Attained the Qualifying Age for State Pension Credit) Regulations 2006 No.214
HB&CTB(D&A) Regs	The Housing Benefit and Council Tax Benefit (Decisions and Appeals) Regulations 2001 No.1002
IS Regs	The Income Support (General) Regulations 1987 No.1967
JSA Regs	The Jobseeker's Allowance Regulations 1996 No.207
SS(C&P) Regs	The Social Security (Claims and Payments) Regulations 1987 No.1968
SS(CMB) Regs	The Social Security (Child Maintenance Bonus) Regulations 1996 No.3195

SS(CMP)A Regs	The Social Security (Child Maintenance Premium) Amendment Regulations 2004 No.98
SS(CMPMA) Regs	The Social Security (Child Maintenance Premium and Miscellaneous Amendments) Regulations 2000 No.3176
SS(PAOR) Regs	The Social Security (Payments on Account, Overpayments and Recovery) Regulations 1988 No.664
SS&CS(DA) Regs	The Social Security and Child Support (Decisions and Appeals) Regulations 1999 No.991

Guidance

References to guidance are given either with the relevant paragraph numbers, or with volume titles and nearest heading.

Guidance for Child Support Agency staff

CSG	*Child Support Guide*
DMG	*Decision Makers Guide for Child Support*
DDMG	*Departures Decision Makers Guide*
EFIG	*Effective Full Maintenance Assessments and Interim Maintenance Assessments Guide*
EG	*Enforcement Guide* (Note: there are two separate guides, one for England and Wales and one for Scotland)
PatG	*Paternity Guide*
PG	*Procedures Guide*
RCG	*Requirement to Co-operate Guide*
TG	*Trace Guide*

Child Support Agency guidance can be obtained following a Freedom of Information request to the Child Support Agency.

Guidance for Jobcentre Plus staff

ISGAP	*Income Support Guidance and Procedure* manuals are a series of volumes produced by the DWP. Volume 10 covers CSA-related action. There is an equivalent set for jobseeker's allowance, but for ease of reference we refer to income support guidance only.

The Jobcentre Plus guidance can be obtained following a Freedom of Information request to Jobcentre Plus.

Index

How to use this Index

Entries against the bold headings direct you to the general information on the subject, or where the subject is covered most fully. Sub-entries are listed alphabetically and direct you to specific aspects of the subject.